THE NAVY:

1939 to the Present Day

THE NAVY

❖

1939 TO THE PRESENT DAY

Max Arthur

Hodder & Stoughton

First published in 1997 by Hodder and Stoughton
A division of Hodder Headline PLC

10 9 8 7 6 5 4 3 2 1

British Library Cataloguing in Publication Data
Arthur, Max, 1939–
The Navy : 1939 to the present day
1. Great Britain. Royal Navy – History – 20th century
2. Great Britain – History, Naval – 20th century
I. Title
359'.00941

ISBN 0 340 68469 0

Printed and bound in Great Britain by
Mackays of Chatham PLC, Chatham, Kent

Hodder and Stoughton
A division of Hodder Headline PLC
338 Euston Road
London NW1 3BH

Foreword

by Admiral of the Fleet
Lord Lewin of Greenwich,
K.G., G.C.B., L.V.O., D.S.C.

Max Arthur's preceding book, *The True Glory: The Royal Navy, 1914–1939*, gripping though it was, left me, and I guess very many others, hanging on the edge of our seats. We came in in 1939. For us covering the period from 1939 reminds us of the television show, 'This is *Our* Lives'. I am particularly pleased that this book, unlike its predecessor, includes the Merchant Navy. For these men who served in the merchant ships showed the greatest bravery and endured the greater hardships and earned the admiration and respect of their Royal Navy contemporaries. To my mind, the two Navies are indistinguishable in their contribution to our maritime history.

We are an island nation, a truism that the Channel Tunnel and the European Union cannot alter. Our national character and our history have been moulded by our dependence on the sea and on our seamen. There was a time when this was instinctively understood, when practically every family in the land had a connection with the sea: fathers, uncles, brothers, nephews, at sea in ships, or working in the shipyards or the docks. That has changed and it needs books like this to remind today's people not just of our maritime past but our continuing dependence on the free use of the sea.

I was stirred by many memories: contributions by old friends, new aspects of operations in which I took part as a very junior officer, the Pedestal Convoy, the Barents Sea and the Atlantic, D-Day: and in later operations – the Falklands and the Gulf – when I proudly followed the achievements of people who had been trained by those of my time. One particular sentence in this book sums it up: 'Captains in the South Atlantic, as they went to war, said they were conscious of ten generations of Naval Officers looking over their shoulders.' That is the heart of the matter.

Contents

Foreword by Lord Lewin of Greenwich   v

List of Illustrations   viii

Author's Preface   ix

Acknowledgements   xi

PART ONE

1. A Brief History of World War II   3

2. From 1939 to Dunkirk   12

3. From 1940 to the sinkings of *Hood* and *Bismarck*   54

4. Convoys, submarines and battleships, 1941–42   97

5. Dieppe to Italy, 1942–44   155

6. D-Day to VE-Day   231

7. The Far East War and Liberation   267

PART TWO

The Royal Navy from 1945 to the 1990s   305

Index   409

List of Illustrations

Section I

Courageous sinks after being hit by two torpedoes from U29
The Royal Navy and an armada of small ships evacuate troops from Dunkirk, May 1940
Glorious, which was sunk by *Scharnhorst* and *Gneisenau*, 1940
Allied landings at Dieppe, 1942
Operation Pedestal, 1942. *Dorset* under fire while bringing supplies to the island of Malta
Captain F. J. Walker on the bridge of *Starling*
The crew of *Starling* search for wreckage and bodies
Walker waits while depth-charges are fired again
Strips of sailcloth recording the hopes and fears of the survivors of the sinking of SS *Lullworth Hill*
The crew of *Seraph* after another good operation, May 1943
D-Day 1944. *Warspite* fires on to the beaches of Normandy
Royal Marines of 4th Special Service Brigade charge ashore on D-Day 1944
Royal Navy Commandos talking to liberated French villagers

Section II

Youth: *Swordfish* aircrew after a successful attack on a U-boat
Maturity: Three long-serving men of a destroyer show that discipline, sheer doggedness and humour will overcome adversity
A Chief Petty Officer in costume for the ship's concert
May 1945. Men of the Royal Navy march through the streets of war-torn Berlin
Searching a Japanese officer, September 1945
Officers and ratings on the casing of U825 at Lisahally, May 1945
Trafalgar Square, VE-Day 1945
Exodus packed with European Jewish refugees, Haifa harbour, 1947
Rocket-assisted take-off from *Ocean*, Korea, June 1953
Suez, 1956. Royal Marines in landing craft with naval helicopters and warship support, launch their initial attack
Sheffield on fire after being struck by an exocet missile, Falklands, 1982
A door gunner in a Royal Navy SeaKing helicopter, Gulf, 1990
Air Sea Rescue crew prepare to lower a dinghy
A dramatic rescue of the crew of a merchant ship

Author's Preface

What I have sought to do with these personal accounts is to capture something of the spirit of the men and women who served with the Royal Navy between 1939 and the present: it is not intended as a formal history of the Royal Navy.

The book is based on taped interviews with those who served during this period. Apart from minor editing, these are their own words. In a few cases, however, a written account by the contributor has been included.

The rank given at the start of each contributor's account is the highest held during the period to which the account refers.

Like in *The True Glory: The Royal Navy 1914–1939* each account is a chapter in itself, a chapter in the life of the person who related it. I have arranged the accounts, wherever possible, in chronological order. Because these are personal accounts, not cold histories, the order in which I have placed them may sometimes seem imperfect. However, wherever possible, I have checked for historical accuracy.

The length of these accounts varies, some take many pages, whereas others select the most affecting moments. In some cases, contributors appear several times to tell of different actions in which they were involved. To give all the accounts an historical context, I have included a short history of the Royal Navy from 1939 to 1945 and another from 1945 to the present day.

The accounts of Lieutenant-Commander Roger Lancashire, the medical officer of *Exeter*, and Surgeon Admiral Sir Dick Caldwell, the medical officer of the *Royal Oak* (and *Prince of Wales*), were an integral part of *The True Glory*. I had no hesitation about including them also in this volume. The accounts from those Marines who have served in Northern Ireland are – for security reasons – anonymous, and have been taken from my book *Northern Ireland Soldiers Talking*. Accounts of the Falklands campaign are taken from my book *Above All Courage*. The dramatic account of the sinking of *Courageous* comes from *War in a Stringbag* written by the late Commander Charles Lamb. The fine account of HMS *Naiad*'s actions is from *The Man Around the Engine*, written by Vice-Admiral Sir Louis Le Bailly.

I was especially delighted with the contributions from Captain Frank Layard and Captain Brian de Courcy-Ireland who both served at the Battle of

Jutland in 1916. Like so many contributors to this book, they have given long and loyal service to the Royal Navy.

One of my main aims throughout this book was to include accounts from those, too often unsung, heroes of the Merchant Navy; I have particularly concentrated their accounts into the chapters on Operation Pedestal (page 135ff.). I hope I have served them well.

For the past four years, it has been my pleasure to meet and talk with those who have served or been associated with the Royal Navy. All had faced the rigours of training, understood the reasons for discipline, enjoyed the camaraderie and, in the face of sometimes appalling adversity, shown the courage, compassion and the humour that this country has come to expect of its senior service. I am certain that tradition will continue.

Throughout the writing of this book it has been my privilege to meet many fine men and women. These are their words – I have been but a catalyst.

Hampstead
London

Author's Acknowledgements

I would like to thank all members of the Royal Navy who told me of their personal experiences and who, throughout the writing of this book, gave me generous support. Sadly, a place could not be found for everyone's story, but all deserved one. I would also like to thank the wives and families to whom I spoke: their stories also deserve to be told.

Throughout the writing of this book I have had outstanding help from many sources and I would like to thank them all: The Department of Public Relations (RN); Captain Bob McQueen of the Royal Naval Association; Lieutenant-Commander Mike Coombes of the Association of Royal Naval Officers; Lieutenant-Commander Mike Lawrence and many others at Fleet Air Arm Officers Association; Commander Jeff Tall, Director of Royal Navy Submarine Museum and his colleague, Gus Britton; Jim Allaway and Anton Hanney and the staff of 'Navy News'; Captain Tony Newing, RM, Editor of *The Globe and Laurel*; Captain Derek Oakley, RM, of the Royal Marines Historical Society for his permission to use extracts from the Special Publication on D-Day. Also Major Mark Bentinck, RM, Corps Historical Records Officer; Matthew Little, Archivist, Royal Marines Museum; Peter Hunt, Brad King and Conrad Black of Imperial War Museum; the late Len Fogwill, secretary of the River Plate Veterans' Association; and Stuart Eadon for permission to use an extract from his very fine book *Kamikaze*.

I am also most grateful to John Winton, naval historian, who kindly read through the manuscript and made valuable suggestions, and Ian Drury, military historian, who has written the historical notes. On the publishing front, Roland Philipps, Publishing Director of Hodder and Stoughton, gave me every assistance and waited patiently. Angela Herlihy dealt admirably with the last-minute changes. My editor, John Bright-Holmes, has overseen my last three books and has throughout offered constructive advice, encouragement and great good humour. I am much in his debt. Sarah Mnatzaganian and Jos Razzell, ably backed by Sacha Baker, transcribed extremely complex tapes and organised the material to make my editing a pleasure. Carolyn Mallam transcribed the remainder of the tapes as she has done for all my books: she has been a steadfast support and I thank her. Linda Brazier did considerable last-minute typing.

Author's Acknowledgements

Vice-Admiral Sir John Roxburgh and Rear-Admiral David Kirk offered sound advice throughout both books and I am most grateful to them. I should also like to acknowledge *The Royal Navy Day by Day* by A. D. Sainsbury (published by Ian Allan in association with the National Maritime Museum) and *Chronology of War 1939–1945* by Rohwer and Hummelchen published by Greenhill Books: both have been an invaluable reference, as has the classic history of the Royal Navy in the Second World War, *Engage the Enemy More Closely* by Correlli Barnett. To the many others too numerous to name, all so important, who have given me information and co-operation, please accept my thanks.

I would also like to thank my dear friends Don and Liz McClen and Fanny and Cecil Lewis who were there at the beginning. Cecil died in January 1997 at the age of 98, but his classic work on flying, *Sagittarius Rising*, is still in print. Finally I must thank Ruth Cowen who recently came into my life: her love, humour and incisive eye have enhanced this book.

This book is dedicated to those who have served, or are at present serving, with the Royal Navy and the Merchant Navy

The Sea and Sailors

The sea – this truth must be confessed – has no generosity. No display of manly qualities – courage, hardihood, endurance, faithfulness – has ever been known to touch its irresponsible consciousness of power. The ocean has the conscienceless temper of a savage autocrat spoiled by much adulation. He cannot brook the slightest appearance of defiance, and has remained the irreconcilable enemy of ships and men ever since ships and men had the unheard-of audacity to go afloat together in the face of his frown. From that day he has gone on swallowing up fleets and men without his resentment being glutted by the number of victims – by so many wrecked ships and wrecked lives. Today, as ever, he is ready to beguile and betray, to smash and to drown the incorrigible optimism of men. . . . If not always in the hot mood to smash, he is always stealthily ready for a drowning. The most amazing wonder of the deep is its unfathomable cruelty.

From *The Mirror of the Sea* by Joseph Conrad

PART ONE

The Royal Navy from
1939–1945

A Brief History of World War II

For the Royal Navy, the events of autumn 1939 bore an uncanny resemblance to those of 1914. Many senior Admirals had served as captains in the Grand Fleet of World War I and from the signal 'TOTAL GERMANY', transmitted on 3 September, there followed a familiar pattern of events. The battleships assembled at Scapa Flow and cruiser squadrons throughout the world ensured that enemy merchantmen vanished from the seas. For a second time this century a British Expeditionary Force was transported to France, with minimal interference from the Germany navy.

Hitler's *Kriegsmarine* was dwarfed by the Royal Navy, but it did possess several heavy cruisers designed for extended commerce raiding. One named after the heroic Admiral Graf von Spee sailed down the Channel on the eve of hostilities. Sporting six 11-inch guns and fitted with diesels that offered rapid acceleration as well as prodigious endurance, the *Graf Spee* had already been dubbed a 'pocket battleship'. While battlecruisers like the famous *Hood* or the French *Dunkerque* could have brought her to action if they had intercepted her, the *Graf Spee* was theoretically capable of outrunning any other ship she could not outfight. And she was not short of sea room. Raiding across the south Atlantic, she emulated *Emden*'s epic cruise in 1914, venturing into the Indian Ocean and forcing the Royal Navy to devote vast numbers of warships to hunting her. Ironically, *Graf Spee*'s luck ran out in the same waters as von Spee's original squadron.

Commodore Harwood's instincts took him towards the river Plate and the raider was confronted by the cruisers *Exeter*, *Ajax* and *Achilles*. Fortune favoured the brave: *Exeter* survived serious damage and the two light cruisers pressed home their attack despite the ineffectiveness of their 6-inch guns against the German's heavy armour. The *Graf Spee* sought sanctuary in neutral Montevideo. Bravery was followed by bluff and the German captain, believing himself blockaded by overwhelming forces, promptly scuttled his ship. Hitler's navy had been very publicly humiliated – the immolation of the *Graf Spee* being reported live on American radio – and Harwood's cruisers returned to an ecstatic reception in Britain.

The same ingredients of British boldness versus German caution seemed to be repeated in April 1940 when British and French forces intervened in Norway. The battlecruisers *Scharnhorst* and *Gneisenau* displayed none of the fighting spirit of their predecessors when they encountered HMS *Renown*; the Germans swinging away immediately, creating a stern chase in which the World War I veteran piled on steam in a vain attempt to overhaul Hitler's two most powerful warships. A German destroyer squadron in Narvik fjord was attacked by British destroyers twice, the second time supported by the veteran battleship HMS *Warspite*. The German squadron was annihilated and a U-boat that tried to intervene was sunk for good measure. Fleet Air Arm dive-bombers became the first carrier-borne aircraft to sink an enemy warship when they swooped on the *Königsberg*. However, the German navy soon had its revenge. *Scharnhorst* and *Gneisenau* ran into the aircraft carrier *Glorious* en route to the UK after the Norwegian campaign had been abandoned. With no air cover – and none of her aircraft airborne – she was sunk despite the heroic sacrifice of the escorting destroyers.

In May 1940 the German army burst through the Ardennes to crush the western allies. It enjoyed no significant advantage in numbers, and was outnumbered in both tanks and aircraft, but in *Blitzkrieg* the German army had a winning tactical method; and for determined professionalism its soldiers and airmen had no equals. It fell to Lord Gort, VC to grasp the nettle and save the British army to fight another day. He ordered the BEF to fall back on Dunkirk, effectively abandoning France to her fate. The Royal Navy confounded all expectations by evacuating the BEF aided in this supreme hour of need by all manner of volunteer craft. Rescuing the soldiers kept Britain in the war, but the German triumph posed the gravest danger to the United Kingdom since the French invasion scares of the 1770s. And conquest by Nazi Germany was a far grimmer prospect than a raid by one of Louis XV's generals. In the event, the RAF prevented the Luftwaffe from achieving air superiority over southern England. Germany's half-hearted invasion plans were abandoned in the autumn of 1940 and Hitler turned his attention to his true enemy: Soviet Russia.

After the fall of France, the German U-boats began to operate from the French Atlantic coast. Freed from the long passage around Scotland, they were able to mount increasingly deadly attacks on Britain's Atlantic lifeline. For three years, under the ruthless direction of Admiral Dönitz, German

U-boats waged a savage war from the Caribbean to the Arctic, the most critical battles occuring in the bleak wastes of the North Atlantic. Beyond the range of land-based aircraft, convoys and their escorts struggled against an invisible foe whose presence was only discovered as torpedoes slammed into hulls. In World War I, from 1916 to 1918, the British Army had shouldered an increasing share of the Allied burden, fighting and ultimately defeating the main body of the German army; but in World War II, in the critical years of 1940–3, Britain's national survival depended on the Royal Navy. No amount of 'digging for victory' in Britain could compensate for the loss of imported food and raw materials defended at such cost by British and Canadian warships.

Pre-war faith in ASDIC (sonar) was confounded by experience. War-time conditions proved very different from peacetime exercises in the Channel and convoys seldom had either modern escort vessels or peace-time-trained crews. In any case, the most daring U-boat skippers ran in on the surface at night, relying on the U-boat's low silhouette to hide them from red-eyed lookouts. Supported by their own long-range aircraft, and as-sembled into 'Wolf Packs', the U-boats were able to make co-ordinated attacks against which the frantic efforts of a few corvettes could do little. Practical military necessity made for a brutal war. Survivors huddled in open boats were often seen at the height of a battle, only to drift into oblivion. Crews of tankers, or freighters packed with iron ore, were lucky to get to a boat if their ship was hit.

The war in the North Atlantic hinged as much on scientists as on seamen, and the pendulum of technical advantage swung to and fro. The British acquired radar to detect U-boats running on the surface, and the early U-boat 'aces' were killed or captured. But German intelligence cracked British naval codes and the U-boats were able to ambush a succession of convoys, concentrating all available submarines against overworked escorts. However, Britain's priceless ULTRA decrypts provided fuller and more frequent intelligence of U-boat activity; convoys were re-routed around the 'Wolf Packs', and Dönitz's men found themselves searching empty sea. The turning-point occurred in 1943 as a combination of very-long-range aircraft, centimetric radar and improved anti-submarine weapons like 'Hedgehog' inflicted catastrophic losses on the U-boats. Had Churchill's cabinet managed to prise a few squadrons of four-engined aircraft away from Bomber Command a little sooner, the U-boats would have been neutralised earlier.

New technology was complemented by new 'scientific' tactics, honed ashore by a 'wargaming' programme, the fruit of pioneering operational research. Statistical analysis of every convoy battle and the first-hand experiences of convoy commanders were combined to create an ever-expanding data base. Following the scheme of 'setting a thief to catch a thief', veteran British submarine commanders added their experience: even ex-submariner Admiral Horton, C-in-C Western Approaches met his match (at the hands of a WRNS officer!) when he tried his skills against state-of-the-art escort tactics at a map exercise in Liverpool.

America's colossal industrial resources enabled merchant shipping losses to be made good, and a vast army could cross the Atlantic, assembling in England for the liberation of Europe. It was fortunate indeed that that army made its landing when it did. In 1945 the technical advantage was suddenly regained by Germany: its Type XXI U-boats rendered most Allied anti-submarine weapons obsolete. A new armada was poised in the Norwegian fjords, but the crews never had time to train. As the avenging Russian army swept towards Berlin, thousands of German naval personnel were thrown into the land battle. The Baltic training areas were overrun and the former commander of U-boats enjoyed a brief interlude as Hitler's successor before the Nazi state was obliterated. Winston Churchill rightly regarded the U-boat as the single greatest threat to British survival: had the Royal Navy failed to defeat Dönitz's submarines, the United Kingdom would have lost the war.

German surface ships made a succession of forays into the Atlantic, in the case of the 'pocket battleship' *Scheer* into the Indian Ocean as well; *Scharnhorst* and *Gneisenau* making a particularly deadly pair of surface raiders. One convoy survived thanks to the presence of the battleship *Ramillies*, two others were granted time to scatter by the gallant sacrifice of their armed merchant cruiser escorts, *Rawalpindi* and *Jervis Bay* respectively. The most famous raider, *Bismarck*, was sent to the bottom on her maiden voyage – without sinking a single merchant ship – but not before sinking the pride of the pre-war Navy, HMS *Hood*. In a ghastly reminder of Jutland, the old battlecruiser blew up and took all but three of her complement down with her. Brought to bay by a handful of Swordfish biplanes, *Bismarck* was destroyed by *King George V* and *Rodney*. The subsequent escape up the English channel of her consort, the heavy cruiser *Prinz Eugen* together with *Scharnhorst* and *Gneisenau* was presented as a triumph by German propaganda. In fact the return of this powerful squadron from Brest to Germany effectively ended the surface campaign in the Atlantic.

As the Battle of the Atlantic intensified, a new and even more savage campaign began in the world's most unforgiving seas. The German invasion of Russia in June 1941 transformed the war. If Hitler could knock out Russia – as the German army had managed to do in 1917 – the Nazi war machine would control the resources of eastern Europe and the oil reserves of the Caucasus. Having carved up Poland in alliance with Hitler, Stalin was suddenly transformed into an ally and the Royal Navy was charged with escorting supplies of war material to Russia's Arctic ports. With the Luftwaffe based in Norway and furiously learning how to launch torpedoes from aircraft – a tactic it had fortunately disdained as impractical before the war – and most major enemy surface units concentrating in the fjords, it was clear that the Arctic convoys would meet with determined opposition.

In the land of the midnight sun, there was no cover from enemy aircraft, but only the seasonal retreat of the polar ice cap granted adequate sea room. In the darkness of winter, the sea conditions were awful beyond description. Convoys were assembled off Iceland and shepherded around Norway to deliver their vital cargoes; with little or no protection against air attack. *Bismarck*'s sistership, the formidable *Tirpitz*, was soon ensconced in her Arctic lair, poised to lead an overwhelming assault on the convoys and their escorts. The mistaken belief that she was about to pounce led to the notorious order for Convoy PQ17 to scatter. Dispersed to avoid destruction by the enemy battleship, the merchantships were picked off by a deadly combination of U-boats and bomber aircraft.

The German surface forces were frustrated again and again as British signals intelligence betrayed their plans. Interceptions that were achieved were defeated by the incredibly aggressive defence mounted by the Royal Navy escorts. Often hopelessly inferior to the powerful enemy cruisers, the escorts' boldness culminated in the Battle of the Barents Sea in which a far stronger German squadron was driven off and the convoy saved. Hitler was so furious that he sacked Admiral Raeder, the German C-in-C, and ordered all heavy ships to be paid off. Thus Admiral Dönitz succeeded to command the *Kriegsmarine*. He preserved some of the major units but *Scharnhorst* was intercepted and sunk by a surface action group led by *Duke of York* in December 1943. *Tirpitz* would remain a terrible menace until cornered at her anchorage by a succession of Fleet Air Arm strikes, and X-craft miniature submarine attacks. She was administered the coup-de-grace by 617 Squadron, RAF, in 1944. Russian co-operation during the Arctic convoys was marred by Bolshevik suspicion: the last time British forces landed in Murmansk they had come to strangle the revolution in its cradle. The unforgiving attitude of the Soviet authorities continued after 1945 when families that had hosted British sailors were promptly arrested by the NKVD. Only in the last years of the Communist regime was the contribution of the Arctic convoys and the sacrifice of hundreds of British sailors finally acknowledged.

The Royal Navy's base at Malta had been vacated by British capital ships well in advance of Italy's declaration of war in May 1940. But before the Royal Navy could take on the powerful Italian fleet, it had the disagreeable task of neutralising its former French allies. There could be no question of the Germans laying their hands on the powerful French squadron based in North Africa. Negotiations having failed, it was Vice-Admiral Somerville's unpleasant duty to sink that which the French would not surrender. The ensuing bombardment of Mers-el-Kebir was the nadir of Anglo-French relations in this century. The battleship *Bretagne* blew up and sank; *Provence* was damaged and over a thousand French sailors died. A similar battle at Alexandria was fortunately averted but a hastily prepared attack on Dakar in September 1940, was driven off by French naval units and aircraft.

In July 1940 the Italian fleet put to sea to cover a large convoy sailing to Libya, carrying reinforcements for their large army in North Africa. The Royal Navy intervened, Force 'H' sortieing from Gibraltar and the aircraft carrier *Eagle* launching its elderly Swordfish biplanes against the Italian fleet. Enemy shore-based aircraft failed to support their fleet and the heavy units clashed briefly in what became known as the battle of Calabria. Jutland veteran HMS *Warspite* immediately straddled the battleship *Guilio Cesare* but contact was broken before long. A belated Italian air strike landed bombs dangerously close to HMS *Ark Royal*.

On 11 November 1940 the aircraft-carrier HMS *Illustrious* flew off 21 Swordfish. They made their stately progress towards the Italian naval base at Taranto, where all six Italian battleships lay at anchor. They achieved complete surprise, dropping torpedoes by the ghostly light of parachute flares as they weaved past lines of barrage balloons. Three battleships were hit and left with their decks awash and keels resting on the harbour bottom. Although Italian shipyards put right the physical damage within a year, the moral impact proved more lasting and subsequent Italian naval activity was characterised by excessive caution.

Subsequent British naval operations went to the opposite extreme, as the Royal Navy first escorted British and Commonwealth divisions to Greece and then rescued them from the inevitable disaster. General O'Connor's brilliant victories in North Africa were cut short on Churchill's orders; the army poised to overrun the last Italian ports was halted and broken up to provide a scratch force in Greece. Hopelessly outnumbered and outclassed by the formidable German army then assembling in Yugoslavia and Bulgaria, this expeditionary force went the way of its predecessors in Norway and France. The Balkan *Blitzkrieg* began in April, German forces taking just over a fortnight to cut their way to the Peloponnese. For the third time in twelve months, the Royal Navy evacuated thousands of exhausted troops from open beaches and minor ports. The Luftwaffe reigned supreme, and to be caught inshore by daylight was to court disaster. Nevertheless, over 50,000 men were brought off safely.

Over 30,000 British troops were posted on Crete. Unhelpfully, the island's main ports are all on the northern coast. Ships were condemned to a long voyage around the island, all within easy range of enemy airstrips in southern Greece. The British garrison was clustered around the three airfields which were left operational despite the withdrawal of the few surviving RAF fighters. On 20 May, the Luftwaffe airstrikes intensified as Ju-52 transports thundered low over the coast, white canopies scattering behind them. Despite fearful losses, the German paratroops managed to secure enough of Maleme airfield to fly in reinforcements. The lodgement survived desperate counter-attacks and continued to expand. Another evacuation loomed. In the last week of May, the Royal Navy extricated the garrison but incessant air attacks sank the cruisers *Gloucester*, *Fiji* and *Calcutta* and the destroyers *Kelly*, *Kashmir*, *Greyhound*, *Hereward*, and *Imperial*. With another three cruisers badly hit and the battleship *Barham* damaged, Admiral Cunningham was asked if the sacrifice was justified. His observation that it takes three years to build a ship, but it would take three hundred years to rebuild a tradition cannot be gainsaid.

Besieged from the air, Malta came perilously close to defeat. Convoys to resupply the island were escorted by the bulk of the Mediterranean fleet including battleships and aircraft carriers. British 'U' class submarines operating from Malta were obliged to submerge during the day, surfacing in the harbour at night when the bombers had departed. The 10th Flotilla's attacks on Italian shipping drove General Rommel to distraction as his Afrika Korps ran out of fuel and ammunition. Enemy ground operations were frustrated and delayed, and the steady attrition of the Italian merchant marine could not be countered by new construction. However, the submariners' own losses were severe too.

On 6 June 1944 the Allied armies landed in Normandy, withstood the German counter-attacks and broke out to destroy the German forces in northern France. By August, German losses in the 'Falaise pocket' exceeded 400,000 and the issue of the war in Europe was no longer in doubt. The D-Day landings were such a spectacular success that it is often assumed that victory was inevitable, provided the Royal Navy co-ordinated the vast Allied armada of some 1,200 warships (almost 80 per cent of them British). Arguably, by the dawn of 6 June the invasion was bound to succeed provided the weather held; Allied deception measures and catastrophic strategic decisions by the German high command left the Normandy area relatively lightly manned with reserves too distant to intervene in time. The success of British and Canadian anti-submarine forces over the previous two years ensured that the German navy was in no position to contest control of the Channel. By the summer of 1944 the Germans had lost the Battle of the

Atlantic. There were 36 U-boats waiting for the invasion in their indestructible concrete fortresses on the west coast of France, but their attempts to get at the troop ships were frustrated by six British and four Canadian anti-submarine warfare groups which included three escort carriers and over fifty destroyers and frigates. Despite desperate interventions by the handful of remaining German destroyers and torpedo boats, the Allied navies conducted over 300,000 men, 50,000 vehicles and 100,000 tons of supplies to the beachheads in the first six days of the invasion.

With the liberation of France underway, the Royal Navy was finally able to release enough major units to the Far East to resume operations against Japan. There is a legendary naval signal from December 1941 when two British convoys met in mid-Atlantic. 'Commence hostilities with Japan' flashed one escort; 'Permission to finish breakfast first' came the reply. Such naval sang-froid masked the disagreeable truth that by the time Japan declared war, the Royal Navy was already at full stretch fighting in the Atlantic, Mediterranean and Arctic. Disastrous government decisions of the 1920s and 30s had seen the naval base at Singapore expanded and fortified but no ships built to operate from it. The Imperial Japanese Navy, created in the image of the Royal Navy and a British ally during World War I, was now poised to turn on its former mentor.

War with Japan had been imminent since the US oil embargo imposed in the summer of 1941. The Royal Navy proposed to send one or two modernised Queen Elizabeth class battleships, plus four of the old 'R' class and a couple of aircraft-carriers, to Singapore. However, the damage or loss of three battleships in the Mediterranean and the damaging of the carrier *Indomitable* while working up in the Caribbean frustrated any sensible deployment. Overruling both Admiral Pound and his chief-of-staff Admiral Phillips, Winston Churchill insisted on sending *Prince of Wales* and the World War I battlecruiser, *Repulse*, without waiting for additional units. In retrospect, it is perhaps just as well that Pound's idea of ordering both Nelson class battleships to the Far East was overtaken by events. 'Force Z', as the battleship group was christened, included five destroyers and was led by the prickly Admiral Phillips, whose opposition to Churchill led him to be ordered from London to Ceylon to become commander-in-chief, Far Eastern Fleet.

On 8 December 1941, 'Force Z' sailed from Singapore to intercept Japanese invasion forces bound for Malaya. The bulk of Japan's naval airpower was on the other side of the Pacific after its attack on Pearl Harbor, and the troopships were escorted by a few cruisers and (as distant cover) two modernised battlecruisers. Air cover was supposed to be provided by the handful of obsolescent RAF aircraft in Malaya. Communications failures, excellent scouting by Japanese submarines and a mistaken report of landings further south led to 'Force Z' being attacked by Japanese shore-based bombers flying from Indochina. Phillips, a dedicated battleship Admiral who had been notoriously sceptical of airpower, had perhaps based his judgement on the often ineffective high-level bombing conducted by enemy forces in the Mediterranean. But Japan's Mitsubishi G-3M twin-enginned torpedo bombers not only had a combat radius of over 1,200 miles – enabling them to strike so unexpectedly – but well-trained aircrew able to deliver co-ordinated torpedo strikes from both beams. Both battleships were sunk, Phillips going down with *Prince of Wales*. His flagship was the first modern battleship to be sunk by air attack while at sea and able to manoeuvre freely – unlike the anchored Italian battlefleet at Taranto a year earlier.

Singapore surrendered on 15 February 1942: the greatest military defeat ever suffered by British forces. The River Plate veteran *Exeter* was among the casualties when Japanese surface forces appeared off Java. Then the Japanese aircraft-carrier fleet arrived in the Indian Ocean, raiding as far as Ceylon (Sri Lanka) and sinking the British carrier *Hermes* in the process. Although the four 'R' class battleships had now rounded the Cape, without a modern aircraft-carrier force, there was little the Royal Navy could do but wait for the storm to pass.

By late 1944 the British had finally assembled an effective carrier task force (equipped with American aircraft) in the Indian Ocean. The surviving King George V class battleships, including the fourth unit, *Howe* and the French *Richelieu*, were fast enough to accompany carriers in action. Airstrikes on Japanese bases in the Dutch East Indies were achieved with the carriers supported by US-style fleet train of tankers. As 'Task Force 57', under the overall command of US Admiral Nimitz, the British Pacific Fleet attacked Japanese island air bases from Formosa (Taiwan) to Okinawa. There they received the suicidal attentions of Japanese Kamikaze aircraft which caused serious damage to several ships. On the night of 15–16 May 1945 the Royal Navy fought its last major surface action, when a destroyer flotilla exploited freak radar conditions to intercept and sink the heavy-cruiser *Haguro* in a classic torpedo attack.

The Royal Navy ended World War II second only in size to the US Navy. There were 864,000 people serving on ship or shore, including at one point 74,000 women in the WRNS. This incredible expansion and the unprecedented number of 'hostilities only' personnel brought inevitable difficulties, but the second German attempt to starve Britain into submission this century had been defeated. The seas were made safe and the armies of the New World could cross them.

2

From 1939 to Dunkirk

LIEUTENANT FRANK LAYARD, RN

In the piping days of peace between the two world wars, when perhaps there were more opportunities and more time for relaxation, life in destroyers was particularly good. There was much inter-ship and inter-flotilla rivalry and competition of course, but when altogether in Sliema, or in Portsmouth, there was also a great entente and comradeship throughout the Destroyer Force which made for a very happy existence.

Wardroom guest nights in particular could be the occasion for much fun and hilarity. After the preliminary consumption of a good quantity of gin, all would sit down to dinner. The food would not be exactly up to Savoy standards but the messman always made a special effort to put on quite a reasonable meal which would be washed down with some of the best red wine. When the table was cleared the port would be passed and the King's health drunk.

After the port had been round twice, the mess President for the evening (who was generally the captain) would order a round of brandy 'à la Russe'. This consisted of a liqueur glass of brandy with a slice of lemon balanced on the top of the glass and a spoonful of sugar on the lemon. When all were served there would be a shout of '*Viva, Viva, Viva, Bungo*', at which everyone immediately took the lemon and sugar in one hand, tossed off the brandy and then immediately put the lemon and sugar in their mouth. The effect was somewhat breathtaking but extremely pleasant and was almost immediately repeated, so that everyone now was gaining good flying speed. The record of 'Night and Day' would then be put on the gramophone which everyone would sing very lustily. By this time all present as they rose from the table were more than ready for some active and strenuous amusement.

There were several ways in which energies could be expended. For instance, chair tricks. The old wooden wardroom chairs were heavy and very strong and would stand up to any amount of rough usage. There could be a race by two or more competitors through the backs of these chairs which was guaranteed to wipe off the front studs of any boiled shirt and would cause excruciating pain to all but the slimmest when their hips became firmly jammed as they tried to squeeze through. There were other tricks which only the more agile would attempt. For example, two chairs would be placed back-to-back about a yard apart with a broom handle stretched across the back and a shoe pushed down over each of the four corners of the chair backs. The competitor would then be handed a walking-stick and would take his seat on the broom stick with his feet crossed in front of him, keeping his balance with the aid of the walking-stick. He now had to try and remove in turn each of the four shoes from the chair backs with the walking stick. As soon as he raised the stick off the deck and lost its support he started to overbalance and so the movement of flicking off each shoe had to be done with the utmost speed and precision so that the stick could be grounded again if the competitor was to remain on his perch.

In another trick the victim had to sit on a chair and then remove a pin from the bottom of the farside back leg with his teeth without touching the deck. Only the most agile could get round and down behind the chair altogether. There were other no less testing tricks requiring good balance which was generally a bit lacking by that time.

'Captain D's shoot' provided plenty of amusement. The person representing the captain of the firing ship was seated at the end of the wardroom table clad in oilskin and sou'wester with five darts in his hand and a dart board representing the target was fixed to the bulkhead at the other end of the table. The staff conducting the shoot then took up their stations. Two each side of the chair, two armed with soda water siphons in front and to the side of the chair, and two with match boxes level with the dart board. At the command 'Carry out the practice ordered' all lights were extinguished, the chair was violently rocked to and fro to represent the motion of the ship, soda water to represent spray was liberally squirted in the captain's face and matches to represent star shells were flicked up from both sides to illuminate the target.

Thirty seconds was allowed for the shoot during which time the captain had to get off his five darts but it was seldom, as far as I can remember, that the target was ever hit.

Another rather expensive game was sometimes played. Competitors were placed with their backs to the ship's side on the port side of the mess and would each be handed a ten-inch gramophone record of the old breakable sort. The scuttles on the starboard side were then opened and the object of the game was to hurl the record through the scuttle. If truly aimed it would pass through comfortably but of course the majority hit the ship's side or the scuttle frame and shattered into many small pieces amid loud cheers from the onlookers. There was of course a limit to the number of mess records which could thus be sacrificed but there were generally enough old chipped and scratched ones which nobody minded breaking.

Another game we had consisted of two players who lay on the deck facing each other, blindfolded, clasping left hand to left hand and with a tightly rolled newspaper or magazine in the right hand. One shouted, 'Are you there, Moriarty?' The other replied, 'Yes' and then endeavoured to avoid the blow his opponent tried to land on his head with the weapon he had in his right hand.

Perhaps today, in the 1990s, this sounds rather stupid, tipsy horseplay. On these occasions we were certainly noisy and excited. A little flushed with wine perhaps. But never can I remember anything approaching drunkenness. Life then was far less grim and earnest than it is today and perhaps there was more scope and opportunity for youthful exuberance of spirit while at the same time maintaining the high standard of keenness and efficiency which has at all times been demanded in the Service.

APPRENTICE MIKE SHERWOOD, MN

I always wanted to go away to sea and my father, who was at Gallipoli, with the Naval Division, encouraged me. Then, when the time came to decide what I was going to do, I went to be a cadet on the *Conway*, the Merchant Navy's training ship on the Mersey. I was also selected to train for the RNR. The training was terribly physical, and there was a lot of schoolwork, but it was a bloody marvellous life.

The *Conway* was an old sailing ship like the *Victory*. First thing in the morning we'd get straight into our gym gear and go right up the starboard rigging, over the top, and down the port rigging. We just wore shorts and gym shoes, no matter how cold it was. Some would then do exercise on the deck while others would go out along the yards and pretend to take in sails for half an hour. We then had a wash in lukewarm water down in the bows of the ship with a bitter wind blowing through the anchor hose pipes.

My cadet training finished in June 1939, when I had just turned seventeen. Then I went off as an apprentice officer to the Merchant Navy. I was a junior apprentice in the Port Line, a branch of Cunard. They had beautiful ships bringing frozen meat back from Australia. You could choose which company you wanted to go to, as the ships were coming up and down the Mersey all the time, so you saw the type of ship in any company and knew their trade routes.

So off I went on the *Port Adelaide*, an old coal burner. There were three apprentice officers on the ship. Port Line was one of the best companies for looking after their apprentices. Other companies used them as cheap labour, but Port Line made sure we learnt everything.

First thing in the morning we nipped down to the pantry where we made our cup of tea or cocoa. There was a big toaster there with fresh bread every morning made by the baker and we used to cut huge great slices off and toast them. Under the counter there were rows of big jam tins. It was sheer hunger. Then out to work at seven o'clock. One of us would be on the wheel and steer the ship with the quartermaster standing by. One would scrub out the wheelhouse on his hands and knees with a bucket and a scrubber, then he'd go all down the wings of the bridge and the other would scrub out the chart house behind the bridge until it was sparkling. Then at eight o'clock we got cleaned up and into our best uniforms for breakfast. On those Australian ships they didn't half feed you, especially at breakfast. We'd start off with fruit, then cereals. The next course was fish: fried, buttered or smoked; then we had meat, a choice of ham, beef, pork or brawn. Then came your bacon and eggs, sausage and black pudding. Next came rice cakes and honey or oat cakes and golden syrup. When that was done there were little brown and white rolls, just made that morning. We would be eating like trojans to get through this lot because we had to be up on deck for 8.30 grabbing rolls, slapping marmalade on them and putting them in our pockets. It was a massive meal, and lunch was the equivalent and dinner at night even more so. But still we were always hungry.

Between breakfast and lunchtime we would work with the crew on deck and if anything interesting was going on we would be put to that. If not there was just the donkey work, like painting and washing down. After lunch we would do the same sort of thing.

We finished at four and then we would have to do our school work. The Chief Officer would probably have us in his cabin for seamanship, the Second Officer for navigation, the Third Officer for signals. They would have us in their cabins, give us a bit of a lecture and set questions and answers. We would have to go back and sit and work at them in our own special notebooks. The officers went through our books on Saturdays. The Chief Officer would check over the seamanship questions and add his remarks in the right hand column in green ink. On Sunday mornings they went up to the Skipper and he put his comments down in the left hand column in red ink. Then, when you got back from your voyage and arrived, say, in London, the Marine Superintendent would ask for the apprentices' books. We were scared stiff of him, but it was a marvellous system, a very good training.

At night when the captain, officers and passengers went down for their dinner, the Fourth Officer took charge of the bridge. We apprentices used to sit with our notebooks beside the funnel which was over the galley and the

Fourth Mate would flash the lamp to teach us Morse. We would have our dinner in half an hour. The old chef used to shout out, 'Have you finished that yet?' 'No not yet.' 'Right we're finished now, chef,' 'Right, hold on.' He would throw a bone, say like a leg of mutton, and we would fall on it like dogs. We had just had a monstrous bloody meal, yet we could still gnaw the bone.

On each trip we had to spend a fortnight in the engine-room under the Second Engineer and the same coming back. On the outward trip we were trimmers in the stokehold. As trimmer you would go into the bunkers and fill a wheelbarrow up with coal, take it into the stokehold and tip it out for the stokers who shovelled it into the boilers. On the return trip we were stoking. I wasn't all that big, but the firemen were bloody marvellous, even though they were such tough guys. They would see you struggling, and then show you how to do the job.

On our way out to Australia war was declared. I remember being on the bridge with the Second Officer, a big tall fellow called Ring. He always had a bit of a sardonic twist to him. He said, 'Well, Sherwood, this will be something for you to write home about: it's war.' I wondered what the hell he was talking about. To me war being declared meant nothing.

When we reached Australia we had to go and be fitted with a 6-inch gun. The gun's crew was made up from us apprentices and various members of the crew. We had to go over to the naval base at Rushcutter's Bay and learn all about guns. When the time came for us to sail they put on board a DEMS (Defensively Equipped Merchant Ship) gunner, a Royal Navy fellow to look after the gun and see that we knew what we were doing. We steamed out to give this gun a trial, out through Sydney Harbour. I was the sight setter. I used to stand at the side of the gun and say, 'Range so-and-so . . .' We loaded it up, the gunner said 'Fire,' and there was such a clatter we weren't ready for it. I was knocked flat to the ground. Everyone else was flat around me. There was a great roar and commotion from below in the deck house where all the stewards and cooks lived because nobody had told them we were firing and all the bunks and everything fell down.

We didn't feel that we were at war.

LIEUTENANT ARTHUR HEZLET, RN

I was not a volunteer for the submarine service. I wanted to be a gunnery officer but the Navy hadn't any volunteers for submarines at the time so they had to choose whoever they could.

There are two great advantages of serving in a submarine. One was that your pay nearly doubled. As a lieutenant you were paid 13s.6d. a day. You got six shillings extra for submarines and three shillings for every night you slept in them, so you were very substantially better off than anyone in general service. The other was that you got a very early command, generally at about the age of twenty-eight. So after a little while in submarines I said, 'Kindly transfer my name onto the volunteers. I will stay now I'm here.' I went off to China straight after doing the submarine course and was promoted to Lieutenant as I got there. I was navigator, and then the torpedo officer of a submarine called *Regulus* in China where we kept one eye on the Japanese and also on problems like anti-piracy patrols.

In 1938, just before the war, I went as First Lieutenant to one of the little training submarines, an H-boat of first world war vintage, which we thought of as being real old Ming. Then on 1 June 1939 the *Thetis* disaster occurred. *Thetis* was a T-Class submarine on trials off the Mersey. In those days a ship wasn't Admiralty property until it had finished its trials. So the firm's engineers controlled everything during the trials and if the trials were successful then it became a warship and the crew took over. But no civilians knew how to dive a submarine so they had to request the Admiralty to take over for the diving part of the trials. With the *Thetis* there was, I understand, a mix-up with the naval crew expecting certain valves to be left in certain positions when they weren't. They let the sea in through a torpedo tube which sank her in a very short time. Four men were saved from this submarine but the rest, 99 in all, were drowned. This total was considerably more than the crew because it had the firm's people on board for the trials. The captain, first lieutenant and engineer of the next submarine, the *Trident*, being built went out in her and were also drowned.

So suddenly, with this frightful crisis, I was sent up to Birkenhead to take the place of the first lieutenant of *Trident*. The *Trident* was completed just after the war began and we went to sea in October 1939 and straight into the war. I remained in *Trident* for the first six months of the war and for the Norwegian campaign.

SUB-LIEUTENANT JOHN ROXBURGH, RN

Come August 1939 it was obvious the war was coming. Convoys for merchant shipping had already started. I was serving in the destroyer *Walpole*. I'll never forget the Prime Minister, Neville Chamberlain, announcing the start of war, at eleven o'clock on a Sunday morning, 3rd September. After that we were at war, our depth-charges were primed and we were ready to go. A quarter of an hour after war had been declared we found a submarine echo which we attacked and dropped eleven charges. We were never credited with a submarine and I should think it was quite likely a shoal of fish or a rock, but it really got one's mind racing. There was I, a young chap of twenty, actually dropping things to kill people. It was quite exciting.

STOKER 2ND CLASS VERNON COLES, RN

My first ship was HMS *Faulknor* under Captain Charles Daniels. The day war broke out we were the leader of the 8th Destroyer Flotilla in Scapa Flow. We all had the wind up, expecting torpedoes all over the place because we were in such a vulnerable position. However we eased down after about ten days, when each day became the same as the next – all part of life's routine. We were at action stations at five o'clock in the morning and again at sundown, so it was rather tiring.

The battle fleet was taken to sea under the command of 'Big Gun Forbes' – Admiral Sir Charles Forbes. The flagship was HMS *Nelson* and we used to accompany HMS *Rodney* and the aircraft-carrier *Ark Royal* too. We'd bring them in and they'd stay in for a few days and we'd go back out again on U-boat sweeps.

I saw my first real action on 14 September 1939. We were exercising with *Ark Royal* and three destroyers off St Kilda. Suddenly, during the mid-afternoon, there were two terrific explosions – we went to action stations immediately. We learnt that a German U-boat had fired two torpedoes at *Ark Royal*. Their torpedoes had magnetic heads on so, when they came within the magnetic field of *Ark Royal*, they both exploded. Otherwise she would have been hit.

We sailed straight down the torpedo tracks, dropped a full pattern of depth-charges and up she came. It was U-39. We took them all prisoner; we rescued the men in the whalers and then brought them on board. They were badly shaken, as anybody would have been on the receiving end of a couple of depth-charges.

Captain Daniels had the German U-boat captain interrogated. I talked to some of the German prisoners. They thought they were going to be shot and they were actually surprised at the way they were treated. We had to communicate with them in sign language, but we gave them cigarettes and things. They were rather wet when they came aboard, so they were supplied with blankets while all their clothes and underwear were taken down to the boiler room to dry off. Their vests all had the German swastika on, so off they came during the night – they were taken as souvenirs. The Germans were most upset about that.

We off-loaded them in Scapa Flow. That was the first U-boat of the war to go down and they were the first naval prisoners-of-war.

LIEUTENANT CHARLES LAMB, RN

HMS *Courageous* sailed from Plymouth under cover of darkness on 3rd September 1939. She was provided with an escort of four destroyers. It was anticipated that the ship would attract U-boat attacks, when the destroyers would achieve the miraculous results with their Asdic which were forecast so confidently. The presence of the ship would also serve to distract the attention of the enemy from the merchant ships and their valuable cargoes and their passengers, hurrying home to the British Isles. The two Swordfish squadrons (24 Swordfish) on board would provide the major deterrent to the U-boats.

If *Courageous* had been a battleship she would have been escorted by a small fleet of vessels, none of which would have been permitted to leave the screen except to hunt in the immediate vicinity. Our four destroyers were there to protect *Courageous*, but they also had to go submarine-hunting and answer calls for help from distressed shipping, and throughout those opening days of the war there were seldom more than two escorts within sight of the ship. *Courageous* presented an easy target.

On board, the attitude of everyone was carefree and casual. We carried no fighter aircraft, and hundreds of miles west of the Scilly Isles there appeared to be no need. We flew on various types of search in answer to the distress calls that came flooding in from all directions. In the aircraft, our only means of communicating with the parent ship, if an answer was required, was with an Aldis lamp when she was within sight.

The transition from peace to war takes time, and in *Courageous* it wasn't until the following Sunday, 17th September, that the ship's company really woke up to the fact that we were at war; and even then we needed a German submarine's captain to bring the fact home. His demonstration was most convincing: at eight o'clock, on a warm Sunday evening, he fired two torpedoes at the ship, which struck us on the port side, almost simultaneously, and we sank in twenty minutes.

At three in the afternoon, on that same Sunday 17th September, eight pilots and observers had trooped into the wardroom for tea. We had been standing-by all day, in case of emergency calls, and there was only an hour to go before the other squadron took over the duty. As our Flight Commander pointed out, if we had to take off before our duty ended at four o'clock, it would be our last opportunity to eat or drink for many hours.

My observer, Robert Wall, brought his sandwiches to the place next to me, and we sat in silence, sipping our tea. All of a sudden our peace was shattered by the blare of the ship's bugler sounding off 'flying stations' on the tannoy. I joined the general scramble out of the wardroom and up the ladders to the crewroom in the island, where we kept our flying clothing. Clad in our overalls and helmets and goggles, we ran to our aircraft. While we ran up our engines and tested the magnetos, the observers were briefed by the Operations Officer. They then sprinted down to the deck to their aircraft, carrying their navigation instruments and Bigsworth Boards – a square wooden frame fitted with parallel rulers to which they clipped a plotting diagram, or a chart, so that they could navigate with the board resting on their knees in the confined space of the rear cockpit. Behind them, facing aft, sat the telegraphist air gunner (TAG), Doug Hemingway, who, as well as manning the Lewis gun when it was needed, also tuned the aircraft's radio to the ship's W/T frequency to keep a listening watch.

When Wall had climbed into the rear cockpit, and attached himself to the aircraft by the safety wire which clipped on to the harness between the observer and the air gunner's legs – obviously known as the 'Jockstrap' – he called me on the voice-pipe to tell me what we were about to do. Rubber voice-pipes between both cockpits connected to the earpieces of all three flying helmets, known as Gosport Tubes, and were very effective. It was surprising how clearly one could hear by this primitive method of communication.

We were the last of the eight Swordfish to take off and while we watched the others roll down the middle of the flight-deck, and clamber into the air, Wall briefed me down the voice-pipe. Apparently a big passenger liner, the SS *Kaliristan*, was being threatened by a U-boat on the surface. The German had ordered the crew and passengers to take to their boats, before it sank the ship. She was thought to be ninety or one hundred miles to the south, on the Atlantic edge of the Bay of Biscay. When I opened the throttle that afternoon I was the last pilot to take-off from *Courageous* – and was to be the last to land.

Two of the ship's four escorts raced off at maximum speed to the reported sighting of SS *Kaliristan*, and *Courageous* altered course in the same direction and increased her speed to 25 knots – almost the maximum. But because of the W/T silence she was unable to inform us. I heard later that the destroyers recovered the passengers and the crew, but met another merchant ship and transferred them, and they all got home safely. An attack was made on the submarine, which was still on the surface, and succeeded in making it dive. Six of the aircraft all landed safely before Robert and I, and the aircraft on our immediate right, had reached the furthermost point of our search.

When we returned there was no sign of *Courageous*, and we began our square-search immediately. We had a questionable forty-five minutes of flying time remaining, but would almost certainly run out of fuel at a quarter to eight. I flew four minutes to the west, four minutes to the north, eight minutes to the east and then eight minutes to the south, and altered course to start the fifth leg – sixteen minutes to the west – with a sinking heart. At the end of that leg, if we reached it, we would have been searching for forty minutes, and might have four or five minutes' petrol remaining. Neither Wall nor I spoke. We were both thinking of Nigel Playfair and his young observer, exactly a week before, and it seemed certain that like them, we too were to disappear without trace. It would be dark within an hour, and the mist which obscured the horizon was deepening with evening shadow. There was no possible chance of rescue out there, five hundred miles west of the Scilly Isles.

At the end of that sixteen-minute leg to the west, flying into the sun, which was only a few degrees above the hazy horizon, I began my turn to the north, cursing the lack of horizon which made accurate flying difficult. The blind-flying panel and artificial horizon had not appeared on the scene then, and all we had to guide us was a Reid and Sigrist Turn-and-Bank indicator, and some red mercury in a small thermometer tube, to tell the pilot whether he was flying nose-up or nose-down. As we began to swing, the setting sun rolled away over my left shoulder and its rays were reflected by something which glinted on the water for a split second, way out on the port beam; I checked the turn and steered towards it. Could it be the ship? There was something there, quite definitely . . . and then I saw it . . . the elongated hull and blunt projection of a conning-tower, sticking upwards – a U-boat – possibly five or six miles away. I yelled into the voice-pipe, 'There's a submarine on the port bow, about five miles away. I think we can reach it . . . it will give us something to do . . .'

'What *are* you going to do?' asked Wall. 'Ditch beside it?'

'We'll attack it first! I've still got the bombs.' I had been reluctant to jettison them until just before we ditched, because without them we would have been flying without any purpose, and would have been quite impotent.

'Okay,' said Robert, in a resigned voice. Like me, he was hating the inactivity of just droning along, waiting for the engine to splutter into silence as the fuel ran out. At least our last moments in the air would have some purpose. Anything was better than just flogging on and on, waiting for the engine to stop.

Putting the aircraft into a shallow dive I throttled back as the speed built up, and set the 'Mickey-Mouse' bomb-release so that they would drop together. This was going to be a once-only attack. There was insufficient fuel for more than one dive.

I stared hard at the submarine. It seemed to be growing in size but not getting any nearer. Then it dawned on me – the visibility distance was much greater than we thought. It was well over fifteen miles away and it wasn't a submarine at all – it was the ship! The conning-tower was the ship's island.

'It's the *Courageous*!' I yelled, and, jettisoning the bombs, I throttled right back, to stretch the dive into a glide.

I could feel the tension of the two occupants of the rear cockpit, craning their heads into the slipstream and holding their breath. Had any one of us looked around the sea on this final approach we might have seen the feathery wake of a U-boat's periscope, for somewhere in the immediate vicinity, with

Courageous in her sights, a German submarine skipper was holding his breath too, and closing in for the kill.

When a carrier turns into wind to receive her aircraft, it seems to be a lazy, leisurely movement to the approaching pilot, about to land. The bow starts to turn, imperceptibly to begin with, and then more emphatically in a graceful sweeping arc. The stern seems to kick the other way, as though resisting the motion, and then gives way in a rush, causing a mighty wash astern. While the ship is turning, the wind across the flight-deck can be violently antagonistic to a pilot who tries to land before the turn has been completed. Since we were about to run out of petrol, the turn seemed interminable, and after one half-circuit of the ship I decided to risk the cross-wind, and the violent turning motion, and get down before it was too late.

'Hey!' protested Robert. 'What the hell are you doing? She's only half-way round, and the batsman's waving us off like mad!' He could not know that the petrol indicator had been showing 'E' for Empty for the last ten minutes at least. The Swordfish has a Bristol Pegasus Three radial engine which obscures the flight-deck – and the ship – in the very last stages of a deck-landing. Normally, by approaching in a gentle turn to port, right down to the deck, it is possible to keep the deck in sight until straightening up; then it is necessary to look between the engine cylinders, at 'eleven and twelve o'clock', when the yellow bats come into view for a split second as the deck swoops upwards at an alarming rate.

That afternoon he was being very helpful – by waving his bats around his head in a frenzied 'go round again' sign – and I could see him all the way down to the deck. He had every right to wave me off. Apart from the obvious danger of landing on a restricted area, which was swinging violently to starboard as the bow swung to port, I was much too high. In case my petrol gave out in the last few vital seconds, I had to keep my height, to remain within the gliding distance all the way down.

The Swordfish has a strong fixed undercarriage, an enormous rudder, and very good brakes. If our landing was rather like that of a clumsy seagull alighting on the water in a rush, it was nevertheless successful. The hook picked up a wire and all was well.

We walked through the hangar and down to the wardroom without knowing that my crab-like landing was the last ever on that flight-deck. As the ship turned out of wind she must have crossed the bows of the U-boat, providing the German with a straightforward beam-on shot. His two torpedoes hit us almost simultaneously, just as Robert and I were stepping into the wardroom. If the core of the earth exploded, and the universe split from pole to pole, it could sound no worse. Every light went out and the deck reared upwards, throwing me backwards, and the hot blast which followed tore at the skin on my face and my clothes. There was something Satanic about it, and unreal. In the sudden deathly silence which followed I knew that the ship had died.

In the wardroom passage the deafening silence was broken by the tinkling of glass, breaking somewhere; and the tiny sound of trickling water. There was also a persistent whisper of noise which at first I failed to identify. Then it dawned on me that it was the sound of men breathing.

The bulkhead behind me was now partly underfoot; and facing aft, I was standing with my left foot on the deck, which sloped upwards to starboard at an amazing angle. My other foot was on the wall. The silence was frightening. I supposed that the ship's engine had been blown to bits.

When the torpedoes ripped open the ship's side and she rolled over to port at such as incredible angle it was obvious at once that she had been struck a mortal blow. In the first few seconds the whole length of the port side of the flight-deck hung suspended a few feet from the sea, crushing the ship's boats which burst through the sea up to the surface, swept from their stowages on the decks below. In those opening seconds, the aircraft in the hangar slid to port, crashing against each other and against the port bulkhead, adding to the uneven top-weight and increasing the ship's list; furniture in the mess-decks broke from deck fastenings and slid crazily to port; petrol tanks burst, flooding down into the decks below, and an evil slick of oil and petrol quickly spread over the calm sea, surrounding the ship with an inflammable mixture which might have burst into flame – and a massive explosion – at any moment; hundreds of men were hurled into the sea from all parts of the ship, some being sucked from their underwater compartments. The ship's ring-main was severed at once, extinguishing all the lights and cutting all power to every piece of machinery throughout, silencing the broadcasting system so that not even the essential pipe, 'abandon ship', could be made, and in one fraction of time a bustling community, humming with life, became a silent floating tomb. The other event had no effect on the ship's diminishing seaworthiness, but was perhaps even more of a blow to morale than any other single factor, for some object – probably a mast aerial – fell across the lanyard which operated the steam siren on the funnel, and as though to counteract the ghostly silence below, a long mournful blast, went on and on and on, as though the ship herself was crying out in her death agonies.

Before I could move from the darkness of the ante-room I heard a voice calling for help. Inside, by groping about, I found that a big, glass-fronted bookcase had fallen on top of the Principal Medical Officer, a huge pot-bellied Surgeon-Commander named Clifford-Brown. With the strength born of the desperation inspired by his cries it did not take long to lift it – just enough for him to crawl out and up. I could see the scuttles were open on the port side too so I propelled his colossal bulk into the passage, which led straight off aft to the quarter-deck. A long way ahead the doorway out to the deck was flooded with sunlight, like a bright light at the end of a long tunnel, inviting everyone to safety. I turned uphill, to starboard, into the intense darkness, to get my Mae West. I had to clamber up the sloping deck. Fortunately my cabin door was open. I then tried to remember in which drawer the silver combs I had bought for the bridesmaids were lying; with them were two fivers and my wedding ring. But at that moment the deck under my feet gave a shuddering heave and lifted uneasily and the slope to port increased, and all the books from the shelves above my desk tumbled downwards, striking me on the head and shoulders. I panicked, thinking she was going to roll over, and before I knew that I had moved I was out in the passage again, the combs forgotten. The bridesmaids would have treasured them even more if they had been rescued from a sinking ship.

When I stumbled out into the fresh air the stern was pointing due west towards the sun. When I looked aft I saw the twin periscopes of the U-boat which had just torpedoed us. The thought that the enemy was lying just under the surface, gloating at the sight of a great ship writhing in her death-throes, was obscene, and I hurried up the sloping deck to join the group on the 4.7-inch gun. Lieutenant Ingram had taken charge. He was trying to train the barrel downwards, by the hand mechanism. 'Do you know how to fire this bloody thing?' he said fiercely. 'I'd like to blast him to hell . . .' But it was no use.

The destroyer on our starboard quarter had spotted the periscopes but the German U-boat disappeared before the ship had moved a hundred feet. The destroyer dropped a pattern of depth-charges over the spot where the U-boat had been, killing all our men then in the water, but failed to damage the submarine. The intentions of the destroyer's captain were sound, but I was glad that I was still on board *Courageous* at the time. Then our Commander appeared and shouted 'abandon ship' several times. His face was grey with anxiety. Men were diving into the water in all directions, some from the flight-deck which was fully seventy feet above sea level. My attention was diverted by a noise above, on the seaplane platform; and looking up I saw that the Royal Marines were falling-in neatly, as though they were attending some parade. A Corporal was in charge. I watched, expecting him to give them the order to abandon ship, but he stood them at ease and then stood at ease himself.

'Look at those Marines!' I said to Kiggell, the adjutant of the other squadron, who was standing beside me. 'They haven't heard the Commander and are waiting for the Captain Royal Marines to tell them what to do. He was blown over the side some minutes ago. I saw him swimming to the destroyer, in his pink mess jacket. Perhaps they don't know.'

To remain in a neat assembly the Royal Marines were forced to stand at an angle to the deck of at least forty-five degrees. They looked like some comic turn on a music-hall stage. 'Silly buggers!' said Kiggell. 'They'll stand there until someone gives them an order and if nobody does, they'll all go down with the ship.' He moved towards the starboard ladder leading up to the seaplane platform. 'Come on,' he said to me.

When we got to the Marines I said, 'You must hurry,' I said to the Corporal, 'The ship is going down' – but they did not move. At this point Kiggell's experience of coping with natives on the North-West Frontier came to the rescue. He took a firm pace forward and with head thrown back and both arms rigid, he bellowed like a bull, 'ROYAL MARINES – H'N! TURN FOR'ARD – DIS-MISS! ABANDON SHIP – OVER THE SIDE AT THE DOUBLE – EVERY MAN JACK OF YOU!' It was the only language they understood, and they reacted at once.

Back on the quarter-deck I saw that the stern had risen even higher and it was time to go. Only the three men from the Reserve Fleet remained at the rails, plus one lieutenant. We discovered that the three Reserve Fleet men were unable to swim and were just standing there, having abandoned all hope of survival, waiting for the ship to take them with her. I offered to take them across, one by one, if there was time, and after a lot of silly argument one of them agreed and Kiggell helped him over the side as soon as I dived in. The sea was warm. The man was wearing yellow braces and I clutched him by these, but was unable to prevent him from putting his face into the sea and making burbling noises. We reached the destroyer in a matter of minutes – ten at the most – by which time he was dead. A crowd of men on board *Impulsive* hauled him up the side, but shook their heads at me, sadly. This upset me, because he certainly hadn't drowned. He was just too old for the shock of the last twenty minutes and I felt angry with the Admiralty for dragging these old pensioners back to sea. We could have managed without them.

On my way back to the *Courageous* from the destroyer, the carrier's stern suddenly rose in the air until the ship was vertical. The quarter-deck was pointing at the sky and it seemed to be hundreds of feet up. Then she was gone.

The sea all round me was a mass of heads, all bobbing about in the calm water. As the ship plunged downwards a great cheer went up from the sea's surface and someone started to sing 'Roll out the Barrel'. It was dark a few minutes later and I had a long swim before I found the destroyer and was very glad when I did. An American liner appeared on the scene at the same moment and picked up hundreds of survivors. During the crowded twenty minutes in which she sank 514 men lost their lives. When a ship goes down there are always more relatives whose lives have been saddened by the tragic events than there are men drowned.

SURGEON-LIEUTENANT DICK CALDWELL, RN

I joined the Royal Navy as a qualified doctor in 1934 on a four-year engagement. In 1938 I thought that I would leave the Navy, but a close friend of mine strongly advised me to stay. He said that he felt war was imminent and that if I left and was then called up later, I'd have to start at the beginning again. So I decided to stay and was posted to the *Royal Oak*. As I travelled up to Scapa Flow, I felt everywhere there was the shadow of war: a feeling of unease. Chamberlain's speech about 'Peace in Our Time' really had a hollow ring to it.

As war approached, I think the thought of going to war was exciting. In September when war was declared, the admiral called us together in the wardroom and gave us all champagne. He gave us the toast 'Damnation to Hitler'!

I thought, well, what do we do now? We went out on patrols only returning to Scapa, that huge desolate place, each time. On the night of 13th October, I had been playing poker and had been listening to gramophone records with two fellows I was never to see again. At half past twelve I picked my way carefully along the darkened quarterdeck to the hatchway leading to my cabin. I undressed and climbed on to my bunk.

We were in harbour – if such a term can be used to describe the wide, bleak waters of Scapa Flow – and after a not unadventurous spell at sea, no thoughts of the impending disaster could have been in anyone's mind, when at ten past one a muffled, ominous explosion shook the ship.

'Lord,' I said to myself, 'I don't like the sound of that much,' and as I jumped down from my bunk I found my heart thumping a bit. I looked into the next cabin and saw my neighbour pulling on a pair of trousers, and out in the cabin flat five or six officers were already discussing how and where the explosion could have occurred. (One must remember the vast number of compartments and storing places in a ship like *Royal Oak*.) Eight minutes passed. It was cold, and one or two men drifted back to their cabins. Just as I decided to do the same, a tremendous shuddering explosion occurred and the ship took a list to starboard. I heard the tinkling of glass falling from ledges and pictures in what seemed to be the awe-stricken silence that followed; a silence that was suddenly shattered by a third explosion. All the lights went out, the list increased, and it was obvious to everyone that we were for it.

I got on to deck in my pyjamas, monkey jacket and one bedroom slipper – I dropped the other and remember deciding not to retrieve it. A fourth torpedo struck us and the mighty bulk of the battleship shuddered again and settled further into the water. These last three blows had occurred in the short space of three minutes, and it was now every man for himself in a sinking ship with the cold, black sea all around us. I suppose all of us have wondered how we would feel in a case like this; I know I have, and I was certainly shocked but, curiously, not frightened as we stood on the sloping deck in the darkness, wisps of smoke eddying round us. One heard shouts of reassurance, even of humour; and a sudden splash as men clambered over the guard rails and dived twenty or thirty feet into the water below. I had no plan. My mind was curiously blank with regard to my personal safety, although I can most vividly recall every thought and impression that passed through my brain; my new and rather expensive tennis racket, a book I had borrowed and promised to return, three pounds in the bottom of my drawer, a ship of this size must surely take a long time to sink (six minutes later it was out of sight), but above all these surprising thoughts: 'This can't be happening to me; you read about it in books, and see it on the flicks, but it doesn't happen, it can't be happening to me.'

The ship suddenly increased her list more and more rapidly. We were now on the ship's side and as she slid over, turning turtle, I lost my footing, fell, tried frantically to scramble up and dive clear and was thrown headlong into the sea. ('I'll be sucked down – that's what they say happens – what a fool I was not to jump sooner.') I seemed to go down and down and started fighting for breath. Then, as I came to the surface, the stern and propeller soared above me, then slipped slowly into the water and disappeared. A rush of water swept me head over heels, it seemed, and I went under again and came up in oil, thick black oil. I gulped it and retched at the filthy taste of it in my throat; oil, thick black oil smarting in my eyes. I swam and floundered about, hoping to find some form of support in the darkness. None of us had lifebelts. I heard cries round me, saw black heads bobbing, and I swam frenziedly again. I tried to wriggle out of my jacket, but found it heavy and slimy with oil. I repeatedly went under until quite suddenly I gave it up and thought, 'I'm going to drown.' Perfectly dispassionately 'I'm going to drown' and in a way which I cannot explain I wondered how to. And I thought of all the people I wanted to see again, and things I wanted to do – that was all I thought of – and then I saw a group of heads and then threshed my way towards them.

Somebody swam quite strongly past me and I caught his leg and tried to hold it. He kicked me clear. I saw an upturned boat ahead of me. How far was it? Or how near? Fifteen yards can seem insurmountable, and then I touched the freeboard, touched it and held on. 'I've made it, by God, I've made it; and to think a few minutes ago I might have been drowned.' I thought what a pity one can't thank inanimate things, I was so grateful to that support.

I tried to wipe the oil out of my eyes with my free hand, and then with my sleeve, and realised how stupid that was. My mind flashed back to a silent picture of Buster Keaton as a diver drying his hands on a towel at the bottom of the sea. I said 'Hullo' to the indistinguishable face beside me, and it said 'Oh, this bloody oil!'

There were about a dozen of us, I think, hanging on round a boat which kept steady as long as we did, but every now and then someone would try to improve his position or make himself more secure by clambering on to the upturned keel. Then slowly but inevitably our support would begin to roll over and back we would slip into the water, clawing frantically for a fingerhold on the smooth surface, and shouting at each other till the movement ceased and we were supported once more. This happened many times and every time meant a mouthful of oil and a thumping heart.

Time dragged on, with no sign of us being picked up. We strained our eyes in the darkness for some glimmer of light, but none came. We sang, 'Daisy, Daisy, give me your answer do.' *Daisy* was the name of the drifter attached to the *Royal Oak*.

At last we saw a mast head light which grew brighter and then the blacker darkness of a boat moving slowly towards us. We shouted again and again.

When she was within twenty yards of us we left our upturned boat and struck out in her direction. She had ropes hanging down, up which we tried to climb. I remember falling back into the sea twice. My hands were numb. I thought 'Mustn't lose now. Come on, mustn't lose now' – but have no recollection whatsoever of finally succeeding . . . I found myself sitting on a hot grating in the engine room, shivering uncontrollably from the cold which I had not previously noticed – most of us had this experience.

I stood up and vomited oil and salt water all over somebody sitting at my feet. I did this three times and apologised each time to him. He didn't appear to worry much, anyway.

We were taken to the *Pegasus* and given hot drinks and helped into hot baths, and splashed and scrubbed. They were very grand to us, and we began to talk and recognise people and shake hands and try not to notice friends that were missing. Over eight hundred were drowned that night.

Of the happenings during the following days before we disembarked and were sent south, I retain vivid memories which now seem so swift-moving and so violently contrasted that they really belong to a different story. The air raids, the shattering noise, a German pilot lazily parachuting down silhouetted against a bright blue sky, while his plane, broken up by gunfire, crashed in flames, on the hill-side; the sinister whistle of bombs from the raiders; the whole-hearted enthusiasm at an impromptu concert the night after we were torpedoed; the marvellous kindness shown to us by the Thurso folk; the sense of relief we felt in the train taking us south (a relief broken almost comically by a train-collision); the gradual acquisition of strange clothing, of odd meals and drinks, and so – at last – London; to find normality almost unreal after chaos.

Leave soon put that right!

LIEUTENANT-COMMANDER RICHARD JENNINGS, RN

In early December 1939 we were patrolling the River Plate. The *Exeter* was well overdue for a refit so it was decided we should go to Durban to have the bottom scraped and the propeller fixed. Commodore Harwood, who had been aboard the *Exeter*, transferred his broad pennant to the *Ajax* because he wanted to stay in the area. He must have known that trouble was imminent.

The *Exeter* set off for Durban, but less than twelve hours later it was learned that the *Doric Star* had been sunk by a German pocket battleship between Cape Town and Freetown. So we were recalled and sent to Port Stanley for a four-day self-refit.

On 8 December the commodore told us to patrol around the Falkland Islands in case the Germans were planning a comeback to mark the anniversary of the Battle of the Falkland Islands in 1914. But nothing happened, so we headed north and joined the commodore in the Plate estuary on the evening of 12th December. We did some steam tactics on arrival, and Commodore Harwood sent for the captains of the *Exeter*, *Ajax* and *Achilles* to inform them of his intentions, should we encounter the pocket battleship. No-one else knew what tactics he was going to pursue.

I had the middle watch that night of 12th December. When I was relieved I went aft, shaved and decided against turning in as dawn action stations was due at 0440. After some more steam tactics we reverted to third degree of readiness. I got into my pyjamas, arranged for a call by the sentry (just outside my cabin door) and turned in, only to be called ten minutes later. I hustled up to my action station in the Director Control Tower. As I was crossing the compass platform the captain hailed me – not with the usual sort of rigmarole of 'Enemy in sight, bearing etc.', but with 'There's the fucking *Scheer*! Open fire at her!' Throughout the battle the crew of the *Exeter* thought they were fighting the *Admiral von Scheer*. But the name of the enemy ship was, of course, the *Graf Spee*.

So the fight was on. It was about 0612. In the DC Tower I was in telephonic touch with the Transmitting Station which, in turn, was in touch with all main armament quarters. I ordered 'Open fire'. The range was then about 20,000 yards and the *Graf Spee* was as large as life on the horizon. Our 8-inch guns could hit any target up to 30,000 yards away.

A shot in one of the early salvos passed through 'B' turret's ammunition embarkation hatch immediately below the bottom of 'B' turret's gunroom, passed through the sick bay, bowling over the Sick Berth Petty Officer and a tray for eight of his special cocktails, and then through the starboard side without bursting, until hitting the water, perhaps. Fragments from one of the early 'shorts' penetrated our side and cut a lot of circuit, including the gun-ready lamps and the fall-of-shot hooter. So it was extra difficult to spot our own fall-of-shot among those of the 6-inch ships, *Ajax* and *Achilles*. Incidentally, the *Graf Spee*'s weight of broadside was 2.5 times the combined weights of our three ships' broadsides.

At 0624 while loading for the ninth broadside, 'B' turret received a direct hit, knocking it right out of action. Not only that but fragments peppered the compass platform leaving only the captain and two others standing. The captain, with his eyes full of grit, decided to fight the ship from the after conning position. We in the DC Tower a few feet – less than fifteen feet – above the compass platform were quite unaware of all this upset. Another round entered the fore superstructure, ran along the deck of the Remote Control W/T office, passed out through my office and burst over the starboard A-A guns, starting fires in the area of the ready-use ammunition lockers where a midshipman and an ordinary seaman distinguished themselves. In the meantime 'A' turret, when loading for our 32nd broadside, was put out of action by a direct hit on the right gun.

It was perhaps the last hit that came in by the Petty Officer's mess and burst in the Chief Petty Officer's locker flat that caused most worry. The flat was above three magazines and a diesel generator was put out of action. The transmitting station was rendered useless as visibility was nil due to white powder used for insulating the space around the Transmitting Station. Breathing was also difficult. The crew was ordered out to join up with the damage-control parties. I left the DC Tower finding, to my surprise, that the compass platform had been abandoned. I went aft to the after control and, with the control officer, decided to put 'Y' turret into local control with me standing on the gun house roof to help with the spotting. While talking to the After Control Officer I failed to notice we had altered course a few degrees and that the guns of 'Y' turret were only a few feet away. When the guns spoke I remember looking down and seeing that my legs were still there!

After perhaps two salvos in local control 'Y' turret lost all power due to flooding and the flooding in the ship grew worse. At this stage Harwood told us to drop out of the action and head for Port Stanley. There was nothing more we could do, for the *Graf Spee* was too far away to ram.

By this time the commander, Bobby Graham, had been knocked out: he was laid up in his cabin with thirty-two bits of ironmongery in his legs. So the next in command to Bell was Jennings. Jennings just busied himself in general. People were working pretty much without instruction. Everybody went about their jobs very calmly. During the three preceding years we had exercised action stations every Friday, so we all knew what to do.

The fire was still burning in the chief petty officer's locker flat. Underneath this were the anti-aircraft ammunition and the small-arms magazines; it was a potential disaster. The damage-control parties managed to get the submersible pump forward into the flat and start it heaving and flowing. Then they opened the scuttle in the ship's side which was about two feet above sea-level – we had a ten-degree list to starboard – so the suction pump and discharge were more or less level with the hole in the ship's side. Even so they managed to put the fire out, which was fortunate.

The action had lasted from 0612 until 0725. It was a long hour and thirteen minutes and certainly the most intense action I saw during my time in the navy. At that time we had no idea whether we'd made any impact on the *Graf Spee* with our guns. We had fired 95 salvos from 'Y' turret before it went out of action. 'A' turret fired 32 and 'B' turret only eight. One had to have respect for the gun layers of the *Graf Spee*.

ABLE SEAMAN LEN FOGWILL, RN

It was 13th December 1939. I was serving on the 8-inch-gun cruiser HMS *Exeter* patrolling the River Plate. The captain was F.S. Bell and we were in company with HMS *Ajax*, which was captained by C.H. Woodhouse and a New Zealand ship, *Achilles*, captained by W.E. Parry. We were known as the South American Squadron commanded by Commodore H.H. Harwood whose broad pennant was aboard *Ajax*.

I'd done the middle watch from midnight until four o'clock in the morning. I was a look-out on the port side of the after-control. The night was warm and, as far as I was concerned, the war was far away. It was known that a German raider was sinking our shipping but we never thought the raider would come our way. What Commodore Harwood thought was another matter.

Directly after the middle watch we went to dawn action stations, which lasted about an hour. By the time I stood down from there I was jolly tired and didn't need much rocking in my hammock. I was fast asleep when action stations sounded. By force of habit I was out of bed and at my action stations before the bugler had finished sounding general quarters. I dashed off with my socks on and my shoes under my arm.

I was in the after-control position and relieved the man on look-out who told me that a ship had been sighted on the port quarter. Just at that moment the challenge lights on the mast lit up and I turned my glasses on the sighted ship. I could just see the mast through the slight haze. Then there was a flash which I took to be the flashing light in answer to our challenge. There were flashes all around us and then the sound of guns. This was no friendly ship. Over the tannoy they announced that we were engaging the German pocket battleship *Admiral von Scheer*. Only later in the day did we learn it was the *Graf Spee*.

Our three cruisers were in line ahead formation led by the *Achilles* with the *Ajax* and the *Exeter* following. Immediately the *Exeter* was turned out of line towards the *Graf Spee*. I was above the after-control, just alongside the after-director looking out with binoculars. I could make out every detail on the enemy ship. The range closed quickly and until we were steaming almost parallel with her.

When we got into our range, one of our first salvoes hit the control tower of the *Graf Spee*. We learned this afterwards because at the time we had very little knowledge of how the battle was going. We only knew we were being attacked! The enemy's firing was extremely accurate and *Exeter* was getting a pasting, steaming straight towards the enemy with the front part of the ship knocked to a shambles.

Shells were passing right through the superstructure. There was shrapnel flying everywhere. In the first ten minutes we lost five officers and fifty-six ratings. 'A' and 'B' turrets, the 8-inch and 4-inch guns, were knocked out very early on, along with the starboard torpedo tubes. The bridge from where the captain was controlling the ship was put out of action, most of the personnel being killed or injured. The captain, although wounded about the face, came aft to the after-control where I was. I had to keep him informed of the *Graf Spee*'s position, as he couldn't see properly.

He sent Commander Graham forward to organise the forward-control parties. They had been badly knocked about by an 11-inch shell passing into the ship on the port side just below 'B' turret. It had passed at an angle from forward to aft and exploded above the 4-inch magazine in the chief petty officer's locker flat, killing nearly everyone. It was one of the worst places the salvo could have hit because it was the nerve centre of the ship; all the cables to the transmitting station and the telephone exchange ran through there. The explosion and the fire put all communications out of action.

By 0650 *Exeter* was in a sorry state. She was taking in water and had developed a list. But I never thought she would go down. All guns were out of action except for two on 'Y' turret. The only steering position was the emergency position right aft where a sailmaker was at the wheel. Orders to him were being passed by a quickly formed chain of men who were drawn from the quarters where they were no longer needed. The chain passed from the captain in the after-control right aft to the emergency steering position. I was running some of the messages. When there was no communication with the after-steering, the sailmaker took it upon himself to steer the ship all-to-starboard then all-to-port, trying to dodge the shells. He used his intuition.

After a while the captain told me to take over as his messenger and I had to run from place to place, delivering messages to all parts of the ship. It seemed as if I bore a charmed life because all the time I was going about, my shipmates were being killed. I was losing friends but was oblivious to it at the time. I was just doing the things I had been trained to do. When I went through the waist, the deck where the torpedo tubes are, I saw injured men lying around dying. Even the padre was down there handing out tots of whisky to the injured. He was a boy for his whisky.

There were bodies everywhere and some of them were in a terrible condition. A piece of shrapnel took the back of our sub-lieutenant's head off. I'd never seen anyone die before. We were a young ship's company; a lot of us were in our teens and early twenties. This was our first action although most of us had been together for nearly three years. I'd say we were members of the finest and most efficient ship in the Royal Navy. We were trained to do our utmost and I'm sure we were doing our duty automatically.

There was shrapnel everywhere. Every one of us had caught a bit. The morale of the men was grand, even with the shells and shrapnel flying about. At one time during the action our wireless aerials were shot away. They fell down across the after-control and got entangled around the after-director and jammed the door shut. I took an axe and broke through the cables, whereupon the door opened and the director layer popped his head out and politely said, 'Thank you very much!'

Then there was a lull in the action. The *Graf Spee* must have suffered as much as we had, since we'd been pumping shells into her for quite a while. During that time we managed to get the fires under control and ditch the amphibious aircraft – which were leaking petrol – into the sea. Every position in the ship had a damage control party. We knew what to do and where to go. We had to rig up emergency lighting and ring mains to supply the after-turret. Everything had to be done with man-power and the fires were put out with sea water. As we worked we learned who had been killed. Somebody said, 'Nobby Clarkson's killed.' He was a great friend of mine, killed in 'A' turret and my cousin was killed as well.

Although the *Exeter* was now on only two guns, we steamed into action with the guns firing on the foremost bearing. The control of the tower was taken on by the gunnery officer Richard Jennings, with utter disregard for his own safety. He stood on top of the turret shouting directions down into the front of the guns.

By now we were in a sinking condition and slowly listing to port. When it became apparent to the commodore that we were in a dangerous condition we were ordered to withdraw from the action and make our way to Port Stanley.

But we weren't in any great hurry to retreat. The captain had mentioned to the ship's doctor that he intended to ram the *Graf Spee* so we were all ready to rig up the Lewis guns, but in the end we didn't have to. Nobody felt particularly relieved that we were out of the action; the general feeling was that we hadn't done enough. It made you kind of bloodthirsty. You felt so isolated from the real activity because it's the shells from the ship which are doing the job, not you. I never really experienced fear, not even in retrospect.

We stopped for lunch and everybody was given a tot of rum. It was my first because I was only just eighteen and under age. The shock of what we had been through sank into us in the form of hunger. At that time there was no means of getting a meal and the only thing we could get our hands on was raw cabbage. We had this and enjoyed it.

Then we set to work to clear away the damage. Some of this work was ghastly because as the debris was cleared away, the great number of dead and wounded was brought to light. I was put on look-out on the wings of the bridge on the flag deck. It was pretty grim because there were still some bodies around. The shell which had passed from port to starboard had sliced right through the deck and chopped off the legs of all the telegraphers who were lined up on a bench. They were all killed instantly. There were over sixty killed and over 120 wounded. During the afternoon our fallen comrades were buried at sea with full naval honours. I know that every survivor thinks with pride of those who were lost and will never forget them.

We were very well cared for when we reached Port Stanley. The *Exeter* certainly did have the worst of the whole encounter; on a memorial plaque I was later shown of the Battle of the River Plate the *Exeter* took up three-quarters of the plaque. The *Ajax* lost seven men and the *Achilles* four.

We stayed in the Falklands for a couple of months and were given leave to come home on 28th February. We had to bury four of the dead on the island. Most of the badly injured were transferred to South Africa. On the way home we called into Sierra Leone. The first person I saw on the gangway was my father who was serving on HMS *Albatross*, a seaplane carrier based in Freetown. He had seen action at Jutland! We went ashore and had a few beers.

Surgeon-Lieutenant Roger Lancashire, RN

The Germans are great ones for doing the magnificent thing on the right day and Commodore Harwood reckoned that on 8th December 1939 they would be thinking of how they could extract their revenge off the Falklands Islands for the sinking of the *Scharnhorst* and *Gneisenau*, twenty-five years earlier almost to the day. So on 8th December *Exeter* went round and round the Falklands looking for smoke or anything suspicious, but nothing happened at all. We then rejoined Harwood who had shifted his flag from *Exeter* to *Ajax*. It was a good thing that he did. Together with *Achilles* we rendezvoused about 200 miles off the mouth of the Plate on 12th December. The obvious thing that we had to do was to get the *Graf Spee* to divide her fire. We were steaming in line ahead when the enemy was sighted.

Harwood had decided what we were going to do twenty-four hours in advance. We detached ourselves and steamed away as fast as we could in order to close the range; but their opening fire was so accurate that in the first ten minutes of the battle we lost five officers and fifty-six ratings killed outright. That was ten per cent of the ship's company. I was squatting on my haunches close to the wardroom door taking drugs and instruments out of a cupboard when the *Graf Spee*'s first salvo fell short and burst on impact with the water. There was a loud crash and a blast of air blew my cap off and threw me backwards. Later on, I found part of an 11-inch shell fuze-cap embedded in the fanlight casing. Had I been standing, it would certainly have beheaded me. Unfortunately, other fragments came hurtling inboard, killing all the fire party assembled in the stokers' bathroom on the same deck.

The next salvo struck 'A' turret and blew up and started a fire right forward. We never saw one of the team of shipwrights again, nor Sub-Lieutenant Morse whose father was C-in-C in Freetown. The second one hit 'B' turret manned by the Royal Marines which was immediately below the bridge. It was lucky that anybody came out of it alive. On the bridge, there were only three survivors and old 'Hookie' Bell had splinters in both eyes and his leg. I suppose there were about ten men on the bridge including those from the plot just aft, one of whom was our sub-lieutenant. The three survivors went aft to control, which was just forward of 'Y' turret. I didn't go up to the bridge, I stayed down in the wardroom. Thank God we had rehearsed 'Action Stations' prior to this battle because we'd rigged up the sick-bay in the wardroom so many times in the last three years, that everything went like clockwork. Fortunately, to take the place of our missing sick-birth attendant, we had an extra war complement from *Ajax*. Some of the wounded were treated in the sick-bay up forward but most of them were brought down to the wardroom. Every now and then the Master-at-Arms, who was part of my team, thank God, would call me up to see if I could identify somebody, especially if he was on his last legs.

The casualties were fairly devastating. There were two or three who literally died in my arms. These were people who I'd been living with, as it were, for three years. There were cases where, if I'd had the facilities and an endless supply of blood transfusions, things might have been different, but it wasn't like that. I did a quick assessment of who was most likely to benefit and then went to work on them. We had no nursing orderlies with us. But the Royal Marine bandsmen came up after their Transmitting Station had been put out of action. I took over 'Hookie' Bell's day and sleeping cabin. A lot of the casualties were in there. There was quite a lot of stitching up and other tasks which merged into one another.

As the day crept on and night fell I had, with the help of the bandsmen, got a good team going. We had a problem with the morphine. Instead of being in bottles with a rubber-topped diaphragm so that you could plunge the needle through, they were in ampoules. That was one of the things that I spent a day complaining about, when I returned to Devonport, with a RNVR Surgeon Rear-Admiral who listed our requirements. The first thing I told him was, that morphine should not be dispensed in the ampoules because to break them open we had to use a file which was very time-consuming. In a hurry it was much easier to use bottles. Thank God we had a ruddy great packing case which we'd had on board since we commissioned in 1936, which was only to be opened in action. A character came along to deliver a message. He was rather badly shot up so I put a few stitches in him and tied him up and made him as comfortable as possible. Then when he had come to, he said, 'Well, let me do something, Doc, for heaven's sake.' So I said, 'All right. Open that crate for me.' Right at the very top was the very thing we wanted; a ruddy great big pair of tailor's scissors used for cutting open serge trousers. It was beautifully planned. I remember putting that down in my report. There was also enough morphine in there. I operated on a fellow called Causton. I was wondering whether I ought to amputate his foot but then I saw that there was a good blood supply. Several of his tendons had gone. I knew that I had three or four ampoules of anaesthetic – which was quite new in those days – to give an injection into a vein. I got them myself in Rio and there was one left up in the sick bay. So I sent a messenger up to get it. With the assistance of the sick-berth PO, we operated on Causton and laid him out on the deck of 'Hookie' Bell's sleeping cabin. I got the finest sutures and needles which we could get hold of and stitched the tendons together again. It was a nice clean wound and kept his foot on for him. In 1943 I was sent out to Durban. I spent a fortnight in the transit camp near Capetown, so I went down most days to the naval hospital and this fellow Causton was still there. He had found work in an office and was walking about with a stick. I felt about ten yards tall.

The only time I left the sick-bay was when I got the message that 'Hookie' Bell and Commander Graham had been blown off the bridge and were wounded in the legs. 'Hookie' went to the after-conning position and the commander went to his cabin. As I poked my head through the hatch on my way from the wardroom to the quarterdeck, a hand shoved my head down again with a yell, 'Port Twenty.' I passed the message on to the chain of men for transmission to the two perspiring heroes who were manning the massive steering wheel way back aft.

On deck I had never seen anything like it before. The immaculate *Exeter* I'd known for three years was an absolute shambles. All the aircraft who had been told to stay on their catapults were now riddled and high octane fuel was pouring out of them. Richard Jennings, 'Guns', was standing on the lid of 'Y' turret giving his orders. Hookie Bell and I went up to see him and he gave me a running commentary of what was going on. It was fantastic. I was spellbound. There in the distance you could see the *Graf Spee*, firing every now and again. The exciting thing was that *Ajax* and *Achilles* had made a smokescreen and they were taking it in turns to dodge in and out of it and give a rapid and accurate six-inch broadside, which the *Graf Spee* didn't like very much. 'Hookie' Bell said to me, 'You see what position we're in: "A" and "B" turret are out of action (which I already knew), so we've only got one gun here in "Y" turret. All the power's gone, so even that's got to be trained and loaded by hand. But it's all we've got now.'

Then he said, 'If he gives me half a chance and heads this way I intend to ram the bugger.'

I fixed up his legs to stop them from bleeding and said, 'Now look, when you can, let me know when you're under control and I'll come and do what I can for your eyes.' At about midnight he came below. We were swinging about all over the place, but fortunately, as part of my job years ago, I'd done quite a lot of eye work, so with the chief steward holding a torch I was able to clear one eye and reminded 'Hookie' that Nelson had managed pretty well with only one. It was not until the following Sunday night, when he was staying as the guest of Henniker-Heaton, the governor at Port Stanley, that I was able to do the other eye under much easier conditions.

There were a number of facial injuries from the battle. I had to stitch an ear back on and there were quite a few scalp injuries. A Royal Marine came in, brought by his mates, and they couldn't think what the matter was. He was the most mild-mannered chap but he suddenly started behaving very oddly and using the most terrible obscene language. So I thought there must be something the matter with him. They couldn't find any sign of a wound or scar so I had a jolly good look at his scalp and sure enough there was a tiny hole in the front. A fragment of shell had gone right through into the frontal lobe like a leucotomy. I left it there like that; that was the cause of his problem. I wanted to take him back home because we could have looked after him and my friend Sir Geoffrey Jefferson who was a neuro-surgeon could have helped. They sent him down to the Falklands Hospital where they couldn't do anything. We took him up to Buenos Aires where he was operated upon and died on the table . . .

I was constantly on the go from that Tuesday and the wee small hours of Wednesday until the following Sunday night. Harwood made a signal to

'Hookie' Bell and said, 'Can you make it to the Falklands?' We had a very dangerous list to port and our main mast was whipping about in a terrible state. We were navigating by a boat's compass.

You see, we had been struck by seven 11-inch shells, three of which passed straight through the ship without exploding. One of them went clean through the sick-bay, through where the heads (toilets) were, removing all the bedpans and the bath. The blast of the things did a hell of a lot of damage. We weren't holed below the water-line but the place was absolutely incredible. The *Exeter* was a damned well-built ship.

When we were down at Port Stanley afterwards, Commodore Harwood sent for me and 'Hookie' Bell. Governor Henniker-Heaton was there and they asked me what we were going to do with all the patients. Some of them could be taken back but they were not allowed unless they were capable of looking after themselves, which was fair enough. So I suggested that since there were lots of fracture cases, they should send out an orthopaedic surgeon. 'Good God,' he said, 'They'll never do that.' I said, 'Of course they would. They'd be most interested to see their injuries.'

They sent a pal of mine who I'd met many times in my RNVR days in Liverpool. They put them all in one of the cruisers, the *Dorsetshire* I think, and took them over to the Cape.

The only reason that I am able to tell this story now is that we in *Exeter* had basically been the same ship's company for three years, so there was a lot of rapport and camaraderie which there wouldn't have been the case if we had been a new commission. Without that, we could not have survived the punishment we took.

MIDSHIPMAN MIKE SHERWOOD, RNR

We got home at the end of January 1940. There was a letter for me from the Admiralty telling me I was a midshipman now in the RNR and I was to join HMS *Escapade* at Rosyth. The Merchant Navy had no option but to release me.* I went up to Rosyth a day or two before my eighteenth birthday. I knew nothing at all about the Royal Navy, and wasn't too sure about the routine and what I was supposed to do.

The *Escapade* was lying alongside the jetty in a row of destroyers. It was a cold winter's night. The quartermaster was there and I said I was the new midshipman and he said, 'Come this way.' He took me down aft to the wardroom and said, 'It's the new snotty, sir.' The captain was just finishing

---

* During the war the Royal Naval Reserve was made up of Merchant Navy officers who were selected by the navy to train as naval officers to be called up into the reserve. Much the same as the Territorial Army except that the RNR were all from the Merchant Navy. The other naval reserve, the RNVR (Royal Naval Volunteer Reserve), was civilian.

dinner. He was a big burly Australian called Harry Graham. The rest of the eight officers were sitting down at the table with him. I walked in there with my idea of Naval routine, 'Midshipman, reporting for duty.' He was smoking a cigarette with a big long holder, a real Noël Coward thing, he was a friend of Noël Coward's, he knew Lord Louis Mountbatten too. 'Ah, Snotty.' he said. 'Sit down there until I have finished my story. Bring a glass of port for the snotty,' and here was I just a port apprentice being treated like that, where in the Merchant Navy the skipper would hardly speak to you.

The crew at that time was the skipper; a first lieutenant, about twenty-five, who was RN; a sub-lieutenant RN who was twenty-one; and there were two other sub-lieutenants RNR; two ex-Merchant Navy – one a P & O, the other from Union Castle Line – myself, and a Warrant Officer Gunner. We were the Third Destroyer Flotilla – all the E's: *Escort, Escapade* and *Encounter*. We used to take a convoy from Scotland, from the entrance of the Fifth of Forth over to Bergen in Norway, which wasn't yet in the war so we had to stop at the three-mile limit, and a Norwegian gunboat would come out and take over from us. She would see them in, and hand over the return convoy which we would bring back to the Forth. It was just normal trade, nothing to do with the war. There were all sorts of different ships in the convoy, Norwegian, British, Dutch, Latvian.

Four destroyers guarded the convoy, one at each corner, protecting against submarines. The routine was that you would steam out an angle away from the convoy until you could hardly see it; but you didn't want to lose it, so then you turned round and came back in again towards them. You just went backwards and forwards like that. This was before radar, so you, with your binoculars, were watching them all the time.

On my second day on board I was on watch with the First Lieutenant on what was known as the last dog watch, a cold night in the middle of February. I wanted to see what was going on so I went up on the bridge with him but I didn't understand a thing because there were different words of command. The First Lieutenant was steaming in at the convoy in the pitch dark and rain. Then he says to me, 'OK, sonny, you take over. I am just going to check on the chart,' whereupon he dives in on the chart table and leaves me standing up there and the ship, of course, is steaming in. He was breaking me in, he knew what he was doing. I was too proud to call him out and say 'What do I do now?' So I said these magic words that he was saying, 'Starboard 20,' to see what would happen. Round she came and I thought, 'Thank Christ for that.' Going out was the worst part, in case you lost the convoy. Anyway that broke me in for that. Come eight o'clock we went off watch and I went down below. The destroyer was built for peace-time and there wasn't enough room for all the officers. I was sleeping in the skipper's day-cabin. He stayed in the sea-cabin and lived on the bridge all the time we were at sea. In port we changed over. It was a lovely big cabin, he had a bed in it, not a bunk. Anyway I got down there at eight o'clock, washed and cleaned myself, clean white shirt on, stiff collar and at about half-past eight went down to the wardroom for dinner. I got in there but there was nobody at the table. The First Lieutenant had already eaten and was sitting in one of the chairs and he and the rest were all scruffy looking like they always were. They had eaten without me because they thought I was being as sick as a dog because everybody who joined a destroyer was always sick. So I was the talking point, all the stewards were looking at me, and it soon spread down the ship about this new snotty who was looking for his grub. It spread amongst the crew too. As things went on if, say, the Chief Petty Officers had made a particularly good duff, or suet pudding with custard, they always used to sent some down to me, a bit for the snotty. So that was my first introduction to those ships.

I was also known as the Rate Officer. Up in the top of the destroyer over the bridge there is the 'director' which controls all the guns. You sit there, the director trains on to the target and all the guns follow electric pointers which are transmitting from this and then you shout down the information – 'Range 3000 yards, inclination, so-and-so, speed so-and-so,' – and it was all mechanically operated and transmitted to the guns. The fellows in the guns just looked at the pointers, they weren't looking at what they were shooting at. I only did any firing once. We were coming down with a convoy from Norway and you couldn't believe there was a war on because everything was so nice and easy. One of the lookouts suddenly shouted, 'Submarine on the port side,' so we looked round and sure enough there was a submarine about two miles away. We all went into 'action stations'. We spun the ship round and were steaming at her, opening fire. We got off half a dozen shells before she dived. Skipper Harry Graham said, 'She must have gone. Back to the convoy.' As we were steaming back, the lookout shouted, 'The bloody submarine is here again.' We looked round and there was the stern of the submarine coming up. So we turned round and rushed back at her firing and down she went. Probably one of the other ships hit her this time as all the survivors were swimming around. Harry Graham detailed one of the destroyers to pick them up. The U-boats had sunk a lot of merchant ships so there was a lot of resentment amongst the crew as we could have given them a good thumping as they came on board.

When the Germans invaded Norway in April 1940, we went up there. It was just a time of chaos. There was a port up in the north called Harstad and we were ferrying troops ashore there from the ships. One lot were the French Foreign Legion who carried two flasks, one of brandy and another of wine.

Maybe they topped up on one of the liners because half our crew were as stewed as newts.

We were being attacked by air all the time. We didn't know where the hell we were going half the time and nothing was co-ordinated. We weren't ordered to go and do this or go and do that or any specific job. We were waiting for something to happen. We were on standby there when *Warspite* came in and went up into Narvik to take on six German destroyers there. We were just around the corner from them and a bit later the *Warspite* was called up again and she went in with another load of destroyers and they had a further battle.

As most of Norway was being occupied by the Germans, we had to evacuate our troops. I was sent ashore to pick up the General. The boat took me in and I said, 'Wait for me there, don't go, no matter what.' The town was practically deserted, the Germans were just over the horizon. You could hear the tanks firing. I followed some rough directions, looking for a hotel where the General was supposed to be. When I got to the crossroads where the hotel was, I could see a tank at the top pointing down the road. I thought, 'Nobody can get over there.' The next minute I was tapped on the shoulder. I jumped out of my skin. There was a big burly sergeant from a Guards regiment. He said, 'What's up sonny? Want to get across?' I said, 'Yes, I want to get over to the headquarters to get the General out.' He said, 'That's the Headquarters up there.' 'Yes, but there is a bloody tank up the road.' 'I tell you what, you wait for it.' He had a Bren gun. He said, 'I'll jump out and have a shot or two at them, while I do, you run over.' Good as his word he opened up and I ran across to the hotel. When I got inside I looked around. There was nobody downstairs so I went upstairs, into a big room which was full of army officers, Bertie Wooster types. I said, 'I have come for the General.' 'Don't know where he is, no sign of him,' they said, completely unconcerned. There were all sorts of bangs and crashes going on as the Germans were shelling the town. I thought, 'bugger you,' and I came out, no General. I got on board ship and it started to steam off. By this time there was confusion. As we steamed off a plane suddenly came straight for us, at sea level. All our machine-guns opened up. A wing fell off and it dropped into the water. When we picked up the pilot we found he was Norwegian, flying one of our Swordfish seaplanes with floats. He had been flashing to tell us he had picked up the bloody General! As I said, chaos, no communication.

By this time we were running low on fuel and there were no tankers nearby so we were shoved into a fjord to await a tanker. It was a very narrow fjord with cliffs up each side. We were put in there because the planes couldn't get their sights on you to drop any bombs. But there were a lot of old wrecks there, which wasn't very reassuring. Eventually a tanker was sent to us and gave us just enough fuel to get back to Scapa Flow. That was the end of the Norwegian campaign. We were the last out.

We sailed back to Scapa and, as we left, I knew it was going to be a slow run. I thought we were going to be massacred, but we steamed all the way down to Scapa and nobody came near us.

Lieutenant Arthur Hezlet, RN

The submarine war didn't really hot up until after Christmas 1939 when suddenly we lost three submarines in succession. People thought there was some great secret weapon that had got them all, but it wasn't, as they've discovered since. It was German anti-submarine craft in two cases. Our submarines were in very shallow water, only 80 feet and the Germans got to them partly by trawling with wires and grapnels.

But with the Norwegian campaign things really began in earnest and the British submarines did very well considering the amount of exercises they had had. The idea in those days was, when war started you stopped exercising – that was for peacetime – but of course later you realised you had to exercise harder in war than you did in peace.

When the invasion of Norway took place, we were off Oslo. We had left harbour in *Trident* before anyone suspected what was going to happen. We had very poor information in those days and the Admiralty didn't believe Norway was going to be invaded until it happened.

The Germans sent about a dozen troopships ahead pretending to be merchant ships and they protected themselves by going up through Swedish and Norwegian territorial waters when we couldn't touch them. We saw these ships going north but we couldn't make them out. We knew they weren't neutral, because neutrals normally had their flag painted beside their names and none of these had. I had quite an argument with my captain who said there was absolutely nothing we could do. He said, 'If we started sinking these things and they proved to be neutral it would be really bad news.' But I felt there was something very wrong and a big action was about to happen.

Then a tanker came out of the three-mile limit and cut a corner across a bay, just where we were. I was on watch and got hold of the captain. He said he was a very uncertain of what we should do and he hadn't been given any instructions. Eventually I got him to agree to stop this ship. He popped up with the gun and ordered it to stop. Not only did it stop, but it scuttled, and he then didn't make a signal to Admiralty which was very unwise. That was the very beginning of the invasion but we then went home because we'd been out for the normal patrol period.

On our next patrol, when we had a new captain, we were off the west coast of Norway. All the enemy traffic was going up inside the islands while we were patrolling outside. We were achieving nothing. This captain was made of really stern stuff and said, 'Well, we must get inside,' which was quite a feat. We went right up Kors Fjord just south of Bergen. We sat there and waited all night and nobody seemed to notice us. The next day a ship called the *Cläre Hugo Stinnes* came along and we drove it ashore. We had to use the gun to do it, so we were on the surface in the middle of Norway and the captain then said, 'I think we'd better get out of this,' so we went down Kors Fjord on the surface and, just as we got to the entrance of it, some aircraft and anti-submarine vessels appeared and we were hunted just outside.

This was early on in the days of submarine warfare and we weren't very experienced. We were quite certain the enemy had hydrophones and could hear us if we made a noise. We therefore tried hard not to use any machinery, to do everything as silently as we could. Of course, if you don't use any machinery in a submarine it will do as it likes and you begin to lose control. On one occasion we went very deep, with the stern down and the captain was saying, 'Hold it,' and 'Don't make a noise.' Eventually we had to do something because the bilge water was getting near the electric motors and he said, 'Well, get some buckets.' We bailed the water out of the engine-room, passing these buckets through the submarine and poured them into the torpedo compartment which made less noise than pumping. This decreased the angle and then a stoker in the engine-room dropped a bucket which made a huge clatter. Everybody burst out laughing, easing the tension. Eventually we got to the stage where *Trident* was still sinking and we had to do something so the captain said, 'I think the best thing is to blow a little into the main ballast to stop her going down.' So we did that. But of course you lose control because, as you come up the air expands and comes more buoyant and after a very short time we were roaring up out of control and burst right out of the sea.

The captain raised the periscope to find the enemy had gone.

ORDINARY SEAMAN DICK COPPEARD, RN

At Portland we were given a night's leave so we went ashore, picked up a couple of WAAFs and took them to the pictures. While we were there they flashed on the screen for all personnel of the ships in harbour to return to their ships immediately. When we got back they were putting sandbags all round the gun positions and the bridge and we wondered what the devil was going on.

Eventually we found out that we were going over to France to pick up the troops. We had heard one or two rumours but didn't know what we were letting ourselves in for. We crossed the Channel with one or two small ships and came up near Le Havre first of all. It was real war: the town was on fire, there was smoke everywhere and oil tanks burning. We didn't go right into the harbour but were told to carry on to Fécamp and embark as many people from the jetties as we could. Most of them were stretcher-cases and walking wounded. They looked like a beaten army – they weren't really, but they looked it. Some were from the 51st Highland Division, a few French, and a regiment from the Midlands.

We cleared the mess decks to make room for the stretchers. The walking cases were pushed into corners. There were two or three hundred of them on board, plus about sixty of us crew. We tried to feed them but ran out of food. At one point we had to take bread off some French soldiers who didn't want to share it around. They seemed shocked and were very, very quiet. I don't think they realised what was happening to them. A lot of them had never seen warfare. We got the chaps off at Portsmouth. Those that could walk marched off the jetty, heads up and shoulders back. Some of them lined up. I don't think many had their rifles with them.

We did three trips in all; the second and third were to St Valéry. Three nights and four days without sleeping, except for a brief kip in the wheel-house. We were unopposed until we reached St Valéry on the third trip. Unknown guns fired on us all the time we were loading: four or five hours in all. The skipper was on the bridge, I was in the wheelhouse and everyone else on the ship was down below helping the wounded. I had to stay in the wheelhouse all the time, in case we had to leave in a hurry. I had to rely on someone bringing me food or drink but I got very phlegmatic in the end and had a catnap now and then. All the time these guns were firing at us but luckily nothing hit us.

Then the skipper shouted down the voice pipe, 'Steer for the harbour entrance, don't wait for orders, just get out.' The guns followed us out of the harbour and we had a couple of near-misses but nobody was hurt.

On our way back from St Valéry a dozen or so German aircraft passed overhead. Luckily they ignored us, even though we were a pukka warship and didn't carry a Red Cross. We had no real anti-aircraft armament except our famous 'steam' mortars. They were a couple of mortars mounted in the stern and connected up to high-pressure steam. You dropped a grenade in and waited until the dive-bomber was coming down and when it was at the right height you opened a valve and the grenade shot up in the air. By the time it got up there the aeroplane was half a mile away. Oh my God, it was funny. That was the desperate situation we were in. It would have been funny if it hadn't been so serious.

LIEUTENANT BRUCE JUNOR, RN

I was serving in HMS *Ajax* who was having a refit after seeing action in the Battle of the River Plate. I was on a short leave when the Commander rang me up to report at once with my boots and gaiters on and prepare to go over seas. I dashed back to Chatham where I and another officer went in an Admiralty car to Ramsgate and boarded an old destroyer HMS *Wolfhound*. J. W. McCoy was Captain of an ordinary crew who had been on convoy duty in the Atlantic.

We crossed the Channel under heavy attack by bombers but we landed on the jetty at Dunkirk. A British Naval Officer was giving the orders but Captain Tennant was in overall charge from a dug-out at the root of the jetty (the landward each of the jetty). I remember four of us went into a building in Dunkirk when a big bomb blasted off and a couple of soldiers who had been out in the open were killed, but inside the building we were alright. We walked about three miles along the front down to the beach where there were a few soldiers and one on a stretcher. There were destroyers lying two to three miles out, because being deep draughted vessels, the water was too shallow for them to come in except at high tide.

I was part of a small group of naval officers who were ordered to report to the jetty. We had to walk through part of the town to reach this long jetty, roughly 400 yards where I was to be for several days taking part in the organisation of the evacuation of troops.

For the first 48 hours I was never off my feet. Soldiers came from scattered units and in small groups under command, all shattered and dispirited from fighting and marching with no food or rest. Montgomery, the Divisional Commander, marched the troops by night and handled the Division so well to manage to evacuate so very many soldiers.

The Admiralty got hold of Dutch schoots which were robust, petrol powered, large, open barges with powerful engines designed to carry cargo in the Dutch inland waterways. For the evacuation they were manned by British Naval personnel and of course were so useful because of their very shallow draft which enabled them to get up to the root of the pier. The destroyers could only safely reach the end of the jetty and then only at high water. The trouble was the range of the tide was 18 feet. This means that the water level between tides changes by 18 feet, thus making it very difficult to get the troops down into the barges at low water. Very early on the Admiral in charge, had sent a signal asking for scaling ladders. Chatham and Sheerness dockyards worked day and night making dozens of schoot scaling ladders to send over to Dunkirk in destroyers.

The evacuation of the beaches was a magnificent bit of organisation but it has gone down in history that the whole of the British Expeditions Force

(BEF) came off on Dunkirk beaches which is nonsense. 30,000 to 40,000 men were evacuated from the beaches by the "little ships" which was a very magnificent effort. It was, however, a drop in the ocean compared to the evacuation by the Royal Navy and the Merchant Navy from the jetty of some 220,000 men.

The destroyers came alongside the deep water side of the jetty to fill up with men, but they were quite unsuitable for that job because they could not take more than 100 men. The schoot barges could take a couple of hundred men. Ferries were also brought from England and Ireland and as they were designed with a shallow draught they did very good work taking off hundreds of troops. We lowered the wounded into the ferries as well as we could, at some points of the tide a number of wounded could be got onto the destroyers. I don't remember many stretcher cases. I dare say some had to be left behind to fall into the hands of the enemy. The men's spirits varied; some straggled down in ones and twos, while some marched on in good order. I expect it depended on what they had been through previously and what sort of officers they had. There were quite a few French colonial troops who were very dignified.

There were air raids continuously and the trawlers had to be quick because of the falling bombs. All the ammunition and oil tanks for the BEF were stored in Dunkirk Harbour, somewhere just across the fareway, and all the time I was in Dunkirk the sappers were blowing up the ammunition and burning the oil.

There was an old paddler that used to ply between London Bridge and Southend Pier for five bob, seasick and back. She berthed at the extreme end of the jetty outside, not inside, and was bombed and sunk. The bombing made three large gaps in the jetty but we bridged them with the brows (gangways) from the old paddler. These brows saved the day. Then the first spitfire I had ever seen came over and they did good work. They drove the Germans off and kept them away and allowing us to keep them away and allowing us to keep the momentum going.

We were at it 24 hours a day getting these chaps off with very little food. After the first 48 hours other chaps working with me simply lay down on the jetty and went to sleep with his head on his cap. He slept for about 15 minutes, then got up, didn't feel much better and said "you go and have a sleep". I lay down on the concrete and put my cap under my head and slept like a log for about 15 minutes. What those 15 minutes did for me was quite incredible. I don't remember any food other than a sandwich at times and, on occasion, being able to scrounge some food off ship whilst the soldiers were boarding.

I was on that jetty about a week when I was shanghaied. I had been helping a wounded soldier down into a trawler when the bombing increased with a bomb landing close by so the skipper thought it best to go and pulled away once I was on board. A bomb immediately fell where I had been standing on the jetty. Armed with one 4-inch gun on the trawler I found myself in Ramsgate. I went to a hotel the Admiralty had taken over which was packed out. I slept in a chair, wrote a hurried note to my wife and bought a pair of socks before getting a lift back to Dunkirk in HMS *Keith*. I did this on my own initiative as I had involuntarily deserted my post. I was there some days more feeling very weary and my feet were sore of going up and down that concrete. We got the bulk of the men off in those eight days and Dunkirk was still burning.

Orders came for me to rejoin my ship, HMS *Ajax*. I think they thought when they sent me back it was finished, no more to be done. After I had gone I heard that they did another day and got a lot more troops off. Then the other pier master, a very nice man who had been working along side me, came off in a landing craft which was bombed and sunk. He was drowned.

I scrounged a lift back to Ramsgate on a ferry '*Ulster Prince*' being used in the evacuation. The skipper said it had life belts for 100 people, but that a good 800 people were on board. I was damn tired, but returned to Chatham and rejoined HMS *Ajax*. We sailed out to the Mediterranean a few days later.

Lieutenant-Commander C. H. Corbet-Singleton, RN

H. M. S. Albury.
9th June 1940.

Sir,

I have the honour to forward the account of proceedings of His Majesty's Ship *Albury* during the days May 28th to June 5th 1940.

2.   I left Harwich at noon on May 23th in company with the Fifth Minesweeping Flotilla, arrived off Zudecotte Beach at 2130 and, anchoring, as close as possible, sent boats inshore to embark troops. The rate of embarkation was then slow as the tide was low and a small surf was troublesome on the beach. The troops were in good spirits though short of rations; I landed a quantity of dry provisions in the skiff.

3.   About 2330 a bomb was seen to drop about one mile to seaward of the ship, but no interference was caused to the work in hand.

4.   At 0230 on May 29th I got under way and proceeded without incident to Margate, where the troops were disembarked.

5.   I then returned to Zudecotte, arriving there at 1930 on May 29th; a considerable amount of bombing was in progress. On arrival the roads were

fairly empty, as we had passed, on the way, a number of loaded ships returning.

6. I made towards a burning paddle-steamer, which had grounded and, being full of troops and survivors, appeared to be in a bad way. All boats and Carley floats were sent away and many survivors were picked up. Bombs were being dropped continually around the ship and the paddle-steamer during this operation, and two machine-gun attacks were carried out. I have nothing but the utmost praise for all concerned, the majority of whom are very young and had certainly never been in action before. Continual anti-aircraft fire was kept up by the Twelve Pounder. I sent a signal for Fighter assistance, which arrived later in the evening.

7. Fifty seven cot-cases alone were brought off, mostly suffering from severe burns; the Commanding Officer and other survivors from His Majesty's Destroyer *Grenade* were amongst those embarked. After having cleared the steamer out as far as was known, I proceeded down the coast towards Bray, and picked up troops from several boats, which they had found on the beach. A Captain Churchill, from the Headquarters Staff, came off and told me that he had to get over to England to see his uncle, the Prime Minister, by 0600.

8. I proceeded to Margate, arriving at 0530 on May 30th, disembarked troops, survivors and Captain Churchill, then sailed for Sheerness for coal and ammunition.

9. I left Sheerness at 0300 on May 31st and arrived without incident off the beach just to the East of Dunkirk, at 0930. The rate of embarkation was slow owing to considerable surf on the beach, but valuable assistance was given by a large power boat. It was necessary for me to leave at 1230 in order to unload and be at my rendez-vous by 2200 on May 31st for the evening operations.

10. I sailed from Margate to comply with previous instructions and proceeded, under the orders of the Senior Officer of the Fifth Minesweeping Flotilla, to my appointed station off the beach; navigation at this period was difficult, as the absence of wind allowed the smoke from Dunkirk to settle over the channel, so that visibility was poor. On anchoring at 2345 a shell from a shore battery landed about a cable to seaward; this was repeated spasmodically. Reports were then received of magnetic mines being dropped in the channel.

11. About 0230 the Flotilla was ordered to carry on embarkation, using

ships' boats. Shortly after dawn a bombing attack took place, and from then on these attacks were practically continuous. Several Heinkel III type aircraft were observed, but the majority of the attackers were identified as Junkers 87 Dive-bombers. Embarkation was carried out, though the rate was slow.

12.   His Majesty's Ship *Speedwell* was seen to be aground; a wire was passed and I towed her off. During this operation the ship came under machine-gun fire from the air, and great credit is due to my First Lieutenant for the speed and coolness with which he carried out the evolution.

13.   I then received orders from the Flag Officer afloat to proceed alongside in Dunkirk harbour, and to complete with troops there. As troops were being embarked, bombs were dropped in the harbour and a machine-gun attack was delivered, but no casualties were incurred.

14.   Just before I slipped, with a full load of troops on board, His Majesty's Destroyer *Ivanhoe* was hit by a bomb outside the harbour. Two ships went to her assistance, so I proceeded at full speed.

15.   While leaving the channel and coming up to the Breedt bank, the most intense bombing attacks were experienced. Repeated near misses were registered on His Majesty's Ship *Gossamer*, ahead of me. His Majesty's Destroyer *Havant*, who had just overtaken me, was hit in the vicinity of number Three gun; continuing at high speed, she described a large circle to starboard, and when last seen was steaming in a Southerly direction. Near misses were also registered on His Majesty's Ship *Albury*; Fighter assistance was requested.

16.   These bombers came in relays and pursued the ship well out to sea. The Twelve pounder was kept in action the whole time, and it was very noticeable that if fire was withheld until aircraft approaching from astern were close, they were forced to sheer off and go round again. Effective use was made of Lewis and Bren guns, the latter obtained from and manned by the troops.

17.   I proceeded to Sheerness, landed the troops, replenished supplies of coal and ammunition, and sailed for Dunkirk at 1600, on June 2nd.

18.   On arrival in Dunkirk harbour at 0015 on June 3rd, I went alongside the Eastern arm. French troops were embarked though there did not appear to be many waiting, and it was necessary to send along the jetty towards the town to collect them. During the time that His Majesty's Ship *Albury* was alongside, intermittent shelling was taking place, apparently directed at the harbour and ships alongside. I sailed eventually about 0215 with Two hundred troops on board.

19.   While returning I encountered a floating mine off 'U' buoy, which I reported to you. It was slightly conical in shape, and from its appearance might have been a Dutch mine. I sank it and proceeded to Sheerness to land the troops and to coal.

20.   I sailed again for Dunkirk at 1630 on June 3rd in company with His Majesty's Ships *Gossamer* and *Leda*, and was detached off 'W' buoy to act independently, in order to arrive at the harbour at 0020 on June 4th. I was ordered alongside the West pier, filled up with French soldiers, and left the harbour at 0130.

21.   Fog was encountered between 'U' buoy and the North Goodwin Light-vessel, and I overtook His Majesty's Ship *Leda*, who had been in collision; I stood by her until relieved by His Majesty's Ship *Kellett*.

22.   In the vicinity of the Elbow buoy, the French Auxiliary Naval Vessel *Emile Deschamps*, crowded with troops and refugees, was passed. I was about five cables ahead of her, and signalling her the course to the North Goodwin Light-vessel which she had missed, when she blew up and sank within half a minute. I turned to pick up survivors, and reported to you that she had been sunk by a mine.

23.   The London Fire Brigade Fire-float *Massey Shaw* was on the spot and assisted with the rescue work. During the operation the Master of this vessel informed me quite confidently that he had seen a periscope shortly before the explosion, so I sent out an Enemy Submarine report. I proceeded to Margate with the survivors, forty of whom, men and women, were severely wounded, and landed them with the troops.

24.   The morale, courage, and endurance shewn by all on board during this period, was exceptional, an encouraging fact as the average age is very low. Sub-Lieutenant F.R.A. Turnbull, R.N. did excellent work on the beach with the boats, and Sub-Lieutenant B.P. Cahill, R.N.V.R. spent long hours on the bridge with unremitting attention to duty. . . .

I have the honour to be, Sir,

Your obedient servant,

C.H. Corbet-Singleton

Lieutenant-Commander
in Command.

The Vice-Admiral,
Dover Command.
(Copy to the Senior Officer, 5th Minesweeping Flotilla.)

PETTY OFFICER PILOT DICK LEGGOTT, FLEET AIR ARM

I joined *Glorious* in April 1940. I had been operating from Wick with another petty officer pilot, A.G. Johnson. Our flight had been led by Lieutenant Charles Evans and he asked us to join him on *Glorious*. However Evans didn't join *Glorious*, and this rather upset us.

We had heard a few rumours about *Glorious* and soon we learnt that things were not at ease between the captain and his air staff, his Commander Flying, J. B. Heath, and Lieutenant-Commander Flying. While we were in northern waters the captain wanted to send our aircraft to help the army, but Heath said it was a misuse of naval aircraft. The outcome was that Heath was put ashore at Scapa Flow. There was a feeling of sadness about it all, for I could understand both points of view.

We returned to collect RAF Hurricanes and Spitfires from off the Norwegian coast. On the way back the captain told us there would be no flying, which flew in the face of proper practice. I believe he wanted to get the RAF planes back as soon as possible. However, there should have been aircraft up keeping a look out for enemy ships, particularly as it was June and it was daylight practically the whole time. As soon as the captain said this, the personnel of Swordfish Squadron 823 started storing their torpedoes away. A number of aviators objected; but they were told by the chief in charge of the operation that they were getting a lap ahead for leave.

On 8th June we had left the Fleet. It was a lovely summer's day and we were accompanied by two destroyers, HMS *Ardent* and HMS *Acasta*. I wasn't concerned because we had done this journey before. We were sitting in the sunshine when we were stood down for tea. I went below and as I was having my tea I saw through the porthole splash, splash, splash. The messman went up on deck and then came running down to tell us that two German pocket battleships were shelling us.

Our action stations were our aeroplanes. I finished eating my Dundee cake and went up to the hangar. When I arrived there I found a few pilots beginning to congregate. On the bridge our two squadron commanders were talking to the captain. They wanted to take off and attack the bridge of the *Scharnhorst* and *Gneisenau*, knock out some of their sensitive equipment and personnel, and then, if *Glorious* couldn't turn into wind, land on *Ark Royal*. But the captain rejected this idea. He told the squadron commanders it would be like rats about to leave what they thought might be a sinking ship. So we didn't get our Gladiators off.

While we were discussing this a salvo came in and shell splinters were splattering into aeroplanes which began to leak petrol. The damage control people arrived and told us to leave so that they could deal with the mess.

I left and stood by a guard rail with my section leader looking out at the two ships. Then I went to get my Mae West. As I was stepping into the ship's island, a salvo came in, killing three or four sailors who had gone ahead of me. I saw a PO Telegraphist and asked him if he'd got a signal off. He wasn't certain, though he thought something had gone off on low power, and he was hopeful someone would have heard it.

Then down from the bridge came a messenger who told us the captain had been killed and that all communication with the bridge had been severed. I was talking with Sub Lieutenant McLaughlan when we were approached by an Engineer Lieutenant. He had been ordered by the Engineer Commander to go round the ship and inform everyone that *Glorious* had not taken a full supply of oil at Scapa Flow. He stressed that all those who survived should tell the subsequent inquiry. At the time neither McLaughlan or myself appreciated the reason behind making this point. At this point, although the ship was burning, there had been no order to abandon ship. I then went with two lieutenants to the lower flying-off deck to arrange Carley floats ready for launching, and at the same time to muster men on the cable deck below. While we were doing this, four sailors emerged from one of the watches looking very anxious. A young Lieutenant ordered them to return below. This upset the men who explained that their officers had either been killed or severely wounded and that their CPO had ordered them on deck while he closed the water-tight doors behind them. The Lieutenant wanted to send them back, but I was joined by two other lieutenants from 823 Squadron who agreed with my view. The four men's faces showed their relief as they moved off to join the others on the cable deck. We wanted to get all the Carley floats into the water so that when people jumped in they'd be there all together. Unfortunately some character called out 'Every man for himself' and with that they all leapt over the side except for a few non-swimmers. We encouraged them to jump telling them their lifebelts would keep them afloat until they reached a float. One asked a young lieutenant to push him over which he did. 'Thank you,' he said as he was falling into the sea.

After everyone had jumped off I was left there with these two young lieutenants. I offered them each a cigarette and we had a few quiet minutes looking out over the sea. Then they asked me to join them on a Carley float. It was like being invited to tea on the vicar's lawn and having cucumber sandwiches.

I swam to a Carley float some way away. I was absolutely exhausted when I got there and was pulled on. I was bitterly cold. There were no other floats nearby. Twelve hours later, we had drifted to other Carley floats whose occupants decided to swim over to our float because they thought we had food and water, when in fact none of the floats had either food or water aboard. As the ship was sinking we had sent stores ratings below to see if they could locate bully beef and tinned milk, but they had been beaten by smoke and flames.

People were hanging on to the sides. I remember clearly one of them hanging on to one of the ropes. I asked him if he was all right. He looked at me and he said, 'Yes.' And with that he slipped away into a very peaceful death. Another said he was going down below to keep warm. I grabbed him, but he persisted. In the end he took one big dive and swam out ten or fifteen yards and then stopped. He looked as if he was sitting in a little shelter, a little shelter in a field. In the beginning I was asked how long I thought we would be on the float. I reckoned eight hours, possibly sixteen. In the end every one of the fifty-odd people we had slipped away and I was left alone with Marine Hellis.

After three days and two nights we were picked up by a Norwegian trawler which later found Squadron Commander, Bing Cross, and one of his pilots, Pat Jameson.

It was hard to say why I survived. I think it's the way that one is nurtured. In nature, animals, plants and humans are the same: if they are well nurtured from an early age they will stand difficult circumstances far better than if they are poorly nurtured. It was also a state of mind: it was no good being afraid, it is a pointless exercise. Why make yourself, allow yourself to be mentally uncomfortable? I kept thinking that my mother would be unhappy if I didn't make it. The other thing was, is it all worth it? I believed that it was, and that helped greatly.

3

From 1940 to the sinkings of *Hood* and *Bismarck*

After the defeat of France in June 1940, the serious question arose over the future of the French Fleet which, now based at Oran in Algeria, might, the British government feared, fall into German or Italian hands.

STOKER 1st CLASS VERNON COLES, RN

HMS *Faulknor* was part of 'H' Force. We met our flotilla at sea with the *Hood* and *Ark Royal*, then together sailed south. *Hood* was flying the flag of Vice-Admiral Sir James Somerville. We also had the *Valiant* in company. When we eventually arrived in Gibraltar, we thought, 'God, there's something happening here.' We were even more convinced when we saw that *Resolution* had arrived – another 15-inch battleship. There were also the cruisers *Arethusa* and *Enterprise* and ten other destroyers.

We began sailing on our own, patrolling off Mers-el-Kebir, near Oran. The French told us to shove off. Because we only had five 4.7-inch guns we withdrew and patrolled on the skyline. The following morning, 3rd July, the entire fleet arrived. Captain Holland, who spoke French, went to present terms to the French commander, Admiral Gensoul. The terms were given roughly as follows: put to sea and join forces with the British; or sail to the French West Indies and there de-militarise his ships; or sail with reduced crews to any British port; or scuttle all his ships within six hours of the offer of the British ultimatum. If there was no answer to this signal, we would open fire at 11 o'clock.

We reckoned that Somerville found this pretty distasteful. However, eleven o'clock came, and we did not hear anything from Admiral Gensoul; but we didn't fire. So the boat went in again with more terms. Admiral Gensoul refused to see the captain. He was told that we would open fire at two o'clock. It didn't happen. Then the terms went in the third time but again they were rejected. Apparently, Churchill was getting a bit hot under the collar about this. So, as there was no reply, five o'clock was given as the deadline and the battle ensigns went up. I was on no. 5 gun so I had a front-line view of the quarterdeck.

At 1755 we opened fire. It was a sad irony. We were not attacking the Germans or Italians, but the Royal Navy's oldest enemy and our twentieth-century ally. The whole fleet was going across and ranging. What a bombardment! I had never seen anything like it. One of our destroyers out on the starboard wing had got so close inshore that she was coming under the range of their 9-inch gun, so the *Hood* just trained her guns to fire at the hill, just below a big fort which was where the firing was coming from. The fort came tumbling down because the blast had undermined its foundations. The French battleship *Dunkerque* was right under a dockyard crane and the *Hood* had to destroy it before she could get at the *Dunkerque*. Her first broadside hit the crane, it was just like a matelot dropping. The second salvo hit the *Dunkerque*. We were firing from a distance of seven or eight miles, which for a 15-inch gun is point-blank range. Our ships sank the *Bretagne*, knocked the stern off *Mogador* and badly damaged *Provence*. Admiral Gensoul then said, 'For God's sake stop firing. You're murdering us.' Over 1100 French sailors had been killed.

The *Strasbourg* got away, along with five large destroyers. We went after her with *Hood*, *Ark Royal* and three F-class destroyers. She had a good start and we missed her. We turned back and joined our fleet. We didn't like firing on the French, but if we hadn't, they might have joined the Germans. Before we got back to Gibraltar the French Air Force came over and dive-bombed us with twin dive-bombers.

SIGNALMAN FREDERICK HUMPHRYES, RN

Mention the Royal Navy in World War Two and people instantly think of the big battleships, cruisers and destroyers. However, at the beginning of the war most of these warships were distributed world-wide, leaving the North Sea and the seas between Scotland and Greenland almost completely unguarded. These waters had to be patrolled for apart from the English Channel, this was the only way out to the Atlantic where the German raiders wanted to attack our convoys. As a result, ocean liners were commandeered by the Royal Navy for this purpose.

The liners were stripped of their luxury fittings and the lower decks and holds packed with empty oil drums in the vain belief it would enable them to remain afloat if holed in an action. These AMCs, or Armed Merchant Cruisers, were then fitted with eight 6-inch guns, many small calibre weapons and, in some cases, depth-charge throwers which made them quite formidable warships, even though most if not all of the 6-inch guns were of pre-World War One vintage, while many were made before 1900. Their main duty was to patrol the area between Scotland, Iceland and the Denmark Straits between Iceland and Greenland (known as the Northern Patrol). Unfortunately they were just as vulnerable to attacks from submarines as any other merchant ship, as they had no sonar or asdic equipment.

I was a signalman on the *Transylvania*, an ex-Anchor Line ship. We, *Rawalpindi* and *Scotstoun* were the first three AMCs to go on patrol, although soon followed by many more. At midnight on 10th August 1940 I was off watch and asleep in my bunk when I was awakened by two very loud explosions, quickly followed by the klaxon for 'Action Stations'. I was up and dressed in a matter of minutes: all the time I could feel the ship heeling over. I raced along the passage to get to the bridge three decks above me and, as I ran, I could see and hear the watertight doors clanging shut, closing off the passages and decks.

When I did reach the bridge the ship was listing well to starboard. Two torpedoes had struck us amidships in the engine-room, a fatal blow as this was the largest void in the ship. The conditions down there must have been appalling; as the ship continued to heel over we could hear the explosive noise of bulkheads and watertight doors giving way under the strain of trying to hold back the sea, and with these noises came a continuous roar, apparently from the engine-room, from ruptured steam pipes and the inrushing sea. The ship was sinking, so the captain mustered his officers on the bridge, thanked them and the ratings on the bridge then gave the order to 'Abandon Ship'. The leading signalman who was in charge of my watch said, 'Go on, boy, off you go and good luck.' I never met up with him again and to this day don't know whether he survived or not.

By now the ship was lying over at an astonishing angle, and the weather conditions were very bad. It was impossible to launch the life-boat port side due to the angle of the ship, and on the starboard side (my boat station) the rough sea and high waves had smashed the boats in the davits. I am a non-swimmer, so it was no use me jumping into the sea. I just clung to a deck hatch. I had no idea what to do, but honestly did not think for one minute about dying as it all seemed so unreal. Eventually, while clinging to the hatch, I heard men shouting to me to jump. Even though it was dark I could just distinguish a small boat, known as a harbour skimming dish, in front of me. I have no idea how I managed to reach the boat – all I remember is that I was in the water with several others clinging to the ropes around the sides of the boat, which was completely full. We soon drifted off away from the ship and in the dark we watched her slowly stand on end and sink beneath the waves, carrying with her very many of the crew. I noticed that, strangely, some lights remained on as the sank. This all happened during the fifteen or twenty minutes from the time we were hit.

I remained clinging to the little boat for the next seven hours. The weather had been so bad that rescue operations had been delayed: by the time they reached the place where the ship had sunk we had drifted quite a few miles away. Eventually we sighted them in the distance and, as I was a signalman, the men in the boat hauled me in and held me upright while I signalled to them with a hand lamp. Fortunately they saw the light and headed towards us. On reaching our position the four destroyers, *Fame*, *Mashona*, *Matabele* and *Ashanti* formed a square in an attempt to create a calmer patch of sea. We drifted toward *Ashanti*, which had lowered her scrambling nets along her side.

As we reached the destroyer's side those hanging on the side of the boat nearest the ship scrambled up the nets first, while we on the other side had to wait until some of the men had left the boat before we could enter it and reach the nets. With the very heavy swell the rise and fall between the boat and the destroyer was considerable; when it came to my turn I mis-timed my jump, missing the net completely. Fortunately the small boat rose on a wave, catching my legs and throwing me up to where a sailor lying flat on the destroyer's deck caught my wrist, hanging on until another sailor helped him pull me inboard.

By this time I was exhausted and numb with cold after all that time in the water. The sailors took me below to a mess where I was stripped of my clothes, given a blanket to wrap around myself and a cup of steaming hot tea, after which I lay down on the lockers for a good sleep. When I awoke I was given my clothes, which by now were dry, and together with the other survivors, a good meal.

We anchored off Greenock and, after thanking the crew members(to whom I am eternally grateful) we were taken ashore. We were met by members of the Salvation Army, who took us to a large hall where we could have a good wash and were given fresh clean civilian clothes plus half-a-crown(2s. 6d.), a bar of toilet soap, a small hand-towel, a packet of cigarettes and a box of matches.

After being debriefed we were sent down to London, where we reported to the RN Transport Office. The chief petty officer said that if we lived within the London area we could have night leave to visit our relations, but only on the strict understanding that we reported back to him by 8am the next day. This we readily agreed to. The following day we were on our way back to Chatham, to HMS *Pembroke*, to await another draft to another ship to continue our part in the war at sea.

Lieutenant Horace Taylor, RNVR

I had volunteered for the Navy at the outbreak of war in September 1939. I was thirty-two and had spent the previous two years doing war service as staff officer to the man in charge of Manchester Central Docks. I was sent a medical form and had to have my ears examined. When I got to the recruitment department they called my name: 'Taylor – Navy rejection.' I felt horrible. So I went home and wrote a letter to the Secretary to the Admiralty. I told them if they didn't do something very quickly, they were going to lose a good chap. My letter went that day and the next my commission came through.

To start with, there were various training jobs to do. I had some funny jobs in my time. At one point I was given a Webley .45 gun and was told to defend the third floor of the Admiralty. I was there until the start of the Battle of Britain. Then I became involved with mine-sweeping, especially magnetic mines. When I first started there were only two of us, but some more chaps came later. We were a very secret society. Nobody knew we existed. We had no Admiralty building of our own, no telephone, no brass plate on the door. The reason for the secrecy was that we were scared stiff that the Germans would find out what we knew about their mines and alter their bombs as a result.

At first the work didn't sound very thrilling to me, but once the Battle of Britain and the Blitz on London began, I realised just how important we were. Magnetic mines were being dropped in their hundreds and London was virtually paralysed. The day I started work, there were 121 unexploded bombs to be dealt with. As the evacuation area for just one bomb was 20,000 people, you can imagine the panic everyone was in. The trouble was, these were the first mines of their kind to be dropped and we had little idea how to handle them. So there were no proper tools. We were working with ladies' hair pins, match sticks, bent nails, a bicycle pump and the bulb of a motor-horn.

My first job was in a big hospital in North London which held 2,000 patients, mostly from Dunkirk. A mine had landed in the front gateway. No one could get in or go out. The mine weighed 2,000 kilos, was two feet two inches in diameter, and nine feet long. Magnetic mines like this one were being dropped by enemy aircraft in the hope of mining the Thames. They had huge reinforced parachutes and when the bomb was released, the aeroplane, now free of the weight, would rise sharply up into the sky. If all went well, the mine would fall into the sea. If it didn't and landed elsewhere, then it wouldn't go off. Or if it did, it would go off when it shouldn't.

These mines had a small fuse, which, if triggered, would go off in seventeen seconds. The mystery of the seventeen seconds was that this was the time the Germans estimated it would take for the mine to sink down into the water. Then the pressure of the water flooding the fuse hole would immobilise the seventeen-second compartment. There was a clock on the other side of the mine which activated it from a magnetic point of view, so that it would stick to a ship's steel hull if one came close enough. Then it would explode two or three hours later. Our job was to take out that little delicate seventeen-second fuse and make the mine safe enough to be moved. Then the army boys would take our mine to somewhere on the south coast where some very splendid scientists would open it up and see how it worked.

It was that little fuse that put the wind up us, because we knew that if we started it, we'd have seventeen seconds to clear out. So part of our drill was to find somewhere to hide, if we realised it was going to go off. That is not as easy as it sounds. And how far can you run in seventeen seconds? But my first job was so important, I couldn't afford to be scared, with 2,000 wounded soldiers and God knows how many nurses relying on me. The responsibility was shattering.

First of all I got my escape hole dug a hundred yards away from the mine. My assistant, Able Seaman Ross, would stay down there, logging my instructions as to what I was doing with the mine. Then, if something went wrong, at least some information could be passed to the Admiralty.

I told the hospital authorities what I was doing, and told them that if I got the small fuse out, I would blow a whistle, so everyone in the hospital could relax. Because the tension, as you can imagine, was colossal. I was working in full view of the hospital; they were all watching through the windows.

I set to work with the bicycle pump, the motor-horn and a bucket of water. The idea was to put enough pressure into the bulb of the horn to make the mine think it was twelve feet under water, which would immobilise the fuse. That seemed to work all right. Then I started to work on removing the fuse. We always expected there to be booby traps behind the fuses, so when I got the locking ring almost undone, I jammed a bit of stick into the ground to hold the fuse from falling out. Then I tied some rope to the stick and walked off, holding the other end of the rope in my hand, so I could pull away the stick from a safe distance. I was walking away, knowing that everyone was watching, very steady and nonchalant, not scared at all. I was just about to get into my little fox hole when there was one hell of an explosion. It felt as if the whole building was shaking. Well, it wasn't the main charge, it was a big one, because it blew a hole in the concrete path four feet across and blew the mine nine feet away.

I walked back very slowly and carefully. I knew that there wasn't any danger from the small fuse so I blew a whistle. I hadn't realised what a stupid thing that was to do. Because in no time at all a tidal wave of nurses came out after us. They wanted my tie, they wanted my shirt, they wanted the German parachute. I was nearly pulled apart and the parachute nearly disappeared, such was the relief of the tension. I must confess to having felt some satisfaction after that job, looking at that huge building full of life, knowing that it would be there a bit longer.

My second job was at the Royal Air Force Depot, Uxbridge. For me, this was an easy one. There were no tidal waves of nurses and the fuses all came free smoothly. I thought no more about it, but I was awarded the George Cross.

A much more tricky customer was in a woodland in Oxfordshire. When we found the mine I thought to myself, 'Now where do I go in seventeen seconds with all these trees in the way?' There was an army unit not far away so I went to the colonel and told him I wanted fifty men to carve a way through the forest. He said, 'Who the bloody hell do you think you are?' I was only a Lieutenant and no proper application had been made by the Admiralty. So I said, 'It really is important. May I telephone the Admiralty?' There was a 36-hour delay on the telephones at this time, but the colonel said, 'Have a go.' He didn't know that our squad had a secret telephone code which would get us through to the Admiralty in two minutes. I picked up the telephone and whispered my code and in a couple of minutes I was through. Five minutes later the War Office phoned back and told the colonel to give me everything I wanted.

When I finally got started on the mine, the fuse came out sweetly, thank goodness, but when I started on the magnetic circuit, there was a loud hiss as I got to the 4-inch locking ring. I thought, 'Hell, this has never happened before,' and I jumped back over a stone wall and landed in a bed of nettles. And then I realised what a clot I'd been. The mine had been filled with hot explosives which had shrunk when they'd cooled. I'd just released the vacuum; that was the hiss.

On one occasion, we had a huge bomb in the Southampton basin. It was lying alongside a wall where three big coal barges were moored. The trouble was that two of the barges had been blown up by another mine and had sunk, burying our mine in God knows how much coal. So we moored two barges together and over the space between them, we built a device to support pulley blocks. Then we sent down divers, weighed down with copper suits, to scrape away the coal. The pulley blocks technique failed to shift the mine, so we got an atmospheric balloon. These balloons were four feet in diameter and were supposed to lift about a ton, so we shackled that on to the mine and waited until low tide. The balloon lifted the mine off the sea bed without any problems. Then we secured the mine to our vessel and set sail with a quarter-mile of rope in between us and the mine, just in case it decided to go off.

When we reached the head of a minefield in the Solent, bad weather blew up and the balloon sprung a puncture, so we were dragging our mine through a mine field. Eventually we got another balloon attached and decided to try to beach the mine on the Hamble Spit. We grounded it and when it had dried out, we could see its vital components. Then we left it on the mud bank and went to an establishment called HMS *Cricket*. We explained to the commander what had happened and where our mine was and that we were going to fire it at noon that day. That was agreed on. However, when we fired there was a bit of a thunder clap. We weren't very popular after that. So we thought it was about time we left.

In all the operations we did, I never felt afraid. It was prayer that kept me going. Every morning at breakfast time I'd ask God to hold my hand steady and deal with that treacherous little fuse. Each time my arm was taken in a firm grip and I was in safe-keeping.

But I did get blown up, once. A bomb I was working on went off and blew me right through two houses. When they found me, I was still conscious. I knew exactly what had gone wrong, and all I wanted to do was to tell my boss what had happened, for the sake of the rest of the crew. But my rescuers wanted to put me into hospital. I was wrapped in bandages. I couldn't see; I thought I was blind, but it was just all the dirt in my eyes. I kept insisting I must go and see the Regional Commissioner but the doctor refused. So I said to him, 'You're obstructing a Naval Officer in the course of his duty.' I suppose he must have thought I was dulally because there was nothing about me to prove I was a naval officer. I didn't have any clothes on because they'd all been blown off.

Eventually they gave in and I was taken to the Regional Commissioner. They let me use the green line telephone and I was able to talk freely to my boss. He was very pleased to know that I was alive and he told me to go to hospital. I ended up in Leamington Spa, in a ladies' ward.

MARINE BILL BISHOP, RM

In the summer of 1940 HMS *Liverpool* was involved in convoy escort between Alexandria and Malta. Those of us who had attained the age of twenty in 1940, were entitled to draw a daily tot of rum, or 3d per day in lieu, and eagerly awaited the bosun's pipe followed by – 'Up spirits.' Invariably some wag would add – 'and stand fast the Holy Ghost.'

Some of the ship's company actually believed that our three-quarter cupful of two parts of water and one of rum, 'Nelson's Blood', endowed us with Dutch courage. As far as I was concerned its value was demonstrated to the full during my very first high-level bombing attack. The loudspeaker suddenly announced 'Enemy aircraft in sight on the port quarter.' Almost immediately a more accurate bearing followed along with the estimated height of the aircraft. It was an estimate too, as along with most of the Fleet the *Liverpool* was not equipped with radar. We relied entirely on the sharp eyes of the aircraft lookouts and the crews of the Director Control Tower (DCT). On the odd occasion we had an aircraft-carrier in attendance, we considered ourselves very fortunate. For most of that unforgettable summer our aircraft protection consisted of three ancient Gladiators from Malta; *Faith*, *Hope* and *Charity*.

Following the enemy aircraft warning, came another terse command; 'All guns load, load, load.' Simultaneously, all four turrets swivelled (manually) on to the given bearing. In a glance snatched between loading, I saw a swarm of Savoia Marchetti glinting like silver birds against blue sky. Those Italian pilots were very canny, and always kept well out of range of our high explosive shells.

We watched the white puffs of smoke from the exploding shells and could see a shower of black dots in the sky leaving the planes. All the while, the quartermaster was chanting 'Bombs falling, bombs falling, lie down, lie down.' I pressed my face hard against the gun deck. I heard the clanging of a thousand fragments of razor-edged shrapnel ricocheting all around me. During those initial bombing attacks, I learned the real meaning of fear.

Immediately after the raid, we scrambled to our feet and waited for the next attack. I looked around me at the haggard faces; and I realised that what I saw was also mirrored on my own. By October the ship's sides and both funnels were literally peppered with jagged shrapnel holes. One 2500-lb. bomb struck the ship dead amidships immediately in front of the semi-circular Compass platform, but was made harmless after striking a triangular projection of the superstructure which wrenched out the fins and detonator. The bomb plunged through three decks and came to rest on the armoured deck of the aircraft bomb room without exploding. The one casualty was a young stoker, who was asleep off watch on top of his locker. His remains were splattered all over the bulkheads.

During those dark days in the Mediterranean I did ask myself how much longer can we go on – how much more can we endure without breaking up? True enough, we'd had our fair share of mixed fortune and only a few casualties, but I felt sure that the worst was yet to come. The knowledge that we were fighting this war for a wage of just over a pound a week didn't exactly boost my flagging ego either. My answer came on the night of 14 October at approximately 1920 hours. There was a glorious brilliant full moon that night as *Liverpool* zig-zagged monotonously on her return journey from Malta to Alexandria with the rest of the escorts.

That full moon ensured that the ship made an excellent target and one that could be seen with ridiculous ease by the pilot of an Italian S79 torpedo-carrying plane. Zooming in from the starboard side, the plane was spotted only after he had released a cylinder of high explosive. I was lounging on the gundeck armed with a king size mug of tea and a doorstep sandwich of margarine and 'Admiralty Ham' (corned beef), when I heard the sound of the plane's engines.

A few seconds later the torpedo struck the starboard bow and set fire to the paint shop. 'Action stations' was called. I scrambled down the steel ladder leading to the steel room of 'X' turret, several feet below the water line. I was hurled against the racks holding the 6-inch shells by a much louder explosion. Violent and distinctly alarming shudders and vibrations reverberated along the hull for the whole of the ship's length. As we squatted in the small compartment, totally surrounded by tier upon tier of highly explosive shells, several minor explosions rippled along the hull. Once again, I knew the meaning of unadulterated fear. Then came the order; we heard, 'Prepare to abandon ship.' There was no panic-stricken rush for the ladder leading to the cabin flat above us and eventually to the quarterdeck. But there we found the heavy armoured hatch had jammed. There was a lot of swearing and grunts and groans as two of us pressed our backs against the hatch, egged on by the other two. The few minutes that elapsed before the hatch moved seemed like an eternity. I was not the only one thinking the ship would capsize.

Thankfully, we all clambered onto the quarterdeck with our lifebelts fully inflated and awaited the order to abandon ship. The order was never given. 'A' turret, against which the fire had been licking furiously, had been quickly flooded to prevent what would have undoubtedly been the death of the ship. To this day, I feel certain that the magazine crew were never given time to escape. Where we stood on the quarterdeck, we could feel the searing heat from what had been the fo'c'sle, as towering sheets of flame leaped above the superstructure. It was unforgettable. As the flames roared around 'A' turret, I could see the turret roof had disappeared and the triple guns pointed at different angles. I also noticed that the whole of the bows forward of the turret was leaning sharply to starboard. The fire parties were doing their best but the foam generating equipment which had been stored in the capstan flat for'ard, had been totally destroyed.

We helped the first-aiders and the Sick Berth Attendants to try to ease the pain of those who were severely burned. Some, however, died as I tried to bandage them. The blackened corpses with their grotesquely distorted limbs were laid out in line along both sides of the quarterdeck. Once the preliminary order to abandon ship had been cancelled we were ordered to revert to Defence Stations, which meant that we Marines closed up around P2 AA-gun. The fire continued to rage for the remainder of that long, long night. Before long, we were proceeding slowly astern assisted by a tow from the cruiser *Orion*. Sometimes our stern rose clear from the water and the sound of her engines seemed to magnify as the screws threshed madly and uselessly. There were two reasons for going astern; one was simply because the skipper had no choice – he could not possibly go ahead; second was the hope that the almost severed 40-foot section of the wrecked bows, would part company from the rest of the ship. Only the stem was holding the damaged structure.

I was the communications number and wearing the sticky earphones when, at 0200, I heard, 'Enemy aircraft approaching from the starboard quarter – believed to be large numbers – all guns load, load, load.' This meant that as the ship was going astern, the expected attack would come from our port bow or what was left of it. For about two minutes silence reigned on the gun deck which was most unusual. It was ruptured by the harsh grating tones of 'Shiner' Wright, 'I don't know about you blokes but as far as I'm concerned, this is bloody well it, don't let's kid ourselves about it boyos, so stand by your beds and muster your kits for the last time.' We all knew full well that the enemy planes could not possibly fail to see us; the ship was a blazing beacon. We heard the drone of the engines getting nearer; we shivered, fully expecting to hear that familiar banshee whine of falling bombs which would surely come.

But to our great relief, the armada of planes ignored us completely. We could only assume that they were returning after a raid on Alexandria. Even then, it would have been a simple matter for the planes to return at daylight. It was mid-afternoon on 15th October when the 40-foot length of our mangled bow finally broke away from the ship. The ship had suffered this torture long enough, and there was a great sigh of relief when the distorted remains of what was once her slender bows, sank slowly into the sea.

We buried our dead that same afternoon. Each body was weighted and, one by one, they were placed on a sloping stretcher on the guard rail. We listened to the melancholy notes of the Last Post, sounded by the Boy Bugler, as one by one our dead shipmates splashed into the darkness.

LIEUTENANT MICHAEL TORRENS-SPENCE, RN

I was appointed to the *Glorious*, the pre-war Mediterranean fleet aircraft-carrier, in September 1937. In July 1939, with the imminent threat of war, the fleet base was moved from Malta to Alexandria. When war with Germany was declared on 3rd September *Glorious* was sent through the Suez Canal to Aden to counter the German surface raider threat in the Indian Ocean. After three months of pretty intensive flying no raiders had appeared. I was then sent home from Aden by P&O. Three new squadrons were required for the new carrier *Illustrious* completing at Barrow, 806 Squadron (Fulmar) fighters and 815 and 819 (Swordfish). In May 1940 the *Illustrious* went to Bermuda to work up with the three squadrons embarked. On 10th June 1940 Italy declared war. This put the Italian Navy and Air Force between Britain and her last army (after Dunkirk) in Egypt. This army had some four divisions facing some fifteen Italian divisions on the Egyptian frontier. The Italian navy at Taranto had two brand new fast 15-inch battleships, with cruisers, destroyers and submarines to match but no aircraft-carriers. The Italian Air Force was deployed in Sardinia, Sicily, the Dodecanese and Libya with numerous fast bomber squadrons (SM 79s) and reconnaissance flying boats. The Mediterranean Fleet had two or three battleships, of late World War One vintage, and one aircraft-carrier, the twenty-five-year-old *Eagle*, with one Swordfish squadron embarked, but she was only good for 20 knots and in need of a refit. In cruisers and destroyers the Mediterranean Fleet was heavily outnumbered. The need to reinforce the Fleet and supply the army in Egypt was critically urgent. The Cape route would have taken far too long. Major reinforcements and supplies, including *Illustrious* and the modernised battleship *Valiant*, were therefore sailed for Alexandria from Gibraltar on 1st September to take on the Italian Air Force and Navy. The operation was a total and unexpected success thanks to *Illustrious*'s Fulmar fighters which shot down the enemy's reconnaissance aircraft. Consequently the Italians were unable to mount any offensive action. The whole force got through completely unscathed.

Admiral Cunningham, the C-in-C, was quick to seize the advantage he now had, amounting to command of the sea, no less. For the next four months the Fleet put to sea every two or three weeks to cover shipping movements between Gibraltar, Malta, and Alexandria. This continued until January 1941 when *Illustrious* ran short of fighters (I will come to this later). The Swordfish attacked the enemy shore bases and airfields by night and provided air anti-submarine patrols whilst the Fulmars dealt with the air threat. By far the most successful and spectacular offensive action by the Swordfish was the attack on Taranto on the night of 11th November 1940. The plan was to torpedo the Italian Fleet at its moorings at a range of 200 miles from the *Illustrious*. We would be up against 21 batteries of AA guns, barrage balloons, searchlights, and underwater torpedo nets, not to mention the guns on the ships we were attacking. Clearly the outcome was going to be anything between a disaster and a famous victory. We would be using torpedoes with magnetic warheads which had just been invented. Up to this point the torpedo had an ordinary contact head which depended on hitting something. This new magnetic head was designed to go off under the ship which would do much greater damage than hitting on the side of the ship. The RAF's Glenn Martin reconnaissance aircraft in Malta had taken some good photographs of where the ships were moored and of the location of barrage balloons and torpedo nets. It was a question of memorising these things and then playing off the cuff when you got there. There was no precedent for judging how it would work. You had to drop the torpedo at a height of 50 feet or less at very close range because of the confined space. Half the aircraft carried torpedoes and the other half bombs and flares. Fifty per cent casualties amongst the torpedo aircraft was probably the general guesstimate. Twenty-one aircraft attacked Taranto. About three weeks earlier we had a fire in the hangar in *Illustrious*. Trying to put in extra fuel tanks, somebody short-circuited a wire and caused a fire which seriously damaged several aircraft so *Illustrious*'s two Swordfish squadrons were short of aircraft. Five were borrowed from the old *Eagle*, she not being fit for the operation.

Lieutenant-Commander Williamson led off the first wave of aircraft at about 2030. My squadron commander, Ginger Hale, led the second wave about half an hour later.

During the attack a hundred thousand rounds were fired at us but only one aircraft was shot down in each wave. I got hit underneath by one half-inch machine-gun bullet. It was the pilot's job to aim the torpedo. Nobody was given a specific target. I dived down in between the moored ships aimed at the nearest big one, which turned out to be the *Littorio*, and released my torpedo. While you're low down over the water and surrounded by enemy ships the comfort is that they can't shoot at you without shooting at each other. I then made for the entrance to the harbour at zero feet and thence back to the *Illustrious*. It's difficult to know whether you have hit the target or not because, once you have dropped the torpedo, you're away. I didn't even see any of the action around me, I was too busy looking for barrage balloons. Once the formation had arrived over the target at about 8,000 feet it was every man for himself. We did not know what damage had been done until the RAF took some photographs afterwards which showed three battleships sitting on the bottom. There was great jubilation aboard *Illustrious* at having had only two aircraft shot down. When we were debriefed they wanted to know if I had hit anything and I could only say that you couldn't miss a big ship at such a short range if the torpedo ran straight. The photographs of that raid appeared in all the newspapers. I was credited with a hit on the *Littorio*. But ships sunk in the harbour can always be refloated. Only one of the three was never repaired. Two were repaired but it took a long time. In March 1941 the Italians still had only one of their battleships in action – the *Vittorio Veneto* – which wasn't hit at Taranto.

The objective of the navy was to try and keep the Mediterranean open for our traffic and to close off the enemy's supply route from Italy to North Africa. In the four months from September to December 1940 there were at least six operations, the whole fleet putting to sea to cover merchant-shipping movements, along with offensive action by the Stringbags. In November and December the Italians succeeded in mounting three or four high-level bombing raids with three-engined SM79s whose Bristol-Jupiter engines were Italian made, the same engines as the Stringbag. They were fast and aimed their bombs at *Illustrious* every time. But we never got hit. On 6th January we were at sea again off Malta to take over a convoy from Gibraltar. We knew that the Germans had sent a Fliegerkorps of Stukas to Sicily, commanded by a Luftwaffe Major-General. Their aim was to sink the *Illustrious*, having appreciated that she was the key to the control of the Mediterranean, but by now we were down to twelve Fulmars, having started with eighteen, and of these only five were serviceable.

I landed one at lunchtime after an anti-submarine patrol and went down to the wardroom for lunch. About ten minutes later a wave of Stukas arrived and a 1,000-lb. bomb penetrated the armoured deck and went off in the hangar above the wardroom. In the consequent smoke black-out, and with red-hot shrapnel flying about, I made a dive for the wardroom door and got up on deck. It transpired later that half a dozen people who were having lunch with me were killed. When the attack developed we had two Fulmars on patrol, but they had been brought down to chase some Italian torpedo-bombers, and three Fulmars on deck, which took off only seconds before the first bomb hit, so the Stuka attack was virtually unopposed. The Fulmars laid into the Stukas after they had dropped their bombs, and shot down a few, but it was nearly a miracle that the ship got back to Malta, having taken five bombs and having the steering gear jammed. I spoke to a chap in hospital who had been in the hangar when the bomb exploded. He said that he had heard a bang overhead as he was standing in the hangar and he looked up and saw this bomb 'dropping like a football'. Those were his words. He woke up in hospital. About 150 men were killed. The Germans thought they had sunk us, which is partly what saved us. The Luftwaffe pilots went back and said 'We have sunk her,' so they stopped sending in more attacks. Funnily enough, when we were in

Greece a few months later, I spoke to a German Stuka pilot, a prisoner-of-war, who had been bombing us a few months earlier. Even then he would not believe that the *Illustrious* had not been sunk.

Twelve surviving Swordfish from 815 and 819 Squadrons landed in Malta and became 815 Squadron. On 23rd January they flew to Crete with the aid of a following wind. The five Fulmars also got to Malta and were left there for the defence of the island. I was then sent to the Western Desert with half of the squadron, to provide anti-submarine escorts for the coastal traffic to Tobruk, but after three weeks of this the whole squadron was sent on to Eleusis, an airfield near Athens. The object was to attack the two harbours in Albania, Valona and Durazzo, through which the Italians were supplying their army on the Greek frontier. To reach these targets it was necessary to refuel at an improvised forward airfield called Paramythia on the Albanian border, near Corfu, but with no intelligence or daylight reconnaissance and only moonlight to see by it wasn't easy to locate targets.

On the first attack on Valona on 12th March Jackie Jago was shot down, which left me to take over the squadron. Our last attack on Valona was on 15th April, whereupon we were obliged to evacuate by the German invasion of Greece. Altogether we attacked Valona three times and Durazzo and Brindisi once each, but this was only possible when there was sufficient moonlight. Damage assessment was virtually impossible except in the case of the last attack which blew up an ammunition ship.

There was one major diversion in the middle of this Albanian exercise, namely the battle of Cape Matapan. On 28th March, when we were refitting at Eleusis because of no moon, I was ordered to Crete with all available torpedo-armed aircraft, which amounted to just two. We landed at Maleme in Crete at about noon and were given a position, course and speed of the Italian Fleet, which was attempting to attack our troop convoys from Egypt to Greece. We took off at 1700 for a dusk attack.

My young observer, Sub-Lieutenant Peter Winter, did a good job and found the enemy. Before attacking we had to circle for a time until the light conditions were right. While doing so a mixture of eight Swordfish and Albacores led by Lieutenant-Commander Gerald Saunt, arrived from *Formidable*, flying in line ahead at low level. The enemy was in very close formation with all ships making smoke which obliged Saunt's aircraft to drop their torpedoes in succession outside the smoke screen.

At that time we still had no radio communication between aircraft, so that, even if Saunt could have thought out a better tactic, he had no means of ordering it. Being free to act independently I thought it would be a better if I climbed up to about 2,000 feet to get a plan view of the formation in the last trace of twilight. This revealed a bit of sea room clear of smoke on the bow of a major target. I descended into this space and aimed my torpedo at very short range at an easily identifiable cruiser of the Pola class.

The Pola cruiser was virtually stopped. The Italian Admiral Iachino detached two other heavy cruisers, *Zara* and *Fiume*, and two destroyers to escort her, and legged it for home with his main body. This included the new battleship *Vittorio Veneto* which had not been hit at Taranto. Admiral Cunningham was then able to overtake the detached force and sink it by gunfire later in the night off Cape Matapan.

It was subsequently confirmed by Italian prisoners-of-war that the Pola class cruiser was hit by a single aircraft attacking in the manner I described some minutes after the main attack.

After the fall of Crete 815 Squadron was sent to Cyprus with orders to fly a daily reconnaissance to Rhodes to get warning of any seaborne attack on Cyprus from there. The then defences of Cyprus consisted of three Hurricanes and a battalion of Sherwood Foresters, but the threat disappeared when the Germans invaded Russia on 22nd June 1941. By that time the Syrian campaign had begun and 815 Squadron concerned itself with attacking Beirut and stopping the Vichy French running supplies into Syria from the west. The latter was accomplished on 15th June when the Squadron sank the big French destroyer *Chevalier Paul* by moonlight between Cyprus and Syria. The French did not try it again.

This ended my war in the Mediterranean. I was flown home in a Catalina from Cairo to Poole via Malta, Lisbon and Foynes (in the Irish Republic), thirty-two hours' flying time, to relieve Dennis Cambell as Naval Test Pilot at Boscombe Down.

Midshipman Ian McIntosh, RN

When war was declared I was in the cruiser *Sussex* as a midshipman which I'd joined at the start of 1939. We'd had a bit of patrolling off the Spanish coast during the Civil War on the Mediterranean side, then around June the whole fleet moved to Alexandria. We were in fact in Alexandria when war was declared. One of the preparations for war, apart from fusing all the shells, was to sharpen the cutlasses for the boarding party. As this was likely to be led by midshipmen, the idea of sailors behind you with sharp cutlasses wasn't a very cheerful thought!

I had come over to Britain from Australia at the end of 1937 to start my training in Portsmouth with the idea of later transferring to the Royal Australian navy. I always wanted to go into submarines but the Australian Navy at that time had not got any. Firstly, I found submarines fascinating on the technical and engineering side; secondly you all lived very close together and knew each other very well indeed and thirdly, you got responsibility very young: So this was an attractive combination to be in.

Because of the war our training class on HMS *Dolphin* at Gosport was only five or six weeks. I was then sent to go out to Alexandria to be spare fourth hand for one of the submarines out there, but I never arrived because my merchant ship, the Anchor Line *Britannia*, was sunk on the way out. She had around 550 people aboard and was heading for the Cape and then Bombay. After Bombay I was to get further transport on to Alexandria. It was necessary to sail round the Cape because the Mediterranean was somewhat dangerous at the time.

We started off in convoy. But had just left to sail independently. I was in charge of the watch of look-outs up above the bridge, and had just taken over early morning on 25th March 1941. I thought something was wrong, because we appeared to be going in the opposite direction given the north-east trades are pretty regular. When I got up on the bridge I was not surprised to find that we were being chased by an armed merchant cruiser – *Raider E*. The first of some hefty shells started landing fairly accurately either side as a straddle. We replied with our one 4-inch gun, but it was hopelessly out of range and was soon out of action from a direct hit. We were then hit midships, and in twenty minutes the ship was very heavily on fire. We managed to get a Radio Signal off before the captain struck his colours and ordered 'Abandon Ship'.

The raider was good: as soon as he saw the signal he stopped firing. My lifeboat was Number 7 on the starboard side aft. Unfortunately the port side one had been smashed altogether. So there were quite a lot of candidates for my boat. Eventually I got everyone stacked in and we managed to shove off. There were four oars so I got people rowing. Others I got baling because there were a number of shrapnel holes in the wooden boat. I gave one man a baler. He looked at me in blank astonishment and said, 'Oh but sir, we're passengers!' So I used some strong sailors' language and he baled quite quickly after that!

I wasn't officially in charge of the boat: there was a Lieutenant West, RNVR Special Branch, who was a fire-fighting expert, and the third mate who was an excellent man, but he hadn't had any experience in small boats whereas, as a midshipman, I had. So I just took charge of the thing because nobody else seemed to know what to do.

We were about 600 miles west of Freetown, about eight degrees north of the equator. There was a fresh north-east trade blowing and quite a choppy sea. On taking a muster we found we had 82 people altogether. The lifesaving capacity according to the Board of Trade was supposed to be 56 so it was a bit crowded. We had had one or two rafts in tow to start off with: I hauled them in and saved all the rope I could. We tried to keep in company with the remaining lifeboats for the rest of that day. However we were so overladen it was difficult, and we drifted much further downwind. By the next morning all the other boats were out of sight.

We patched the holes with flattened out condensed milk tins which I nailed across the holes with nails extracted from packing cases. I did three of those from the outside hanging upside down with somebody holding onto my legs, the other I had to do from inside because I couldn't reach it. That just about kept the water out. We got the mast and sail up: it was a dipping lug cutter type of sail, just a straightforward sail, very low naturally. You couldn't sail her at all close to the wind. I discussed with the lieutenant and the third mate which route we should take. I thought we should take advantage of the trade winds and sail west for Brazil instead of trying the east. This route was twice the distance, but it would take us less time. Everyone agreed. I had read a book which mentioned the doldrums getting narrower when you got further west: one merchant sailing ship had crossed the doldrums at 33° West. So I said, 'Well, we'll sail due west until we get to 33° west by my estimates and then we'll go southwest and should pick up the southeast trades to make the coast on it.' All this confidence from a book I read!

I reckoned that we ought to ration things for 28 days. Each day a person had an eggcup full of water, one ship's biscuit which was terribly hard to eat, and two tins of condensed milk shared amongst the 82. That helped you to get the biscuit down. After that you could have your water which was marvellous. Throughout the voyage we never managed to catch any fish or birds although one flying fish gave itself up and we tried putting that on a bent pin. Oddly enough after about three days I don't think anyone felt hungry.

After about a week or so some of the crew started dying; the deaths then became really fairly frequent. The odd thing was you could see who was going to die two or three days before they did. You could see when they'd given up hope and, once they had, they died. It didn't matter whether they were lascars, or Goanese or Sikhs or Europeans: it was all the same. It was very peculiar, somehow it was the despairing look about them that gave it away; those who hadn't run their 'three days' picked up all right when we smelt and then sighted the land. They were 38 by then.

We were all suffering from these boils: the cramped conditions, salt water over you the whole time. In the hot periods we poured water over ourselves to help us cool down. When we were in the doldrums we had very heavy rain squalls just before night fall which used to leave us terribly cold. I had read Captain Bligh's account of his time in an open boat when set adrift by the mutineers of the *Bounty*. He wrote that by removing your clothes, rinsing them in the salt water, ringing them out and then putting them on again you were able reduce the chill. I had everyone follow this advice and it worked.

Contrary to the views of those days I was a great admirer of Bligh: he was a marvellous seaman.

After about a fortnight when we came to the southwest we had about three days in light shifting winds. We were very short of water and our lips had become thick and caked. We were forced to suck on our buttons, anything we could find. Then to my delight we picked up the south-east trades. During that time we did get the first of a few showers. We desperately gathered all the water we could from the sail. After that and several other heavy showers water ceased to be a problem: we were able to have half a condensed milk tin each twice a day. Then on the 22nd day I smelt land and the water changed colour. This was rather earlier than I was reckoning on, but I knew there was an ocean current drifting us in a favourable direction. However I did not know whether it was good for five or twenty miles a day. I therefore thought it best to ignore it in my estimates. The steering was mostly on the direction of the wind – very regular, and at night you could steer on the stars, which was much the best way. I tended to be on the helm for about twenty hours a day because I found handing it over to some of the others led to the boat being luffed up into the wind. This meant you couldn't get her off the wind; and sailing again without getting an oar out to pull her round was very exhausting.

At about noon we sighted land, a long low sandy shore backed with trees with a few fishing boats. There was a very severe surf running and I wasn't going to try to land in that: we were all fairly weak by this time. So I ran along the coast up to the north-west and then stood out to sea for the night. The next morning we were terribly lucky, it was very calm and we ran into a bay and beached about 200 yards off the shoreline. Everyone made their way ashore. Lieutenant West and I had a general search around the boat and took out anything that was useful. Then we too finally waded ashore. Even though it was only some 200 yards with the water no higher than thigh level, it took us a long time because our legs by then were weak.

We found fresh water which was good, lit a fire using local wood and cattle droppings – a cheerful sign also. We spent that first night lying out and enjoying being able to stretch our legs for a change and drinking the water which we boiled up in a tin. The next morning I divided the boys up a bit: some went to look for shellfish, others to gather firewood, two of the stronger seamen accompanied myself and West to explore inland a bit and see what we could find. We didn't find much in the way of fruit, just a few berries. Making our way back we met two native boys who signed at us. We followed them to a fisherman's village of half a dozen palm-thatched huts housing about thirty people.

We found out we were in northern Brazil, on the north-east coast. We got a message through and arrangements were made to gather us up. We spent about seven hours in canoes travelling up creeks and then a couple of hours in cars and trucks to the state capital, São Luis, where we were looked after very well. Having entered the county illegally without any papers or documents we were first taken to the prison yard where a group photograph was taken of us. Then we were moved off to various hospitals where we were bathed and ailments such as salt water boils were attended to. Within two hours you wouldn't have been able to recognise anyone from the photograph! It wasn't until we were in hospital when they fed us small amounts over short intervals that I did feel hungry. I had lost about three stone in twenty-three days. It was an odd feeling having a shower: one's earlobes were like pieces of paper and of course bones were sticking out everywhere.

They looked after us and fattened us up for six weeks. During that time the fishermen came to see us twice bringing with them presents of fish and mangoes. By then I was able to speak sufficient Portuguese to thank them personally and we gave them some cartons of cigarettes and other things: they were terribly nice people as we found all the Brazilians to be. Theoretically we should have been interned, at least the naval personnel should have been. Basically they consulted Rio, and I think what they roughly said was, 'Well it *was* a British merchant ship, wasn't it?' and we said 'Yes.' They said, 'Well therefore you *must* be distressed British seamen' and we said, 'Yes, we are.' So they said, 'Therefore we *can* repatriate you', and we said, 'Yes, please!'

In the lifeboat I was quite confident, come what may, that I was going to get to the other side: I had very good reasons because I had only just met my wife a little while before: in fact we were sunk the day before her birthday. So I was quite determined that I was going to get back. I was twenty-one at the time.

ABLE SEAMAN THOMAS BARNHAM

Before I joined the Navy I was a professional boxer, lightweight. In the Navy I was trained as a gunner and within three months of war breaking out I was on my first ship, the *Voltaire*. She was an Armed Merchant Cruiser, and they'd put eight 6-inch guns on her, but they were 1901, old stuff. We picked the ship up at Portsmouth and went to Malta where they put us on contraband control. We just toured around the Greek islands for about five months.

Then we got word that we had to go to Canada to escort a convoy. This was 1940. We were the only escort for fifty or sixty ships right over to the Irish coast. Then we had to travel back to Canada on our own for the next convoy. The round trip took nearly three weeks.

We were doing convoys for nearly twelve months. I saw nothing of the war, the only time we saw action was the day we got sunk. In March 1941 we got word that we were going to Freetown. So we set off for Freetown all on our own from Canada. We put in at Trinidad for two or three days and started making our way to Freetown again. Early on 4th April the alarm went off. We could see this ship coming and we kept signalling it, 'who are you, what are you doing in this area?' but it still kept coming and never signalled. All of a sudden up came her guns and they opened up. We all got to our guns but where our shots were falling short, hers were catching us. Within a few minutes we had orders from the officer to split the crew and go down to man a gun in the well deck. When we got down there we found everyone lying dead and when we got up on the gun we couldn't focus it round because it had a direct hit. So we came back up on to our other gun and we just fired away but she kept hitting on us and all of a sudden we went over and the officer said 'Abandon ship.' I didn't abandon ship, I went right through the boat to the stern. I had one or two mates there on other guns. On the way I saw mates of mine lying dead. I went up to the captain who was at the stern, with about twenty other people. He asked me and another kid, a fellow called Ginger McInnes, to go in to the workshop and get some wood to use as floats.

While we were in there a shell came in and Ginger was peppered with everything. I finished up with a nasty cut on the elbow. We came out and all of a sudden the ship just turned over and slung us all into the water. I'm in the water and I see two boys struggling, trying to get on each other's backs. I got in between them. One of them was McInnes and the other a boy called Scott. Neither of them could swim and they were trying to hang onto this piece of wood, so I said, 'Now, cut it out, let me in the middle and we'll just hang on and see what happens.' Then McInnes says, 'Look, Tom', and he held his arm up and his hand was gone. We were in the water about thirty minutes when the boy behind me drowned.

Now all I've got is McInnes, myself and this boy that's drowned behind me. An officer had a life jacket on – you could see his head and shoulders above the water – I shouted to him, 'Pardon me, sir, do you mind coming over here and giving me a hand with McInnes?' He said 'I'm sorry Barnham but I can't swim.' That finished the boy. He kept putting his head on his plank and there was nothing I could do for him. Another lot of lads came by on bits of wood so I went with the other boys and after about two hours the German ship, who'd sunk us, came back.

You could hear t-t-t-t-t like a machine-gun coming from the ship, and we thought they were shooting at us. We had been given to understand that the Germans were right villains and took no prisoners. One of the best swimmers, a boy from Wembley, just gave up and drowned when he heard the machine-guns. But then the Germans put boats down to pick up the survivors. They brought us back to their boat and bathed us because we were all covered in oil. They had a German officer who spoke English, 'You were given to understand we were firing on you in the water but we weren't, we were keeping the sharks away from you'. Then they took us to the bottom of the boat, gave us a blanket and everybody went off to sleep. Everybody was woken up after a while, given soup and the wounded were attended to while we were there, I think we buried about three or four of our lads. Our officers conducted a burial ceremony but while they were doing that we had all the machine-guns on us.

The Germans worked hard on the wounded and we were well looked after on the ship, in fact Easter came round while we were on board and they sent a bit of chocolate and a bottle of beer to the prisoners. But we were dispirited. I'd lost all my friends on the *Voltaire* and there were quite a number of wounded amongst us.

We were taken to Bremerhaven and then on to a German naval base. We were there roughly three or four months. They supplied us with a shirt, I had a woman's overall and they gave us a handkerchief-like holder for our socks and we had clogs. They had us all working in different parts of the barracks. About nine o'clock in the morning they'd put us in a room all day peeling potatoes. After we'd been there about a fortnight to three weeks they would come in, call one of us out and take us to be interrogated. Once we'd finished with our interrogation they would put us back with the other boys. When I went up for interrogation the German officer offered me a cigarette (if you didn't want a cigarette he'd offer you an orange) and then all of a sudden he started on me – How long had I been in the Navy? Was I a conscript? How many brothers did I have in the services, what were they, naval men, Air Force or Army men. What part of the country did I come from – London? Then all of a sudden he finished up saying, 'Well, tell me who do you think is going to win this war?' Naturally I said, 'We are.' So his reply was, 'Tell me what makes you think you are going to win the war?' and then he goes on and says 'Look, I'll tell you why you can't win the war. We've chased you out of France, we're chasing you through the desert.' Everything he said was correct but nevertheless I still said, 'We're going to win the war.'

After the interrogation two cars would take you to another room where all those who had been interrogated were. They asked you what you'd said and they'd all been through the same procedure as I had. Then after everybody had been interrogated they drove us off to a naval camp, all naval ratings and, on the other side of the camp, the Merchant Seamen's Camp. From there we got into shoes and English army uniform. We were there about five or six months. We used to play football to keep our spirits up and there was always something to do.

Then one morning they had us all out early on parade and a German officer came up and said, 'That lot over there, go back to your barracks and get all your belongings, you're leaving.' There must have been about two hundred of us. They put us in cattle wagons and we finished up in an Army camp, Stalag 344, the biggest camp in Germany.

LIEUTENANT (E) LOUIS LE BAILLY RN

With the evacuation of Greece ending in late April 1941 and with the need to reinforce Crete, we had to tear into boiler cleaning, change evaporator coils and make good the usual defects. Captain Berthon, my erstwhile chief in *Hood*, gave us particularly useful advice:

> Make sure of your steering gear, that everyone knows what should be done if the primary steering system fails; but above all try and ensure it never fails. Bomb dodging is an art your captain and navigator, if they are lucky, will quickly learn. To be successful, instantaneous reaction to speed orders from the bridge and a reliable steering gear are essential.

Everyone assumed that Crete was to be the next big battle. And so we worked hard, preparing for an ordeal which we guessed would try us and *Naiad* to the very limit.

Hardly had *Naiad* come to her buoy in Alexandria early on 12th May than my chief was told we had barely 72 hours to bring all the machinery to immediate readiness. After 19 days of watch-keeping and several severe bombing attacks this struck us as a bit hard: we had not appreciated the Mediterranean pace to which we would have to conform. A run ashore had just been organised when orders came to raise steam for our first operation. By 16th May we were in position north of Crete with two other groups of light forces.

By then the bombing of Maleme and Heraklion airfields had started and we could guess at the soldiers' ordeal as we swept along Crete's northern coast. The German assault seemed to be delayed while the softening up process went on, so we returned to Alexandria to top up with fuel. By 20th May we were back in the Aegean furnace. Our task, the captain explained, with two other groups, was to prevent enemy forces from reaching Crete by sea. To accomplish this would mean spending many daylight hours with little RAF fighter support within range of German airfields in Greece and Rhodes.

History now records that in the first three or four days some 24,000 German troops were to arrive in Crete. Besides 500 troop-carrying aircraft with towed gliders there were more than 800 torpedo and dive-bombers, fighters and reconnaissance aircraft under General von Richthoven, a cousin of the world war one air ace. The airborne attack started early on 20th May. As we fought off dive-bombing attacks we saw Junkers 82s towing gliders and disgorging parachute troops on to the Cretan airfields. That night we swept inshore to assist the army but, though we could see the fighting, we were unable to distinguish German troops from ours so there was no chance of intervening. So close were we that the scent of wild garlic permeated even the boiler rooms. To this day that unmistakable smell recalls those hectic hours.

We engaged six Italian motor torpedo boats and sank or damaged four. As dawn came we withdrew to the southward. High-level bombing attacks pursued us and while on deck I saw *Juno*, one of our destroyer escorts, receive a bomb in her magazine which sank her almost immediately. During the night of May 21/22 Rear-Admiral Glennie with *Dido*, *Orion*, *Ajax* and four destroyers met an Italian escorted convoy. Within two hours the transports were sunk and some 2500 German seaborne reinforcements left to drown or swim ashore. Glennie was lucky. The darkness, during which the Germans had hoped to sneak in reinforcements by sea, was the navy's ally. The Germans quickly realised our night-fighting skills and swopped tactics. They dispatched the next large convoy by day, to become *Naiad*'s target on 22nd May.

Admiral King's force consisted of *Naiad*, *Calcutta*, *Carlisle*, the Australian cruiser *Perth* and three destroyers. It should have been joined by Admiral Glennie's force but he had had to return to Alexandria almost out of ammunition. On 21st May the German airforce had concentrated on the land battle. Next day the Mediterranean fleet was their main target. The attack on *Naiad* and the rest of the squadron started at dawn and continued for 15 hours. At 0830 a caique full of German soldiers was sighted and sunk as was another small troopship an hour later. We then sighted a collection of caiques and small merchant vessels escorted by a destroyer and a motor torpedo boat. The destroyer managed to lay a smoke screen and escape but the other escort and several caiques were sunk, while the convoy was forced back to Milos.

By 1100 we had been in action for five-and-a-half hours against high-level, dive- and torpedo-bombers. Our decks had been machine-gunned with phosphorus-tipped bullets inflicting terrible wounds on our short range weapon's crews and setting some of the ready-use ammunition alight. Our high-angle (anti-aircraft) director tower had been hit and a near-miss blew in our starboard side for'd well below the waterline and flooded the small-arms magazine. The inrush of water, for we were at full-speed, burst open the hatch to the messdeck above. The water taken in there brought *Naiad* down for'd and more water started to pour through the splinter holes (400 were later counted) in the ship's side, holes which the damage control parties had not yet had time to plug. A large messdeck was in danger of filling up and I was sent to help the shipwright shore down the hatch through which water continued to gush. So with the survivors of the local damage control party, sometimes up to our necks as the ship heeled under full helm to avoid the next stick of bombs, we wrestled to stem the flooding. Not the least of our difficulties were the mangled bodies of those killed by splinters and the clothing from broken kit lockers which blocked the suction hoses lowering the water level. In the end we had to ask the bridge to slow down for a few moments: no sooner had the squadron's speed eased than *Carlisle* was hit.

By now 'X' turret (aft) had used up its ammunition and 'A' magazine (for'd) still with some left but the turret itself temporarily out of action was flooding up through a damaged bulkhead from the adjacent small-arms magazine, wide open to the sea. So the magazine crew, up to their knees in the rising water and in semi-darkness had to pass ammunition manually from the magazine, along the messdecks and then down into the empty 'X' turret whose guns remained serviceable. Air attacks came from every angle but we were lucky: one air-launched torpedo passed harmlessly under our stern. Another had punched a hole through our stem without exploding.

When the German troop convoy turned back, Admiral King, aware that his squadron's ammunition supply was practically exhausted, retired towards *Fiji* and *Gloucester* who had been sent to support us. Tragedy almost immediately ensued. The destroyer *Greyhound* was sunk by a salvo of bombs. *Kingston* and *Kandahar* went to pick up survivors and Admiral King sent *Fiji* and *Gloucester* to give them cover. In hindsight, this was a mistake. The admiral was unaware that both cruisers were also desperately short of ammunition. The gallant *Gloucester* was hit by a salvo of bombs which sank her. *Fiji*, by now down to firing her practice ammunition, correctly left her and dropped all her Carley floats to help *Gloucester's* swimmers in the water.

The situation was desperate and a brave and determined Admiral Rawlings, commanding the battle fleet, brought it into the Kithera Channel to support the cruisers, but the cost was heavy and *Warspite* and *Valiant* were both damaged. Next *Fiji* was attacked by a single plane and an unlucky hit blew in her side abreast the engine-room. Then another aircraft scored a further hit and *Fiji* rolled over and sank. Unlike *Gloucester* however, whose survivors were machine-gunned and mostly killed in the water, many of *Fiji's* ship's company, even without their Carley floats, were picked up after dark by *Kingston* and *Kandahar*.

On 22nd May Admiral Cunningham made the signal: 'Stick it out. Navy must not let Army down. No enemy forces must reach Crete by sea.' But the price of preventing seaborne forces reaching Crete had not yet been fully paid. That night, *Kelly*, with Mountbatten in command, together with *Kashmir* and *Kipling*, was sent to intercept more seaborne troops trying to filter on to northern Crete. After sinking two caiques full of soldiers and bombarding the German-held Maleme airfield on to which troop-carrying aircraft were still landing, the small force turned for Alexandria at full-speed. At about 0830 they were attacked by a posse of 24 dive bombers and *Kashmir* was sunk almost at once. *Kelly*, at 30 knots and under full helm, was hit by another stick of bombs and turned turtle. Her commander (E) and those of the engine-room crew still alive, found themselves in an air-lock, so fast had *Kelly* turned over. Several contrived to swim down through the engine-room hatch and so to the surface. Many of *Kashmir*'s and *Kelly*'s people had been killed in the original bombing; many more were machine-gunned in the oily water. Courageously *Kipling*, despite three hours of intensive attack, rescued a large number of survivors, including Captain Mountbatten.

During a prolonged bombing attack such as we endured, engine and boiler rooms resemble the inside of a giant's kettle against which a sledge-hammer is being beaten with uncertain aim. Sometimes there was an almighty clang; sometimes the giant, in his frustration, seemed to pick up the kettle and shake and even kick it. The officer detailed to broadcast a running commentary suffered a breakdown during the battle so we heard little below, but through the noise and heat of the machinery spaces we came to understand something of what was happening on deck. Suddenly more speed would be called for, then we would hear our 5.25-inch turrets opening fire which told us aircraft were attacking. Next the bridge telegraphs might move to Emergency Full Speed and we would see the rudder indicator go to hard-a-port or starboard at the moment of bomb release. This would be followed by the sound of *Naiad*'s short-range weapons as the bomber pulled out of its dive or the torpedo-bomber dropped its torpedo. We learned to interpret, by the ensuing shake or shudder or clang, the success or otherwise of our navigator's avoiding action. Occasionally the damage control officer would ring me with reports of damage received or casualties suffered; occasionally my valiant chief stoker would report the fuel expenditure and his plans to keep the boilers supplied as our fuel reserves dwindled or seawater contamination from near-misses adjacent to some tanks showed up in his scrupulous testing.

From time to time my chief or I would visit the boiler rooms. Here, for hour after frightening hour, with ears popping from the air pressure, the young stokers knew and heard little of what was going on apart from the obvious near-misses and the scream of the boiler-room fans. On their alertness, as they watched for orders to open or shut off oil sprayers to the furnaces, depended the precise supply of steam available to meet the sudden changes of speed ordered from the bridge, on which *Naiad*'s survival depended. The more imaginative amongst them, no doubt, tried not to think which would be worse, to be boiled by superheated steam, cremated or drowned. Commander Marshall and I, in our respective engine-rooms, spoke often by phone and when not visiting the boiler-rooms one or other would go round the damage control parties and tell the bridge of the situation down below . . .

One irreparable loss was Chief Stoker Whittle, the regulating chief stoker I had selected on my first day as senior engineer. The next six months, in the general air of stability on the stoker's messdecks, confirmed the wisdom of my choice and now he was gone, killed towards the end of the action by a stray splinter as he went about his other task of ensuring the continuity of our fuel supply. He fought for his life for many hours, but when I went aft at night to see him buried with a shell at his feet, the commander broke the near unbelievable news that *Hood* had blown up. That there was another world outside the conflict in which we were engaged was difficult enough to comprehend, that the navy should be fighting two such great sea battles, so many thousand miles apart, was almost beyond understanding; but that the ship in which I had been weaned and I had come to love should have disappeared in seconds was a kick in the stomach.

It was hot and sultry in Alexandria harbour when *Naiad*, well down by the bows, limped in. Overhead was a German reconnaissance aircraft. No doubt the observer could see the masses of shipping in the harbour but he could hardly have distinguished the two large hospital barges which secured on either side of *Naiad*; nor could he have seen the torn bodies lying white-faced on their stretchers or heard the half-stifled groan or tight-lipped jest as they were manoeuvred down the narrow gangway. Nor could he have heard anything from the other barge for, from the dead, lying at last in peace, there could come no sound.

As the last of the wounded were carried down the gangway, we mustered on the quarterdeck. After a service in remembrance of those taken away by the barges and those buried at sea we gave thanks for our own deliverance. Our drawn and rather haggard captain, his arm in a sling, spoke to us of the gun's crews who had fought their guns till they dropped, of the magazine crew who had worked in the dark in a rising flood of water, of the signal boy who had twice swarmed aloft and re-rigged wireless aerials twice shot away and of the Royal Marine who had ditched the burning ammunition from a ready use locker. The captain said: "There was a moment when, due to casualties and damage Stukas dived on us unopposed; no guns were firing. We are here because when I asked for Full Speed, I got more than full speed; and when I caused the wheel to be put over, we turned like a taxicab in a London street. Indeed I would say that, occasionally, during last Thursday, we on the upper deck had moments when we could pause and take stock. But if, for a moment throughout that long action, the engines had faltered or the steering had not functioned, we should now be with those friends we have left lying beneath the sea around Crete."

When our army in Crete could fight no more the Mediterranean fleet, now reduced from four battleships, a carrier, 12 cruisers and 30 destroyers to less than a quarter of that number, had to remove from the rugged southern Cretan shore whatever soldiers were left, in the face of overwhelming air attack.

Just as Cunningham began to believe there were no more evacuation tasks for his battered ships, a personal appeal from New Zealand's prime minister, then in Egypt, triggered one final desperate operation. The fleet's last serviceable squadron, *Phoebe*, *Abdiel*, *Hotspur*, *Jackal* and *Kimberley* was sent to bring off the brave New Zealanders who had fought their way across Crete to Sphakia. Amazingly the squadron suffered no loss, but *Calcutta*, with her brilliant fighting record was bombed and sunk after being sent out from Alexandria to help fight off air attacks against the other ships so heavily laden with soldiers.

Except for those of us who had to remain to keep the coal-fired dock boilers alight to maintain steam to work the pumps (the Arab stokers having sensibly fled) most of *Naiad*'s crew were sent ashore until a parachute mine, lodged under the floating dock in which we lay, had been defused. Thereafter, with the help of the repair ships, we set about welding a great plate over the huge hole for'd and repairing the multitude of splinter holes and other damage. Many of the sailors were helping to restore *Orion* and at the same time remove the remains of the 300 soldiers killed when a bomb penetrated a crowded messdeck during her last trip from Crete. Then, unexpectedly, the French turned on us in Syria and *Naiad* was needed quickly on the Lebanese coast. So, our repairs more or less completed, we undocked, re-ammunitioned, re-fuelled and steamed at full speed to Haifa.

SUB (A) LIEUTENANT PAT JACKSON RN

We did our training at Portsmouth in *Frobisher*. I was a midshipman. Next we went to the *Courageous* as an introduction to aircraft-carriers, after which we went to flying school and I started flying Tiger Moths at Gravesend on 5th May 1939. After tonsillitis I caught up with the course at Peterborough, which was an RAF base. We all had cars and in the evenings we'd meet our girlfriends. Life was fun in those days. War broke out while I was there.

We went down to the south of France for deck landings. First the instructor took us down onto the deck in a Gypsy Moth, just to show us what it looked like. Then we were put in a Swordfish and had to go out and do it alone. People always think deck landings are difficult, but I never found them much of a problem. I drove my car faster than I landed a Swordfish.

Then we came home to torpedo-school at Gosport. I was there until the invasion threat, when everyone was called into active squadrons. I went to join 825 Squadron which had had quite a few casualties, including their Commander. Lieutenant Commander Esmonde, the new commander, arrived shortly before me and almost immediately we went to the Norwegian coast in *Furious* for bombing and anti-shipping strikes. That was in 1940.

In May 1941 the squadron joined the *Victorious* on a convoy out to the Med. We had taken on some new crew, RNVR chaps who had not done any deck landings so we went to sea to give them some experience. On our return to Scapa Flow, we saw the most wonderful sight: the *Prince of Wales* and the *Hood* going at high speed into the sunset. We thought something must be up, they were going so fast and sure enough, as soon as we moored up, the *Victorious* was ordered to follow them out and ploughed across the North Atlantic. We were after the *Bismarck*. She had sunk the *Hood*.

I must admit, there were butterflies in my stomach. The prelude to our Air Strike was horrible, sitting and waiting your turn to get into the ring. You feel, 'God, I'd get out of this if I could,' but once you get into the cockpit and start up and fly in formation, you're just doing what you're trained to do. Just going across the Atlantic at vast speed with little to do except check your aeroplane, through one had butterflies galore floating around. I wouldn't say only in the stomach; almost visible, they were!

Eventually the *Bismarck* was sighted and we were sent off to try to slow her down and do as much damage as possible. It was 24th May, the day before my birthday. We took off at about ten o'clock at night. It was getting dark, the sea was rising and the weather forecast was not good. There were nine of us in the air. We staggered up through the cloud and got an echo on the ASV, so we came whistling down through the cloud and there was the *Prince of Wales*. Fortunately we didn't attack her because we recognised the four guns in the foreward turret. So we pulled away and she sent a signal by light that *Bismarck* was 15 miles from her starboard bow.

We went off, trying to get a bit more height. Then the *Bismarck* saw us and started to let fly, it was chaotic as we went in for the attack. Heavy flak bursts all around and the stench of burning explosives. It was at this moment I felt a tapping on my shoulder from the rear cockpit. I thought someone must have been hurt, so I put my head back and heard Lieutenant 'Dapper' Berrill's calm voice wishing me a very happy birthday. I looked at my watch; it was 0003 on 25th May.

Then we headed back to the carriers. We found them in the dark, purely because Captain Bovelle, bless his heart, used his signalling lamps to make a signal to the flagship. We all landed safely, even though it was dark, with rain and a pitching deck which was good because half the chaps hadn't landed at night before.

The next day, we heard that the German ships had slipped clear of our radar net, so an air search was organised. We lumbered into the air, each on a different bearing from the *Victorious*. The weather was bad, and wherever we looked, all we saw was a small circle of breaking waves immediately below us. Eventually at the end of our search we had to head back as we were running low on fuel. But there was no sign of the *Victorious* where we had expected to find her. We were lost halfway across the North Atlantic and the nearest land, Greenland, was well out of range of our fuel tank, which was nearly empty. All we could do was carry on the search, using the weakest mixture the engine would accept.

I was brought up a Catholic and when I saw the petrol tank register show 'E' for empty, I said three 'Hail Marys' pretty smartish. Then I heard Dapper Berrill shout and saw his glove hand pointing downwards. Below us was the outline of a submerged ship's lifeboat, with waves breaking over it. Someone was looking after us all right.

When someone gives you a lifeboat in the middle of the Atlantic and says, 'Get on with it, chum,' you don't muck around, you get on with it. I decided to ditch immediately, and dropped a smoke float to show which way the wind was blowing. I came down as if I were doing a deck landing and landed in the water about twenty yards upwind of the lifeboat. I stuffed my flying boots full of Verys light pistols and cartridges, and Dapper brought his compass. We had to release the dinghy manually, and it was blowing so hard that it was like trying to control a rather frisky horse. In the struggle with the dinghy, the air gunner, Leading Airman Sparkes, forgot to bring the fresh water bottles.

We got into the dinghy and it took just a few moments to drift downwind to the lifeboat, which was submerged. All we had to bale with was our flying boots, so we set to until there was enough freeboard for us to get on board and get some shelter from the freezing wind. As soon as we were on board, we all felt sick and retched up what was left of our breakfasts. Then we explored the boat, which had come from a Dutch ship, the *SS Elusa*. There was a bundle amidships which we thought at first might be a dead body, but turned out to be a sail bag with a lug-sail and a fore-sail. There were sweeps and a mast lashed to the thwarts. There was also a rusty axe and knife, a suit of clothes and trilby hat, a water-logged tin of 50 cigarettes and a bottle of 1890 Napoleon brandy. There were hard ship's biscuits and a water beaker in the boat's lockers.

We had a tot of brandy to revive our spirits, but it was rather strong on an empty stomach. Then we began to rig the mast using the lashing lines and cut the blade off a sweep to make a gaff, put a splice round it and hauled it up. The boat heeled over and took on steerage, which was a great relief. Now we had to decide what direction to steer. The wind was westerly, force five or six and I thought I remembered from school that the prevailing wind over the Atlantic was westerly, so we headed East.

That night we were swamped by heavy seas and had to bail out non-stop. And the wind kept changing all the time; we were in centre of low pressure. I tried to stay calm and sail with the wind, but then you'd find you couldn't make headway. It was like being in a cave. The three of us in a small boat with nobody to push us through. Sometimes I felt the world had given us up.

Dapper was a great comfort. I couldn't have asked for anyone nicer to share discomfort with. He was a Catholic, too, and he kept saying, 'Don't worry, chaps, I'm saying a prayer. You watch it, nine days and we'll be saved.' But Sparkes was a different story. He built himself a little igloo up in the bows using the aircraft dinghy cover and he sat under that saying, 'Why bother? It's only prolonging the agony.'

Since Sparkes had given up and Dapper hadn't much experience under-sail, it was up to me to handle the boat. I didn't sleep for the first four or five nights and I started to hallucinate. I thought we were sailing around the moon and the British consul on the moon had called me ashore and said, 'Would you like a hot bath?' and I said, 'Damn right I would,' and I started to walk ashore. Fortunately old Dapper pulled me back into the boat and told me I probably needed some sleep, so I left him to it and slept.

Eventually the strong winds lessened and we concentrated on sailing in a westerly direction, hoping to reach North America. Then we spotted another boat. Everything about it was black. The crew had black rings around their eyes. The officer in the boat shouted across that they were Norwegian, the only survivors from a convoy which had been torpedoed fourteen days before, and there were several dead men on the bottom boards. They were heading for Greenland but had been driven back by gales. He suggested that some of his crew should join us and that we should sail in company to the North. It was a hard decision, considering the state they were in, but I had to refuse. Our boat was lighter and faster than theirs and we would have more chance of survival alone. We gave them the cigarettes and some biscuits and went our separate ways. They were never seen again.

The weather alternated between fresh and gale force winds and during the storms we lost two sea anchors and our rudder. We were all suffering from the cold and the damp. We had to ration the water so we were thirsty all the time. Eating biscuit soaked in cold water gave us terrible toothache and the circulation in our feet and legs slowed right down. Dapper and I kept our flying boots off so we could move more freely and because we needed them for bailing. Although our feet were cold, we kept their circulation going by moving around the boat and whichever one of us was not at the tiller would massage the other's feet.

Sparkes insisted on keeping his wet flying boots on and because he sat in his tent and didn't move around, his feet became much worse than ours. Eventually he crawled aft, saying, 'Christ, I'm in agony.' I looked at his legs and they were going black from the feet up. When I massaged them, they were like bags of ice. He was in serious danger of getting gangrene, so we decided to make for the nearest landfall – Greenland, even though we had little chance of landing near some habitation. We altered course to due North, hoping to spot some mountains before coming too close to the shoreline, and then sail along the coast to an inhabited area. On our eighth day in the boat we spotted some sea birds, then three geese landed on the water near us. We felt sure land couldn't be far away. There was a lot of wreckage in the water and at one point I thought I spotted the periscope of a U-boat and panicked. But it was just a table leg bobbing past.

Then the weather worsened into an Easterly gale, and without a sea anchor and with just a steering oar, all we could do was run before the wind. On our ninth morning in the boat it was sleeting and we were sailing through crashing high waves. Dapper was struggling to steer with the oar and the sails had started to split. It was utterly miserable. I was sitting amidships, thinking, 'Well, I've asked the dear old Holy Mother to look after us and if she's given me this, I can't really ask her again, so I'd better start preparing to meet my maker.' Then, as we were sitting on top of one of these huge breakers, I saw this funny little ship, and thought, 'Oh gosh, I'm hallucinating again.' Like the chap in the desert seeing the palm tree. But the next time we were up on a breaker I saw the ship again. The wind was blowing its smoke in horizontal lines.

I then started panic stations and fired off all the Very lights we'd got. It looked as if the ship would pass without spotting us, but the last smoke puff went off with a louder 'pop' than usual, and they saw us and blasted on their siren. It was music to our ears. They dropped me a line over our bow which I made fast around our mast and this pulled us in under the lea. Some chaps jumped from their deck into the boat to help us. I could stand up but Dapper's hand was frozen to the oar; we had to lever his fingers up. Sparkes was unable to stand at all, so these three husky Icelanders hauled him on board.

Dapper and Sparkes were taken to the sick bay, but I felt fit, I just had tingly feet. Then there was some explaining to do. 'Where are you from? What are you doing?' They thought we were survivors from a German ship. Once I'd convinced the Captain we were not German, he couldn't have been more charming. From then on it was all comfort and good food.

They took us to Reykjavik where a Michael Bratbee came on board to check our identity. Dapper and Sparkes were taken to hospital and Sparkes lost his toes. I went to see the British admiral because I wanted to tell him about the Norwegian boat we saw. He sent a search out, but they didn't find anyone. He also sent a signal to the Admiralty that we'd been found, and some kind civil servant rang up my mother and said, 'You'll probably be glad to know that your son has been found.' She said, 'I never had any doubts about it. I went to a seance the other day and the medium said, "Your son's doing what he likes best: sailing."'

CHIEF PETTY OFFICER BILL LOWE

I joined HMS *Hood* in January 1930, and stayed on her until August 1933. My first impression of the *Hood* was of amazement: she seemed to go on forever. However, she was in a mess, as the inspecting admiral had noticed. The captain of the ship gave us six weeks to clean her up, make her look like a warship. He said, 'When I carry out my inspection I will not take one day, two days, three days, it'll be four days. I shall visit every cubby hole that's in this ship.' It must have taken four tons of paint to paint her. It was recognised that she had as much steel as the Forth Road Bridge. She carried 1,400 men, and was an oil burner.

I had various different jobs. My harbour job was with motor-boats and launches, in charge of the machinery. I was also the tankee, or water handler, for a while. I used to have to keep all the ship's company supplied with water, control the gravity tanks. We carried about 260 tons of fresh water and 4,000 tons of fuel. That's over fourteen miles of freshwater pipes – twelve miles of steel ladders.

We had all the sports on board; the quarterdeck was quite big enough for hockey. We used to play games against each of the staff, football teams, hockey teams, ukkers teams, ludo and swimming. However there wasn't a lot of games played in those days, except by the officers who used to play quite a bit, but we never used to worry about them.

We hardly knew anybody other than who was in our own department. I would see fresh faces everyday and I wouldn't know them. Every time we went abroad and went into harbour there was about fifty of us go ashore to go back to England for courses and about another fifty joined – that's how it was all the time. Branches used to keep to their own.

A full ship's company wasn't assembled very often, but when the gaffer or captain wanted to say something serious they cleared lower deck. The quarter-deck could take 1,400 with the surrounds. Edward VIII came down once and inspected the ship's company. They built a dais on the quarterdeck for him and we had to march by, everyone in the ship, and salute him. You could imagine what the lads were saying to that. He wanted to see everybody and he did.

Nine years after I left, I was out one evening with my father going along London Road in Brighton to our usual pub. Just as we got near the door a chap came out and said, 'The *Hood* has been sunk.' My father looked at me and I looked at him and I said, 'No! No, I don't believe that.' When we got in the pub everyone was talking about it. It was devastating news; nobody could believe it.

She was the ship that made the greatest impression on me.

LEADING SICK BERTH ATTENDANT SAM WOOD, RN

The first time I saw the *Prince of Wales* I had come from the Isle of Man, straight from the training ship *St George*. She was the sort of ship you dreamt about as being part of the Royal Navy. It looked awful, frightening – I felt like a little ant. It was greyish blue, and even though it was December, the sun was shining and making everything look even more colossal. The deck was covered in pipes, leaves, portable generators, all sorts. Everything was humming and flashing blue lights. There were lots of people working on it, about 1,300, more frenzied than normally because it was the ship's final days in the dockyard. I was part of the medical personnel in the sick bay, one level down, and the first to arrive. The rest came about a fortnight afterwards, hundreds of them.

One evening we were all sitting down to supper when the tannoy went. The captain was speaking. He told us that two enemy capital ships had been reported leaving Bergen in Norway, and emphasised that one of them was the *Bismarck*. Then he gave us a resumé of what he expected the *Bismarck* was coming out for and said we were going to intercept if possible. He said the *Hood* and the *Prince of Wales* would give a good account of themselves. He then wished us the best of luck.

We had been sailing for a couple of days. The seas were fairly rough. One night it was terrible, awful, high waves, yet nobody was sea-sick. Before that some people had been sick on training exercises. They used to come to the sick bay to try and report sick – we would kick their arses and tell them to get on with it. On this occasion, before we even met *Bismarck*, no one reported sick, probably due to the tension.

When we were organising the battle stations for the medical personnel, I was told to go and pick out a suitable place for myself. I found a position exactly over the 'B' turret, a good twenty feet up in the air from the deck, which was at sea level. The waves were splashing over us. I had a smashing view, better than being at the pictures. It was an armoured wheelhouse with slots in it, some looking to port, some to starboard. The main one was looking forward over the turrets and the bows. All I had to do was move around and look where I wanted, I was the king of my own castle. At the time, with the view, I thought I couldn't have picked a better position. Actually, the way it turned out, I picked the worst place on the whole ship.

My orders were to wait and see what happened, to attend casualties and to get them down to the main clearing stations. There was another leading seaman there with me. We just waited. Every now and again the captain broadcast what was happening and what *Norfolk* and *Suffolk*, who were shadowing the *Bismarck*, were doing, and what signals had been received. Finally, he told us to expect to be in contact at dawn next morning. We remained closed up at Action Stations that night. The steady hum of the ship's engines seemed to calm everyone.

Dawn broke on the 24th May and looking out to the North East I watched the sun's golden orange light rising from the horizon and fusing itself into the dark blue of the night. The first thing I saw of the ships were two smudges on the far horizon. The *Bismarck* fired first. I just saw this orange flash come from her and this cloud of smoke and then the *Prinz Eugen* opened fire. I heard these horrible whistling noises like a train and then, as I looked, a great water spout appeared near me. Even then it didn't dawn on me that it was explosive power, it was as though I was watching a picture. The reality struck when the *Hood* went up.

I was watching the orange flashes coming from the *Bismarck*, so naturally I was on the starboard side. The leading seaman with me said, 'Christ, look how close the firing is getting to the *Hood*.' As I looked out, suddenly the *Hood* exploded. She was just one pall of black smoke. Then she disappeared into a big orange flash and a huge pall of smoke which blacked us out. Time seemed to stand still. I just watched in horror. The bows pointed out of this smoke, just the bows, tilted up and then this whole apparition slid out of sight, all in slow motion, just slid slowly away. I couldn't believe it. The *Hood* had gone.

The armoured wheelhouse we were in had a door which was closed by a big ratchet, nine-inch thick and made of iron. I thought, 'I'm not going to get trapped if this ship is going blow up like the *Hood*.' So I opened the door and headed for the bridge. Just as I was going up to the bridge this shell landed. It came through the front part of the bridge, passed through, and exploded on the compass platform itself. I was sucked up and seemed to float across the bridge and finally came to rest on the deck amidst a shambles of torn steel fixtures and bodies.

That was the first time I had seen casualties to that degree. First-aid parties came up to help me. They were formed of marine bandsmen, writers, and suppliers. There was a multitude of injuries including Lieutenant Esmonde

Knight, blood pouring from his face. He was a well-known actor in the pre-war days. While we were looking after them another shell hit the radio direction room, and killed many more people.

When the bridge had been cleared of the wounded, I sat down and reflected. I was covered in dirt and blood and my head was throbbing. In my mind I could see the *Hood* sinking and felt I should have reached and grabbed the bows as they were disappearing. It was crazy thinking, but everything was crazy that morning.

We put a smoke-screen up after we had been hit, but we continued to shadow the *Bismarck* all that day and part of the next. I think we lost her in the evening time. I had just one small glimpse of her afterwards, when she fired at us – that was when she was making arrangements with *Prinz Eugen* to separate, to cause distraction.

I was about three hundred yards from the *Hood*. I will never forget it. I can see it now, even see the paint on the sides of it. We didn't try to go back for survivors, as we had to keep in contact with *Bismarck*. A destroyer went to pick up survivors. There were only three.

ABLE SEAMAN BOB TILBURN, RN

I was born in Leeds and when I was ten we went on holiday to Portsmouth to visit relations. It was Navy week and we went round all the ships. From then onwards, it was my one ambition to join the Royal Navy. My father was a policeman and it took me a lot to persuade him to sign the forms, but he did eventually, and I joined when I was sixteen.

After training I was sent to Portsmouth to join the *Iron Duke*, an old battleship used as a sea-going training ship. A few months later there was the Munich panic and I was sent out to Gibraltar to join the *Hood*.

On the *Iron Duke* we were still boys training. But on the *Hood* we were part of a ship's company, doing a job. Our captain, 'Hookey' Walker, had a hook for his left hand. On Sundays he used to change his silver hook to a gold one. In those days you were not necessarily frightened of those officers, you were in awe of them. Because they were so far above you, not only in the mental scale but in the social scale as well. It was still very feudal. Ratings could get as far as a warrant officer but that was it. I once knew a fellow whose father was a Company Sergeant-Major. His father said, 'The men underneath me are more frightened of me than anything else, and that's a good idea because if I told them to do something they'll do it. Rather than being frightened of what they were going to do, they're frightened of me.' With hindsight, I could see the logic of it.

We were involved with the Spanish Civil War, patrolling mostly; joined the Home Fleet for exercises and did one Russian convoy, operating mostly from Scapa. Then we were sent to the Mediterranean for the unfortunate action against the French fleet in Oran. We were all horrified on board. Personally I think that French admiral should have been boiled in oil.

We then came home, went into Liverpool to repair a turbine, and then back up to Scapa Flow. We now did North Atlantic patrolling. The North Atlantic in bad weather is very, very tough. On one occasion there was a very bad storm and we lost all the other ships even though we were using searchlights to try and signal. Four days later, ships were sighted ahead of us. So, general panic stations. In fact it was our tankers, which should have been three miles to the stern of us. The destroyers had disappeared. It was one of the worst storms I've been in. The waves were recorded as being 60 feet high. One wave came over and moved 'A' turret around. 'A' turret weighed 1000 tons.

When I first started off on the *Hood* I was in the shell room of 'A' turret. But later on when I was made a seaman gunner, and when they got rid of the 5.5-inch guns and put the 4-inch dual purpose AA guns, I was on the anti-aircraft guns.

I loved it. I loved watching the water, seeing the waves, seeing the power of the water. I thought it was tremendous. And how the seabirds, the seagulls would fly alongside us against and amongst all these howling gales. And you'd throw a piece of bread up in the air and down they'd swoop and grab it.

I always thought it was tremendous, the sea, but mentally, life at sea was numbing. I started reading navigation handbooks and I got some books about the stars. I would write down how far a star was away, multiplying the speed of light by so many million miles. Just to keep the mind going.

Our food was very, very good, when it was in the fridge. But by the time the chefs had had a go at it, and it was on your plate, it wasn't too good. The *Hood* could carry food for three months for 1,500 people. You weren't living out of a tin of beans or anything like that.

On 22nd May 1941 the *Hood* set sail with the *Prince of Wales* in pursuit of the *Bismarck* and the *Prinz Eugen* which were on their way to attack Atlantic convoys supplying Britain. The *Prince of Wales* had only just come out of the makers' yard and still had some civilian employees on board working on her gun turrets. We went over to Iceland and refuelled there. All the time we were wondering which way the *Bismarck* was going to come. There were three possible ways she could break out: via the Denmark Strait between Iceland and Greenland, or either north or south of the Faroe Islands. The *Norfolk* and *Suffolk*, 8-inch gunned cruisers, were keeping a look out in the Denmark Strait. The next morning, 23rd May, *Suffolk* spotted the *Bismarck* and *Norfolk* and *Suffolk* shadowed her from then on.

The *Bismarck* was approximately 300 miles away. We set off after her and at 2000 went into action stations because we expected to pick her up at midnight. Then the weather deteriorated and at midnight there was a blizzard, so we couldn't see anything. But we still had reports from the *Suffolk* saying in which direction they had last seen her. We switched off our radar in case the *Bismarck* could pick up our transmissions and know there was somebody shadowing her. We were travelling at full speed, about 29.5 knots. Then between 5.00 and 6.00 on the morning of 24th May, we sighted the *Bismarck* in the distance, turned in towards her and opened fire at about 25,000 yards. I was manning one of the 4-inch AA guns on the port side. The *Bismarck* answered immediately with three shells, getting closer and closer and closer.

Then the fourth, fifth and sixth shells hit us. Everyone, even the gun crews, was ordered to go into the shelter deck. There were three of us from our gun who didn't take cover. Then a shell hit the upper deck and started a fire. The ammunition in our ready use locker was on fire and started exploding. The gunner's mate told us to put out the fire, but we said, 'When it stops exploding, we will.' He went back inside to report to the gunnery officer and at that moment a shell flew into the shelter and killed the lot – 200 blokes. We three were still alive, lying flat on our faces on the deck with everything going off around us.

The next shell came aft and the ship shook like mad. I was next to the gun shield, so I was protected from the blast, but one of my mates was killed and the other had his side cut open by a splinter. It opened him up like a butcher and all his innards were coming out. Bits of bodies were falling over the deck and one hit me on the legs. I thought, 'I'm going to be sick,' so I got up and went to the ship's side to throw up. Then I looked up and saw the bows coming out of the water. The *Hood* was turning over. I jumped on to the forecastle which was nearly under water and started to strip off: tin hat, gas mask, duffel coat and all the rest. By then the water had reached me and I was swimming.

I had my sea boots on and a very tight belt. I paddled around in the water and took my knife and cut my belt so I could breathe properly. Then I looked around and saw the ship was rolling over on top of me. It wasn't a shadow, it was a big mast coming over on top of me. It caught me across the back of the legs and the radio aerial wrapped around the back of my legs and started pulling me down. I still had my knife in my hands so I cut my sea boots off and shot to the surface. I looked up to see the *Hood* with her bows stuck in the air. Then she slid under.

It was 6.00 in the morning. It was dark and cloudy but there was good visibility. A heavy swell, about 15 or 20 foot. There wasn't anybody in sight.

Further away I could see a lot of clobber in the water, so I swam over. I thought I would get myself one of those little rafts, made of wood and about a metre square. But they were in a fuel oil slick and I didn't want to go in. So I paddled around and I was getting really very cold by then. I spotted two other survivors on rafts, Ted Briggs and Midshipman Dundas. But there was nobody else, nobody else. No bodies, nobody else alive or dead. Just we three.

Eventually, I was getting tired and cold so I got one of these rafts, laid my chest on it and paddled over to Briggs. You know, someone to talk to. He wasn't feeling very well because he had swallowed some of the oil fuel. But Dundas was sitting on his raft, He'd been on the bridge, 40 feet up in the air. Tell me how he did it? He must have flown.

I tried to sit on my raft but every time I pulled it down the other side came up and so I packed it in, because it was falling on my face all the time. We were on three separate little rafts, Dundas, Briggs and me. Where could we go? I mean, the nearest land was one mile straight down. You can't swim, you've just got to hope for the best. An aeroplane came over once but obviously didn't see us.

I'd read one or two of Jack London's books, where in the very cold conditions of Canada you go to sleep and you die. So I thought I might as well go to sleep. So I actually tried to go to sleep on this thing that was tossing up and down. I thought, if I'm going to die, I might as well die in my sleep. And then Dundas shouted, 'What's that?' and I woke up a bit and looked behind me and there was this destroyer coming, the *Electra*. What a beautiful sight. Then it went straight past us. But I could see the signalman on the bridge who was looking aft and he suddenly sighted us and gave the flash and told the skipper and he turned to pick us up. That was a marvellous sight.

They dropped a scrambling net over the side and two or three of them came down. Waist deep in water, they just grabbed a hold of us. Shot me over the guard rail like a sack of spuds. I was so cold I couldn't move my arms or legs or anything. They took us down below and put us on the mess deck table. They had stacks of blankets. They were expecting to pick up about two or three hundred survivors. We were lying on warm blankets on the mess deck table and the doctor said, 'Right, off with the clothes, blankets on top,' and gave them handfuls of cotton wool to rub us down, to get the oil off and also to get the circulation going. Then one bloke said to the doctor, 'Are we all right to give them a cup of tea?' and the doctor said, 'Oh yes, ideal,' and then went to his locker and brought back some rum and said, 'Drink that.' I was old enough, I was twenty. I was able to swallow it in a cup of tea, half tea and half rum. It was wonderful. I could feel the heat going down inside. I was able to talk, but not very much. I was so cold, numb. I couldn't move my arms and legs. They had to lift my head to give me tea.

Then they put us into the sick bay. Orders came down from the captain: 'We are going into Reykjavik to refuel. Do you want to go ashore into hospital or do you want to stay aboard while we go and sink the *Bismarck*?' He was quite serious, the captain. They were going to go and sink the *Bismarck* when they found her. The *Electra* had half-inch plate and I'd been on the *Hood* with 15-inch plate. 'Oh,' I said, 'I've got to go.' So we went right to the hospital, all three of us.

As I walked into the ward in the army hospital, there was a bloke in bed who said, 'Hey sailor, it's just been on the radio, did you know the *Hood*'s been sunk?' I'm afraid I wasn't very kind to him. Well, I'd been up nearly forty-eight hours. We'd gone into actions stations at 8.00 o'clock at night and we were at action stations all night. We were sunk at 6.00 the following morning. We were in the water for two and a half hours. The water temperature was about 5° centigrade. Just a few degrees above freezing. We went into hospital that evening and the first thing I asked for was a hot bath because I was still covered in oil. Then I went to bed and I was just bang out.

The next day I was very shaky. We were told we must not talk to anybody until we got back to the Admiralty. Don't say anything to anybody at all. I prayed a lot. But there must have been an awful lot of other people who prayed on that ship as well. Ninety per cent at least – why me?

We three were separated, for different reasons. I had been clobbered on my knee when the yard arm hit me, which I didn't realise at the time because I was cold. It wasn't until I actually started to walk on the destroyer that I found I'd been clobbered. Briggs, of course, had oil in his stomach. And Dundas was all right, he got up and walked.

I had been told there were only three of us survivors and more than fourteen hundred had died – but it didn't sink in for a long, long time. That was peculiar. It sunk into me that I was still there, I was alive, I wasn't one of them down there. I think I got, up to a point, happier. Well, it's better being in a hospital than on a ship at sea in the war. The surroundings were better, nicer, warmer, happier.

We were in there about five days and we were sent back to the UK. Our orders were; 'You go on this ferry from Reykjavik to Greenock. You go into your cabin, keep your trap shut, don't talk to anybody. Your food will be brought to your cabin. Don't go out of your cabin. You'll be met at Greenock.' Briggs and I had a cabin together but Dundas, being an officer, had one to himself.

We arrived at Greenock on 29 May and travelled down to London on an overnight train. We were picked up in King's Cross and taken to the

Admiralty. After the de-brief, Vice-Admiral Whitworth said, 'Do you want to go to the barracks and get kitted out, or do you want to go on leave until the court of enquiries which will be held very shortly?' So we said, 'Leave,' and went on leave. I was on leave for three months.

After the *Hood* sank my parents got a telegram from the Admiralty, 'Missing, presumed killed.' When I went to hospital in Reykjavik a second lieutenant from the West Yorkshire regiment, came to see me. He said, 'I know who you are, and I know what you are. I'm in the personnel department.' He said, 'I'll send a telegram to your family, give me your name and address.' All I put was, 'Quite safe, I'll write soon. Bob.' They got the telegram saying I was dead and two hours later they got the cable from Reykjavik.

For a long time I was in a state of suspended shock. It took me a long while to get over it. We knew immediately there were no survivors. There was no-one in the water. What I couldn't understand was why there were no bodies. No people drowning or anything, which you'd expect. That is what has puzzled me ever since.

I returned for the board of enquiry. The Rear Admiral in charge of the board of enquiry was 'Hookey' Walker. He asked me something and I said, 'Excuse me, sir, but you'd know more about the *Hood* than I do because you were captain when I first joined it.' They asked me a few difficult questions, the fire for instance. What colour was it? The explosions, what type? Were they like Japanese firecrackers? I said, 'I don't know, I've never heard a Japanese fire cracker.' What colour were the flames? They were trying to establish exactly what was on fire. Which really had no bearing on the actual sinking.

I had no theory at that time. I just told them what I could see. Ted Briggs, he was on the bridge, he could tell them a lot about the bearing, the water temperature, air temperature, signals that were made. I could tell them what had happened on the upper deck. Dundas was also on the bridge.

The *Bismarck* hit us. There was no doubt about that. She hit us at least three times before the final blow. But they were lucky in the fact that they found a weak place. You normally expect the Germans to hit you first, because their range-taking and firing is much better than ours. But once we get a hit we hold it.

In 1943 I went to America to join the HMS *Queen Elizabeth*, which was one of those ships that were clobbered by the Italians in Alexandria and went across to America to get repaired. Then she went home and straight on to the Far East.

The crew didn't treat me as a freak or anything. I'd been lucky, that's all. I kept quiet about it. I thought to myself: my mother, my father, my two sisters, my aunts and uncles, had all thought I was dead. Now, 1418 people were killed, so why should I boast about being alive when each of those 1418 had seven or eight relations who were saying, 'Why you? Why not my son, my brother, my husband?' So I kept quiet about it for a long, long time.

TELEGRAPHIST AIR GUNNER LES SAYER, RN

I joined the Fleet Air Arm as a TAG (Telegraphist Air Gunner). The training was just over a year. You did radio theory, semaphore and Morse Code. Then you did the air gunnery side, shooting, towing and bombing. It was good training but in those days it was run by the RAF not by the Navy, so our pilots were officers and all the ground crew were RAF.

We did our training in Blackburn Sharks and Westland (Wappity). I loved it, my first flight. Another 2s. 6d. a day, and it was a challenge.

My first job was on 811 Squadron. Then I got drafted to 825 Squadron, where Lieutenant-Commander Esmonde was the CO. All the time I knew Esmonde I don't suppose he ever spoke more than twenty words to me, not even in the cockpit. There was just no communication between the ranks. We formed up in the Orkneys. We'd only just got together. There was a nucleus of experienced people, about three pilots and maybe a couple of observers and maybe a couple of TAGS. All the others were brand new and straight out of training.

Normally you would spend at least a couple of months working up, practising torpedo attacks, but no sooner had we got together than we were shunted on to the *Victorious*, because that was when the *Bismarck* came out. She was out to get the convoys. So it was considered absolutely imperative that we got her first. We were the only squadron available and *Victorious* was the only carrier available in that area. *Bismarck* was much too far out of range for land-based aircraft, and most of our squadron were virgins.

The TAGs were not briefed. All we knew was what the ship's company knew, that we were chasing the *Bismarck* and that when we got within her range then the Swordfish would be launched. So we were at the sort of readiness stage, all nine of us TAGs stuffed into a little briefing room. Then we got the call, 'All right, we're away'.

The Swordfish is a three-seat open cockpit design. So the pilot is in the front, the observer is in the middle and the TAG at the back. We could only fire backwards. The weather was terrible. We climbed in a loose formation to about 10,000 feet. We got a blip on our primitive radar and came down to have a look at what it was, thinking it might be the *Bismarck* but unfortunately it was only an American coastguard cutter. However, the *Bismarck* was just beyond that and we had given our position away. So we had to do a low-level attack, and in we went. I was flying with Lieutenant Percy Gick who never spoke to me, but he was a good pilot.

As we went in I was sitting in the back, looking down between my feet. I could see the tail of our torpedo through a hole in the fabric in the bottom of the aircraft. It was like a red fin. I'm sitting there waiting to see that red fin disappear, then I know that the fish is gone and we're away, taking avoiding action. We did a run in and they were letting everything loose from the *Bismarck* and we were fortunate they didn't hit us, mainly because their range finders couldn't get down to speeds that were less than 100mph and our speed was roughly 90 knots.

Gick told us over the speaking tubes that he wasn't lined up and that he was going round again. So we went out to about 25 miles and came back again on our own: all the others were on their way back. So we came in right down at sea level. I'm standing up looking forward at the *Bismarck* and she's getting bigger and bigger and still they didn't see us. I thought to myself, well, they've only got us to aim at, they're bound to hit us, this is your lot anyway, so forget it. But we went in and dropped the fish and turned away and it was only then that they saw us and they let us have everything. Gick was very good. When they started firing their heavy stuff at us we had to count from the time they fired and take avoiding action. Another hazard was the huge waterspouts made by their shells. You could go through the splashes and get pulled down. We did fly through one of these splashes. It came up underneath us and ripped all the underside of the aircraft out so it was a bit draughty! We kept at about ten feet above sea level.

We felt relief when we turned around. I remember saying, 'It's bloody cold back here' because all the fabric had been ripped away, but it was only hazardous from the point of view that we probably didn't have much petrol. I could hear the pilot and observer talking to each other about courses to steer.

We thought we'd hit the *Bismarck*. There was only one known hit and that was amidships, and we thought we'd got it. It jammed the *Bismarck*'s rudders and she was seen to make two big circles. I suppose it was the beginning of the end for her.

When we got back to the *Victorious* it was dark. We had been flying for about four hours and we were right at the end of our endurance. We all got back safely even though, for some of the pilots, it was the first time they had done a deck landing at night. When we got back we were given bacon and eggs for the first time ever, and also a tot.

She was finally finished by *King George* V, *Rodney*, *Norfolk* and *Dorsetshire* with a loss of 2000 men on 27th May.

4

Convoys, submarines and battleships, 1941–42

LEADING TELEGRAPHIST PERCY CULLUM, RN

I joined the battleship *Barham* to work on the upper deck in an attempt to obtain a RN commission. (In those days it was necessary to transfer to the Executive Branch.) I could easily have qualified as a Leading Seaman because they gave me an excellent training course. I was on the foc's'le for entering and leaving harbour, and was involved in the streaming and recovery of paravanes. Generally I learnt all the things necessary to be a good seaman, which included forming part of a 4-inch gun crew and taking part in shoots, but at the same time I lived in the telegraphists' mess.

Barham was the only canteen messing battleship in the navy. Having spent two years in destroyers I was a godsend as far as they were concerned, because I could make 'duffs' and things like that.

The navy used to dish out tins of meat and vegetables and, because they were given away, the caterers tended to regard them as being no good, but they were actually very good indeed. One evening I said to the mess caterer, 'What have you got for supper?' and he said, 'Ham.' I said, 'You can't afford to give these people ham, because that costs about threepence a man. Have you got any tins of meat and veg?' They had, so I sent someone up to the galley for a big pot and got some flour, water and suet. Then I put all the meat and vegetables in a pot and made about twenty-four dumplings. It was marvellous, something they hadn't had for a long time.

On the day *Barham* was sunk, I was in charge of the watch of cooks. We were about a hundred miles south of Crete, between Crete and the north coast of Africa, and we were doing a sweep up and down over that area to check for anything crossing. The date was 25th November 1941, the time 4.30 in the afternoon. We had *Queen Elizabeth* and *Valiant* with us, they were the other part of the battle squadron, and eight destroyers were out on the screen.

We had just finished tea and I said to one of the fellows, 'I want you to go up to the canteen and get some bacon which we are going to have for supper,' when the torpedoes from the U-boat hit us and the ship began to list. There were about 150 of us on the mess deck and there was one ladder out.

We all made a scramble for the ladder, and at the top was the 6-inch gun battery. By the time I got to the top of the ladder the ship had gone over to the port side and some of the fellows were actually tumbling down into the 6-inch-gun battery. When he saw what was happening the padre stood astride the hatchway and grabbed hold of people, turned them around and put them on to the ladder which led to the upper deck. I was one of those the padre grabbed by the scruff of the neck. He was a very brave man, that padre. He didn't survive.

By the time I got on to the upper deck the ship was well over on her port beam. The feeling was not one of panic, but shock. I knew where some floats were stored, so, with a couple more I scrambled up to try and get them free. But the ship was keeling over all the time so we decided to give it up as a bad job, scrambled up the sloping deck to the ship's side and over the guard rail. Then we slid down the ship's side and stood on the bilge keel. That was when the after-magazines blew up and was the last thing any of us knew.

My own theory is that many who were already in the water were killed by stuff falling on them; most of the people who were close to the explosion were killed by it, and it was only some of us who had been shot into the air by the explosion that survived. When I came to, I was about 150 yards from where the ship had gone down. I was in complete darkness – even though it was half-past-four on a bright sunny afternoon – and my first thought was that I had gone down with the ship. So I held my breath for as long as I could in hope of coming to the surface. I am told that if you are drowning you breathe water in as if you are breathing air and you don't know the difference.

When I couldn't hold my breath any longer I took a deep breath and, much to my surprise, breathed in air. I assumed I had gone down with the ship and was in an air bubble somewhere below the surface of the water. So I took another deep breath, but this time it was water and fuel. It was beginning to get clearer and then I realised that the darkness was in fact smoke, and I was on the surface of the water which was thick with oil fuel. You can't swim in oil fuel, so I collected bits of wood and anything else I could find to keep myself afloat. I saw a boy sitting on a motor-boat cushion, so I shouted out to him and he pushed another cushion over towards me which I grabbed hold of and tried to get on top of, mainly because I could feel underwater explosions. I thought, God, they are dropping depth-charges, and having got this far I am now going to be killed by depth-charges. But, being thick with oil, every time I reached to get hold of this thing it just flopped over the top of me so eventually I gave up and hung on to the side of it.

Then after about an hour or so our destroyers came to pick us up. A whaler came over to where I was but by this time I was feeling quite fit. I could hear people screaming and crying in the water around me, so I said to the coxswain of the whaler, 'Go and look after people who are injured because I am OK, you can come back for me later on,' which they did. By this time they had got quite a lot of other people in the boat. The whaler had ropes hanging down its side so I hung on to one of those. My eyes had got full of oil fuel and I couldn't see but somebody leant over the side of the boat and wiped my eyes and as we got clear of the oil fuel they pulled us in towards HMS *Hotspur*. I had always been a good swimmer, so I let go of the whaler and struck out for the ship. It wasn't until then that the reaction started to take over and I could feel myself losing my grip, somebody grabbed hold of me, pulled me on to a scramble net and hoisted me up on to the upper deck of the *Hotspur*.

As soon as we got on board the destroyer they stripped our clothes off us and gave us a piece of soap and a piece of cloth and sent us to have a shower. When I put my hands out to wash myself the water hurt my hands so I said to somebody, 'Will you rub me down? I think I have been burnt.' I had thought I had been caught in the flash of the explosion. This fellow said, 'I'm the same,' and when we got the fuel off our hands we found that, as we had slid down the ship's side and steadied ourselves with our hands, we had torn all the skin off our hands on the barnacles.

We washed as best we could and then, being a wireless person, I went along to the wireless office. There I was joined by a PO cook who had come down the ship's side on his bottom, so you can imagine that the poor man could hardly sit down. The *Hotspur* took us overnight back to Alexandria. The next day they told us not to mention the fact that we were from *Barham* because they didn't want it broadcast. They took us aboard the *Resource*, which was a store ship in Alexandria, and cleaned us up and those who needed medical attention were seen to. They then sent us to a camp in the desert and sent us back to Alexandria a week later. They rigged us all out with as much uniform as they could. Then they decided who should be sent home. If you had been a survivor twice or if you had been on the station for more than three years, you were entitled to go home. I was doubly qualified: having been a survivor twice and having been away from home for nearly three years.

They sent us to Port Taufiq, at the bottom end of the Suez Canal, and there we picked up the troopship which brought us home via Mombasa and three glorious weeks as guests of the citizens of Durban.

LIEUTENANT PERCY GICK, RN

On the morning of the sinking of the *Ark Royal*, 13th November 1941, I gave Bird, one of our fliers, a bollocking because he had recently made several bad deck landings and had broken aircraft, including mine. I virtually told him that if he didn't do better he'd be out of the squadron. That afternoon he was the last to land. I had got up to the bridge by then: it was the most beautiful landing I'd ever seen. At that moment the torpedo hit. He leaped out of his aircraft, white as a sheet, and said, 'Christ, what have I done now?!' It was a bloody great bang – nobody knew what had caused it.

Of course we had already got full rudder turn to port, and what with the flood of water and natural heel from the turn, she just went up on her end, then on and on and on . . . When she got to the critical angle of 27 degrees, the captain gave the order to abandon ship which they promptly did. Norfolk, my observer, and I went straight down to the quarterdeck, his abandon-ship station, where the fourteen-foot dinghy was. We got that over the side and asked the first destroyer that came along if they'd pick it up and put it on board. Then we went to my abandon-ship station – one of the cutters of the upper side. Three Engine-Room Artificers had turned up so, while they were sorting out the boat, Norfolk disappeared, then came back with a crate of beer. He'd kicked the wardroom bar-door down. They got into our cutter while I lowered it. It went down nicely enough but ran out of wire about four feet above the water. Nobody had thought of the ship being heeled. So I got an axe and chopped, first the aft wire, then the forward wire, then I shinned down a rope.

We pulled away from the ship and drank a lot of beer. We had duly abandoned ship and we didn't see what else we could do which would be of much use. By the time we had finished the beer, we began to think this was a bit stupid, so we rowed back and, with enormous difficulty, shinned up the ropes to get back on board. We were greeted by the commander with: 'What the hell are you doing? You were supposed to abandon ship!' Anyhow, there we were. Naturally we found some more beer – it was a hot day and by noon we were rather thirsty again. We sat around until *Legion* came alongside, then we duly took some ropes from her. Meanwhile the gunnery officer and a few other chaps had gone to the foc's'le, thinking we might be towed.

One of the troubles about the ship was that you could only get steam if you had electric power, and the only generators were steam-driven. Unbelievable, there was no diesel generator on the ship. The senior engineer, Oliver, who had stayed on board was still down below. So we did the only thing we could to get the boilers going again. We used some ropes to pull two great big wires up from *Legion*. There wasn't one of us on board that had the slightest idea of what we were doing, but a bloke on the *Legion* was shouting to us, 'Find some big terminals, you must have some.' We found a red one and a blue one, then had to put the appropriate wires on. I distinctly remember one of us trying to test connections while someone else was shouting 'Put some electricity on this thing!' So we did some odd tests with bits of thin wire, found our terminals were connected to something and screwed in the wires and asked *Legion* to switch on. And, by God, we got our lights back! Then we just sat around, drank some more beer, standing by in case we were needed.

At that stage we had the pumps going so we weren't worried about sinking suddenly. She wasn't filling any more – she'd steadied up. The critical angle was 27 degrees – by the time she had levelled off she was at about 23 degrees. Of course, no-one at that time knew about counter-flooding so there was no damage control on the ship at all. We wouldn't have known, as air crew chaps, but if we had counter-flooded we'd probably have been able to get her upright and save her.

When we got the power back Oliver was able to get the steam up as he had a few chaps down below to help him. They got her steaming at about three knots back towards Gibraltar, and we were debating about whether we could get to Gibraltar when there was another bloody great crunch. This was the funnel uptake which went under the hangar deck, then up to the starboard side to the funnel. This angle got under the water and suddenly collapsed so that there was another gush of water and she lurched over a long way. She was now over the 27 degree mark. The last few blokes got off, except the poor old gunnery officer and his chaps who were up on the foc's'le – they didn't get the buzz to leave.

A rope was attached to *Legion* and my team and others slid down it. When it got to my turn I told the captain that I wanted to go forward and shouted to see if anyone was around. I crept forward with a small torch shouting now and then. That was the frightening bit. The only noise was ticking clocks and squeaking rats, and an occasional crunch when she went down a bit further. It was really very eerie and frightening. Fortunately someone heard my shouting. A splendid chap sitting in his action station, he hadn't got the buzz about abandoning ship – up he came, but told me he would not leave until the captain told him so I led him off. In the end there was only one man killed. Apparently when the ship's water-tight doors were closed some men used to doss down where they worked instead of groping their way back to their messdeck.

After checking the ship, I shot over down the rope, followed by the captain. That was when we saw a flashing torch on the foc's'le and found we'd left the poor old gunnery officer and his mates up there, so we had to go back to pick them up. Once we were on board the destroyer I went down below; I couldn't bear it. Hours later, she rolled right over – I didn't want to see. It was an awful loss. *Ark Royal* was so important.

SERGEANT TERRY BROOKS, RM

My first sight of the *Prince of Wales* was when I walked through the dockyard at Liverpool, turned the corner and got a view of her stern. I looked at her and thought, God I've done it at last, this ship is never going to sink.

We had no guns on board so they took her out of Liverpool right round to Rosyth where we were fitted with guns and ammunition. We had an air-raid attack there. Then we went round to Scapa Flow. It was the bleakest place we had been to but I thought it was wonderful.

It was from there that we sailed forth to do battle with the *Bismarck* and the cruiser (*Prinz Eugen*). I can't remember being frightened at all. We were expecting to sink the *Bismarck* and at 5.30 that morning the old chaplain said a few words of prayer, God bless you and the best of British. *Bismarck* fired first then we turned in towards her, flat out. The range wasn't much more than fifteen thousand yards and that is point-blank. We were about a thousand yards behind the *Hood* and I was watching the *Hood* through my own personal periscope in the forward 5.25-inch gun turret. There were shots astern, one shot landed in the *Hood*'s 4-inch gantry and all the 4-inch guns went up in the air and so did the ammunition. It was the fifth shot that did for her. It hit her in the turret, a blue spark as it hit. One second she was a beautiful battle-cruiser going flat out towards the *Bismarck*, then a massive flash of red gold, yellow, black. I kept on saying, 'The *Hood* has gone,' but the lads in my crew wouldn't believe it. We carried on banging away until our turrets went out of action. Then we shadowed the *Bismarck*. We'd hit her once or twice but not badly enough. Then we were told to return to Iceland because we'd been damaged and the whole fleet was after her. We got back to Reykjavik, blocked the hole with concrete, came back to Rosyth and got leave. Then back to Scapa.

One night, later on in the year, we heard that a piano party was coming aboard. Everyone said, 'Piano party? What are they talking about?' Anyway a boat came alongside and who should come aboard but Winston Churchill and off we sailed for Newfoundland. I shared duties with Superintendent Thomson of Scotland Yard, Churchill's bodyguard. I lost the old devil one day, couldn't find him anywhere. In the end I found him on the forward mess deck with the sailors, playing Ludo. Funny small man. Half-way across the Atlantic, Churchill was on the bridge – somebody had made him a little box to stand on so he could see – and we came to one of the biggest convoys I've ever seen. Old Churchill raised a signal somewhat similar to

Nelson's signal and we belted at high speed right through the middle of the convoy. He was like a little boy, 'Let's do it again!' All the convoy was hooting at him and he was waving his great cigar.

We went back to England, and leave. Then out to Colombo via Cape Town, and then Singapore. This was December 1941. Somebody had told us that the Japs were landing at two places in Thailand, Singapore and Petani, and at Kota Bhara just over the border in Malaya, on the east coast. We went in but there was nothing there at all. We had no air cover, which surprised me. As we turned back to Singapore we got caught by bombers. The *Repulse* sank first. I fired and fired and fired, anti-aircraft guns. Their planes came from all angles, very clever, high-level, low-level, firing torpedoes – two different directions at once. They were bloody good. They got us in the after-end on the port side and buckled the screws so we were going round at about five knots in a wide circle and all we could do was try to defend ourselves. I couldn't move my turret because of the extreme list to port. I had a block and tackle round my guns trying to shoot. Eventually I got my gun facing outward and if any aircraft came within range I opened fire. Then I went to check on my best chum, Taffy Thomas. By the time I got back, the electric cables were on fire.

There is a strange silence about a ship that's stricken. I can't describe it, but you know it's finished and I wasn't the least bit surprised when my phone rang, and I was ordered to abandon ship. I mustered all my lads on the fo'c'sle. I wanted to know that they were all there and had a feeling that people were missing, so I went and found a couple more below decks. When I had them all on the fo'c'sle I said, 'Undo your bootlaces, take your boots off and blow your life belts up.'

Then I ordered them to jump. It was about sixty feet to the water. I went straight in feet first wearing an overall suit and a cork life belt. Christ knows how far I went down but I came up like a bloody cork. When I came up I didn't have an overall suit on and my cork life belt had gone. I didn't hang about to see where it went because I didn't want to get sucked under. I was a fairly good swimmer. Eventually I got picked up by a destroyer.

There were 400 people lost on the *Prince of Wales* and about 700 on *Repulse*. A lot were trapped below in the engine-rooms. I could hear their screaming for years.

SURGEON-LIEUTENANT DICK CALDWELL, RN

We had left suddenly from the west coast of Scotland on 25th October 1941, and headed out westwards and then turned south. There was much conjecture and below-decks gossip as to our destination and plans. We arrived on 5th November at Freetown and, after a short stop there for refuelling, continued southwards and despite the grim war situation we staged the traditional and light-hearted 'crossing the line' ceremony.

It was now fairly obvious that we were heading for Cape Town and it subsequently transpired that President Roosevelt and Stalin had already been informed by Winston Churchill, 'We are sending our latest battleship *Prince of Wales* into the Indian Ocean as a deterrent to the Japanese . . . it can catch and kill any Japanese ship.'

We sailed into Table Bay on 16th November, but our stay in Cape Town, much to our disappointment, was brief, and two days later we set off again with some urgency for Colombo. Secrecy had now broken and the newspaper headlines flared the news 'Britain's newest battleship for Singapore'. Ten days later at Colombo, having called at the tiny wartime base of Addu Atoll in the Maldive Islands, we joined up with *Repulse* and the four escorting destroyers. Incidentally, during out passage out we had heard that the aircraft-carrier *Indomitable* had damaged herself in the West Indies and would not be available as planned to join and support Force 'Z' (as it was to be designated) and no replacement for the aircraft-carrier would be provided. This was a bitter and ominous piece of news.

When we arrived at Singapore on 2nd December the city was brightly lit and certainly, on the surface at any rate, confident that the advent of the two large ships would counteract and lull the now insistent sabre-rattling of the Japanese war-lords. The arrival of *Prince of Wales* in particular, to which the newspapers had already attached the adjective 'unsinkable', was greeted with great enthusiasm and the local press went so far as to state somewhat euphorically, 'the Japanese are caught in a trap of their own making and neither by land nor sea nor in the air do they have a glimmer of a chance of victory . . .' (It subsequently emerged that Japanese minesweepers were already laying massive minefields in the northern route from Singapore and Japanese submarines were already deployed in the same areas.)

The night after our arrival in Singapore a large party was given in our honour. Old friends were met and new friends made and future plans discussed of meetings, of tennis and golf; but these were not to be for early the following day, all leave was stopped – the date was now 6th December.

It was about 3.30am on the fateful Sunday morning of 7th December when I awoke hearing 'Action Stations' shouted and sounded off on the ship's loudspeakers. As I reluctantly got up and dressed I thought it was probably only an exercise, but on arriving at my action station on the bridge I quickly realised from the general atmosphere of tenseness that this was not the case, and on questioning someone I was told that several almost certainly hostile aircraft were reported flying in towards Singapore. The first grey light of dawn was just visible as we stood there – whispering, waiting.

Suddenly someone shouted 'Look!' and pointed. There, far away and very high over Singapore itself, just dots moving in a searchlight beam, were several aircraft. I watched them fascinated. We knew now they were Japs and as I watched them I thought, 'What everyone hoped and prayed would not happen is about to happen now, for just as soon as they drop a bomb, or we fire a gun it's another war to spread misery, death and destruction.' Even as I was thinking this I heard the crump, crump, of bombs answered almost instantaneously by the flaming roar of our guns. So it had happened!

Later, as we gathered round a crackling oscillating wireless set in the wardroom we heard of the fury and treachery of the Japanese strike at Pearl Harbor, and of battered ships and airfields. And I think most of us felt 'Well, the Americans are in! It's round one to the Japs – but now they are for it.'

Gradually we began to get news of the locust-like infiltration of the Japs, and of convoys moving south and of the landing and fighting in the northern tip of Malaya. Late on the afternoon of 8th December we heard the orders we were all expecting and, as *Prince of Wales* followed by *Repulse* led out to sea to whatever was in store for us, we were proud of her – powerful, sombre and sinister. I felt and recognised apprehension – not fear – but tension coupled however with a deepened comradeship with one's shipmates and, hateful though war and its implications undoubtedly are, one experiences a self-lessness and this comradeship which is difficult to define. I and many of my friends were aware of this as we stood in groups in the darkness talking, and conjecturing what might be lying ahead of us, and how the Japs would respond to our surprise attack – it was well for our peace of minds that we did not know.

Later there was a sudden silence, then the loud-speaker buzzed into activity. The captain's well-known voice began; there was a large convoy of Japanese ships unloading men and material in a bay in North Malaya. They were escorted by at least two battleships, half a dozen cruisers and many destroyers. We were going to attack them at dawn on 10th December. We had the vital element of surprise. We could do great damage, but we would have to be prepared for quick retaliation and subsequent heavy aerial attack by the enemy.

Well, that was it. Someone said he had heard the names of the enemy battleships and this caused a run on 'Jane's Fighting Ships'. How many guns? What have their cruisers got? We steamed steadily northward, well out to sea in cloudy poor visibility, admirable for our purpose. Then about an hour before the onset of darkness, unfortunately and ominously the clouds lifted, the sky cleared, and shortly afterwards the news flashed round the ship that a Japanese float-plane had been spotted far off on the horizon which was quite obviously shadowing us from a distance and reporting details of our course and disposition. Alas, we had no fighter aircraft available. Our surprise attack was no longer a surprise, and we cursed the fact that sheer chance had revealed us in that short clear period before darkness fell.

We were to be at our action stations all night then, and I wandered down to my cabin, collected a few things I would need, and as I went out took a last look at my cabin with all its personal belongings and wondered vaguely 'What the hell will you look like this time tomorrow?'

My action station was on the signal deck on the bridge. I had first-aid outfits and bamboo stretchers stored there and a telephone communicating with the other below-deck medical stations – there were two of them. I stood there for a long time just leaning over the bridge, looking down at the dark sea with the foam creaming its way aft on our bow wave, not thinking of anything much, and occasionally drifting in and out of the upper conning tower where we could smoke and just distinguish forms to talk to in the eerie blue light. I sat on the deck and leaning against a stretcher, dozed and woke and dozed again. Then somebody shook me and said, 'There is a broadcast just coming through.' It was from Admiral Phillips, the new C-in-C, telling us he had reluctantly decided to cancel our dawn attack. He knew how disappointed we would all be but unpleasant preparation for our reception would now be too great to justify our going in and he intended to alter course and turn south immediately – that was all. I didn't quite know whether I was a bit relieved or disappointed; but I did think that it must have been a hard and also a brave decision to make.

Next morning, as we steamed back south, we received news of suspected Japanese landings further down the Malaysian coast and a destroyer was sent in to have a look. Our reconnaissance aircraft was also catapulted off the ship to explore and report back. However, nothing was found. The morning wore on. Suddenly about 11.20 am we resumed first degree of readiness, and shortly afterwards echoing over all the ships' loudspeakers came that harsh and insistent bugle call, 'Repel Aircraft'. Galvanic in its effects on everyone and dramatic in its results! Every man has his post of duty and gets there by the shortest and quickest route probably plugging cotton wool in his ears and jamming on his tin helmet as he runs.

We were steaming very fast now, *Repulse* and ourselves with our destroyers spread out well ahead of us. Suddenly I saw puffs of smoke coming from one of them. She had opened fire. Looking for the puffs in the sky I saw more and more Jap planes and our own guns started up. A signalman shouted, 'Look at that bastard coming in at us.'

I saw a heavy twin-engined bomber fairly low over the water coming straight in at us, the noise was unbelievable, the roar of all our 5.15-inch armament, the cracking detonation of Oerlikons and Bofors and the chattering ear-splitting rhythm of the multiple pom-poms. They rose through a frenzied crescendo as the bomber approached. I watched him get nearer and nearer, bigger and bigger, I was horribly fascinated and kept thinking, 'We must get him, we must get him.' Then I saw his torpedo fall from the belly of his plane, splash into the sea and then its tell-tale line of bubbles heading for us.

Simultaneously the ship swung round to port to avoid its track and I found myself holding my breath and gripping the rail like a vice as the torpedo passed harmlessly on its way. They were attacking us from high-level too and a stick of bombs came screaming down ahead of us, throwing up huge pillars of water as they exploded in the sea. We avoided another two torpedo attacks on our starboard side and as the second plane banked away there was a cheer from the gun's crews – or rather a roar – as in smoke and like flaming newspaper it dropped lower and lower until it hit the sea and disappeared. A huge oily column of smoke marked its end.

We saw another plume of smoke rising from the sea three or four miles astern. It was certainly nice to know that anything crashing into the sea was Japanese. Then there was a slight lull. So far so good. We sent a signal to *Repulse* asking her if she was all right and her captain replied, 'Yes, we have already avoided 19 torpedoes.'

I had not had time to finish the cigarette I had lit when 'Repel Aircraft' sounded off again and I saw more aircraft heading in our direction from both sides.

The guns roared again and I heard a shout, 'They've hit *Repulse*.' I looked across and saw smoke and flames rising from her amidships. It gives you a nasty jolt to see another ship hit. I went to the intercommunicating telephone to tell the others down below and, as I clicked the receiver back on, there was a dull heavy shuddering explosion.

The 35,000 tons of *Prince of Wales* lifted and then settled with a slight list – a horrid sickening feeling. Verbal comment seemed superfluous. A young marine standing near me said 'W-was that a t-torpedo?' and started, quite automatically I'm sure, blowing up the inflator on his airbelt. Our speed dropped. The whole set-up was changing and I didn't feel awfully happy. I wondered how the medical parties between the decks were getting on. The indescribable din continued. *Repulse* had been torpedoed two or three times now and was travelling very slowly listing badly on fire, but her guns still flashed defiantly. As I watched her there was another heavy sickening jolt – hard to describe – like a sudden earth tremor I imagine. Another torpedo struck us and a huge cascade of water drenched us on the bridge. I went into the upper conning position to use the phone and find out if I was wanted below but it was out of order.

My job was upper deck casualties, so up till now I'd nothing to do but watch it all happening. The commander came scrabbling up a ladder, said 'All right here?' and gave us a grand tough smile.

The ship shook to another explosion. The high-level bombers had hit us with a heavy bomb which crashed through the catapult deck and exploded between decks. My impressions after this were a jumbled medley. I saw the battered *Repulse* hit again and again, list over more and more and slip below water leaving hundreds of bobbing heads, boats, Carley floats and debris.

I saw the track of a torpedo approaching, and realised that in our crippled condition it was going to hit us. It seemed a horrid inevitability waiting for the explosion that followed. I thought if only it was going to get dark soon we might escape but it was only midday. We gave a great lurch again as the torpedo tore into us. We were now practically stationary and listing heavily to port.

I realised that we could not last much longer and had a sudden vivid flash-back of our short-lived but exciting commission in *Prince of Wales* – ten months full of incident, full of highlights, his Majesty the King coming on board; the *Bismarck* action with *Hood* blowing up and sinking just ahead of us; the thrill of taking Winston Churchill across for the Atlantic Charter; his meeting on board with the American President, Franklin D. Roosevelt, and these two great men in our wardroom; grimmer memories of fighting, escorting a convoy to Malta, then the sudden trip out east to Singapore, to this. And inevitably my mind went back to my own previous escape from the *Royal Oak*.

There were casualties on the upper deck now and several had been brought up inside the superstructure. They were attended to and given morphine, and those that were unable to look after themselves were carried and placed inside floats or rafts for it was obvious now that we were going to sink soon. I went up top again for more morphine and, looking aft through the clouds of smoke, saw one of our destroyers manoeuvre alongside us and take off many wounded and as many others as she could manage. She slid clear as our list increased.

There were now hundreds of sailors standing on the sloping deck, they had been driven up from below by the increasing list and the encroaching rising water. We enlisted several of them into first-aid and stretcher parties. With the badly wounded the best we could do was to put them into Carley floats and launch them into the sea on the port side hoping they would float clear or be paddled clear before the ship slowly turned turtle, with its vast superstructure presenting an obvious danger.

On the starboard side men started climbing over the rails and diving and jumping thirty or forty feet into the sea below; but diving off the high side of a sinking ship (although a sound precaution) is a euphemism.

I took off my cap and my shoes and looked carefully round for somewhere to place them (an extraordinary action which I have read and heard of other people doing). I stood for a minute in the orderly crowd waiting their chance and heard a sailor say to his pal, 'Come on, chum, all the explosions will have frightened the bleeding sharks away.'

The ship was heeling over more now and I climbed over the guard rails and slid down to a projection on the ship's side. I stood there and looked down on dozens of heads, arms and legs in the water still far below. Then I said to myself, 'Please God don't let me be drowned,' took a deep breath and jumped out and down into the oily water.

A few minutes later *Prince of Wales* rolled over, her bows rose in the air and she slipped out of sight beneath the waves.

MARINE PETER DUNSTAN, RM

I was detailed to the *Prince of Wales*. As we marched out of Plymouth barracks to Devonport railway station the band struck up with 'God Bless the Prince of Wales'. I wish He had.

The Navy has a traditional saying that, if a ship is launched in blood she is a hoodoo, and there was a dockyard matey killed when the *Prince of Wales* went down the slips on her launch. She was a hoodoo from then on. A week before we went on board the Germans had dropped a bomb between the side of the ship and the dock and it burst under the boiler room, causing some flooding. After we came aboard they decided to take her across to Liverpool for patching up. We got halfway across the dock gates and she jammed. If she had gone a bit further she would have broken her back so we didn't go into Liverpool but went straight up into Rosyth. One or two incidents happened there. While they were putting machinery up on the bridge some silly so-and-so slipped and fell the whole length of the bridge and was killed. Another jumped in the dry dock and committed suicide.

In October 1941 we were detailed off to the Far East. Every time we stuck our nose out, something happened, so if that wasn't hoodoo, I don't know what is. I don't remember much about our last battle because I was down below transferring shells from the magazines on to a slide which went round to the guns. The guns were firing like mad but I was blind to what was going on. We found out afterwards that the torpedoes were coming at us twenty at a time. The first torpedo hit us just between the port propellers and it blew one of the propellers off and jammed our rudder. We were going around in a six-mile circle. We had had it.

When the order came to abandon ship Sergeant Brooks, who was the turret captain, lined us all up on the fo'c'sle and counted us off. Three of the gun crew were missing so we stood there while Sergeant Brooks got the three up from the magazine. Then he gave the order to jump. From where we went over the starboard bows to the water was roughly seventy feet. Let's face it, I won't even jump in the bath today, it's too deep. But as a Royal Marine you are trained to obey an order and when Sergeant Brooks said, 'Jump!' we jumped and didn't think about it.

Even today I cannot remember the transition from going down to coming up but I remember breaking surface. We had rubber lifebelts around us. I swam towards a cork float raft and we pushed it towards the destroyer, *Express*, one of our escorts. She was tied up to the *Prince of Wales*, getting casualties off. But the *Prince* started to turn and they had to sever the ropes with axes. I remember lying on my back and hearing them shout, 'She's going!' and watching her turn over with a number of officers in white sitting on the top of the bridge as she went over. They didn't make any attempt to get off. The undertow as the ship went over would have sucked them down. I was pulled aboard *Express* by a big hairy stoker who gave me a tot of rum. There was a second one a short time later and altogether I had four tots by the time we got to Singapore.

After a short time approximately 170 Royal Marine survivors from the *Prince of Wales* were detailed for guard duties at the Royal Navy wireless station at Kranji, while about 120 Marines from *Repulse* were sent to guard the Naval Base and the stores complex. But the fighting in Malaya was coming closer every day.

Surgeon-Lieutenant Maurice Brown, RN

It was lovely sunny afternoon in January 1942 when the destroyer *Gurkha* slowly made its way down the swept channel from Alexandria harbour and out to sea. I was on the bridge with the captain and several other officers and it was cold enough to wear a great-coat. In the distance two destroyers could be seen coming towards Alexandria in line ahead. They appeared to be very close together and soon it was evident that the second destroyer was being towed. Our curiosity increased as the distance separating us decreased and shortly afterwards I saw one of the many naval casualties in the Mediterranean at this time. It was obvious that the stern of the second destroyer had been blown off, but the water-tight doors had held and she stayed afloat.

'Must have been an acoustic torpedo,' someone said. 'Follows the bloody ship around till it finds her.'

The two destroyers were now very close and the smoke of a smouldering fire could be seen coming from the exposed stern of the second destroyer. 'Everyone in that part of the ship must have been killed for a certainty,' I thought, trying to picture the incident. These people certainly had had their baptism of fire, and I hoped I would acquit myself well if and when my time came.

My thoughts were interrupted by the captain shouting, 'Let's give them three cheers.'

A line of matelots rapidly formed along the deck and, as the two destroyers drew abreast, three resounding cheers went out from the *Gurkha*, led by the captain from the bridge. I felt that, as each cheer rang out, each and every man on board was expressing the admiration, sympathy and fellow-feeling for those of the wounded destroyer.

After three hours sailing, the captain announced that we were to pick up a convoy and take it to Malta.

There is practically no medical work on board a destroyer for the medical officer which most of them carried. When there is action with numerous casualties several months' work is crowded into a few hours. It was only natural, therefore, that the MO should be asked to do non-medical work like censoring correspondence and decoding messages. The decoding, at sea at any rate, was a not unimportant duty and the messages were usually reports on how many U-boats there were in the vicinity.

That evening after dinner, as was the custom, we spread ourselves round the wardroom either reading or snoozing or just talking. Inevitably two or three officers would start on some topic, anything from philosophy to prostitutes, and before long there would be a free debate in which the whole wardroom took part.

I went to my bunk shortly before midnight. I had one of four cabins, about seven feet square each, which were beside the wardroom. The wardroom occupied the whole width of the ship and, with the pantry, made up a watertight compartment. The four cabins, two of them on the port side and two on the starboard side had a wide passage, or cabin flat, in between which was also a watertight compartment. To get from the wardroom to the cabin flat one climbed a ladder out of the wardroom, through a man-hole on to the main deck, then along the deck a few yards to another man-hole and down a ladder which led to the cabin flat. This arrangement of watertight compartments localised damage to the ship.

I was awakened by the loudest explosion I have ever heard and thrown out of my bunk. I landed on my feet facing the curtain door of the cabin and was very wide awake. The door-way of the cabin was criss-crossed with burning planks. 'This is it,' flashed through my mind and, without stopping to think for a moment, I proceeded to lift the burning planks away in order to get into the cabin flat. My action was purely automatic, actuated by an irresistible urge to escape from the tiny blazing cabin. I never knew the real meaning of 'irresistible urge' before. As I grasped the planks I could feel the heat of the flames in my face and hear the sizzling of the burning flesh on my hands, though I was not conscious of any great pain. The planks were removed surprisingly easily – they had just been stuck to the varnished doorway by the heat – and I was out in the cabin flat. The flames rapidly died down, and in the ensuing darkness, I could not find the ladder which would take me up through the man-hole on to the weather deck and safety. In the darkness I moved about, groping for the ladder. Several times I crossed the few square yards where the ladder should have been and realised, with a sinking feeling, that it had disappeared. The only means of escape had gone and I was trapped in a watertight compartment. I groped my way round the other three cabins calling their occupants, but nobody answered. Never did I feel so lonely. I could hear the hiss and crackling of a terrific fire, interrupted every now and then by the explosion of the anti-aircraft pom-poms situated high up on the after superstructure.

The wardroom, just on the other side of the bulkhead from the cabin was on fire. Beneath me were the fuel oil tanks, and beneath the wardroom depth-charges and 4-inch shells were stored. Good God! Would the heat of the fire ignite the oil tanks or set off the ammunition and blow the ship to pieces? And I was trapped in a metal box. I could do nothing but wait, and pray that if the ship did not blow up, and the fire was put out, I would be found.

Suddenly I heard a loud clanging noise. It came from beneath my feet. I soon recognised it as the engines trying to turn the propellers, but the propeller shaft was loose in its seating and, after a crescendo of clanging metal, during which I was afraid the whole propeller shaft was going to come hurtling up through the deck, the engines stopped and all was quiet again.

I called for help, but I could hear no voices, and presumed everyone was out of earshot. In any case, no-one could get to the cabin flat because of the fire. Then I heard a voice, the thin piping voice of the midshipman. It came from the wardroom on the other side of that bulkhead which was keeping the fire from me. How could he be alive in that inferno? He was shouting 'Gun lights'. (He wanted the commissioned gunner to get the electric lights working again.) He called three times. In the middle of the third call there was the sound of a heavy object falling and the call was cut short. I felt more lonely than ever. The thought that I might not be rescued hit me. The fear that the ship might blow up at any moment was almost unbearable.

I was aware now that there was a gentle roll of the ship and that, as it moved from side to side, water was swirling around my ankles. I had no idea where this water was coming from but its presence gave me the one thought, 'this ship is sinking'. By now I could vaguely make out the outlines of the cabin flat and presumed it was daylight outside. I had no idea of the passage of time,

17 September 1939, two weeks after the outbreak of war, the 22,000 ton aircraft carrier, *Courageous*, sinks after being hit by two torpedoes from U-29. In this single, brief action, the Royal Navy had lost 518 men and one-sixth of her strength in large carriers.

May 1940. The Royal Navy, and an armada of small ships, evacuated over a third of a million troops from Dunkirk. Churchill eloquently spoke of the catastrophe that had been averted. 'The whole root and core and brain of the British Army, on which and around which we were to build the great British Armies in the later years of the war, seemed about to perish upon the field or to be led into ignominious and starving captivity.'

9 June 1940. The proud *Glorious*, seen here on an earlier occasion, with no air cover and no look out in the crow's nest, became a sitting duck for the *Scharnhorst* and *Gneisenau*. Also sunk, after the bravest of fights, were the escort destroyers, *Acasta* and *Ardent*. In this action 1,501 men were to lose their lives, only 41 survived.

19 June 1942. After the abortive raid on Dieppe, the dead lie covered alongside their destroyed landing craft and tanks. Of the 6,100 men who took part in the raid, the majority of whom were Canadians, 1,179 were killed and 2,190 captured.

10 August 1942. Operation Pedestal. Fourteen merchant ships, accompanied by the largest armada of Royal Navy ships, miraculously, the tanker *Ohio* survived intense enemy action to bring vital oil supplies to the stricken island of Malta. *Dorset*, seen here under fire, was sunk on 13 August. During the period 1939 to 1945 the British Merchant Navy were to lose nearly 2,500 ships.

Captain F. J. Walker CB, DSO and three bars, on the bridge of *Starling*. A U-boat has submerged: the search is on.

Walker has ordered depth-charges to be fired. The crew of *Starling* search for wreckage or bodies.

Depth-charges are fired again: Walker waits. He was the most renowned of all escort group commanders. With his personal technique of 'creeping attack' he destroyed 20 U-boats. He once hunted his prey for 38 hours. His early death on 9 July 1944, was attributed to his naval service.
'Pleased with danger when the seas ran high, He sought the storms.' Dryden.

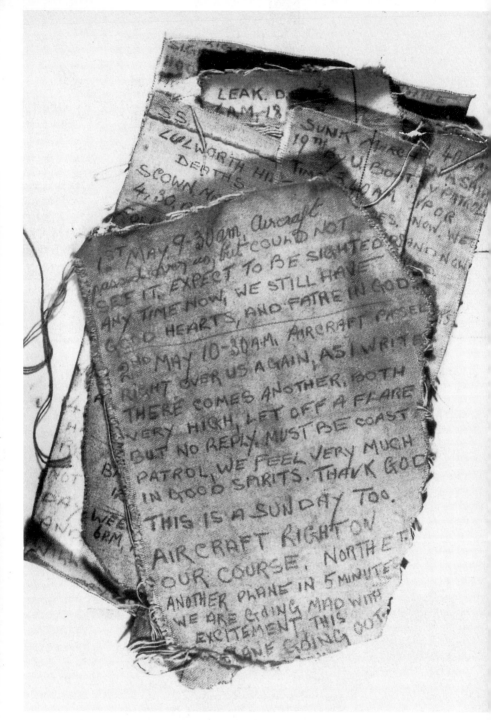

May 1943. After fifty days on a raft, on which fourteen men died, ship's carpenter Kenneth Cooke and Able Seaman Colin Armitage were the sole survivors of the sinking of SS *Lullworth Hill*. Cooke recorded their hopes and fears on torn strips of sailcloth before they were picked up in the South Atlantic.

May 1943. *Seraph*, commanded by Lt Bill Jewell, after another particularly good operation. Prior to Sicily landings, as a decoy, the body of 'Major Martin RM' (the man who never was) was floated from *Seraph*, off the Spanish coast.

6 June 1944, D-Day. The mighty warrior *Warspite*, opens fire onto the beaches of Normandy.

D-Day. Royal Marines of 4th Special Service Brigade charge ashore near St Aubin-Sur-Mer.

Royal Navy Commandos talking to liberated French villagers. Note their khaki uniforms.

it all felt so interminably long. Now, when I touched the metal bulkheads, in my half-blind groping in search of the ladder, I got what seemed like a mild electric shock in my fingers. I could not understand this until I felt something hanging from the end of my fingers. I tried to pull this away, too late to realise it was the burnt skin of my own hand which had folded outside like a glove and was anchored at the nail bed. Now I knew that even if I did find that ladder, and could reach the man-hole, I could not undo the strong clasps which held it in place. The water was now up to my knees.

Suddenly the cabin flat was ablaze with light. A sheet of flame spread across the water and set me alight. Automatically I splashed the water I was standing in up over my head, and, as quickly as it came, the flame disappeared. A film of oil on the water had been ignited by the heat of the bulkhead next to the wardroom.

Inexorably the water rose, and my hopes of escape sank. Now I could no longer make out the outlines of the cabin flat. The fire had blinded me! When the water reached my waist and I was still standing helpless and blind I felt a sudden surge of heat and realised that I had again been set on fire. Splashing the water up round myself again soon extinguished the flames.

The water was slowly rising up my body. I calculated I had about fifteen more minutes of life left. When it reached shoulder height I began to have a most irrational, but none the less real, fear that the ship would sink while I was still alive, but trapped inside it. To be drowned in the cabin flat with the ship still afloat seemed a much less horrible alternative. So strong was this feeling that I began devising means of ensuring that I would not be taken down with the ship alive. There was a rack of revolvers in a case on the bulkhead between the two port cabins, but by the time I thought of them as a means of escape, they were already under water. In any case my hands were now incapable of handling a revolver. When the water reached my neck I was swept off my feet with the gentle roll of the ship. This really seemed the end and I yielded again to the lure of self-destruction. The thought of drowning myself occurred to me but even at that moment the instinct of self-preservation proved too strong and the mood passed so that I only got as far as dipping my face in the water once. I was now afloat in the water, which, with the roll of the ship, swished from side to side carrying me with it. I could still see nothing but imagined all the debris of burnt planks, cigarette ends, oil and filth which floated around me. The very fact that there was now no possible escape, no strain of hoping for a miracle to happen, left me wonderfully and illogically calm. I thought of the people who would miss me – the ones who would really grieve for me. I was humbled to discover how very few there were. My mother, my fiancée, my best friend Charles.

How long now? I looked up to see how close my head was to the upper bulkhead. I could not believe it! I could see, and what I saw was a tiny triangle of daylight about ten feet above my head. I immediately swam over to it. When I got there I found a space where solid deck should be. Using my elbows (I could touch nothing with my hands) I climbed through what could only have been the main weather deck of the ship, and found myself in the small-arms ammunition store. A case of ammunition had exploded against the bulkhead and blown a hole in it. I looked at the jagged edge of the metal and shuddered as I thought of touching it with my hands. The hole looked far too small to crawl through. I knew that if I got stuck, or my jersey caught on those jagged edges I could never free myself and would be left half in freedom and half in prison. Squeezing myself into the slimmest possible shape I put my head and shoulders through and found, to my relief, that not only did my jersey not catch, but I was able to lean my elbows on the torpedo tubes out on the open deck, in the clean fresh air and daylight. The contact was unbelievable. Despair was replaced by hope; darkness by light; and the nauseating smell of crude oil, burning clothes, hair and flesh, by the smell of the sweet, pure air. I took in great lungfuls of it as though I had never experienced the sensation before. I was sprawled across the torpedo tubes about four feet above the main deck. Not having the use of my hands, I wriggled down off the torpedo tubes, but as my feet touched the deck I realised my jersey had caught on a projection on the torpedo tube and I hung half suspended and powerless to do anything about it. The main deck (my former ceiling) was awash and the ship was badly down by the stern. I saw sailors up forward and rejoiced that the ship had not been abandoned. My blindness in the cabin flat had obviously been due to the oil in my eyes and not burns.

Then a hand shot out from nowhere and unhooked my jersey. What with the suddenness of the action, my oil-covered feet and a roll of the ship which sent a wave over the deck, I fell and slithered down the sloping deck into the scuppers. Luckily the guard rail prevented me from going overboard.

Willing hands were now helping me, but after walking a few yards my legs gave up and I sank down on the deck. I saw the Sick Berth Attendant passing several times on his duties and each time asked him for morphine. At last he stopped when he heard my voice and said, 'Good God, it's the Doc.' He could not recognise me for I was literally black from head to foot with thick tarry oil. With the aid of a matelot's big strong shoulder under my bottom I climbed the steps to the sick bay. I remember lying in the sick bay and the Sick Berth Attendant trying to clean the burns, but I must have fainted.

My next recollection was of lying outside on the deck, up forward, being strapped into a Neil-Robertson stretcher, a series of bamboo-like slats of wood interlaced and held together with rope. Everything was being done at the double and I realised I was a last-minute job before the ship was abandoned. Owing to the haste, only a simple loop was put round the middle of the stretcher, instead of securing the rope to two tie points, and I was swung out on a davit. As soon as I was swung clear of the ship, my head and shoulders, the heavier half of me, tilted downwards and I was in danger of sliding out of the stretcher on to the whaler waiting to receive me in the sea some twenty feet below. I hung on to the foot of the cone-shaped stretcher with my toes to prevent me sliding out head first. At the same time someone saw the danger and shouted 'lower away'. This matelots did with a will and I went down at high speed and crashed into the whaler coming up with a wave. Immediately I was in the boat the sailors pushed off from the now sinking destroyer. We had only gone about one hundred yards when someone cried, 'There she goes.' I craned my neck up over the gunwale of the whaler to see the ship getting lower and lower by the stern and the bows rising up higher in the air. She seemed to hang, poised like this for some time as though in one last defiant gesture, before sinking slowly, stern first. It was a sight I will never forget.

We were picked up by a Dutch destroyer, crammed with survivors from the *Gurkha*. (Unfortunately, most of the officers were having breakfast when the torpedo struck the wardroom. Only the captain, 'Guns', and a sub-lieutenant who were on duty on the bridge at the time survived.) At last I was lying down, and, glorious relief, an injection of morphine. Never did I revel so luxuriously in the enveloping arms of Morpheus. The thought of the U-boats still crossed my mind but the injection eased my fears as well as my pain and I was soon asleep.

My last memory of that place is of lying on a stretcher near the water's edge in a row with scores of other casualties. There was a clear blue sky and the sun was shining, although the air was cool. Standing off from the shore was a large hospital ship to which the casualties were being taken in relays. I hoped that when my turn came I would be left on one of the upper decks as I was now not a little adverse to dark places below decks. But, alas, immediately we reached the hospital ship I was taken straight into a lift which went down and down until I thought it could go no further. At last, it stopped, but from here I was taken through such a maze of corridors that, even had I been particularly fit and active, I would have had difficulty in finding my way back. Knowing that I was too weak to make any effective escape, I decided that if anything happened to the hospital ship I would not even try. From my position in the bowels of the ship I could hear the anchor being weighed, the slow turning of the propellers and the general familiar noises of a ship getting under way. Soon, to the steady throbbing of the engines, I fell asleep.

LIEUTENANT JOHN ROXBURGH, RN

I left the *Tribune* with my captain, Lieut-Commander Bob Norfolk, who took me with him as his second-in-command, or First Lieutenant (No. 1), to build a submarine called *Thorn* at Birkenhead. After completing its trials we went out to the Mediterranean. I remember being sent for by Norfolk. He was looking rather solemn but there was a twinkle in his eye. He told me a letter of mine had been returned, marked 'Unsuitable'. I read it and it described our farewell party when we left Birkenhead. We had a jolly good thrash and booze-up and afterwards one of our ratings had gone around the control-room swigging all the half-empty glasses. He then got up on deck with a bucket full of gash to hurl over the side, but he was so well tanked up, he forgot to let go and followed the bucket overboard. Fortunately he was rescued. I had described this vividly in my letter to a girlfriend in Canada which had been picked up by the censors as being an 'Unsuitable letter', letting information go to the enemy. The captain laughed and gave it back to me. No action was taken.

We had quite an interesting time out in the Mediterranean in *Thorn* (which unhappily was lost with all hands in August 1942). On 30th January 1942 we were off Dubrovnik where we had surfaced to shell a ship, to save our torpedoes. In the middle of this action the shore batteries opened up on us and we dived quickly near a lighthouse in the middle of a spit of rock offshore. There were shells bursting around us so the captain ordered us to 200 feet. As we were going down we suddenly all fell over without any sound having been made. It was a most uncanny feeling. The captain had ordered 'Starboard 30 (degrees)' but the course ordered to be steered hadn't got through to the helmsman due to the confusion reigning at the time, so we had done a complete circle as we went down and rammed the base of the lighthouse. Thereafter we surfaced and there was the lighthouse keeper looking down on us pretty excited.

The shore batteries opened up again so we dived and withdrew. When we surfaced that night I went up on deck with the second coxswain to inspect the damage. The whole of one side of our torpedo tubes had been bent round at right angles: the torpedoes were intact but could not be fired due to the blanking off by the bent tubes.

As there was no other damage we continued on our patrol and went up to the port of Pola near the top of the Adriatic, where we encountered a destroyer, an Italian submarine and supporting aircraft on exercises. We watched the destroyer giving the submarine practice attacks. That night, the 30th January, we sank the submarine as it returned to harbour, even though we only had half our torpedoes available. We found out later it was called the *Medusa* with a training class of a number of aspiring submarine COs on board. We had sunk the odd merchant ship before but it was our first warship sinking.

The next day we returned and there was a floating crane over the top of the submarine, trying to raise it, and there were a number of destroyers patrolling in defence. Norfolk wanted to try and sink the crane which I thought was a bit 'dodgy'. It would be very difficult to sink, particularly in face of the strong anti-submarine patrols, and why not let those poor buggers down there survive if they can? But I think most of them perished.

On that patrol we had a group of Yugoslav agents on board whom we were going to land. They were led by a delightful British officer called Major Atherton who had been the Balkans correspondent of the *Morning Post* before the war. They were going to help General Mihailović, as opposed to Tito, and they carried gold sovereigns defaced by a cross from a knife. Unfortunately after we landed them they were picked up by Mihailović partisans who butchered all but one of them, who escaped, for their money.

LEADING AIRMAN DONALD BUNCE, RN

In late March 1941, the German battleships *Scharnhorst* and *Gneisenau* returned to the port of Brest, on the west coast of France, having sunk 22 Allied ships totalling 116,000 tons. They were joined, after the sinking of the *Bismarck*, by *Prinz Eugen*. Their continued presence at Brest was a severe threat to North African and Atlantic supply convoys, and the Admiralty were forced to divert precious capital ships to protect these routes. These three very powerful enemy ships, at large on the High Seas, could have forced us to our knees, so it was imperative that this threat be countered.

A war cabinet meeting, at about this time, concluded that our naval commitments were too widespread, and the task of neutralising these ships should rest with the Royal Air Force. The raids on Brest left the warships damaged, but by no means crippled, and they remained a threat.

During April, high level meetings concluded that it was highly probable that the Brest ships would attempt a dash through the Channel, and this was one month before the German High Command came to the same conclusion. Clause 7 of the Allied Directive which became known as 'Fuller', stated, 'It is unlikely that the enemy would pass through the Straits (of Dover) in daylight'.

Admiral Otto Ciliax was in command of the German fleet, and his planning, with his countryman, the fighter ace Adolf Galland, was meticulous. Weather forecasts and tides indicated the night of 11th February 1942, at 1930, as being the ideal time to sail. A delay of two hours would be acceptable, after that the operation would be postponed.

In brief, the series of events which followed were so bizarre, they beggar belief.

First, the RAF mounted a night raid on Brest at 1930, which, of course, delayed the ships' departure. This, in turn, meant that the submarine *Sea*

Lion, on regular nightly patrol off Brest, ran out of time, and, at 2000, retired to recharge her batteries, thus missing the big ships and their destroyer escort, when they sailed at 2130.

The next line of observation was three RAF Hudson reconnaissance patrols, covering the area from Brest to Dieppe. The first Hudson was attacked by a Ju88 night-fighter, switched off its radar and escaped, but then discovered that it could not get the radar to start again, and so the aircraft returned to base. The second Hudson also developed radar trouble, and, likewise, returned to base. When its radar had been repaired, this aircraft got stuck in the mud at the airfield and was not back on station until 2248. Another miss! The third aircraft was working OK, but was recalled to base one hour early because of fog at the airfield. It was now 0630 on 12th February, and the Germans could hardly believe their luck; so, at 0830, the Senior Officer – Escorts – gave their position to German HQ.

It was usual, each morning, for the RAF to fly weather sorties of two Spitfires, but they had strict instructions to maintain radio silence. At 1020 Flight Lieutenant Oxspring took off with Sergeant Beaumont, and at 1030, Group Captain Beamish took off with Wing Commander Boyd, but from different airfields.

Both saw the Armada of ships, which had now swollen to 63, including minesweepers and E-boats, all protected overhead with a constant cover of fighters. Beamish decided not to break radio silence, but Oxspring did, and, amazingly, there is no record by the British that this signal was received; but the Germans logged it and, from then on, expected trouble. It took another hour to convince the British High Command that the danger existed, and, at 1135, Air Vice-Marshal Leigh-Mallory ordered 'Fuller' into action, sixteen-and-a-half hours after the ships had left Brest. At 1155 MTBs (Motor Torpedo Boats) left Dover. At 1210, South Foreland batteries opened up with 9.2-inch guns and fired 33 rounds, and, at 1235, the MTBs attacked, both without doing any damage.

As the British had expected a night passage through the Straits, this meant that everyone had now stood down. This applied to the Swordfish of 825 Squadron at Manston. At 1105, a Wing Commander Roberts, on the Admiral's staff at Dover, began to suspect the worst, and he telephoned Lieutenant-Commander Esmonde, 825's CO, to warn him. He, in turn, brought 825 to readiness. Roberts then attempted to arrange a fighter escort, five squadrons to support 825 and two to attack the German E-boats. At Biggin Hill RAF airfield, the Intelligence Officer was on leave, and had taken the key of the safe with him, so no one knew what 'Fuller' meant. At 1218, No. 72 Spitfire Squadron left for Manston, to escort 825, not aware of the full implications of the action in which they were involved.

As we made our way to the dispersal on that February day, the weather was no different to the previous days, bitterly cold, with snow covering the grass airfield. Blissfully unaware of what was ahead, what dominated our minds was that a planned night attack was now to take place at midday. As usual, TAGs (Telegraphist Air Gunners) were excluded from the briefing sessions and had to rely on the Observer for any 'Gen' (or information). Four TAGs, one former pilot of mine, one Observer, and, of course Esmonde himself, had taken part in the torpedo attack on the *Bismarck*, from HMS *Victorious*, and we were only too aware of the implications of a daylight action. This time it would not be in the middle of the North Atlantic, but in the Straits of Dover, and a warning was ringing in our ears from the RAF types in the mess: a new German fighter, the Focke-Wulf 190 was now operational.

We took off and formed up over the coast, and I exchanged a 'thumbs up' sign with fellow TAG 'Ginger' Johnson, just before seeing Spitfires overhead, and assumed all our escort had arrived. Soon after, we were headed out to sea, in line-ahead formation. I was in the first flight of three, with Esmonde leading, our aircraft bringing up the rear. The second flight was some distance from us, still in 'V' formation. I began to prepare the Vickers Gas-Operated machine-gun, loading a magazine and then sitting down and waiting. The weather was overcast, with low cloud and poor visibility, and the Spitfires were just below the cloud base.

Then it all happened: tracer from a destroyer 'floated' our way, that is, until it came close, when it took on the characteristics of an express train, and in came the FW190s. I don't know how many there were. I was just concentrating on those that were on our tail; it seemed endless. As soon as one peeled off another was in its place, with tracer speeding toward us. After a while they lowered their under-carriage and flaps in an attempt to reduce speed and prolong the attack.

I began swearing away and at the same time fired as much of the feeble .303 tracer in front of the 190s as I could, stoppages permitting; all drill in this respect went overboard, as indeed went any malfunctioning magazine. There simply wasn't time for anything else. From my backward viewpoint, it was developing into a practice shoot for FW190s, and we were the drogue target; they were coming so close, as they peeled off to the port I had a sideways clear view of the pilot. I had a quick visual image of the shells hitting the water, giving them perfect alignment to hit the old Swordfish.

Yet despite everything I had no impending sense of danger or injury to myself. I just considered myself 'fireproof'. Just as suddenly as it had started, the fighters left; presumably our torpedo had been launched, one is usually aware of the drop, but not on this occasion. Now I could look around. I tried to send some kind of distress signal, but the wireless set was dead. However, the IFF worked, and I immediately switched to the distress position, but as this relied on radar contact, at sea level this was a useless exercise.

I turned to the Observer, Mac Samples, to ask if he was OK. He reached down with one hand and brought it up covered in blood; his leg and foot were badly injured. The pilot, Pat Kingsmill, was also wounded in the leg.

Below us I saw some small boats which I thought might be MTBs. As we closed, their true identity was revealed: they were E-Boats and their gunfire immediately began hitting us. But Pat, with great skill, began to crab away, and I, with further oaths, emptied my last magazine in their direction. Then, suddenly, great flashes streaked down the port side; a large square hole in the upper main plane meant that the dinghy had been shot away. We had also lost two cylinders from the engine but we still managed to fly. Not for long. With the tail well down, we ditched perfectly.

On impact, I hit my harness release button and threw it off, then literally, stepped overboard into the Channel, to help Mac. A jerk on my head told me that I had forgotten to unplug the headphones! Thank God a motor launch was alongside. I was grateful, for it was extremely cold! Once aboard, I was bundled down below, to lie between the giant diesel engines, given dry clothes and a cup of 'pussers' rum. Pat was in the wheelhouse, and Mac lay on the after deck, a big matelot attempting to keep him warm, for his injuries were quite severe. The passage to Ramsgate harbour, at full speed through a choppy sea, must have been a nightmare to the other two. The rum helped me, but the roar of the engines precluded any conversation, leaving me with my own thoughts.

An ambulance was waiting on the quayside and quickly whipped us off to hospital. I wanted news of my mates. At base Edgar Lee (Observer in the second aircraft) told me his pilot had severe back injuries but, to my dismay, his TAG, 'Ginger' Johnson, had been killed early in the action. There was no news of the rest, but there was still hope. Next morning, it became increasingly evident that we who had made it back were to be the only ones!

I was in a daze and it didn't help when, along with the PO Fitter, we were ordered to assemble and pack the kit of the other five TAGs. Stowing photographs and other personal items was very traumatic, but it had to be done, and rather by me than anyone else.

I learnt later what had happened. In the engagement Lieutenant-Commander Esmonde, who was leading the first flight, was jumped on by fighters, as well as being fired on by the enemy ships, and his aircraft was severely damaged, but even with most of his lower port wing lost, he flew on, until he finally crashed into the Channel.

The second aircraft, piloted by Sub-Lieutenant Rose, was attacked in the same manner, Rose was badly wounded and only with the encouragement of his Observer, Sub-Lieutenant Lee, did he manage to keep the damaged aircraft flying, make his attack and, finally, ditch safely. We had managed to get inside the destroyer screen and release our torpedo at about 1,000 yards before ditching.

The second sub-flight of three aircraft was not heard of again, and all nine people were lost.

Even more mishaps were to occur that afternoon. The RAF mistakenly attacked the only destroyer raid we could muster. The only success was that the *Scharnhorst* twice hit a mine and the *Gneisenau* hit another.

Air losses, during this time, were heavy; RAF attacks on Brest had cost them 43 planes. Losses on 12th February were: RAF 37 planes, and the RN six Swordfish.

For the Germans, the whole affair was a major propaganda coup; for the British, after the initial despair, a realisation that one threat to vital Middle East convoys had been removed.

How big a 'fiasco', or 'cock-up', it was can be judged by the fact it was one of only three events during the 1939–45 war that was subject to an 'Official Enquiry'. I would imagine inter-service co-operation improved dramatically when the War Command received the report.

PETTY OFFICER THOMAS GOULD, RN

On 16 February 1942 we were inshore in shallow water. We could have just about dived, but the Germans were looking for us at sea. We had just sunk a very heavily escorted merchant ship which was escorted by aircraft, MTBs and destroyers off the north coast of Crete, in Suda Bay. *Thrasher* had suffered about three-and-a-half hours of depth-charges, how many I don't know. I don't know if anybody had nerve enough to count them. This wasn't the first time: we had had it before. We were there primarily to map the mines being set by the Germans and then relay the information back.

We surfaced as night-time came and were close inshore on normal duty watch. The skipper, Lieutenant Mackenzie, came down off the bridge and went to his cabin. I went to my Mess but just as I was about to get into my bunk I heard rolling noises outside. I thought, nothing of mine is out there – it sounded to me like the gun-casing, the parapet of the gun. The skipper also heard it because it was just above his head. Anyway I went and reported to the bridge, and he sent the lookout over, Daisy Adams, a gunlayer, who was responsible for the gun, to have a look at what was going on.

Daisy came back to say that there was a large black object on the forecasing in front of the gun platform and a great hole in the super-structure of the platform itself. They told me to come up and have a look for myself, so I did. Lieutenant Roberts was also asked as he was responsible for the outside as well, and was responsible for discipline over and above myself, the coxswain. We took some sacking and heaving lines and when we got through we found it was a bomb.

First Lieutenant Roberts took sketches of the bomb, where it lay on the forecasing while I held it still, as the boat was rolling around. At any moment it was in danger of rolling off the casing on to the saddletank below and exploding. Between us we managed to wrap the bomb in the sacking and tie it with the heaving line. It was too heavy to be thrown clear of the saddle tanks – it weighed about 100 lbs and was about three feet long. We had to manhandle it overboard, really slowly and carefully. I don't think the pilot had enough time to set the fuses. The explosion sounded as if a depth-charge had gone off. If it's very close to the submarine it shrinks the boat and then you hear the steel of the boat coming back to its normal size and shape again: it sounded like sand landing on a tin roof.

To get to where the second bomb was we had to wriggle forward through the outer casing of the submarine. In that confined space there were angle irons to hold the superstructure up, battery ventilations (which are rather large tubes) and drop bollards as well. When we got through I saw that it was another heavy bomb, again 100 lbs, and I picked the bomb up and passed it through to Roberts who came in behind me. I then laid on my back with the bomb on my stomach, and held on to it while he laid on his stomach with his head to my head pulling me by the shoulders. I was being pulled forward with the bomb on my stomach. Every time we moved it made a nasty twanging sound like a broken spring, which it may well have been. Finally we got to the grating.

All this took about an hour. It took us twenty minutes to wriggle in and a bit more to slowly wriggle out holding the bomb. We passed it up to the sub-lieutenant, who was waiting on the forecasing. I certainly think he should have been awarded something more than a mention in dispatches. We passed it up to him, and he laid it down on the forecasing. We wrapped it up with sacking again and put a couple of heaving lines around it. Then he walked forward to the highest point at the foremost part of the boat, and gave a signal to the bridge with a dim light to go astern. As with the first bomb, the boat moved astern as we lowered it gingerly over the bows. When we knew it was on the surface of the water and the boat was moving we let it go, heaving lines as well. Then we ducked and waited for the next explosion, but nothing happened – it obviously couldn't have been primed.

Lieutenant Roberts and myself were awarded the Victoria Cross for what we did. At the investiture at Buckingham Palace King George said, 'How long were you in there?' and I said, 'Oh, about an hour, sir' and he said, 'I bet it was cold.' I said, 'Yes, Your Majesty, but I didn't notice it.' Then he shook my hand and pinned on the Victoria Cross. I wasn't nervous until I saw my wife sitting at the front. We came out of the palace with my wife holding our baby.

LEADING SEAMAN TOM PARSONS, RN

I had been on the *Prince of Wales* when she was sunk and was taken back to Singapore. I was then detailed to patrol the Johore Straits in small boats, doing hit-and-run raids. On 12th February 1942 I was sent to HMS *Li Wo*, a converted Yangtze river steamer weighing 1000 tons. Out of a mixed crew from all the services I was the only trained gunlayer on the main armament, an old 4-inch gun made in Japan, which was situated in the bows. The chief bosun's mate, CPO Charlie Rogers, was the captain of the gun and Lieutenant Thomas Wilkinson, RNR, was the ship's captain.

We left harbour on Friday 13th February. Local residents thought the steamer was being used for evacuation, and there were scenes of panic as we left. We headed for the Straits of Bangka and were attacked many times by lone aircraft, but we came through. On Saturday 14th February we dropped anchor close inshore, hoping that we would not be spotted by enemy aircraft, as the captain intended to go through the eighty miles of the Bangka Straits in darkness. We were spotted by a Japanese seaplane just as we got under way again.

At about 4.30pm we sighted smoke on the horizon off the port bow. It was a convoy, about ten miles away. Lieutenant Wilkinson asked if anyone could recognise Japanese warships and I told him I was familiar with them as I had spent two years on the China station. So I went up to the bridge and he handed me his telescope. I saw one Japanese light cruiser and two destroyers and without looking any more I told the captain the convoy was Japanese, no doubt about it. It later turned out that a heavy cruiser was at the rear of the convoy.

The captain addressed the crew and said, 'There is a Japanese convoy ahead. I am going to attack it and we'll take as many of those Jap bastards as possible with us.' These are words I will never forget. We headed for the convoy and the captain selected a troopship of about 10,000 tons as the target. I had a mixed bag of ammunition in the stand. Six semi-armour-piercing shells, four graze fuse shells, and three A A shells, plus three practice shells.

At about four thousand yards, we opened fire. The first SAP shell was over target, but at least three of our remaining SAP shells were bang on. Fire immediately broke out on the troopship and she was soon blazing furiously and the several thousand Japanese troops aboard were jumping into the sea. Within a few minutes I had used all our ammunition, so Wilkinson selected another target, the transport ship nearest to him, and rammed it at full speed and sank it. I will never forget an RAF sergeant who was manning the Vickers Lewis gun. His deadly accurate fire completely wiped out the four-man gun's crew aboard the Jap transport we rammed. The enemy's gun was about 40 mm and it was this gun which caused our first casualties. I was wounded in the chest. Then as we pulled away, the transport ship sank.

The RAF sergeant opened up on another transport about 200 yards away but the convoy cleared away from us and we came under fire from the Japanese warships. It was a fearful experience as it took them five to ten minutes to find our range, their gunnery was so inaccurate. We heard their shells whistling overhead, always expecting the next one to land inboard, knowing we had to just sit there and take it, helpless and unable to do anything about it. When they eventually found the range, it was all over.

The *Li Wo* listed to starboard and sank stern first. The captain stayed on the bridge but I and many others jumped into the water and started swimming towards the life rafts. The Jap transports closed in, picking up their own survivors, as we expected they would then come and picked us up too. But we were in for a shock. They came right at us and deliberately rammed our rafts. We realised just before they hit us what they were doing and quickly dived into the sea. Then I watched that transport go among a group of survivors and manoeuvre amongst them with their churning screws, killing at least a dozen. They machine-gunned us as we tried to get away from the sinking ships. Then they threw grenades and even lumps of coal and wood at us in the water. Out of a crew of over one hundred, only ten of us got ashore alive. Seven lived to celebrate VJ day.

Bandsman George Lloyd, RM

I was one of fourteen Royal Marine bandsmen who worked in the Transmitting Station (TS) of HMS *Trinidad*, a wonderful, incredibly fast cruiser. We'd been trained to operate the computer which controlled our main armament. The TS was right down near the bottom of the ship below an armour-plated deck. On one side were the ship's oil fuel tanks, and, on the other, the magazine.

On 29th March 1942 we were escorting a convoy on its way to Murmansk. We were crossing the Barents Sea when we picked up three unidentified ships on our radar screens. It was 6.30am. In those days no-one could trust radar 100% and we didn't want to attack one of our own convoys or Russian destroyers that were in the vicinity. Visibility was poor, so we had to wait until we were close enough to identify the suspect ships. When we were less than two miles away, visibility cleared and the three ships were identified as German destroyers. Immediately the captain gave the order to open fire and we hit the leading ship with our first salvoes.

Everything seemed to be going well until, suddenly, there was a huge explosion on our port side and our lights went out. We had been hit not by the German destroyers but by one of our own torpedoes. Something had gone wrong with it, and it came round full circle and exploded into our port side.

There were twenty-one men in the Transmitting Station when the explosion happened. I was working the switchboard close to the ladder which was the only way of getting in or out. Straightaway our band corporal vanished up the ladder and out of the hatch. He just did a bunk.

Then the emergency light came on and we found that the explosion had broken communications between our computer tables and the turrets, so Warrant Officer Gould, who was in charge, shouted to me to try to telephone the bridge. But the lines were dead. Gould then ordered a signal sailor to go up to the bridge and report that all the lights were out and our lines were completely dead.

By this time oil from the oil fuel tanks started pouring down through the open hatch. I moved a few yards to the other side of the room to get away from it. Then the oil became a strong cascade and Gould shouted, 'Shut the hatch!' But no-one moved. Everyone seemed to be completely paralysed with fear and stayed glued to his position. Just like so many hypnotised rabbits, standing waiting to be drowned. No panic, no movement.

Again, Gould shouted, 'Shut the hatch, shut the hatch!' The oil was now up to our groins. Thomas Barber ('Lou') went to the ladder and tried to climb it but he was knocked back by the force of the oil. I went over to help him and suddenly I became really angry. I said to myself, 'God, you can't do this to me, I have work to do, music to write.' It was that anger which saved me. When Lou tried again to get up the ladder, I went after him and pushed. He couldn't move so I shouted, 'Shove, Lou, go on, shove!' and then he moved a little bit. I thought of my wife, Nancy, and started to climb the ladder.

I have no memory of what happened after this until I crawled out of the hatch two decks up. They later found that another sailor had tried to get out after me, but the hatch had come down and broken his back. So I was the last person to get out of the TS. All the rest were drowned in that cold black oil.

My next memory is of trying to haul myself out of the hatch leading on to the mess deck. Lou had disappeared. I lay on the deck totally exhausted and unable to move. Then I crawled across the mess deck and up some iron stairs to an upper deck where I again lay down. I felt like a burnt-out cinder. On the deck below there were first aid fellows and security people. One was standing above the ladders going down to the lower decks and shouting, 'Anybody there? Anybody below?' I wanted to shout that help was needed in the TS but I couldn't speak. I had no strength.

I was just lying on the deck, saturated with oil, when a sailor came along and said, 'Get yourself to the bake house, Bandy,' so I crawled to the bakehouse where somebody gave me a blanket. That's when fear overcame me. Quite frankly, I was scared out of my mind. Just lying there in a state of shock, no reserves left, I couldn't stop shivering.

Somehow, the damage control parties managed to save the ship and we crawled to Murmansk. Everyone around me was terrified that we would be a sitting target for the U-boats which ambushed convoys coming into Murmansk. But the destroyers, *Oribi* and *Fury*, maintained an anti-submarine screen around us and the armed minesweeper *Harrier* went ahead of us all through the night. When we arrived in Murmansk the next day, people seemed to come to life again with the sheer relief of arriving safely. But I couldn't keep still, and shivered all the time.

They could do nothing for me. In those days, they didn't understand shock. I managed to walk off the ship but by the time I reached naval hospital in Scotland six weeks later I had reached total collapse. Almost comatose. My wife came to see me and the doctors told her I was a hopeless case. I would have to spend the rest of my life in hospital. So she said, 'If you can't do anything with him, you'd better let me have a try.' For years, she didn't get a wink of sleep, I was always screaming. But eventually I recovered. She saved my life. And I did write music.

But I am still haunted by the picture of those silent men standing motionless, the tiny emergency light bulb giving its dim light, the cold black oil engulfing their bodies. It is a picture that will always live with me.

Ordinary Telegraphist Alan Higgins, RN

I had joined the *Edinburgh* as a boy telegraphist in April 1941. For the next year we were engaged on monotonous patrols of the Denmark Straits, separating Iceland and Greenland, as well as two more exciting Malta convoys, and a desolate time on a Russian convoy.

The *Edinburgh* was sunk on 2nd May 1942. Our troubles started, ironically, when *Edinburgh* left her convoy during U-boat activity.

I vividly remember the moment we were first hit. It was 29th April, just after 4 p.m., when the afternoon watch were settling down for tea. I was perpetually seasick, so whenever I was off watch I needed a place to lie down. Space was at a premium because of the wartime complement, so I was stretched out on top of some clothes lockers. A voice from the mess deck table had just told me I was poaching his billet, when there was a terrific explosion and blinding flash, then darkness and cries from the injured and dying in the next compartment, a scant eighth of an inch steel wall away.

Emergency lanterns lit automatically. The ship felt as though it was clasped in a trembling hand which was turning it over to its starboard side at a steep angle. Oil had spilled on to the cork lino – I was the last in a queue of Royal Marines and communication ratings, unable to keep my feet on the slippery deck. The queue moved painfully slowly as the men squeezed through the one small hatch one by one.

Because of the number of men engaged in running a wartime cruiser, the Admiralty had issued an order that, in the event of a ship listing to one side, the crew were to muster on the opposite side, providing a small adjustment of the list. I finally emerged on the side nearer the water to find that my eight stone was urgently needed on the high side of the ship. The list was so steep that I had to crawl across and up the catapult deck. There I found that a number of men had thrown a Carley float over the side, but in their haste had forgotten to hold the line securing it to the ship: they were standing watching it drift away. The sea was extremely cold, and one could only have expected to survive a few minutes at most on a raft in any case.

Someone asked for volunteers to fight a fire aft. Arriving at the scene, I found only a bit of paintwork making a small blaze, so went aft to where the real damage was. I thought we had only been hit by a torpedo amidships, just forward of my mess deck, but on going aft I could see that thirty to forty feet of stern had been completely blown away, while the quarter-deck had curled up like a sardine tin lid, enveloping the two six-inch gun turrets so completely that the guns were actually protruding through the quarter-deck, itself rendering them completely useless.

Feeling cold, I went to find a pair of overalls. While I was on the starboard side one of our torpedo men fired the four 21-inch torpedoes into the sea, lightening that side by about eight tons. Also on that side was our only lifeboat, which had warped launching gear and wouldn't launch. This was just as well as it was grossly overcrowded, and if launched could easily have caused between twenty and thirty more casualties.

The *Edinburgh* was now not only on her own but also only just buoyant. A number of men had been battened down to die in order to create this buoyancy. This buoyancy was achieved by making the mess decks and other compartments airtight. However hard a course this may seem, it was choice of either all lives (some eight hundred men) or perhaps fifty, and the answer was too obvious even to consider.

The torpedo that hit us amidships on the starboard side had destroyed our two main wireless transmitter rooms, leaving us with only a small emergency transmitter in the remote-control office behind the bridge. This was now our only means of communication with the convoy escort, but thankfully it did what was desired of it, although it was hours before two destroyers, *Forester* and *Foresight*, arrived.

With no steering the ship could only limp along in one big circle – cold comfort with a U-boat lurking about. She was very quiet except for the deep sound of a loose part, probably the starboard propeller shafts banging against the hull. If ever a death knell was heard, this was it.

The two destroyers were a very welcome sight; if the *Edinburgh* sank there was an outside chance of being picked up. Then the situation changed dramatically as three 'Z' class German destroyers arrived. They had guns far larger than our destroyers', and we on *Edinburgh* were unable to fire our guns due to our instability.

Soon the three British ships – *Forester*, *Foresight* and *Edinburgh* – were disabled. I remember thinking that it was safer to stand on the side at which the Germans were firing, so that if I was hit it would be directly by a shell rather than by shrapnel from an exploding shell.

The next incident made me feel very proud. Three small minesweepers, *Harrier*, *Gossamer* and *Hussar*, each armed with a 'pop gun', charged the three powerful German destroyers and although they disappeared at times in a welter of German salvoes they miraculously emerged to pop away at the Germans, as spirited as ever. The German destroyers made away, and hours later a Russian tug, gunboat and two or three larger destroyers arrived to reinforce our sorry group.

Through skilled repairs the two British destroyers were again made action ready, although unfortunately the captain and some others had been killed in a direct hit on one destroyer's bridge and engine-room, and the other also had casualties. However the situation looked brighter, with the two British destroyers towing and steering *Edinburgh*, which was, incredibly, still using her engines and one propeller. In this way the group began making for Murmansk.

In our relief we had reckoned without the German destroyers, who returned to have another go at us. The Russian ships had disappeared by this time, so once again we were in a desperate state. I had gone below in the hope of buying a bar of chocolate from the canteen when the third torpedo struck us. It struck the port side, almost exactly opposite to where one of the torpedoes had struck in the first attack on the starboard side, thus almost blowing *Edinburgh* in half.

This explosion occurred almost beneath me, blowing me off my feet and leaving me in a dazed condition amongst the debris of dust, cork linings, vent shafts and dislodged pipes. Through the dust and dim light I saw a white shrouded figure making his way aft, disappearing without a sound. I later found that this was the chief cook, CPO Gray, who was the only fatal casualty from that torpedo strike.

After gathering my wits, I found I was alone; the deck outside the galley had collapsed and the hatch above me was battened down. I remember thinking, 'What silly sod closed the hatch?' Closing it was quite useless, as I was on the upper deck which would only flood if the ship was already sinking. Luckily it was not long before the hatch opened and a face peered through, asking, 'What are you doing down there?' In retrospect I have thought of many answers, but at the time all I wanted was to get out into the open.

I went straight to the hangers and applied liberal dollops of thick grease about my ears and hands, after the fashion of channel swimmers, thinking I would have a better chance of surviving if I did go into the water. The ship was settling deeper but incredibly the third torpedo had hit the place exactly opposite to where the first torpedoes had created so much damage. Luckily this latest damage was not quite so severe, although she must have been near to breaking in half.

We were carrying a number of wounded merchant seamen on board so our Admiral, Bonham-Carter, ordered two minesweepers alongside – I also vaguely remember a Russian gunboat being present. A number of our crew then boarded the minesweepers to help off-load the wounded seamen. I remember a coder called Kneebone helping me with one stretcher case, a Lascar seaman who could not move. The *Edinburgh* and *Gossamer* were moving apart and I could imagine this poor chap's feelings as he was passed over the gap between the two ships which gradually yawed open, and closed again. I am glad to say that we did not lose a man in these operations.

At one stage Kneebone and myself were carrying a stretcher across the flight deck when our forward 6-inch gun opened up. It was such a shock that I almost dropped the stretcher. Fine on the port bow I could see this German destroyer firing on us, then we hit it and set it on fire. I saw it disappear in a cloud of smoke.

Only at this point was the order to abandon ship given. I was surprised to find that there were very few left aboard. I went aboard the *Gossamer*, as did the Admiral. We made several attempts to sink our old ship: first we dropped depth charges below it, then we fired point blank into her magazines. I remember now either the pompom or the ready-use 4-inch shell magazines blowing up, but she seemed almost indifferent to our efforts to sink her. A few of us were going to ask the admiral if we could go back aboard, as the old *Edinburgh* seemed almost unsinkable, and after all a sailor gets very attached to his ship. However, the thought of a humble ordinary telegraphist daring to approach a Rear Admiral was too great to contemplate so I stayed on the stern and watched whilst one of our destroyers, either *Foresight* or *Forester*, delivered what might only be described as the coup-de-grace. By now the ship had been hit by two torpedoes amidships and one aft which meant that she was sound forward and in the engine- and boiler-room, but flooded else-where. When the final torpedo hit her, it was in the boiler room, a cavernous space stretching from the keep to the upper deck, with no saving watertight deck levels. She finally went down in seconds, stern first, vertically until the bows were perpendicular, curtsied when the water level reached her forward gun turrets, and then slid quietly out of sight.

I went below where neat rum was being issued. After a tot I went forward and passed out, waking with a fearsome headache and wincing at the glare of sun on the snow at Polyarnoe, which was to be my home until September. The action had lasted for about two days. I suppose the thought of dying affects people in various ways; all I could think of at the time was how my parents would take the news.

After a while I was posted to a 'Y' station at Polyarnoe. One day during some air activity I climbed on to the deck to look at some Ju88s which were approaching. Jock Gillies, one of the telegraphists, warned me of the danger of flying glass should bombs be dropped. All I remember from then on was lying on the floor in an outside passage and peering out of a low window in time to see a huge flying boulder, then the roof being blown off the building. I ran like the wind over the hill away from the scene, accompanied by another telegraphist who had a bucket over his head to protect him from all the flying debris and shrapnel.

I was brought up short by a very determined Russian soldier, guarding a 30-gallon drum of oil. As he gesticulated with his bayonet, I cried, 'Angliski Matrosk' (English soldier); what he said in Russian I didn't understand but its meaning was obvious, so I departed promptly. On returning to the now blasted 'Y' station I saw the Irish stoker-come-handyman, covered in blood but laughing his head off. The blood turned out to be the red syrup from a box of tinned damsons which had been smashed by the bombing, showering the syrup over him.

LIEUTENANT-COMMANDER ROGER HILL, RN

On 24th June 1942 we got a cypher from the Admiralty ordering us to sail that night for Hvalfjord in Iceland. We were to join the Russian convoy PQ17. I was then in command of *Ledbury*, a Hunt class destroyer. After a wild two hours' oiling, storing, getting spare gear and reliefs and topping up with extra ammunition, we were under way. The feeling on board seemed to be one of cheerful excitement, as well as some trepidation.

We arrived in Hvalfjord on 26th June and the next morning I went ashore to the convoy conference. The large room was filled with all those taking part.

Admiral Hamilton who commanded the four cruisers was there, small, quiet and courteous. I knew him from Combined Operations days and reckoned nothing would ruffle him and he would never give up fighting.

Then there was Jackie Broome, the close escort leader from the *Keppel*. From the fleet destroyers there was Alistair Ewing in the *Offa*, whom I much admired, Jock Campbell in *Fury*, and Adrian Northey in our sister ship *Wilton*.

The masters of the 35 merchant ships sat in rows with bundles of books and charts on their laps. There were a large number of American merchant ships and at least one Russian, the tanker *Azerbaijan*. These ships all carried war material and this convoy would have supplied a complete army and airforce of, say, a small Balkan country. There were some 500 aircraft crated and on deck, as well as tanks, guns and ammunition of all sorts.

The Western Approach destroyers included the ex-American four-stacker *Leamington* and there were three corvettes, three minesweepers and four old trawlers. Two anti-aircraft ships, the *Palomares* and *Pozarica*, a 'Ranger' tanker, three rescue ships and two submarines made up this fleet.

The conference was well run, the explanations were clear and the emphasis was on the defence the escort would give against air and submarine attack. I had a brief chat with Douglas Fairbanks, Junior, who had a liaison job on one of the American cruisers. He was a most unlikely person to meet in Iceland enroute for Russia.

I returned to my ship full of confidence in our leaders, and, as we steamed down the fjord, I briefed the officers and ship's company. I told them we would have some really good shooting at high-level and torpedo-bombers with quite a chance of a go at some U-boats. I tried to pass on the confidence I felt in Admiral Hamilton and Jackie Broome. I told them we would be in three watches in order to give them as much rest as possible, since, when anything happened, we would go to action stations.

On the afternoon of 30th June we sighted the great mass of shipping in their orderly nine columns. I was on the starboard quarter of the convoy, with *Offa* in the next square to me and *Leamington* next to her. The evening and night passed peacefully. Daylight lasted all through the night and from now on there was no darkness.

At 0900 we were well inside the Arctic Circle. It was still a flat calm, with scattered patches of fog, and the big merchant ships hardly seemed to be moving on the cold, glassy sea. The little escorts were zigging and weaving about, sniffing at suspect echoes like gun dogs. I swept the horizon with my binoculars and saw a U-boat on the surface about six miles away. We turned towards her, signalling *Offa* and *Leamington* to join the chase. I planned to open fire at ten thousand yards, but *Offa* fired too soon and the U-boat crash-dived. We did a square search for an hour, but got no contact, and at 1045 *Offa* ordered us back to the convoy.

I was bitterly disappointed; it was the first U-boat I had sighted on the surface during the whole course of the war.

At 1130 on 2nd July we sighted the returning QP13 convoy. It was obvious the Germans were saving all their fire power for us, the loaded convoy. At 1300 a Blohm and Voss shadowing seaplane joined us and flew round the convoy in a big circle, just out of range. Sometimes he would fly ahead and land on the sea, to save on diesel, and lumber off as the leading ships approached. It was a nasty feeling to know that our exact position was always known to the enemy. We fired an occasional single round at him if he got a bit careless. We wanted to perfect our very low-angle fire to be ready for the torpedo-planes.

At 1630 we sighted a flight of Heinkel 115 seaplanes manoeuvring astern of the convoy and trying to get in with torpedoes. Six attacked on the port quarter but did not press home their attack. Surprisingly, there were no more attacks that afternoon or during the 'night'. The feeling in the ship was that we had beaten off the air attacks without loss, and everyone was very cheerful. I was puzzled; previous convoys had been attacked about every six hours when at their closest to enemy airfields in Norway.

At 1300 on 3rd July when we were steering east to pass between Bear Island and Spitzbergen, *Leamington* sighted a U-boat and asked me to join her. We spent the afternoon playing hide-and-seek with U-boats until 1700. By then we were thirty miles astern of the convoy, so we headed back.

Suddenly, coming clear of the fog, there was a U-boat going at full speed after the convoy about seven miles ahead of me. He was making 17 knots and as I turned to bring all my guns to bear when he was five miles away, he crash-dived. We searched for him without success; I think there was a layer of colder water that they dived below and the asdic did not get through.

The convoy was attracting U-boats like a magnet, and if only there had been hunter groups to spare, what a killing we would have had. But this was 1942, and there was no ship or plane to spare anywhere. The U-boats had never been so bold; I had seen seven on the surface in the last two days. By midnight we had rejoined the convoy, topped up with 88 tons of oil and were zigging in our square, wondering what in hell was going to happen next. The night hours were peaceful, except for the usual asdic contacts and depth-charging. We were now past the nearest point to the enemy air bases and were nearly 300 miles from the North Cape. I felt, if we got through 4th July without serious loss, we were almost home to Archangel.

At 1600 on 4th July we started to get aircraft on the radar screen and soon sighted some Heinkel 115s flying around the stern. A torpedo from one of them hit and sank the *Christopher Newport*. Then a few Junkers 88 appeared and did some high-level attacks; no ships were hit, but this proved to be merely a diversion. At 1819 we sighted six or seven aircraft low on the horizon. I closed the convoy, thinking this would be a bombing attack, when suddenly the whole horizon on our side was alive with planes. We counted up to 26 but there was no time to count more. I saw they were Heinkel 111K which carry two torpedoes each, and we opened out to meet them.

They came at us like a cavalry charge, so hard and fast that they could not turn away, but after dropping their torpedoes, continued through the fire of the fifty ships and away the other side. We started firing at a group going from left to right, and then saw a single plane coming right at us. Our shots were bursting all around him and I think he crashed, but just then two torpedoes were coming straight at me and I went hard-a-port to dodge them. Then a plane came over from the other side of the convoy and I put the oerlikon onto him. I could see the shots going into his wing and the fire starting. The plane swerved to port and *Offa* blew him to bits. Now a great mass of smoke and flame went high in the air as torpedoes hit the tanker *Azerbaijan* and two other ships.

The whole sky around the convoy was a mass of bursting shells. Tracers were going in all directions and the sea was boiling with the falling shrapnel. The noise of the gunfire was continuous, and in the centre a great pall of black smoke was slowly rising where a ship loaded with arms and ammunition had been hit. Suddenly the firing stopped. The planes had gone. The damaged ships were falling back, with the rescue ships and escorts standing by. For the size of the attack, the losses were small. We reckoned we had won this battle, and the enemy had really taken a beating, but in fact only three aircraft were brought down against three ships hit. The R/T was full of instructions from Jackie Broome in *Keppel* to the ships astern. *Azerbaijan* was rejoining, having put the fire out. The tone of the talk was cheerful and it was felt that the enemy had done his worst.

At 2025 the Commodore hoisted a string of flags. The yeoman knelt down and, using his big telescope, called out the letters for someone to write down. Then he looked them up in his code book and said to me, 'The Commodore's Chief Yeoman has made a proper balls-up this time; that signal means, 'Convoy is to scatter.' 'Put the answering pendant at the dip,' I replied (which means, 'Your signal not understood', and makes the originator check it). I saw that the destroyers near me had also got the answering pendant at the dip. The Commodore's ship lowered the flags and then hoisted the same ones again, and at the same time Jackie Broome in *Keppel* came up on the R/T, 'To all destroyers "Strike", repeat "Strike".' 'Christ,' I thought, 'here we go, surface attack by the *Tirpitz*,' and I searched the horizon with my glasses. I called for the first lieutenant and steered for the head of the convoy.

In fact three signals had arrived in close succession from the Admiralty. The first ordered the cruiser force to withdraw to westward at high speed, the second ordered the convoy to disperse due to threat from surface forces, and the third, 'Most immediate' signal said, 'Convoy is to scatter'. Because these messages had come from the Admiralty we never doubted that the *Tirpitz*, *Hipper* and some large destroyers were just below the horizon, and about to open fire on the convoy.

As we steamed through the convoy to join *Keppel* the crews of the merchant ships cheered us and we waved back. A paragraph from some naval action orders kept going through my mind, idiotically, 'The ship's company should change into clean underwear before going into action so that wounds are not contaminated.'

From way over on the edge of the ice, the four cruisers came streaking across the bows of the convoy. *Wilton* and *Ledbury* were stationed astern since we could only do 25 knots, which was the speed of the fleet. Adrian Northey made some rude signals to me, and I insulted him back, feeling comforted that he was with me in this hopeless battle. For our cruisers had only eight-inch guns and virtually no armour, and would be blown out of the water before their guns were inside the range of the 15-inch guns of the *Tirpitz*.

My plan was to join the torpedo-carrying destroyers and give fire support as they went into the attack. We would turn as if firing torpedoes, and throw some big armour-piercing shells over the side. Privately, I decided that, if we got that far, we would go on and try to ram the *Tirpitz*. I piped the port watch to supper and tried to eat a sandwich, but it stuck in my throat. I think my stomach was three decks below.

The puzzling thing to us all on the bridge was that no-one, Admiralty, Admiral Hamilton or Jackie Broome, had given an enemy position. We searched the horizon with the big director telescopes and all the bridge binoculars, but it remained a hazy, empty line. We never doubted for one moment that we were going to attack a bigger force to save the convoy, but, eventually, hours later, we realised that no surface action was going to take place after all and that we were running away. We were leaving the convoy, scattered and defenceless, to be slaughtered by the U-boats and aircraft.

At about midnight the most terrible and harrowing signals started coming up to the bridge from the radio office. They were coming through on the Merchant Navy wavelength. 'Am being bombed by large number of planes.' 'On fire in the ice.' 'Abandoning ship,' and, 'Six U-boats approaching on the surface.'

I discussed with the pilot whether we should quietly slow down, turn round and go back to look for the survivors of the convoy. I thought for months afterwards this was what I should have done. But discipline is strong, our orders were clear, we were miles away by then, and, the ever-governing factor, almost out of fuel. So, bitter, bewildered, tired and utterly miserable, we stayed with the admiral and the cruisers. Underneath the bitterness was the sneaking relief of having survived, of which I also felt ashamed.

I have always felt that, as the merchant ships were going to almost certain destruction, then we should have gone back and taken the same chance and we would have got some of them to Archangel. Even though we would probably have lost the destroyers as well once the oiler was sunk – still we would have tried. As it was 23 of the 34 merchant men were sunk by U-boats or aircraft. Never will I forget how they cheered us as we moved at full speed to the attack; and it has haunted me ever since that we left them to be destroyed.

OPERATION PEDESTAL

By the summer of 1942, the Germans and their allies were in control of most of Europe. Malta was the unconquered British bastion of the inner Mediterranean and the whole Allied cause depended on its successful defence. But by August 1942 Malta was on the verge of surrender. Only five merchant ships had reached the island that year, three of which had been sunk in the harbour at Valletta before they were discharged.

Operation Pedestal, the despatch of fourteen merchant ships to Malta in August 1942, marked the turning-point in the siege of Malta and of the war in the Mediterranean. The story of the operation is told by six survivors.

LIEUTENANT-COMMANDER ROGER HILL, RN
(Hunt class destroyer *Ledbury*)

Operation Pedestal was the last all-out attempt to get a convoy of merchant ships through to Malta. Their food was running out and they had no aviation fuel, no submarine diesel and nothing for the dockyard. Malta had virtually stopped.

If the convoy failed, Malta would have to surrender. The Governor of Malta, Lord Gort, said to me, 'You can make the garrison eat their belts, but the three hundred thousand civilians have to be fed or evacuated.'

The convoy of over fifty ships left Gibraltar on 9th August 1942. Thirteen merchant ships and the 10,000-ton Texaco tanker, *Ohio*, steamed in four columns. They were all big, fast ships and the speed of the convoy was 15 knots. Around them was a screen of 26 destroyers. Close round the convoy were the anti-aircraft destroyers, like my *Ledbury*, and the battleships *Nelson* and *Rodney* each of which had nine 16-inch guns, steamed astern of the two outside columns. The anti-aircraft ship *Cairo* had a roving commission near the convoy and *Jaunty*, an ocean tug, followed along behind.

Three aircraft carriers, *Victorious*, *Indomitable* and *Eagle* followed the convoy inside the destroyer screen. They carried a total of 72 fighters and were constantly altering course into the wind to fly off and land on the patrols. The cruisers *Sirius*, *Phoebe* and *Charybdis* careered about keeping an anti-aircraft guard on the carriers. Finally, there was the old aircraft-carrier *Furious* with her own destroyer screen, whose job it was to fly off 38 Spitfires when we were about 500 miles from Malta, as reinforcements for Malta's depleted squadrons.

As we approached down the Mediterranean we were entering a cauldron of attack. Crete and Greece were in German hands and would be used for air attack, then of course the long toe of Italy, Sardinia, and Sicily was all aerodromes. About 20 submarines and 40 E-boats were also waiting for us. It was just like another Charge of the Light Brigade.

Officer Cadet Frederick Treves, RN
(Merchant vessel *Waimarama*)

We were at action stations as soon as we got into the Med on the evening of 9 August so I would have been up in the fo'c'sle with Bowdrey. He was the oldest man in the ship and I the youngest. He was looking after me. He even held my hand when we were being bombed.

The sea was very calm and the convoy was going very slowly. It was a moonless night and we were in total blackout when I saw all these twinkling lights strung across the sea like jewels. I asked Bowdrey, 'What are those?' and he said, 'I think they're Spanish fishing vessels. They're probably telling the Germans we're just coming into the Med.'

The first action I saw was late on 10th August. Some spotter planes went over and the fleet put up a terrific anti-aircraft barrage, especially the 16-inch guns on the *Nelson* and *Rodney*. I think no 16-inch gun had ever been fired at that angle before and the whole sky was puckered with little puffs of smoke cloud. It was an enormous umbrella of fire, absolutely terrifying. The feeling of terror it evoked is impossible to describe.

As well as this huge barrage of anti-aircraft fire we could hear the scream of the destroyers, that extraordinary wailing scream destroyers made when tearing around trying to find the submarines which had been detected somewhere. The next day, 11th August, I saw the *Eagle* go down. I heard two or three huge explosions so I rushed out of the fo'c'sle on to the forward well deck and saw the *Eagle* on its side. It had been torpedoed by a submarine.

There were little tiny dots like ants all over the side of this vast belly coming out of the sea. It was all the crew trying to get into the water from the side of the ship. In the distance all the destroyers were rushing around in circles trying to find the submarine, their sirens blaring. Even above this noise you could hear the people on the *Eagle* screaming as the ship sank.

It was an enormous blow, but 800 people were saved from the *Eagle* and they were taken back to Gibraltar by the tug, *Jaunty*, which was having trouble keeping up with the convoy.

After the *Eagle* sank things began to liven up much more. They started to bomb the convoy constantly and I don't know how many ships went up in the next forty-eight hours. The noise was just indescribable, bombing day and night, torpedoing, and the firing of guns in retaliation. The Stuka dive-bombers would dive on the ship and the siren on the plane's bodywork would make this banshee noise which increased and increased and increased as they did a kamikaze-type dive on the target and then released the 500-lb bomb. We suffered that for days.

LIEUTENANT-COMMANDER ROGER HILL, RN
(*Ledbury*)

The *Ledbury* was fitted with a loudspeaker system and on 10th August the telegraphist tuned this to the carrier fighter control officer. We listened to the calm voice of the control officer talking to the fighter leaders. This served as a useful early warning of air attack, as the carrier's radar had a greater range than ours, but we also became very interested and involved with the fighter pilots. Our favourite was a Red Leader who was a real comedian and sometimes put on a Yankee drawl.

On the evening of 11th August we heard the fighter control vectoring the fighters on to approaching enemy bombers, and heard the excited voices of the pilots as they attacked: 'From Red Leader, large number of bandits below me to port – attacking, I say again, attacking.'

The first attack was from high-level bombers. We had a nice steady shoot at them and as the shellbursts increased around them, they dropped their bombs well away from us and turned away, chased by our fighters. At 2000 about forty Junkers 88s attacked in shallow dives, but no-one was hit in either attack.

The fighters were staying up until the last minute and we could hear them saying, 'I've got no petrol, I've got no petrol!' and they were landing on the aircraft carriers with their tanks empty. One or two crashed on to the carrier and burst into flames. As the planes crashed they were just thrown over the side to keep the carriers clear.

Before dawn the next day (12th August) we could hear our fighter planes warming up and the first patrols took off at first light. At 0915 there was an attack by about thirty Ju 88s. They pressed on right through our gunfire and dropped their bombs all amongst the convoy. This was the first time I had ever seen bombs in the air dropping close to the ship. One was close enough to wet a gun's crew as it landed in the sea. Rather frightening.

All that day we were bombed. At 1300 the merchant ship *Deucalion* was damaged and later sunk. That afternoon we were listening to our old friend Red Leader going for some 'bandits'. Then control called him, 'Red Leader, Red Leader?' but there was no reply. Then 'Red Two' came up, 'Red Leader has just been shot down.' We were heartbroken.

Then I saw a parachute coming down and I thought, 'Blimey, that might be Red Leader,' so I rushed over to pick him up. I hung over the side and said to my first lieutenant, 'What is he, Jimmy?' and he said, 'A fucking Hun, sir. Three more parachutes coming down to starboard.' 'Let them go to hell,' I replied.

That evening our troubles really started. A flight of dive-bombers came in, supported by fast German fighters and our Fleet Air Arm chaps were completely out-gunned and out-speeded. The dive-bombers were targeting our carriers like a disturbed wasp's nest, screaming down almost vertically, one after the other. And our fighters were following them right into their own ship's fire, trying to shoot down the dive-bombers. It was the most spectacular sight I'd ever seen.

Captain 'Eddie' Baines, RN
(Hunt class destroyer *Bramham*)

On 12th August the bombing started in a big way and at around 1300 the *Deucalion*, one of the merchant ships, got hit by one bomb and had a near-miss with two others. She was not vitally damaged but she came to a halt because she was making water and they wanted to see what was wrong with her. *Bramham* was a 'rescue' ship so we came up alongside her.

We were greeted by the sight of the *Deucalion's* boats being lowered in great panic and people tumbling into them and rowing over to us. The officers and particularly the captain standing on her bridge were absolutely apoplectic with rage and saying, 'Send the boats back!' which I would have done, anyway.

So when the boats came alongside our scrambling nets, we jumped on the men's knuckles as they came up over the edge. They called us a few choice names but we invited them to choose: either they could get back into their boats and stay there or go back to the *Deucalion*. So they thought better of it, recovered their nerve and returned on board.

Deucalion now could only make 13.5 knots so we were ordered to escort her to Malta by what was known as the inshore route, along the coast of North Africa. It was just as unpleasant on the inshore route as anywhere else and we got bombed on the way. Then at dusk a couple of torpedo-bombers came out of the murk and popped a torpedo into *Deucalion* and blew a bloody great hole in her stern. She was burning down below and there was obviously no hope for her, so the captain gave the order to abandon ship.

Then we had to sink her by going up close and dropping depth-charges. We didn't want her to get picked up by the enemy as a propaganda prize. The scare was that she would blow up as we went alongside, as all the merchant ships were carrying high octane aero spirit and huge amounts of ammunition. She seemed to be settling by the stern so I left her, and when we'd been steaming at 23 knots for about an hour I saw an explosion astern and it was the *Deucalion* blowing up.

Junior Radio Operator John Jackson, MN
(Merchant Vessel *Waimarama*)

During 12th August we had a number of alarms but our fighter protection saved us from direct attacks. But that evening at about 1835 I saw a flight of Stukas coming out of the sun, flying very low, peeling off one after the other and diving straight on to the carrier *Indomitable*. There was no other target they were going for. They were going for the *Indomitable* and they were going to have her.

Nelson opened up with her 16-inch guns and we all fired our guns. The ship rattled with the vibration. But nothing seemed to stop these planes and they continued to attack. A lot of bombs missed, but about the fourth or fifth plane coming down scored a direct hit and did a lot of damage. We saw terrific clouds of smoke and spray and *Indomitable* vanished from view in the smoke.

We were getting close to the Pantelleria Straits which were too narrow for the heavy warships to manoeuvre in. At about 1900 the aircraft-carriers, the battleships *Rodney* and *Nelson*, and several cruisers turned around and we were left with a fairly small cover: the cruisers *Manchester*, *Kenya*, *Nigeria*, the light cruiser *Cairo* and a number of escort vessels including the *Ledbury*, *Bramham*, *Speedy*, *Penn* and five or six others. So we continued, a bit deflated. But at that time everything was intact, apart from losing *Deucalion*. If all went well, we'd be under the cover of the Spitfires from Malta by the next morning.

As we reached the Pantelleria Straits it was getting dark. The convoy started to form into two columns to pass through the narrow channel swept for mines by the destroyers. Then, without any warning, we heard a loud explosion and saw that the Admiral's ship *Nigeria*, in column ahead of us, had been hit amidships by a torpedo from a U-boat. She heeled over to starboard in a cloud of smoke. A few seconds later, *Cairo* was torpedoed and hit in her stern and she swung round to port, seemed to settle in the water and stop. A second later the tanker *Ohio* was hit amidships and caught fire. This was bad news. The *Ohio* was the most important ship in the convoy because what Malta needed most was oil.

The whole convoy immediately took evasive action and carried on at full speed. From then onwards, right through into the night it was just like Dante's Inferno. It was unbelievable. Half an hour after the U-boat attack there was a big low-level bombing raid. We were alongside the *Clan Ferguson* at the time. She was carrying the same cargo as us: aviation spirit in five-litre cans on the foredeck and lots of ammunition and petrol for Malta. Then she got hit by a Ju88 and it was just like someone holding a piece of rag soaked in petrol and putting a match to it. A terrific sheet of flame shot up into the air about half-a-mile high. She went down very quickly and how anybody survived I don't know, but they did. About sixty people were rescued.

So we knew what we were facing. But, funnily, we didn't really think about it at the time. We thought, 'Poor old people on the *Clan Ferguson*, but it's not going to happen to us, we're not going to get hit.' If you didn't think like this you could never go on.

CAPTAIN DUDLEY MASON, MN
(Texaco oil tanker *Ohio*)

Minutes after *Nigeria* and *Cairo* were hit by torpedoes, there was a bright flash and a column of water was thrown up to mast-head height. A second later, flames shot up into the air. We had been hit amidships on the port side, halfway between bow and stern. There was a hole in the port side 24 feet by 27 feet, reaching from the main deck to well below the waterline. The deck on the port side was torn up and laid right back inboard almost to the centre-line and was buckled beam to beam. The flying bridge was damaged and the pump-room was a shambles.

I immediately rang 'Finish with engines', as the pump-room had caught on fire and flames were bursting out of the kerosene tanks, whose lids had blown off. I had previously told the chief engineer that he was not to stop the engines whatever happened unless I gave him the order to do so. I gave the order now because the pump-room was on fire and the men were in danger.

The gunners were still firing, ignoring the flames and the bombs which were falling all around the ship. Some men were running for the boats but I told them, 'Come on, let's get that fire out.' They grabbed fire extinguishers and set to work.

It was then a case of fighting the pump-room fire. At first I thought it was a forlorn hope, but we went to work with foam fire extinguishers and managed to put out the flames much more easily than I had expected. We also put out the flames in the kerosene tanks and replaced the tank lids, although these could not be screwed down as they were badly buckled.

While we were fighting the fires the air attack was still going on. The planes were diving to mast-head height to drop their bombs, and we had several near misses.

I sent for the chief engineer to ask him how long it would take to raise steam, as the steam had dropped back while we were stopped. Fortunately, since we had a diesel generator, we were able to raise steam again within ten minutes, instead of the usual three or four hours.

I had been forced to stop not only to fight the fire, but because our steering was out of order and we were turning in circles, making us a danger to the *Nigeria* and *Cairo* which were lying stopped near us. We tested the main engines and found they were all right, but stopped until we rigged up the emergency steering gear aft.

I had a signal from Admiral Burrough, who had been taken off the *Nigeria*, asking how we were getting on. I told him we should soon be able to get under way again, but since our gyro was wrecked, I requested a destroyer to lead us once we were under way. The *Ledbury* came to lead us on with a blue light astern and we got under way at about 2130 and followed her throughout the night.

Steering was rather difficult. The chief officer took the wheel aft and was directed from the forward bridge by me using a telephone line which, fortunately, was still intact.

A merchant ship ahead of us was burning to the water's edge and I was afraid of catching fire from her so I requested the *Ledbury* to steer further away from her as our kerosene tanks were open to the sea. The chief engineer reported all well in the engine-room and we were now averaging 15 to 16 knots, following the *Ledbury* round the minefield past Cape Bon. I had been concerned that the speed might break the ship's back, but the hull was showing no undue strain.

LIEUTENANT-COMMANDER ROGER HILL, RN
(*Ledbury*)

After being damaged by a U-boat torpedo at 2000 on 12th August, the *Nigeria* turned round and went back to Gibraltar with far too many destroyers escorting her. As far as I was concerned it didn't matter a tuppenny cuss how many cruisers we lost; our job was to stay by the merchant ships. I was horrified when I saw how few destroyers we had left.

After the U-boat attack there was a very clever attack from high-level bombers combined with a low-level torpedo attack. The *Clan Ferguson* on my starboard side was hit and blew up and another, the *Empire Hope*, was set on fire. After these attacks the convoy was in disarray, with several ships on fire and many others going in the wrong direction. I went alongside them with a loud hailer to get them going on the right course again. Then I came across an American ship, the *Almeria Lykes*. The captain was a bit stroppy and said he was going back to Gibraltar, he didn't see there was any point in going on. So I told him he wouldn't have a hope in hell without an escort and if he joined up with the others he would be in Malta tomorrow. He came round like a lamb and joined up with the convoy. But he was sunk later on.

As I went to rejoin the fleet, I came across the *Ohio* lying stopped in the dark so I went alongside and called out to Captain Mason. He seemed very cheerful and in control. He said they'd put out a fire and had set up emergency steering gear, but they had no means of navigation. So I said, 'Well, I'll put a dim light on my stern and I'll lead you.' So they joined in astern of me and I led them right into the coast because I reckoned that was the safest place to go. Soon we were belting along at 16 knots, which was great.

We had hot soup, stew and cocoa served up all over the ship and apart from people manning the telephones, the whole crew slept on deck at their stations. As we rounded Cape Bon and steered south there was a spectacular sight ahead of us. Tracers tearing through the dark, star shells bursting and heavy gunfire. Italian E-boats from Pantelleria were attacking the convoy. We were lucky we were missing it all. Four merchant ships, *Wairangi*, *Santa Elisa*, *Glenorchy* and *Almeria Lykes* were sunk that night and we received a signal from the cruiser *Manchester* saying that her engine-room was flooded and she was on fire.

Early the next morning we led *Ohio* back into line with what was left of the convoy.

Officer Cadet Frederick Treves, RN
(*Waimarama*)

The night of 12th August was horrendous. Bombings, emergency turns to starboard and port, flames, ships going up, huge explosions. I saw our sister ship, the *Wairangi*, go up in a sheet of flame. Like us, she was loaded up with high octane aero spirit, 500lb bombs, oerlikon shells, pom-pom shells and a bit of food for Malta.

There was a slight lull on the morning of 13th August. I went to the saloon and found that some of the chaps had been getting at the liquor locker. The chief steward was way beyond recall. Then the sirens went and I rushed to my quarters on the fo'c'sle, right across the well deck. As I got to the door at the side of the fo'c'sle, a bomb fell and I was blown through the door onto some bags of lime and my old friend Bowdrey fell on top of me to protect me. I thought I was going to die and I started to get very numb. But Bowdrey moved off me and I managed to get up and went out onto the well deck. It hadn't quite dawned on me that the ship had been hit.

There was black smoke everywhere, flames were burning aft of the bridge and the deck was slanting to starboard, so I thought, 'Well, I'm being a terrible coward, but I think I'd better go.' I made a very quick decision and darted to the port side of the ship, forgetting the rule that you should always leave the ship on the side nearest the water. I tore up the tilting deck, grabbed the side rail and dived into the water. I had a helmet on, which was lucky, because the water was full of debris, and a kapok life-saving suit. The wind had been blowing to starboard, but as I dived it changed direction and fanned the flames away from me and towards the rest of the crew. The flames were 600 feet high.

I bobbed up to the surface like a cork. There was debris and people screaming all around me, 'I can't swim, I'm drowning!' I was quite a good swimmer and I felt terribly calm and tried to organise everybody, telling them to stop wasting their breath by screaming for help. And I kept blowing my whistle in morse code, trying to give them instructions. This pathetic little whistle playing, 'de de de de'. Stupid thing to do; they couldn't hear me. I saw the wireless officer, Jackson. He couldn't swim and I pulled him out because the ship was sucking him up back into the flames.

Then I saw my friend and mentor, Bowdrey. He was standing on a raft, his arms were outstretched and he was screaming for help, he couldn't swim. It was a picture I'll never be able to forget. He was drifting back into the flames on this raft. I started out towards him, but I realised he was very near the flames and the raft would be too heavy to stop. So I turned over and swam away. That has haunted me all my life. I was a coward. He'd done everything for me and I didn't do anything for him. That affected me greatly.

The *Ledbury* came into the circle of flames to pick up survivors. They were still being attacked and we were being machine-gunned in the water by German and Italian planes. Captain Hill talked to us all the time through his loudhailer. Eventually they lowered a wooden boat and dragged me on board.

JUNIOR RADIO OPERATOR JOHN JACKSON, MN
(*Waimarama*)

On the morning of the 13th I was talking to the liaison officer in the chart room. He said, 'Jacko, I reckon we'll be in Malta in four or five hours. We'll be all right.' And then we heard aircraft approaching and headed for the port side of the bridge where both our action stations were. As the liaison officer stepped out ahead of me there was the most enormous explosion and a wall of flame came between the two of us. An absolutely solid curtain of flame. That was the last I saw of the liaison officer.

The captain's steward had just brought his breakfast up on a tray and stood there in the middle of the chart room. He was only a lad, sixteen or seventeen. I shouted to him, 'Come on, let's get down the companionway to the next deck,' so we jumped down the companionway and got out on to the port side. It was a sight you can hardly describe, thick black smoke, flames and the ammunition exploding. The ship had started listing over to starboard and I could see about twenty men already swimming around in the water. The ship was enveloped in flame except for the small patch where these men were swimming around, so I shouted to the captain's steward to follow me and I jumped feet first over the side. I don't like water and I couldn't swim – it had to be pretty hot to get me to do that.

As I came up I saw the ship's bows sinking and I struggled away as best I could. The water was full of wood and debris and the fire was very very close and it was getting very hot. As I was floundering a young cadet, Freddy Treves, came up to me in the water and said, 'Jacko, lie on your back and don't move; I'm going to tow you away.'

Now the one thing I'd always heard was that drowning people always struggle, so I told myself, 'Don't struggle, Jackson, this guy's going to tow you away.' And so he did. He got me by the arms and pulled me, very slowly, away from the flames, which were increasing all the time. Then a whacking great spar of wood came along side and he said, 'Can you grab that spar?' and I did and I heaved myself on to it. And he said, 'Right, are you OK now?' and I said, 'Freddy, I'm fine, you carry on, off you go.' There was no question, he was a very brave lad.

So I found myself paddling away from the flames. I was quite confident. All around me people were shouting and screaming. A lot of people perished in the flames. Then I saw the *Ledbury*, a little destroyer, approaching. They put a whaler into the water and played a hose on it as it went in and picked the people out of the flames. And then Captain Hill put the bows of his ship into the flames, picking people out of the water, it was unbelievable. The captain was a brave man, but my golly, so were the people in the whaler.

I was in the water with the cook and another person nearby. Then the *Ledbury* picked the whaler up and started to move away and the cook said, 'They're going to leave us, they haven't seen us'. I remembered my whistle, and I blew it and they spotted us and swung the ship around and the three of us got up the net and scrambled aboard. Then they doped us with morphine to take the shock away.

ABLE SEAMAN LESLIE HOLLANDER, RN, ABLE SEAMAN ARTHUR KEEPER, RN AND ABLE SEAMAN ERIC GARDINER, RN
(Gunners on the *Waimarama*)

Keeper: I was on the very topmost part of the ship and I had a battery of rockets. They were lethal things because they went off in a fantastic flash of flame and if anyone was near when you pulled the trigger they'd lose all the hair on their bodies. But I never got to see how effective they were because, before we knew it, the bombers were down on us. My first impression was of being on the concrete gun platform with flames all over the deck below me and the ship listing badly. I simply slid down the ship's sides and into the water where the main hazard was the flames because the sea was alight.

Gardiner: I was on a more forward gun than Les Hollander and I can remember calling back to him, 'Here they come, here they come!' And these Junkers 88s came out of the sun, pounding the ship and the ship was hit on the bridge near my turret. Fortunately, I was strapped onto the turret but my gun's crew were blown away. There was one boy left on the bridge and he was on fire.

I unstrapped myself and looked aft. There was nothing left of the ship and the bow of the ship was stuck up in the air. So down I went and met Leslie in the water and we started to strike out to safety with the fire following us. We swam and swam as fast as we could to get away from the ship.

Hollander: I was a station above Eric Gardiner and I managed to get down to his level. There were a couple of chaps there who were alight from head to foot, as though somebody had thrown a couple of gallons of petrol and put a match to them. We said to them, 'The best thing you can do is get on your feet and backside and slide down the side of the ship.' We couldn't do anything for them whatsoever, you were scrambling for your own life.

I slid halfway down the bow of the ship and stopped. I could see that the sea was fully alight with the high octane we were carrying. I thought, 'I've got to jump in the water, it's no good hanging on to the ship because I'll be sucked down.' So I jumped into the water and found Eric. The water was alight to the right and left of us and we knew if we didn't get through this opening we would be engulfed by the flames. The debris of the sinking ship, deck cargo, planks of wood, were shooting up through the water like rockets. It was frightening, thinking you might get caught by one of these things and be blown out of the water.

So we swam off together. At one point we had to swim under the water to get away from the flames. We came up with our mouths full of oil, and spat it all out. Eventually we got away from the fire and I said to Eric, 'Are you all right?' and he said to me, 'Yes, I'm fine.' All we had on was a little pair of khaki shorts, a tin helmet, sunglasses and sea boots. I threw my tin helmet off and kicked off my boots. It was a beautiful morning, the sun was shining, the sea was calm, but we couldn't see any ships at all. I was singing, 'Oh what a beautiful morning.'

It seemed like ages we were swimming, and then Eric had a plan. 'If you go to starboard, I'll go to port. If you get picked up first, you'll come to my rescue and if I get picked up first, I'll come to your rescue.' So we said our goodbyes and shook hands, he went his way and I went mine. I thought to myself, 'I'm swimming nowhere.'

Keeper: How long I was in the water I have no idea, but the flames were very close and you could hear chaps yelling all around you. Suddenly the *Ledbury* appeared, she came into the flames. Her bows were alight and they had to put high pressure hoses on them to put the fire out. Then they put scramble nets down the side and some of the ratings came down, stuck their feet in the net and put their hands round me and hauled me aboard.

Gardiner: We'd been in the water at least two hours before the *Ledbury* arrived on the scene and picked the pair of us up. We were taken aboard and believe you me, we were more than welcome. They took us down to the mess and got out the rum and we rummed up, fell into some bunks and out we went, because we'd not slept for a few days.

LIEUTENANT-COMMANDER ROGER HILL, RN
(*Ledbury*)

At 0730 on 13th August about a dozen torpedo-planes came in low from the port beam and a flight of Junkers 88 came out of the sun. A stick of bombs hit the *Waimarama* and she blew up with the biggest explosion I have ever seen. The flames were about six times the height of my mast. The *Melbourne Star* was 600 yards astern of the *Waimarama* and she couldn't avoid going right through the flames. The people who were aft in the *Melbourne Star* all jumped over the side because they thought their own ship had been hit, which gives you an idea of the intensity of the flames. The Admiral made to me, 'Survivors, but don't go into the flames.' Now, you've got to realise that I had been on PQ17, a convoy to Russia which had been ordered by the Admiralty to scatter because they thought the *Tirpitz* was about to attack. I was a close escort of that convoy but the Admiral signalled to us and told us to take up station to protect him against submarines. We all queried this and flashed at him, 'Could we go back to the convoy?' but he said, 'No, take up your station.' So we left the merchant ships at high speed and it was simply terrible. Something I have never ever got over in my life, not even now. That the navy should leave the merchant navy. The merchant ships were nearly all sunk. And it was in the Arctic and if a man was twenty seconds in the water he was dead.

My crew had felt just as badly about this as I did. So when we were going with this convoy to Malta I said, 'As long as there's a merchant ship afloat we'll stay alongside it and to hell with any signal we get from anybody.' And I got all sorts of signals telling me to go back to Gibraltar and to do all sorts of things, but I just threw them over the side. I was determined to stay with the merchant ships. When the *Waimarama* blew up and I went into these flames I felt I was redeeming myself for the disgrace of leaving the ships on the Russian convoy.

So we went towards the flames. I did not think anyone could have survived but as we approached there were heads bobbing about in the water, black with oil. I put down a whaler and she stayed outside the flames and picked up all the people she could find. I spoke to those we passed through a loudhailer, saying, 'I must get the ones near the fire first,' and they shouted back, 'That's all right.'

I took the ship into the flames. The fire was spreading outward over the sea, even to windward, and it was a grim race to pick up the men in the water before the flames reached them. When we got into the flames you couldn't see very much in all the fire and smoke and the heat was tremendous. Even on the bridge I had my hand over my beard because I thought it would catch on fire. I wondered how long my ship could stay there without blowing up. There was the odd survivor in the water and my sailors put a strap round their waists and jumped over the side and pulled these chaps into the landing nets. Terribly burnt, some of them. Then they were rushed along to the sick bay where the doctor looked after them.

We got everybody we could see and I thought, 'Well, thank God, I can't see any more, I'm going out astern.' So I started to go astern but the coxswain called up the voice pipe, 'There's another man over there, sir.' And I said, 'Coxswain, all I can see is flames and smoke.' He said, 'No, I saw him raise his arm, he's over there, sir.' So I had to go in again which I didn't want to do at all. We picked up this chap, Jackson, a wireless operator.

When we finally got out of the flames we found we had picked up a total of 45 survivors, only 19 from the *Waimarama* and the rest from the *Melbourne Star*.

At 1115 we came up to the *Ohio*. She was lying stopped, with *Penn* dropping depth-charges around her. About half-a-mile away, the big merchant ship *Dorset* was also lying stopped with *Bramham* standing by. The convoy was about ten miles away being bombed.

I suggested to *Penn* that I should take the *Ohio* in tow, but just then I received a signal from the Admiral at Malta telling me to go in search of the cruiser *Manchester*. I decided to obey the order, even though it meant leaving the *Ohio*. I think what decided me do this was my shortage of fuel; I thought the *Manchester* would be able to give me some fuel during the night.

We set off and relaxed into two watches to give the hands a chance to bath, eat and sleep. I felt I must get some sleep, but after just about an hour there was a cry of, 'Captain sir, enemy aircraft, enemy aircraft!' I ran on to the bridge and there were these two planes coming towards us. At first I thought they were Beaufighters from Malta, but they were Italian torpedo-bombers.

I spoke over the loud hailer to my eager pom-pom crews, 'Now you're going to get these. Wait, wait, let them come in. They think they've surprised us. Let them come in. Right, open fire on the left one.' And they opened fire and you saw all these little bursts of flame on the front wing of the left plane and he went straight down. I said, 'Shift target right-hand,' and they fired at him and he went right down. Everybody was cheering and shouting and singing.

Then there was a great cry; the second plane had dropped a torpedo and it was coming straight for us. I went hard to port and it missed the stern by what seemed a few inches. Then I thought, this is a terrific boost to morale. So I said, 'Splice the mainbrace, stand fast the Hun.'

We failed to find any sign of the *Manchester* so we turned towards where we thought the *Ohio* might be.

CAPTAIN DUDLEY MASON, MN
(*Ohio*)

At 0700 on 13th August we caught up with the convoy after being led through the night by the *Ledbury*. The convoy was now in two columns, our position being at the end of the line, owing to our defective steering. At 0800 the heavy bombing attacks started again. We sustained many near-misses, but there seemed to be no damage to the ship. Then the *Waimarama* had a direct bomb hit and blew up. The *Melbourne Star*, following her, could not avoid the flames and steamed straight through them. The *Ohio* just managed to clear the edge of the flames by going hard to port.

During these attacks we were constantly receiving orders by wireless to make 45-degree emergency turns. It was quite impossible to execute these in the time given. These orders were also transmitted over the radio telephone, and the wireless orders were always several seconds behind, thus causing misunderstanding and confusion.

At about 0900 a Junkers 88 crashed into the sea close to our bow and bounced on to our foredeck, making a terrific crash and throwing masses of debris into the air. A little later the chief officer telephoned me from aft in great excitement to say that a Stuka had landed on the poop. Apparently this plane had also fallen into the sea and bounced on to our ship. I was rather tired, having been on the bridge all night and I'm afraid I answered him rather curtly, saying, 'Oh, that's nothing. We've had a Junkers 88 on the foredeck for nearly half an hour.'

At about the same time a near-miss right under our fore-foot opened up the port and starboard bow tanks, buckled the plating and flooded the forepeak tank. The *Ohio* vibrated violently forward to aft, amidst a deluge of water.

Despite these problems, we were making good headway. The weather was fine with good visibility, smooth sea and light airs, and we were steaming at 13 knots, steering approximately east. At 1000, when we were 100 miles west of Malta, a large plane flew right over us at about 2,000 feet, banked slightly and dropped a salvo of six bombs, three falling close to the port side and three close to the starboard side. The *Ohio* was lifted right out of the water and shook violently from stem to stern. The *Dorset* was hit by bombs at almost the same time.

At 1030 the main engines stopped as the two electric fuel pumps were out of commission. The steam pump remained intact, but it was practically impossible to keep the vacuum with this one pump. We managed to get the main engines going again, as there was only a little water in the engine-room, but we could only do about three to four knots. Then one of the boilers blew out and extinguished the fires. Enemy planes continued to bomb, but our gunners and crew kept up a deadly and accurate barrage, and no further damage was done.

Ledbury offered to take us in tow, and we reckoned that with our own power we would be able to make 12 knots. But at 1045 the second boiler blew out, extinguishing the remaining fires, and the vessel stopped. The *Ledbury* then signalled that she had to leave us to go to the assistance of the cruiser *Manchester*. Bombing was still going on.

At 1130 the *Penn* came alongside and we gave her a 10-inch manilla tow rope from forward, but the attempt to tow from ahead was hopeless as the ship just turned in circles, finally parting the tow rope. I signalled to the *Penn* that the only hope of towing the *Ohio* was from alongside, or with one ahead and one astern to steady the ship. We were still being bombed while stopped, so I asked the *Penn* to take off my crew until more assistance was available, to which he agreed, and at 1400 the *Penn* came alongside and took off the whole crew.

At 1800 two motor launches and a minesweeper, *Rye*, came out from Malta to assist us. I called for a small number of volunteers to return to the *Ohio* to make the tow ropes fast, but the whole crew voluntarily returned. The tow ropes were made fast to *Penn* and *Rye*, both towing ahead. The bombing attacks were still going on and at approximately 1830 a plane dropped a bomb directly on the fore part of the boat deck, which passed right through the accommodation into the engine-room, exploding on the boiler taps. It made a shambles of the after-accommodation and the boiler-room, and the crew were blinded and choked by the powder from the asbestos lagging. The engine-room ventilator and falling debris fell on Gunner Brown, causing numerous internal and external injuries.

I did not see any use in remaining on board the stopped *Ohio* with the consequent risk to life from continuous air attack. As the attempt at towing was proving unsuccessful with the assistance available, I ordered the crew to the boats, from which they were divided between the motor-launches and destroyers, and I lost track of them.

During the night the destroyers tried to get the *Ohio* in tow again, with the assistance of the destroyer *Bramham*, which came alongside in the night. But they were not successful. During the night some of the crew of the destroyers went aboard the *Ohio* and manned the guns through that night and the next day. Also during that night the 400 survivors in the destroyers took advantage of the stores and clothing on the *Ohio* and had also took away most of the wreckage of the two planes on the foredeck and the poop as souvenirs.

In the early hours of 14th Gunner Brown died and we buried him from the stern of the *Penn*. At about 0800 enemy air activity recommenced and continued. The *Ledbury* returned after a fruitless search for the *Manchester* and offered assistance. I was now in one of the motor launches about three cables astern of the *Ohio*.

At 0900 a near-miss fell just astern of the vessel, carrying away the rudder and holing the vessel aft, putting huge strain on the main deck which had already been weakened by the torpedo hit in the pump-room. The *Ohio* began to settle by the stern as the engine-room flooded. I watched the ship settling aft and sent a message to the *Penn* for my chief engineer and chief officer to assist as much as possible with the air compressor gear. I assumed these people were on board the *Penn*. The reply was, 'Come aboard.'

It was then about 1030. The *Penn* was towing alongside the *Ohio* on the starboard side and the *Bramham* was alongside on the port side and the ship was making headway. When I got on board the *Penn* I found that thirty of my crew, mostly officers and engineers, had been taken to Malta by a motor launch when it had developed engine trouble. I was left with only two firemen, two greasers and two other seamen belonging to the *Ohio*. So I boarded the *Ohio* and made a complete examination of the vessel with the assistance of these men.

We sounded all the empty spaces and tested the air compressor gear. The empty tanks were still intact and dry, but the kerosene was overflowing from the port tanks and the water was flowing in through the hole in the ship's side, forcing the kerosene up with it, as all the lids were buckled and nothing could be done with the compressed air. *Penn* was endeavouring to keep the engine-room pumped dry but the water was gaining six inches per hour. The mean free-board of the *Ohio* was now 2 foot 6 inches and the stern half of the vessel was expected to fall off at any time as the ship was now buckling more in way of the pump-room. She was drawing 40 feet aft instead of 29 feet.

From this examination I came to the conclusion that the ship could still be saved and would last at least another twelve hours, provided she did not break in half at the main deck where she was buckling, in which case the stern half would probably have fallen off, leaving the forward section still afloat and salvable. I passed this advice to the senior naval officer and also told him that if the after-end did part, towing operations would be easier and we should still get 75% of the cargo to its destination. This conclusion I continued to impress on all those interested, insisting that it could and must be done.

CAPTAIN 'EDDIE' BAINES, RN
(Bramham)

I was standing by the damaged *Dorset* when, about three or four miles away, I saw the problems that people were having with the poor old *Ohio*. The *Penn* and the *Rye*, a minesweeper that had come out from Malta, were trying to get the *Ohio* moving and I could see without even using my binoculars that they had got it all arse about face and really were not achieving much. Then the *Dorset* was sunk and after picking up the survivors I made my way over to the *Ohio*.

I went up to the *Penn* and said to him over the loud hailer, 'Wouldn't it be a much better idea to tow with one destroyer on either side rather one ahead and one on the stern?' He agreed and decided that, come dusk, we would do that.

At about one o'clock in the morning I went to the starboard side of the tanker and *Penn* went on the port side. Unfortunately on the port side of the ship there were some big flanges sticking out which had been blown out by a torpedo. The *Penn* was bigger than my *Bramham* and his stern overlapped this flange. He was very frightened that he would damage his own ship by bashing it against this flange, so he said he was going to cast off. I said, 'Look, can't we stay put and get on with it? The sooner we get to Malta the better.' But he said he didn't want to get to Malta with a ship with just one screw. I saw his point so we both cast off.

At first light *Ledbury* arrived back from her search for *Manchester* and offered her assistance. I went alongside the port side and positioned myself so the flange was clear of my stern. *Penn* went to the starboard side and so we secured and made tracks for Malta.

Through trial and error we discovered that if the *Ohio* took a swing to starboard the *Penn* should increase speed by a third of a knot which would very slowly check that swing and would bring her back again. And the swing would go past the right course and come towards my way so then I would increase speed slightly. So in fact the actual course was a zig-zag, but it worked extraordinarily well.

At 0900 a bomb holed the tanker aft and she started sinking. By this time the remaining merchant ships in the convoy, the *Port Chalmers, Rochester Castle,* and *Melbourne Star* had safely reached Malta with their escorts. Leaving us poor sods with this old crock, tied together with cobwebs, sinking slowly in the middle of the sea.

LIEUTENANT-COMMANDER ROGER HILL, RN
(*Ledbury*)

On the morning of 14th August we headed towards where we thought the *Ohio* would be but she was much further behind the rest of the convoy than I had expected. We found her in the company of *Rye*, a minesweeper which had come out from Malta, *Penn* and *Bramham*. *Ohio*'s boilers had blown up and there was no hope of getting her engines going. So we had three destroyers and a minesweeper circling around the damaged tanker, whose cargo was intact and Malta less than a hundred miles away.

It was absolutely vital to get the tanker to Malta but the difficulties were immense. She was slowly sinking and she had this great big plate sticking out and, as you tried to tow her, she turned to port all the time. I put a wire onto her quarter and when they tried to tow her I pulled on this wire to try and keep her straight, but I put too much power on and the wire broke. So then I went and took her in tow with a big manilla rope. *Rye* took a line from my fo'c'sle to keep my bows up. *Penn* lashed herself to the *Ohio's* side to keep her straight. This was fine and we were off, making about two knots.

Then a crowd of nine dive-bombers came screaming down at us. It was horrible to be held by tow ropes at each end, moving at two knots and quite unable to dodge. We all lay down on the bridge as a 500-lb. bomb whistled over the top of the bridge and splashed alongside the fo'c'sle. Luckily for us, it did not explode; it was an oil bomb, designed to set the tanker on fire. *Ohio* had a near-hit in the raid and started to settle by the stern.

Just as the bombers were flying away, we spotted some Spitfires from Malta chasing the Stukas over the sea. We had radioed Malta to report the dive-bombing attack, but the Spitfires had only arrived in time to chase the Stukas away. Unfortunately, none of us had any radio with which we could talk to them directly.

When the attack was over, we were in confusion. The *Ohio* and *Penn* were pointing towards Malta and *Ledbury* and *Rye* were pointing in the opposite direction. The chaos of wires, ropes and cables hanging down into the sea had to be seen to be believed.

We finally got ourselves disentangled and then *Bramham* lashed herself on the port side of *Ohio* and by shouting to each other she and the *Penn* got the *Ohio* moving and kept her on the right course. The destroyers alongside were about half the length of the tanker and she was very unwieldy. When she swung badly I put my bows against her and pushed her round.

The afternoon dragged by slowly and we longed for darkness when there would be no more threat of attack from the air. I felt if we had any more bombs around I would lie down on the deck and burst into tears. That evening at dusk we spotted the cliffs on the south side of Malta. All the sailors and survivors on deck cheered at the sight. Now we only had our own minefields to get through and perhaps an E-boat attack to face in the night. We stayed at action stations all night with permission for everyone to sleep except the man on the phone.

In the night there was quite a circus act. A tug came out from Malta with masses of people on her bridge all shouting at once. Then she rammed *Penn*, made a hole in her wardroom and disappeared into the night.

During the night *Ohio* made several attempts to blow herself up on our minefields as she swung off course, but each time the destroyers alongside pulled her up and I gave her a push in the right direction. As we were pushing her round the last point for the run to Valletta, the coastal defence opened fire. They thought they had spotted E-boats. We made signals to try and stop them firing but they kept on. So eventually I got a big light flashing and I said, 'For Christ's sake, stop firing at us!' and they stopped.

In the early morning as we approached Malta I walked round the ship and looked at the sleeping members of my crew. They were lying in duffle coats, one head on another chap's tummy, faces all sunburnt and lined with the strain of the last few days. I felt proud of them, and grateful we had got through it all without a single casualty. The pom-pom's crew were closed up and ready, training their guns. I climbed up and said, 'Good morning, aren't you going to get any sleep?' and they said, 'Oh no, please sir, just one more attack, can't we have one more attack?' I said, 'Christ almighty, haven't you had enough attacks?' They were great people.

At daylight we came round the corner to the entrance to the Grand Harbour. I pushed the *Ohio* round with my bows and followed her in. It was the most wonderful moment of my life. The battlements of Malta were black with thousands of people, all cheering and shouting and there were bands playing everywhere. It was the most amazing sight to see all these people who had suffered so much, cheering us.

The *Ohio* was pushed by tugs to the wharf to discharge her oil. Her stern was so low now that water was washing over her after deck. Within five minutes they were pumping her out in case she was sunk by enemy bombing.

We berthed the *Ledbury* in the French creek. I went quickly around the ship, looked in on the wounded, then got some dope from Doc, took off my clothes and then, oh boy, did I sleep.

Junior Radio Operator John Jackson, MN
(*Waimarama*)

After the hell of the past three days it was unbelievable joy to see the entrance to Malta's Grand Harbour. I went ashore with the survivors of the *Waimarama* and the *Melbourne Star*. The fourth officer of the *Melbourne Star* was sitting opposite me in the stern of the whaler as we went into the harbour. I saw his face as he caught sight of the *Melbourne Star*, and he burst into tears. He was tough, he wasn't a baby. It was as if he had seen a ghost. I'll never forget his face.

Then I saw the other surviving merchant ships, the *Brisbane Star* with a great gaping hole in its bows, the *Rochester Castle* and the *Port Chalmers* lying almost discharged of their cargoes. A band was playing and crowds were lining the quayside, cheering. It was real *Boy's Own* stuff. You actually felt you had done something.

Captain Dudley Mason, MN
(*Ohio*)

At 0600 on 15th August, when we were in the Malta Channel, two tugs made fast fore and aft, but the destroyers remained alongside. At 0800, by magnificent seamanship on the part of the two destroyers, the ship entered Malta Harbour and discharged its cargo safely.

5

Dieppe to Italy, 1942–44

ORDINARY SIGNALMAN LES SELDON, RN COMMAND

I joined the navy on 5th December 1941 and trained at HMS *Collingwood* which was about two miles away from my mother's house in Gosport. I wanted to be a signalman and it was a six-month course. You take four exams before you pass out as an ordinary signalman, which is the lowest of the low.

My first draft was at HMS *Dundonald*, the combined Operations HQ. I joined on 10th July 1942. There were fifty from Portsmouth, fifty from Chatham and fifty from Devonport. We were put through a ten-day course of dealing with wireless sets and radio telegraphy. I was a visual signalman so I had been taught Morse, mechanical semaphore and flag signals. We had to learn the meaning of ninety-seven flags. Some of those were the same flag with a different meaning depending on whether we were in port or at sea. We were taught codes on top of that and we did the basics in code-breaking.

After a fortnight, they got us on the parade ground and read out a list of thirty names, including mine. They said, 'You gentlemen have volunteered for the Naval Commando.' As it turned out, only one of us had actually volunteered. We were kitted out with uniforms and clobber and were told we were going for specialist training near Oban. However somebody grabbed hold of me and said, 'A signalman has gone sick, so you're wanted in B6 section.'

I joined my new section, rather bewildered. We left the camp and marched about two miles up the road, some of the lads pushing a wireless barrow (a double-ended, tubular-framed pram, with a Type 22 Set built in) to Brassie railway station and caught the next train to Glasgow. We were then put into a lorry, driven for several hours, and dumped way out in the Scottish countryside. We were supposed to practise various signalling methods and survive on our own, sleeping rough with one army blanket each. Luckily, it was early August and the weather kept fair. We were in contact with Dundonald via the 22 set and after a couple of days we were called back, only to find that we were leaving the next day for the south of England.

We travelled to London by train, then in the back of a lorry to a village called Crondall, not far from Aldershot. Sub-Lieutenant Evans, who was running the show, told us we were to wear our naval uniforms whenever we were in the village because the information had been put around that we were all survivors of sunken ships and had been brought to the countryside for recuperation. I don't know who they thought they were kidding.

The next day we were all in battle dress. The more experienced men told 'little lambs' like me that we were preparing for the Dieppe raid. I didn't have a clue what they meant or where Dieppe was. I learnt later on that the aim was to take Dieppe, hold it for a few hours and destroy anything of military value.

Every day that week we fell in with the wireless sets and signalling equipment, drew a packed lunch each, jumped into lorries and drove out into the open country. I had no equipment and nothing to do and one hot sunny day I was so bored I fell asleep. The next thing I knew was a kick in the ribs and a voice saying, 'What the hell do you think you're doing?' It was Sub-Lieutenant Evans who was on a motorbike, checking up on each station. I asked him what I was supposed to do, with no signal gear and nobody in sight. He mumbled, 'Well, bloody well stay awake,' and drove off.

The following Monday we were told we were going down to Salisbury Plain to put on a big exercise for Mr Churchill. All the lads said, 'Don't be so bloody daft. We know we're going to Dieppe.' My friend, Keith, showed me the Smith Wesson Colt 45 and bullets he had been issued with and told me he was leaving the next morning to join a tank landing-craft. We left the next morning by lorry and at six o'clock that evening we arrived at Newhaven. We'd had nothing but water all day so that night they gave us a delicious hot stew. Blokes were joking and calling it 'the condemned man's last meal'. How right they were.

We left for Dieppe at 10pm that same night on a naval motor-launch which was acting as an escort for four or five R-boats (motor minesweeper). I was on the bridge with a telegraphist. Commander McClintock was in charge of the landing-craft throughout the raid and we were sent on board as his communication. It was a beautiful moonlit night. As we came out of New-haven we could see all the landing-craft heading out to sea. There were dozens and dozens of them.

Halfway across the Channel, one of our R-boats broke down and all the commandos on board were yelling at us. We took them in tow until they got their engine going and then carried on. The commander explained to me that the moon would soon go down and we would be in darkness, which was ideal. It took about six hours to get across. As we were approaching Dieppe, an array of lights suddenly went up in the sky. The commander said, 'What the hell's that?' I thought it must surely be the Air Force bombardment and the ack-ack going in. But he said, 'No. The bombardment has been cancelled; were not getting one.'

We were looking at the lights which were on our port bow. It looked just like pretty fireworks going up in the sky. I was using my binoculars and suddenly I saw a boat coming up to us flat out. It was a German armed trawler and it passed our bow by about thirty feet. It could easily have carved us right in half. She was so close that I could actually see the chap at the wheel. As she passed us we started bucking and dipping in her wake and I thought we were going to turn over. We had five little landing-craft behind us. How the hell they survived it, I'll never know.

Then the commander said to me, 'Oh good. They've left the lights on on the harbour mole.' There was a point just along the coast which also had a light on it. So he had an exact fix of where he wanted to be. We had to drop our commandos in a gully in the cliff. We went right on to the beach and grounded our bow while the five landing-craft and No. 4 Commando emptied out.

It was absolutely dead quiet. The men wanted to go up the gully but their radio operator told mine that it was full of barbed wire. They were just wondering what to do when another message came through to say that somebody had found that by using the fixings at the end of the barbed wire as ladder steps they could get around the wire and in. So the lads went in to take on the guns that Lord Lovat and his commandos were attacking. We were on Orange Two beach and Lovat was just around the point on Orange One beach, trying to go around the other side of the gun emplacement.

We left them and went back along the coast past Pourville, where they'd made another landing. Commander McClintock had to get back down to White beach at Dieppe itself to see about the others, because once the commandos had done their job, they'd be off.

At White beach, where the casino was, all hell was let loose. I saw plenty during the war, but never anything like I saw there. There were bodies lying on the beach, massed up, and bodies floating right in by the shore. They were mainly Canadians. Their bodies were dragged down by their helmets and boots, but the big pack kept them floating on top. Those that were still alive were huddled up by the sea wall. A bit later on in the day, the edge of the water was absolutely red with blood.

Many of the lads who should have got ashore never made it. It was impossible. There were machine-guns all along the front, coming from the hotels. There were hundreds of windows in the casino, each seemed to have a machine-gun. Then there were rifle men up on the cliffs throwing stick grenades over. The front of Dieppe itself is quite flat. I went back there for the first time in 1986 and saw the distance between the hotels and the first road and the bloody beach; it's something like two hundred yards with a lot of shingle. That's the ground they would have to have covered. I stood there and thought, 'That was murder.'

All this time I was attempting to send signals to the lads of the Naval Commando ashore, but they were all dead by then. Then I was sending light signals back to the First Destroyer Flotilla, some way out to sea. *Calpe* was the headquarters ship and *Fernie* was the deputy-headquarters ship. So I was signalling back to them. The commander was trying to tell them it was impossible to get ashore because the gunfire was so heavy and all the communications were knocked out. We were requesting what to do. They were still sending landing-craft ashore. There were some German landing-craft in the inner dock in Dieppe. The Royal Marine Commandos' job – once the town had been taken – was to go in, get those landing-craft and bring them back to the UK. So the Marines were laid off ten miles offshore, in some French Chaucer boats (which were like little gunboats), awaiting their opportunity. At around 11.00 am some silly bugger sent the signal – I actually saw it – to send the Marines in. It would just have been murder. They had a big smoke screen down and Colonel Phillips, RM stood on the stern of the landing-craft as it was going in and realised that he was getting pounded to hell. He signalled to the others to get back and not attempt it. I think two landing-craft got in and got hit and Colonel Phillips was killed. I saw the Marine boats going into the smoke, but you couldn't really see anything because the mortar fire was like hailstones.

On the beach people were just cut to ribbons. My own best mate, Keith, I was told later was bending over attending to a wounded person and he got hit and fell on a big boulder. Then another mortar bomb hit him and he was so smashed up he couldn't be recognised.

Our craft was attacked. The commander and I were were on the bridge along with a New Zealand sub-lieutenant, when a German plane came down. Everyone was banging away at everything by this time. We all ducked down and right alongside of me was a spare oil drum full of oil. I heard this 'thwuck' right by my ear. I didn't take any notice. I stood up and oil was running out of the drum. One of the crew took the oil drum down and found this bloody cannon shell in there. If it hadn't gone into oil, I would have been blasted to kingdom come.

From eleven o'clock onwards the commander was sending landing-craft in to try and get men and the wounded off. They would load up with wounded and get away from the beach and then get shot to pieces in the sea. A hell of a lot of them went that way. A couple of destroyers went in to try and re-lay smoke but they had to turn away before they met each other which left a big gateway in the middle. All the German guns were firing out through that gateway and all the British guns were firing in through it. Two RAF aircraft came from opposite ends of the beach right down to sea-level and laid smoke from their exhaust pipes to fill that gap. I have always thought those two pilots should have been given VCs that day because, although they were getting gunfire from both sides, they still flew through it.

A Spitfire was shot down and a parachute came down a little way out to sea. We went out to get him and, as we went to pick him up, the parachute got wrapped around one of the propellers. We got that pilot on to the *Calpe* before she sailed. She was absolutely loaded with wounded all over the decks. We started to leave too, but a mile or so away from the beach, the commander said to me, 'Do you think this boat could tow a landing-craft on one engine?' I stupidly said yes. So we turned back 180 degrees and went back to the beach. I wondered why I hadn't kept my mouth shut. We got back to the smoke and came across a MLC (motor landing-craft), which was for carrying lorries, loaded with troops. Its engine had broken down and they were waiting, stranded. There was speculative firing going on around the smoke screen. We got a tow-rope and started to tow her. We had to turn to port to go along the beach a bit to swing back out to sea. Lo and behold we came across another MLC loaded with troops so we got another tow-rope and tied them on. Then we put straight out to sea. I thought, 'Thank God. Let's get home.'

It was one or two o'clock in the afternoon. I'd had no sleep, nothing to eat and nothing to drink. I hadn't even had a pee since six o'clock the evening before. We saw that the *Berkeley* – a destroyer – was sinking. She'd been hit with bombs. I flashed the signal and the *Albrighton* – another destroyer – replied that it was okay, they'd got the survivors off and they were going to sink her because there was no way they could tow her.

There was absolutely nothing else in sight, just an open sea. We felt isolated. It was a boiling hot day. The sun was beating down and I thought I was imagining things, because I looked out to sea and said to the commander, 'I don't know if the sun is baking me brain, but I can see a fire in the water.' He turned slightly to port and headed towards it and it was a little landing-craft. Its engines had caught fire. There were about five blokes on it who wouldn't have stood a chance. We went alongside of them and let them climb into the MLCs. Just after we left it, the burning craft went 'gurgle, gurgle' and sank. So I thought to myself, at least I'd had a mission, saving some of the lads' lives.

There must have been at least fifty or sixty lads on the landing-craft we were towing. We got back to Newhaven and the commander asked me to make the signal requesting them to open the gates. The reply came back: 'Port closed. No more entries.' I reported that to the commander who was standing alongside me and he said, 'Make to him, "Open the gates or I open fire".' So they opened the gates and let us in. The port was absolutely massed with tank landing-craft and there were ambulances and wounded all over the jetties.

As we got into the port, my telegraphist was talking to the ship's telegraphist and I was standing by the bulkhead when my legs started giving way. He said, 'What's up, Ginge?' I said, 'I'm going to sleep. I'm bloody knackered.' The telegraphist asked me if I'd had anything to eat. I said, 'No.' Two seamen got hold of me and gave me what I thought was a banquet. It was sausage, egg, bacon, mash, tinned tomatoes and a lovely hot, sweet cup of tea. When I'd finished that my head was nodding on to the mess table, they slung me on to one of their bunks and I went straight off to sleep. I slept all night and they woke me up the next morning. I went up on to the jetty with the telegraphist and one of our officers was there. He said, 'Where the bloody hell have you been?' We'd been reported missing because we were asleep and hadn't reported in.

We went back to Crondall and got our leave passes straightaway. The next day we were on leave. In the pubs at Crondall that night, they put some of those old white enamel pails on the bar, full of booze. All the lads had to do was help themselves. Quite a few drowned their sorrows.

I had ten days leave so I went home to see my mother, father, and married sister. When I got in my mother said, 'Oh hello, boy. What're you doing home?' I told her I'd been to Dieppe and she said, 'Oh have you, son? That's nice.' She didn't have a clue what it meant. When I got back to Newhaven, some old lady gave me a pre-war photograph of the casino at Dieppe. I carried that in my wallet all through the rest of the war.

WREN DORREE SPENCER (née ROELICH)

After reporting to the training base I was told that I was to become a cook. 'Ha ha,' I said, 'pull the other one. I want to be a driver or boat's crew, or something like that, and in any case I loathe cooking and even my soft boiled eggs are hard.' It wasn't a joke though. The navy had decreed in its wisdom that I was to be a cook, so that was that; and after the first shock, I thought, it might not be so bad. I could learn to cook delicious dishes, and surprise my family when I went on leave.

The second shock came when reporting to Portsmouth Barracks, eyeing with delight all those delicious sailors who, for some reason, seemed to be running. Perhaps it was the cold? Suddenly my companion and I were hailed in a loud voice by a man in a different uniform, who turned out to be a Warrant Officer. 'Well,' we thought, 'this is great. We are rising in the world already.' But when he reached us, as we kept sauntering on, we saw to our amazement that he appeared to be very angry and red-faced.

'Why aren't you wearing your raincoats?' he shouted. 'Well, it isn't raining,' we replied in surprise, thinking he was a bit touched. He went on, 'It's the rig of the day. If you had bothered to look at the notice board, you would have known.' Feeling a bit deflated by now, especially as the sailors all appeared to be smirking, even though they were still running, we apologised, thinking to humour him, but he still seemed to be angry and demanded to know why we were actually walking on the quasterdeck. To us it looked like ordinary paving stone, and we said so. The poor man seemed to be having some sort of fit, but after a few minutes of silence, when he seemed to be trying to swallow, he said quietly, 'Everyone runs on the quarterdeck, it's a tradition.' Well I ask you, to be running in a thick coat when it wasn't raining seemed absolutely potty, but rather than upset him again we set off at a run.

The third shock came when we were told to report to the galley at six o'clock. Thinking that was all right by us, we were absolutely horrified to be enlightened that it was 6 am and not 6 pm. 'You're joking,' we wailed, 'we aren't awake by then!' 'Don't worry,' we were told, 'you'll be awake all right.' And so we were, to shouts of 'Wakey, wakey, rise and shine, the morning's fine!' How the heck they reckoned we could rise and shine at that hour in the morning was beyond us, but we made it, reporting to a freezing galley, to be confronted with piles and piles of carrots and potatoes to be peeled.

Talk about penal servitude. We felt like convicts, especially as there didn't appear to be any cups of tea arriving, and we had had no breakfast. Feeling cold and a bit let down, we set to without a will, with stomachs rumbling, to peel those horrible spuds, which seemed to be leering at us with their beady eyes. Suddenly there was a commotion. One of the rookies had fainted. The officer in charge rushed to get her a cup of tea, whereupon the crafty so-and-so opened one eye and winked at us. We begrudged her every sip of the tea she didn't deserve and, with mouths drooling, all decided to do a faint the next day. Needless to say, we couldn't find the courage.

Our first training fortnight soon passed, not as bad as we first had imagined, and with lots of laughs, and we toughened up very quickly. It was quite sad when we were all drafted to different bases and had to part company.

My first base was Stamshaw camp which was composed of Nissen huts. Our hut was bitterly cold, warmed only by a small coke stove in the centre. We used to draw lots to see who would sit in front of it; the poor girls right at the back were really cold and had to wear their outdoor clothing, while the front ones could almost sit in pants and vests.

I was absolutely horrified on my first duty morning shift to have to report to the galley at 4 a.m., walk through a deserted camp, with frost thick on the ground and wrestle with an old-fashioned stove which had to be raked out and lit with wood and paper. A bit different nowadays, I think. Have you ever tried washing up huge greasy pans with cold water and fingers too cold to feel anything? They bred them tough in those days!

Warmth though did arrive, when the sailors poured in for breakfast queuing up for the bacon and eggs, which we poor mugs had been slaving at for hours, only getting grumbles for our work. I remember the Indian sailors I served with for a year were the most courteous. Always very polite, they gave us perfume which they stuck in their own ears on cotton wool, providing us with lots of giggles.

We used to stand outside in the moonlight, and watch our bombers going over, knowing that many would never return, 'Silver wings in the moonlight' was the tune of the time. Then at Christmas 1940, about six months after I'd joined the WRNS, my first fiancé, Elvin, was killed over Hamburg – he was an air-gunner. He was my childhood sweetheart and we were going to be married in April on my twenty first birthday. After he was killed, I had a bit of a breakdown, and they decided to send me up to train at Westfield College in London as a switchboard operator. I hated that job, being inside all the time. My first appointment was at the Admiralty – it was all underground. I got into trouble there straightaway – they said, 'You do this, and you do that,' which I did, and this voice said, 'Can you put me through to so and so?' So I said, 'Who shall I say?' 'Just say Ike,' and I said, 'And I'm Minnie Mouse.' Actually it was General Eisenhower. He was very sweet over it, he said don't make anything of it, but I got really pulled over the coals.

I decided that job wasn't for me, so I put in for another category, as a driver. I hadn't driven before. Halfway through my driving course they decided that I was to be drafted. I said, 'But I can't, because I don't know how to drive! I'm only half-way through the course.' 'You can do it, you can do it, you're a driver.' And they sent me to this place at East Meon in Hampshire. I was petrified, I knew I couldn't drive.

I went up to one of the Canadians there and said, 'Look, I keep telling them that I haven't passed the driving test, but they want me to take a bus-load a sailors into Portsmouth tomorrow! I can't drive!' And he says, 'Get into my lorry, we'll see.' Of course I got into the lorry, we went round and round the camp and the poor blokes in the back were jumping backwards and forwards because I was stalling and starting so much. When we came out he said, 'No, you're quite right, you can't drive.' I was sent back to Portsmouth to my intense relief, and continued my driving course – passing first time.

Of course, I knew a lot of the Canadians who took part in the Dieppe raid. August 1942, it was. I served for a while at a combined operations depot where they trained at East Meon. It was a sort of a hush-hush place, you weren't allowed to talk about anything that was happening there. So many of them were killed. They were lovely chaps, they seemed to be all big and tough and lots of laughter – it was a tragedy.

During Dieppe, when our soldiers were stranded on the beaches there, I was at HMS *Mercury* at Portsdown Hill; it was a signal school. I was a captain's driver; I had to drive him down to Southampton. I can remember standing out there at dawn. It was quite a thick mist, very eerie because it was so silent. I saw all these little boats going out to rescue the stranded soldiers.

I was engaged then to a chap named David and he was killed at sea that day. He was on one of the bigger boats which couldn't get close into the shore. The rowing boats and small boats were ferrying the chaps from the shore out to the bigger boats, and his boat got a direct hit, with a line of soldiers waiting to get on board.

I remember being drafted to HMS *Lizard* late at night. It was a shore base in Hove, opposite HMS *King Alfred* where the officers were trained. I was met by a 'Wren', Ruth Brown, dressed in a duffel coat, hat and pyjama trousers. You're not supposed to change into pyjamas on night duty. She'd forgotten to put on her bell-bottoms, just rolled out of the bunk!

I have many happy memories of HMS *Lizard*. Being an MT (Motor Transport) driver by then I used to serve at night in the MT rooms, so of course there was no bathroom, and we weren't supposed to bath or get undressed. But the mother of one of the drivers had found this hip bath, and sent it to us – it was really luxurious, filled with hot water, in front the open coal fire. One night, however, the duty officer was doing her rounds early, accompanied by two male ratings. We rushed to the poor girl in the hip bath, trying to hold towels in front of her. We didn't manage to cover her before they got there. I think the sailors really thought it was their birthday! I could see their eyes bulging. We all had a dressing-down the next day, and weren't allowed to use the hip bath again.

In spite of everything we had such fun. Perhaps we were aware that it might be a short life, and we were determined to make the most of each day. There was such an air of comradeship everywhere, we were all pulling together, helping those who had been bereaved, so many in such a short time.

I met my future husband, Jack, at HMS *Lizard*, because he had been put on shore-based duty having contracted asthma while returning on a ship from Singapore. He could have chosen to be invalided out, but he loved the Navy so much he spent a year driving lorries instead. He died in 1977, aged fifty-eight, I have never found anyone else. You have to put a brave face on, the war taught me that.

When the war was over I went to live in London and work at Harrods. It was like stepping into another world. When we were in the navy we didn't have to worry about fashion books, clothing coupons, so in that respect we were spoiled; and we always had plenty to eat. I remember making cocoa in a saucepan at night and it was so thick the spoon almost stood upright in it! I'm not saying we didn't work hard, because we did. But returning to civilian life, missing all the companionship and laughter, took a lot of getting used to. In spite of everything, I wouldn't have missed it for the world.

ORDINARY SEAMAN DICK WILDER, RN

I joined *Impulsive* in Southampton after that it had had a major refit. *Impulsive* was the last of the many I-class two-funnelled destroyers built between the wars. The ship had four 4.7-inch guns, a high-angled gun, four torpedo tubes and multiple 0.5s on the searchlight between the two funnels. The speed was about 35 knots. Radar had just been fitted and we had asdics, or sonar as it is now known.

After a brief work up in Scapa Flow we set off for Valfjord, near Reykjavik, in Iceland and acted as part of the escort for the capital ships there. After two months we set off for Seydhisförd to join the escort for the Russian convoy PQ18.

The main section of PQ18, comprising 32 merchant ships, had assembled in Loch Ewe and sailed with a small escort to rendezvous off Iceland with a joiner section of eight ships. The Convoy Commodore was Rear-Admiral Bodham-Whetham in the freighter *Temple Arch* whose master, Captain Sam Lamont, had already completed two return runs to North Russia. The close escort was under the command of Commander Russell, in *Malcolm*, and he had with him two 'A'-Class destroyers, three ocean minesweepers and four anti-submarine trawlers.

For only the second time in the war, a light Escort Carrier was to accompany the convoy – this was the *Avenger*, under the command of Commander Colthurst. Three Swordfish aircraft were embarked for anti-submarine patrols and, for air defence, there were twelve Hawker Hurricanes. The carrier had its own escort of two 'Hunt' class destroyers.

To protect the convoy from attack by heavy surface units, there was a fighting escort of 16 Fleet destroyers, of which *Impulsive* was one. Also as a protection against surface units there were two submarines, P614 and P615. If the enemy units were detected, the submarines would leave the convoy, submerge and attack. Also in the escort were minesweepers and corvettes.

To boost the air defence capability, two anti-aircraft ships were stationed with the convoy. The *Alynbank* and *Ulster Queen* were former merchant ships armed with eight 4-inch AA-guns.

The convoy was made up of forty ships, mostly British and American. In addition there were two oilers for refuelling the escorts and one rescue ship, the *Copeland*, a former passenger-carrying coaster owned by the Clyde Shipping Co. Also, in tow of three escorting trawlers, were three MMs, 105-foot craft armed with close range weapons and with a rescue capability.

In command of these forces was Rear-Admiral Bob Burnett in the cruiser *Scylla*. This was a brand new vessel designed to carry eight to ten 5.25-inch Dual Purpose guns but, due to wartime production problems, she had been completed with eight 4.5-inch AA-guns and had been nicknamed '*Toothless Tiger*'. However, she provided a useful addition to the convoy's AA capability and was an excellent command ship being fitted with the very latest radar equipment and good communications.

Long-range protection against surface forces was provided by heavy units of the Home Fleet patrolling in the Iceland-Spitzbergen area in such positions as to be able to steam towards and hopefully intercept any enemy ships approaching the convoy from the Norwegian coast. These forces were commanded by Admiral Bruce Fraser, Second in Command, Home Fleet, in *Anson*.

To support all forces afloat were two oilers anchored in Bell Sound, Spitzbergen, which supplied bunkers for the fighting escorts. A force of destroyers was detailed to protect them.

Along the Norwegian coast were six of our submarines (five British and one French) lying in wait to catch any German unit leaving the safety of the fjords to harass the convoy. Air cover was provided by long-range Catalina flying-boats based on Sullom Voe in the Shetlands, and a squadron based in Northern Russia. They carried out long-range reconnaissance and anti-submarine patrols. The entire operation was under the command of Admiral Tovey in *King George V* at Scapa Flow.

These units totalled 65 warships and, with the convoy and auxiliaries, there were 110 ships participating in the operation. They were formed up in a conventional formation of a broad front of ten columns, with 4 or 5 ships in each column, with the AA ships, oilers and the rescue ship being allocated convoy positions. The convoy stretched across the ocean for miles. Its speed was 8–10 knots. The convoy left Iceland for Archangel on 2 September 1942. The route was designed to keep us 330 miles from the Norwegian coast but this didn't stop the Luftwaffe making concentrated attacks.

During the whole passage we remained at defence stations, four hours on, four off. My place of duty was on the 4-inch high-angle gun just astern of the after funnel. This meant that when we came off the bridge having done half an hour's stint as lookout we had some shelter to thaw out a bit and doze off for a while, because lack of sleep was probably the hardest thing to bear. Even though it was only September there was ice forming on the guns and upper decks and to counter-act the cold I wore three jerseys, long johns, no.3 trousers and my overalls, topped with a duffle coat, cossack hat, scarf and gloves.

The cold was only one of our hardships. In *Impulsive* we were luckier than some because we were able to sling our hammocks and get spasmodic sleep. Fortunately too, the mess decks were reasonably dry and the only leak we had was cured with the Chief Stoker's chewing gum.

On 8 September, PQ 18 was sighted by a Focke-Wulf long-range bomber on patrol and from then on we were constantly shadowed, mainly by BV138 flying-boats. First blood was drawn on 12 September when *Faulknor* successfully attacked and sank U-88. This U-boat had penetrated the screen, was detected by the destroyer's asdic and sunk by the first five depth-charge pattern set at 150–250 feet.

The next day, 13th September, Hurricanes from *Avenger* attempted to drive off a BV138 shadowing the convoy and were appalled to see their .303 bullets ricochetting off the plane as it dodged into the clouds.

A Swordfish spotted a U-boat on the surface twenty miles astern of the convoy at 0815 but it dived before an attack could be made. However, U-408 and U-589 had worked themselves into an attacking position and successfully torpedoed *Stalingrad* and *Oliver Ellsworth*, the third and fifth ships in the starboard column. This was at 0900. I heard the 'crunch' of the explosions and saw for the first time ships being sunk. The feeling of fear this aroused in me I have never forgotten.

Meanwhile, air activity was building up. At 1100 a Swordfish observed a BV138 dropping an object into the sea fifteen miles ahead of the convoy. This was reported as a possible mine and the commodore then ordered an emergency turn to 45° to port. The same Swordfish sighted a U-boat surfaced ten miles ahead of the convoy but the attempted attack was thwarted by a BV138. Another U-boat was sighted twelve miles on the port side at 1400.

At 1435 radar detected a large group of aircraft and for the next hour it was apparent that aircraft were massing for attack. Hurricanes constantly drove off small groups of Ju88s expending much ammunition without apparent success and had to return to *Avenger* to refuel and rearm.

The main attack developed shortly after 1530 when a force of 28 Heinkel 111 torpedo-bombers and 17 Ju 88 torpedo-bombers came in from the starboard quarter followed by 20 Ju 88 dive-bombers. The torpedo-carrying aircraft appeared in waves over the rim of the earth like a swarm of locusts, flying just above the waves. The commodore ordered an emergency turn of 45° to port. Then all hell was let loose as the merchant ships and escorts opened fire with every gun which could be brought to bear. We fired as many rounds as we could under maximum elevation. It was hard pushing rounds up the spout like this but when the devil needs, you do your utmost. While we were firing I did not have time to be afraid, but looking over the side during a lull and seeing torpedoes speeding by was frightening to say the least. Our firing, although erratic, caused the aircraft to drop their torpedoes badly, some appeared to nose-dive, others either bounced off the waves or hit tail first, but some ran true. With more than forty aircraft, each carrying two torpedoes, inevitably some torpedoes found their target. One of the first ships to be hit was the *Empire Stevenson*. The torpedo detonated her cargo of munitions and she went up in a tremendous explosions, a yellow flash, then a great red cloud ascended to a height of more than 3,000 feet. The next astern, the *Wacosta*, bore the burnt of the blast which devastated her upper works, then, as she steamed on, the burning remains of the *Empire Stevenson* descended, much of it falling on *Wacosta*. Whether she could have withstood this onslaught will never be known because she was then struck by a torpedo. Other ships fatally hit were *Afrikander* in column 9 and *Oregonian*, *Macbeth* and *Sukhona* in column 10, also *John Penn* in column 7 and the lead ship in column 4, *Empire Beaumont*.

Having dropped their torpedoes, the enemy aircraft swept over the convoy or to be more accurate, through the convoy weaving between these ships making it difficult to fire at them without hitting our own ships. They came so low and close that the aircrew could be seen. Passing one destroyer the airmen waved and this was returned by the seamen in the form of two fingered gestures and advice. Then, down through the clouds, the Ju88 dive bombers made their attacks. To see an aircraft aimed directly at you and knowing that it is the pilot's intention to blast your ship to pieces is somewhat disconcerting. It was, therefore, the aim of every gun's crew to dispatch as many projectiles as possible into the aircraft to reverse the position. The attack ended in stalemate. No ships were hit yet some suffered superficial damage. No aircraft were shot down but many were hit. The aircraft flew away pursued by *Avenger*'s Hurricanes which had been caught replenishing when the Luftwaffe commenced their attack. The convoy steamed on, licking its wounds and astern was a scene of desolation: four sinking freighters, the sea dotted with lifeboats and life-rafts and the surface covered with wreckage and, slowly moving around searching for survivors, were the three ML-MMs who had slipped their tows and were doing sterling rescue work.

The respite was short – only a hour. Nine Heinkel 115 float planes attacked but were repelled by the Hurricanes. Sadly, one Hurricane with its pilot was lost. Then the last attack was made at 2030 by twelve Heinkel 115s. The guns of the escorts repelled the attack and two aircraft were shot down.

And so ended at last the first day of major assault on the convoy. The big attack was the most devastating torpedo attack of the whole war, eight ships being sunk or destroyed in less than eight minutes. The gunners in the escorts and convoy had fought hard and several aircraft had been destroyed and more damaged.

The next day, 14th September, U-boats were active in the early hours. U-587 was detected but eluded attack by *Impulsive* and torpedoed the tanker *Atheltemplar*. Later a Swordfish sighted and vectored *Onslow* to a U-boat which was then attacked and breaking up noises were reported. Aircraft made several attacks and appeared to be concentrating on *Avenger*, but all were beaten off. Twenty-two HE 111s and eighteen Ju 88s attacked at 1400 with torpedoes. *Mary Luchenbach* was hit and blew up in a similar fashion to the *Empire Stevenson*, her only survivor was picked up half-a-mile away. Seventeen torpedoes were fired at *Avenger*. Her Hurricanes destroyed 5 bombers and damaged 17.

Similar attacks continued throughout 15th September but no ships were hit and no successes were reported by our forces. Forty-five aircraft took part in the heaviest attack. Several submarine contacts were attacked but there was no evidence to support a kill.

However, early next day, 16th September, soon after the convoy had altered course to the southeast, *Impulsive* picked up a firm contact, which was U-457. John Whittle was officer of the watch at the time. When he got an urgent message from the asdics he rang the alarm bells, reduced speed and fired the depth-charges. On the previous day I had been deafened by the gunfire and could literally hear nothing. At the time I was the port after-lookout on the bridge and heard nothing of the excitement going on around the bridge, not even the alarm bells. I had no idea anything was happening until I saw the depth-charges being hurled into the sea and then the terrific volume of water erupting from just beyond our stern! Then oil and wreckage came up to the surface; we had destroyed the submarine.

PQ 18 was now almost out of range of the Luftwaffe so at 1600 Admiral Burnett left the convoy with part of the fighting escort of destroyers to rendezvous with QP 14, a convoy of 'returned empties', many of which were survivors of PQ 17. Later *Avenger* and *Alynbank* joined QP 14 leaving one AA-ship, *Ulster Prince* to continue to provide support for the remainder of the convoy's journey to Russia.

On 17 September the weather became foggy and the ships were once again within range of land-based aircraft and they were shadowed by Ju 88s from Norway and supported by a Catalina from Russia. U-boats continued their harassing tactics and once more the bombers attacked. The *Kentucky* was hit by a bomb and disabled and the minesweeper *Sharpshooter* took her in tow but she was again attacked, set on fire and then blew up. The remainder of the convoy, now reduced to 27 merchant ships with their escorts, continued towards the North Russian ports in deteriorating weather and experienced problems due to inferior pilotage, groundings and further air attacks before reaching harbour on 19th September.

TELEGRAPHIST AIR GUNNER LES SAYER

I did PQ18 in the *Avenger*. There must have been about forty merchant ships and forty escorting ships. It was a hell of a big fleet. PQ18 was one of the most horrific experiences of the war for me. It was all right until we got within range of the Luftwaffe in Norway and then we were under constant attack by high-level bombers, torpedo-bombers, dive-bombers and submarines. I don't know how many ships they sank. It was something like eleven on the first few attacks.

We were flying Swordfish on anti-sub patrols so you could be airborne while these attacks were on or you could be on the carrier which was under attack anyway. On the *Avenger* there were three operational Swordfish at any one time and a half a dozen Hurricanes. The Hurricanes did a great job but they had difficulty in dealing with 42 torpedo bombers coming in one attack. We spotted subs almost every day and some were sunk, caught by depth-charges. We carried a couple of depth-charges so we could have a go as well. We would sight them and report them, but if you got within range of the Braum and Vas seaplanes you would be pretty anxious because their cannon could get you at ninety knots without too much of a problem. The Blohm and Voss was a big type of seaplane which they used for shadowing duties.

The German pilots had bags of courage, looking at it from a purely airmanship point of view. Each of those 42 aircraft had two torpedoes, not one. Some of them carried the torpedoes that went round in ever-decreasing circles so if they miss you the first time they might get you the second time.

We lost a couple of destroyers but on that convoy it was the merchant ships that went down. The Liberty ship, an ammunition ship, was hit and went up just like a mini atom-bomb. We just had to keep going, we couldn't have stopped. It's terrible when you see debris floating around, upturned dinghies or lifeboats with no-one in them. It's very cold out there; you don't last very long in the water.

One thing which stands out in my mind is standing on the flight deck of the *Avenger*. An enemy plane had been shot down, I suppose at the head of the convoy, and the German crew were sitting in their dinghy and were floating down in between the lines of the ships. They came right along side the *Avenger* and they were shouting, 'Comrade!', and the guy next to me said, 'Die you bastards, die.' And I thought 'No, that could have been me.'

It was obvious that PQ18 wasn't going very well but the previous convoy PQ17 had been an even bigger disaster. They didn't have sufficient ships, they scattered. But PQ18 stayed together, and did much better than PQ17.

We didn't go all the way to Murmansk. We turned around because the captain of the *Avenger* said the Swordfish crews were so fatigued that he wasn't going to guarantee their safety. You did three hours in the air, three hours on standby and three hours off. You did that for about three days and fed on Benzedrine tablets to keep you going. You didn't notice the tiredness until afterwards when the whole thing was over.

When I got back I was emotionally drained and found it very difficult to relax. PQ18 was the one experience which rammed home to me the futility of war. All those people, all those innocent people, and all those ships, lost. It's the utter waste.

Chief Engine-Room Artificer Trevor Lewis RN

On Sunday 13th September 1942, we slipped out of Haifa in company with our sister ship, *Zulu*, carrying three hundred and fifty Royal Marine Commandos and soldiers, bound for an unknown destination but obviously prepared for a landing on some stretch of enemy held coastline. Both *Sikh* and *Zulu* were painted Italian grey with red and white recognition stripes on the foc's'le, presumably to hoodwink enemy aircraft. To us simple sailors, known to be superstitious, this was another bad omen and gloomy forecasts were flying around on the lower deck as to what could happen going into action under Italian colours. Still no-one on the lower deck knew our destination, although we were informed that the ships would enter the outer harbour of Alexandria, for last minute topping up with fuel, under cover of darkness.

It was dark when we entered harbour in Alex, and fuel lighters were soon alongside – it was then we learnt our destination. The Arab crewmen on the lighters were shouting up at us 'You go Tobruk eh?' – another bad omen of things to come. After fuelling to the limit we sailed immediately for what we now knew to be a Combined Operations raid on Tobruk, described later by Admiral Harwood as 'a forlorn hope'. The plan was for *Sikh* and *Zulu*, known as Force 'A', to break the boom at Tobruk, enter the harbour and destroy all shipping, landing the Marines and soldiers who would capture the town. Our guns were also to silence the German batteries at the mouth of the harbour. The Long Range Desert Group would then come in from the landward side to attack the garrison, who would be caught between two fires. So much for the plan, which turned out to be a disaster; the Germans had been forewarned of our arrival through the criminal lack of security in Egypt; as every Arab seemed to know the whole plan.

We arrived off Tobruk around 3am, stopped two miles offshore and began lowering our assault craft with the Royal Marine Commandos. They set off for the beach and were soon involved in heavy fighting. The second wave of assault craft turned back, much to the annoyance of Captain Micklethwaite who slated the CO on the upper deck, before ordering him and all his detatchment for'd on the messdecks. We had moved a mile inshore when at around 5am a searchlight picked us out, wavered for a moment, and then held us as all hell broke loose. The German 88mm guns in the batteries concentrated their fire on what was I suppose a sitting target.

As *Sikh* began to circle to seaward, shells from the German batteries found the range and with a terrific explosion a salvo of 88mm shells exploded in the gear room. In the engine-room we saw the oil pressure fall to zero, and immediately closed the throttles to stop engines. Another salvo of shells landed aft and wrecked the steering gear, and 'A' gun for'd blew up with all its ready ammunition after a shell scored a direct hit: the Royal Marines who had been sent for'd to the messdeck suffered a dreadful fate and were burnt to death. Attempts to flood 'A' and 'B' magazines to put the fire out were hopeless.

I reported to the bridge, 'Lubricating oil pressure failed, Sir, Main engines stopped,' and Captain Micklethwaite himself came to the voice pipe. In a calm, authoritative voice he said, 'CERA, we must try and get out of range of the shore batteries – half ahead both engines.' We both knew what the result would be – seizure of the main engines, which would be the end of us all. Another violent explosion rocked the ship, and I went aft to the gear room, up the hatch and along the upper deck to see if anything could be done to restore lubricating oil pressure. Dropping down the gear room hatch, it became obvious that nothing could be done: the port and starboard fuel pumps had been smashed by the force of the explosion, the compartment was four to five feet deep in oil and water, and both the Leading Stoker and Stoker who had been on watch appeared to be dead. Clawing my way through the oil and water and clambering over twisted metal I reached both bodies and saw they had been killed outright: I had to confirm this before returning to the engine-room.

On the upper deck it was a shambles; twisted torpedo tubes and jagged pieces of metal littered the deck. Some of the Royal Marines had escaped from the for'd messdeck but had been caught in the blast of the explosions. They were screaming from terrible burns, with their skin from neck to fingernails trailing behind them. Some leapt over the side in their agony.

Miraculously when I dropped down the engine-room hatch again we had still not received a major hit in the engine-room. The Chief Gunner's Mate Harry Seymour was still firing back at the shore from 'X' gun in the after turret, but this was the only bark *Sikh* had left, all the other guns having been put out of action. The main engine throttles had been opened to Half Ahead and the ship began to move: with my senior ERA, we tried desperately to bring a small auxiliary oil pump into play to supply oil to the main engine bearings.

We soon found that the ship was going round in a circle, as the salvo of shells landing near the Tiller flat had destroyed the tiller mechanism. The Engineer Officer went down with a small party to try to connect the hand-steering gear but it was impossible. After a few minutes of watching the engine-room tachometer turning ahead, there was a loud rumbling noise, tremendous vibration throughout the ship and then a violent booming. At first we thought we had been hit in the engine-room, but then realised the port and starboard main turbines had seized up solid from lack of lubrication.

After reporting the situation to the bridge we got the Captain's reply, 'Thank you CERA, stand by for further orders.' He was an inspiration to us all with his cool, calm way of giving orders in times of crisis, and this was reflected in the behaviour of my engine-room staff. With two ERA's, a Leading Stoker and two Stokers they all carried out orders without question right to the end: both boilers were still keeping up a head of steam and the generators in the engine room were still providing light. The worst thing for us was the failure of the forced draught fans when the temperature on the engine-room plates rapidly rose to well over 120°F; with hot metal and escaping steam all round us, breathing became difficult.

Sikh was now helpless, stopped and unable to move again under her own power, when the message came down from the bridge that *Zulu* would come alongside and tow us clear of the shore batteries and out of range of the guns. *Zulu* closed and a line was passed; all the time shells were still whistling around us, some exploding in the water, some causing more damage both forward and aft. *Zulu* was hit but not disabled, and after frantic efforts on both ships the line was secured and *Zulu* began to take the strain and pull us clear. I remember thinking my chum Charlie Manship would be down in the engine room of *Zulu*, and silently urged him on; sadly it was not to be. An 88 mm shell hit *Zulu* on the quarterdeck, carrying away the bollard and towing wire, whereupon Captain Micklethwaite ordered *Zulu* away. She laid a smoke-screen between us and the shore and headed off for Alexandria at about 0700.

'X' turret continued to fire back at the enemy, but it was obvious we were finished as we could not get out of range of the guns on shore. Enemy aircraft appeared and dropped a few bombs, but it seemed they were more interested in *Zulu* than in us. It was not until much later that we learned that *Zulu* had been sunk, after being hit in the engine-room by a stick of bombs, and Charlie Manship killed. Ironically, *Sikh*, having been blasted both fore and aft, suffered not one major explosion in the engine-room.

Soon after 0730 Captain Micklethwaite himself rang the engine-room with the order, 'Abandon Ship, CERA.' We left the engine-room together after a last look round and shook hands all round at the top of the engine-room hatch. By this time the ship was settling in the water, and as the shelling seemed to have stopped for the moment Alec Sutton and I decided to see if we could salvage anything from our mess before going over the side. A shell had exploded on the bridge immediately above our mess and the blast had ripped through the Mess Flat, bursting open lockers, cupboards and doors. I found my old reefer jacket with snapshots of my wife and children in the inside pocket. These were to be a source of great comfort in the next few months. Strange though it may seem, a small bottle of rum was still intact. We drank a couple of tots of neat rum each, after which I think we could have taken on Rommel and the whole of the Afrika Korps single handed.

It was time to go, so clambering down to the break of the foc's'le on the starboard side we jumped into the water and swam away from the ship: most of the survivors were already in the water. When we were two or three hundred yards from the ship we saw our captain haul down our Battle Ensign from the foremast, then walk down the starboard side to repeat the process at the aftermast, before jumping into the sea. He was the last man to leave the ship.

It was not long before the end came for *Sikh* as she heeled over to starboard and finally sank. We were left feeling alone in the world, shocked, afraid, yet still struggling to survive. It is a solemn, heartbreaking experience to see the ship you have loved going to the bottom.

The survivors now gathered together in small groups, some clinging to mess tables or benches they had managed to throw over the side, others, hanging on to the Carley floats. The badly wounded and those who had been burned, we managed to put into the Carley floats whilst those of us who were uninjured trod water and hung on to the side ropes. Fortunately the sea was fairly calm and we tried to cheer each other up, though men behave very differently in such circumstances: some cry – usually the result of shock, not weakness; some curse with a long tirade of abuse against everyone else; some laugh and try to crack jokes – 'Where's that bloody taxi I ordered?', or the most standard Naval joke, 'If only Mother could see me now she'd buy me out.' And some just give way to despair and slide away into the depths. It's difficult to stop them when you are clinging to your own life, as it seems at the time, literally by a thread. After an hour or so the cold starts to creep in, even in the Med, and with the cold a kind of despair as you begin to resign yourself to the inevitable.

The bombing and shelling had stopped and all was quiet and peaceful, but with no friendly ship in sight all hope of rescue seemed to have gone. You just wonder how long it will be before the end come. The laughter, the cursing, the joking, gradually die away as men struggle to keep afloat: many a silent prayer is offered.

Suddenly someone shouted 'A ship!', and we saw a large landing-craft type vessel bearing down on us, together with a high speed launch, both flying the German Swastika. Fear of another kind came to us: these were Germans, our enemies.

They came alongside each group of survivors and hauled us out of the water. The wounded were handled carefully and with compassion, and two or three dead bodies were taken up with a degree of reverence. Those of us who were uninjured were hauled inboard and laid out on deck like so many stranded fish, then they came around to each man with a tot of brandy, stuck a cigarette in our mouths and offered us a light. The wounded were taken below for treatment.

These were the men of Rommel's Africa Korps, and when we were taken inshore to Tobruk it seemed as though the whole of the Africa Korps were there to see us being brought in. We heard afterwards that Field Marshal Rommel himself was there to greet our captain who, thank God, had also been rescued and brought ashore with four or five other officers. We were taken first of all to Navy House for interrogation, after a brief word from Captain Micklethwaite to survivors of the ship's company. The officers and men were separated. We were very much prisoners-of-war.

Our interrogations were conducted by the Italians, watched over by the Germans, and it soon became obvious that they treated us prisoners with more respect than they did the Italians, their own allies. The Italian officer interrogating me took my snapshots of the family and was about to throw them away when I protested. The German officer holding a watching brief barked at him, looked at my snaps and handed them back to me with a click of his heels.

COMMANDER E.A. GIBBS, RN

In December 1942 *Pathfinder* was sent out from Mers-el-Kebir with several other destroyers to provide additional escort for a big troop convoy. The troops were embarked in a number of large passenger liners which we met near Gibraltar, and escorted them eastward. During the hours of darkness, the convoy and escort divided, some ships standing on towards Algiers, whilst we joined the screen of the Oran section.

We had not long separated when, away on the eastern horizon, we saw two white rockets climbing into the sky, and knew that one of the ships for Algiers had been torpedoed. We delivered our section at Oran at daybreak, and as soon as the liners were safely in, the destroyers *Quiberon*, *Lightning*, *Panther* and ourselves stood out to sea again to help the 23,000-ton P & O liner *Strathallan*, whose distress rockets we had seen the previous night.

We found the liner in tow of the flotilla leader *Laforey* who was towing with two enormous short hawsers that must have belonged to the *Strathallan*, and making four or five knots through the water: as a pair, they looked like an ant with an elephant in tow. Except that she had an appreciable list, the *Strathallan* did not at that stage appear to be in danger. She was heading towards Oran.

We all took up our stations around the tow to guard against more submarines, and for a while all went well. An old V-class destroyer, a fine veteran of the previous war, arrived from the northward with about 1,000 people picked up from *Strathallan's* boats. The boats had held many nurses, and other members of the Women's Services.

Presently we realised that something must be wrong, for the *Panther* was ordered alongside *Strathallan* to embark troops. She laid her bows against the big liner's quarter so that the soldiers could transfer from one ship to the other, and after a while sheered off and steered towards Oran.

Then we were ordered to take off troops, and followed the *Panther's* example which had been so successful. With our bows laid against *Strathallan's* quarter, and our engines turning at about one knot more than the liner's speed to hold us there, we lashed the two ships together with wire hawsers. The sea was quite calm, and we rode quite comfortably: in the course of the whole operation we suffered no more than a few slightly buckled plates in our forecastle. Once we were alongside we could see why the troops were being taken off. The *Strathallan* was on fire down below. We could see smoke curling out of her ventilators.

The soldiers began coming on board, down ropes and rope ladders from the *Strathallan's* deck far above us, down onto our forecastle. It was a most cheerful and orderly proceeding, but it was clear that the troops were not used to ropes or rope ladders. We had not long been secured alongside when these was an extraordinary sound, a deep 'who-o-o-of', and with it a pillar of fire seemingly incandescent, shot out of her funnel, climbed perhaps a couple of hundred feet, and hung there. Her funnel was a long way forward of us, and its top very high above us, yet the heat on our bridge was scorching to the face. The pillar of fire died down, and disappeared back inside her funnel. But it was obvious that something very bad had happened down below, and the volume of smoke pouring out of her ventilators increased rapidly.

This made no difference to the soldiers' demeanour, there was no sign of hurry, and the embarkation went on as before. Steadily they poured down on to our forecastle, and kept moving aft. The captain had decreed that no troops should go below decks: they would be no safer behind our thin plating than they would be on deck.

The senior army officer on board was leaning calmly over the *Strathallan*'s rail, chatting casually to our captain. At length he said there were only a thousand more troops left in the liner. We had already embarked a great many more than that, and our decks were jammed with people; and as the *Lightning* was standing by to relieve us we cast off, and she took our place.

Our forecastle and upper deck presented a remarkable appearance, solid khaki except for little islands left clear around our guns so that we could fight them. We had embarked 1,379 soldiers, an extra top-weight of about one hundred tons, so that the ship was definitely tender on the helm.,

The *Lightning* took off the last 1,000 people, and then she, too, cast off. The *Strathallan*'s own officers and men had of course remained on board, but as soon as the *Lightning* left her the fire broke through to the liner's upper deck. A Fleet tug ran alongside to embark her ship's company, and she in turn had barely cleared before the *Strathallan* was blazing furiously from stem to stern.

The liner sank, and the destroyers returned to Oran to land the troops. By that time we had taken part in so many rescues that we quite expected to be offered honorary membership of the RNLI.

Lieutenant John Harvey-Jones, RN

In late 1942 I was appointed to a destroyer called the *Israel* which was just re-fitting at Portsmouth. We covered the North Africa landings and then went up to join Force Q, an advance force of three cruisers and three destroyers which was to hold right up close to the front line and, whenever the Germans or Italians ran convoys over, we would go out and sink them. We moved up to Bône just two days before an operation when they bombed us and hit us and the ship sank in harbour. There were a few casualties but not a lot. We were put ashore and I had a miserable week. I had lost all my gear. We were used as spare soldiers. We were given a ball of string and told to go and blow up these little butterfly anti-personnel mines. I hadn't joined the navy to be a soldier and I was fairly scared and not enjoying it very much and so the next time the force came in I asked my captain if I could transfer to one of the other destroyers and he said 'yes'. So I went aboard a ship called *Quentin*. The captain was Percy Noble and when I went to see him he was very courteous, looked at me rather quizzically and said, 'OK, get your gear aboard, we sail at five o'clock.' So I got my gear aboard, was shown my bunk and action station, and we duly sailed.

We were in action until three the following morning and had an extremely successful operation in which, along with the rest of Force Q, we completely obliterated a convoy en route from Trapani to Tunis, and sank all the escorts. We then methodically sank all the merchant ships which were full of soldiers. Not a very sporting action but we were all pretty chuffed with ourselves. I was the officer in charge on the quarter-deck. I turned in and went to my new cabin, and at six in the morning there was a huge great bang and all the lights went out, the cabin door jammed and the deck buckled. Eventually I managed to get out of the cabin and I went up top to see what had happened. We had been hit by a destroyer in the engine-room which was next to the officers' cabin space. Having already been sunk once I knew exactly what needed doing, so I got hold of a damage control team and we started shoring up the double cabin. Nothing very much seemed to be happening and I sent a sailor up top to see what was going on. When he didn't come back I poked my head up on the deck in time to see our troops on the fo'c'sle just about to jump into the next destroyer, so we ran like hell and just made it onto the next destroyer. Again, no wet feet but no kit.

And so back to Bône and back to England. I felt fairly heroic. I felt that I had done my stuff but I was mildly ashamed of being sunk because that is not the object of the exercise. My girlfriend thought I was a little hero.

Then I was appointed to the *Duke of York* at Scapa Flow. It was a battleship but it didn't do anything; you might as well have been in a floating barracks. When I finished there I was sent to do a sub-lieutenant's course. That was really when you got your proper professional training. You were taught signals, torpedoes, gunnery and electrics and a lot of special navigation. At the end of our course we had to choose what we wanted to specialise in and I chose to go to submarines. I hadn't much enjoyed it when *Quentin* was sunk because there were quite a lot of wounded people. I'd always been scared stiff of being wounded anyway though not particularly frightened of being killed. I'm a coward and don't like the idea of pain. One of the great attractions of a submarine was that either everybody went or nobody went. Also I was still in my heroic mood. I reckoned that submarines were continuously in action and I wanted to do my stuff. The last thing I wanted was to be pushed into another battleship. The only way you could be sure of being in a small ship was to be in submarines.

They were very short of volunteers for the submarine service at the time and many of my friends volunteered too. I went to train at Blyth in Northumberland for three months and that is where I met my wife who was in the WRNS. She had been detailed to turn out as cannon fodder at a dance, I met her there and fell heavily in love but she didn't fall in love with me. She thought I was a mess. I was not as un-selfconfident as I had been before, but gradually submarines gave me much more confidence in myself. It was in submarines that I really found myself.

I joined the submarine *Trusty* in December 1942. I was nineteen and it was all a great adventure. We considered ourselves to be heroes because most civilians' reaction was 'Heavens, I wouldn't go into submarines for all the tea in China.'

There was a lot going for it – plenty of action and plenty of pay, but there were drawbacks. The regulation white jumper was absolutely essential, because the submarine under water takes the temperature of the water around it. Submarines operating around Norway were bitterly cold for those were the days before massive insulation. We just had a steel hull and then a bit of cork insulation on the surface, which fell off as soon as you were depth-charged. Equally, if you were in the Far East where the water was hot a submarine was like being inside a can of beans being boiled in a saucepan. The physical conditions in submarines were very uncomfortable too. You couldn't take even a suitcase aboard a submarine. The total stowage I had for all my personal kit was much less than a two-foot-square cupboard. We had no frozen foods, there was no air-conditioning, we had one ordinary domestic fridge and, once that ran out, you had had it. All the butter and everything else was skimmed. We had to bake our own bread every day, but for a young man it was one continuous picnic by comparison with the rest of the navy. There was no dressing-up and taking shifts for dinner. We would tumble down the hatch and eat dirty great wodges of corned beef.

Trusty initially went to Norway and had a couple of patrols which were absolute misery because we were stuck in the middle of nowhere, well out of sight of land and had no idea where we were. The weather was so appalling that, when we surfaced to re-charge our batteries, we had to steer into the weather just in order to avoid being totally swamped. A submarine has no stability, it rolls excessively, and we had to lash ourselves on to the bridge which at the best of times was only about twelve foot above the water. Effectively you were under water almost as much as you were above it.

We had protective clothing called Ursula suits. These were waterproof suits but even with about three towels round the neck you were still getting continuously soaked in the freezing sea water. You couldn't keep your binoculars clean, so everything depended on the people on the bridge seeing anything else before they saw you. You couldn't use radar – we had only just been fitted with radar anyway – because it would be picked up instantly, so you were still fighting a sort of First-World-War war. In fact, under the rough conditions, it was very doubtful, if we had to fire a torpedo, whether it would have run. I remember once when we dived, we were still rolling at a hundred feet down. That was diabolical, but it was good initial training except that nothing happened. We just sat there. If we had been able to engage or had a chance of firing that would have been great, but we simply had two weeks of hanging around in that sort of misery and then slinking back to Lerwick which, though, was a gorgeous place. The Shetlands were a marvellous jumping-off place for patrols.

I had done a very short time, about three or four months, on *Trusty* when I joined a submarine called *Voracious* which was going out to the Mediterranean. That was my first properly operational submarine. There were four of us; Freddy Chavis was in command; the first lieutenant 'Tubby' Whitehead; I was the third hand and the fourth was John Marks, RNVR. The submarine itself was tiny, even by wartime submarine standards. We operated out of Malta and in the Aegean. It took four or five days to get to the Aegean from Malta and it wasn't a highly dangerous passage but the Aegean itself had been entirely blocked off by minefields. Getting through a minefield was quite exciting then. We had a short transmission unit on the asdic which allegedly picked up a mine ahead. The submarine went through the minefield at about two knots so you'd pick the mine up when it was about a hundred yards away. It made you feel good but it was really by guess and by God. Once you got into the Aegean there were plenty of targets albeit rather small ones, mostly kites. The Germans were still garrisoning all the islands but we had a lot of irregular forces there. There was an Anglo-Greek schooner squadron, who used to all be dressed up as Greek sailors. The identification sign would be a fishing net over a port quarter and a lantern in the barn but of course all the Greeks had fishing nets over the port quarter and lanterns in the barn. We found ourselves continuously boarding these villainous looking craft with the most appalling looking ruffians on board and they'd all pull out naval papers.

By September 1943 the Germans and Italians were beginning to pull out of the Aegean. It was just before the Italians switched sides but the Greek islands were still German-occupied. The surface ships were schooners with an auxiliary engine. These kept the Aegean alive, because the Aegean is a mass of islands and the only communications were by sea. The boats had these ageing two-stroke engines which went bop, bop, bop, bop . . . and piddled around at four knots. We used to board them, take the crews off and either blow them up with a demolition charge or gun them down. I had been sunk before but never had any direct contact with the enemy. Naval officers rarely saw the enemy.

Then the Germans started to evacuate the islands one at a time. Eventually there really wasn't any longer a need for submarines – so we were sent out to the Far East.

LIEUTENANT JOHN ROXBURGH, RN

In December 1942, while serving as the spare Submarine Commanding Officer in the Tenth Flotilla at Malta, I was summoned to take over command of P.44. later named *United*, when her Commanding Officer went sick. I was all of twenty-three at the time and the youngest CO in the flotilla.

I sailed in *United* on my first patrol in command and had a bit of luck. Ships were pouring across the Narrows between Sicily and North Africa with supplies for Rommel. It was a very hot area which we dubbed 'the Cauldron'. From Malta one had to go along the south coast of Sicily to Cape Bon and the Tunis area. Normally the first patrol of a submarine CO was a quiet number in a quiet area. However at this stage of the North African battle ashore it was essential that every submarine available was sent there to intercept Rommel's supplies, and we had a pretty lively time. We didn't sink anything but we were troubled with depth-charges.

I well remember my first attack in earnest. It was on a heavily escorted convoy of three or four supply ships. I had manoeuvred *United* into a firing position on one of the convoys when I found myself in the direct path of an oncoming escort. I went deep to duck under the destroyer as I ordered 'Fire'. Just then the escort dropped a pattern of depth-charges as it passed over the top of us. In the ensuing 'kerfuffle' the order to fire was late in reaching the torpedo compartment. We missed!

Depth-charges didn't bother me too much. You assumed you were going to escape them, and if you didn't, it would happen very quickly. I would be much more frightened as an infantryman in a battle with bullets flying around than being depth-charged.

We encountered 29 destroyers and 15 other targets on that patrol. Apparently the crew were all horrified at how young I looked. The other thing they wanted to know was: was I married? Because my predecessor wasn't married and was obviously after a VC, they reckoned that, because I was married, I might want to live: this gave them confidence!

On the way to that patrol we'd been down off Bizerta and we were moved up to Trapani in the north-west of Sicily (the principal base of the Italians' anti-submarine patrols). We were to join Commander 'Tubby' Linton, VC, on that patrol line with two other submarines. We were moving up at night on the surface and it was glassy calm, dark with mist on the horizon. You couldn't see much and there were E-boats patrolling in the area. Silent passage in such conditions was imperative; at the same time I had to charge my batteries and run the engines which, of course, was noisy. We compromised by proceeding slowly charging the batteries as quickly as possible whilst listening for the E-boats. This delayed us reaching our appointed position. Because I failed to reach that patrol line, a ship got through. When I saw 'Tubby' Linton afterwards he ticked me off for not making my position in time. I told him there was a lot of phosphoresence in the water. When it was flat calm, porpoises darting around like torpedoes can be pretty frightening. There we were going along quietly when suddenly two enormous great white tracks, phosphorescent as hell, came hurtling towards us. These were genuine torpedoes. I thought, 'This bloody torpedo is getting pretty close; I had better clear the bridge and get below.' Then I thought, 'It will pass in a second, and if it hits, well, at least I have slightly more chance than if I am down below.' So I stayed on the bridge for an extra second. I often wonder if I wasn't being a bit of a coward but I stayed there just to watch the result of the torpedo. The track actually went under the submarine which meant that the torpedo had passed ahead. The second track went astern which meant the torpedo had probably passed under us. Then I got the hell out of it. The next day I had an encounter with a merchant ship. It was an eventful first patrol in the 'Cauldron'.

In those days in the Med, we had no air-purification system in submarines. With 33 crew and a very small hull, at the end of a normal 15-hour-day's dive you were not gasping for breath but you were breathing deep. At the end of 18 hours it was uncomfortable. On 17th January 1943, on my second patrol, we were again in the 'Cauldron' and off the island of Marettimo, where we attacked and sank an Italian destroyer *Bombardiere*, which got in the way of a salvo of torpedoes I aimed at a supply ship in another heavily escorted convoy. We were subsequently depth-charged quite severely and then hunted all through the night; there was no way we could surface and draw in fresh air, so come the dawn we had been dived for over 24 hours, and I could see us facing another 18 hours submerged next day. We went deep and I ordered all activities to cease: no cooking, no reloading of torpedoes, everyone was to turn in, no activity, nothing. Which we did. We heard a convoy pass overhead and by the end of that time it was bloody uncomfortable. We were gasping for breath. Some of us had to do some work, but most of the chaps were straight out. While most were sleeping the navigator worked out the time when it was OK to surface – obviously as soon as it was dark. We came to periscope level at about seven o'clock. The setting sun was still glowing on the horizon. There was a huge groan when I announced we would have to stay down at least another half-hour.

Because we had fired torpedoes the air pressure in the submarine was high which makes breathing carbon dioxide more lethal. As soon as I was confident it was dark we surfaced and opened the conning tower hatch to relieve the air pressure in the submarine; this was after 36½ hours submerged. When I came to open the hatch I ordered the signalman who was following me to hang on to my legs so that I was not blown over the side with all the air escaping from the submarine. I realised as I climbed up on to the bridge that if the enemy were present we would have no alternative but to scuttle the submarine and surrender. I just couldn't see how we could fight. I had not told anyone this, it was just in my mind. As soon as I was on the bridge I had the most agonising splitting headache. I felt as if my head was going to burst. I threw up. I was as sick as a dog, totally useless, as everyone else was down below.

However, we soon recovered ourselves with the engines running, sucking precious fresh air into the submarine and starting to charge our flat batteries, when after half-an-hour an aircraft flew overhead and we dived in a hurry. This half-hour on the surface undoubtedly saved our lives.

When we returned to Malta twenty-four hours late we had been given up as overdue and lost. One of my first steps was to go into the wardroom and order my ration of one can of beer per month from the Maltese steward. To this he replied, 'Oh Senor, Lieutenant Stevens thought he would drown his sorrows and considered your beer would be better for him on earth than for you in heaven, so he drank your beer.' Steve and I were just friends at this stage; subsequently he became godfather to my daughter and after the war I was best man at his wedding and godfather to his daughter. But just then I could have strangled him – alas, he had already sailed on patrol!

The medics worked out the dosage we would have been under for CO_2 poisoning and it was very high. We had a young Commando officer on board, because we were going to blow up trains and sabotage tunnels. We didn't in fact do it on that patrol but it was one of our plans. He was physically fitter than we were. I put in my patrol report that he was the least affected on board by the CO_2 poisoning. Most people were very quiet and sleepy most of the time. No-one did anything silly. No after-effects.

On another occasion I was patrolling off the toe of Italy at the entrance to the Straits of Messina. It was flat calm. One used to go deep, then come up for a periscope look, and then go deep again. One could not stay at periscope depth in the clear waters of the Mediterranean because aircraft could see you. The first lieutenant was on watch whilst I slept. He stayed deep a little too long and when he came up there was a U-boat coming straight at us on the surface. He called me and I rushed to the periscope and turned to get off the U-boat's course on to a firing track. The U-boat was pretty close and by the time I had got on to the track it was too broad, too fine an angle and too long a range to fire. The bastard was going past when I had a clear view of about six chaps on the bridge, stripped to the waist and wonderfully sunburnt, the German swastika ensign flying in the breeze only 500 yards away. She was a sitting duck if only I could have got on to her track.

I was beastly to the first lieutenant after that and subjected him to a routine, for the next hour-and-a-half, of going down to 125 feet and returning to periscope depth at regular intervals just to make sure he didn't stay deep too long whilst on watch. He became a novelist after the war and put this incident in his book!

On another occasion off the toe of Italy we sighted a ship about 7,000 or 8,000 yards away, very broad on the bow. I roared in at it for three-quarters of an hour flat out, got very close, fired four torpedoes and sank her. She was escorted by a destroyer and an aircraft and they both clobbered us with bombs and depth-charges.

When I returned to Malta and made my report, the RAF sent me a series of photographs recording the whole attack. It was quite extraordinary. A RAF pilot in a Spitfire flying at 25,000 feet returning to Malta from a photo reconnaissance over Taranto had witnessed and photographed everything. Below him he could see the picture unfold. He had photographs of the torpedoes roaring across the ocean towards the ship; two torpedoes hitting, two more going on into the blue; the aircraft coming in to bomb me and the destroyer turning round and roaring back to depth-charge me. The whole picture. He was even able to confirm the range I had fired at accurately!

ABLE SEAMAN JACK HUNT, RN

On Christmas Day of 1942, HMS *Saxifrage* was diverted to Aruba in the Netherlands Antilles, off the north-west coast of Venezuela. Our task was to escort three tankers to Trinidad. On 28 December we left Trinidad for Gibraltar (some 4,000 miles away) with a convoy of nine tankers carrying essential fuel supplies for the North African offensive. The escort consisted of the destroyer HMS *Havelock* and corvettes HMS *Pimpernel*, HMS *Godetia* and HMS *Saxifrage*. We were the junior ships who, traditionally, were the general dogsbody in any group's workings. Dash here, dash there, rescue survivors; investigate suspicious sightings (real or imaginary) and as always try to persuade skippers to stay in convoy. This was a never-ending task really as each skipper's instinct seemed to be to keep as much distance between him and his neighbours as he could get away with. But then, sitting on 10,000 or so tons of aviation fuel must be somewhat unnerving.

In the days and weeks that followed we were to lose the 'Lucky Saxi' epithet gained on our first convoy to Russia, but not before we were detached from the convoy in order to intercept and search a suspected blockade runner. We off-loaded a number of crates from the neutral merchantman, creating problems of stowage on the *Saxifrage*. Not until well into the voyage did some enterprising matelot find that one crate contained expensive Swiss wrist-watches. At £5 a time most of the ship's company soon owned at least one. The more affluent bought a boxed set of five, at the appropriate rate of discount of course.

The first few days were fairly uneventful, though attempts to top up fuel tanks from the only tanker carrying fuel oil was only partially successful. There seemed to be some technical hitch with connections. The journey facing us would tax our endurance to the very limit, so it was imperative we re-fuelled whenever an opportunity presented itself. We had been advised from various sources that several U-boat packs had been diverted from more northerly convoy routes to reinforce the pack we knew to be shadowing us.

We were the first convoy to attempt the run from Trinidad to Gibraltar direct, so we would be the sole target of the packs following and racing to intercept us.

This produced a bizarre occurrence. The attacking U-boat actually passed between us and the stricken tanker on the surface, heading for the open sea astern of the convoy. Machine-gun fire from the tanker was indiscriminate and a positive danger to all in her vicinity. Some hit the hull of the U-boat, but to what avail I could not see from the W/T office. Our own light guns, Oerlikons and pom-pom 2-pounder, could not immediately be sufficiently depressed because of the safety railings around each gun; these were designed to avoid members of the crew going about their duties on the upper deck getting their heads blown off by some slap-happy gunner. The last I saw of the U-boat was a dim shape partially illuminated by star shell, disappearing behind the stern of the *Vigilance* with tracer rounds ricocheting from her upper works, followed by the most ferocious cursing from our gunners.

To a man, the all-pervading feeling was fiery frustration, a towering rage that our enemy, whom we rarely saw, had been near enough for us to spit at, and on the surface. There was also a covert guilty feeling we had not been about our job as we should have done. The very fact we were unable to locate the U-boat with our asdics after the attack further dismayed us. We were instructed to return to the tanker and rescue survivors. Several boats had been launched and in the area astern of the tanker there were a number of small lights in the water indicating others who jumped into the sea and were being kept afloat by their rubber lifebelts.

We had to manoeuvre alongside first one boat and then the other, as they did not appear to have any means of propulsion. As with other rescues we had been involved in, the effects of shock were the main reason little effort was made by the survivors to help themselves, though not all were helpless. Some were doing their best to use the oars in the boat, but not enough co-ordination was applied. In one boat there were a number, six or seven, huddled together shivering and shaking, not speaking but now and then one could hear a mournful whimper.

A further search was made to recover those who were in the sea, marked by their little red rescue lamps on the life jackets. Most of these were badly affected by fuel oil and some had frightening burns. Manhandling those covered in fuel oil up the rescue nets and over the ship side was very difficult. All hands who could be spared were on the rescue nets helping with the lifting and pushing, and, indeed with the cursing and swearing. We managed to rescue 27 of the crew of 57.

Further misfortune befell us two days after we, the escorts, topped up our fuel tanks from the oiler. It was torpedoed and sank very quickly. Almost at the same time another tanker was torpedoed and set on fire. When the hunt for the U-boat(s) was called off we stood by the *Havelock* whilst she recovered the survivors from the dual sinkings.

It is not entirely clear to me now what our thoughts and feelings were. After all, we had escorted numerous convoys with very few losses but we had suffered four losses in ten days! There was despondency as well as the feeling we were not doing our job properly. Each day now we were confronting the uncomplaining survivors living with us while not being able, it seemed, to justify our existence, to them most particularly, but also to ourselves. We took these losses in a very personal way.

Following the sinking of the re-fuelling tanker there was daily check and report to *Havelock* of fuel stocks, which restricted the time we could expend on offensive sweeps around the convoy. It also governed the time a contact could be pursued and depth-charge attacks maintained. It became apparent that the U-boats appreciated our limitations, as they surfaced during the day, charging their batteries and clearly visible with binoculars but just out of range of our armaments.

Our survivors from the *Vigilance* endured their suffering with a patience that was remarkable. Our Sick Berth Attendant (we did not carry a doctor) performed minor miracles with the facilities at his command. One day, watching him gently removing black burnt skin from the hands and neck of one poor soul while whispering comforting words to relieve the agony, I found myself quite overcome and had to go and find a corner to myself.

We shared our bunks and hammocks with our 'guests' gladly as we did our rations and what clothing they needed. Their unspoken gratitude for their lives and their care was almost embarrassing at times. Our own demeanour at this time could have been a little more cheerful, but such a prolonged period of a routine of four hours on duty followed by four hours off, frequently interspersed with continuous spells of 'Action Stations', did not do a great deal for morale.

Following the sinking of the *Oltenia* we experienced three days of almost non-stop U-boat attacks. Five more ships were torpedoed in this period. The state of the escort fuel supplies reached a critical level. We had a further 33 survivors on board by this time and living conditions were chaotic. The basic ration of food was supplemented by the meagre stocks of tinned specialities most of the crew had bought either in Trinidad or New York, intended as gifts for the folks at home. Fresh water was very strictly rationed, ironic in that great expanse.

We were too tired to take time to contemplate our predicament. The time off watch was spent snatching sleep wherever there was space to lie. The survivor 'guests', those that were able, prepared what food was available and helped with the re-ammunitioning of guns and depth-charges, but they were a great embarrassment when we were called to 'action stations'. They congregated on the upper deck hampering the movements of those who had duties to perform. Their fear of being trapped down below was stark and understandable. Their own officers were continually having to clear them back down below, but without a great deal of success; back down one hatchway, then swiftly up another.

The saga of Convoy TM1 ended when three destroyers from Gibraltar joined the escort, re-fuelling the corvettes. We finally reached Gibraltar on 14th January, with just two tankers left of the original nine. Whatever else I learned from that convoy I was convinced those tanker crews were a breed apart. They were the true heroes.

LIEUTENANT BILL JEWELL, RN

I joined the submarine HMS *Seraph* while she was being built at Vickers in Barrow. I was there for about six weeks during which time we made one or two changes. We carried out the necessary trials, did a three-week work-up and on to Holy Loch to prepare for war. At the end of 1942 we sailed to the Mediterranean to patrol the North African coast during the November landings. General Mark Clark and a team of Americans joined us for a short trip – it was his first time in a submarine. We put them ashore on a bay near Oran for a conference to arrange the landings in North Africa.

Having got back I was sent to collect General Giraud from the south of France; Captain Jerauld Wright, USN, came aboard as nominal captain. We had to wait for at least a couple of days before we could go in to Miramar. Giraud had great difficulty in getting down to the coast because he was always being followed by the Germans. He eventually came off in a fishing boat from the shore. They came alongside and we put a plank across for him which he promptly fell off! Our wireless broke down as we turned back to Gibraltar but fortunately a seaplane was sent out, picked them up, and took them to Gibraltar. We followed in slow time, arriving four days later.

On one patrol we were sent to Cape Bon to look at Galita island, the only lighthouse in the area which the American Texas Rangers were planning to take. We went around the island with the colonel and two of his staff officers for some time, looking at everything. We must have been seen because they kept the periscope up for too long. Night was falling when we started off back and shortly afterwards an Italian submarine came up close by us. We both fired torpedoes and we both missed, but we rammed them at about 200 feet and surfaced immediately afterwards. The bow was seriously damaged so we had to head off back to Blyth for repairs.

Halfway through these, I was sent down to the Admiralty, to meet Lieutenant-Commander Ewen Montagu in the Intelligence Department. Briefly, they were trying to think up ruses to disperse the enemy. After the North African landings the next obvious target was Sicily, indeed it was so obvious that, as Churchill said, 'Anybody but a damn fool would know it is Sicily.' Operation 'Mincemeat' was devised to hoodwink the German High Command that Sicily was only a cover target, the real objectives being Sardinia in the west and Greece in the east. Montagu dreamed up the idea of putting a body into the water so it would be picked up. 'Major Martin' was supposed to be a Royal Marine officer on Mountbatten's staff. The corpse could carry what purported to be vital secret documents to ensure that the other side was misled in predicting where we were going. Among them was a personal letter to General Alexander from General Archibald Nye, which was actually written by him.

I just looked at it as another job to get on with, I really had no feelings about it either way. I'd done some fairly clandestine operations already so it seemed only logical that they should consider me the right man for the job. I enjoyed going down to London to see my parents because until then I'd only seen them for about two weeks throughout the war. Montagu asked me how long the boat was going to take to repair, and I had really no idea but I put it at about a month. He seemed to think the whole operation would go well and we decided that he would arrange everything until we'd got to Holy Loch after our repairs and a brief work-out.

In Spring 1943 Montagu and an Air Force officer came up to the depot ship at Holy Loch to deliver 'Major Martin'. They came alongside with a refrigerated canister about six foot long and about the width of a man's shoulders. It looked like a small torpedo. We lowered it into the fore-ends and hung it on the torpedo rails. Nobody except myself knew what was going on and there was quite a lot of speculation about what this thing could be. There were rumours that it was a secret weapon. We sailed within an hour of taking delivery and set off for the Mediterranean. We had no real problems apart from being bombed twice, which was par for the course anyway.

On 30th April, 1943 we arrived south of Huelva where Spain and Portugal meet. Intelligence hoped that the canister would drift inshore from this position where it would surely come to the attention of the Spanish authorities. By this time the crew had decided that the canister was some form of meteorological device for predicting the weather. I explained that they were on no account to talk to anyone about the matter, either then or in the future.

When it was really dark, we got as near as we could to the estuary. The first problem we encountered was an enormous fishing fleet which came out, passed over us and beyond. We closed into the coast and lifted the canister on deck on to the fore-casing. We shut everyone else down below and put the hatch down. All the other officers and I went down on to the casing, unscrewed the lid of the canister and took the body out. Both my father and brother were doctors so I didn't have a problem handling the corpse. The poor devil had died in a lunatic asylum in London and was about thirty-eight. That was the macabre aspect of the whole scenario. I was supposed to check that he had all his private impedimenta about him. He was dressed in a Royal Marine uniform and all his letters and documents were in a case attached to a chain which led to the pocket of his great coat. They'd been able to find someone who looked very like him in the Admiralty, so they were able to take a photograph to produce his official pass.

Intelligence had taken every precaution to ensure the authenticity of their decoy. As well as the false plans, he was provided with passes, theatre ticket stubs, keys, money and personal letters, including two from his fictional fiancée, Pam. These rather imaginative love letters had been written by some of the girls at the Admiralty who probably had plenty of experience in writing to absent loved ones. Poor Pam had been so naive:

Your letter came this morning just as I was dashing out – madly late as usual! You do write such heavenly ones. But what are these horrible dark hints you're throwing out about being sent off somewhere – of course I won't say a word to anyone – I never do when you tell me such things, but it's not abroad is it?

Previously I'd had a look through the prayer book and got some idea of how the burial service should be. You never do burials from a submarine and I'd never done a burial at sea before. So we read this out over him and pushed him quietly over the side. We ran the propellers full out astern to move his body towards the shore and sent him on his way having no idea whether he would get there or not. We then set off to Gibraltar. Absolutely everything had gone according to plan. The greatest difficulty we had was getting rid of the canister because it was designed to be refrigerated and had tiny compartments all around it. We started off by putting a charge inside the thing, but nothing happened. The charge went off but the canister didn't sink. Then we tried firing machine-guns through it but it took about 400 rounds and still didn't sink. So we had to blow it to small pieces with another charge and eventually it went down.

As we tied up in Gibraltar, somebody came on board and handed me a folded piece of paper. I opened it and read it. It said that the body had arrived successfully. Really that was the last I had to do with it. The enemy must have swallowed 'Mincemeat' whole because they mobilised a lot of troops to Sardinia. Believing the Allied forces were coming up through Greece, the German High Command moved all the armoured divisions from Sicily to Greece. When the time came, there were very few troops in Sicily and the loss of life from the invasion was minimal. 'The Man That Never Was' (as he came to be known) really changed the tide in that area.

From Gibraltar, I was sent straight to see General Patton in Oran. I was to be a marker submarine for the landings in Sicily. I found Patton very arrogant. He seemed to think that nobody but an American was good for anything at all, but after the troops were ashore in Sicily, he did get into a boat and come and see me to thank me for everything we had done.

ACTING LEADING SEAMAN EYNON HAWKINS, RN

I was a senior gunner in charge of the army and naval gunners aboard the tanker *British Dominion*. It was nearly 10,000 tons. We had a 4-inch gun, a twelve-pounder, two Oerlikon-guns and two machine-guns. There were four naval gunners and five from the army. We went on a convoy across to New York. From there we went down to the West Indies and Trinidad. We formed a convoy there of seven ships, all tankers, bound for Gibraltar. Two more tankers joined us two days after and then there were nine tankers altogether. Of course we were sitting targets. Only two actually got through to Gibraltar. Seven of us were sunk by submarines.

This was the first time I came under attack from torpedoes and submarines. We were under attack for ten days. They always attacked in the night, we couldn't do anything really. We had two corvettes as escorts and they really had their work cut out. We saw the fires on the ships in front of us, we could hear the men screaming in the water asking for help but we couldn't stop. I was on the 4-inch gun when the Oerlikon guns opened fire to draw the escort's attention because they had seen a periscope. The corvettes charged them to draw them away but they kept coming back. We had to just keep ploughing on through.

We were the last to be torpedoed. I was very lucky to be on watch on the 4-inch gun right on the poop deck. The first bang was amidships where we were hit by three torpedoes. We were carrying benzene and it went up just like striking a match. Luckily most of the people were sleeping on deck.

I swam away from the burning ship but then I heard someone crying for help. It was a man we used to call Maltese Joe. He was in a terrible state, and so was his lifebelt. I pulled him away from the ship and got my face and hands burnt in the process, luckily not too badly. I was trying to swap my lifebelt with Joe's to keep him afloat when I heard someone else crying out. So I left him and swam back over and pulled another man over. When I got back, Joe was dead. I don't know whether it was from shock or burns.

There were seven or eight men in the water near me and they were all in a panic and swimming like hell. I took charge and told them to keep together so we'd have a better chance of getting picked up by the corvette when he came back for us. They listened to me because I was a senior gunner. I think they realised that we had a better chance if we stuck together. I kept telling them the corvette would come back when she'd chased the submarines away. I'd seen the corvettes go back when other ships had got sunk before us. They were still dropping depth-charges and that is what I was most frightened of. I could hear them coming near and I could feel the explosions in the water. The ship was still blazing.

We were an hour and a half in the water. The water wasn't too cold; the sea was calm, not choppy. We all had these lights and I asked for volunteers with me to put their lights out to make sure the batteries would last longer. Then this corvette came back picking up the survivors. They saw our lights. As the ship came alongside we were shouting, 'Help, help!' and they were telling us to keep quiet because submarines could pick up our noise.

I was very tired when I got on to the ship. They wrapped us in blankets, we had a drop of rum and then we had to go and be interviewed by the corvette captain. That was the first time I had seen our captain, Captain Miller. He had a bandage round his head and a cut on his neck. He was very pleased to see me. He had lost thirty-six out of the fifty-three crew.

I was glad to be on board that corvette. Then it sunk in about the loss of my shipmates. We were all like pals aboard on one ship. They must have had a terrible death; we could hear them screaming. The people asleep in the cabins didn't have time to get out. Even some of the crew asleep on the deck didn't make or, because it happened so quick. It was a quick decision I made to jump. I didn't know whether I would be picked up, but if I hadn't jumped I would have been burnt to death. I didn't have time to think which is the better, to drown or be burnt? They dropped me off at Gibraltar. A week in hospital, a little time in barracks being kitted, and then they sent us back to England on the *Renown*. I came back to Devonport, got rekitted and was given a month's survivor's leave. I got the Albert Medal, which in 1971 became the George Cross.

Sometime later I was up in Hull, doing a gunnery course. I had to go in front of this officer and he snapped at me and said, 'What's that ribbon you've got on there?' I said, 'The Albert Medal, Sir,' and he said, 'You've got it on the wrong side.' 'Well,' I said, 'that's where he put it.' 'Who put it there?' he asked. I said, 'The King,' and he said, 'Oh, we had better leave it there then.' I left the navy in 1946.

ABLE SEAMAN KEN OAKLEY, RN

On the night of 19th December 1941 Italian two-man submarines got into Alexandria harbour unseen by following a ship in, and managed to plant explosives under *Queen Elizabeth* and *Valiant*. Very daring and well executed too. This meant that the Mediterranean Fleet was now deprived of all of its major battleships. Morale in the Fleet was devastated.

Back in England after this disaster, I was sent to barracks in Devonport. Then I received a draft chit, 'You lot from here to left, Scotland, number 1 . . .' At Glasgow we find a lorry waiting outside the station, which takes us to a little place called Baigh and there, under canvas again, we were told that Lord Louis Mountbatten had issued a signal on taking over Combined Operations.

He wanted naval men to be on the beach with the first wave of assaulting troops, naval men who would speak naval language to people who were coming in to commit the ultimate 'crime' of beaching their craft. They were to be trained in all commando techniques, etc. This meant we forsook our blue suits and wore khaki and army boots, but we wore sailor's hats with the khaki. At first it was Combined Operations, then it became Royal Navy Commando. We trained very hard up there, working with the army. Eventually we moved in with the Yankee army, at Inveraray and ended up with them in Algiers.

In Algiers one of our chaps went on a little sortie with one or two friends, found a bar, had a few drinks and they were coming back when they were challenged. They didn't know the password so the next minute a hail of fire was descending on them. So my friend, John, pulls out his .45 and returns fire, at which stage someone shouted in English, we are American soldiers, that of course ended that. When the smoke cleared one of the Americans was lying wounded. He wasn't dead but the bullet had grazed his head. So my friend goes along and puts on a dressing and, while he was doing this, all the others slipped silently into the night and disappeared. The next thing he knows he has been arrested and thrown into jail for shooting this American soldier.

He stays in jail overnight and then our Senior Naval Officer, Commander Ranson, visited the jail to find out what it was all about, and on being told he said, 'Well you must release the prisoner to my jurisdiction. He will be dealt with on board.' The Americans let him go and, on getting him back on board, the commander gave him a kick in the pants and said, 'Behave yourself, make sure this never happens again. Get on with your duties.' John was very lucky to get away with that.

After further training back in Scotland, we set off in January 1943 in a troopship to the Middle East for the invasion on Sicily. We went round the Cape then up the coast and landed at Port Taufiq at the end of the Suez Canal on the Red Sea. We now had to do exercises with the assault group we were going to land with in the bay.

After one such sortie we had a medical inspection. When the medical officer got to me, he asked, 'Mm, what's that? Can't you pull the skin back any farther?' I said, 'No Sir.' 'Mm, I don't like that at all,' he said. 'I think you'll have to have something done about that. If you put that back on the beach and it grows over any more you would be in serious trouble. I think we had better send you ashore to be circumcised.'

So I went ashore to an army camp and the medical officer came in, stripped me to the waist and told me to sit down in the chair. I was sitting down, with a local anaesthetic. He said, 'Now let's have a look'. The scalpel out at the ready, he added, 'I'm going to show you something you've always had and never seen. It is easy making the first cut with the scalpel, just like skinning a banana.' Second cut, third cut and as he is speaking so he is doing it until he gradually cut it all off, and there I am, exposed. 'Put the dressing on, now you better go and have a rest.' I was looking at it while he was doing it; I was just sitting in the chair. What an experience. I stayed in hospital there under canvas in the desert for about three days. Oh, it was painful. Then they sent me back to the ship and of course all the lads were ready then, all raring to go. I told them what had happened. They all wanted to see.

Over the past few months the great assault ships had been loaded with men and materials. We had crept up the Suez Canal one at a time and assembled at Port Said. Early in July 1943 we were ready to sail for Sicily.

We were spotted by enemy aircraft four days before 'the day' but they didn't attack us; in fact it was a lovely cruise. At midnight on 9 July we were at anchor eight miles from Avola on the south-east coast of Sicily, our immediate objective. After a good meal we put on our equipment and manned the assault boats. I was sitting right in the stern of the boat. At last the order came 'lower boats', and we were away. The sea was so rough that our boat was thrown against the ship. Away went the 2-inch mortar, swept over the side. One soldier said, 'It's time they supplied us with umbrellas,' as another great sea swept over us.

Then came that very difficult time between ship and shore when you wonder if you will survive what's up ahead. The boats were tossed all over the place and the soldiers were seasick, but they had cardboard boxes to vomit into and this helped them a lot. Suddenly a flare burst over us – we'd lost the element of surprise, but we still had about a mile to go. Our formations split up and made for their own landing places, with fire from enemy machine-guns directed at us. There was also anti-aircraft fire and light machine-gun fire and the occasional shell.

Our Bren guns engaged the enemy machine-guns and we began to get our bearings. We had landed in almost exactly the right place so it didn't take us long to set up lights and signs to call in the second flight. We waded out along the length of the beach, finding the best landing places. We could not find the beachmaster. I was detailed to find him and make a report, so off I went towards the Marina D'Avola. I joined up with four more 'B' Commandos but still couldn't find him.

We were approaching the marina tower when a sniper opened fire at us. We took cover and shot back. Our cover was a ledge towards the top of a small cliff and in order to get back to the beach, we had to cross a lot of open ground. We had decided to make a dash for it when the sniper opened up again at a man coming from our beach. He appeared to be hit – he rolled in the water and floated away. Later on we found out that it was the assistant beachmaster who was playing 'possum'.

A little later we made a run for it and got back to the beach safely. No other 'B' Commandos had landed and the beachmaster had not appeared so we did our best to get the craft in and direct the avalanche of men ashore.

About this time, nearly an hour after 'H' hour, a battery in the hills began to shell us. A landing-craft carrying about 250 men was the target. It was beached and the men were pouring off down two ladders, but near-misses and one hit were making things hot. I waded out and told the men to jump for it as the water was not very deep. A few jumped and I steadied them as they fell. My gunnery training said straightaway that the next one was going to be on target. Then it came. A terrific explosion and I felt myself fading away into oblivion.

I came to under the water. I felt numb and shocked: had I been wounded? Or maybe some limbs were missing? I couldn't tell, but then felt someone clutch my legs and drag me down again. I lost all reason and kicked like mad until I was free and shot to the surface. A body floated by, its limbs still kicking, it must have been the man who clutched me. There was skin where people had been blown out of their skin – if you ever had tripe that is what it was like, arms, legs.

I staggered through all this to the shore and collapsed there for a few moments, then looked around, completely dazed. My comrades were fleeing for cover and in the water men were crying for help. I went back into the water again to help a man whose arm was hanging on by a few bits of cloth and flesh. He said, 'My arm! Look, it's hit me.' I didn't say anything but managed to get him to the beach and lie him down. I collapsed then, exhausted, those shells still coming down far too close for comfort.

Then I heard a voice crying, 'Help me, oh God, help! Help!' I looked up and on the gangplank was an army captain I had been speaking to earlier. I ran to him up the ladder and saw both his legs had shattered and were dragging in the water. Goodness knows how I got him to the beach. He was a dead weight. I shall never forget the way he thanked me as I lay there almost sobbing at all these terrible sights; so this was war!

I pulled myself together, and saw that the landing-craft had been hit almost directly above where I was standing. How did I get away with it? A man or the remains of him was splattered all over the side.

A few more 'B' Commandos landed but the beachmaster still hadn't turned up and only one assistant beachmaster was there to take charge. Craft were coming in all the time.

Then the beachmaster turned up. I went out to take a line to another landing-craft that had beached on a false bar – a hill of sand made by water movement – a little way out of the beach, the men were coming into deep water in full kit. I took a rope out to give them some assistance. One man clung onto me and I said, 'Ditch your helmet, ditch your bag.' 'No I mustn't,' he said. 'I must hold on.' So he is holding on, he is holding on to me and pulling me under. Anyway I kicked clear of him, I was exhausted at this stage. I was quite a way out and Commander Ranson came up in a boat with one of our chaps. I was in dire straits. I hailed him with what little breath I had left and they threw me a line, but I missed. So I was left until they had picked up two soldiers and then they threw me a life-belt and towed me to the beach, where I collapsed again.

I came to and swilled my mouth out with fresh water; it felt as if I had swallowed half of the Med. In the meantime along came an LCA, a Landing craft (assault), and I am getting the people off there and one of the chaps, his nerves gone completely, clung to floorboards, 'No, no I can't, I cannot do it.' I said, 'OK,' to the crew. 'Take him back.' They had to take him back on board the parent ship. He was an army chap, in really bad shock.

There were plenty of guns and ammunition lying about on the beach. So I set up a Bren gun on a tripod as an anti-aircraft weapon and when a Messesschmitt 109 came over to strafe the beach I opened up on him with it. I don't know whether I hit him but I certainly put up some opposition. He was having too much of his own way. In the end all visible signs of enemy resistance disappeared and our troops and equipment started pouring ashore.

At dusk the enemy bombers returned; this became their practice for the next few days. After four and a half days of night and day work on the beach amongst all that carnage, we boarded a Landing-Craft (tank) and sailed to Syracuse, then to Malta, and on to the dear 'Old Country'.

All the way back, I couldn't get those terrible sights out of my head, they would keep coming back.

CORPORAL JOE HUMPHREY, RM

I was a member of 40 Commando. We were sent up to Ayrshire. The idea was to train across the sand-dunes of the seashore at Troon. Over the weeks we learned to move very fast, taking our equipment with us to the edge of the water, over the sand-dunes, and on to the main road. Really hard work, but we gradually got used to it. And we wondered why.

Very soon we were told. We got on the trains, we were down to Gairloch, where we boarded the troopships – I was in the *Derbyshire*. In there too was 1st Canadian Division – we had taken the 2nd Canadians into Dieppe. Our Chief of Combined Operations, Lord Louis Mountbatten, spoke to 40 and 41 Commandos, on the shores at Gairloch. He told us we were going on the greatest amphibious operation of all time, and as soon as we struck anchor sailing down the Clyde we would be told, and we were: it was the invasion of Sicily.

We got going immediately: looking up plans, maps and illustrations. We all had books with some Italian language in, while the NCOs had to study the beaches and their approach. They took us all the way down to the Bay of Biscay, straight to Gibraltar and along the Mediterranean, and finally, on 10th July 1943, we were there.

We had a very long run in; they reckoned it was seven miles. As we approached the beaches the sea got very very rough indeed and our boats were scattered. Every Marine Commando was feeling so sick, I don't think I could have cared if the whole German army was waiting for us on the beaches. However, I was on the boat carrying No. 1 Platoon, and I was No. 1 Section, so I was going to be first out of the boat. On board with us was our troop commander, Captain Michael Ephraums. We had got to like him so much that we would follow him to hell and back – which we did, more than once.

When we hit the beach, we hit this shallow bit. We had to go up on top of that and then back into deep water, up to our necks, away and up the beach. There we were, on Lake Dia; this was an unopposed landing.

Our first objective was an Italian barracks. We surrounded that, caught them absolutely unawares, got them outside and took them prisoner. Then we began to run into a bit of trouble, but not too bad – there wasn't too much fight in the Italians, and we began to round them up.

One or two sad things: the countryside was so rough there that they couldn't use motor vehicles, and their guns and mortars were towed by horses. Well, unfortunately, to stop them we had to shoot the horses, and it was a terrible thing that couple of days, because this hot sun was beating down on these dead horses and dead men. The Italians would sooner not fight at all, they gave themselves up in hundreds, but we also learnt a hard lesson there.

When they would move a white flag – or white handkerchief or whatever – we would go across the fields to bring them in. We very soon stopped that because those that had some courage were acting as snipers, and picking our fellows off. We very quickly learnt to wave them in, make them come across the fields to us.

We tore across the country, and this is where I had perhaps my biggest thrill of the war. We were advancing in arrowhead formation; I was the man right in front, with my Bren gunner and the rest of my section right beside me. But my goodness, I never was more alive than then: I was watching every window, every doorway, every bush, the brow of every hill, wondering all the time if the enemy was there.

However, we got down into Syracuse and gradually we had the whole thing under control. At first the Italians, obviously enough I suppose, were very shy of us; they not only shut all their doors, they pulled down all their blinds, nobody appeared on the street, and we went through these deserted streets. Finally we got to the main square of Syracuse, and we started cooking up – meat and vegetable stuff out of tins.

Our next big target was a port called Augusta, which at that time was behind the enemy lines. Our ship was the *Ulster Monarch*, and 40 Commando was now led by Colonel Manners, who had been a lieutenant in Dieppe. Our orders were to take the port of Augusta, the harbour installations, the signal stations, and berths. 'A' troop, the troop I was with, were ordered to take the railway tunnel before the Germans or the Italians could blow it up. It was away up the mountainside, so we had orders to be on our toes and first ashore. We had to run, not double, but run, double file, right through the docks, right through the town of Augusta, and up this awful hill: it was stony, shingle, potholes, scrub, bramble, weeds, nettles, you name it. We had to save this railway tunnel at all costs.

When we eventually got up there, we stopped. We could hear voices in the tunnel. So we surrounded it with our Bren guns and rifles at the ready I called out (in English because I didn't know anything else), 'Come out or we'll open fire!' Eventually two men and a woman came out, holding a white handkerchief. It's as well we didn't open fire, because in that tunnel was practically the whole population of Augusta. They knew that the 8th Army was approaching, they could hear the guns in the distance and the bombers had been over, and they had all gone to the tunnel for safety.

We left some men in charge of them, and went up over the top of the tunnel, up over the hill. I must say, it was there I nearly met my end, because a German rifleman opened fire and I swear I felt the bullet go past my head. We started shouting and roaring, then a young German officer and six Germans appeared. I think to this day it was a complete mistake on their part. They spoke English, and called out, 'Comrades!' I shouted out, 'Put down your guns and come forward!' and they did. When they came forward and saw that there was only five of us, he was furious. But that was it – his guns were behind him, and we had six prisoners.

We held on at Augusta until 8th Army came up. Augusta, as a port, was secured without any damage. We didn't have much more action in Sicily after that. We then went up into the hinterland south of Messina which was full of trees but behind the enemy lines – we'd come in from the sea and tucked our boats into the shore – we hid among the long grass. Out on the road we could see Italian and German soldiers passing up and down, but we weren't ordered to do anything, just to lie low and stay put.

The next thing we knew was that Sicily had been taken. The Americans had gone round the other side, and they had taken Palermo and eventually reached Messina. That was it; all over. I must say we were all smiles, because the sand-dunes on the shore where we landed weren't anything like those at Troon, they were far less hazardous. After I hit the beach and then the road, I gave a great yell of delight, I was so surprised. It was a great feeling.

LIEUTENANT JOHN BRIDGE, RNVR

Up until June 1940 I taught physics at Sheffield Grammar School. When war broke out I felt that I could take no active part in killing another man. So, when the navy wrote to me in May 1940 asking me if I would like to volunteer for bomb disposal I immediately said 'yes', because you needed an honours degree in physics for the job and it didn't involve taking another person's life. In fact the whole idea was to save lives, so it fitted in with my philosophy.

I was interviewed on 6th June 1940, was commissioned on 13th June and joined the first group to be trained in naval bomb and mine disposal. There were eight of us; six were physics teachers, one was the son of an admiral and the other was an explosives expert with ICI. I didn't get to know them very well as the training courses were so short. The first course with the RAF lasted five days, and the second course in mines lasted just three.

We were lucky with our RAF lecturers. The one who taught us about bombs was a civilian called Harrison who had solved the problem of how the electrically operated German fuses worked. The other lecturer was good on shells, which were easier to handle than bombs as they didn't subject you to the same threat. By the end, I felt they had taught us all they knew and was fairly confident about handling electric fuses. However, all of us learned far more later, on the job, than we did on those training courses.

After training I was stationed in Plymouth and was responsible for defusing bombs in the south-west. My responsibility was naval, meaning bombs or mines in dockyards or naval establishments, as well as any found below high-water-mark on the beach. However, there was an understanding between the RAF, army and navy and the vast majority of bombs which I rendered safe were not actually naval responsibility.

I tackled my first bomb on 6th July, just seven days after being stationed in Plymouth. It was 50 kilos in weight, about six foot six inches long and 8 inches in diameter and was lying on the surface in a back street. As it was my first bomb I was a bit cautious. The first thing to do was find the fuse and get at it without disturbing the bomb. If you shook the bomb, you were in trouble because it could be fully armed.

If you could see the fuse, you'd look for the number, which would tell you the sort of fuse you were dealing with. In this case it was ELAZ 19, an electric impact fuse. For these fuses we used a discharger to drain away the current, after which the fuse was safe and you'd unlock the locking screw and remove the fuse. After that the bomb was relatively safe; it only contained high explosive. Luckily, my first bomb was no trouble and I rendered it safe in a few minutes.

Over the next thirteen months I disarmed about 110 bombs, not to mention incendiaries. The most dangerous I faced was in the Plymouth blitz of March 1941, when we had to deal with fifteen bombs in three days. One had fallen in Devonport dockyard and, when I arrived, I found its delayed action fuse was ticking. It was the first time I'd met a bomb with a ticking fuse. Normally I'd have applied a magnetic clock-stopper while removing the fuse, but this was a big bomb, 250 kg, so it had two fuse pockets, one at the back with the ticking clock, and a second, booby-trapped fuse at the front. I had to immobilise the booby trap fuse before I dealt with the clock, because if I put the clock stopper on the clock, the magnetic field might have affected the spring in the booby trap and she would have blown up.

This was a nerve-wracking business. I knew the bomb could blow up at any time, yet I had to immobilise the front fuse – which took at least five or ten minutes – before I could stop the clock.

I immobilised the front fuse without any trouble and then turned to the second fuse, put on the clock stopper and pressed the button. But the clock carried on ticking merrily. So I reversed the current but the clock just would not stop. There was only one thing to do: to go up from the bottom and take the whole thing out. I don't mind telling you, it was frightening. There I was, sitting on this bomb with my spanners, taking the fuse out and thinking, 'I hope this doesn't go off while I'm sitting on it.' All that took about an hour, the worst hour of my life. I was looking death in the face the whole time. Only recently I had seen my first corpses, a husband and wife who'd been beheaded by an unexploded bomb that went through their air raid shelter. It really made you think.

Another tricky customer was in May, two months later. A bomb had dropped into a valve chamber which controlled the flooding of a dry dock in Falmouth. We arrived at low tide and found the bomb lying in six feet of water at the bottom of this chamber, which was 35 feet deep and 6 feet square. I stripped off some of my clothes, climbed down the girders to have a look at the bomb and tried to get my thoughts together. I had no idea how I was going to tackle it.

The bomb had been in the water for two days, so the chances were that the salt water had drained its electrical charge and made it relatively safe. So I prodded the bomb with a boat hook and found that it had been damaged; there was a hole in its side. That gave me a clue. If I lashed a good rope to the boat hook, I could get the hook in the hole and we might be able to lift the bomb to the surface. This would save me diving in and attaching a rope to it underwater. Luckily, it worked and the men hauled the 250 kg bomb to the surface. I watched to make sure it didn't snag on the girders. When we got it to the top, it was a simple matter to defuse it. For that I was awarded a Bar to the George Medal.

After Plymouth I spent six weeks in Portland, and then went to Scapa Flow for the winter. It was bleak and cheerless there. There were no bombs and only a few mines to deal with. I spent most of my time going around the ships, teaching them how to deal with unexploded bombs. During the six months I was there I visited over a hundred ships. Even so, the navy thought I didn't have enough to do so they sent me to lecture to ships' companies on how to behave if taken prisoner-of-war. The amount they knew at that time could be written on the back of a postage stamp. I found it less than satisfying, because I hadn't got a real message to put across.

So it was a God-send for me when they sent me to Simonstown in South Africa. It was a gorgeous life; the Cape Peninsula is one of the finest spots in the world and there was no rationing and no blackout. I lived in a hotel and had plenty of spare time, so I read some confidential documents about the development of underwater weapons. I realised that there was no-one in Simonstown who could tackle such weapons, so I thought I'd better get trained to be a diver, just in case. I put the idea to the admiral in Simonstown and he said, 'Yes, good idea, arrange it forthwith.' So I started training immediately.

On my first dive I only went down 12 feet and my left ear started to bleed. I went to see the doctor and he told me to lay off diving for three weeks and to go down slowly next time. I did, and it was fine. Diving was a novel experience and I enjoyed it. The water was clear and warm and the diving suit was very substantial, which gave me confidence. You had a big helmet with a pipe going up to the air pump, a safety rope around your middle, and a thin line which was the only system of communication in those days. Every fifteen minutes they'd give the line a tug on the surface, and you'd tug back, to show you were all right. Eventually I became a fully qualified diver, and it turned out to be quite fortunate that I was.

In 1943 I was sent to the Mediterranean as the Allies were due to make an assault on the Italian mainland. Many of the nearby ports had been mined and were unusable. News came that a bomb disposal party had been sent to do a recce at Messina harbour in the northeast of Sicily. They had spotted some underwater charges and, unfortunately, five out of the seven men in the party were killed when they tried to tackle the charges. My captain turned to me and said, 'I want you to go to Messina, find out how this accident occurred, what the present situation is and how you are going to tackle it.' Just like that. Clear cut. He was a man after my own heart.

So off I went to Messina, which was still being shelled from across the Straits, but was otherwise fairly safe. I went to see the two survivors who were still in hospital. They said they had located bunches of charges lashed together about forty feet down in the water. They had tried to pull the charges up the surface using a thin line with a hook at the end, with a derrick and a lorry to do the pulling. But while the lorry was moving, the charges had snagged on something, there was an almighty flash, and the consequence was five men dead, two injured.

So that was how the accident occurred. What was the present situation? Fortunately there was a small rowing-boat available and I got one of the ratings to row me around carefully about five yards from the quay so I could look over the stern and down at the bottom. I could see at least two more groups of charges and other things I couldn't identify. So that was the present situation. How was I going to tackle it? The answer was: get me a diving suit; I'm not going to do it the way they tried.

The diving suit arrived on a Sunday and the Allies were due to invade Italy on the following Thursday. In my squad were two qualified divers. One of them was Warrant Officer Stone. He had been trained in the navy and the navy does things by rote: you do this, then you do that, and then you're allowed five minutes for a cigarette. Petty Officer Woods did one dive, but to me the whole thing seemed too slow. So when he came up and took his helmet off, I said, 'From now on I'll do the diving.' I knew it wouldn't go down very well because officers don't usually dive and these trained divers had to be my attendants, which went against the grain. I was well aware of this and ignored it. When Stone didn't call me 'Sir', I didn't bother him. I just told him what to do. And from that point I did all the diving.

I planned the whole of the operation while lying in bed, which is where I did most of my planning. I'd found that the underwater charges were in two parts: three charges and a new mechanism, lashed together with wire. The biggest challenge was to lift them out of the water safely. So I asked W/O Stone and the ratings to make me a special four-legged 'tripod' to support a pulley block. I put four wires around the pulley, one for each part of the underwater charge, and positioned the 'tripod' at the water's edge.

The next challenge was to separate the four parts of the charge. I could have cut through the steel wire with a hacksaw, or I could use a one-ounce charge instead. The method was of considerable importance, so I explained the pros and cons of both to the naval officer in charge, Captain Campbell, who immediately decided I had to do it with the explosive charge (the other method would have been very risky for me). I was heartened to hear his decision. So I went down and put on an inch of plastic explosive, came up and blew it from a safe distance. It worked beautifully; the wire was cut and the charges and the mechanism were all splayed out on the sea bed. So we pulled the mechanism to the top. It consisted of two cylinders with a cable between them. The top mechanism was for firing and the bottom mechanism was a charge, and my hunch was that, if you could just separate the cable, the danger would be over. I called for a volunteer to do the cutting and told him (A/B Peters) to cut the cable strand by strand. It worked. We pulled the three depth-charges to the surface with a lorry and then moved on and retrieved the other set of charges safely, using the same technique and on the same day.

Over the next few days we dealt with 207 depth-charges and unidentified objects. By this time Warrant Officer Stone was calling me 'Sir'. I'd done over twenty dives by the Wednesday morning and the harbour was almost clear. All that remained were some unidentified objects. Captain Campbell came up to me and said, 'You've done enough. You should rest now.' I knew that, with luck, I could finish the job so I disobeyed him and dived again on Wednesday morning. By noon on Wednesday I was able to go to the captain and tell him the harbour was clear.

As a result of that they were able to use the harbour for the Allied landings in the toe of Italy and the invasion went off far faster than planned. At one point they were three days ahead of their schedule. That gave me great satisfaction. For that operation I was awarded the George Cross, POWoods and A/B Peters were awarded George Medals, and W/O Stone a King's Commendation.

It was an amazing war altogether. And all eight members of my original training group survived it. Absolutely incredible.

Engine-Room Artificer Vernon Coles, RN

I left HMS *Faulknor* and went back to Portsmouth to do my trade test for engine-room artificer (ERA). I passed, became an ERA and went over to Victory Barracks which I didn't like very much because, after all the action we'd seen, life was dead. I had a couple of drinks one Sunday and foolishly volunteered for submarines.

I got over to HMS *Dolphin*. I performed the joining routine and medical on the Monday, the Davis Escape in the tank on the Tuesday and, on the Wednesday, I was on the train up to Scotland and Holy Loch. I arrived on board the *Forth* – the submarine parent-ship. The engineer commander said, 'Now you people think you're going to be sat in a classroom, learning all about submarines. Well, you're the first class to arrive and the training for ERAs has changed because we've lost so many. You'll have to do your training at sea, in the boats.'

It was frightening the first time I heard the water rushing up around us in the quick diving tank. After about four or five months they asked for volunteers for Special Underwater Services. Again it was on a Sunday, just after tot time, so I volunteered. That night I was on the train back to *Dolphin* in Gosport. They gathered us on the Tuesday morning. About nine of us had volunteered and we all had to be ERA submariners. So far we'd done a few trips and sunk a couple. That wasn't much, just coastal stuff; nothing to write home about.

We had to go to a selection committee with Lieutenant Hezlet. He was a man's man. We did five days in the tank getting used to being underwater. We used to play ludo on the bottom of the tank on a big steel board and the dice were about four or five inches square. We used to toss them in a bucket and then go swimming after them to see what score we had. On the last day's diving they put wooden blanks in our goggles so we couldn't see anything. We were sent down for two or three hours just to give us confidence in the units.

We used to wear Sladen diving suits. They are very loose and you get in through the apron in the stomach. Then you bring the top down like a jumper and seal the hole with a jubilee clip. The helmet was a soft-top built into the suit. There were eye-pieces like those in a gas-mask. The oxygen supply came through a mouthpiece which was strapped onto a harness on the back.

We were taken over to Portsmouth dockyard but, at this stage, we still didn't have any idea what we'd let ourselves in for. One morning we got into a boat with Lieutenant Hezlet and were given a strict escort to a room in a shed while they phoned for permission to open the inner door. We went into a building and saw our first midget submarine. X3 was the first X-craft but she was already in use for training in Loch Striven, Strathclyde; the one we saw was X4 and she was lying all opened up, her total length when finished was 51 feet. They used to build them in three sections. The bow section was built in Hull, the control room in Portsmouth and the tail in Devonport. We had a good look at her before she was bolted together. It was a little frightening.

We went up to Scotland to Port Bannatyne, on the Island of Bute. We took over a hydropathic hotel there, and a shooting lodge at the top of Loch Striven called Ardtarig, which had belonged to Lord Geddes. The beauty of this was that in 1922, at the time of the 'Geddes Axe', Commander Varley and Commander Bell were among two officers who were kicked out of the Royal Navy, so they had started building their own boat. They were the ones who started the midget submarines. So they had the greatest delight in kicking out Lord Geddes in order to take over his shooting lodge for the midget submarine base.

The ERAs started intense training. We had to carry on diving in cold water. We used to dive in our helmet suits off the old sloop *Tedworth*. We overcame our fear within days. When we went out in X4 for the first time, it was just like sitting in an aeroplane. There were scuttles you could look out from. We soon got our confidence in them.

We had to chop down trees for winter fuel at the loch. They were all owned by Bryant and May so they were not very happy at the end of the war to find the trees gone. We spent half the day training in a midget submarine and the other half chopping down trees.

We all lived in the shooting lodge together. There were lots of officers there, and they took all the rooms except for one. That was for the ERAs to eat and sleep in. It was our mess. They had a delightful bar down below but we didn't have one. Commander Bell did give us the privilege of having a bucket of beer a night. We used to take a cup to our room and quaff it.

We had an advanced training base right up on the north-west coast of Scotland at Loch Cairnbaan. That was known as HHZ, and was where the final training took place. Meanwhile the X-Operational class had been designed and built down in Barrow. When they came along, we could see they'd been thrown together, they were so noisy. They looked delightful though. We had three in a crew; two officers and an ERA.

I wasn't chosen on the first operation, but I was chosen for the passage crew on the X10. That went very well. These new boats were a vast improvement on X3 and X4 but they weren't good enough to go when the time came. We all had to go on to a floating dock. Meanwhile, one chap chucked his hand in, and I got a job with an operational crew. Everybody was entitled to throw their hand in right up to the last minute. Three of them did that, so a few of us had to jump in immediately and take over. This was poor management. When we heard the list of ERAs who had been chosen to go, we knew damn well in our mess that some of them wouldn't make it. If you spoke with an Oxford accent or your father was an officer you were in, never mind whether you could use a spanner or not. It was seamanship officers who were making the decision. They even chose a Frenchman to go – that was foolish because if he'd been taken prisoner he'd have been executed. He decided not to go at the last minute.

Our mission was to attack the German Fleet. They were in Trondheim at that stage but then they moved to Altenfjord. When the German ships came in from the sea, it was noted that they always moored tied up fore and aft, so they were always on the same compass bearing which made the attack easier. The object was to lay two-ton charges, one under the bow and one under the stern to break her back. There were two tons of explosive in each charge. If she didn't sink it was just too bad; she would still be no good as a fighting unit. We were going for the *Lützow*, the *Scharnhorst* and the *Tirpitz*. The explosives were carried in two charges secured to the side of the boats, but they had their own ballast tanks so that when you released them, it didn't make any difference to the trim.

We knew very well that three men couldn't manage. It meant that, if the diver had to go out to cut himself through nets, it left only two men in the boat who could neither carry out the attack successfully nor get the boat back home again. The boat had two control positions. The forward one was the steering position where the ERA sat. He opened the main vents and kingstons to dive and surface the boat. He also had the HP airline and the chart table to his left. In practice, the captain did all that himself. The after control position was where the first lieutenant sat. He had a set of hydroplanes and could steer from that position. He was responsible for the trim, and he controlled the trim and compensating pumps. He also had the engine and tail clutches and the engine and air compressor controls. The captain was at the periscope. If the ERA went out, it just couldn't be done.

Just before the attack the staff decided to put in a fourth member. He was a diver from the Chariots. That improved the situation but also reduced the diving time because the extra man would burn off twenty-five per cent of the oxygen. We couldn't generate oxygen at all.

Then somebody on the staff took the ERA out of the passage crew. When we went on passage, we were due to surface every six hours to run the engine, dry the boat out and put a charge in. It meant that with three in the boat, they were four hours on watch and two hours off. The tow to the *Tirpitz* attack was ten days. That was hell. I've no idea why they did it because the oxygen supply wasn't an issue.

During exercises we used manilla tow-ropes, which had been breaking wholesale. So we tried out nylon tow-ropes and had no trouble whatsoever. When the day came for the big attack, three boats had nylon ropes and three had manilla. The three with nylon ropes were all 'wavy-navy' (RNVR) and the three with manilla were Royal Navy. I don't know why there was such a discrepancy. Don Cameron, VC, was with the Royal Navy Reserve. He was a sea-going man but he was still considered 'wavy-navy'. He wouldn't go unless he had a nylon rope. He knew what he was doing.

The great day came and we sailed. The first boat was X6 under tow to the *Truculent*. We followed half-an hour after behind the *Syrtis* under Lieutenant Jupp. We were sailing at half-hour intervals. Four days out, the first tow-rope broke. That was X8 and she was lost for about thirty-six hours. They got her to the surface and Captain Jack Smart decided to press on on the same compass bearing. He bumped into one of the other towing submarines who then reported back to the Admiralty that he'd got this other boat alongside. Captain Lt. J. P. H. Oakley turned the towing-boat back and they renewed contact. In so doing, X8 bumped against her as they tried to pass the second tow-rope across. It sent one of the charges ticking so they jettisoned it very quickly and tried to make a quick get-away. It was set at 'safe' but it exploded and caused so much damage it set the other charge ticking. They had to drop that one quickly and get away. They scuttled X8, so that was the first boat lost.

X5, X6 and X7 were to attack the *Tirpitz*, X8 and X9 the *Scharnhorst* and X10 the *Lutzow*. X9 was due to surface at eight o'clock in the morning for fresh air so the *Syrtis* slowed down. Our telecommunication with the passage crew X9 had broken down after the third day out, so we had to throw three hand-grenades over the side to tell her to come up. We did that and she didn't surface. All we had was the broken part of a tow-rope to pull in. Our boat hasn't been seen since – she must have gone straight down. Paddy Kieron was the captain, 'Darkie' Heart the able seaman and 'Ginger' Holitt the stoker. They were three damn good people. That was a shocker for us. We reckoned it happened at about six o'clock in the morning because we checked the engine-room register. The ERA on the throttles didn't report the sudden increase in revolutions. That meant that the *Scharnhorst* was out of the attack.

On the sixth day out Godfrey Place's tow-rope broke. He and one other survived but First Lieutenant Bill Whitham and the ERA Bill Whitley went down. X6 and X7 got the *Tirpitz* but no other boats were taken. X6 was taken with Don Cameron, John Lorimer, Dick Kendall, and the ERA, Eddie Goddard. X5 had nylon tow-ropes and was under Henty Creer, but she was lost. He got into the fjord all right but one can only conjecture about what happened to them. So one-and-a-half crews were killed, one-and-a-half were taken prisoner and three got back.

We'd have got them all if we'd had nylon tow-ropes. It was a good attack, but it could have been fantastic. It could have changed the course of the war. We were very depressed because, after all that training we'd been through, we found that everything had gone up in smoke. The whole flotilla was wiped out. We only had six boats and they'd all gone down. There were six more being built.

Later on we picked up X24, which is now outside the museum at Portsmouth.

We were later sent to Scapa Flow to test the defences. There were so many people there to observe us being caught on asdics, or whatever, but we just sailed in with no trouble at all and surfaced in the Flow. They were staggered when they realised they had no defence at all against the enemy, despite the earlier loss of the *Royal Oak*.

After testing the Scapa defences we went into Bergen to attack a floating dock but through sheer bad luck and a multitude of small boats traversing Bergen harbour, Max Shean the captain, had very little opportunity to use the periscope so we got under a large merchant vessel, the *Barenfels*, and sank her instead. The date was 14th April 1944.

LIEUTENANT GODFREY PLACE, RN

While *Unbeaten*, in which I was serving as first lieutenant, was refitting in November 1942 – the captain of the 12th Submarine Flotilla asked me, 'How would you like to join us and sink the *Tirpitz*?' I said that sounded a good idea and the next thing I knew I was preparing for Operation 'Source'.

The 12th Flotilla consisted of midget submarines known as X-class. They were designed by a man called Farley, a submarine captain of the First World War. The boats were just over fifty feet long, weighed 35 tons, and could dive to 300 feet. Each craft carried two huge mines on the outside of the pressure hull, each of which contained two tons of explosive. The method of attack was that you would drop these huge great charges underneath a ship and hope to get away in time before the clockwork timers detonated the mines.

We spent the summer of 1943 training in Scotland. The original plan was for three of the six X-craft in the fleet to attack the *Tirpitz*, two the *Scharnhorst* and one the *Lützow*. All three ships were lying in inlets off Altenfjord, an area of Norway which wasn't terribly well known. We had good pictures taken by reconnaissance planes, but we didn't appreciate what type of anti-torpedo nets they would have to protect the harbours. We assumed they would be similar to the English nets which went down only to about 40 feet and, always with a gap underneath them. On the last practice run all six of us 'escaped' undetected. We really thought it shouldn't be too difficult.

The plan was for the submarine fleet, manned by passage crews, to be towed across to Norway by orthodox submarines and slipped when in reach of Altenfjord. All the X-craft were to go by different routes, so that we couldn't be found together. The attack crew for my craft – the X7 – was to be myself, First Lieutenant Bill Whitham, Lieutenant Bob Aitken and the ERA, Whitley. The X7 left on 12th September, just three weeks after I had married my wife, Althea.

The first two boats to leave had five-inch tow wires, but there were only four-inch wires available for the rest of us, and they all parted at some point during the tow. One boat, X9, was lost on passage. The X8 broke away, unknown to its parent submarine, and paddled around in rough weather until being picked up, but it had taken such a buffeting that it had to be scuttled. So that left just four X-craft: ourselves in X7; my best man, Henty-Creer, in X5; Cameron in X6; and Hudspeth in X10. As we'd lost a third of the fleet on the tow we were ordered to forget the *Scharnhorst* and the *Lützow* and attack just the *Tirpitz*.

I decided we should take over from X7's passage crew on 18th September, although the weather was bad. Just as our parent submarine, the *Stubborn*, got under way again the tow wire parted, so Bill Whitham and I spent three exhausting hours struggling to set up our only remaining spare, a 2.5-inch wire.

The next day we spent mostly sleeping, until the evening when the weather cleared and we came up to the surface to charge our batteries. During supper we heard an alarming noise from up forward. I went up on deck and saw a green and black German mine caught in our tow wire and bumping against the bow. One of the mine's horns had already broken so I quickly pushed it off with my foot while I freed its mooring wire from our tow. I breathed a sigh of relief as I watched the mine floating astern and when I got below we toasted Minerva – the mine with the crumpled horn.

We slipped on the following evening, 20th September, just after dark. I wasn't particularly aware of the other three X-craft, but I assumed they would be somewhere nearby. The going was easy and all the warnings we'd had about tides and the difficulty of finding where you were didn't seem to apply at all.

At dawn the next day X7's internal exhaust pipe split and the fumes had to be extracted with the air compressor. When we entered Altenfjord I could see the *Scharnhorst* at anchor out in the middle of the fjord. It was a tempting sight, but I had to ignore it and carry on to attack the *Tirpitz*.

That evening we cleaned up the boat while Whitley made rough repairs to the exhaust and charged the batteries. Then at 0100 we dived and made our way to the entrance of Kaafjord, where the *Tirpitz* was lying. We found a gap in the anti-submarine nets at the entrance and entered at a depth of forty feet. Just as we were coming up to periscope depth to check our position, I caught sight of a motor-boat and we were forced to dive again, still uncertain where we were. After a reasonable pause I brought X7 up again, but we hit a torpedo net at 30 feet and stopped dead. The water was so clear I could see the mesh of the net through the periscope. It was a double thickness of six-inch square mesh, nothing like the nets we used in England. We tried going slow speed astern but with no success. It took an hour of struggling backwards and forwards to break through the net. Then we sat on the bottom for a while to let the giro steady itself before we pressed on. We were already well behind schedule.

At 6.40am we sighted the *Tirpitz* at a range of about a mile. My plan for the attack was to dive down deep about 500 yards from the target, pass under the torpedo nets at 70 feet and lay the charges, then escape under the nets. At 0705 I took X7 down to 70 feet for the attack but we hit a net and had to disentangle ourselves. We tried again at 90 feet, but got even more firmly stuck this time. When we finally came clear and rose up to the surface I saw that, somehow, we had got under the net and were now about thirty yards from the *Tirpitz*'s port beam. We actually broke surface at that point but no-one spotted us, even when we gave the target's side a glancing blow. So we slid underneath and dropped one charge forward and one aft. As we dropped the second charge at 0720 we heard the first sounds of counter-attack from the enemy. It was not directed at us, as it turned out, but at X6 which had been spotted after dropping its charges.

Our charges had a time delay of about an hour but the timers had proved unreliable so it was imperative we escape through the nets as quickly as possible. The charges dropped by the other X-craft might go up at any time after 0800. For the next three-quarters of an hour we nosed around just feet from the sea floor, looking for a gap in the nets and rapidly losing all sense of our exact position. We tried most places along the bottom of the nets, and even broke water sometimes, but couldn't find a way out anywhere. The HP air was getting dangerously low and eventually the situation was so desperate that I decided to try going over the top of a curtain net between two buoys. We surfaced, gave a strong thrust and flopped over the net. Then we dived down to the bottom and tried to get as far away from the *Tirpitz* as we could before the charges went up. But at sixty feet we hit yet another net and while we were struggling to get free the explosion went up, a continuous roar that seemed to last whole minutes.

The explosion shook us free of the net but also damaged X7, so I took her down to the bottom to assess the damage. The situation was not promising. Water was coming in through the hull glands, but none of the pumps worked and our HP bottles were empty. When we surfaced to check our position our night periscope was hit by enemy fire, and at this point I decided to abandon ship. As the Germans were dropping depth-charges we decided to try a surface surrender. With some trepidation I opened the fore hatch just enough to allow me to wave a white sweater. The firing stopped immediately so I climbed out on to the casing, still waving the sweater. We had surfaced close to a battle practice target so I thought, 'That's fine. I'll hold on to the practice target and bring the crew out.' Just then, the X7 bumped into the target and the curved side of the target forced our bows down, letting water into the hatch before I had time to close it. Unfortunately the boat hadn't got enough buoyancy to stay on the surface and she went down, leaving me standing on the practice target. I felt fairly confident that the others would get out all right but, as it turned out, the only one to escape alive was Aitken, who was a trained diver, and he was picked up in a comatose condition. Whitham and Whitley had run out of oxygen before they could escape.

So there I was, standing on the battle target, wearing just my under-clothes, sea boot stockings and army boots. I felt ridiculous as I was taken on to the quarter-deck. The *Tirpitz* was in chaos. One chap kept running up to me and saying, 'How many boats?' and 'You will be shot.' I had a sudden vision of Gabby, the town crier in a cartoon film of *Gulliver's Travels*, saying, 'You can't do this to me, you can't do this to me – I've a wife and kids, millions of kids.' What I actually said was, 'I'm an English naval officer and I expect to be treated with due courtesy.' But I wish I had known at the time that the likelihood of my being shot on a crowded deck was very small.

Also aboard the *Tirpitz* were Cameron and the crew of X6 who had scuttled their craft and surrendered after laying their charges.

I spent the rest of the war as a POW in Germany. Initially I was taken to the Naval Interrogation camp. This was a complete waste of time because the only secret about the operation was the fact that small submarines were able to breach their defences at all.

I reached the POW camp nine days before Christmas 1943. There I was, at the ripe old age of twenty-two, thinking, 'I'm going to get out as soon as I can.' So a group of us attempted a wire-cutting escape in about the second week of January. When it failed we were all given a month in solitary confinement which was very pleasant because you could have a bath in front of the stove, on your own. When I got back to the main camp everyone was saying, 'Silly young fool, he's only been here five minutes'.

By that time it was clear that Germany was going to lose the war, so I decided to sit it out. We had a radio and could listen to the news from everywhere. I heard about my VC in February 1944 when it was announced on the news. There was a little bit of a celebration, but I was too busy feeling hungry and thirsty to care very much about the award.

It was only when I flew home at the end of the war that I heard what had happened to the rest of the X-craft. X-10 had got lost in a fjord and was picked up by one of the parent craft, and X-5 was lost with all hands, no-one knows when or where.

Eventually I went to receive my award from the King and the Queen. This was the first investiture she had attended so we were given a special briefing. The chap said, 'The Queen will probably ask where you got your award and all you have to tell her is in which regiment or squadron and give the theatre of war.' The Queen actually asked, 'What are you doing now?' I was then working on future X-craft designs which was supposed to be super-secret, so I couldn't think of anything to say. Then I remembered that the King had been to see us a little time before, so all I said was, 'His Majesty knows!'

LIEUTENANT HENRY LEACH

By early 1943 the real contribution to the war of continuing to run convoys to Russia had decreased markedly. On the other hand the enemy threat in those Northern waters had been maintained at much the same level. For although the U-boat threat had been reduced the surface element (now the battleship *Tirpitz*, the battlecruiser *Scharnhorst* and the pocket battleship *Lützow* together with destroyers) was stronger. Thus the military case for further Russian convoys now turned mainly on their value as 'bait' to tempt the German surface forces into action. The convoys ceased.

But there were also political considerations and by the autumn it was decided to re-start the convoys later that year. Paradoxically the conditions for the reception of the ships at the Russian terminal were hopelessly inadequate. It appeared that the Russians, far from being grateful for vital war stocks run through at considerable risk and at the cost of many brave lives, went out of their way to be difficult and obstructive.

The merchant ships berthed at Murmansk, one of the gloomiest towns in the northern hemisphere. Repeatedly bombed by the Germans from airfields just across the Norwegian frontier, it had been reduced to a state of rubble and dejection. In winter the uncaring inhabitants shuffled about like ghosts. In summer the whole town stank with a stench so vile as to be hardly bearable.

The disorganisation, muddle and inefficiency on the part of the shore authorities were incredible and the effect on the morale of the seamen was deep.

Conditions were no better for the escorting warships. They were allocated an open anchorage at Vaenga, to seaward of Murmansk in the same Kola Inlet.

Being in Kola was like being in a trap with the knowledge that it might be sprung at any moment. The amount of rest and relaxation obtained was commensurate and nearly everyone was glad to put to sea again where they felt that at least they were 'in with a chance'.

Admiral Sir Bruce Fraser, Commander-in-Chief Home Fleet, knew all this from his Commanding Officers. Now, with the restarting of the convoys, he determined to visit Kola to see things for himself and to try to sharpen the Russian Commanders into doing better. Flying his flag in the battleship *Duke of York*, he sailed from Scapa Flow with the cruiser *Jamaica* and four destroyers to provide distant cover to Convoy JW 55A which had left Loch Ewe on the West coast of Scotland on 12th December.

At that time I was a young Lieutenant of twenty in *Duke of York*. My action station was Officer of the Quarters of 'A' Turret – four 14-inch guns each firing a shell of over 3/4 ton to a range of 18 miles and each manned by fifty men.

A few days before departure our own captain (Brian Schofield) after only three weeks in command, had hurried south to stand by his wife who was desperately ill. Twenty-four hours before we sailed Guy Russell transferred to us from *Nelson*, an unusual occurrence which led the discerning to suspect that something out of the ordinary was impending. Guy Russell was a big man in every sense of the word – physically, in leadership, in charm and in his understanding of human nature. He had a well-developed and unique method of registering commendation or reproof to his subordinates, based on his intimate knowledge of London. For the former he would grin and drawl 'Bond Street', while a coldly growled 'that was pretty Whitechapel' had the opposite effect.

The visit to Russia, though the first of its kind by a British battleship, was unremarkable. We entered in a howling snowstorm and left a few days later in another one. *Duke of York, Jamaica* and their escorts returned south to Akureyri in Iceland to refuel. On the night of 23rd December they put to sea again in distant support for the next convoy which had sailed from Loch Ewe three days earlier. It was this latter convoy, JW 55B, leaving as the slower earlier JW 55A arrived at Kola, that it was hoped would provide irresistible bait to the German surface forces lurking ready to pounce in the North Norwegian fjords. Further bait was provided by a third convoy, RA 55A, sailing south from Kola on 22 December with a heavy destroyer escort. To the north additional distant cover came from the cruisers *Belfast*, *Norfolk* and *Sheffield*. This British trap was now set; would the Germans spring it?

The weather had deteriorated and even a great ship like *Duke of York* was bucketing about in a manner which precluded anyone lying on a camp bed for long. Few slept much. Over all hung an air of expectancy and uncertainty. What was the enemy up to? When would we meet him? Would we meet him at all? Doubts on the latter generated the greatest anxiety.

We did not meet him that night. But soon after the black dawn of a long, dark, storm-ridden Boxing Day, cold and fatigue were ameliorated by definite news of our impending target and for the first time the real prospect of action that day. *Scharnhorst* had attacked the convoys but had been successfully intercepted and had withdrawn, later to attack again from a different quarter and again be driven off. This was a much-needed tonic.

Scharnhorst turned south, pursued by our cruisers. This presented the Commander-in-Chief with a dilemma: would she attempt to break out into the Atlantic to carry out further raiding operations like the *Bismarck*? Or would she return to her Norwegian base? Instinct inclined the C-in-C to the latter view and he adjusted course to intercept accordingly. Events were to prove him right.

Bruce Fraser's tactical plan was clear. Unless the enemy opened fire first, *Duke of York* would not engage until the range had closed to 12,000 yards; *Jamaica* would illuminate the target with starshell and was disposed accordingly.

Then came the long-awaited order:

'All positions stand-to.'

In an instant tiredness, cold and seasickness were shed and all hands became poised for their individual tasks.

'Follow Director,' and the huge turrets swung round in line with the Director Control Tower.

'All guns with armour-piercing and full charge load, load, load.' The clatter of the hoists as they brought up the shells and cordite charges from the magazines. The rattle of the rammers as they drove them into the chambers of the guns. The slam of the breeches as they closed. These were music to all.

Then a great stillness for seemingly endless minutes, disturbed only by the squelch of the hydraulics as Layers and Trainer followed the pointers in their receivers from the Director.

'Broadsides' and the interceptors completing the firing circuits right up to the Director Layer's trigger were closed.

A glance at the Range Receiver whose counters were steadily inexorably ticking down until . . . 12,000 yards . . . the fire gong rang 'ting ting' and . . . CRASH, all guns fired and the Battle of North Cape had started.

It is an indifferent view through a turret periscope, especially in rough weather, but two things of significance stick in my mind. The first was that when *Jamaica*'s starshell illuminated the target, *Scharnhorst*'s turrets were clearly seen to be still trained fore and aft. Astonishingly, after being trailed by our northerly cruisers for the whole of that day, she was caught completely by surprise by *Duke of York* and *Jamaica*. I heard later that the captain and admiral on *Scharnhorst* were obsessed by the risk of RDF transmissions being intercepted by Direction Finding equipment with which the British were known to be equipped. Although they had considerable faith in the effectiveness of their RDF, they preferred not to use it for this reason.

The second incident was that at an early stage in the action my no. 3 gun misfired, so reducing my turret's output by 25%. The rules for this were unequivocal: wait 30 minutes, open the breech, remove the cordite cartridges and drop them overboard. Entirely prudent for peacetime but arguably too rigid for a war situation in which time and output were crucial to success. I compromised – waited five minutes and ordered the gun to be unloaded and the charges ditched. The God of Battles was with me.

Scharnhorst turned east and, despite the best endeavours of *Duke of York*'s Engine Room Department, it became clear that she had the legs of us in those conditions. Steadily, gallingly, the range counters clicked up as the enemy drew away. I cannot adequately describe the growing frustration of those few who were in a position to realise what was happening: to have achieved surprise, got so close, apparently done so well, and all for nothing as the enemy outpaced us into the night. To conserve ammunition fire was checked when the range ceased to be effective on an ahead bearing where the ship's movement generated the greatest fire control errors. The resultant despondency was profound.

Suddenly the range steadied, then started to close. Had we done it after all? We gained rapidly; our own secondary armament of 5.25-inch illuminated with starshell and fire was re-opened with the 14-inch. We closed right in to point blank range. *Scharnhorst* was ablaze from end to end. Men could be seen leaping over the side into the icy sea, and death within minutes, to escape the inferno. It was a terrible sight. Thirty-six survivors, including one Petty Officer but no officers, were picked up by the destroyers and later transferred to *Duke of York*. It was over.

One's feelings? Almost a blankness of shock at what had been done. Some relief that it had gone the way it had. Little exultation – the closing scenes were too grim for that and the remoteness of actions at sea precludes hate between sailors. Pride in achievement. And a great weariness. It had been a long day's night.

CORPORAL JOE HUMPHREY, RM

With all the reinforcements coming in, we moved over to the other, western, side of Italy, and started training on the hills around Naples. These were very steep hills with orange and lemon groves. We would climb these steep hills and then run down them at full speed. The coming-down business meant you took two or three steps and jumped! Land and run again, jump! And run again. It sounds dangerous, but it was good fun.

This was January 1944. Eventually on about 14th or 15th January we moved up to the front line in front of Monte Cassino. Monte Cassino was the strong point of the Gustav line, and it was manned by German paratroops who were well entrenched behind barbed wire fences and minefields. In front of that was the Garigliano river. We were to open up the big assault on Monte Cassino.

We had to go across the Garigliano in rubber dinghies. The river was in full flood; by the time we got to the other side we were slightly downstream to where we should have been, but we eventually got on to a sunken road and then all hell was let loose. This time, instead of being in the front, my section was at the back. In all the other raids we had led them in. In this one we were at the back, and we began to take casualties. The first one to go was a good friend of mine, Tom Ockwell. He stepped on a mine which killed him, and Sergeant Shea, coming behind as platoon sergeant, was blinded. And the fellow in front was torn up the back.

We did what we could for them, but there wasn't much we could do, because we had to go on, but we left them a couple of extra field dressings in case they were needed. Then another good friend of mine, Lance-Corporal Taffy Hastings, also stepped on a mine, and was killed. That night lots of our friends were killed either by mines, hand-grenade or bullets. And eventually I was hit in the shoulder myself, by shrapnel from a hand-grenade. I fell, and Jimmy Steedman, got over to me. 'All right?' he asked. I said, 'No. I can't see.' I just couldn't believe it. He said, 'You must . . .' I said, 'I can't see!!' Little did I know, but that was me on the way back to England.

It was explained to me later on in hospital at Naples that the shrapnel had hit my shoulder, but that the suction of the grenade had taken my eyes. I was told that if a bomb was up against a window, it'll blow it in; if it's a certain distance from it, it'll suck it out. Well, it had sucked my right eye out, and squashed my left one. So, I was on my way back, thinking I was a prisoner, because I was being carried by Germans. Eventually I was put down and this English fellow spoke to me, asked me how I was. I asked him, 'Are you a prisoner too?' He said, 'You're not a prisoner!' I said, 'Those Germans are carrying me.' He said, 'No no no. They brought you in, you're their passport.

We're going to get you back across to Garigliano now.' They took me across the river, and I was lying in this house called a casualty clearing station, where this German was screaming something I couldn't understand. I said, 'Oh, for Christ's sake, shut your big mouth.' I'd seen our fellows killed, and wounded, I knew all hell was being knocked out of them up there. Then a RAMC bloke came over to me and he says, 'Look, you have to, er, leave him alone. He's a German soldier, he's just lost a leg right up to the hip.'

We went back to Naples, to hospital there, and the casualties were so vast that every bed was full; there were stretchers up the middle aisle. Two days after I was in, the Matron came stumping up the ward. 'Corporal! Is that yours?' She put a condom in my hand. 'That's disgusting,' she said. I said, 'Wait a minute'; she didn't, she went away, so I said to the ward sister later, 'Would you ask the matron to come and see me?' I had to explain to her that when we were doing the commando landings, we put our paper money in one of these things and tied it in a half hitch. I was forgiven after that. But, a few days later, she came to me and said, 'Do you know a Sergeant Shea?'; I said, 'I do, he's my platoon sergeant.' She said, 'Well, he's in a side ward, and he's not too well. There's another bed in there – would you mind sharing it with him, because we think that if there's somebody there he knows, it will help.' The funny thing was, when I did join Bill Shea in the side ward, he went quiet. He'd been shouting, 'Share that among you!' and all this sort of thing, trying to throw hand-grenades all over the place. He'd been heavily hit, and he was delirious.

Eighteen of us flew out on a plane from Naples to Tunis, all eye cases. The RAF bloke in charge of the plane told us that a German fighter had come up. Our plane was marked with a Red Cross and this German fighter circled right round us and then let us go. We finished up in military hospital in Tunis, for about a week, and then we went up by hospital train to Algiers.

Sharing the eye ward there were quite a few blokes who later became St Dunstaners. On the way home the physiotherapists were working on my shoulder, which had been pretty badly damaged, and I began to hear of how a blind person could work as a physiotherapist. And that is what I became.

LIEUTENANT BILL JOHNSON, RN

I first met Captain Walker when I was on the secretarial staff of Captain 'D', Liverpool. It was a shore base with a lovely big house; from there we used to administer all the convoys going in and out of Liverpool across the Atlantic and to Freetown. I was the CB officer, in charge of the distribution of confidential books and ciphers to all the ships on the convoys. We used to get reports of proceedings in from all the senior officers of the escorts. The reports from HMS *Stork*, the 36 Escort Group commanded by Commander Walker soon came in to prominence. At one point while under attack by U-boats, Commander Walker found he had to make a vital decision: whether to leave the convoy only partially protected while he (and possibly another ship) went off to hunt the U-boat, or to stay with the convoy in order to give it full protection. He decided that the only way to stop the U-boat sinking any further ships was to put it out of action, so he went over and sunk it. We always looked forward to reading his reports of proceedings – they were written in his own inimitable style, lots of touches of humour.

Eventually, after doing this trip, the powers that be thought he needed a rest. So they promoted him to Captain and made him Captain 'D' Liverpool, a shore-based job, so then I was actually on his staff. He lived quite close to me and we got to know him socially. While he was captain there, we also formed a concert party which we took to hospitals and service establishments. We called it the 'Shakers' and he was one of our fans, always coming to our shows. During that time he managed to get the ear of the Commander-in-Chief, Sir Max Horton, and was able to put some of his somewhat revolutionary ideas to him. Eventually he got his way, and support groups for the Atlantic convoys were formed. The problem was that the convoys had to go across the Atlantic with escorts, and there was a black gap in the middle where there was no aircraft cover. The U-boats knew this and they used to indulge in wolf-pack tactics, forming-up in order to attack the ships going across this unprotected area. The function of the support group was to protect the convoys and their escorts going across that two hundred miles gap. If a U-boat popped up we could detect it up to a hundred miles away by HFD (high frequency direction finding), and go off and hunt it as a group, still leaving the convoy fully protected. Captain Walker was made Senior Officer of the new founded second escort, or support group, in *Starling*, an AA-sloop, now called a frigate. The others were *Wren, Wild Goose, Cygnet, Kite* and *Woodpecker*, all sloops.

In the first four months in the *Starling* they sank five U-boats. At this point I had spent about two and a half years on Captain 'D's staff at Liverpool and I was asked if I had any ideas about moving on. I said, 'Well there's only one job I'd like and I don't suppose that I've got a hell of a chance of getting it, and that is secretary to Captain Walker.' Before I knew where I was I was at sea in HMS *Wren* in order to get my sea legs, which I thoroughly enjoyed. We had one of the waiters from the Savoy as our wardroom steward, so everything was done very well, silver service and everything. We were to go down as guinea-pigs to try and find a defence against a new weapon – the first guided missile, called a 'Chase-me-Charlie'. These were mounted on small gliders and released from the parent plane which directed it by radio towards the target. We had a lot of scientists on board to try and work out a defence – they hoped that we'd be attacked by it. The only defence they had discovered was an electric razor – it messed up the radio-control! So we all brought up a lot of electric razors so that, if one of these planes appeared we could switch them on in the hope that the baby 'plane' would turn around and blow its parent plane up.

At that time the U-boats had also developed acoustic torpedoes which were attracted by the noise of the screws (or propellers) attacking the ship. They would home on to those screws. One way to stop them was to reduce speed to seven knots. However, the *Starling* had also got a new secret defensive weapon called the Foxer. The idea of this Foxer was to make lots of noise well behind the screws by towing lots of rusty old iron behind the ship. The *Starling* tried it on but they got caught up with the wires, so they let it go and Captain Walker refused to use a Foxer again.

The Foxer put the *Starling* slightly out of action, so he sent a signal across to *Wren* saying that he was changing commanding officers over and coming across so he could carry on the operation from *Wren*. He came aboard with his staff. He had another secretary with him at the time who came over as well. I was more or less a passenger at that point; it wasn't until we got back to Liverpool for the next trip that I officially took over duties as his secretary.

The night before I took up the job, I'd arranged to have a farewell party ashore. It wasn't until that evening that I discovered I was supposed to be on board right then. So I transferred the party from ashore to the ward room of the *Starling*. Everybody turned up and whilst we were having drinks before dinner there was a knock on the ward door, and there was Captain Walker. 'I'm sorry to interrupt your party but my steward is ashore; may I have dinner in the wardroom?' Needless to say, we were only too delighted. We put him at the head of the table, we thought naturally he would sit there, but he said he wouldn't hear of it. He said, 'This is your party, I'm only a gate-crasher.' He went down to the end of the table with some of the Wrens and we had a hilarious evening – that's when I saw him do his party trick of standing on his head and drinking a glass of beer. He would then invite people to do the same thing and when they were upside down he would pour a pint of beer down their trouser leg.

On the first action I was involved in, we went to sea in October 1943. We were in the *Starling*. We had some very rough weather, we were hove to for about four days. I was thrown out of my bunk into about twelve inches of water in my cabin. After that I slept in a hammock, immediately outside the captain's cabin and below the bridge. Not only was that more comfortable on the rough sea, but it meant that if any signals came in for the captain I could take them in to him. That is how I knew, particularly on the sixth trip, that he never had more than four hours consecutive sleep, because I was the chap who had to wake him up with the signals.

Walker was in charge on the bridge. He was a very strong disciplinarian, but a very caring man. He always took requests for compassionate leave very sympathetically. He liked to be on the bridge as much as possible, because he liked to be seen by the ship's company in order to give them confidence. He was also a shy man, he didn't show his feelings except occasionally when people didn't do as he hoped, then he would throw his cap on the ground and jump on it.

On that first trip, on 6th November, we attacked a U-boat with a 'creeping' attack. The *Kite* had picked up a radar echo and the lookout spotted the U-boat as it came out of a patch of fog about five hundred yards ahead. It was in such a good position to have a shot at the *Tracker*, which was a small aircraft carrier, and made a good target. *Kite* fired some charges immediately. The U-boat did fire a torpedo, but with the dropping of the depth-charge and *Tracker* turning away, it missed. *Starling*, *Kite* and *Woodcock* were stalking the U-boat; we were in asdic contact. We got reports from the cabin on the bridge. I was on the other side of the bridge making notes of what was going on. The timing was particular, if we increased speed too much we would have become targets of one of these 'gnats', these acoustic torpedoes. However, we had to increase speed so as to drop depth-charges without blowing ourselves up.

On this occasion it was pitch black, but they had a steady asdic contact of the ship. We followed the U-boat and then at dawn, *Woodcock* was instructed by Walker by loudhailer to switch off his asdic. He then directed *Woodcock* to a position over the U-boat. The U-boat knew when they were being pinged; they could hear the attacking ship as the pings on its hull got more rapid, and take evasive action. It was busy concentrating on the steady pinging of the *Starling*, which was some distance away. So then the *Woodcock* increased speed, and it wasn't until the depth-charges dropped that they knew she was there: they never knew what hit them. It was so simple. That was the 'creeping' attack which we did very successfully.

You could hear the underwater explosions and very often you could smell the diesel oil. Bodies eventually came to the surface. There were no survivors. The only thing there was the headless and tailless torpedo which came to the surface. We had to pick up bits of wreckage, as evidence, and we had to find human remains in order to claim a kill. At first the doctor had to pickle these human remains, but when they arrived at the Admiralty it was opened by a Wren who passed out on the spot, so they didn't think that was quite such a good idea. However, we had to take some evidence back.

The *Kite* said it had been a large U-boat, a 'Milch cow', used to supply the other ones. We spliced the mainbrace and I put on a show over the radio to celebrate.

That was the first U-boat, sunk at 7.30. At 1.00 we got a HF/DF bearing on another U-boat, about twenty miles away. Now it was their turn, the *Woodcock* and *Kite*, to look after and shield the aircraft carriers. The *Starling* went in with the *Wild Goose*. *Wild Goose* had a good contact but *Starling's* giro compass was thrown out of action by a shallow depth-charge explosion. When this had been repaired, Captain Walker directed *Wild Goose* into another creeping attack, to fire twenty-six charges. Something went wrong and she only fired ten. Walker was in a fury at his own mistake, because his most trusted ship had let him down and because, in the middle of the attack, he was told that his giro compass was not two degrees out of line but nine. He threw his cap on the deck and jumped on it. *Wild Goose* only said, 'This is most unusual.' He started to send a rude signal to them when he was interrupted by a loud underwater explosion and the asdic operators reported unmistakable breaking-up noises. Diesel oil came to the surface and, believe it or not, up popped another headless and tailess torpedo. So, instead of sending this stinker to the *Wild Goose*, he sent a message to splice the mainbrace. In his report of proceedings he said, 'I would have staked my last penny that the attack was bum, and I should have lost my money.'

The sixth trip of the second support group was in January 1944. This time we were with two aircraft-carriers, the *Nairana* and *Activity*. The *Starling* had with her the *Wild Goose*, *Kite*, *Wren*, *Woodpecker* and *Magpie*. The captain would issue very brief orders to all the commanding officers, as he didn't want people signalling to ask him for instructions. They were to do as they thought best, but tell him what they were doing. They knew exactly what they had to do anyway because we had the plan of campaign; as soon as we got the U-boats, the black flags went up and we were off. We also knew exactly what the other people were doing. We worked very much as a team.

Captain Walker didn't like working with the carriers. However, we were instructed to take our own aircraft with us as we couldn't get aircraft support across the middle of the Atlantic, which in theory was absolutely splendid, but the mid-Atlantic can be a rough sea. It is extremely difficult to get planes off a heavy deck and almost impossible to get them back on again. But they did make jolly good targets for the U-boats and acted as a bait.

This was to prove itself when on 1 February, the *Wild Goose* suddenly got a shout from the bridge that there was a submarine echo to starboard. It looked as if the U-boat was trying to get a shot at the *Nairana*. Commander Wemyss from the *Wild Goose* immediately ordered, 'Hard to starboard, full speed, hoist the attacking flag, tell leader on radio that I am attacking.' The *Wild Goose* attacked; *Magpie* went to go in with her. *Wild Goose* told the

Nairana to get out of the way, then dropped a ten-charge pattern to scare the U-boat off before it could target the aircraft-carriers.

Captain Walker then told the *Kite*, *Wren* and *Woodpecker* to screen the *Nairana*, while he went in to join the *Wild Goose* and *Magpie*. *Magpie* tried an attack but without success, so she went off to assist in screening the carrier. The *Wild Goose* and the *Starling* carried on hunting. Walker said, 'When the *Magpie* left to join the remainder of our force, *Wild Goose* handed me an asdic contact with the Boche on a plate.'

They were in contact with the U-boat by asdic when they carried out an operation 'plaster'. This involved attacking abreast: they went in at five knots, dropping in all some sixty depth-charges set to explode between 500 and 700 feet at five-second intervals. You can imagine the explosions. They were terrific, throwing from the stern and away from the stern.

After dropping the depth-charges all sorts of things came up: oil, clothing, planks of wood, pulped life jackets, books and the mangled remains of bodies. That was U-502. Again we sent out our boats for the remains and spliced the mainbrace.

Five days after the attack on the *Nairana*, we joined forces with the west-bound convoy, SL147. We were told that, by virtue of seniority, Captain Walker was not only senior officer of our group, but also of the escort. He was in charge of all the ships in the convoy. It was a terrific responsibility – there were eighty-one ships and two aircraft-carriers. Joining a convoy at sea is quite an experience. You go for days and days seeing nothing else but the five or six ships that you're in company with, and then suddenly on the horizon you see the silhouettes. As you get nearer, it's rather like coming into a town: it looks like civilisation. This particular convoy seemed pleased to see us. We had signals that there were at least fifteen U-boats converging on them. Actually there were twenty-six, although we didn't know that at the time.

Wild Goose was six miles ahead of the convoy in the port quarter when her port bridge lookout sounded an alarm which rang through silence, to be repeated in dozens of ships spread across miles of the Atlantic. Their lookout had sited a U-boat on the surface with only the conning tower showing, about a mile and a half away. Walker ordered the convoy to alter course. The U-boat was preparing to ram, but realising he had been sighted he crash-dived. But instead of diving deep and taking avoiding action, he stayed at periscope depth to keep track of *Wild Goose*'s movements. Again, the same Able Seaman who spotted him drew attention to this, but they couldn't get the depth-charges to bear on it. All they could do was fire with the machine-guns. This eventually persuaded it to down periscope and dive away.

Wild Goose then got an asdic contact and directed the *Woodpecker* into a 'creeping attack'. When the last depth-charge had exploded the *Starling* came up. Walker took one look at the surging water left by the depth charges and sent a signal across to the *Woodpecker*: 'Look what a mess you've made.' They did a cross-check and Walker then directed the *Woodpecker* into a creeping attack. She dropped twenty-six sets of depth-charges to explode at maximum depth, probably about 700 feet, although they could have gone much deeper. (As the depth-charges were improved over time they were able to go deeper and deeper.) There was a tremendous explosion – we had got it!

We fired snow-flake rockets so we could see the wreckage. We picked up a German coat and some other things. From Naval Intelligence later on we were able to recognise it as the U-762, a big one. Sometimes the wreckage gave us clues as to what it was. We spliced the mainbrace that day.

The next U-boat was ten miles ahead of the convoy. It was found through HF/DF signalling by wireless on the surface at 6.00am the next day. Walker sent *Magpie* and *Kite* to investigate. *Magpie* was still some distance astern of *Kite*, who was racing to catch up. However, she sighted a U-boat as it came out of a patch of mist, steaming fast toward the convoy and only 800 yards away. Fortunately the commanding officer realised the danger of being attacked by a 'gnat', or acoustic torpedo, so as the U-boat crash-dived he did the usual drill, reducing speed to seven knots and firing a single depth-charge in the hope of counter-mining a gnat before it could strike home. A second or two later a violent explosion threw a column of water twenty yards on *Kite*'s port beam. The depth-charge had actually counter-mined the 'gnat' warheads, causing a double explosion.

Kite then increased to full speed and ran over the diving position to fire a full pattern of ten depth-charges. She got no result, so set off to hunt the U-boat. At the moment when *Kite* and the U-boat sighted each other, *Wild Goose* obtained a radar contact with another U-boat which was little more than a mile away on the convoy's port bow. Also fearing a gnat torpedo, she reduced speed to seven knots and fired off a starshell. The first shower revealed the U-boat about to dive. Then there was an explosion – the gnat, having failed to pick up on the propellers, had exploded at the end of its run.

We couldn't see what was happening. We didn't know at that time what they were doing. It wasn't until we joined *Wild Goose* at about 8.30 in the morning that Captain Walker was again handed the asdic contact 'on a plate' by *Wild Goose*. He directed *Wild Goose* on two creeping attacks. These gnats were all about, and another went off at the end of its run.

After we'd fired the depth-charges on the second creeping attack, oil came to the surface, although there was no other sign of damage. The carriers which had been diverted steamed near the *Starling*, and the senior officer there signalled Walker, 'Good Luck. Hope to see you again.' Walker replied, 'We seem to have nabbed a couple of particularly tough babies, will be rejoining soon.'

Just as the convoy was moving away, a shallow-running torpedo was suddenly spotted racing towards the ship. There was no time to pick up speed or take avoiding action. Walker immediately ordered, 'Hard to Port, stand by depth-charges, shallow setting, fire!' The U-boat had come up to the surface, fired this torpedo and then gone down again. We all fully expected to be hit – many sailors were flat on the deck but, incredibly, the depth-charge counter-minded the torpedo, which exploded only five or ten yards from the quarter deck.

The ship seemed to leap in the air. A huge wave rolled over her. The compass went out of action, electrical switches were thrown open, but the greatest tragedy was that every bottle in the wardroom was shattered into fragments.

There wasn't time to be frightened. This situation illustrated the discipline that the captain was able to exhort. If they'd paused to think, if they hadn't been so disciplined, they would have said that the captain must be crazy firing a depth-charge at this slow speed. But thanks to the training and discipline they immediately did exactly what they were told and saved our lives.

Almost without a pause more depth-charges were thrown out away from the ship while we went hard to port. Then *Starling* went with *Wild Goose* for more briefings and attacks. We followed up with another 'operation plaster' at about 10.00 in the morning, which finally produced human remains and wreckage. Captain Walker then went on to see what was happening to the *Kite* and the *Magpie*, which were ten miles ahead. They hadn't had any joy in attacking, although again on one occasion a gnat had been fired in self-defence as the *Kite* had stepped in to begin her depth-charge barrage. Again the depth-charges immediately counter-mined the gnat torpedo. From the *Starling* we could see this terrific crash, and through all the water that was in the air it looked as though *Kite* had been hit. Then when the splash died down we could see that she was still there. So, the attack was continuing. It was close enough for us to see.

Next, the *Magpie* went in with a creeping attack but got no results, until Walker suddenly remembered that the *Magpie* was equipped with a hedgehog – a multi-barrelled mortar bomb thrower that could destroy only if one or more bombs scored direct hits. He directed the *Magpie* into a hedgehog attack, which was from the head of the ship instead of the stern. It actually scored a direct hit. According to his report of proceedings, 'I was highly tickled by this hedgehoggery. Complicated instruments are normally deemed essential to score an occasional hit with this weapon. But under my order over the RT, *Magpie* steamed into attack and fired off her bombs when told, as if firing depth-charges for a creeping attack. To score two bullseyes, like that first shot, with somebody else's 'hedgehog' a thousand yards away was, of course, a ghastly fluke, but amusing considering no instruments at all were used, for his gyro compass had been put out of action from that other attack. That was the fourth attack of the day and Walker had been in command for thirty-six hours without a break. There were 81 merchant ships depending on him, two aircraft carriers, a close escort of six and our own sloops. And we did it without any loss of ships.

By this time we had been in action quite a long time, but we were getting sandwiches and cocoa. He snatched his first two hours' sleep for nearly three days after the fourth attack when we'd run out of depth-charges. We had a Norwegian tanker come alongside us so the lieutenant could take over the bridge while the captain was resting. We went along in line abreast with this tanker and they transferred all these depth-charges at sea. The ships were both rolling heavily but had to be twenty-five yards apart, and we had to keep them at that distance while the charges were hauled over singly by hand. This was a very dangerous operation, as each roll of the tanker threatened to capsize the sloop. Sometimes the depth-charges sank below the surface or were carried away to bump dangerously across the ship's side. With the very last depth-charge they sent along a bottle of brandy, which we were glad to see.

While we were loading the depth-charges, *Wild Goose*, *Woodpecker* and *Magpie* had gone to protect another convoy, HX278. On the next day, 12th February, they came across a U-boat creeping up on the convoy from the stern. *Wild Goose* as usual made contact and then went in with the *Magpie*. After an hour's attack, during which some fifty-odd depth-charges were dropped, *Wild Goose* made firm contact at last and the commander, Captain Wemyss, tired of what he called this 'grouping around and dot-and-carry-on business', went in for a full blooded plaster attack. They duly heard breaking-up noises, so we were sure that was a kill. We were still some way away. At first there was some doubt as the doctor was not sure the remains were human – sometimes the Germans sent up animal carcases to fool the attacking ships. But we all went back to inspect the site, and it was clear another U-boat had been sunk – U-424.

After a couple of days without much action Captain Walker decided to sweep astern of the next convoy we joined, ON224. The Admiralty, however, told him to rejoin the convoy. At that moment the *Woodpecker* put up her black flag indicating she'd found something. So Captain Walker did what another sailor had done, saying that he didn't see the signal. He went off to attack this U-boat with the *Woodpecker*. From what I can remember we spent all day attacking this boat with no luck. Eventually the captain said, 'It's got to surface to charge its batteries so we'll just wait.' About 5.30 in the evening the lookout in the crow's nest couldn't get the words out quickly enough. He pointed and we saw the U-boat on the surface. We opened fire and got several hits: soon they were all abandoning ship. The U-boat engineering officer went back down with the scuttling charges and it was blown up.

All the survivors came aboard, although we wouldn't let them on until they gave us the number of the U-boat and the name of the captain. What I used to do with those chaps was to take off all their diaries and personal effects. As soon as they were all dried off I would lay them out on the table, having extracted any stuff which might be useful for the director of Naval Intelligence, and I got them to come in one by one and claim their belongings.

In the report of proceedings Walker said he signalled the group to splice the mainbrace and he wrote, 'The enemy threw in the towel after receiving a big wallop in the belly from *Starling*'s last creeping attack.' This was on 19th February at 5.00pm. That was the sixth sinking.

Then *Woodpecker* reported having her stern blown off by a gnat. It hit her, and the depth-charges went up by her sinking stern as we formed a screen around her. The *Starling* went alongside and threw a tow-line over to take her in tow.

On the way back one of the officers on *Woodpecker* woke up and found the sky over his head instead of the bulkhead. We took off all the ship's company, and eventually a tug arrived to take her in tow to Liverpool. Then unfortunately a storm sprang up when she was practically in the sight of Land's End, and *Woodpecker* sank.

Finally we arrived at Liverpool. It was 9.00 on a very dull morning. Before we got into harbour we got a signal from the Admiralty saying the Prime Minister and the War Cabinet wish to convey their congratulations. Then the First Lord of the Admiralty, A.V. Alexander, went by in the *Philante* and passed by us signalling a personal congratulation, then we came into Gladstone dock. We were cheered into the harbour. There were hundreds of people there. There were 2,000 officers, sailors and Wrens lining each side of the dock. Military bands were playing, 'A-Hunting We Will Go'. Captain Walker's wife was at the side, and his son and my wife were there as well. The First Lord made a speech which compared the trip that we'd done with the battle of the Atlantic, considering the effect upon the enemy. He compared it to the Battle of Trafalgar. Captain Walker was awarded his third DSO and two years' extra seniority as Captain. And if he'd lived he'd have been in the running for Flag Rank.

When he formed the Second Support Group, Captain Walker wrote: 'Our job is to *kill*, and all officers must fully develop the spirit of vicious offensive. No matter how many convoys we may shepherd through in safety, we shall have failed unless we can slaughter U-boats. All energies must be bent to this end.' No-one doubted that by the time he died – on 9th July 1944 of cerebral thrombosis, brought on by overstrain, overwork and war weariness.

First Officer Diana Barnato Walker, ATA

When the war started I joined the Red Cross, but some friends in the Air Transport Auxiliary (ATA) said I should join them – they needed pilots. I had learnt to fly in a Tiger Moth but hadn't done any flying for years.

The ATA trained in their own way. They categorised aircraft into six classes and you learnt one in each class, then you could fly anything in that class. We flew dual control, then solo, had classroom lessons and were even taught a little engineering. Once you had trained on twins you were sometimes a taxi pilot and sometimes a delivery pilot. Taxi pilots fetched and carried everybody to and from the beginnings or end of link-ups of their jobs. Delivery pilots ferried aircraft to where they were needed. I delivered many types of aircraft but flew more Spitfires than any other type – by the time I was twenty-two I had flown 260 Spitfires as well as many other different types of aircraft.

On 6th May 1944 I married Wing Commander Derek Walker. Marriage didn't stop me, or him, flying. After our honeymoon Derek returned to duty with the 2nd Tactical Air Force while I went to my ferry pool. On that historic date – 6th June 1944 – I delivered an AOP Auster from Hamble to Tangmere to replace theirs which had been blown over by gales. Later that evening I flew a Fleet Air Arm Albacore from Hamble to Eastleigh. Whilst I was tootling along the coast, I saw tanks moving on the roads, on their way to being loaded on to ships in the ports. Bailey bridge sections were also ready to be towed with the ships.

On 27th June, three weeks after the Normandy invasion, my CO at Hamble called me to Operations. 'Diana, your return job! I want you to be very careful and if you don't like it, don't take it. Go around it very carefully, run it up, test everything, then leave it if there is anything suspicious.'

She added that after my flight up to Hawarden in a Vultee Vengeance IV (an American single-engined two-seat dive-bomber used by the RAF and Fleet Air Arm), the ferry pool there would fly me to Royal Naval Air Station, Burscough, north of Liverpool, where the RAF were sending in a special ground crew for an aircraft which two naval pilots had disliked. The first pilot had done a precautionary landing there while the second had aborted his take-off because, he said, something was wrong.

I couldn't wait to get to Burscough. When I did, I found the aircraft in question was a gull-winged naval thing with elbow-bent wings, standing forlornly by a blister hangar with its ground crew, plus transport, in waiting. I looked around it as I spoke to the senior airman. He said they couldn't find anything wrong with it at all. They, and the other ATA pilot who had flown me over, were all waiting on my whims. Will she, won't she? – I could almost hear them thinking.

At first I thought it was a Corsair, but reading my delivery chit I saw that it was a Grumman Avenger I, an American torpedo-bomber used by both the American Navy and our Fleet Air Arm. It was a big aeroplane, weighing nearly 11,000 lb. empty, 2,000 lb. more than the Corsair.

With great relief to everyone, I agreed to take it. I opened up very slowly, taking off while watching the speeds and temperatures closely. When I reached 5,000 feet I throttled back to cruising revs and boost, and flicked the switch over to check the supercharger, whereupon the revs and boost disappeared downwards. So, nearly, did the Avenger and I.

Something, as the FAA pilots had reported earlier, definitely wasn't right. What was wrong was now obvious – to me. The supercharger was linked up the wrong way round. Knowing this, I was able to fly all the way to Worthy Down in Wiltshire with the switch in its wrong position, but we didn't blow up.

Margot Gore, my CO, called me to her office the next day, telling me the 'authorities' had rung through to ask her to commend the pilot on finding the fault on their Avenger that had mystified the male sex. I grew at least an inch in stature after that interview, thinking to myself, 'There you are, the ATA training must be better than the Navy's!'

I got hold of another Navy plane a few days later. I was at Speke, near Liverpool, having to fly a Blackburn Skua to Eastleigh. The Skua had been used by the Fleet Air Arm since before the war, but by 1944 it had been relegated to training or target-tugs.

I didn't even take the trouble to read all the makers' handling notes. After take-off the undercarriage came up and the red lights showed it was locked up but the undercarriage warning horn still blew! I was condemned to fly the one-and-a-half-hour trip with the horn trying to deafen me.

When I landed the mechanic in charge told me if I pushed a test button for the horn once or twice the horn might have unjammed. 'It was in the notes, Miss!' If I had taken the trouble to read them all I wouldn't have gone to bed with a raging headache and ringing in my ears. It was an unpleasant flight. I didn't like the Skua at all.

Large flying-boats were the only type of aircraft women pilots were not allowed to fly. We could fly the Air-Sea Rescue single-engined amphibious Walrus and Sea Otters off land, but not off water. Margot Gore said the high-ups at ATA thought that if women pilots got stuck out for days with large flying-boats in some far northern place with Navy or RAF crews all sorts of antics might ensue.

I flew my first Walrus on 3 July 1944, a Walrus II belonging to 277 Squadron at Shoreham, flying it to Wroughton. It was a my least favourite aircraft. It was difficult to get into; either a climb and hoist up the outside of the cockpit or a crawl along the inside of the hull, past anchors and cables. They were awash with paraphernalia that was murder for elbows, knees and finger-nails. After opening for take-off nothing much seemed to happen at all, it just rolled along with everything clanking in the back. It didn't get airborne before the control column had biffed you in the bosom several times over the bumps. When you hauled back, nothing much happened either, until it felt like getting itself airborne. Then it wallowed and flew much more like a boat than an aircraft.

It took a lot of elbow-grease to wind up the undercarriage. This made only two knots difference in its dreary cruising speed of 83-88 knots, so we usually left it down. It climbed at 75 knots, approached to land at 65 knots, and clanked on to the ground at 53 knots. Not much scope, with its speeds in no way critical to the pilot – provided the engine worked.

ATA handling notes said the rudder and elevator were very sensitive during take-off. As far as I was concerned, nothing was sensitive about that clattering lump of flying machine.

The Hamble girls cleared the factory at Cowes, Isle of Wight, and flew – if you can call it that – the Walruses to one of the various Fleet Air Arm stations or maintenance units. My friend Anne Walker didn't like the Walrus either – who did? Except, of course, the people who were saved or collected from the sea by virtue of its amphibious characteristics.

Anne took off one day in a cross-wind, a hazardous performance with all that double-wing. She swung, finishing up at the end of the take-off run in a haystack. She was knocked out and the whole caboosh, aircraft and haystack, went up in flames. Fortunately, a baker's delivery boy was cycling along the lane beside the aerodrome boundary. He pulled her out of the conflagration, then rescued his bike plus a lot of burnt loaves of bread. Bread was rationed but he offloaded some of the singed stuff. Anne brought it back to the cottage we shared for tea. We said that when we had guests to stay, she should do it again.

Philippa Bennett was a first-class pilot with a four-engined rating: very reliable, and really good. On a rare occasion, for her, she was given a Walrus, and meticulously pumped up the wheels en route. However, she forgot to pump them down again. She made a really beautiful, gentle landing, as she always did, with everything, but on the two underwing floats.

The ground crew jacked up the Walrus and pumped down the wheels. The landing onto the smooth grass of Eastleigh aerodrome had been so good (unlike most of mine) that the floats were not even dented.

A male pilot from another ferry pool was in a Walrus flying north towards the Wrekin in Shropshire. He was over the Severn River where it winds through a deep-sided culvert with forests on either side, when he had a complete engine failure. He didn't have much choice, but, rather than crash into the tops of the trees, he pointed into the narrow cleft and landed on the water. He threw out the anchor and waded ashore. The pilot was highly commended for saving his aircraft, but the Walrus proved to be slightly damaged when the tide receded.

At Hamble, on the misty afternoon of 29 October 1944 Alison King, the Ops Officer, peered round the mess door and said, 'Oh, Diana, if you're not doing anything, there's a Vengeance here for Gosport. Would you like to pop it over? We'll send a van to collect you.' Although it was a request, one never refused.

Gosport, a Fleet Air Arm station, was only around the corner from Hamble so although the weather was foggy, it wasn't far to fly. Signals told me that there was some work going on at Gosport, so I had to be careful of any runway obstructions.

I had flown over there a few days earlier and had spotted a lot of road-work signs with red danger lanterns, so I was going to have a good look before landing anyway.

I was just about to start up when Alison came rushing towards me. 'Diana!' she shouted, 'do you know it's only 400 yards?' 'Mmm, yes!' I replied casually, nodding, then started up. Alison, looking a bit nonplussed, shrugged her shoulders slightly before turning back towards the ATA hut. I wondered why she had worried to tell me. After all, surely she knew that an old hand like me wouldn't ever go off, even for ten minutes without first checking with Signals for anything unusual, which is why they had told me about the works and the runway length. I knew you could land very short with a Vengeance, so I'd have more than enough room.

When in the air, I found it really was very poor visibility indeed. It was also already starting to get dark. I was able to fly very low along the coast, then into the circuit at Gosport. There, to my amazement, through the ever-increasing fog and darkness, I could just make out that there was absolutely nothing at all blocking any part of the runway. It was completely clear.

When I got back to Hamble, I gave my delivery chit to Alison, saying, 'You know, it wasn't only 400 yards, but the entire length of the runway was clear. What were you going on about?'

She said: 'The latest Met. report came in after you'd left the mess, showing that the weather was deteriorating, and it was already down to 400 yards in the fog there, and decreasing fast. I just wanted to warn you to stop you going. You wouldn't take any notice of what I said. It was the visibility, you goose, not the runway length!'

Derek survived a terrible war only to die in an air crash in the circuit of RAF Hendon. He was buried eighteen months after we married.

I continued to fly after the war and by 1969 I had more than doubled the flying hours I had done when the war ended. I have flown over 120 different types and mark of aeroplane. I wouldn't have missed a single type, a single hour or any one of those flights. Not even the Walruses!

LIEUTENANT-COMMANDER IAN MCINTOSH, RN

Early in May 1944 I was in command of *Sceptre* and sent down to the Bay of Biscay with a list of six ships to sink: they were running iron ore from Bilbao to the French Atlantic ports. They had been unmolested for a long time. I studied weekly intelligence reports for the previous two years or so from which I gained a clear idea of their turnaround time, the state of the tide they would sail as well as knowing the ships themselves. None was terribly big: the largest was a 7,000-tonner. I was given all sorts of restrictions: I wasn't to offend the Spaniards, hurt them or damage Spanish property or ports. However I could go into territorial waters, as long as I wasn't caught.

Just to the east of Bilbao, heading towards the French coast, I got my first ship in a night attack as she had just sailed after loading: it was about the third or fourth biggest. She was in territorial waters but I was outside, so that was all right. It was, I must admit, rather a lucky shot.

This action rather stirred the Germans up. They had anti-submarine patrols sweeping along the coast trying to look for me. I followed the second largest as it came out of Bilbao and went along the coast a little way to the west to Castro Urdiales where there was a loading gantry. He certainly was in territorial waters, but he was under way when I started my attack on him. I didn't regard that place as being a Spanish harbour, not within the full terms of the reference. He had just got a picking-up rope on the buoy when my first torpedo hit him; I then put another one in to him to make sure he settled firmly on the bottom. That really did stir things up.

The biggest chap of the lot was in Bilbao and was due to come out. I was longing to get at him but obviously they had delayed his sailing a bit. Escorts kept sailing up the coast: I counted about a dozen. Although I was keen to get this bloke, I was anticipating a lot of trouble from the escorts because the water conditions were on their side. I might have got him but I was sure to be hammered. However at that stage I was hauled out. I went down to Gibraltar with the idea of doing another patrol in the Bay on the way back, but by then the second front of D-Day had happened, so I was taken back up north well clear of all that brouhaha.

When I finally got back to England I was sent for by Admiral Cunningham, the First Sea Lord who said, 'Well, McIntosh, you've got something to explain, haven't you? Tell me about it.' So I told him and I said that I had perhaps stretched the rules a bit during the last attack, but I thought it was near enough all right. He listened and finally said, 'Well, the bloody ships are sunk. Well done!' Two months later when I was down in Submarine Headquarters the Chief of Staff said, 'By the way, McIntosh, we told the Foreign Office that we'd severely reprimanded you. Have another gin!'

6

From D-Day to VE-Day

CAPTAIN J.H.B. HUGHES, RM

The cruiser, HMS *Danae*, on returning from the Eastern Fleet, then based on Mombasa, was re-gunned in Rosyth prior to working up for *Operation Overlord*. She was then based at Greenock on the Clyde. This period was devoted to bombardment and air-spotting drills with three Spitfire aircraft.

Nominated as a member of the In-Shore Bombardment Squadron, the ship's company was addressed on a freezing quarterdeck by the commander. His comment that we had the honour to be expendable was smartly countered by 'Fuck that for a lark' from the rear ranks of the stokers' division!

We sailed down the Clyde on the afternoon of 1st June in company with *Mauritius*. In St George's Channel we picked up an assembly of vessels including the Dutch cruiser *Van Tromp*, which were to be sunk to form the Mulberry harbours. It was off Land's End that we received the postponement signal and we doubled back into the Bristol Channel to resume our journey the following day.

Passing Exmouth on 5th June we took station with *Mauritius* leading, behind four fleet minesweepers. During the night we were passed by heavy bombers, gliders and towing aircraft, a number of which were shot down by heavy flak. At 2am *Mauritius*' radar went unserviceable and we took over the direction and lead of the Eastern Assault Column. Before dawn on the bridge we all had a tot of the most superb 1812 brandy from a bottle laid down by my great-grandfather in 1821 – sent to me by my father with the comment, 'You may find this of some use in the near future.' Just after dawn the navigator and I reported to the captain, 'Enemy has opened fire, sir.' His reply of 'Not yet, boys' was followed by us being bracketed by six shells. As Air Defence Officer I then immediately opened fire with window shell (containing metal strips) from the twin 4-inch guns aft. This was to confuse the German radar. It appeared to be successful as no further shells bracketed the ship.

We then commenced the operations for which we had been trained, namely engaging and knocking out three enemy batteries. This took about two-and-a-half hours during which we lost two of our Spitfires – shot down! At about 10 am we closed the beaches to knock out the opposition to the landing forces in the Ouistreham area. Our open 6-inch and twin 4-inch guns went into independent fire – the guns being laid, trained and fired by the crews stripped to the waist. This was real 'Nelson Stuff'. We knocked up a fantastic rate of fire. My sergeant-major told me he thought that 'X' and 'Y' guns were firing at least 19 rounds per minute on occasion! We all joined in, jumping in to relieve the exhausted crew members where we could.

It was exhilarating beyond description with even my thirteen-year-old Boy Bugler firing 'Y' Gun with the lanyard while the captain of the gun, a corporal, leapt to get more charges into the breech.

Suddenly it all came to a halt. As we swabbed down the red-hot pieces of artillery, the afternoon Despatch Boat made its way from ship to ship in the age-old tradition of the Royal Navy. *Danae* was totally out of ammunition and, with the RM Detachment and its Lewis and Maxim guns supplying an inadequate anti-aircraft defence, we sailed at about 5 pm at 23 knots for Portsmouth to re-ammunition.

The Executive Commander, Noel Findlay, took the White Ensign from the main gaff. He claimed it as his right as he had flown the same flag from his ship at Jutland! After all, having been chopped by the 'Geddes Axe' and come back from retirement when serving as Managing Director of Whitbread's Brewery, he had ensured that we had beer at all times including even on D-Day!

LIEUTENANT-COMMANDER ROGER HILL, RN

At 1900 on 5th June we were in position convoying Group G9, which carried the assault troops for Gold Beach – the 50th Division. It was a great moment – at last we were under way and off for France to finish the war. Even if ships were sunk all round us, we were going on to the beaches with anything that stayed afloat. I felt a sense of relief that our object was crystal-clear and there were no difficult decisions to make when casualties started.

All through the night we overhauled the line of shipping which was now an endless stream. 'We have built a bridge of ships from England to France,' Admiral Cunningham had said and we passed it all keyed up for explosions and losses, ships on fire and everything that goes bump in the night, but nothing happened.

The mine-sweepers had done their job and the coastal batteries and the mined beaches had been plastered by Bomber Command during the night. At daylight 900 Flying Fortresses came over high and dropped their bombs in the same area. As the roar of their engines and noise of the exploding bombs died away, there was a sudden pause and quiet.

We had all studied aerial photos and knew that our target was an 88-millimetre gun and a concrete pill box which enfiladed our beach. At 0625, when we were just over four miles from the beach. We were working on the right-hand English beach – Gold – to our right the cliffs rose to Port en Bessin. I turned into the tide, to bring our six 4.7-inch guns to bear, and opened fire. At this moment *Jervis* was truly at the sharp end of the war.

Since we were the first to fire we were able to spot the explosions of our own shells and to move on to the target: we continued to plaster it, but I felt sure we had knocked out the gun. It was necessary to make absolutely certain, lest they lay low and then opened fire on our people as they went up the beach. So we kept firing for thirty-five minutes. We wore earpads on the bridge, since the noise of the guns was really painful, and all orders had to be shouted in the few seconds between salvoes. The cruisers joined in from further out to sea and all the destroyers on either side were blazing away. Each ship was flying a big battle white ensign. It was a thrilling moment.

At about 0715 the rocket landing craft appeared and lay off our Green Beach. Suddenly she fired, and we could see the six hundred rockets fly through the air. Each of these was the equivalent to a six-inch shell. No-one could be alive in that beach and most of the beach mines must have been exploded. We all increased to rapid fire for ten minutes and watched in awe as the shore and low hills around the beach leaped and rocked in the hailstorm of shells. The big gun seemed to have stopped firing at us, but the 88-millimetre persisted and kept landing right alongside the bridge, but we could not see the flash of the gun. At 0730 the tanks were going over the edge of their landing craft and swimming ashore.

Suddenly we could see them on the beach, like little models – moving forward, stopping, firing, and moving forward again. Coming in from the big ships were the flotillas of the landing craft, and as we watched (the guns still blazing away), they formed in line abreast and were rushing for the surf line of the beach. I found myself banging the bridge with my clenched first, 'By God, we're ashore in France, we're back in France again.'

Now the craft approaching and landing on the beach were continuous, mostly landing tanks.

They went in at an angle to the beach because of their slow speed and the strong tide. I saw *Saumarez* lead four other destroyers right into the shore and they all plastered some strong point in a village. Suddenly, as I watched through binoculars, I saw flashes of explosions from below a church as shells hit the craft on the beach and one was soon on fire.

We opened fire with two forward turrets; the first salvo was over, the second short. The guns were then brought 'Up two hundred'. We turned to starboard to bring the after turret to bear. The six guns were firing beautifully, the right guns loading with armour piercing, and the left with direct-action high-explosive. We could see the concrete emplacement and the shells were bursting on it and all around. It was a wonderful sight and I let the guns go on for fifteen minutes. Then we lay, loaded and ready, to see if they fired again, but there was no sign of life or of gunfire.

Marine Stan Blacker

606 Flotilla (Landing Craft (Mechanised), or LCM, Mk111), E Squadron, Royal Marines, was formed without craft at HMS *Westcliff*, a Royal Navy Shore Establishment at Westcliff-on-Sea in December 1943. In January they moved to HMS *Cricket* on the banks of the River Hamble to await the arrival of its craft and to join 'E' Squadron.

Our training for landing craft had been very rushed over a short period of time and, as a Flotilla, we had only ever done one beach landing in practice with training landing craft and Dutch troops when we had carried out an early-morning landing on a small island in the Blackwater River.

Each flotilla consisted of 16 craft with six flotillas to each squadron. Each craft had a crew of four, a coxswain, two deck-hands and a mechanic. Every fourth craft had a signalman. Our flotilla had three officers. In February the 16 LCMs duly arrived up the River Hamble. Seeing them filled us with dismay and left us wondering if we would ever reach the beaches of France! These LCMs had been brought back from the landings in North Africa and Sicily and were in a terrible condition. Each craft had cracked welding and engine trouble. Out of all the 4,200 landing craft that took part in D-Day, the LCMs were the smallest craft to make their own way across. Each was powered by two 9hp marine diesels giving each craft a maximum speed of 9 knots. The well-decks were open to the sky and provided no protection whatever against weather. The maximum load was one tank or 30 troops with kit. With the naval maintenance party working flat out and all ranks of the Flotilla's own efforts for some six weeks before D-Day our LCMs were as good as we could possibly get them.

On 3rd June we were ordered to parade and Captain Gooding, RM, our CO, informed us that the hour of action was drawing near and to remember that we were Royal Marines and that our Country depended on us. He then told us that all identity must be removed. I can remember amongst my belongings dropping in a picture of my mother and sister taken in the garden at home and wondering if I would ever see the picture, or them, again. Our only identity was now the two identity discs on a piece of string around our necks.

About 3pm on 5th June we were ordered to stand to. The Padre appeared and asked us to take off our helmets and kneel in three ranks. He then said, 'The Hour of Battle draws near and the thoughts and hopes of the Free World are upon you. Please God give you all the courage to face and beat the enemy.' We all said the Lord's Prayer and then marched through the camp to the Landing Craft. The men of the Royal Artillery on the AA guns all wished us good luck.

And so we sailed in a drizzle and under heavy clouds to the rendezvous point off the south coast of the Isle of Wight, St Catherine's Point. Because of the bad weather, all the LCM flotillas began to lose formation and the signalman in every fourth craft received orders for us to make our way independently across, and to follow the bigger landing craft and merchant ships to our destination!

Before we sailed we had been issued with chewing gum to prevent seasickness, but with the rough seas and our craft being flat bottomed, the continuous buffeting made a lot of the troops, and some of the crews on board, seasick.

As dawn appeared our flotillas had again become badly scattered, but the first rays of light enabled us to see a small merchant craft which told us of a minefield ahead and that the path through it would be marked with green flags on small buoys, which we soon saw too. Had it not been for that very small merchant ship, our flotillas would have sailed quite happily into the minefield. Shortly after clearing that minefield one of our LCMs signalled that they had broken down. We replied that we would turn back to take them off on to our craft. However they said that they would stay with their craft and try to get the engines going again. This proved a bad decision as they could not get going again and they drifted into Le Havre, where they were taken prisoners-of-war.

We could now see the mass of shipping ahead of us. Our flotilla had now become so scattered that, out of the 14 craft left, only two were in contact with one another. As we approached the beach we saw that the whole coast was ablaze and I thought 'My God, we will never get in there alive.' With all thought gone of being the third wave in, with our scattered formation and late arrival owing to the terrible crossing, we headed, together with some other craft, for the Red section of Gold Beach. As we approached, the beachmaster waved us back. We circled for some time until the beach was clear, then we were called in to hit the beach with ramp down and off went the lorry. As we hit the beach we saw two dead soldiers being washed by the sea: poor buggers.

By 11am all 14 of the flotilla had arrived and unloaded. We continued all day ferrying troops and ammunition, our LCM taking load after load of 25-pounder shells in cases of two. When arriving at the beach, these had to be unloaded by hand, back-breaking work after the tiring journey across.

Each time we landed at the beach, we could see the long white strips of tape marking the tracks through the mined beach which had been laid by the Royal Engineers. When the tide receded we saw how lucky we were that the tide was high enough to carry us in, as the obstacles on the beach were everywhere – row upon row of wooden poles, each with an explosive charge attached. The pole was anchored by a chain to the seabed to allow the pole to float up and down with the tide and, should you hit one, the charge was sufficient to blow at least the bottom out of any small landing craft and sink it.

That first day was a very long one.

ACTING LIEUTENANT-COMMANDER EDWARD GUERITZ RN

My Army opposite number, the Beach Group Commander, Lieutenant-Colonel D.H.V. Board, and I took passage in LCH185 which was the 'flagship' of Commander E.N.V. Currey, Deputy Senior Officer of the Assault Group and leader of Group S3 under Captain Eric Bush (who had carried out his first assault landing at Gallipoli when he was fifteen). During the training period in Scotland they had been responsible for working up the Assault Group, and not least the skills of the units which were to provide the close-in support for the assault troops.

Royal Naval Commandos wore khaki battledress and the same load of equipment and weapons as other units in the Beach Group. We had distinguishing marks on our helmets for easy identification; as a Principal Beachmaster my helmet was painted blue. My own contribution was a red scarf and a walking stick.

The scene on a beach in the early stages of an assault landing is seldom encouraging. The situation on Red Beach, Queen Sector of Sword Area, was therefore much as expected, not least the fire from enemy guns, mortars and some small arms. Of two tank landing craft beached to give fire support on the eastern edge of Red Beach, one was on fire, and some wounded were crawling up the beach.

A number of armoured vehicles were standing halfway up the beach, some firing; flail tanks were operating to explode beach mines; beach exits were jammed with vehicles impeded by soft sand and mine explosions. The sharpest impression, as always, was created by the sight of bodies scattered on the beach from the water's edge. One of these turned out to be my immediate superior, Commander Rowley Nicholl, who was Deputy Naval-Officer-in-Charge of the Sword Assault Area, not dead but severely wounded, having insisted upon accompanying the leading beach parties.

We had been right to expect casualties among the early landings of the naval beach parties, and each of the first reconnaissance parties suffered losses. A little later a beachmaster was killed when a mine exploded. As I stopped to talk to Commander Nicholl, Colonel Board went on. We did not see him again until we found his body in the evening only a short distance along the beach lying beside his dead escort.

The task of No. 5 Beach Group and its associated Royal Naval parties, including Commando Fox RN was to bring order out of chaos, or at least to organise the chaos as far as possible. As soon as we landed we had to reconnoitre the beaches and set up signs to mark the beach limits, approach channels, and navigational hazards. Landing Craft Obstruction Clearance Units (LCOCU) cooperated with Royal Engineers to clear beach obstacles, explode mines and booby traps, and mark potholes and quicksands. Landing Craft Recovering Units (LCRU) with waterproofed or amphibious vehicles brought help to damaged or stranded craft.

While this was going on the Beach Group, with its many specialised units, began marking the beach exits, carrying out mine clearance, laying beach roadway across soft sand, recovering drowned or damaged vehicles, ministering to the wounded and directing the ever-increasing flow of traffic. We had to keep everybody moving: momentum had to be maintained. It was sometimes necessary to speak sharply to keep groups of men moving to clear the beach, even in one case some military policemen.

On Queen Sector circumstances conspired to create very considerable congestion on the beach and just inland. Traffic congestion impeded the forward movement of the Intermediate Brigade, 185 Infantry Brigade, which came ashore hot on the heels of the assault brigade at about 9.30am. This Brigade had intended to press forward with the tanks of the Staffordshire Yeomanry to attack Caen. Also 41 Royal Marine Commando had landed on Queen Green Beach to swing right towards the Canadian Sector, while 4 Commando of 1 Special Service Brigade, led by Lord Lovat, moved briskly over Red Beach to swing left and join 6 Airborne Division over the River Orne. Commandos were easily distinguished by their berets, whereas everyone else wore a steel helmet. It had not been possible to clear many of the obstacles from the approaches to the beaches before the tide, accelerated by the wind, had swept over them. When the Naval Officer-in-Charge, Sword Area, Captain W.R. Leggatt came ashore, it was decided to hold off incoming flights of landing craft to enable the beaches to be cleared. The Reserve Brigade, 9 Infantry Brigade, did not land until mid-afternoon.

As the day went on there was sporadic shelling and mortar fire on the beaches; the first air raid, by a lone Focke-Wulf, came at 5pm. Barrage balloons were flown by many ships, but later they lost their popularity among those on the beach when it was realised that German gunners were using them for ranging on beach targets. Some further enemy air action occurred later causing confusion as the airborne reinforcement and re-supply flights for 6 Airborne Division flew in towards the River Orne. These flights necessarily passed close to the ships lying off the Beach and there was a good deal of trigger-happy firing.

During the afternoon 6 Beach Group, accompanied by RN Commando, arrived ashore and we were able to reallocate responsibilities within the Sword Area. The commander of 6 Beach Group took command of both Beach Groups until he was wounded during the night, as was his second-in-command who relieved him.

By the end of the day it was reported that 130,000 Allied troops had landed by sea, including 50,000 Americans and 75,000 British and Canadians. The Sword beaches contributed 29,000 men, second only to Omaha, together with about 2,000 vehicles and 1,300 tons of stores. Nearly 8,000 British troops were landed by air. Total casualties among the British forces were reported to be 4,300.

The work of landing men, vehicles and supplies continued on Sword Beach for the next three weeks of the Build-Up phase, interrupted by a violent storm which lasted for four days and caused havoc in the whole Allied landing area. In spite of powerful fire support from battleships and cruisers offshore, German mobile guns continued to inflict damage and casualties in ships and craft and among those working in the Beach area. I was wounded in the head during the evening shelling on 'D-plus-19' (25th/26th June).

Marine Bernard Slack, RM

I joined the Royal Marines six days before my eighteenth birthday. I wanted to find a bit of excitement – although I wondered if I had done the right thing.

I trained at Chatham; we were trained specifically for D-Day, they absolutely crammed us, moved us all over the place. I was trained for landing craft. There were several types of landing craft; I was in a Landing Craft (Mechanised) or LCM, the largest of the minor section, which weighed only twenty tons. We were the smallest craft to sail over there under our own steam. We had a crew of four, and could carry either one three-ton lorry or one hundred troops.

We were in quarantine prior to D-Day for two or three weeks. Finally we left from the river Hamble at Bursledon carrying a three-ton lorry and three engineers. We came down to Ver sur Mer. I think the official figure was that 1,126 landing craft took part along the coast – they were all over the place. When we touched down there was all sorts coming at us. The noise was horrific: people were shaking. At the time, all my training came together, and I thought, this is what it's all about. I fell into the pattern of things in a matter of seconds. There wasn't time to worry or whine.

Where we landed we found what they call the tetrahedra – the 'Rommel's asparagus', as we called it. It was four triple bars, and triple wooden stakes, and on the end of every one was an 88 mm percussion cap shell, strapped to blow the bottom out of you. There were what we used to call 'can-openers', great big shards of metal sticking out, but of course the Royal Navy beach commandos went in first and cleared pathways. I couldn't believe it on the first trip in: I'm there and one or two more of the lads were standing up when we hear a shout from the beachmaster, 'Stick yer bloody heads down.' I says, 'What's the matter?' He says, 'They're sniping at yer.'

D-Day was just chaos, organised chaos. Everything was coming at us: we were getting dive-bombed and all sorts. The troops unloaded the lorry. We got orders then from the beachmasters, no more vehicles at all, just troops. So we went back out to get them. That first day, you couldn't count how many times we went back to those ships. We had to go four, five, six miles out, pick these pongos up and very often when we landed them they were sea-sick, poor devils.

We took thousands in, that first day. We just kept going and going. Day three, day four, we were still at it, night and day, night and day. Rommel had said, 'The first twenty-four hours will be very decisive. If we can knock them back into the sea then we've won.' But he didn't. He tried everything, attacks from the air, the lot. Our way of thinking was that the more troops we got in, the quicker they would push the trouble away from us.

On that first night, and for the next week or so, we had to snatch sleep when we could. One of us would get down between the engines; we could all do each other's jobs. They said that for three miles out you could walk on ships and not get your feet wet. This was their way of putting it. So you can just imagine the barrage of guns when they all opened up. It was unbelievable. We weren't hit, but we had some very near misses, believe me. As soon as we hit the shore we got in reverse while the men were still getting off. While we were on the beach we could see men getting shot down. Not everyone got hit – some of them made it right up the beach. As callous as it seems we didn't bother, although we saw some terrible sights, because it was nothing to do with us. I saw some of my mates from the Royal Marines die. We saw the hospital ships lifting them up on the stretchers, on to the decks to tend them, but you don't bother, you just get on with your job. This is what you're trained for. However, we did have to go out and pick up men from ships that had been sunk. Very often we even picked them up on the run in.

There was a massive amount of equipment floating about, and bodies and everything. If it got round your props, you couldn't clear them; what you had to do was try to ram yourself on to the shore and stay there until an ebb tide got you off – it was a damn dangerous position to be in. Everything was going. There were rocket ships; they were terrible things, firing over us just inland at the batteries. They were actually shelling and bombing in front of us. One of the most frightening things was when we thought the RAF had let us down. We cursed them as we were going in – 'oh Christ, not turning up again' – and all of a sudden there was this roar, and you can imagine being in the Channel on a twenty-ton craft and wall, to wall, there are bombers going in, bombing just off the beaches where the troops were going back. Some of them got hit with big bombs, goodness knows what. It kept the adrenalin going. We used to get into the beach in the least dangerous place and then get off again as quick as we could.

However, as the troops advanced, so the trouble was being pushed further and further away from us, and in the finish we were only getting sporadic, happy-go-lucky fire from the German in-shore batteries. We could hear them coming, we knew when to get going and when to get out of the way.

Between a week and a fortnight after we first arrived they towed over the Mulberry Harbour and put it in front of Arromanches. They put an admiral in charge and things got more orderly, but no less busy. There was a terrific off-shore current, it was causing no end of problems to our ships, so the first thing they did was get 62 old and useless merchant packets and sink them off Arromanches. Then they towed the Mulberry Port and put it at the back. We wondered what the hell was happening – we had no idea, as it was such a secret. We could see it easily, although we were a couple of miles away.

Then, when they got the port established, we moved in. They got all us waifs and strays together, and they got the job tidied up. We were working absolutely independently, free of anyone, for about three or four months. At night time the enemy still came in with his Stukas and his Focke-Wulfs – he was trying everything.

I was there for six months. Montgomery said that he did not want to stretch his supply lines, so as the ports got taken the British quickly got them up and running. He also said Mulberry Harbour would last six months, which was about right. So after three months there was less and less happening for us because they were bypassing Mulberry. Then all of a sudden the big nobs back in London realised. 'God Almighty, we've got all these bootnecks swinging round over there, doing nothing.' So they sent us back.

The way I look at it, after all that happened, it's actually great that I'm still alive.

Youth. Swordfish aircrew after a successful attack on a U-boat. Left to right: Sub Lieutenant (A) Laing, Sub Lieutenant (A) Beresford and Leading Airman Beech.

Maturity. Three long-serving men of a destroyer clearly show that discipline, sheer doggedness and humour will overcome adversity. These men, and men like them, were the backbone of the Royal Navy.

With the war ebbing towards its end, even a Chief Petty Officer can submit with a smile to make-up and costume for the ship's concert.

May 1945. Men of the Royal Navy proudly march through war-torn Berlin.

September 1945. A Japanese officer being searched. The facial expression of the naval guard speaks volumes.

May 1945. Officers and ratings on casing of U-826 at Lisahally. The commanding officer is standing in the foreground. The U-boat in the background is the infamous 'Black Panther' U-1105. Of the 1,162 U-boats built, 782 were lost. Of these 521 were sunk by British Forces.

VE-day 1945, Trafalgar Square. A time for love; a time for laughter. Nelson would have approved.

July 1947. With Britain holding the mandate for Palestine, the number of Jewish refugees allowed to enter the country was restricted. The Royal Navy was given the onerous task of preventing ships, such as the *Exodus*, seen here with 4,500 refugees, from entering Haifa.

June 1953, Korea. By July 1950 a combined British and US naval task force had been set up to counteract the North Korean invasion of the South. The Navy's carriers, *Triumph*, *Ocean*, *Theseus* and *Glory* with the allies, took the war to the enemy by attacking the lengthy lines of communication in the North. Pistol engined Sea Furies (seen here taking off from *Ocean* with rocket assistance) and Fireflys, performed remarkably well. Despite being 200 knots slower, a Sea Fury, piloted by Lieutenant Carmichael shot down a MIG.

November 1956, Suez. In summer of 1956 Egypt nationalised the Suez Canal. Following a successful Israeli offensive, the British and French launched their own offensive. Here Royal Marines in landing craft with naval helicopter and warship support, launch their initial attack.

4 May 1982, Falklands. The Royal Navy rapidly assembled a vast task force for this operation. It was to lose two Type 21 frigates, *Antelope* and *Ardent* and two Type 42 destroyers, *Coventry* and *Sheffield*.

1990–1991, Gulf War. The Royal Navy deployed nearly 3,000 personnel afloat and over 500 ashore. WRNS served for the first time in HMS *Brilliant*. Mine clearance by divers proved particularly arduous. Seen here is a door gunner in a Royal Navy Sea King helicopter.

Today and every day. A Royal Navy Air Sea Rescue crew prepare to lower a dinghy.

Chief Petty Officer David Wallace and Steve Wright helped rescue the crew of the merchant ship, *Murree*, before leaping 90 feet into the sea, as the ship was sinking.

ORDINARY SIGNALMAN JACK (BUSTER) BROWN, RN

Having joined the Royal Navy as a 'Boy, second class' under the direct entry scheme, in 1944 I found myself as a very young ordinary signalman on HMS *Kellett*, a fleet minesweeper. Our flotilla was sweeping in Lyme and Swanage bays, when our captain received the signal ordering the flotilla to 'in sweeps' and to proceed to where there had been some action, to do what we could to help.

As it transpired, we were being sent to the catastrophe off Slapton Sands, where German E-boats had attacked a fleet of US Landing Craft who had been rehearsing for the D-Day landings. I remember the dozens of corpses covered in fuel oil floating in the sea, and our ship's boats being lowered to recover them. We had about seventy brought aboard, but only one was still alive and he died shortly afterwards. The flotilla returned to our base at Portland where the dockyard abounded with ambulances, but there was not much that could be done for the poor blokes. There were 638 killed.

Shortly afterwards, in May, German planes came over and dropped mines right inside Portland Harbour. Most shipping had to 'stay put' until the small sweepers cleared them up. On 5th June we sailed for an unknown destination but, owing to bad weather, we were forced to return. On the following day we sailed again, and this time it was the real thing. The flotilla was placed under the command of the US Admiral on board USS *Ancon*, who ordered us to sweep as far into the beaches of 'Utah' and 'Omaha' as possible. Suddenly, during the early dark morning of 6th June, there was the most almighty crashing and banging: our sweep cable had fouled another one. We were no more than a few hundred yards from the occupied coast. Our captain asked on the intercom what the racket was all about. When told he made a swift decision: 'Tell the silly bastard to cut the fucking thing adrift!'

As daylight appeared I saw what was, to me, the most fantastic sight I have ever seen. The sea was completely covered in ships of all shapes and sizes, the sky full of planes towing gliders with the now white-striped identifying marks. Shortly before 6am every ship that had guns opened up with a barrage of fire, so the whole of the French coast as far as the eye could see appeared to be bathed in one long, continuous concussion wave.

The landing having been successful on our part we sailed back to the south coast where we promptly ran aground on the rocks and stove a great hole in the bow. The poor *Kellett* was finally helped into Portsmouth. As we came in belching black smoke (she was a coal-burner), and with a huge list to port, HMS *Arethusa* passed us in the opposite direction taking King George VI across to France. *Arethusa* made a 'well done!' signal to us to which our first lieutenant replied, 'They're round and they bounce'!

PETTY OFFICER JAMES HINTON, RN

I was an electrical artificer on HMS *Scourge*, a fleet destroyer. We arrived in Portsmouth on 27th May 1944, my twenty-first birthday. All those in the PO's mess gave me their tot of rum and I got a bit sauced. For the last few days of May we were allowed restricted leave ashore but then leave was abruptly cancelled. We began to stock up on ammunition and waited for orders. On the afternoon of 4th June we set sail, but the sea was too choppy and the invasion was postponed for twenty-four hours.

After lunch the next day our captain told us that we were going to be in the vanguard, leaving that afternoon. We would be escorting the minesweepers through the British and German minefields and taking part in the initial bombardment of the French coast. There was some apprehension and a lot of excitement at this news. The captain would always hold a little service before we left to go on a convoy or other action. He had his own version of the Breton prayer and he would say, 'Dear God be with us. Our ship is so small and the sea is so great.' He was Lieutenant-Commander Balfour, a magnificent captain, very approachable yet very stern, and respected by the crew.

We set to work preparing the ship for sea. As an electrical artificer I had a lot to do. Warships are heavily dependent upon their electricity supply and checks needed to be made on the condition of the generators, switchboards, emergency power supplies and gun-firing circuits, amongst other routines.

At 1535 we hauled in the anchor and set out for France. The crew was very alert, tensed up, proud and excited. We were a young crew with an average age of nineteen. At twenty-one I was the youngest petty officer aboard. As we set out for France many of us looked back at the English coast with mixed feelings; what were we heading for and would we see England again? How would we cope with a mass attack from the air and how well would we be able to defend the British land forces and armour in our care? Would the E-boats and U-boats come out to engage us from their lairs on the French coast? We thought of our loved ones and friends. I had just heard from my wife, Mary, that we were expecting our first baby in December.

As we crossed the Channel, we were in constant fear of attack by enemy bombers. We saw a plane circling in the far distance, and prayed it was not the enemy to give warning of what was taking place. At last dusk fell and the chance of being attacked diminished. But there was soon another hazard to face: the minefield ahead. At 10.15pm we closed with the minesweepers and reduced speed to about three knots. The captain ordered all not working below decks to muster on the upper deck. We could see quite well around us for it was a moonlit night and the sea was very bright. We watched loose mines bobbing threateningly close to the ship's side. Two or three rubbed the ship's side and one fellow put his fingers in his ears. It needed only one of those horns to knock against us for the ship to be obliterated.

A welcome distraction from mine-spotting was hearing a heavy continuous drone overhead and watching our airborne troops fly over in gliders towed by their tug planes. Quite a few silent prayers were said for them.

After we got through the minefields we separated from the minesweepers and headed for the French coast. We were the first warship to arrive off the Sword sector, two miles off Ouistreham on the extreme left flank of the British invasion area. Then we helped to guide through some of the bigger warships, the *Warspite* and others, to their bombarding positions. At around 0430 we saw one of our sister destroyers, *Svenner*, torpedoed. She had a Norwegian crew. As she went down her bow and stern stuck up like a defiant V for victory. We were not allowed to pick up survivors, but one of our sister ships, HMS *Swift*, was nearer to *Svenner* and the captain could not bear to see the crew struggling so he let his engines idle, drifted towards them and picked up a hundred people.

As dawn broke we could see the enormous size of the armada that had made its way across the English Channel. Literally, the sea was full of ships, like huge stepping stones, going seemingly all the way back to our home ports. We could also see some enemy movement ashore, but I don't think they had seen us. We all felt very impatient for action. Eventually *Warspite* opened up and the bombardment began. We had a major who went ashore and directed our firing and we knocked out our first target, a German gun position, quite quickly, although shrapnel from its return fire came too close for comfort. Then we lost contact with the major, so from that time on our Gunnery Officer was solely responsible.

I had a free warrant on the ship and went around checking gun circuits, searchlight and signalling lamps and, if there was a problem, I was there to fix it. I watched the bombardment. The most impressive were the multi rocket-firing ships. They were firing their rockets over the heads of the troops going in, we were firing over the top of those and the *Warspite* was firing over the top of us. So there was terrific fire-power. It was exhilarating.

By now the sea between us and the shore was filled with craft carrying tanks and men, all passing our starboard beam and heading for the beaches. We were instructed to go in and lay down a smoke-screen and give covering fire for these small craft. We went in to about a mile from shore which was too close because we were being out-gunned. The Germans had 6-inch guns and ours were 4.7-inch. We saw some landing craft which failed to get there and we saw some of the tanks going down. The noise was terrific, and all the flashes; it was like make-believe. You really couldn't believe it was happening.

Then we went back to our fire position. We watched the action on the beaches through our binoculars and rangefinder. Our troops had very good support from the special tanks which set off the mines with great flailing chains and others which threw flames into the German gun-posts. These tanks gave our forces a good start. The wounded, and survivors from sinking craft, were being picked up by the landing ships and craft which had managed to get their weapons and people ashore. The wounded were taken back to hospitals which had been set up all over the south coast.

We kept up our fire for two-and-a-half hours and then we were ordered to break off and go along the eastern flank to protect *Warspite* and *Ramillies* from attack by E-boats and U-boats. Although we were still at action stations the crew was a little more relaxed and hot drinks were taken around to everyone. We protected the warships for two hours and then resumed our bombardment of enemy gun positions. One post after another. There was a lot of debris and shrapnel flying around, but we were lucky and there were no casualties.

At 2200 we were sent out to patrol the sea lanes and were twice attacked by Junkers dropping high explosives. The first two just missed our stern and, about half an hour later, a string of six high-explosives straddled our beam, three on each side, but missed us. The explosion sent vibrations right through the destroyer's structure and drenched the bridge.

When D-day was over at midnight, we thought, 'Well, thank God, we had a lucky day.'

Able Seaman Ken Oakley, RN

We came back to England after the invasion of Sicily and then we started training for the Normandy invasion. I was part of the Beach Brigade. Our role was to get the beach organised so that the troops could move inland as quickly as possible. Close co-operation with the army was absolutely essential.

We went for training to Lossiemouth in Scotland, which was a Fleet Air Arm base, and from there in November/December 1943 we went to do a simulation invasion exercise at Burghead Bay, which lies across country west of Lossiemouth. Afterwards we could see why we were trained there, for it was almost a miniature replica of the Normandy coast.

It was the most awful exercise. The weather was bitterly cold and we were in the water and had to survive for three days as best we could on our rations. There was no food coming in from the outside and none on the beach. We were allowed to go slightly inland, about half a mile or so, to catch a rabbit or whatever. We made tents with tarpaulin or capes; nothing else was provided.

When we came back from the exercise we were pretty well knocked up. After a short time we had a leave just prior to Christmas and on that leave I think I ate more than I have ever done. I ate all my rations and my family's too.

It was good. We came back up to Scotland afterwards, with more training and more exercises. And learning too to drive all the vehicles which might pass through the beachhead. We didn't pass a driving test on civilian standards, only on naval standards. Rod McDowell, an ex-chauffeur, taught me how to drive. After that I was allowed to drive the jeep.

At this time I was the bodyguard and driver to the beachmaster, Lieutenant John Church, and we formed up with the rest of the Beach Brigade which consisted of Army and Naval Commandos, RAF, and Engineers and their armoured vehicles. We started to travel down south in April/May. When we reached the outskirts of Wellington (Shropshire) where I had been brought up – we stopped in a huge field just outside the town. So I said to the Naval Officer in charge of our unit, 'Could I go home for a couple of hours and wash and brush up?' My home was five miles from here. 'Yes,' he said. 'You can go.' So Rod and I went in the jeep to my mother's place. She was totally amazed to see me. At that time we didn't have a bath in the cottage so my mother sent me to my aunt's house to have a good wash.

The next morning the convoy drove through Wellington and Dawley. All the people were waving and I saw a girl I had gone to school with. She recognised me and waved. In a few moments we were through and down the hill, and then we drove right the way down south and camped outside Portsmouth. There it was just a matter of keeping fit and waiting for the big day.

We were all in a sealed camp, no leave was allowed unless it was absolutely imperative. I was allowed out, as the batman to the beachmaster, to collect his library books. We had lots of visits from various VIPs, telling us how great we were and that we had been chosen to spearhead the attack. Monty came across best of everyone. He had the ability to put things over. Finally the day came when we were assembled and drove down to the dockside at Portsmouth. There wasn't a lot of anxiety; we had done our training. We had passed through Sicily and knew roughly what to expect. We had been well briefed on the defences and what one could expect to see, various points of recognition. We had been shown mock-ups of the beach defences, what the type of sand was on the beach and how far it was to the road. Everything was very well prepared. The most dangerous gun emplacement was the Merville battery which was in the hills to our east side and that was going to be dealt with by the Airborne Forces. We boarded the HQ ship but the operation was postponed for bad weather. I wouldn't have liked to have gone ashore that day: the wind was howling.

The next day we were told the operation was on, and we sailed. We stayed on the ship for twenty-four hours, passing time as best we could. On the evening prior to the landing we were given a briefing by the senior arms officer and I will always remember his final words: 'Don't worry if all the first wave of you are killed,' he said. 'We shall simply pass over your bodies with more and more men. This landing must be a success, whatever it costs.' What a confident thought to go to bed on! I was in the first wave. Of course the Padre, Bishop Maurice Wood, said a few words.

We were called very early the next morning, around three o'clock, to stand by our boarding stations. We were in position for the launch and boarded the Landing Craft (Assault) which was tossing about very badly because the weather was still blowy. We had a gangway down to ours. It was awkward to get into because the LCA was pitching and tossing. Finally we were all loaded. About thirty of our unit were in this craft. We were all split up so that, if there were any losses, we didn't lose the whole unit.

The landing craft made for the shoreline some five miles distant, which is quite a long trip. It was still dark at this time and I remember, after we had proceeded some way, that I could see the star formations in the sky. However we could hear the bombardment passing over us, huge shells from the battleships hurtling ashore, the screams of the different types of shell and, as daylight broke, I saw a rocket ship discharge its full load of rockets towards the Merville battery area. It was fantastic; the whole scene was a sheet of flame. Incredible.

All around the sea was one mass of craft, landing craft of all kinds, shapes and sizes. A lot in our immediate area were LCAs because we were going for the initial assault. There was a good feeling as we went forward except that most of the army were seasick. I wasn't very happy myself. However when we got within sight of the shore we were getting spattered with light gunfire, nothing very heavy at this moment. Finally we got within sight of the stakes, the dreaded stakes, with the shells and mines on, which protected the beaches. Our coxswain did a marvellous job. We were headed straight for this stake and I could see the 56lb. shell lashed to it. In just the last second, he missed it. He got it just right. He steered us in between the stakes and got us ashore without touching one of those shells.

At the order 'Down Ramp' we were all surging ashore. We were in a few inches of water. All around were craft beaching and chaos and more gunfire was pouring down on us. We ran, under fire, up to the top of the beach where we went to ground, about a hundred yards from high-water. People were going down and screaming and crying all around us. As we hit the sand at the top of the beach we took stock of our bearings and realised we had landed almost exactly in our correct positions. We landed on Queen Red One, Sword Sector, Colleville sur Orne.

To our left the patterning of mortar fire seemed very intense but we seemed to be just under the arch of fire so that we were relatively safe. The main part of the mortar fire seemed to be to our left, further down, which suited us fine but for the people that were in it, it was awful. A commando was screaming, 'Help me, help me,' and I looked at the beachmaster as if to say, 'Should we go to help him?' but we couldn't. My duty was to stay with the beachmaster; he was my prime responsibility. The commando had a huge pack on his back anyway which would protect him from various splinters and shrapnel. It didn't look good at all, but he wasn't the only person who was in dire straits all around us. The mortar fire was very intense. Some people were filtering through, only some, not many. Then behind us came the roar of a tank. A Duplex Drive tank had managed to get ashore. He pulled up behind us, opened his hatch and fired, and that was the end of the mortar fire. One shot, honest, no more than that one shot screamed over our heads, whoosh, and it must have gone straight down into the bunkers. Fantastic, I thought, a great job.

We were then able to proceed. There was still some odd light machine-gun and rifle fire coming down. The tank was off and gone, he was in the business of getting through and knocking the next one out. It was great, because the DD tanks were able to float the last few hundred yards, they had the propeller hood all around and they could switch from the track to a propeller in the tank itself. So they were launched off the LCTs – Landing Craft (Tank) – some two hundred yards or so from the beach and floated in under the drive of their propeller. As soon as they hit the beach they switched back to their tracks, cast off the flotation skirt, and they were in business. And there you are, one of these chaps comes in with this damn great tank and makes the mortar look like a pea shooter.

We were now left with the business of organising the beach, getting everything moved off the beach and getting the signs laid. The beachmaster's responsibility was to get that beach cleared, get it organised, and he was the senior officer on the beach, irrespective of rank – whether the army guy was a general or whatever, he was the man in charge of the beach. He sent his various teams to do the clearing, get the stakes out, get the roads laid down for the heavy vehicles. After some time one of our chaps came up to me and said, 'Oh, Ken, can you help me? Sid is down there, very badly wounded.' Sid was an old friend and we had gone on leave together. He had been the assistant beachmaster's bodyguard and his duty was to put the left-hand extremity sign for our section on the beach at the beachmaster's order. This sign was a huge great pole with a flag on it. So I went along to Sid who was lying some two hundred yards away. He was severely wounded. The assistant beachmaster said to me, 'He caught it across the back. His kidneys were hanging out. I've pushed them back in and shoved on this dressing. Can you get him to the first aid post?' I said, 'Yes. Will do.' We had to half carry him, half drag him. The fire was not too bad; the mortar fire had subsided but we got the occasional rattle of machine-gun fire. We got Sid to the first aid post and left him there under a bit of canvas. He was going to get some attention and be looked after. Then I had to go back to my duties at the shore line. More and more craft were coming in continuously and I was directing them. The trouble was, when the soldiers came ashore their first reaction was, 'Let's group up and have a little check and then we'll have a cup of tea.' We had learned on exercises that you must not allow this to happen, you must keep the beaches clear and the momentum going. If the beach is clogged up the whole impetus is lost. You have to keep it moving. There is no other way. This is what we were doing, chasing them, telling them to get off the beach, that is your exit, that is *your* exit, over there, over *there*.

The beachmaster, Lieutenant Commander Gueritz, had a complete list of everything that was coming in and the designated signs to be put up. So all that was well in hand. The troops were a bit bewildered and a bit sea sick and one of our assistant beachmasters had been wounded in the shoulder, so he had used his white waistcoat to serve as a sling for his arm. The army had decided that if the assistant beachmaster wore a white waistcoat they would be easily recognisable, forgetting that the white waistcoat would also make him a prime target for the Germans.

Suddenly the air was split by a piercing sound of bagpipes. Along the beach, some hundred yards away, a piper was marching up and down. There was Piper Bill Millin filling his bag up and getting his wind. Lord Lovat had asked him to play a few tunes. Lord Lovat came up behind Bill, formed up his troops and they marched off in parade ground style, straight up into the village of Colleville. It was amazing. How could he have the pipes on the beach amidst all this battle noise? Shells screaming and fire all around. And silently, as the sound of the pipes died away into the hinterland of the beach, we got back to work bringing the landing craft in. That was a real high point in the whole landing.

In the early afternoon the beachmaster came to me and said, 'Ken, I've arranged for Sid Compston to be taken to Arromanches for medical attention. We can get him on to a hospital ship from there quite easily. He'll be better looked after than staying here in the first aid. Would you go with him to look after him?' Sid was pretty ill by now with an infection, but we had penicillin powder to put on his wounds which killed off the infection. Sid survived and recovered; he was later best man at our wedding.

We were still getting shelled at various times from the area of the Merville battery and their mobile guns which they were firing at intervals to disrupt our work.

On the third day the beachmaster said, 'Ken, I want you to go as the representative of our unit to a funeral this afternoon of all those that were killed on the beach. They are being buried today.' The Pioneer Corps had been designated to clear the beaches of dead bodies and put them in canvas bags. The burial took place in an apple orchard. The bulldozers had scraped out three huge trenches between the trees to a depth of about three feet. The bodies were laid side by side. The smell was appalling. We stood with bowed heads and the padre of each denomination read the prayers. I will never forget that funeral. A lot of good men were killed and buried there. It seems an ironic place to bury the dead, in an apple orchard, but it is still there today.

So back we went to the beach and we were still getting craft in. The beachmaster's responsibility was to get material in which the army particularly wanted. If they wanted armour-piercing shells of a certain size they had to come in in preference to food supplies or anything else. The beachmaster had immediate contact with the ships offshore through beach signals. We had a beach signals chap with us all the time with a radio to pass messages.

Our main difficulty was the food. We had to scrounge what food we could by watching what was coming. We would simply take a case to keep us going. There was no provision made for us.

One day I was going about my business and needed to urinate. I went to the back of the beach and I was just finishing when a voice said, 'Oi, what are you doing then?' I looked round and there was an army sergeant. He said, 'You are not supposed to do that there.' I asked why and he said, 'There is a proper place over there, look.' I said, 'How long has that been there?' He said, 'We just put it up.' I said, 'Well you should put signs and tell everyone.' He put me on a charge. I had to go to the beachmaster to explain why I was urinating in an improper place. Pioneer Corps sergeant. He had come in about D-Day plus three. He hadn't seen any action.

Telegraphist Alan Higgins, RN

The day before we sailed for the D-Day landings we, and a few more Landing Craft ship's companies were mustered in a large boatshed in Newhaven. A Royal Navy captain gave us a pep talk which went something like this: 'You men have done a great job at Pantellaria, Sicily, Salerno and Anzio and have earned the reputation of being "the cream of landing craft". As such, the Admiralty had seen fit to reward you.' This caused great speculation amongst the assembled crews: medals, leave, promotion? However, all such speculation was crushed as he continued, 'You have been given the honour of landing on the extreme east flank of the landings at Sword beach, which is expected to be the most hotly contested, and I know that you will conduct yourselves commensurate to the occasion.' Well, with that bit of information under our belts, we realised that we were in for a hot time.

For the invasion we were flotilla leader and carried a Lieutenant-Commandet, RNVR, in addition to our two-ringed skipper, Harry Collinge, and a sub-lieutenant, RNVR, who was the no. 1. After loading the troops, we anchored in Shoreham Bay, whilst the powers-that-be decided whether or not the invasion was on or off. The accommodation for the troops, however, could at best be described as primitive, consisting of rows of wooden, ribbed seats, just like park benches. It doesn't stretch the imagination to envisage what conditions were like after a few hours of being packed like sardines, with all the equipment, weapons and webbing required for landing and storming the beaches. The stench of vomit alone was terrible, most of the troops being seasick. However we duly sailed that evening.

As dawn broke, the sheer size of the operation became apparent. There were battleships, cruisers, destroyers and dozens of other types of craft all going south; hundreds of all types of ships with one purpose – to land and support an army in Normandy.

Through the ring of bombarding vessels we sailed and, as the beach grew nearer, one could see splashes as shells and mortars homed in on and near the landing area. As we reached the beach and began unloading the first casualties were sustained. Orders were for all wounded to be landed on the beach. There was one soldier being helped by two others, his left foot and boot as one, in a mingle of flesh and leather. I shall never forget the almost apologetic look he gave me as he passed by.

A Landing Craft (Tank) shot alongside us and on to the beach with its cargo of tanks ablaze and ammunition exploding. AB Harry Gee, a Yorkshireman, was on our foc's'le blazing away with his Oerlikon 20 mm-cannon – a brave effort, bearing in mind that the air was alive with bullets and shrapnel.

As I ducked back into the wireless offices, we sustained a direct hit. The usual smell of cordite and the cries of wounded men came from the packed no.3 troop space, where a shell had entered and exploded, leaving wounded and dying men as the shrapnel made its exit from the port to the starboard side. Our skipper shouted down the voicepipe for me to see if no. 3 troop space was cleared. This I did with great alacrity, as I knew from past experience that as soon as we had disembarked all our troops, we could kedge off the beach, and reach the relative quiet among the offshore fleet. However, as I was halfway down the ladder, a soldier who was sitting on the bench with his back to me, turned and said, 'Come and help my mate, Jack.' I replied, 'You better get off quick, mate, all the rest have landed.' He replied, 'I can't – my leg has had it – help my mate.' The water was pouring in and although not deep as such, it became a hazard to wounded troops, who were in danger of drowning, as well as making their injuries worse when the ship was rolling.

As I came to the soldier who had called out, I saw that his leg was hanging off below the knee, so I opened the tin of morphia ampoules and jabbed one into his thigh with the attached needle. Turning to his mate, who was semi-conscious, I undid his webbing and tried to set him on the seat next to his wounded mate. He was a big chap, and his gas mask kept catching under the seat. I said, 'Try and help yourself, mate,' but all I got was a vague, incoherent mumbling. I finally got him seated and saw that both his legs were shattered below the knees, so I jabbed a needle of morphine into each of his thighs. These tins of morphine were flat, contained six to eight ampoules, each having a needle attached which could be used by removing the cap from the needle and then squeezing the drug into the casualty.

By now, some other crew members had arrived in the troop space, and the task of getting the dead and wounded up to the deck above began. One soldier looked all right at first, but a closer look revealed a hole of about one inch in diameter behind his ear. He just sat dribbling in a semi-haze. The total extent of his injury wasn't known, and he and the rest of the casualties were put aboard a destroyer, which carried a medical officer. We had only one wire stretcher, so most of the wounded were carried up the ladder, one man supporting the shoulders with his hands under the arms and one man supporting the legs. Not the most satisfactory way of handling wounded men, as the one supporting the shoulders would be kicking the wounded man in the back as he struggled up the ladder.

One of the men I was helping must have had internal injuries, for his face was a leaden colour and he just sighed and gave up the ghost as we reached the top of the ladder. The skipper had told us to try to comfort the wounded as best we could, but just what can one say or do under those circumstances? It was a mercy that we found a destroyer with medical facilities aboard in very short time. The dead and wounded were placed all along a narrow passage on the port side, and the wounded were kept as comfortable as was humanly possible.

After passing all the dead and wounded to the destroyer, we sailed directly back to Newhaven where, when the tide went out, we were left high and dry on what was called a 'gridiron', a wooden platform on the bed of the harbour. Some workmen from the Southern Railway pumped us out and welded dozens of patches of shell damage in a very short time. That night we were loaded again, and thus began what was to be a daily shuttle to the beachhead, the only 'respite' being riding out of the five-day storm, which caused severe damage to all the unloading facilities.

I must record my admiration for the courage and fortitude of the British 'Tommy'. At Anzio, I had expressed these feelings to one particularly brave soldier. He turned to me and said, 'Jack, let me tell you something: I couldn't get off that tin box ship of yours quick enough.' Horses for courses?

Ordinary Seaman Ronald Martin, RN

On *Warspite* we started preparing for D-Day with a practice in Scotland, then we sailed down the west coast to England. D-Day was postponed for twenty-four hours so, having got to the English Channel, we spent another half-day steaming up and down the Bristol Channel until ordered to go back. Eventually on 5th June we were off. We stopped at Plymouth to embark a Russian admiral, a Russian general, a whole pile of war correspondents and photographers and a fat Chinese naval officer. Why he appeared on the scene I'm not quite sure, but he was appointed to my director.

As twilight approached there were 6,000 or 7,000 ships off the south of the Isle of Wight, which was a magnificent sight. The soldiers, poor devils, were so sea-sick, they were leaning over the sides of the landing-craft. Led by a fleet of minesweepers we crept very slowly towards Gold Beach at the eastern end of the beach-head. We arrived just as dawn was breaking and at 0530, or just before, we sighted what we thought were torpedo E-boats coming out from Le Havre to attack us. I opened fire with the port armament. Almost at the same time the 15-inch guns opened up against our first shore battery. So the *Warspite* lays claim to firing the first shots of the invasion. We sank one of the E-boats and the rest retired to Le Havre and didn't come out again. During the next five or six days, we continued bombarding all our targets. There were a few sporadic air attacks but we had air supremacy so there was nothing to worry about from that side. We were helped by both shore spotters and Fleet Air Arm spotters; they were very accurate. We demolished all our targets successfully.

On D-Day itself no-one was having any meals. Instead we had action rations, a big paper bag containing a Cornish pasty – or 'tiddy oggy' as we called them – a couple of apples, a bar of chocolate and that was it. They passed seven packages up to my director and the Chinese officer whom we'd taken on board presumed that they were all for him, so he ate the lot. As a result we had nothing to eat on D-Day. The paymaster commander brought the captain's parcels up on to the bridge personally. The captain took one bite from his tiddly oggy, and said, 'I must say this is very wholesome,' then threw it straight over the side.

One unique situation arose when a German tank commander, hiding with a whole fleet of Panzer tanks in a wood, covered in bushes and twigs, made the mistake of lighting a cigarette while sitting on top of his tank. He was spotted by aircraft. We pin-pointed the target and gave an order unique in naval gunnery history of '15-inch, fifty rounds, rapid fire. Commence.' That was almost impossible because of the time it took to load the one-ton shells, follow their pointers and so on. However, there was a method in that madness because the first broadside fell slap in the middle of the wood and then as the succeeding ones started, because of the human error and the time lag, the shells were chasing the Germans as they started to run away. We got reports back from the aircraft that it was very successful. We could knock a chap off a bicycle at twenty miles.

We then ran out of 15-inch ammunition after nearly four hundred rounds. So we went back to Portsmouth where we loaded ammunition all night. Halfway through the night we got a signal saying that the Americans had got themselves into all sorts of bother down on Omaha beach. Their bombarding wasn't going very well and they had specifically asked for *Warspite* to go down and sort them out. We went straight there to bomb the German troop emplacements with the aid of aircraft and spotters. They would communicate by radio to give the map coordinates. Then we went back to our original bombarding positions and carried on bombarding.

We were told that we had to go up to Rosyth because the 15-inch guns had worn out. We set sail on our own, through the Straits of Dover and up the east coast. Just off Harwich we hit a radio-controlled mine on the port side and that stopped the ship in her tracks. It shifted the port propellers forward by about six feet and put them all out of gear. We limped up to Rosyth and the engineers in the dockyard did a magnificent job. The old crate could still do fourteen knots if pushed. We were sent back to Portsmouth.

Brest had been occupied by the Germans, but they had fallen back into several forts for a last-ditch stand. In August the *Warspite* was asked to go and help shift them. So we went down to Brest and bombarded the shore forts and the British Armoured Corps with their Churchill flame-throwing tanks were also doing the job ashore. Between us we got the Germans so annoyed that they finally gave up and Brest was liberated. We suffered very few casualties at that time. Most of them were only wounded by splinters. There was nothing serious. We were under artillery fire from the shore occasionally, but not for long because we put all their batteries out of action.

We were then asked to go along to Le Havre to help the British army take over the town, so we bombarded their shore batteries. Finally, the dear old lady's last sortie was to Walcheren in the Schelde estuary in Belgium where the commandos and the rocket landing-craft were going to attack the Germans. By then the poor old ship, after two world wars, had really had it. We finally limped back to Portsmouth where she was put into reserve.

LIEUTENANT-COMMANDER IAN MCINTOSH, RN

By the late summer of 1944 some submarines were effectively using radar to detect aircraft and certainly my own submarine *Sceptre* was equipped with it:

I found it worked well. This was despite the general theory amongst submariners that as soon as you switched radar on you were liable to get harried and attacked. I think this was based on a sheer coincidence. Some submarine captain in the Indian Ocean had switched on his radar and shortly afterwards a whole mob of Japanese aircraft had come over the top. The captain had put the two things together. Well, I didn't quite believe this: I was using mine and getting no troubles as a result of it.

One night I was patrolling off Norway and picked up some echoes which turned out to be a convoy which I tracked. The bearing accuracy of that radar set was about plus or minus 20 degrees, but the range was good. By plotting the ranges and getting a rough idea of the bearing I eventually got quite a good plot of their course and speed. So I was able to go in with the angle already set on my night sights to aim off. I made the attack on the surface. It was only when I was about 1,500 yards off the target that I suddenly realised that it was not the convoy but its two escorts. So I had to swing round and alter course to get away from them. Very soon however we picked up more echoes which turned out to be the convoy. We were well clear of the escorts and by then had got into a good attacking position. I closed in and was luckily able to fire by eye as I wouldn't have liked to fire by radar, because it was too inaccurate. We had a good course and speed and I think we hit three ships.

My final patrol was off the same south coast of Norway. This time, shore stations repeatedly jammed my radar, so I had to switch around quite a bit. But much as I tried I couldn't pick up any information. However on the night of 14th October we sighted up a convoy. This time I attacked by eye entirely. We got two on that occasion.

This was the end of my time with *Sceptre*: she was going to be converted. I was put ashore. I was very cross about this because she was working very well. Everything was going fine. My eye was just in. However it wasn't until I was ashore for a while that I realised, after two years in command, that I was pretty tired, without being conscious of it.

Because of our radar attack, which I believe was the first of its type that a submarine had done, they all thought, 'Well, McIntosh is terribly keen on radar and knows all about it.' So I was sent to the Admiralty Signal Establishment at Haslemere as a sort of project leader for the submarine radar set that was being designed. It was a very interesting posting because there were some marvellously good scientists and designers there. But it was not really where I wanted to be.

ACTING LIEUTENANT-COMMANDER JOHN ROXBURGH, RN

At the beginning of 1945 I was given command of a brand new submarine *Tapir*, fresh out of Vickers at Barrow-in-Furness. On 12th April we were on anti-U-boat patrols off Norway. I was trying to sleep after a night on the surface charging our batteries when Donald Duckers, who had been with me in the Meditearranean and was my tried and tested anti-submarine sonar operator, reported yet another diesel engine noise. I had been called by him before that morning and it was usually a small fishing boat, so I got pretty rude. Finally he called me over the intercom, 'Captain in the control-room, Captain in the control-room, U-boat surfacing.' I rushed in and there was a U-boat (U-486) surfacing at 3,000 yards. I fired eight torpedoes and sank him. No survivors from that one.

A week before I had heard a submarine surfacing in my patrol area. I followed it to the surface and identified it as a U-boat moving away. I gave chase and was closing the range on an apparently unsuspecting target on a straight course. Just as I was getting into a firing position I was astounded when my quarry suddenly flashed a bright aldis signalling lamp at me with the message, 'Don't shoot, Steve here.' This was the Lieutenant Stevens (now in command of *Turpin*) who had pinched my solitary ration of beer over three years before in Malta when he thought I had had it. He had inadvertently, in thick foggy weather, been patrolling in my area off Bergen and had discovered his mistake from star sights that evening. He was naturally trying to get the hell out of it as fast as he could and was pretty certain it was *Tapir* which was after him. He was lucky.

I then went out to the Far East sailing from the Clyde just before VE Day. I wanted to get my hat-trick. I had sunk a German and an Italian submarine and I was now keen to get a Jap. I got out there but within a fortnight the war was over. Whilst I may have been glad when the war started, I was even more glad when it was over.

Marine Noel Barker

At our POW camp at Landsdorf the Germans were in charge. Our officers didn't have command over us, as command goes: when you are POWs you are all the same. I don't know what happened to the officers, whether they got taken in transport or not. I never saw them after we were all captured at Calais in June 1940.

I only saw my own mates. We were sleeping in fields and in barns. What food we had was inedible half the time. One time there was a barrel standing in the gateway of the field, full of this meat which was green and crawling with maggots. We ate it because there was nothing else to eat, just wiped the maggots off and ate the meat. People were getting ill, but no-one died that I know of, although it is possible that I didn't hear. Several were shot trying to escape and roughed up as well. You got the butt of a rifle round your head if you said anything out of turn. I wasn't one of those, I managed to escape that.

Then I got sent to the coal mines with a couple of my mates. I had never been down a coal mine before, so I hadn't the faintest idea what it would be like. I remember the first day: we went down in the cage. It was a bit scary to start with. It was a long way from the pit shaft. We went in on trucks: actually one of our blokes got killed on that. It was run by overhead electricity and because it was bare, they warned you to be careful when you got out.

The coal seams weren't level; they were on a slope. There was this chute that the coal used to come down and a bunker controlled the flow of the coal into a truck underneath. They put me on clearing up the coal; a lot of it fell off the chute and, if you didn't keep it clear, it would all choke up. Quite often I would just sit there and let it choke up. I would put my light out and make out it had blown out. It quite often did get blown out when they fired.

I got on a good job going round oiling all the machinery, and that's where I really got my own back. All this stuff that was shunting backwards and forwards had to be kept oiled but, before pouring in the oil, I put a handful of coaldust in first. That wore the bearings out. They were always changing parts. The whole damn lot had to come out. They never did twig on, so I had them there. One of my friends got taken away after throwing a cup of hot coffee in the face of a guard one day, I never saw him again.

We weren't that far from the pit head, but they always counted us a dozen times on the way over. Coming back we used to have a shower. We had working clothes but the footwear wasn't very good; we had wooden clogs which were damned uncomfortable. The only thing they were good for was killing the rats in the hut: they used to come over your bed and run all over you.

There wasn't much hope of escape, we just didn't have the facilities. There were stories about having passports made and God knows what else. I don't know how they did that but I certainly couldn't do it where I was. We used to play a game called Ukkers (Ludo) in the evenings. Also we played chess and bridge: they were the two games which I learnt while I was there. And we had a bloke who actually carved a set of chess men.

We also set up our own theatre. I was keen on electrics before I joined the Marines so I did all the electrics. We had several good actors dressed up for all the parts. They even managed to get dresses somehow for the women's parts. The Germans didn't watch these shows: they knew we had the stage, but we were OK until the Gestapo came round, and smashed everything.

The actual guards weren't too bad. The chap in charge of us when we first went there was an old chap. He was very good, he turned a blind eye to lots of things. I don't think he had a lot of time for the Nazis. But he hadn't been there all that long and there were so many escapes that they took him away and pulled a new bloke in. He was a really hard bastard: when he looked at you his eyes went right through you. He said, 'The next man that escapes from here I will bring back and shoot.' That night two blokes went over the wall. They were away for about a week and when they did catch them, this bugger was out there on the pit head waiting. He pulled his pistol out and shot one. The other managed to get away, but the other guards knocked him down. Then the bloke shot him. They weren't satisfied with that, so they pulled the two bodies back into the compound, laid them out and left them there for a week or more. The Geneva Convention made no difference to him. There weren't any more escapes after that.

We worked seven days a week – no weekends. We were allowed out in the compound after we got back from work. I didn't do much in the way of outdoor activities, though we would walk around the compound for a bit of exercise.

We didn't have any news coming through. The Germans used to supply us with a monthly magazine about all the British planes they had shot down and all the ships they had sunk, which we ignored. It wasn't until just before D-Day landings that I managed to scrape together enough bits and pieces to make myself a wireless set. I made it with cats' whisker and a bit of crystal. The crystal was easy to get because it was in the carbide lamps. It was the other bits and pieces that were more difficult. I managed to get a couple of ear phones from the telephones down in the pit, I pulled them off the wall. But I needed a plug. I thought, well I'll have that bugger off the wall – it looks a bit loose. So I yanked it away. All of a sudden my body started going in and out, then I was flung off right between a load of trucks which fortunately weren't moving. When I got up I felt bloody marvellous. I don't know if I have felt so bloody good in all my life. Anyway I got my plug and a bit extra: I was lucky really. I got my wireless working so I was able to hear of the advance of our troops through Europe. Someone had drawn a map, so we were able to see how the advance was going. I used to lie in bed at night listening to it: one night I fell asleep with the damn thing on and it was only the guards, making such a bloody noise which warned me in time to grab the lot and put it under the bed.

I had two operations while I was there. I had my appendix taken out. In hospital you couldn't have been treated better, they were marvellous. Later on in the war I had something wrong with my inner ear. They didn't have any general anaesthetic, so they did it with a local anaesthetic. They had to cut the

257

bone out of the back of the ear using a hammer and chisel. I remember every second of that. By Christ it was like a sledgehammer banging into my head. Those doctors were fantastic.

We lost a Jewish lad, not from the British army. He had a tumour on the brain. You wouldn't have expected they had much time for him, but they did everything for him. He could speak several languages: when I sat up with him when he was in a coma and dying, he went through the whole lot of them, ending up speaking Yiddish. The doctor came to verify his death. He covered him over, stood at the end of the bed and, making the sign of the cross, said a prayer. I wouldn't have believed that of a German to a Jew, but he did it. I am not a religious man myself, but that was very moving. He must have known about the concentration camps. Everyone knew.

We were moved out of the camp because the Russians were closing in on us. We only knew when they told us to pack up all our stuff and get out in the middle of the night. It was dead of winter and bloody cold out there. We were marched all together covering 1,200 kilometres south into Germany and all the way down to Vienna. We were on the move for four months.

We passed Auschwitz when the Jewish prisoners were being moved out: they were literally like skeletons and were so bloody hungry they were asking us for food. They were literally skin and bone. It was terrible.

Many died on the march from frost-bite and one thing and another. I never thought I would get through it. The worst I got was a fungal infection, Chinese foot. My heels were like rhinoceros hide. We had the same pair of clogs all the way through. I didn't have socks, only a piece of rag to wrap around my feet. It was cold. We couldn't bury anyone that died, we didn't see what happened to them, we just kept marching – they wouldn't let us stop.

When I was first captured a French priest came round asking for our names and addresses, saying he'd write down and let 'them' know where we were. I gave him my address. In the meantime the navy had put out my name as 'lost, presumed dead', at Calais in 1940. Which my family read. They didn't know until about twelve months later that I was actually alive and in a prison camp. Then they had another four more years to wait. I was able to write to them and I got letters back.

We eventually met up with the Americans – General Patton's Third Army. We saw them coming in the distance, a whole column of tanks. He was sitting up there in the front tank. When they came up to us in the village they disarmed the few guards who were left and the first thing the Yanks said was 'Do you want a gun to shoot these bastards?' If they had been the guards that had been there originally, I would gladly have shot the buggers but they changed them over before we got there. These ones were as good as gold. How could you shoot them?

General Patton sat up in his tank and said 'Go and knock on any door and make yourself at home for the night.' It was a little village somewhere in Germany or Austria. Me and my mate went and knocked on this door and asked if we could stay and they said 'Yes, come in.' They were nice and kind. They couldn't speak any English but we could talk German. In five years we had learnt it. It was only a bed we wanted really. We didn't have a bath. They only had the one bed and they insisted that we both had this bed with a duvet: I had never seen a duvet nor even heard of one. You can imagine what happened when we got under: what with the heat and the lights there were fleas all over the bed by the morning. I felt terrible because I didn't want to take their bed but they insisted. I mean, even though they were Germans, I still didn't like to. They gave us breakfast and we were then moved off.

We were marched to an aerodrome. This was the first time I had been in an aeroplane. It was a Yankee plane, a troop carrier with seats down the sides – a Dakota. We went up in this thing and suddenly—oomph! We came down about three hundred foot. Then it went up and down again; what a blooming trip that was. They took us to France where we got into one of our own Lancaster bombers. It could carry quite a few in the body. I managed to climb up in the centre gunner's cockpit and I had that all to myself. All was fine until we came over England and were about to land. Then one of the bloody engines cut out. I thought 'Oh no, not all this bloody way just to be killed just before we land.' Anyway, we did land all right.

That was it. They sent us back to Chatham. I was eighteen when I was captured so I was twenty-three by this time. We were only there long enough to be checked out and put in new uniforms, then we were sent home on eighty-three days leave after five years.

My Dad was at Chesham station to meet me. Mum was at home because it was late at night. It was the first time my Dad ever kissed me. When I wrote to him, he had replied, 'It might seem a long time now, but once it's over it won't seem too bad'. We walked back from the station and met my younger sister and Mum at the front door – she was over the moon. I was pretty thin, around nine or ten stone, having been about twelve stone when I went away.

ABLE SEAMAN THOMAS BARNHAM, RN

When we arrived at Stalag 344, in 1942, it was full of army personnel except for one compound which had a few Air Force lads. Those that weren't

NCOs had to go out to work, working on farms, all different jobs. Some were billeted out permanently, some of them worked in coal mines or brick works. At this camp we had a boy who was an Imperial Amateur champion boxer. Another camp asked for him to go and box at their camp, which the Germans agreed to. But he wouldn't have it, he said, 'I'm a regular in the Services and if I get beat I've got to live with it.' So one morning we got up early, I had a couple of mates with me, an English officer and three Germans. We set off and we travelled half the day and I boxed at this camp and won.

The Germans had the front seats. After that I had it made. We had roll-call at seven in the morning, but when they came and said 'Aufstanden,' which means 'Get up everybody,' they said 'Boxer, bleiben, you can lie in, stay,' so I never used to go on roll-call. Only a silly little thing but I appreciated it, and that's what happened every morning after a boxing match. They'd never cry 'Well done,' but they'd always give me a lie-in, which was real luxury. And I never lost a match.

We were treated reasonably well. First thing in the morning you'd either have black coffee or mint tea. At 11.00am you'd get four or five jacket potatoes and a black loaf between seven with a bit of butter and a bit of meat; then about 12.30 you'd get a pea soup or Sauerkraut. That was your lunch and at about half past two or quarter to three you'd either get your coffee or your tea again, that was your meal. That was all you got, but fortunately we used to get one Red Cross parcel a week each from England. But if we ran out of them we could go probably two months before they'd come in again. I was very fortunate because of my boxing. An English army officer said to me, 'What food do you get, my friend?' I said, 'I get the same as you, sir' although I knew he was living a lot better than I was. So he says, 'You've no extras at all?' and I said, 'No, I get Red Cross parcels the same as the rest of them,' and 'Oh,' he said, 'Something's got to be done about this,' so he gave me a chit so that I could get an extra Red Cross parcel a week. But there were a lot of hungry lads, so whatever I got went in the middle and was shared out, so it hardly meant much.

Towards the end of the war the Germans brought thousands of Russian prisoners in and put them in the camp next to us. There was only barbed wire in between. We watched these people walking and they looked at us as though the wind was blowing through them. They were starving. Typhus broke out and a lot of them died. There was a Russian kid there who was about sixteen and any time we ever threw any bread over to him, which we often did, before he could get it all the other Russians had it. So I said, 'I want to get that kid and bring him into our camp'. One day I cut the wire, brought the kid in and put him in English uniform. He stayed with us two months in our camp. Couldn't speak a word of English, but we used to sit him on our bunk and say, 'What's your name?' and we'd teach him to say, 'Monty Banks' in English; 'Where have you come from?' 'London.' 'Where were you caught?' 'Arnhem.' Four or five little questions which he knew the answer to. An English officer came to me one day and he said, 'We'll toss him back, because if typhoid breaks out in this camp I'm going to hold you responsible and put you on a court martial.' But if you've been a prisoner for four-and-a-half years you don't care, so you can guess what I told him to do.

I must have been at that camp about two and a half years and then they shifted us to a camp in Obersilesien and while we were there the Russians came in.

The Germans put the whole camp on a march, bar those that were sick. I suppose there were a few thousand on the march and there was thick snow. I pretended to be sick so I didn't have to go. About three weeks later they sent off everyone who remained on cattle wagons and we travelled for about five or six days and finished up near Munich.

The Yanks were coming towards us so then everybody had to march, sick or not. We marched all night and slept during the day. Our guards were all old men, seventy or more and they kept falling asleep on the march and we had to wake them so they could take us on. After the first night I'd had enough – I had huge blisters on my feet. So I planned to escape with seven mates of mine, including Monty. An officer came to me and said, 'I hear you're going to bugger off tonight,' and I said, 'Yeah, I'm not having any more of this.' He said, 'You're taking the Russian, with you?' and I said, 'He wants to come,' and so he said, 'Well look, do yourself a favour and the boy a favour, don't let him come because ninety-nine percent, you'll get caught and he's got no chance. You being English, you'll get away with it, but if they know he's a Russian they'll shoot him.' So I left Monty behind with a mate of mine. He later told me Monty was taken off by some Yanks, but I don't know what happened to him after that.

The rest of us got away and finished up in a barn. Some German farmers looked after us for a while, but we were getting a bit restless, so we went out and nicked two cars, a BMW and a Mercedes-Benz, and half of us went in one car and the other half in the other. We drove right through Germany and into France. Whenever we got low on petrol, English or American lorries would give us cans of petrol. We finished at a place called Nancy and when we got there the Yanks pulled us in and put us on a plane home.

When we landed they put us on a train and we finished up at the naval base at Havant in Hampshire. They supplied us with a naval uniform, and gave us our back pay, which was about £200 or £300. Enough to buy a house with in those days.

CORPORAL BERNARD SLACK, RM

Six months after leaving Normandy we went into the Commando base to be reformed, as part of the 116 and 117 Brigades. I was in 33rd Battalion of 117 Brigade. At the time no-one knew that there was only five months to go before Germany capitulated and the war ended. First 116 Brigade went. Then we were getting ready, when out of the blue they picked out 33rd Battalion. We'd done all this training, we'd unstitched all identification, green-painted every bit of brass, so they put us all on one side, saying hang on a bit, we'll tell you what's happening later on.

They sent the 33rd Battalion back into France, under a commando brigadier of Czechoslovakian descent. In France we were doing infantry training, keeping it up, and all of a sudden, one night along comes a transport and we are taken to an airfield in Belgium. Nobody knew what was happening. I always remember the brigadier. He gave us an hour's 'Any Questions?' It turned out that, although under the armistice agreement the German Army had surrendered, the German Fleet had not, but the general public didn't know this.

The German Fleet was ordered off the high seas and, depending on their tonnage, their ships were told which port to make for. The big battle wagons were told to make for Kiel where I was, with the Royal Marines detachment there.

A boom had been thrown across the main harbour. We were outside the boom on landing craft, and our job was to board them; the Royal Navy was inside the boom. There were nine or ten of us on the boarding party – we were lucky, we'd got a German-speaking officer with us. We had to board them cold – mind you, it was handy that we each had a Thompson sub-machine-gun under our arm. The German ships had been told to have either the steps or the rope-ladders down ready, and no hanky-panky.

The very first thing we always did was to take the skipper off for interrogation ashore. They always say that the Germans are OK when they're being led. We always used to make sure the crew could see him being taken ashore. Imagine you've been a gunner in the German navy. You've looked after your gun, you've polished it, there's not a speck of dust gets on that gun, then along come a load of boot-necks and blow the ruddy thing up! So what's your re-action? Not surprisingly we lost some men.

Our CO would go aboard the ship, relay the skipper ashore, leaving about six of us on board, and then he'd come back for us. We had to go down the line of crew and take everything off them which had got the eagle and swastika on it. And then we blew the breeches on the guns fore and aft to make sure they couldn't fire. We left a skeleton crew on and the rest were taken off by Royal Navy patrol boats, and then, and only then, was it passed through the boom into the inner harbour for the Royal Navy to put about a hundred men on and go through it with a tooth comb. We weren't the real demolition party – our job was to see that there was no mucking about. Their weapons were supposed to be all piled up, but when we went over the side we had no idea if they'd obeyed us! We were hoping to God they had done.

We tried to make the crews keep standing to attention while we were on there, but some of our men had to fire into the deck of the ship at their feet, to get them to keep still, or fire into the air to let them know we were there. We didn't bother what was done: the Marines teach you to use your own discretion.

The U-boat base at Kiel had got a town actually underneath it. The biggest problem wasn't the German navy, which we were taking into internment, it was the DPs, the displaced persons. There was a big torpedo shed, with all the torpedoes on cradles waiting for the British experts to check. The torpedo fuel was wood alcohol, which was 98% proof. These DPs had got keys to the shed, and they were draining the fuel into cups and drinking it! We had to deal with all this; we used to mount patrols through this underground place and shoot. We just used to fire down halls and let the bullets ricochet; they'd soon stop, but you could still hear them moving about.

Kiel was terrible. There was shipping, railway, warehouses, big cranes, all rolled into one. It was totally demolished. Going through Hamburg was just as bad – people were living in tin shelters on the street.

Back in France we were all issued with a little handbook by the Intelligence Corps. Inside it said, 'You have the honour of being the advance guard of the army of occupation. Your future conduct will most likely influence the round-table conference, you're ambassadors for Britain.' Yet there we were in Hamburg dodging the bricks. You didn't look round for something bigger to sling back at them, you just bit your lip and kept your composure. Hamburg was like looking out from the top of a hill, and all you could see was bricks. There were trolley-poles sticking out of the rubble, bus roofs showing – it was shattered.

The Royal Marines were ordered to keep a riot squad on 24-hour call. To be a member you had to be over five foot eleven inches tall. I was six-foot-one.

We got called out to these camps outside Kiel where the DPs were. Once one of the DPs killed a deer, out in the forest. They brought it back and there was a fight going on, the guns were out, the knives were out, we had to go out there and deal with it all.

They shot one of our officers and dumped him in the canal. He was twenty-two years old. I was in the funeral party. They did find out the farmer who did it. I believe the main thing he killed him for was his shoes. That's what we were up against.

Another time, we were trying to clear a river, which was full of boats upside down with their propellers showing, and lots of other rubbish. On this river were these brothel barges for the German soldiers. There was a hell of a 'do' going on there, murders and gunfights. The girls were out of work, and were only too happy to accommodate any man. I had to go there and clear them out, shut them down.

They were big barges with beds in – sea-borne brothels. We got propositioned ourselves, but we had more damn sense than that.

ERIC WILLIAMS
Official Naval Reporter

As an official Navy reporter, I was the only journalist permitted to witness the official end of the U-boat war. It took place on Thursday, 10 May 1945, at Loch Eriboll, a narrow inlet in the north coast of Scotland. At seven o'clock that morning I stood on the crowded bridge of a frigate with Captain M. J. Evans who was in command of the operation, and scanned the sea for signs of approaching U-boats. The frigate's crew were closed up at action stations, in case there was any trouble.

At last we spotted a blob and mast and a faint smoke haze on the horizon and the black hull of U-1109 slid towards us. Our guns ranged on her and the U-boat's crew came into focus. I noticed their grey-green uniforms, unkempt beards, pallid skins and the peaked caps of the officers. This was the face of the enemy I had never seen in four years at sea.

I had met a U-boat before in the mid-Atlantic. It had sunk the ship I was on which was carrying old women and children. Since then I'd had a personal interest in U-boats.

We looked for the swastika, but it was not flying. Instead, a ragged green flag of surrender flapped at the mast. Our armed guard leapt aboard and mounted the bridge. The U-boat's commanding officer offered a lame Nazi salute and a few seconds later the Royal Navy's white ensign stood proudly on the conning tower.

Another U-boat had been sighted and, as it approached, we went alongside in a launch and I boarded her. Our guns were trained on her bridge. I asked the sullen CO what had made him join the U-boat service. He drew himself up and said, 'All Germans want to go to the front. I wanted to do it; it was doing more for my country.' He sounded as if he was repeating a vow.

More U-boats came in to surrender and, as I talked to their crews, I built up a fascinating impression of these brave, clever and determined men. Discipline was the backbone of their character – implicit and unquestioning obedience. They preferred to be known as soldiers, not sailors, and they obeyed automatically. When I asked one officer whether he would obey an order he knew to be wrong, he smiled and said, 'But that would not happen. We do not get wrong orders.'

After surrender the U-boats were inspected and then sailed in escorted convoy over to Lisahally in Northern Ireland, where the official surrender was to take place. I sailed over in U-293 in the care of its commandant, Leonhard Klingspor, and a small armed guard. Klingspor was 27, dark, virile and energetic, and he spoke very good English. I stood with him on the tiny bridge on the first evening and talked.

He claimed to have sunk ten ships since 1942. He was very pleased about that. He said he thought it would have been much better for Britain to have allied with Hitler against Russia. When I told him about the concentration camps he smiled and said, 'Propaganda – all propaganda!'

It was a pleasant evening and I felt relaxed and happy. Klingspor gave a quick cheerful command down the conning tower hatch and a few seconds later the sound of Mozart came floating up. Later it was Wagner.

I turned in at about midnight, but was woken a few hours later by the roll of the boat and the crash of water down the conning tower. I put on oilskins and struggled up to the bridge to find a gale blowing and seas breaking over the boat. Klingspor was on the bridge. 'When I say, "Watch out" get under the bridge,' he said. I realised I was now dependent on the seamanship of a U-boat captain. Klingspor gave me a belt which I clipped onto the bridge. He was in his element. He said, 'I like this weather. It is good for attack. The escorts can do nothing.'

He described how he would chain himself to the bridge and ride a following sea, letting the waves break under him, riding in to the attack. I could only admire his courage, but I felt sick and went below.

Later, Klingspor told me about his family, his wife and two children whom he had not seen for fifteen months. He launched into a diatribe about Germany's persecution by the rest of Europe and finished up by saying, 'See, we shall make you a good Nazi yet!' His self-assurance was baffling.

As we approached Culmore Point we heard the packed crowd singing,

'Rule Britannia'. It was a wonderful moment. I looked at Klingspor for some reaction but he did not seem to know the words or the music. As he left for the prison camp I said, 'I am glad you'll now have the chance of finding out the truth for yourself. You will see how false your propaganda was.' He looked at me with a small smile and said, 'I wonder.' And so did I.

7

The Far East War
and Liberation

LIEUTENANT JOHN HARVEY-JONES, RN

When *Voracious* arrived at Colombo we found that our role was to be a training submarine for anti-submarine destroyers. That of course was a necessary job but no fun at all. I was very lucky because, when I arrived, it was decided that I should go immediately to another operational submarine. So I shifted to an S-Class submarine called *Sea Scout* which was 750 to 800 tons and had a crew of 42, and the usual complement of four officers.

Initially we worked off the Andaman Islands and Penang. There was an occasional target you could coast to, but mostly our job was intercepting junks and searching them for contraband or, if there was no contraband and virtually everything including food was contraband, you took the crew off and blew the junk up. The difficulty was that the Japs had quite good anti-submarine vessels and they had also a good number of aircraft in Malaya. Also the Gulf there was very very shallow so you didn't have a lot of water to get under. There were two good things about the patrols, first of all going across the Indian Ocean to the Andamans and back was absolutely fantastic, day after day with just a diesel pumping along, and those marvellous clear nights with only the sky and the stars. It was a nice temperature and during the day we had the opportunity to get some sun. Since we were continuously at war stations we couldn't all slope around on the upper deck or the casing of the submarine, so it was only possible when you were on watch, but nevertheless the passages were an absolute joy and when we were actually on patrol on most days something happened. The captain had a curious view – he didn't trust the two junior officers to run watches on their own, particularly when we were on the surface, and so the first lieutenant and I were worked watch on watch which was very very tiring. Submarine practice was that you only did a two-hour watch so we had two hours on and two hours off for very long periods.

Then it was decided we should go out to Fremantle to operate off Indonesia. The Japanese were beginning to be beaten but they were still fighting in New Guinea. We were there for a while going up into the South China Sea.

The patrols were very long and the only way you were allowed back was if you had fired all your torpedoes. We used to pray for a target which would justify torpedoes but very seldom did we see anything. We did see large craft from time to time but we never sank anything of any notable size.

It was very rare to get through a patrol without being depth-charged. Being depth-charged is particularly unpleasant. First of all it makes a hell of a noise. It is rather like having your head inside a pail with somebody hitting it with a stick so that it clangs and reverberates. Secondly, when you are depth-charged what happens is that lights go out and little spurts of water start to come in. So you have darkness and the sound of water coming in. You can't tell whether it is a lot of water coming in or a little water coming in. The real trouble with being depth-charged, unlike being bombed, is that when you are bombed you are never quite sure it is you they are aiming at. If you are being depth-charged there is no doubt about it. It is almost personal.

After every operational patrol you got some sort of break, and indeed you needed it. It isn't that the patrols were horrendously rough and tough – in comparison with fighting in the trenches it was a doddle. With submarines, it was the absence of daylight and never being in the open air that really got to you. Many of our sailors went down into the submarines and wouldn't actually breathe or see fresh air outside the submarine until they got back into harbour. In the Far East that could be for two or three months. You always had to be ready to dive at a moment's notice, in fact your only protection was to dive, and so we were always very restricted on how many people you had up top. You could have two or three in the conning tower but that was it. The submarines in those days only had the air they went down with and we didn't have any way of generating fresh oxygen. We had a few cylinders of oxygen that could be released if you were kept down for a long time, say for twenty-four, even thirty hours. At the end of thirty hours you were getting very very short of oxygen indeed, and then of course behaviour would change. Being short of oxygen is a bit like being drunk, you feel that you are totally in command of everything but in reality your control of your actions has gone. Then, when you eventually did surface, the fresh air used to some in and actually getting real fresh air with a full oxygen quotient you felt absolutely light-headed.

The longest such spell I had was a bit over thirty hours and that was very unpleasant. Then everybody who wasn't actually needed to work the submarine would lie down to save oxygen. The fear in those situations was that, if you went to sleep, you might not wake up again, though that isn't a bad way to go!

LIEUTENANT-COMMANDER ARTHUR HEZLET, RN

We left for the Far East just after D-Day in *Trenchant*, which had just been completed at Chatham dockyard. We were rubbing our hands, as there were likely to be plenty of targets. Unfortunately the Americans practically sank most of the Japanese fleet before we got there. We arrived in the Far East and made our first patrol outside Sumatra, mainly as an air/sea rescue operation for a B29 bombing raid on Palambang. We had various kinds of electronic gadgets to tell us when they were going overhead so that wasn't a very exciting patrol except that two small Japanese vessels came along, and we popped up with our gun and sank the pair of them. It was quite an exciting battle for they put up a fairly good fight with their machine-guns. But our 4-inch gun soon mastered them.

Although we knew the Japanese normally had no intention of being taken prisoner, we tried to cut off a section of them from what was obviously the commanding officer, and managed to get a few prisoners. We brought them back just in case they were of some use for intelligence purposes and I remember we suspected they were Korean and we thought, 'Let's see what the intelligence books say.' The book said the way to tell a Japanese from a Chinaman is by the big toe. The Japanese always use the one-thonged sandal which means the big toe is completely separate from the others; but we couldn't notice any difference in their toes. The other test of a Japanese (this is scarcely believable but was in the books) was to give them a banana to peel. Apparently a Japanese has a special way of peeling a banana: he cuts it diagonally in half and then he squeezes the ends out like toothpaste. But the trouble was that no-one in Great Britain had seen a banana for four years and where they thought we were going to get a banana from I don't know. Anyway we brought the prisoners back. We decided we didn't like the idea of Japanese being loose in a submarine so we kept them in the torpedo compartment with two armed guards all the time. That was the first time I had come face-to-face with the enemy.

For our second patrol we were sent inside the Malacca Straits with a body of eight commandos, commanded by a major. They were equipped with explosives and four fall-boats, and they were going to try and blow up a bridge in Sumatra which had a road and rail running over it. We found the bridge eventually and we went in that night and launched the commandos. But they found the current in the river too strong and they could make no headway at all. They were very upset having gone all that way for nothing, so after a conference with the major we decided to try again. The next night we landed them on the beach half a mile away from the bridge and they laid their explosives very satisfactorily. But as they withdrew they came across a native chap. They didn't want him to follow them but they didn't want him to tell the Japanese about the changes either. The major said, 'We'll have to knock him out and leave him on the beach.' So they turned to the sergeant and said, 'Knock him out.' The Sergeant tried, but this chap just shook his head, he couldn't be knocked out. So the subaltern hit him on the back of the head with a pistol and even that didn't knock him out. Then they thought, 'This is a bit much, we've been really rather nasty to this fellow,' so they gave him all the counterfeit money which they'd been given in case they were taken prisoner and left this poor half-stunned fellow on the beach by the bridge and started paddling off. They were supposed to come out on a compass course and after so many paddle strokes they were supposed to stop. However they paddled on past us out to sea and I couldn't see them anywhere. It began to get light to the east and I thought, 'I'm afraid they've had it,' and turned around and headed out to sea, practically running them down from behind. We got them all on board and by that time the bridge had been demolished by the explosive charges. This patrol was eventful. Subsequently we laid a minefield off Sumatra and then sank U-boat 859 off Penang on 23rd September.

Eventually the whole flotilla moved to Fremantle in Australia. The war was getting pretty close to the end – this was well into 1945 – and we did a patrol up into the East Indies from Fremantle. We knew that the Japanese were pulling their troops back into Singapore from all the outlying places in the East Indies with the intention of making a fighting retreat up the Kara Peninsula into Siam. They were using two cruisers from Singapore to fetch these troops. While we were passing through the East Indies one of these cruisers, the *Ashigara*, was seen going into Batavia by two American submarines. At that time I was very nicely placed to intercept I made a signal to the American command (it being an American operational area) asking permission to intercept in the Banka Straits, which was approved. We went into the top of the Straits at the same time as another smaller British submarine, an 'S' Class, did the same thing. We went alongside at night to discuss what we'd do. I said, 'The best billets are obviously inside the minefield and what we've got to do is put one submarine on each side of the minefield.' I was quite prepared to toss a coin for whoever went in for the better place and he began to say, 'Oh, I don't think you could go inside there.' I didn't give him another chance. I said, 'Right-o, you stay outside,' and we went round the end of the minefield, very close to the rocks. The depth of water in the straits was 15 fathoms, about 80–90 feet, fairly shallow but quite enough to dive under a ship if it tried to ram you. We waited on the surface to charge the batteries and got a report from the American submarines that the *Ashigara* was on her way north and that she had one destroyer with her. So for the rest of that night we waited on the surface and we sighted something at about three in the morning. It was quite dark, and we couldn't see whether it was the cruiser or the destroyer. I didn't want to dive because if you dive on a dark night like that you can't see through the periscope and you've lost the whole initiative, so I was determined to stay up until I'd solved this question and fired the torpedoes. I let him get far too close but there was nothing I could do about it. We were bow to bow and, as he went by, we swung to keep end on. I heard after the war that he did see us and thought we were a junk, but by keeping bow on to him we didn't give a submarine-shaped silhouette. But we got very, very close and I could hear his boiler room fans as he went past. Then I couldn't keep the swing up and he saw what we were and opened fire. All the shots went right over the top so I turned away and fired a stern torpedo at him. He saw it coming and turned away from the torpedo and the range opened stern to stern, very fast. I was still looking for the cruiser but there was no sign of her. Luckily we shook the destroyer off and went on with the patrol while he went on out to sea.

When daylight came we dived and waited and soon after daylight the *Ashigara* came in sight coming up the Sumatran side, without the destroyer. The destroyer had gone out to sea and this colleague of mine in the 'S' Class had a shot at him and he then turned on the 'S' Class, dropped depth-charges and probably said to the cruiser, 'I've got him, come on by. I'll sit on him while you go by,' not realising there were two of us.

The *Ashigara* then came up on the Sumatran side and we fired a full salvo of eight torpedoes, five of which hit her. She capsized after about half an hour and sank and 800 men were drowned: she had 2,000 troops on board. I let a lot of the ship's company have a look through the periscope and we stuck up so much periscope that the *Ashigara*, which hadn't sunk by then, saw it and opened fire with her anti-aircraft guns. Then we squeezed out past the minefield.

PETTY OFFICER AIRMAN ROY GIBBS, RN

The month of June 1945 saw the British Pacific Fleet licking its Sakishima wounds and replenishing in Sydney, Australia. *Indomitable* was relieved by

Implacable, fresh from its day and night operations against the Japanese held island of Truk. At last the British Pacific Fleet had its highly trained night operating carrier.

On the *Indefatigable* most of the surviving TAGS (Telegraphist Air Gunners) of 820 Squadron were replaced with new faces. Those drafted had been operational through the raids on the *Tirpitz* in Norway, Palembang in Sumatra, and the Sakishima/Formosa campaign. Those of us lucky/ unlucky to remain were placed with senior crews such as the CO and Flight Leaders.

The Fleet set sail from Sydney on 28th June. Very little flying time was available for the new crews to work up. In fact my records show only two dive-bombing practices and four dummy strikes with my new two ring, flight-leader pilot, before we went into action on 24th July. Our first target was a Jap escort carrier in Shido Wan harbour in the Inland Sea.

We settled down to a similar pattern of strikes as at Sakishima, but with more interesting targets. Extracts from my log book record: 'STRIKE. Ships and coastal installations south of Kobe. 2 ships sunk. STRIKE. Shipping Sata harbour, 1 ship and installations left on fire.' 'STRIKE. Maizuru Naval Base, northern coast of Japan. Heavy flak to and from target.' Once again the Jap was proving to be an unpredictable enemy and the defences of targets varied from strike to strike.

For this operation we were designated Task Force 37 and unlike Sakishima, were very much an integral part of the American Fleet. We were even beginning to get mentioned by the British press. One quote said, 'At the end of July it was announced that 1,230 Japanese ships and 1,257 aircraft had been destroyed in 22 days by the Third Fleet, of which the British Pacific Fleet is part. On 9th and 10th August the Fleet sent more than 1,000 planes in strikes against Northern Honshu.'

The opposition was slowly being beaten down, suicide bombers were still attacking, but were mainly piloted by young, new pilots and were becoming less effective.

The first Atom Bomb was confirmed as dropped on 7th August and the second on 11th August. Our Firefly Squadron CO, Major Cheesman, later wrote 'Some people today condemn the use of the Atomic Bomb, but we who were out there at the time owe our lives to the use of these two bombs.' The British Pacific Fleet was in desperate straits, short of fuel, stores, planes, bombs and all the things needed to maintain the type of action in which we were involved.

Since the Japanese had already asked for peace terms Admiral Rawlings decided to withdraw the main body of the Fleet. On 12th August they left, leaving the *Indefatigable*, *King George V*, two cruisers and ten destroyers to carry on the fight. On 13th August we were over north Tokyo, the flak was ferocious but, with our fighters, we shot down 21 Jap planes. We refuelled from a US Tanker on 13th August and on 15th August came the final madness. Although peace was certain that day, the powers-that-be decided on one more final strike with our remaining serviceable aircraft, 6 Avengers, 4 Fireflies and 8 Seafires. The target, Kizarazu Naval Airbase, Tokyo Bay. They went and met a lot of opposition with a loss of aircraft and lives. Even as they were fighting their way back the ceasefire was declared. A stupid unnecessary waste.

We 'spliced the mainbrace' and out came the saved bottled tots in the mess. One CPO Seafire pilot got so stoned that he walked off the side of the flight deck. On his return, the commander threatened to charge him with 'breaking out of ship and breaking in'.

As if we hadn't had enough trouble, on 28th August we were hit by a terrible typhoon. After it was over the American Carrier *Wasp*, with 30 feet of its flight deck hanging over the bows, signalled, 'How did you weather the typhoon?' Our skipper replied, 'What typhoon?'

Until 1st September we flew over Japan looking for POW camps, with some success. All this time we stayed at Action Stations because of the danger of renegade suicide bombers. This gave rise to the famous signal 'It is likely Kamikazes will attack the Fleet as a final fling. An ex-enemy aircraft attacking the Fleet is to be shot down in a friendly manner.'

Finally, as the peace had been signed we sailed into Tokyo Bay on 5th September 1945. When our troopship finally got into Southampton, not only we, but also the many Japanese prisoners-of-war, were turned over by the Customs.

Welcome home, lads. I wonder what they thought we were trying to smuggle?

We had had some success: the Palembang Oilfields had lost two-thirds of their production as a result of our strikes and we had destroyed 68 enemy aircraft but had lost 41 of our aircraft. At Sakishima and Formosa 57 enemy aircraft, excluding probables, were destroyed and the Japanese were success-fully stopped from attacking the Americans in the rear at Okinawa. But altogether the British Pacific Fleet lost 203 aircraft out of a total of 218, which meant a 93% replacement during the operation. It made it difficult to be seen as the Forgotten Fleet. Altogether 356,760 tons of enemy shipping were sunk or damaged.

SUB-LIEUTENANT DICK REYNOLDS, RN

On 10th March the *Indefatigable* sailed from Sydney for the invasion of Okinawa. En route we disembarked at a US air-station at a remote Pacific

Atoll called Ulithi. When we arrived there it was full of American naval and marine squadrons. We had been sworn to silence before we disembarked, so we were very conscious of security, but the Americans were talking quite freely about the invasion. They said, 'It's all right, you are in Ulithi and there is no communication between us and the outside world so you can say what you like.' We were soon briefed by them. A young intelligence officer got up – his words have stuck in my memory to this day. He said, 'You chaps have been fighting in the European theatre, there is one big difference. Those goddamn Germans fight to live, but now you are out here these bastard Japs fight to die.' Those were his exact words.

After sailing north, our task was to subdue all air movement of the Japanese on the islands of Sakishima Gunto. We entered operations there on 25th March. Avengers, Corsairs, Hellcats and Fireflies struck the various airfields. Seafires of 887/894 Squadrons provided low and medium defensive combat air patrols (CAP).

As most suicide attacks came in at very low level, the American system was to keep at least two squadrons of fighters on station to protect the fleet, rather than scrambling aircraft at the last moment. So you could at least be at the right height and, if you were correctly vectored, you would be in the right place. On April Fool's Day, 1st April Peter Roome, our batsman, came up to me before take-off and said, 'What a glorious morning Dick, I envy you being up there.' Everybody on deck was in shorts and sandals! After lunch we were told there was a raid developing to the west. Our senior Fighter Direction Officer, Ian Easton, an experienced pilot and FDO, had always placed us in a good attacking position on previous engagements. I always felt very confident with Ian as he had always got it right. On this day sure enough a big raid did develop but we didn't intercept it until it got into the fleet because they came in very low. The first the radar boys knew about it was when they were only ten miles away.

I got on the tail of a Zeke after he had already dived on *King George V*. I remember quite distinctly, he pulled up, I got on his tail again and managed to give him a burst. I clipped his port wing, he rolled over on his back and dived straight into a carrier which was enveloped in smoke and flames. I thought, you poor bastards. What I didn't realise was that it was my ship; as you can imagine, from 2,000 feet four fleet carriers look exactly alike. I then got on the tail of another Zeke who dropped a bomb on the destroyer *Ulster*, and hit her in the engine-room. He then turned for base but I stuck on his tail, overhauled him and shot him down with a long burst from dead astern. I remember flying past and seeing the pilot slumped in the cockpit – he went straight in the sea so that was that. Returning to the fleet, I was getting pretty low on fuel, but another Zeke appeared on our opposite course, I pulled around, got on his tail, gave him the rest of my ammunition and he went into the sea. So that was 1st April 1945, a day which will always be in my memory.

We had a method of identifying our ship on returning. We had a pivot ship, a cruiser, from which we would take a bearing to our own ship. The ships were always in the same relative position. When I landed I leapt down and there was this blackened flight-deck with a bloody great hole in the Island. That was the first time I realised the situation. The ship recovered all its aircraft safely, in spite of some arrester wires and barriers being out of action.

The sight on deck was unbelievable; a lot of chaps had been killed. The tragedy was that in those days we had our 'ready rooms' in the ship's Island which of course was the nerve centre of the ship, and that is how we lost so many fine people, including the ship's doctor and some very good aviators. Many of the pilots who were at readiness were killed. From that day our new ships, like *Ark Royal* and *Eagle*, all had their 'ready rooms' under the armoured deck. Our armoured flight deck had been pierced, only just, but that meant that the whole blast from the impact had gone through the softer 'flesh', for want of a better word, and had blown up most of the Island. Had it been an American carrier with a wooden deck it would have been a total disaster.

I went to report to the captain who was on the bridge with full whites and medal ribbons, as was the form in those days during actions stations. He looked at me and said, 'Well done.' He heard the R/T relayed to the bridge. I then went down to the wardroom and had a couple of gins. I had lost my cabin mate and best friend. But I couldn't think about it, I daren't. I flew that afternoon.

SUB-LIEUTENANT IVOR MORGAN, RN

I was a pilot with 894 Squadron aboard *Indefatigable*, The sun shone in a cloudless sky at 0500 on 1st April 1945. I was not to fly that day, being temporarily grounded by an ear infection. My job that particular morning was that of Duty Pilot, to supervise flight deck movements – including the ranging and striking down of aircraft – noting the number of each as it took off (and, hopefully, as it returned), acting as liaison between the captain and Air Branch, and generally assisting Commander (Flying) Pat Humphries, known universally as 'Wings'.

As we waited for the fleet to turn into wind, I was struck by the fact that only the captain was correctly dressed in naval uniform. In order to afford some sort of protection against fire we all wore long trousers and long-sleeved shirts – blue for the ratings, khaki drill for the officers. Dominating the scene was the resplendent figure of Captain Quentin Dick Graham, in his high-necked Number Ten tropical white uniform, complete with medal ribbons from 1914 onwards.

'Wings' gave the order to start-up and soon the aircraft were roaring up the deck. Everything went smoothly, not a single machine was U/S and the spare aircraft remained on the deck until such time as they would be taxied forward preparatory to landing-on.

The first inkling I had of trouble was the sound of aerial firing and, looking upwards, saw two aircraft in a tail chase about 2,000 feet above the ship. At first I thought they were two of ours and it had only just registered that the leading machine had a radial engine, whereas our Seafires had in-lines, when it turned on its back and I distinctly saw the 'Rising Sun' roundels on its wings as the pilot commenced a power-dive directly at the spot where I was standing!

By this time all hell had broken loose. All of our guns, from 5.25s to pom-poms and additions, had opened fire, people were yelling. The captain gave a helm order, I rushed on to the main bridge, closed the armoured door behind me – and flung myself down full-length on the deck, together with everyone else.

We waited. The engine roar got louder and louder. There was no escape. This was it, this was how it was going to end. Pity, I thought, life is so enjoyable on the whole. I felt no fear, only a vague disappointment that the curtains were about to be drawn.

And then another thought struck me. I'd like to be there, as some sort of disembodied spirit, when my father opened the telegram. He was a dogmatic person, who would never entertain any arguments but his own, some of which were quite preposterous, nor would he ever admit to being in the wrong. I suppose to hearten me he would always say, 'They couldn't get me at Ypres, they won't get you either.' The sheer illogic of this used to annoy me intensely.

Well, at last, he'd be proved wrong. Yes, I did so hope that there was some way in which I could be a fly on the wall when he learned that I had been killed.

Then came the crash, followed immediately by flame and a searing heat. I choked. I could not draw breath. I believe I lost consciousness. I next remember opening my eyes to see all the recumbent forms near me. All immobile. All dead, I thought I must be dead too. I tried to raise my shoulders and found that I was able to move although no-one else followed suit. Oh well, if this was being dead it wasn't so bad after all. Interesting to find that there was indeed a life hereafter, a fact in which I had never had much faith.

'Port fifteen.'

The captain's voice brought us to our senses and we shambled rather sheepishly to our feet. He above all, in his 'ice cream' suit, had remained erect and in command. This was the moment for which he had trained since joining the navy as a thirteen-year-old cadet in 1914. And he did not fail.

From then on things moved fast. With certain communication lines out of action I was ordered below to assess damage and casualties, for we could now see that the kamikaze had crashed into the bottom of the island at flight deck level. Flames engulfed both forward and after bridge ladders so I swarmed down the thick, knotted manilla rope which had been rigged for just such an emergency.

As I made my descent I saw Pat Chambers staggering aft, his back covered with blood. Someone ran forward and guided him to safety. An Avenger, in the process of being taxied forward, had collided with the superstructure, engine and cockpit blown to smithereens. Of the pilot, there was no sign.

The Damage Control party was already hosing the flames and I could now see a gaping hole where the island sick bay had been. Being of small stature I was able to crawl through the wreckage and there they were, my comrades Al Vaughan and Bill Gibson, showing no sign of injury but both killed by the blast, which had removed most of their clothing. In the passage between the sick bay and the Fighter Ready Room lay Lieutenant Leonard Teff, also killed by the blast which, miraculously, had left untouched the man on each side of him. Looking upwards I realised that the bridge mess was no more.

On regaining the bridge I was relieved to see Pat Humphries on the flight deck. A last minute dash to his cabin for some forgotten article had undoubtedly saved his life.

'Sandy' Sanderson, our Flight Deck Engineer, and his party were already rigging a replacement for No. 3 barrier which had been destroyed. Twenty minutes later we were landing-on, Sub-Lieutenant Dick Reynolds of 894 Squadron holding aloft a gloved hand to indicate two victories.

As soon as I was relieved, I went below to the hangar where maintenance crews were working with every sign of normality. They had thought their last moment had come when, unable to see what was happening, a terrific explosion occurred right above their heads. Flaming petrol ran down the hangar bulkhead, presumably through a fissure in the flight deck, threatening to engulf men and machines alike. Under the leadership of CPO 'Jimmy' Green the fire was brought under control without having to resort to sprinklers.

'Right lads. Show's over. Back to work.' The Jimmy Greens of this world are worth their weight in gold.

I proceeded to the sick bay, where the Principal Medical Officer Surgeon-Commander Yates and his team – Surgeon Lieutenant-Commando Henry Towers and Surgeon-Lieutenant Musgrave, together with their 'tiffies' – had been working non-stop since the kamikaze struck at 0730. With over forty casualties dead, dying and/or seriously wounded, accommodation was hope-lessly inadequate and the adjoining messdeck had been pressed into service as an auxiliary ward. There, upon mess tables, lay men too badly injured to survive. A steward with a hole in his head the size of a cricket ball, loosely plugged with cotton wool, a man with both legs missing. Between them were other casualties – men unrecognisable due to the burn dressings which covered head and body alike – and even as I looked for any of my own chaps, some were quietly slipping away into eternity.

I did find one, however, Able Seaman Gay, 894 Squadron's messenger, who was well into his forties when he joined up. Quiet, polite, conscientious, he was popular and respected by all. He sat, staring at nothing, in an advance state of shock.

If it had been the captain's moment, so had it been for the PMO. After fifteen hours at the operating table, he was ordered by his superior to take some rest. His reply was to order Captain Graham out of the Sick Bay in which, as a non-medical man, he had no authority. Only when, at 2300, it was obvious that he could do no more, did this fifty-five-year-old consent to turn in. The final toll of eleven dead and thirty-two injured but surviving, was in large measure due to his skill and leadership.

LIEUTENANT-COMMANDER T. V. BRIGGS, RN

On Wednesday 9th May the bulk of the East Indies Fleet had just returned to their base at Trincomalee on the east coast of Ceylon, after extended operations in the Andaman Sea covering the Army's recapture of Rangoon from the Japanese. Just before entering harbour, in the early hours of that day, we had listened to the King's broadcast on VE-Day and in a state of great exhilaration were looking forward to celebrating onboard and ashore.

We had hardly finished securing to our buoys when Rear Admiral Walker, sent for me and told me to arrange for every ship to sail as soon as possible – a 'Top Secret' signal had been received that a Japanese cruiser had sailed from Singapore on a mission thought to be to relieve the Japanese garrisons in the Andaman Islands. After a feverish day and night of replenishing with fuel, stores and ammunition (though with just enough time to celebrate VE-Day by splicing the mainbrace), the Fleet sailed at daylight the next morning, Thursday 10th May. We headed for Car Nicobar, the central island of the Andamans, to cut off the cruiser before she could return to Singapore.

That night submarine reports were received that a Japanese 'Nachi' class cruiser and a destroyer had passed through the One Fathom Channel at the north end of the Malacca Straits on a northerly course at a speed of 17 to 20 knots. From this it was clear that we would have to maintain a speed of 17 knots to achieve an interception if we were to pass the Ten Degree Channel, south of Car Nicobar.

The next morning, Friday, the *Shah,* one of the four Escort Carriers, broke down and had to reduce speed to 8 knots. Along with an adverse wind for flying off this made it clear that we were unlikely to achieve the necessary rate of advance.

Then, at about midday, a 'bogie' was reported on radar 80 miles to the eastward (220 miles west of Car Nicobar), and we became almost certain that the Force had been sighted by Jap reconnaissance aircraft. Our course was altered to the southeast to make for the southernmost channel into the Andaman Sea – the Six Degree Channel, between Great Nicobar and Sabang at the northernmost tip of Sumatra. This would give us a better chance of intercepting the cruiser on her return southwards, and less chance of being sighted again by Jap recce aircraft.

At nightfall a Fast Force consisting of *Cumberland, Richelieu* and the 26th Destroyer Flotilla, were sent on to be fifty miles ahead at dawn so as to increase our chances. However the next day, just before midday, as no reports of the enemy had been received, it was decided to haul off to the southwest, and the Fast Force was recalled.

Then, at 6pm that evening, a report was received from the submarine *Statesman* that the Jap cruiser, escorted by three destroyers, had passed southwards into the Malacca Straits. This was a severe blow to our plans, but not unexpected, as we thought we had been sighted by the Jap recce aircraft the day before. Our only hope now was that the cruiser would try again, and come north from Singapore.

Sunday was spent in a position safely to the west of the Sabang Channel fuelling destroyers from the Four Escort Carriers so as to be ready for any eventuality. The plan then was to move at our best speed towards the Six Degree Channel during the night so we would be as close as possible to the southern Andaman Sea, which our quarry had to pass through. Then we were to reverse course in time to be clear of recce aircraft by daylight. Fortunately there was good weather cover.

On 14th May, the Fuelling Force (Royal Fleet Auxiliary *Easdale*, escorted by *Paladin*) arrived in the area, and we rendezvoused with them during the night – *Tromp* was fuelled. At midnight, both Forces were about 220 miles west of the Six Degree Channel, steering east towards it.

We were now coming towards the end of the fifth day in Operation Dukedom. I was fully occupied day and night dealing with the operational requirements. Important decisions had to be made almost every hour. At the back of my mind was the awareness that at last we in the East Indies Fleet had the chance of combating a large Japanese surface ship – after over a year keeping the Japs occupied with air and gun bombardments and supporting the army in Burma in the Indian Ocean whilst the Americans battled with them in the Pacific. It was a great and timely opportunity to prove our mettle: we must not fail. All eyes were upon us and one could feel the expectancy of everyone in the Fleet. My position was a key one, advising the admiral on the spot. I had been on the admiral's bridge and had not slept for four days.

As soon as it was dark that Monday night, the admiral told me I must get some sleep. I remonstrated with him and said I would prefer to keep awake as I would be in no condition coming out of a deep sleep if the signal came with the intelligence we were all waiting for. But he insisted, and at about 8pm I lay down my clothes on the floor of my cabin which was nearby and immediately fell into a deep sleep.

Then of course it happened.

At 2am I was awakened by the admiral. He showed me the 'Top Secret' signal, and wanted to know what we should do about it. It was information that the 'Y' Party had intercepted a Jap signal indicating that some action was taking place at Sabang. A ship, probably an Escort vessel, was being sailed from Sabang. This was a real conundrum, and here was I trying to regain my full senses but, after being aroused, feeling very egg-bound.

This was not the clear-cut signal we had hoped for giving us information about the cruiser's movements. And there was a particularly difficult problem known only to me. I had a pact with Captain Power (D26), who had dropped into the Staff Office to see me after he had been summoned and briefed by the admiral on the day before we sailed. Our pact was that, if we sent him a signal ordering him to a position, it would signify that we had received the 'Top Secret' intelligence giving the cruiser's movements into the Andaman Sea. To launch him now with only a rather sketchy report that an escort had sailed would be contrary to that agreement. However, if the Jap cruiser was to try again, it seemed to me that the timing would be right for her to do so, and that if she did not do it now it would be unlikely that she would try at all. Furthermore, we had been at sea for five days after being in harbour only twenty-four hours after a previous twelve days operation – we could not stick around for much longer. Also the chances were becoming more and more remote. My training had taught me that when you get an enemy report you should send out your forces at full speed to intercept without delaying an instant. Usually you could call them back if it turned out to be a false alarm: however, in this case we did not want to have to break W/T silence and give the whole scheme away. The chance of this would have to be accepted. I therefore advised that if we could not get the cruiser, let us get the escort, or whatever was there. It would be better than waiting for the cruiser which might never come. I advised the admiral that we had better act now, and he agreed.

With some effort, as my mind was still clearing, I drafted the following signal:

To ... D26 (R) AC21 CS5   From ... BS3
PROCEED FORTHWITH WITH TWENTY SIXTH FLOTILLA AT 27 KNOTS TO SEARCH FOR AUXILIARY VESSELS CENTRE LINE 06 DEGREES 10 MINUTES NORTH 97 DEGREES 25 MINUTES NORTH 98 DEGREES 17 MINUTES EAST AT 2130GH 15 MAY. RETURN BY SAME ROUTE TO RENDEZVOUS WITH FORCE 70. AIR SEARCH AND STRIKE FROM CARRIERS WILL BE ARRANGED. THE ABOVE ORDERS MAY BE CANCELLED.

The search indicated was the best estimate of where the enemy might be if they sailed from Sabang, and would lead us about as far south as possible without chancing the Force being seen from the shore. They had 400–500 miles to go. I picked 27 knots as I knew from my destroyer days that they could go this speed with two out of their three boilers, and thus as economically on fuel as possible at high speed.

We supplemented this signal with another sixteen minutes later: ...

IF CANCEL 'MITRE' IS RECEIVED FROM C-IN-C EI OR BS THREE REJOIN ME.

This let the destroyer know that there was some question about the validity of the intelligence.

At 4am Operation Mitre was implemented by BS3, who then told CS5 to take command of Operation Mitre as he was taking the *Queen Elizabeth* back to fuel and rejoining on completion. We rendezvoused with the oiler at 7am and started fuelling at 8.20.

The subsequent chain of events was incredible.

To my utmost dismay a signal was received at about 0600 from AC21 saying that he was sending out an air search at 0820 of four Avengers. We had said in our operating signal that *we* would arrange air search. However we had not intended to do this before about noon, so as to enable 26 to get well to the eastward position where they could cut off any enemy forces in the area from retiring into the Malacca Straits. Unfortunately AC21's search would alert them and give them more time to escape. We wrongly thought we would have come to the same conclusion.

I should have made our intentions clearer. Now the damage had been done and, as the Carrier Force was now out of TBS touch it was better to leave things as they were and not break W/T silence – this with a heavy heart that my omission would prejudice our chances of success.

The next blow was the receipt of C-in-C, East Indies' signal at 1100 to cancel 'Mitre'. Before this, from about 0945 onwards, reports had come in from the air search that small enemy vessels had been sighted and attacked with bombs. At 1108 CS5 signalled to D26 to sink these enemy ships before returning. We received this signal in *Queen Elizabeth* at 1203, and immediately cast off and headed back to the Six Degree Channel at best speed.

Then, one of the search Avengers reported the presence of a heavy cruiser and destroyer, confirmed half an hour later as a '*Nachi*' class cruiser and '*Yubari*' class destroyer. The position given was about 150 miles east of the Six Degree Channel and 100 miles north of the Sumatra coast.

This was utterly unexpected and a great surprise. It was not thought that the cruiser could have passed northwards through the Malacca Straits without being sighted by our submarines, although from 12 May the patrol had been reduced from two to one. No intelligence signals had been received that a cruiser had sailed from Singapore. This was a devastating setback as the cruiser could regain the Malacca Straits at 20 knots, and D26 were not far enough advanced to intercept her. The early air search had, we considered, wrecked the operation.

D26, on receipt of C-in-C East Indies' signal to cancel 'Mitre' at about 1100, had continued on but at a reduced speed of 15 knots whilst he tried to sort out the conflicting orders. From BS3's operating signal, and with our pact in mind, he was under the impression that the cruiser was definitely there. On the other hand the C-in-C was the fountain of Ultra intelligence. He had also certainly received some of the air search's reports that auxiliary enemy vessels were in the area ahead. His action to carry on was therefore correct, and later was confirmed by CS5's signal at about noon to go on. Shortly after this he received the air search's report that the cruiser had been sighted, and exultingly went on again at once to 27 knots. As a result, only about 15 miles of advance had in fact been lost, which in the event did not prejudice the operation.

We pressed on through the Six Degree Channel to our rendezvous for the next morning, and as the night went on became more and more depressed when no action reports or sightings were received. Admiral Walker remarked to me, 'I shall probably be given a final shore job as a Rear Admiral and you will see out your time as Commander before we are retired.' Then at 0215, the signal office reported that part of a faint signal had been received '. . . cruiser, sinking . . .' at 0140. Suddenly our hopes were raised, but on reflection, having not received any action signals or sighting reports, we concluded that it must be some mistake, or the Japs planting a signal to deceive us. Our spirits drooped again, and it was not until about 9am we knew the truth, when we received a signal from the Commander-in-Chief congratulating us on sinking the Japanese cruiser *Haguro*. The hot damp air of the on-coming monsoon had deflected all D26's action signals upwards except that one faint one, so that we heard nothing through the night.

There was tremendous jubilation, especially as our casualties and damage were so small, and great pride that the East Indies Fleet had succeeded in the one major surface operation that presented itself, and in such a brilliant, epic night action by our destroyers, and the FAA operating as they were under the most difficult and hazardous conditions from Escort Carriers. As an operations officer, one learns that things seldom turn out as expected. Operation Dukedom was no exception. It was particularly nice, later, to receive a congratulatory signal from Admiral Fraser, the Commander-in-Chief of our British Pacific Fleet.

LIEUTENANT IAN FRASER, RNR

In June 1943 I was appointed as first lieutenant of an H-class submarine which was refitting in Sheerness. Eventually we sailed but where should we end up but in Londonderry! A boring bit of grey area as far as I was concerned.

We received a signal from the Admiralty asking for volunteers for special and hazardous service. I thought to myself, well, I'm married so they are not going to send me on anything particularly dangerous, which was a fallacy, of course. My navigator, Sub-Lieutenant David Carey, said, 'I'm fed up too. I'll volunteer with you.'

So we found ourselves in Rothesay and they said to me, 'Right, you're in command of an X-craft midget submarine. We want you to do six week's training at the top of Loch Striven. Which I did.

These submarines were 57 feet long. You could stay at sea in them for three weeks and they had a range of over a thousand miles. But I couldn't stand up in them and I'm only five foot four. Fortunately at that age I didn't get backache. These X-Craft had a speed of 6½ knots and if you went any faster you dived and couldn't stop diving. They were built in three pieces, each held together with 164 bolts so that it was possible to take the pieces apart, put a new battery in and even a new front end if you wished.

There were two methods of attack for X-craft. They had great long detachable tanks on either side, each of which held two tons of high explosive, which is what Godfrey Place* used. Place was a figure in the past by now, a prisoner-of-war. On our more advanced craft we also carried six 200-lb. limpet mines which the diver would attach to the bottom of the target's hull.

The crew of an X-craft consisted of four people, the captain, the first lieutenant and two others, one of whom was a diver. We also had two more

* see p.206

crews of four people known as passage crews because to get the X-craft from A to B you had a passage crew which stayed on board during the tow.

When we finished training we all went up to Eddrachillis Bay which is up in the north-west of Scotland. The X-craft were carried on the depot ship, HMS *Bonaventure*, which was an ex-Clanliner. They chose a Clanliner because it had very heavy derricks and could lift weights up to 27 tons out of the water. For six months we played about in and out of the Western Isles and the Orkneys and Shetlands, practising different things.

Then it was Christmas 1944 and the war looked nearly over. We didn't expect to go into action now. But all of a sudden they decided to send us out to the Far East. So the *Bonaventure* loaded six X-craft submarines, two down in the forward hold and four more on the after-deck, all cased in to look like deck cargo, all very secret. My wife was very anxious about me because the first time she had seen an X-craft she nearly had a fit because it was so small.

We sailed from the Clyde in January 1945. The voyage was like a world cruise. We went to the West Indies but we weren't allowed ashore because of all the secrecy. So we went to a secret bay where we swam and picked coconuts. Then we went through the Panama Canal, up to San Diego in California and on to Honolulu. After a month in Hawaii at a big rest camp, we went on to the Philippines.

All this time the Captain of the *Bonaventure*, Captain W.R. Fell, was flying all over the place trying to get us some target to attack. Eventually, in Sydney, he got together with Admiral Fife, the commander of submarines in the US Seventh Fleet. The Pacific war wasn't yet over then, and they came up with the idea of cutting submarine telegraph cables which the Japanese used to send their signals between Saigon, Hong Kong and Singapore.

On VE-Day we were in Brisbane, having a marvellous time. Then we went out on the Great Barrier Reef and practised cutting these cables. It seemed a waste of time to us. The divers used a hydraulic cutter to cut the cables and pure oxygen in their breathing apparatus, which can be very dangerous below a depth of about 32 feet.

We were waiting for a diver from the *Bonaventure* but they were taking so long that I said, 'Come on, David, I'll have a go,' and David Carey said, 'No, I'll have a go'. So he got into his diving suit and dived. The water was as clear as a bell so I watched through the night periscope as he cut the cable and gave the thumbs up and put his equipment away. Then he turned round and gave the thumbs down sign, which meant he was in trouble. He must have been poisoned by oxygen. Immediately I started to blow the tanks but he jumped off the side and we never saw him again. I had lost my First Lieutenant whom I had been with since we volunteered together.

When I got back to the *Bonaventure* they gave me another first lieutenant,

'Kiwi' Smith, a New Zealander. He was a brilliant number one and I was amazed how quickly we got on together.

Captain Fell was still trying to get us something to do. The American navy suggested we attack two Japanese cruisers: the *Takao*, which was lying at the top end of Singapore with its guns pointing up the Malay peninsula where the British army were advancing and the *Myoko* which was half a mile further up the Straits. Our boat, the XE3, was to attack the *Takao* and the XE1, led by Jack Smart, was to attack the *Myoko*.

So we were towed 600 miles by S-class submarines to the Straits of Singapore. Then we took over from the passage crew and were towed for about another twelve hours before slipping about 35 miles from the entrance to the Strait. There was an old British boom across the entrance, but when I got to it the gate was open, so we went through. Then we had eleven miles up the Strait to get to the *Takao*. Navigationally it was a bit worrying as there was nothing to get a fix on and we had to guess our course, more or less. Eventually I saw the cruiser through the periscope about a mile away, so I let each of the crew have a look: Kiwi Smith, Leading Seaman Jamie Magennis who was the diver, and Charlie Reid who was steering.

The *Takao* was lying in very shallow water: eleven to seventeen feet at high water and just three feet at low water. It would have been impossible for us to get under her, except that there was a five-foot depression in the sea bed, 500 feet wide and 150 feet long, over which the *Takao* was lying. The plan was to skim across the shallows, slip down into this depression and under the cruiser's hull. But I really didn't think it would be possible.

About 400 yards from the ship I put the periscope up to have a look around and saw a Japanese liberty boat with about forty men aboard only ten feet away. They were so close I could see their lips moving. We went deep immediately, but I'll never know why they didn't spot us.

Then we scraped along the sea bed towards the ship with only ten feet of water above our heads. We were hoping to go down into the dip at any moment, but suddenly there was an almighty crash as we bashed straight into the side of the ship. I felt sure the Japs must have felt the crash.

We were all sweating hard by this time, especially Magennis in his diving suit. After a breather we started the motor but the boat wouldn't budge. We were stuck – either in an anchor cable or jammed under the ship's curved bows. It took ten terrible minutes of straining at full power forward and back to free us. Then we came out 1,000 yards from the ship, turned around, and started a second attack.

This time we slipped down into the hole and under the *Takao*'s keel. I looked through the periscope and saw that the hull was only a foot over our heads and covered in thick weed. Magennis could hardly squeeze himself out of the hatch. Then we had to wait while he laid the mines. He seemed to take forever and each time he made a noise I thought the Japs would be bound to hear it. He was only gone thirty minutes but it seemed like thirty days. I was very anxious to get away as it was already nearly four hours after high water. But all we could do was watch him through the night periscope and drink pints of orange juice. It was sweltering down there.

At last he got back and we could start to release the side charges. As we worked, he told us what a terrible struggle he'd had, fixing the mines. He'd had to cut away the thick weed and scrape away a thick layer of barnacles before the magnets on the mines would stick to the hull. He had stuck on six. He was exhausted.

The port charge fell away from the boat all right, but the starboard charge would not budge. The tide was falling so quickly that I decided we should get the hell out from under the ship and then free the starboard charge. So we set the motor at half speed ahead, but the boat wouldn't budge an inch, even at full speed. I was in a flat spin. I was sure the *Takao* had settled on top of us in the falling tide and we'd be stuck there for good.

For half an hour we went full speed astern and full ahead, with no success. I made a mental plan to abandon ship before the charges went off in six hours' time. But just as I was despairing, we felt a movement, and the XE3 climbed out from under the ship. It was such a relief to see daylight through the periscope.

Now we were sitting less than twenty feet down in perfectly clear water. Anybody looking over the side of the *Takao* would have thought, 'What's that bloody great rock down there?' I offered to go out in a diving suit and release the starboard charge, but Magennis insisted he could do it. So out he went with a bloody great spanner and for a couple of minutes he made a hell of a noise freeing the charge. They were the most anxious minutes of my life. All the time I was cursing him, cursing Captain Fell, and, more than anything, cursing myself for having volunteered for this madness. In the end the charge fell away and Magennis got back into the hatch. We were all exhausted but at last we could go. 'Home, James,' I said, 'and don't spare the horses!'

After that it was plain sailing. Down the Strait, through the entrance and out to sea where we picked up our parent submarine dead on time and were towed back to Singapore. Jack Smart in XE1 had failed to attack the *Myoko* as he'd been held up by Japanese patrol boats, so he'd dropped his side cargoes alongside the *Takao* and had come back.

When we got back to the *Bonaventure* I went up with the captain to look at the charts and the aerial photographs. The captain said, 'The aerial photographs show this cruiser with oil all over the place, but it hasn't sunk.' I tried to point out that it only had to go down two feet and it'd be on the sea bed. But he said, 'You'll have to go back and have another go at it.' So I said, 'All right, in ten days' time.' We weren't very happy about that, of course.

Two or three days later, when I'd rested up and written my patrol report, we were on deck watching a film. The film suddenly stopped and the captain said, 'I've stopped the film, Gentlemen, because the return to Singapore has been delayed. They've dropped a bomb on Hiroshima.' I thought, 'Thank Christ, it's been delayed.' Then, lo and behold, five or six days later they dropped the second nuclear bomb and the war was finished. So we didn't have to go back.

Later on that year I was awarded a VC. On my way back home they asked if I'd like to go to Singapore to see the *Takao*. So I went with a Japanese interpreter who took me on board the hulk. He opened the hatch and I could see that the whole ship had been blown to bits. It had virtually no bottom.

Jamie Magennis, who was also awarded a VC, and I went together to Buckingham Palace to collect our awards. Our wives came too. I've no idea what King George said to me; all I can remember is that he talked with a lisp.

ENGINE-ROOM ARTIFICER VERNON COLES

In 1945 a new flotilla of midget submarines was formed and numbered 14th Flotilla. These comprised the new X-submarimes, the XEs, the 'E' meaning for operations in the Far East against Japan.

In July 1945 we were told that XE1 and XE3 would enter Singapore and attack two cruisers. At this stage the Allies had broken every Jap code and the enemy knew it. So as to retain secrecy the Japs used ocean cables. One ran from Singapore to a shore station in Saigon. Another cable came out of Saigon and ran to Hong Kong and on to Tokyo.

The Americans asked if we could cut them and the immediate response was 'Yes'. We then had to think about how we would do it.

The boats chosen to do this were XE4 for Saigon and XE5 for Hong Kong. The crew of XE4 was captained by Lieutenant Max Shean, an Australian with Sub-Lieutenant Ben Kelly, myself as the engineer and two divers, Sub-Lieutenant Briggs and Sub-Lieutenant Adam Bergius. These boats were so small, we were packed in like sardines.

When we knew we were close by the cables we dragged a grapnel along the sea bed and after a couple of false alarms became anchored on to the first cable. Ken Briggs went out and cut it and came back into the boat with a smile on his face and approximately two feet of the cable to prove to the authorities that it had been done. The only problem for Ken was that he was operating in about 42 feet of water which was considered very dangerous to his breathing oxygen and helium. But he did it. The deepest one should operate was 32 feet.

We then moved position approximately ten miles to where the other cable was thought to be located and after a short while it was a repeat performance except that, on this occasion Adam Berguis went out and brought a length back in. When we arrived back at the depot ship HMS *Bonaventura* in Brunei Bay, Labuan, we learned that XE1 had missed her target, the cruiser *Nachi*, completely. Max was asked if our crew would go straight back into Singapore and attack it. We said we would go, but we were a little anxious as the element of surprise had been lost as 'Tich' Fraser in XE3 had made a successful attack on *Takao*, for which he and Micky Magennis were awarded VCs.

Thank goodness the Japs packed in just as were about to sail.

Many years later we were told that the main purpose of cutting the cables was for the Americans to get a feeling about whether the Japs would fight on after all their recent reverses. They sensed the Japs would; they made up their minds and dropped the Atom bombs.

Some months later I had returned to large submarines and joined *Timeless* and in our journeying around Japan we visited Nagasaki where I saw the damage the bombs had caused. I had no compassion for the Japanese having seen at first-hand what they had done to British and Australian prisoners. But I do believe to this day that the dropping of the bombs saved my life and many, many thousands more.

Marine Peter Dunstan, RM

After the sinking of the *Prince of Wales* and *Repulse*, and as the fighting in Malaya came closer to Singapore, we Marines were marched to the barracks of the Argyll & Sutherland Highlanders. Colonel Stewart of the Argylls stood on a soapbox on the parade ground and welcomed us, saying, 'The Royal Marines and the Argylls had fought side by side in the annals of history and would do so again.' So we became known as the Plymouth Argylls Battallion. But about four hours later we were at fighting stations in the NAAFI. As we had lost everything when the ships went down, we had khaki jungle uniform given to us, and that was our sum total, along with a rifle or bayonet.

We did commando work up behind the Jap lines for about a week. After that we were withdrawn back to Singapore. By this time the Japs were advancing down the north-west side of the island and they started to mortar our barracks. There was an Indian hospital alongside our barracks which was on fire and I was helping to evacuate it when I caught a mortar bomb splinter in the hand and shoulder. Out east, wounds go poisonous within the hour, and my hand blew up. I was given a Bren gun but I couldn't use it. So I had to hand it over and was sent to Singapore General Hospital. While I was there I used my good hand to help the eye surgeon.

About a week or ten days later we were told that we had surrendered. The

Japs came in and said, 'Everybody out of the hospital within forty-eight hours.' Two of my marines died the following day. I was taken up to the prisoner-of-war camp at Changi Jail. On the way we were told to line up along the road because a Japanese general's car was going to pass by. As the car passed us, I felt completely numb. At the camp the feeling was just numbness, too. We just got on with it and kept our noses clean. We thought it would not last long.

Then the Japs said they were moving us to a new place where there would be hospitals and plenty of food. All lies, of course. They put 600 of us on each train, 35 men to each covered steel truck. Inside the trucks the heat was unbearable, you couldn't lie down and if you wanted to go to the toilet you got your mates to hold on to your hands and you stuck your behind out as the train was going. It took five days to get from Singapore to Ban Pong. When we arrived we were ordered off and marched, walked or struggled to the prison camp. On the way some Thais had laid out some wicker baskets full of food and they told us to take it and eat it. We'd hardly eaten for five days.

When we got to the prison camp it was under nine inches of water so we were ordered further up country, where we were set to work on the railway. Our base camp was at Tarsao and then we carried on to a camp called Kanu, which was where we did most of our construction work.

Almost the whole railway was constructed with hammer and chisel. The Japs would say, 'Right, start down here, hammer and chisel, two men, one hole, half a metre, finish – yasmi – rest.' So the chaps would hammer away and in a couple of hours they'd finish. So the Japs said, 'Ah, right, two men, one hole, one metre.' The men were still finishing a bit fast so, 'All right, two men, two holes, one metre each . . .' and so it would go on.

We lived in huts made of bamboo which we had to build ourselves. Just a bamboo platform eighteen inches off the ground and a palm-leaved roof over the top. No sides, so the mosquitos had a whale of a time. No blankets, except what you owned yourself. No clothes or food utensils were issued. So it was a pint mug of rice in the morning, then we were marched out of the camp and on to the railway before dawn. At midday they would let us stop for some more rice, then we carried on working until it was dark and we were marched back to the camp. For three months I never saw the camp I was living in. If it poured with rain, you carried on working, boiling sunshine or monsoon, you just carried on. We liked the monsoon because we had a bath.

At times we were made to carry blokes to work. They demanded so many men a day and if there weren't enough, they would go into the sick hut. If a man had an ulcer he was excused, but if he had malaria he was out on the track. We carried many men out on bamboo and rice-sack stretchers and they had to lie out on the side of the track, breaking rocks to make ballast. This was normal procedure. We couldn't see any future for our lives.

We had nicknames for all the Japs. One little swine was known as Silver Bullet because he had a bullet on his belt. At this particular cutting the chaps were working on bosun's swings, drilling the rocks for dynamiting. Silver Bullet would stand right on the edge of the cliff and if he thought you weren't working hard enough he would throw a rock at you. One day he slipped and landed in the river about two hundred feet below. It was very strange, how he slipped.

We had one we called the Mad Mongol. He was a Korean and the Koreans were worse than the Japanese. I was going to the toilet one night and I didn't bow or salute and he knocked the hell out of me. But it was a question of suspended animation. You just avoided any trouble that you could. I only got bashed twice in three-and-a-half years; I was lucky, I kept out of it.

The other occasion was when we were cutting down trees. I was working in a group of fourteen people, all of average height. I was six foot six. This Jap thought I was slacking because I couldn't get under the tree properly so he started to knock the stuffing out of me with a lump of bamboo. What made me do it I'll never know, but I clenched my fist and drew it back. When I realised what I was doing, I put it behind my back, but he had seen it. So he broke two other bamboos across my back which knocked the hell out of me. Then he dragged me up to this bridge and got two of my mates to lift a massive piece of wood onto my shoulder. He told me to take it up to the bridge. We were by then used to carrying heavy weights, so I did it and went back and said to him, 'OK, another one?' 'No, no, no, finish.' Physically they beat us but psychologically we beat them.

Just two days later I was up on the bridge which was known as the Pack of Cards because it collapsed five times. I was up there banging some nails in when it collapsed. I got scissored by this log above me. Even today I can't feel my leg. The best of it was that this little swine that had bashed me up two days before was the first one up on the bridge with the saw and he cut through this log and got me down.

Soon after that I got malaria and beriberi. That was two years after capture. We had no drugs, no quinine for malaria. The two doctors we had could do virtually nothing. I was sent down country to Tarsao and I got over the malaria somehow. I was one of the lucky ones; I had malaria four times in all, but my body reacted well and I got away with it. Other chaps are still getting malaria today and they still can't treat it. I got over the beriberi by drinking some fermented wine made from jungle leaves. I was lucky. But we lost a hell of a lot of people from cholera and malaria.

We saw only two parcels from the Red Cross in three-and-a-half years.

When the war was over and we opened the Jap storehouses they were stacked high with Red Cross parcels. The Japs had been looting them. If they had allowed those parcels through, three-quarters of our boys would not have died.

It was a struggle to survive. You had a mate; if you didn't have a mate you didn't live. He looked after you and you looked after him. We were getting a few cows through at that time, one cow between six hundred and that was a month's supply. The cows were only the size of a large English calf.

Everything used to go into the pot except the tripe, for some reason. I used to get hold of it sometimes, take it down to the river and clean it. Then I'd boil it and eat it. We used to catch the blood from the beasts and let it congeal and slice it up and cook it on the fire. If nobody was looking we whipped the tongue out.

We were paid ten cents a day by the Japanese when they felt like it. An egg cost 25 cents when you could get it. Unfortunately we had chaps who thought that what was yours was theirs and so what I used to do was spend my money on bananas and sit there and peel the lot and scoff the lot. It was the only way. It was like a very bad dream.

When I recovered from malaria I learnt that there was a party going down river and I thought there might be a chance of escaping my present situation. So I swapped with this other marine and took his place. We got down river to where this railway repair workshop was, five kilometres from the (real) bridge on the river Kwai. I worked there for a while and then got a job in the sawmill, which is where I stayed for the last ten months of the war.

In early 1945 one of the first indications we had that things were really going our way was when we heard the sound of aircraft and saw our planes flying between the clouds and the sun. You can imagine the magnification of the planes in those conditions. It gave us the greatest pleasure to say to the Japanese, 'We've got bigger ones than that coming, you stand by.' That was the first time we were able to start getting back at them and give them a little bit of a wigging.

Then one evening we heard the sound of aircraft and saw twenty-one planes away in the distance. It was nearing sunset and as they turned the sun caught them and they lit up like little balls of fire. They formed a circle over the bridge on the river Kwai and they were playing ring o'roses. They took it in turns to dive down, drop their bombs and come back up again. We heard afterwards that they were Liberators and they'd missed the bridge and hit a prison camp and killed thirty-five of our own boys and nine Japanese.

Some time afterwards we saw a plane approaching so low that we could see the rear-gunner waving at us. The plane waggled its wings to say, 'All right, boys, we know you're there.' No. 2 and no. 3 came across with their bellies open and we watched as they dropped their bombs and glided away. That time they managed to hit the bridge and also a Japanese troop train quarter of a mile from our camp. The feeling of elation in our camp was something I'll never forget.

A Japanese officer in the workshops had a radio which had been doctored so that he could only receive Japanese broadcasts, but it kept going wrong. They found a prisoner in our camp who could repair it who also knew how to fiddle it and tune into the news on Radio Colombo. That was how we heard that the atomic bombs had been dropped. Then a Liberator came over dropping leaflets which told us the war was finished. Two or three days later a jeep came into our camp with a British Indian Army lieutenant and a sergeant, loaded up to the gunwales with food and ammunition. We had never seen a jeep before; we didn't know what it was. Within hours they were in contact with Rangoon telling them what supplies we needed.

One of my mates, Sergeant Tommy Locklin, was dangerously ill with cerebral malaria at the time and the padre came round and said, 'Come on, Locklin, you've got to pull out of it now, the war is over.' Tommy told the padre where to get off in a pretty unrepeatable way. But one of the first cases dropped by the Dakotas had fresh blood on ice for him and other prisoners. Tommy was given some of this blood and today he is as fit as I am.

Sergeant Terry Brooks, RM

The Commanding General in Singapore ordered us to surrender. I was on the Thompson Road manning a defensive line with my lads when I surrendered, sitting there with a rifle in my hands. The Japs gave orders to form a column and march to Changi Jail over fourteen miles away, which we did. The line of men was as long as the bloody trek. As a prisoner you have got nothing. You just accept the inevitable. You have had a go and you have failed and you expect to be treated as a normal prisoner-of-war but of course we weren't. They tried to make us sign an undertaking not to escape and we refused. So they put us all on the concrete parade ground until we agreed. People were beginning to die and the officer in charge of all prisoners-of-war said, 'We'll sign it. I don't care what you put on it.' I put B.M Lever on mine – Breach Mechanism Lever. Then five months later we went off up into the jungle. There were no losses in Changi because we were relatively fit, but our troubles began in the jungle.

Our destination was the camp called Ban Pong which was built on a dried up rice paddy which as soon as it rained, had a foot of water in it. Someone had been there before and they hadn't had a good time either. The vultures were walking up and down the street outside the camp – waiting for us to die.

We had to build our own huts out of bamboo and we didn't have a clue how to do it. We learned later of course. The very first morning the camp was flooded and there were millions of ants floating around. Right in the middle of the hut was a huge great python and we all took off. Five months later, if the same sort of thing happened up in the jungle, the snake wouldn't last more than five minutes. We'd kill it and eat it. I was there four days and I caught sand fly fever – dengue – which is worse than malaria. I thought I was dying. I had to wait until it wore off. There was a doctor but he had no drugs, nothing. And then we started to walk to build a railway. We built the railway up to Kanchanaburi and then we crossed the river. For the next two years I was building and repairing the bridge over the River Kwai.

Eventually in 1944 they took all the officers away. A week before they went a senior British Officer came to me and said, 'I want you to take charge of the camp when we leave.' I said, 'Why me for God's sake? You have got army grades senior to me, Australian Army, Indian Army.' He said, 'I want you.' I said, 'What the hell for?' He said, 'Well, you are a Royal Marine.' I said, 'Give me forty-eight hours to think it over.' I weighed it all up. The first thing in my mind was survival. I thought that if I was in charge I would have less chance of being sent on to the railway again. So I said 'yes' and took over command of the camp. There were 8,000 men at the time but they got whittled away. Some were sent by ship to Japan. I was due to go, but wasn't fit enough. The ship was sunk. I lost two of my best corporals on that.

It was a nice job being in charge. As far as I was concerned there was only one crime and that was thieving from your mates and I instituted a rule that anyone found thieving from their mates would be given a damn good hiding. It happened once but not at my instigation! However, 'jungle law' prevailed and he was punished by his mates. There were some very strange moments. One day a man called to me and said, 'Cheerio, Terry,' and I said, 'What's the matter?' but there was no sound. I wasn't very well but I managed to get out to him and he was dead. In his pack there was seven pounds of rotting bully beef.

One day we were on parade, Tenco, five o'clock in the evening. I heard aircraft. Somebody said, 'Look up,' and I looked up and there were 27 Liberators coming over, very low. I could see the bomb doors open and all the bombs as they fell. They went for the bridge, bang, bang, bang and I thought, 'God that one was near,' and I looked over and saw that our Number One hut was blazing. I dragged one lad out but for three days after that we were digging bodies out. We lost about nineteen men in that raid.

A short while later they wanted a party to build airstrips further down the isthmus and I was one of them. We marched 200 miles barefoot. It took us a fortnight. By this time I was pretty low. I think I was in a daze. I was down to six stone seven. The lads used to carry me to work because if you didn't work you didn't get any rations. I went blind for three months. It was frightening. That was the worst time. The lads used to go out and collect wild peanuts for me which was the only way to treat the disease. Somehow somebody got me on to a truck back to the main hospital. I laugh when you call it a hospital camp – you went there to die. There were Scottish doctors, Australian doctors, but hardly any drugs at all. I didn't think I was going to die; it never occurred to me.

But then came the day when I was standing at the door of the hut and the Japanese were marching along, changing their reliefs. There was something funny about them, I couldn't quite place it. So I decided not to come to attention – but they didn't notice. I thought, 'You bastards, it's over.' The next minute the British officers came and said, 'It is over.' We all sang 'God save the King,' and 'Abide with me'. Then we heard explosions all over the place. The Japanese soldiers and Korean privates and corporals were committing hari-kiri by blowing themselves to pieces. All the Japs we hated were dead. We saw them dead. We had to make our way to Bangkok, about sixty miles away. When we arrived they put us in a hangar. We were sitting there and we heard a sound which we all recognised but couldn't put a name to. It was the sound of a tea trolley being pushed along. In it came and it was pushed by a lovely blond German girl. Very embarrassing for her because no-one could keep their eyes off her as she went round and round, poor girl.

One morning the Dakotas arrived and flew us off. They took us to an open air hospital and said, 'Get rid of all your clothes, keep your personal belongings and destroy everything else.' Then they gave us a pint bottle of beer each. I saw all the lads through. Then a nurse said, 'All right, Sergeant, you are in now.' I went through to the ward. I'll never forget the sight. A row of beds with mosquito nets all folded up and on each was a man sitting in his brand new green jungle clothes, crying. Never forgot it. We have all tried to forget, but we will carry these memories to the grave.

PETTY OFFICER ALF HUNT, RN

I was a Petty Officer in change of the radio equipment in a flotilla of 8 MTBs. On 17 December the Japs started to land in Hong Kong. We were sent into Kowloon Harbour, a narrow stretch of water between Kowloon and Hong Kong. Two boats were sent in at about eleven o'clock that morning. I was on No. 12 boat. No. 26 went in with us. Of course the Japs were waiting for us. No. 26 caught fire and blew up. There were no survivors. We carried on down the harbour and fired torpedoes at Kowloon where they were embarking from the jetties but we got hit as we turned to come out. The Japs were firing at us from Hong Kong as well as from Kowloon. We had taken on aviation spirit for our engines and so we caught fire, but we were going at full speed, crashed straight into the jetties at Kowloon, and blew up. The skipper was alongside me on the upper deck and he took the brunt of the blast. The explosion blew me overboard. I was the only survivor.

I swam to Kowloon, a distance of about a hundred yards. There I got into a typhoon drain with a six-foot diameter. I was up to my waist in water. I had been hit; a bullet through my steel helmet had grazed my forehead. I still have quite a big scar. I was also hit on the arm and back and twice in the left leg with machine-gun bullets. I could just about hobble. I had a 45-revolver and ammunition. They had told us the Japs were taking no prisoners, but to be honest I hadn't got the guts to shoot myself. You have to be insane to do a thing like that, or very brave, and I was in between.

After twenty minutes or so I saw a little boat come along with three Japanese soldiers in it. So I took off my bandoleer of ammunition and my revolver and flung them into the water. They came and picked me up with a lot of shouting in Japanese and tied me up with barbed wire around my wrists, even though I was wounded. I still have those scars too.

When we got to land they put me on the back of an old lorry and took me to their headquarters in Prince Edward Road. It was a European style house, beautifully decorated. They had knocked holes in the ceiling downstairs and holes in the roof, and they had a fire burning in the corner. It is cold in Hong Kong in December. That was my first night as a prisoner.

I felt very lonely. When I was interrogated on the first day they said, 'If you want to tell us anything you needn't because we know all we want to know about Hong Kong.' The only thing they didn't know, I didn't know either, which was what the naval Commodore's name was. He had been there only about six weeks.

I was treated reasonably well. The Japs used to bring me cigarettes or chocolate bars or something to eat, and would try to talk to me in English. The chef was Japanese, an army chap, but he looked after me very well and brought me plenty to eat. I was there about four or five days, I suppose. Then at eleven o'clock in the morning there was one big whoosh and a 9.2-inch shell from Fort Stanley came and knocked the house down. The only bloke I was sorry to see killed was the chef. Quite a few of the Japs were killed too. They whipped me out – I was still on a stretcher because I had a gammy leg – and into the Argyll Street prisoner-of-war camp. I was there for a month. There were a couple of doctors in Argyll, one Canadian and one British.

Hong Kong had surrendered by then. I had heard very little about the fighting. The Japs were putting out propaganda on loudspeakers. There was still quite a lot of shelling going on from Hong Kong on to the mainland by the British.

After about a month I could get around, and after Argyll Street I went to Sham Shui Po in Kowloon, a prisoner-of-war camp. It had been an old army camp but the Chinese had looted it and there was no wood left in it. We slept on concrete floors. There were about five or six thousand there. After only a few days we were sent to North Point on Hong Kong island. The camp had had mules or horses in it and was infested with flies. We were there for a couple of weeks and then got sent back to Sham Shui Po. It was quite a march – ten miles each way.

In Sham Shui Po the food was awful. It was just rice and maybe a few bean sprouts or a bit of vegetable. Just a couple of meals a day and watery soup – enough to survive on, that's all. We did nothing in the camp for the first three or four months. We were just wandering around, walking round the electric fence. Most of the lads were captured with kit on them but I didn't have any. I just had a pair of shorts but I did scrounge bits and pieces off other lads. I had a pair of boots I took off a dead Canadian officer.

We were in Sham Shui Po until 27 September 1942. During that time we went on an outside working party on half a dozen occasions. We went to Kai Tak airport, the airport for Hong Kong, and were set to work extending the runway into the harbour, carrying big lumps of rock and dropping them into the harbour.

It was hard work. We worked from dawn to dusk. They didn't really beat me but you had to keep at it. Several of the lads got a good walloping. They hit with a cane or rifle butt, anything like that. We lost a lot of men. Diphtheria killed several hundred men. They attempted very little treatment for that. There were some 'Pot Pomang' crystals to gargle with but that was about all. English doctors looked after us. We had a Dr Jackson who was a navy doctor.

I was down to eight and a half stone from 12 stone 7lbs. I had beriberi and pellagra, which is like a scurvy complaint, but most of the lads had that. We ate just the same food every day. I don't think we ever had any meat. Once or twice they sent stinking fish and we had some rotten eggs – some of these hundred-year-old eggs, covered in mud, which are dug out of the river bed. There were no Red Cross parcels. But there was plenty of water.

Morale was always pretty good. If anyone said, 'We shan't ever get out of this,' they were dead in a couple of days. We slept on a concrete floor all those months. Eventually I got a blanket.

The Japanese told us to sign a form to say we wouldn't escape. At first we refused to sign it, so they paraded us on the parade ground, and wouldn't let us off that parade ground until we did sign it. They then fetched all the sick people out of the hospital. In the end the officer said 'We'll sign it and say it is under duress,' so that it didn't mean anything.

Then they split us into groups of ten and if one of your group escaped they'd shoot the lot of us. Quite a few did get away. They went in groups – to China, into Bias Bay. A New Zealand navy lieutenant got away and so did one of my colleagues, a petty officer called Maxwell Holroyd.

In our free time we were just wandering around doing nothing. We had a pack of cards and we played crib. We weren't allowed to write home. My mother didn't know anything until the war finished. The first thing she knew was that she had a card from the Australian Red Cross that I had written after our release to say I was safe and free. She didn't know for three-and-a-half years.

On 27 September we left Hong Kong for Japan on the *Lisbon Maru* which was a 6,000 or 7,000-ton freighter. Conditions were awful: there was no room to lie down. They couldn't push us into the for'ard hold so we were the ones into the main hold, right down in the bottom of the ship on top of the ballast. There were some terrible cases of chaps with dysentery and diphtheria on board. Several died during the next five days. We were allowed on the upper deck in groups, to go to the toilet. The food wasn't too bad. We did get bully beef and rice. I didn't see any element of compassion from the Japanese.

At seven o'clock in the morning on 1st October we were torpedoed by USS *Grouper*, an American submarine. She fired five torpedoes at us and only one hit, but that was right in the coal bunkers in the middle of the ship. It killed about eleven of the Japanese crew, but none of the POWs.

There were about 1,500 Jap troops on board. They were taken off during the following night. We were about one hundred miles outside Shanghai, near the Tusan Islands when they put all the hatch covers on stretched the tarpaulins over and battened us down. A few Japs were left on board with machine-guns to make sure we didn't escape. The conditions were hard to describe. Chaps dying there from diphtheria and dysentery. There was no air and the stench was terrible. I was right on the bottom of the ship yet I seemed to get fresh air. I don't know whether it was coming down a ventilator or what, but it wasn't bad right on the bottom. Our water bottles were empty and some of the lads were begging for water. You can cope without food but without water it's terrible. Eventually the Jap guards opened the hatch cover and dropped a bucket of piss down. That was the type of people they were.

About one o'clock the next day the ship took a list and started to sink. One of the lads got a knife and he stuck it up in between the hatch covers and split the tarpaulin. There was a mad rush as everyone pushed out and got on the upper deck. The first half a dozen were machine-gunned by the Jap guards on the bridge. Some of the lads in the aft didn't even get out, they were still battened down. I jumped overboard and they fired at us in the water. They were picking chaps off, using them for target practise. Then the guards were killed by our lads. I would think there were about eleven ships in the area within a mile radius. Small and bigger ships, navy boats and civilian boats – Japanese. But they didn't make any attempt to pick anyone up. They were just churning our chaps up with their screws, going in and out amongst them and firing at people in the water.

There were islands about four miles away and I thought, I am not going to get picked up, and I swam to these islands. I reckon I was ashore within an hour and a half. There was a hell of a tide going inshore. The problem was that some of the chaps went inshore and were swept in-between the islands and back out to sea again. They couldn't land. There was about 1,870 on board originally and 840 went down with her and about another 200 died within two weeks. About 200 of us got ashore onto Steep Island. There was a big lighthouse there and the first thing I saw on it was 'Chance Brothers, Smethwick, Birmingham, England'. This was on the side of the lighthouse. It was reassuring. There was a Chinese village on the island and they picked up quite a lot of the lads in sampans. It was brave of them because they didn't know what the Japs would do to them. We went to this little village and they gave us all the spare clothes they had.

When I got ashore I was terribly thirsty. On the beach there was a beautiful clear trickle of water coming down the rocks from above the cliffs. When some of us got there we lay on our stomachs and drank. It was beautiful, like nectar, and we climbed up the cut-out steps in the rocks. When we got to the top we found it was a toilet – all the Chinese used it as a toilet – but to us it tasted like nectar.

We were there for about four or five days. I think we just felt exhilaration at being alive. Three men got away. I had the chance but I said no, I would rather stick with the main crowd. The escapees went by sampan or junk to the mainland. Of course they told the whole story of the *Lisbon*.

The Chinese on the island fed us and did us proud, but they were frightened of recriminations. We gave them back all the clothes. They put us on a Jap navy boat and took us to Shanghai. The Jap navy, I must say, was very, very good. They gave us corned beef, condensed milk and blankets. The skipper of our boat spoke very good English because most of the Japanese navy were trained by the British.

We got to Shanghai about seven o'clock in the morning. Then we stood on the jetty until midnight and it was freezing. There were blokes who died on the jetty. Then they put us on board an old Japanese drumsteamer, the *Shin Se Maru*. It had already been on the bottom. It had cockles and shellfish on its inside, we didn't know if we would make it or not. Anyhow, it was uneventful and we got to Moji in Japan where they put us on the train. On this train they gave us what they call a 'Binto', which is like a little wicker basket with rice balls and dried fruit, fish and vegetables. It was quite good accommodation too. The train took us to Osaka.

I was among twenty-six of us taken off at Hiroshima where there was a military hospital. We were all ill with dysentery or diphtheria and only six of us came out alive. I had dysentery. I was passing a lot of blood too but I never gave up hope. I never ever once thought that I wouldn't make it. If you gave up the spirit, you didn't survive.

I then went to Osaka from there, into a hospital underneath the big baseball stadium and then I went into the main camp with the rest of the lads. They were all survivors from the *Lisbon, Maru*, between four and five hundred of us. They did feed us up a little bit and then we went out on working parties. I was in a steel works for a time, breaking pig iron, which was a very hard job – lifting big chunks of iron and throwing them down to break them up. I was down to about seven stone by then. Not everyone was emaciated – some wore it better than others.

Then I worked on the docks for about two-and-a-half years. We fared reasonably well. We never did any fishing. We could have a swim in the midday break but that was about all. The Japanese civilians weren't too bad at all. The Koreans guards were bastards. I suppose we lost between thirty and forty men. There was no contact at all with the outside world – no wireless, but some of the lads could understand Japanese and they read the newspapers.

My worst moment in those two-and-a-half years was being bombed by our own people. We got hammered in five different camps. These B.29s used to come over at about 40,000 feet and they looked like white ghosts in formations of twenty-seven. The next day they would be over at roof-top height. I saw three shot down. A couple of the crew were picked up as prisoners. They were treated badly. The Japanese weren't very friendly after all that heavy bombing. One of the lads got stabbed in the street. An old woman dashed out of the crowd and stabbed him. It didn't kill him, though.

We worked with women and I learnt the lingo pretty well. I shall always remember, just before the war finished, we were working on a barge and there was an elderly lady there having a midday meal. She had a chunk of meat, picked it up in her chopsticks and gave it to me – that was probably her month's meat ration.

The Japanese brought a lot of sugar from the islands and used it for aviation spirit. We used to unload it in two hundred kilo weight sacks. By now I was down to about six stone seven, that was the lowest I got down to.

We were then told that they had dropped a bomb on Hiroshima and Nagasaki. We knew that something important had happened when the emperor spoke over the radio. Then the American planes started coming over and we knew it was over. They parachuted a couple of blokes into our air camp about 25th August, who were the scruffiest blokes I have ever seen. They hadn't had a shave or anything. Then they started dropping supplies and that was almost worse than the bombing. There were leaflets that warned us not to eat too much because our stomachs had shrunk.

We arrived in Southampton on 5 November 1945. I had six brothers, four of whom were pilots in the RAF and they had all survived. As a family we were very, very lucky. They didn't recognise me at first when they met me at the station. There was a lot of hugging. Then they took me home.

I was invalided out and given nineteen shillings a week pension. Then we got our compensation off the Japanese, £74.

Even after all these years I still get nightmares. I suffer from tinnitus. I am also claustrophobic and I can't stick it on public transport. Sometimes I relive the bit on the motor boat and see the skipper covered in blood. On *Lisbon* I see the water rising up around us and feel the terror.

Lieutenant Ronald Neath, RNVR

In 1945 every available battleship, aircraft-carrier, cruiser, destroyer, store-ship and tanker was despatched from Britain to the Pacific theatre to join the Americans in the final assault on Japan. Although US forces had been taking the brunt, and would continue to do so, it was considered vital that there should be a strong British presence in the area when Hong Kong and Singapore were liberated.

The 35,000-ton battleship *Duke of York*, which I had joined in the previous winter as a junior gunnery officer, left Liverpool in April 1945. We celebrated VE-Day in Malta – not too exuberantly, I recall, for many of us were apprehensive about fighting the fanatical Japanese for perhaps a very long time to come.

After nearly going aground in the Suez Canal because of our heavy armament, we had a most unpleasant passage through the Red Sea where the frightful heat and funnel fumes brought on a lot of sickness, particularly among the engine-room staff. We were instructed to sunbathe as much as possible so as to avoid prickly heat and boils. Skin cancer was not treated seriously then.

Admiral Lord Louis Mountbatten spent time on board with us in Colombo, mingling with the whole ship's company by day and usually partying in the wardroom by night until the wee hours.

We received a great welcome in Australia but soon moved north, past the Great Barrier Reef and across the Coral Sea to Manus in the Admiralty Islands where we embarked our Commander-in-Chief, Admiral Sir Bruce Fraser. Then we moved on to the American base at Guam in the Marianas.

The Americans on the island entertained us royally. For a colleague and myself our allocated hosts on the first day ashore were none other than Henry Fonda, then a US naval officer, and a well-chosen female escort. Fleet Admiral Nimitz came on board two or three times, likewise Admiral 'Bull' Halsey, commanding the US Third Fleet, and General Carl Spaatz in charge of the US Army Airforce.

Nimitz and Fraser were the most impressive wartime leaders I met. Both were quiet men, with a great sense of humour, and were totally approachable, irrespective of rank. Fraser did not sleep much at night and when we were in harbour he would sometimes come up on the quarterdeck, where I, as a junior RNVR officer, frequently had the middle watch. If I was not busy he would engage me in a long friendly conversation, rarely talking about himself, but asking about me and what I hoped to do after the war.

Every day while we were at Guam the skies were full of planes, mainly US 'Superforts', mounting a constant air offensive on the mainland of Japan. There, too, we heard the sensational news of Hiroshima and Nagasaki.

We were at sea on VJ-Day, 15th August. The celebrations going on in London were broadcast over the ship's tannoy system but many of us felt resentful and had little inclination to listen, because we were sweltering in our anti-flash gear, closed up at full action stations in case Japanese kamikaze planes attacked the ship in a final fling.

We had to wait several more uncomfortable days, even having to scurry out of the way of a threatening typhoon, while waiting for General MacArthur to make up his mind about how and when the formal surrender should take place.

British warships had to cope with many problems in the Pacific. They did not have the same mobility as the ships of the US Navy. Even in a big battleship we seemed always to be short of fuel and fresh water. I was made aware of this when I managed to get myself invited for a relaxing day on board the USS *Iowa*.

On 27th August the *Duke of York* was the first British ship to enter Japanese home waters since the war had begun. That evening, together with the US flagship *Missouri* and the largest fleet of warships ever assembled, we dropped anchor in the shadow of Mount Fujiyama. Later, when the minefields had been cleared, we moved into Tokyo Bay and were given the place of honour next to the USS *Missouri* where the surrender ceremony was to take place. We had to lend our comfortable wardroom chairs for the VIPs to sit on, as well as our smart admiral's barge for Nimitz to make his various official visits.

In these final days the *Duke of York* as flagship overflowed with senior staff officers. There were also scores of press reporters, newsreel men and photographers on board all vying for accommodation – and a shower. In the scramble I had to give up my cabin.

As cities, Tokyo and Yokohama were terribly smashed. On two brief visits ashore we saw burnt out factories, wrecked machinery, huge craters filled with water and mountains of ashes and rubble as far as the eye could see – a wasteland of ruins.

During one of those days of waiting I found myself on duty in one of the destroyers which had anchored further up the bay close to the Tokyo waterfront. Suddenly, approaching the ship in a cloud of spray, a landing-craft was sighted which was full of figures waving frantically. As it drew near, an outburst of cheering was heard, getting louder and louder. These were the first Allied prisoners-of-war to be released, dirty, unshaven, haggard, yet exultant. Some waved in a bewildered sort of way, as if they could not believe we were real, or that what they saw was true. Scrambling on board, helped by dozens of willing hands, these men shook hands and embraced us wildly. But there were others who could not speak or move. Several were on makeshift stretchers – an awesome sight.

The Japanese made their formal surrender aboard the *Missouri* on the morning of 2nd September 1945. With a grandstand view we were able to see the arrival of General MacArthur, Admiral Nimitz, numerous Allied and Commonwealth personalities as well as the top-hatted and bemedalled Japanese representatives. Admiral Fraser signed for the United Kingdom, and the ceremony ended with a great display of Allied air power in which massed formations of B29 Superfortresses, Avengers, Helldivers and Corsairs zoomed low over the assembled ships.

In the evening there was an impressive and moving ceremony aboard *Duke of York*. Admirals Nimitz and Halsey, our own Commander-in-Chief, General Spaatz and almost all the Allied leaders were present on the quarterdeck to witness it. This was the ceremony of sunset. Allied and Commonwealth flags flew from the ships' yardarms and a massed band of the Royal Marines was drawn up under the great 14-inch guns of the after-turrets. As the sun went down, casting a pink glow over the peak of Fujiyama, Royal Marine buglers sounded the sunset call and then, to the accompaniment of rolling drums, the ensigns of all the Allied nations were ceremoniously lowered; last of all, the *Duke of York*'s own White Ensign, the flag which had flown over every Royal Navy ship by day and night since the beginning of the war, was gathered in. The guard presented arms and the band played the hymn 'The day Thou gavest Lord is ended'. All around us the great American ships were silent, their crews facing towards the British flagship, and saluting. This was a magic moment and few of us dispersed without a tear.

On 9 September we left for Hong Kong, stopping at war-torn Okinawa on the way, then on to Manila to help with the evacuation of released POWs and, finally, a month later, our ship returned to Sydney. There, to my astonishment, a telegram awaited our bemused Commander saying that I could now be released from Naval service (under Class 'B') because I had won a university Arts scholarship before being called up in 1940. The Commander commented that he was not aware I was an artist!

Some weeks later I was transferred to a destroyer under the command of the then Prince Philip of Greece (now Prince Philip, Duke of Edinburgh) for an early passage home, but I changed places with a fellow officer and reached England in a fast and not uncomfortable liner just in time for Christmas 1945.

PART TWO

The Royal Navy
from 1945 to the 1990s

Historical Note – Corfu – Palestine – HMS *Warspite* – HMS *Amethyst* – Korea – Coronation – Nuclear testing – Suez – Tristan da Cunha – Borneo – Northern Ireland – The Falklands – Search and Rescue – The Gulf – *Envoi*

My sea had been black; black and grey with great lumps of roaring white water crashing over our bows to rush swilling along the lurching deck. Often I had stood, gloved hands gripping a rail or a stanchion, just gazing, awed by this immense world of black and brutal water. Northern waters had been our lot, and from the Western Isles of Scotland we had sailed out through the Atlantic, the Irish Sea, the North Sea, the Pentland Firth, the Skagerrak, the Kattegat, the Baltic Sea and the Gulf of Bothnia. Nippy it had usually been, with rough weather the main feature, but there had been times of stillness, times of friendship, times of thoughtfulness, vigorous times, uncertain times, hilarious times and times of wonder and great beauty.

Able Seaman Peter O'Toole, RN (National Service)

Historical Note

W hen the dropping of atomic bombs on Hiroshima and Nagasaki rendered the planned amphibious invasion of Japan thankfully unnecessary, the Royal Navy's longest and costliest war was finally over. The U-boats that had come so perilously close to cutting the Atlantic lifeline lay in ports around the North Sea, awaiting disposal; hardly a single major surface unit of Hitler's navy had survived to surrender. The few Japanese warships to escape destruction swung at anchor, lacking fuel to put to sea; their greatest battleship *Yamato* had met her end in a final Kamikaze style run to Okinawa, sunk by massed American aircraft. The enormous quantitive and qualitive superiority of the US Navy was obvious to all, especially to the sailors of the British fleet in the Pacific. The Americans' apparently limitless supplies of everything from fighter-bombers to ice cream, and the fleet train that sustained such massive operations so far from shore bases, contrasted sharply with the spartan conditions still endured by the British. The Royal Navy could look back with justifiable pride in its victory, but the end of World War II ushered in an age of uncertainty which has arguably still not ended.

President Truman's Secretary of State, Dean Acheson, observed that 'Great Britain has lost an Empire and has yet to find a role'. The frequency with which he has been quoted does not detract from the basic, if uncomfortable truth of his message. In 1945 Germany and Japan lay in ruins, but Britain was the world's largest debtor nation with sterling liabilities vastly exceeding her gold reserves and dwindling stock of US dollars. While the debate over the causes of Britain's economic nosedive in the next fifty years continues, there is no denying the long-term malaise which has led to Britain having a smaller fleet than France for the first time since the American War of Independence. Although the recipient of enormous sums of American aid, the twin demands of a global military posture and the unprecented welfare programmes demanded by the post-war electorate combined to drain the economy further. Then fashionable economic theory suggested that it was possible to mortage the future to pay for current expenditure; so both the nation and the navy were living on borrowed time.

The immediate post-war years were not without action. The new Albanian communist regime mined two British destroyers, *Volage* and *Saumarez*; the establishment of Israel forced new and distasteful tasks on to the Mediterranean fleet, and the North Sea had to be swept of the thousands of mines laid during the war. Communist forces triumphed in China too, their attempt to seize HMS *Amethyst* leading to her celebrated escape down the Yangtse in the finest traditions of the service.

The Royal Navy remained in the vanguard of technological development: pioneering the use of jet aircraft from aircraft carriers, with the angled decks and landing systems required for their operation. New sonar and new radar systems further extended the reach of naval forces. Late war Japanese suicide aircraft had already spurred the development of anti-aircraft missiles. Work began on the first British naval surface-to-air missile, the Sea Slug, in 1948; it went to sea finally in 1962 and saw its first and only combat use twenty years later off the Falkland Islands.

The Communist invasion of South Korea in 1950 suspended planned defence cuts. A British task force centred around six aircraft-carriers supported the UN troops ashore. Piston-engined Fleet Air Arm Hawker Sea Furys tangled with Russian MiG-15 jet fighters, shooting one down although not without loss to themselves. At the Spithead Review for Queen Elizabeth II in 1953, the Royal Navy was able to assemble nearly 200 warships with 300 aircraft flying overhead. Yet in 1956 the Anglo-French-Israeli assault on Egypt exposed the grim truth: for all its apparent strength, the Royal Navy would never be able to mount a major operation overseas without the consent of America. This politically controversial action, the landing of British troops in Egypt, involved the first mass helicopter assault in history. Westland Whirlwinds of No. 845 Squadron landed 45 Commando, Royal Marines from *Albion* and *Bulwark*. The two aircraft-carriers were subsequently converted to 'Commando Carriers': able to land troops further inland, over the heads of any opposition on the beach, this was a new and very useful capability for the Royal Marines.

If the Suez campaign witnessed a number of 'firsts', it also included some significant 'lasts'. HMS *Newfoundland* was fired on by an Egyptian frigate during the night of 31 October: radar-directed 6-in gunfire sank the *Domiat* in a few minutes: the last Royal Navy surface action of its kind to date.

Unfortunately for the British government, the US administration demanded an immediate end to the Anglo-French invasion. And since both nations owed their continued financial existence to the US Treasury, neither could defy the President's wishes. While the Royal Navy would retain the capability to mount major operations outside European waters for another thirty years, US political approval was now a required precondition.

The 1957 Defence White Paper was the first public attempt to bring Britain's armed forces into the nuclear age. Although many assumptions made at the time (for instance, the idea that manned fighter aircraft could be replaced by ground-launched missiles) proved premature or entirely false, it did entail sweeping cuts in the naval budget; Duncan Sandys' 'Axe' was still wielded with an eye to past glories. While all surviving battleships were ordered to be scrapped and research and development concentrated on new missiles, the Royal Navy was still committed to maintaining several carrier groups, with one such Task Force based at Singapore.

The first British nuclear-powered submarine, HMS *Dreadnought*, was laid down at Barrow in 1959, but her powerplant was American and US constructors assisted Vickers. The first British-built nuclear submarine, *Valiant* was laid down in 1962. In February 1963 it was announced that the Royal Navy would assume responsibility for Britain's nuclear deterrent: a class of four (the bare minimum required) boats armed with the American Polaris intercontinental ballistic missile. Carrying sixteen nuclear missiles, HMS *Resolution* put to sea on the first operational patrol in 1969. Since then, the Royal Navy has maintained a continuous patrol with one missile-armed submarine, twenty-four hours a day. Two crews are provided for each submarine, taking turns to man them on their necessarily isolated missions (the crews have no contact with the outside world, the boats must remain hidden for the deterent to be effective). The first of *Resolution*'s successors, HMS *Vanguard*, commissioned in 1993 carries the American Lockheed Trident missile system.

Royal Navy submariners spent the 1970s and 1980s fighting the Cold War. In the North Atlantic, under the Polar ice cap and sometimes sportingly close to the arctic lair of the Red Banner Northern Fleet, British submarines shadowed the Russian missile boats and attack submarines in conditions sometimes dangerously close to actual war. Honing their skills in the internationally renowned training course, the 'Perisher', Royal Navy submarine captains earned the grudging respect of their Soviet adversaries. With upwards of 300 Soviet submarines poised to fight another Battle of the Atlantic if NATO and the Warsaw Pact ever did come to blows, the Royal Navy came to concentrate ever more resources on ASW (Anti-Submarine Warfare). The Macmillan government announced as much as early as 1958, although retaining carrier battle groups in the Atlantic and Mediterranean.

In 1966 the Defence Secretary Denis Healey proposed the abolition of the Fleet Air Arm, the cancellation of the long-planned new aircraft carrier, and the scrapping of all existing ones. (At the same time, the cancellation of the TSR.2 bomber dealt a near mortal blow to the RAF and the British aviation industry.) The new policy called for the Royal Navy to concentrate on ASW in the North Atlantic, with the RAF providing air support for the fleet (from shore bases that had yet to be built). Although *Ark Royal* was kept operational at enormous cost until 1978, there would be no more fleet carriers in the Royal Navy. In their absence, 'through deck cruisers' were developed in much the same way the US Army ordered 'Combat Cars' in the late 1930s when forbidden by its political masters to order actual tanks. Thus the *Invincible* class light carriers were available in 1982, together with the veteran *Hermes* when a Task Force had to be hastily improvised to recapture the Falklands. With a handful of the unique BAe Sea Harriers, they steamed for the South Atlantic with no-one aboard able to predict what would happen when they met the 200 jet fighter bombers available to Argentina.

It is salutary to reflect that, had the Argentine *junta* stayed its hand for another six months or so, the Royal Navy would not have been able to mount 'Operation Corporate' and the Falkland Islanders would have been governed by a regime that had already murdered 15,000 of its own citizens. Defence Secretary John Nott applied all the naval knowledge one can obtain as an infantry subaltern to plan the notorious 1981 naval cuts. Under the same disingenuous banner as the later 'Options for Change', his paper 'The Way Forward' proposed selling one of the three 'Invincibles' immediately, the other two to be mothballed; the number of destroyers and frigates was to be reduced from 50 to 32; all amphibious landing ships were to go and the Royal Marines were to be entirely disbanded.

The Argentine *junta* rescued the Royal Navy. With Admiral Sir Henry Leach injecting some much needed backbone, the Cabinet ordered the fleet to the Falklands. Despite the heavy odds, superior training and weapons systems enabled the Sea Harriers to more than hold their own. The enemy leadership had staked all on an immediate political solution, and the Argentine forces were woefully unprepared for the campaign that followed. The airfield at Port Stanley was not extended and could not operate fast jets; only half a dozen missiles had been delivered for their navy's Etendard aircraft, and their only major warship to be lost, Pearl Harbor survivor *Belgrano* (ex-USS *Phoenix*) sank after only two hits from World War II-era torpedoes fired by the submarine HMS *Conqueror*. Any British complacency was rudely shattered when the first Etendard attack hit HMS *Sheffield* with a single Exocet missile; the name entering popular jargon then and there. Later bombing attacks were pressed home with great gallantry by the Argentine pilots, but they were driven off and the troops safely landed, there to defeat the Argentine garrison.

Sad to say, the sparkling re-affirmation of the Royal Navy's professional capabilities did not lead to a change of heart at Westminster. Defence planning during the later 1980s culminated in 'Options for Change': a renewed onslaught on all three service budgets in 1990. It is impossible to resist the conclusion that this was a Treasury-inspired cost-cutting measure made without regard to political reality. The stated logic, that the collapse of the USSR and the subsequent instability of eastern Europe and Asia made the world a 'safer' place, was soon proved wrong. Iraq invaded Kuwait that summer and, thirty years after British warships landed troops in the Emirate to forestall a similar Iraqi attack, British forces played a major role in the US-led coalition. A Chinese guided missile fired at the American battleship *Missouri* was shot down by HMS *Gloucester* and Fleet Air Arm helicopters sank the flotilla of Iraqi missile boats before it even posed a threat. Today, Sea Harriers are flying over the Balkans to support the beleaguered UN forces engaged in the difficult task of keeping peace in former-Yugoslavia. Yet if the British government's taste for overseas adventures has survived, the British capability to mount them has not. Unnoticed by the government or the nation, the British merchant marine has now shrunk so far that Britain cannot launch any significant military operation outside mainland Europe without other nations providing the shipping. At the time of the Falklands conflict in 1980, there were 1,145 British-registered ships of over 500 tons displacement; by mid-1995 there were just 258. International shipping owners were willing to charter their vessels to the British government during the Gulf War (and receive almost whatever fee they proposed) but the operation was conducted under American control. Iraqi forces posed no more threat to Coalition shipping than the Sudanese Dervishes could have stopped Lord Kitchener's arrival in Egypt in 1898. Another time, against a more capable opponent, they may not be so willing.

Without a coherent foreign and defence policy, the ship of state drifts rudderless. In the age of CNN and the Internet it seems to have been forgotten that 98 per cent of British trade is still carried by sea, and that a rail tunnel between Dover and Calais does not stop Britain being an island. If it took too long for Whitehall to grasp the idea that British overseas commitments were too extensive in the 1950s, that the vestiges of Empire could not be maintained on a shrinking industrial base, in the 1990s the wheel has turned full circle. Ships are decommissioned, Shore Establishments closed and British ship builders allowed to go bankrupt.

The Royal Navy has protected this island from invasion since the sixteenth century and saved it from starvation and defeat twice in this century. From the Heligoland Bight in 1914 to the current Balkan *imbroglio*, the men and women of the Royal Navy have done their duty. During the battle of Crete in 1941, Admiral Cunningham remarked that it took three years to build a ship, but three hundred to build a tradition. Several RN captains in the South Atlantic said they went to war, conscious of ten generations of naval officers watching over their shoulders. This priceless legacy should not be discarded lightly.

CORFU

LIEUTENANT EDWARD GUERITZ, RN

The Corfu Channel lies between the coast of Albania and the Greek island of Corfu. It has long been recognised as an international waterway through which the innocent passage of ships of any nation is accepted as a right. The Germans had minefields in the area during World War II, but Allied minesweepers had checked the swept channel when Mediterranean hostilities were over. In May 1946 two British cruisers made the first post-war passage: *Orion* and *Superb*. The latter was a newcomer to the Mediterranean Fleet, one of the first of the somewhat ill-starred *Minotaur* (or *Tiger*) Class. The flagship by contrast had seen much service in these waters in the recent war. Nonetheless, the admiral and his captains were as shocked as they were surprised when shots were fired by Albanian coastal artillery. No hits were scored, but His Majesty's Government protested forcibly to the Albanians.

Even when the initial diplomatic heat had cooled it was thought necessary to check that normal international practice would be observed in future. In August the Commander-in-Chief of the Mediterranean Fleet, Admiral Sir Algernon U. Willis, was informed by the British Admiralty that ships of his fleet could use the Channel. Armament was to be in the fore-and-aft position, but if fired upon ships were to fire back. In September it became evident that our government would welcome the opportunity to test Albanian good faith. Such an opportunity was created by Admiral Willis as his fleet began to assemble for the Fleet Regatta at Argostoli on the island of Cephalonia. Admiral Kinahan and two of his cruisers were supported on this occasion by two destroyers, HMS *Saumarez* and *Volage*.

At 1330 on 22 October Admiral Kinahan's group formed single line ahead, in the order *Mauritius*, *Saumarez*, *Leander* and *Volage*, and proceeded through the swept channel. Ships' companies were at Action Stations with guns trained fore-and-aft. Asdic (sonar) equipment was manned in the destroyers, but not operating. Paravanes were not streamed from the cruisers. At 1453 a heavy explosion, accompanied by a bright yellow flash and a great column of smoke, rent *Saumarez* under the bridge. All of us on the bridge were thrown about, three officers being seriously injured.

It was subsequently established that the ship was in the middle of the swept channel. Damage centred on No. 1 Boiler Room with a gaping hole in the ship's side stretching forward to the vicinity of 'B' gun. Fire broke out on board, and the situation was not helped when fuel oil escaping on to the water was ignited. A brisk wind was blowing us on to the inhospitable shores of Albania. Every effort was made to get steam on the main engines, but these proved unavailing. This was not a happy situation. However, HMS *Volage* manoeuvred into a position in which lines could be passed to tow *Saumarez* stern first. Captain Selby had taken his position at the after steering position on the platform between the torpedo tubes. The torpedo gunner and his quarterdeckman wrestled with ropes and wires until the tow could be secured. At the second attempt *Volage* discreetly took the weight of her unwieldy consort. She was down by the bows and the fore part of the ship was moving appreciably sideways back and forth.

At this point there was another heavy explosion, and the fore part of the *Volage* disappeared as far aft as 'A' gun. These were anxious minutes when the weight of metal hanging down threatened the ship's stability. One officer and seven ratings of the Damage Control party lost their lives when they were caught by the explosion while repairing a hole in the ship's side resulting from an earlier contact with *Saumarez*. By this time *Mauritius* and *Leander* were out of sight. *Saumarez* and the waters of the Channel were still on fire, and it was evident that the two British destroyers were in a minefield. Even if *Volage* regained power of manoeuvre, hidden dangers to the two ships could still exist.

Happily, the damaged section of *Volage* broke away, and she righted herself. She was then manoeuvred so that a fresh tow could be passed between the stern of *Saumarez* and over her damaged bow. The jagged edges of the shattered forecastle were a boatswain's nightmare, but the first lieutenant of *Volage*, Scott, and his company worked wonders with shot-mats and towing hawsers, acquired with prudent foresight in the past. Success was achieved and with great skill, but some lack of naval dignity, the tow back to Corfu began, both ships proceeding stern first. Although the other warships had been out of sight, the Fleet had not been idle. As the long dark evening wore on, *Saumarez* and *Volage* were joined by HMS *Raider* whose captain manoeuvred her close alongside *Saumarez* to play hoses on the fires blazing in her forepart. It was a fine feat of seamanship in the dark considering the slowness of the two, and the irregular swinging movement of the forward half of the damaged destroyer. Fire-fighting in *Saumarez* was a highly demanding task, tackled with courage and steadfastness both by experienced hands and 'Hostilities only' ratings alike. The magnitude of the explosion and its effects took a significant psychological toll, immediately and in the longer term; and it was particularly felt by those who believed they had put their wartime experiences behind them. Reinforcements of fire-fighting parties and equipment arrived by boat from the aircraft-carrier *Ocean*, together with the welcome supplies of tea and sandwiches. More welcome still was help for the wounded. From the time of the first explosion, the Flotilla Medical Officer, Surgeon-Lieutenant O'Riordan, and his Sick Berth Attendant had worked tirelessly to relieve the sufferings of the wounded, some badly burned, some with fractures and some with multiple injuries. The waist awnings were rigged over the torpedo tubes to provide some shelter on the Iron Deck where the casualties were lying. The *Ocean*'s boats were used to transfer some of them to the relatively sophisticated medical treatment available in an aircraft-carrier. The hospital ship *Maine* was on her way to Corfu and many of the casualties were ultimately treated in her. For some no treatment could be sufficient. These and their shipmates killed in the explosion were buried in the cemetery on Corfu with the full naval honours of the Mediterranean Fleet. The death toll of *Saumarez* ship's company was 36 including Petty Officer Cook Salvatore Zarb, who died in Malta two weeks later, bringing the total fatal casualties in the incident to 44. Added to these tragic losses were the injuries suffered by other men, of a wide span of ages, and left with permanent disabilities.

On 12th and 13th November, 1946, a minesweeping force led by *Welfare* carried out sweeping operations in the Corfu Channel. One mine exploded in a sweep, two mines were recovered for examination and twenty were cut from their mooring. Those recovered were in good condition without evidence of lengthy immersion and with grease still on their mooring wires. They were identified as German mines of the GY type and subsequent enquiries established that a large stock of such mines would have fallen into the hands of Yugoslav forces when Germany capitulated. There was no evidence that such mines had been obtained by Albania nor that she had the means to lay an effective field of at least 25 mine, aligned as it was in an established 'swept channel'.

Failing to obtain satisfaction by direct negotiation with Albania, Britain lodged a complaint with the newly created Security Council of United Nations. In this early skirmish in the Cold War Albania was supported by the Soviet Union and Poland. When the Council voted on the issue, resolving by seven votes to two, with Syria abstaining, that Albania was responsible for the deaths of 44 British seamen, the resolution was vetoed by the Soviet Union. Thereafter Britain submitted her case to the International Court of

Justice at the Hague. Britain sought an admission of responsibility, an apology and compensation. The claim for the latter was set at the modest sum of around £843,000. By eleven votes to five the court found in favour of Britain after a trial lasting months. A crucial factor was the evidence of a defector from the Yugoslav Navy. This Lieutenant-Commander claimed to have seen two minesweepers converted to minelayers with rails loaded with mines one day and unloaded some days later, at dates which fitted the pattern of events. With the benefit of knowledge about the activities of Soviet agents in British Diplomatic and Intelligence Services it is now easier to understand how the mine laying operation was carried out to create a trap for the British ships in such a timely fashion. It must be noted that the International Court found that Britain had infringed Albanian sovereignty by the minesweeping operations in November 1946.

PALESTINE

CAPTAIN BRIAN DE COURCY-IRELAND, RN

Briefly, the role of the British naval forces, based on Haifa in 1946–48, was to stop the illegal flow of Jewish immigrants into Palestine. From all over Europe, from Russia and the satellite states, from the ghettos, refugee camps, concentration camps and hiding places, the immigrants were trying to find their way by whatever means they could towards the Promised Land. Blind to almost everything but the dream, and with little idea of what lay ahead of them, they allowed themselves to be driven by determined fanatics intent on getting as many of them as possible into Palestine. After what they had survived can you wonder that they were prepared to submit to almost any hardship? They were often exploited, robbed and treated with callousness by the 'organisation'; and yet they came. In leaky, unseaworthy craft, jammed in by the hundreds, half-starved, short of water, frequently diseased, exposed to the sun, the storms and the sea, they crawled out from little ports in southern Europe; and making for Palestine tried to slip our blockade. For it was Britain's task, as the Mandate Power, to intercept them and escort them into Haifa to be put in camps under guard. A quota of 1,500 a month had been set under an agreement with the Arabs, and the Mandate Power tried to enforce it and allow only that number to settle. And so the numbers in the camp built up. Some illegals did slip through. They just beached the craft and everyone on board – men, women and children – were forced to jump into the water and make their way ashore. Inevitably some never made it and drowned.

After three days' steaming we in HMS *Ajax* made our landfall off Haifa. The *Ajax*, which was my command, was to relieve HMS *Liverpool*, so, as soon as *Liverpool* was clear the next morning, we weighed anchor and berthed in the harbour. We dropped two anchors, turned on them and lay at right angles to the breakwater arm with wires out to it. Thus we faced the port with a clear view of Mount Carmel to starboard. Anti-sabotage sentries were posted day and night, and in addition quarter-pound charges were thrown into the water alongside the ship at frequent but irregular intervals during dark hours. These charges would have the most painful effect upon any frogmen trying to attach limpet mines to the ship's hull; in fact to any swimmers in the vicinity of the ship. They also had the effect of disturbing our sleep; for every time one went off, it was just as if someone had belted the ship's side underwater an almighty blow with a large hammer.

The month that followed was a varied and eventful one for us. Once I had been connected up to the shore telephone system I made contact with the District Commissioner, the Naval Officer in Charge, the Brigadier commanding 1st Infantry Division and his HQ on Mount Carmel, the Naval Liaison Officer (SOO) attached, and so on; and, of course, Captain D14 and the COs of the destroyers and frigates who came to call on me.

On 13 August 1946 I had been put in charge of escorting two large merchant ships – the *Empire Rival* and the *Empire Heywood* – full of illegal immigrants who were being deported to a new camp in Cyprus under armed guard. By the following evening I was very tired and angry since we had been unable to disembark the refugees because of political problems. We had been lying there all day with the temperature over 90°F on deck, and with so many people packed in the holds of the merchant ships. The *Empire Heywood* had 210 men, 148 women and 177 children on board, while the *Empire Rival* had 448 men and 310 women, all well organised under the Haganah leaders.

I sent what medical staff I had to both ships as the conditions were appalling. God knows what the heat in the holds was. There was only room for a few on the deck at a time. The two doctors had been working pretty well non-stop for sixteen hours and were grey with fatigue and dead beat, so I sent them off to get some rest. Our doctor and his staff treated over 500 cases out of the total of 535 men, women and children in the *Empire Heywood*. Almost every child was suffering from skin disease, malnutrition or other ailments and at least three had pneumonia. The sick berth staff worked in those stinking holds with the temperature over 100°F, surrounded by a mob of hysterical people, many lousy and clad in rags.

Of the many memories of that time, one in particular stands out in my mind. It was that of a little Jewish nurse. She had come forward out of the mob and volunteered to help. We learnt later that there were several Jewish doctors among the illegals: none of them came forward. I watched her as she worked, calming the people, organising them, interpreting (she spoke English, French and Yiddish), and helping the doctor. Very competent, very professional. She had been pretty – very pretty – once; but hardship and suffering had lined her face, and she looked ill.

'You know that little nurse, sir,' said the doctor to me, 'she was magnificent. Do you know what she said to me as we finished? I said to her with relief, "Well, I think that's the lot, Nurse." She smiled: "No, doctor, I am afraid there is one more case." '

' "One more?" ' I asked in surprise.

' "Yes," she replied, "it's me." '

I knew the strain she had been under and how she had been driving herself, but I had been too busy to realise how ill she looked. Apparently she had had pleurisy for two days and had been working continuously with a temperature of 104 degrees. We landed her and half a dozen other stretcher cases that night. The main disembarkation was fixed to start first thing in the morning.

On 10th July 1947 the C-in-C sent for me and briefed me on the role I was to carry out in the interception and seizure of the illegal immigrant ship *President Warfield* (the ship was renamed *Exodus*). One of the destroyers (*Cheviot*) was being sailed to pick her up northwest of Malta and shadow her. I was to sail on the morning of 13th July to rendezvous with *Cheviot* and take over, thereafter trailing her to her destination – obviously Palestine. Her actual seizure would be carried out by destroyers. My task was to act as cover and in active support of the destroyers, and to stop the refugees beaching the ship on the Palestinian coast or trying any 'funny business'.

Five hours after setting sail we sighted *President Warfield* and *Cheviot* approximately seventy miles west-north-west of Malta. I took over and we both settled down to shadow or 'escort' her. She was heading to pass down the Malta channel midway between the Maltese and Linosa islands, and then coming round to the east. But her steering was erratic, so her speed averaged about 12 knots. She made sudden alterations of course – at times coming straight at us – but her various attempts to shake us off were only of minor nuisance value.

At 1630 on 16th July I closed on *President Warfield* to have a good look at her and to pass an official warning by loud hailer:

'This is *Ajax*. What port are you making for?'

I repeated this several times, but the only reply I got were jeers and shouts of defiance and abuse. When it died down I continued:

'As you will not tell me I warn you that illegal entry of your passengers into Palestine will not be allowed and your ship will be arrested if you try to do so. We do not want to hurt anyone, but if you resist, force will be used and people will be hurt. If you are wise the sensible passengers will restrain the hotheads.

I repeat, force will be used if our sailors are attacked. Your leaders and all sensible passengers must stop the hotheads from futile resistance. Resistance will not help your cause.'

However, still the *President Warfield* continued. She kept us guessing about whether she would try to beach at Rafah or on the Gaza strip. Two more destroyers with boarding parties arrived to join us.

At 1420 I transferred our boarding parties to *Childers* and *Chieftain* to augment theirs. Finally at 2130 the air escort arrived and circled overhead. The destroyers were now keeping *President Warfield* illuminated periodically. The stage was set for the final act.

At 0200 on 18th July the signal 'Hands to Boarding Stations' was made and the destroyers moved in. The next three hours were hectic. As the destroyers made their runs either singly or in pairs with one on each side, *President Warfield* jerked violently. The whole exercise was fraught with danger to life and limb and particularly hazardous for the *President Warfield*. She was an old American lake steamer with single funnel, high freeboard, four or five decks and much top hamper, including a line of life rafts and Carley floats along each side immediately below the boat deck. Her sides were also perforated to within a few feet of the water line with large square ports and embarkation doors, most of which were open – presumably to give ventilation to the 4,500 men, women and children packed into her.

The destroyers had been fitted with makeshift boarding platforms each side of their bridge superstructures, but they were not an unqualified success under the conditions.

We had heard rumours that the immigrants had one or more 'secret weapons' and we were expecting stiff resistance from the hard core. It is very difficult to board a ship at sea and gain control over a mob of several thousand people. They were packed like sardines and many of them were prostrate through seasickness or illness. The boarding parties soon learned what they were up against. Those that got over were assaulted from all angles; steam jets were turned on them; the side decks were coated in oil fuel to make them slippery; smoke bombs, fireworks and a variety of missiles were hurled at them and tear gas canisters were thrown.

One young Ordinary Seaman gave me his account:

I don't know exactly which boarding I went over with but it was the one after Lieutenant Soames got over. I jumped on to a sloping raft 15–25 feet above the funnel starboard side. The raft was on skids and as soon as I was on it so were six thugs from inboard. They had been hiding behind the raft and so escaped notice. One hopped right past me to the outboard side or lower end of the raft, which was a silly thing to do as I booted him over the side. After I had cleared the raft I became the target for pretty much everything, bar the mess kettle. I tried to get inboard three times but there was too much opposition. I was forced to draw my revolver and fired eleven warning rounds. One of the last shots, however, I used to stop a lad of seventeen or eighteen from collecting my scalp with a meat axe. He got it in the stomach. I am sorry about that, but it was him or me. When they slipped the raft I must have passed out, although I remember jumping clear of the raft in mid-air. The *Cardigan Bay* (which had been stationed as long stop) picked me up at 0430.

When *Cardigan Bay* sighted the raft, he was on it, conscious and grasping his torch but badly beaten up. His face was in a mess, both eyes closed and he had two cuts on his head. But he was cheerful and soon recovered.

The 'battle' continued for nearly three hours. The destroyers found it almost impossible to remain alongside for more than a few minutes at a time. There was quite a swell and with the violent manoeuvring of *President Warfield* and the opposition, the boarding parties found it difficult to get across. Moreover both destroyers developed slight leaks. A total of about four dozen boarders had got across, and one party led by Soames had fought their way to the wheelhouse, only to discover that the ship was being controlled and steered from some secret position. He was more or less besieged in the wheelhouse.

I had been keeping between the ship and the shoreline ready to head her off if she made a dash for the beach, but shortly before 0500 I decided that I must take action. It was a difficult decision to make. A destroyer is one thing but a heavy-armoured cruiser is quite another. If I had severely damaged her or pushed her over, the consequences could have been disastrous. I had no wish to go down in history as the man responsible for losing hundreds of lives; I knew that the politicians would be running for cover and disclaiming all responsibility as fast as they could.

Still, there it was – I must take the chance. I instructed the commander to muster as big a show of force as he could. At 0510 I began my approach. Five minutes later I was within one and a half cables. A photograph of the *President Warfield* taken at this point shows clearly the state she was in and the exhaustion of her passengers. A few seconds later the white flag of surrender went up. It was all over and I stood off.

As soon as we had got things organised we set course up the coast for Haifa. The refugees had been controlling the ship from a sort of armoured citadel below the boat deck aft. It would have been a difficult nut to crack.

After breakfast I sent over a medical team to help the Jewish doctors with casualties. We arrived at Haifa at 1500 and at 1800, and when the Army had taken over, recovered our boarding parties.

While all this had been going on, the Great Powers were haggling over what was to happen to the *President Warfield*, and by the time we arrived at Haifa a formula had been worked out. The refugees were to be transferred to merchant ships and taken back whence they came, if the French government agreed. So as soon as they were able, the army started the unenviable task of transferring the illegals into three chartered merchants ships, our old friends *Ocean Vigour* and *Empire Rival*, plus an older ship, the *Runnymede Park* – approximately 1,500 people per ship.

The C-in-C signalled me to take charge of the convoy and we set out the next day with orders to press on as fast as the merchant ships could make it. I had two frigates under me to assist, *Cardigan Bay* and *Brissenden*, and a promise of two minesweepers later. There were armed guards in all three ships.

We had our problems. *Runnymede Park* could only make eight knots. The refugees started a hunger strike. The masters of the merchant ships had been told roughly where they were bound for; the military guards and doctors (one per ship) had not, such was the army's craze for secrecy. They thought we were bound for Cyprus, twenty hours steaming away! The result was that the doctors had practically no instruments and few medical supplies. With many refugees suffering from TB and other diseases and injuries, as well as pregnant women, they were really up against it. There were sixty births in just four days. The doctors were rushing from ship to ship. They said afterwards that they had never helped bring so many babies into the world in such a short time, nor were they likely to again. The idea was that one person became two or more after entry – only this time it hadn't worked out that way.

I had to send an urgent signal to the C-in-C for additional medical assistance. I then received a signal from the Admiralty saying the French government had agreed to accept the immigrants, and another from the C-in-C saying that the *Troubridge* (D3) was being sailed to relieve me and would take the convoy on to its destination. Joe Selby came panting up in the *Troubridge*, loaded with medical supplies and I turned the convoy over to him, thankfully. My signal had been passed to the C-in-C's shore staff at Malta, as he was at sea carrying out a fleet exercise. It had caused quite a flap and not a little hilarity, with the *Ajax* being in the thick of it once again. What with sixty babies in four days, they were all wondering what we would get up to next.

All I can say is that I was very thankful to get shot of that particular job.

On 28 July 1947 all three ships anchored outside Port de Bouc. France informed the refugees that any volunteers who left the ships would be welcome. The refugees refused and for three weeks the impasse continued. The British government would not back down and return the refugees to Palestine or Cyprus. On 21st August the ships left for Germany disembarking their human cargo in Hamburg – returning them 'in fact' them to the country responsible for their condition. The British Mandate in Palestine ended officially on 14th May 1948.

HMS *WARSPITE*

ORDINARY SEAMAN RONALD MARTIN, RN

After the war, in 1947, the *Warspite* was on her way to the ship-breakers in Scotland. However, she had a mind of her own under tow, running herself aground in Prussia Cove off Saint Michael's Mount in Cornwall. There she lay – eventually they had to break her up on the rocks. Bits of her can be seen sticking up in Marazion to this day. She wasn't going to go to the ship-breakers. The Warspite Association had a big memorial plaque of Cornish stone made and in 1992 we all went down there with the town council, television and press to unveil this stone in memory of the *Warspite*.

It was very sad for me when, early in 1945, I was sent out to Australia to join the Pacific Fleet. I left *Warspite* before she was towed away. She was an incredible ship. She was built in Devonport dockyard and whoever built the hull really knew what they were doing. She was hit twenty-nine times at Jutland, severely damaged at Crete, and then again at Salerno. They say that the *Warspite* was the best value-for-money warship that the Royal Navy ever had. She was a Queen Elizabeth Class battleship, completed in 1916 in time for Jutland. She was a smaller ship than *Hood* or *Prince of Wales*. She was the next down in size until the Anson class came along. None of them had her record.

HMS *AMETHYST*

ORDINARY SEAMAN GORDON 'SHINER' WRIGHT, RN

On 20th April 1949, during the final phase of the Chinese revolution, the frigate HMS *Amethyst* was fired on by communist guns on the Yangtze-Kiang river while sailing up with supplies for the British community in Nanking. Although it was unclear why the vessel was attacked and detained by the communists, the general assumption was that it was intended as an assertion of Chinese sovereignty over an international waterway.

In April 1949 the *Amethyst* was called back from exercises in Mirs Bay on the Yangtze River to stock up with food, ammunition and general supplies. The sailmaker was told to make a couple of big canvas flags, but none of us knew why this was happening or what was actually going on. It was only after we set sail for Nanking that we were told we were to relieve the destroyer *Consort*. We were also told that the communists would be crossing over the river at mid-day that day.

My own opinion is that somebody made a bit of a mess-up, because even with the British flag on the sides of the ship, they started to fire at us that morning. I thought, my God, what the hell's happening here? They started to fire first, and because I was down in the Mess Deck when it happened I don't know whether they missed us or what, but there were no casualties in the early firing.

'Action stations' was called. My action stations were on 'A' gun and yet my sea duties were as helmsman. Of course I went up to 'A' gun, ready to load up the ammunition into the gun hold. The only trouble was, our gun couldn't bear round to where the firing was coming from. Only 'X' and 'Y' guns at the rear of the ship could fire there and those were the two guns that got hit.

All we could see was the smoke coming up from the forward banks; we couldn't actually see the guns that were firing. So, of course, we were just firing in the direction the smoke was coming from. Because we couldn't even bear our gun captain decided, 'Right, down below.'

When I went down into the Mess Deck, I couldn't believe my eyes. There were injured people just lying around. One chap had his ankle shot off, and one of my very best friends, who I used to go ashore with, had had half of his face blown off. I put a big bandage into his face to try and stop the bleeding. It was a big rip, right out. Part of the other side of his face was going as well. He had lost so much blood that there was no hope for him really. I thought, 'Why can't I do something to save him?' Tears were in my eyes, and he was squeezing my hand. I said, 'It's me, Gordon, it's me Gordon, Shiner.' He tried to open one of his eyes and he couldn't see properly because it was all swollen up. As I felt him squeeze my hand I thought, well, he must know he's going to die, although he didn't actually go till later.

I felt so inadequate not being able to do anything to help any of them. That was the first time I'd seen anyone really hurt like that, with shrapnel. Lieutenant Weston, the no. 1, had a bad chest and stomach wound. He was still alive, holding his stomach, and the blood was coming all over his arms. By now *Amethyst* had gone aground on the river bank and was fast in the mud.

We were told to abandon ship. I thought, well, do I go or not? But they kept telling us to go. I thought, well, there's all these wounded here. They said, we'll get the wounded off. I went to swing through one of the safety holds and I saw the river being hit by bullets from the bank. The people who had jumped out and got past the rear end of the ship were being shot in the water. Just as I was thinking: 'this is going to be the lesser of two evils here, I'll stay on board,' they asked for volunteers to stay, so it turned out that I was able to try and help the injured after all.

One of the boats which hadn't got blown up had got ashore, but they were firing at it so much they had to turn round and come back. Some people managed, however, to get ashore on the Nationalist side. The casualties had been dead for two or three hours, and because of the heat they were all smelling badly. We had handkerchiefs around our faces, and were wrapping the bodies up in all the old blankets and hammock covers, whatever we could find.

They were still firing when we went aground. You could have jumped off the foc's'le on to the bank if you'd been that way inclined. Anyway, this is when we started to get some of the wounded ashore. We did get most of them off although, in the meantime, the doctor and his assistant were killed. What made this even worse was that none of us knew anything about first aid. Not that first aid would have helped much because the injuries were so severe, but we could have tried to do something. Luckily for us a Chinese Nationalist doctor, and a Royal Navy one who had been flown in, came on board, and did a really wonderful job.

We felt really relieved when the *Consort* came down from Nanking to try to pull us off the bank, but she got hit very badly. About four of us ran out with a hawser for them to grab hold of and pull us off, but the firing of the snipers was so bad we couldn't do it. They were firing on her too, and she took a lot of casualties. She went back down towards Shanghai, and then we felt very much alone.

We weren't too fearful for our own lives. At night time, I suppose, I used to think about it, but during the day there was so much to do, getting all the people ready for burial at sea. We now had Lieutenant-Commander Kerans who came aboard from Nanking to replace Lieutenant Skinner; he was a naval attaché. We were off the bank by then, more or less out in the middle of the river. They were still firing at us and then they would stop for about an hour. We managed to anchor again close to the south bank, but realised the Communist guns were sited to cover every foot of the river. We felt there was no escape. Commander Kerans began negotiations with the Communists for our safe passage – but they kept refusing.

We were there from 20th April until 31st July, 1949. Over three months. The provisions started to get low, but we had built up a rapport with the communists, who told us we could buy food from the local people, peasants, as they called them. They brought the food on board the ship. The trouble was, we had to pay exorbitant prices: but if we didn't buy it, we went without. At least we were getting green vegetables, vital foods – that's what kept us going.

When the firing first started we had brought bags of flour up to all the open spaces to block the firing. Of course, in the end we had to take those bags of flour back and the chef had to make bread with this flour, which was full of weevils. Of course, we still ate it. It was terrible. And we were drinking distilled water as well, which goes right through you if you drink it all the time. Makes you feel sick.

Actually morale was very good: the chaps knew that the commander kept going ashore for meetings. Every time he went we said this is it, we're going to get a free passage down. But it never worked out because he wouldn't sign this vital paper saying that we had fired first. No way would he do it.

One day all the main officers, the POs and chiefs were called to the captain's cabin. He said, 'Right, we're going to make a break for it. I want you to get all the canvases you can. Put them over the ship. Make the outline different to what it is. Paint it all black. We'll be leaving at ten o'clock.'

During the long sit on the ship Leslie Franks, the coxswain, put me in charge of the wheelhouse. He said, 'I want you to keep the wheelhouse spick and span, get up there every day, polish the brass-work and keep yourself busy.' The first thing I did was clear off the blood.

After that meeting with Commander Kerans Leslie Franks said to me, 'Get all the hammocks, mattresses, whatever you can. Stick them into the wheelhouse. Pile them up against the door.' So I said, 'You don't mind me asking, Blackie, but what's the problem, what's happening?' He said, 'We're going to make a break, Shiner.' I said, 'You must be joking. We'll never make it out of here. We've got 150-odd miles to go and there are bloody communists either side of us.' 'Well,' he said, 'we're going to try, so you hide behind the wheel.' I said, 'Fair enough.' He told the crew to wrap the anchor in grease and canvas, so when it was slipped it wouldn't make a noise. They slackened it off and let it slip through, putting sacks over the hawser pipe where it goes out. We also stretched great sheets of canvas along the sides to alter her silhouette as much as possible. We slipped anchor just after ten in the evening. We had to do a full turn.

That was the most frightening part of all – we could easily have been blown out of the water by their 75 mm and 105 mm guns. I was in the wheelhouse all the way down: I'll never forget that turn. We didn't create very big waves, in fact we turned very slowly, very skilful navigational work. My Divisional Officer was Sub-Lieutenant Hett, who was only twenty or twenty-one. He was working with charts that were ripped and covered with blood, and he had no charts of the river at all, they were all lost. He really should have got more recognition because he got us through even though he wasn't a navigation officer.

So there we were, going down the river in the dark. We passed a local boat which had all its lights on. The communists started firing at this boat. They must have been quite stupid – if we were going to escape we would never put lights on a ship. The skipper said, 'Right, we'll go on now. Let them take it.' You could hear the shells come over the ship. Franks said to me, 'Now, Shiner, if anything happens to me you get on this wheel.' I said to him, 'It's being so bloody cheerful that keeps you going.'

When we were halfway down, just before we got to Kiang Yin, there was a boom right across the river. I heard Commander Kerans say to Hett, 'There's a boom here, we've got to more or less guess which side to take, and hope for the best.' I think they decided to go on the starboard side. In the wheelhouse we were lying on the deck so that if anything happened we'd already be on the deck. Luckily they chose the right side.

It was still dark, it didn't start getting light till half-past five in the morning. I then heard Kerans say that if we got to Woosung Fort it would be the most critical point of the breakout, because they had 9-inch guns which could blow us out of the water if they caught us in their searchlights. Then we heard him say, 'Woosung in sight.' I had my fingers crossed. We got past them, they must have been asleep or something, or the communications were bad. Their big guns did not fire. Kerans then came over the intercom: 'I want every man to give everything for the last leg.'

While we were passing Woosung HMS *Concord* was there. They had been told that if Woosung ever started firing at us they were to blast at its guns. There was cheering, of course, when it came by. I don't know how we did it I never thought for one minute we were going to make it, it was beyond my wildest dreams. I said to Franks, 'Never thought we were going to make it,' and the tears were pouring down my face. I couldn't stop shaking. Open sea at last, fresh air. I can't really put it into words how I felt. Relief, relief to think we were going to have some fresh food, plenty to eat. When we got alongside the boys in *Consort* they said, with great smiles on their faces, 'Right, what do you want to eat? We'll bring some stuff over.' The sirens were going, the hooters were going.

Believe it or not, if it had taken half-an-hour longer we would have run out of fuel. We just had enough. But we had lost 23 out of a ship's company of 183.

Lieutenant-Commander Kerans sent out one final message: 'HAVE REJOINED THE FLEET. AM SOUTH OF WOOSUNG. NO DAMAGE OR CASUALTIES. GOD SAVE THE KING.'

KOREA

Lieutenant John Winton, RN

The Korean campaign lasted over three years, from June 1950 until the armistice in July 1953, and involved the land, sea and air forces of over a dozen United Nations countries. It has always been a forgotten war.

Politicians, at the time and since, persisted in referring to the Korean war in peace-time language, as though it were really only a very minor 'brush-fire' affair. Yet it actually caused total combatant and civilian casualties of nearly four million people – almost twice as many as in the Vietnam war.

As a sub-lieutenant in need of a watch-keeping certificate I volunteered for HMS *Birmingham* based in Korea. We went out in a trooper which was straight Kipling – she was one of those 'steamers white and gold' which used to go rolling down to Rio. Only now she took us to Port Said, Aden, Colombo, Singapore and Hong Kong: even the names are a roll call of the imperial past.

We dressed for dinner every night, with stiff shirts and bow-ties, except when we reached the tropics and were allowed to wear open-necked shirts. On the first night out from Southampton, I happened to sit down to dinner with a friend of mine in the Royal Fusiliers, not knowing that, by trooper custom, where you sit first you sit all the way. But it did me good to be the solitary sailor amongst seven pongoes and to have my leg pulled all the way to Pusan, in South Korea.

At Pusan we were greeted by an American negro band on the jetty and a great sign, 'This is the Busiest Military Port in the World'. It looked a bleak, grey place, bleak grey buildings and a background of bleak grey hills. The soldiers disembarked here, and I did not envy them. I remember thinking at the time that perhaps Korea was best left to the Koreans.

Meanwhile, we all went to Kure, on the Inland Sea of Japan, to wait for our ships to come back from 'up the coast'. We stayed at the rest camp, HMAS *Commonwealth*. The wardroom bar was kept by three Japanese, who might have been triplets. One had green patches sewn on the lapels of his jacket and was addressed as 'Starboard-san'. 'Port-san' had red patches. The third, with one green and one red patch, was 'Midships-san'.

We joined *Birmingham* in the southern island of Kyushu. The ship sailed at once. We newcomers soon found that the Korean war might only be a non-event at home but it was deadly serious here. We kept defence watches, darkened ship religiously, and went to dawn action stations in case something unpleasant had crept up on us in the night.

It never did, but several times we had aircraft alarms, and went to 'repel aircraft' stations – waiting apprehensively in our anti-flash gear for what seemed like hours, and then hearing that some landing craft had been shot up closer inshore. Once a floating mine was spotted drifting down on us. I can still see the Mate of the Upper Deck, standing up in the whaler, poling the thing away from him with the butt-end of a boat-hook.

We spent a lot of time off the so-called 'strategic' islands of Chodo and Sokto, in the north, above the 38th Parallel. They were held by the United Nations. We used to bombard from time to time, especially at a place called 'The Hole in the Wall', where the Chinese had a fairly big gun in an emplacement set in the cliffs.

The Chinese used to run their gun out in the very early mornings, then we would fire back. It was literally a case of the 'fastest gun in the west'. My cabin was somewhere under 'Y' turret and I got used to being tipped out of my bunk and having all my books and belongings thrown on to the cabin deck by the shock waves.

They must have decided that our 6-inch guns were not enough. We were joined by the battleship USS 'Mighty Mo' *Missouri* who used her 16-inch guns to pound the mainland near Chodo. Ships used to go into action with the UN flag at their foremast and their national ensign at the main.

Korea means 'Land of the Morning Calm' and it often was astonishingly peaceful and beautiful from seaward. There were distant blue mountains with snow on them, and closer hills which sometimes wore mysterious layers of mist, so that their slopes rose up like the turrets of a magician's castle.

Occasionally we would anchor in a bay in the evening and find in the morning that more than five hundred fishing junks had arrived during the night. It must have been a similar sight to those Marco Polo saw. And when they all set sail together, it was like watching a huge meadow suddenly bursting into bloom.

We used to do seven- or ten-day blockading patrols 'up the coast' (the west coast; the US Navy took the east coast), alternating with our sister ship *Newcastle*. There was a light fleet carrier operating on the west coast, either *Glory* or *Ocean*, who also took turn and turn about. And there were many smaller ships such as *Cockade, Charity, Cardigan Bay, Whitesand Bay, Opossum, Mounts Bay, St Bride's Bay*, the Canadian *Athabaskan*, and the NZ *Kaniere*.

In spite of our involvement, I still felt we at sea were curiously detached from the reality of war. I used to look at the shore line and think about my army friends in the trooper. One evening I was standing on the quarterdeck, drinking a cup of coffee after dinner. It must have been late April. The days were lengthening and there was a touch of spring in the air, but the Yellow Sea was still bitterly cold. I was watching a couple of flights of US Marine Corsair fighter-bombers bombing and strafing some unfortunates ashore. As I looked, one of the Corsairs was hit by ground fire. The pilot obviously saw us and, already streaming smoke, turned towards us. When he passed overhead, he was starting to flame. We steered a parallel course and lowered the sea-boat to the water-line. He pitched only two or three cables on our starboard bow. Away went the sea-boat, and never did sailors bend their backs to their oars with more enthusiasm.

He must have been in the water only a very few minutes. But it was long enough. The cold had penetrated deep into the core of his body, and he was dead by the time they got him back to the ship. When I got back to the quarterdeck, my coffee was still warm.

We spent Coronation Day (June 2nd 1953) in Hong Kong, and I still remember the dragon processions in the streets, watching the fireworks from a Star ferry crossing the harbour to Kowloon, and how the ferry listed most alarmingly, first one way and then the other, as the Chinese, who are besotted by fireworks, rushed from side to side to see the display.

Most of our shore leave was spent in Sasebo, a shanty town full of bars and massage parlours where we danced curious ritual dances with grubby little Japanese girls and pretended – just as they did – they were geishas. The base was run by the Americans. They were very generous in lending their films and landing craft to take our libertymen ashore, but they had little of our sense of humour.

In July 1953 we were anchored off the coast, at ten minutes' notice for steam, for twelve days, while the politicians talked interminably about an armistice. It was finally agreed, but the talks at Panmunjon went on. I have a son, who is older now than I was then, and those talks are still in progress.

So, what good came of it at last? Was it a famous victory? It certainly was a vindication of sea power. Without that the United Nations, forced down into the Pusan pocket in the early days, would have been driven right off the peninsula. Without sea power the Inchon landing would have been impossible, and the Marines could not have been brought off from Hungnam. Almost all the United Nations' reinforcements and supplies came by sea.

Above all, Korea showed the politicians, who badly needed the education, then as now, that traditional principles of sea and air power, as demonstrated again and again in World War Two, had *not* been made obsolete by nuclear weapons.

Nursing Sister Ruth Stone, QARNNS

The Navy required people with three qualifications and a year's experience in some other field, so it took me five years just to qualify for entry. I joined the QARNNS in 1947. We weren't young – we went in at twenty-four and twenty-five. It was a sensible requirement because we had to turn our hand to any sort of nursing.

We worked hard and played hard – we had only one weekend off in three. I did not fall in love with any of the doctors – you couldn't afford to do that when you had embarked on a naval nursing career. You loved them and left them. And I did leave them because I went to sea to Korea.

There was a lot of activity alongside dusty Pusan harbour; fleets of field ambulances arrived carrying wounded from the hospital trains, weaving their way through stacks of yellow-ringed bombs and other sinister-looking hardware. We came alongside the shore to meet the hospital trains which brought the injured from the battlefield to the quayside. Not only were the wounded crowding the quay side but stacked high were yellow painted napalm bombs. It was a chilling sight.

At the bottom of Her Majesty's Hospital Ship *Maine*'s main gangway, the senior medical officer and wardmaster assessed the gravity of each man's general condition and the appropriate ward was allocated accordingly. The dangerously and seriously ill were directed to the only ward with air-conditioning; the less critically injured to the adjacent wards and the walking wounded to the waterline wards a deck below. Simultaneously, two surgeons would operate on as many urgent cases as they could (occasionally ashore in field hospital tents), while loading was underway. There were often amputations, since gangrene was the great enemy, and, of course, it was not always possible to operate in really rough weather at sea, especially as in early autumn typhoons presented a further hazard.

With immediate treatment and medication instructions written on luggage labels attached to the casualties' wrists, together with scanty previous notes scrawled by doctors in the forward casualty clearing station, South Korean soldiers carried the stretchers to the wards and the loading of the weary and bedraggled wounded was usually achieved in twelve hours. The sailing time back to Japan through the Shimonoseki Straits and into the Inland Sea normally took two to three days. It was impossible to reduce this period as the Allies had not yet declared the Japanese-swept channels free of mines.

This part of the journey was the most strenuous time for the medical division, complemented and equipped as we were for peace-time duties. The two-day sisters and nurses rarely found their work done before midnight and the sole night sister made her weary way to her bunk at about midday. The theatre sister was on duty or on call continuously. The six VADs staffed the officers' ward and the sick berth staff were magnificent during the crisis. At the height of the conflict they stood watches from 8am to 2am, followed by five hours off, then from 7am to 9pm, with additional skeleton night staff.

Our matron, Miss Barbara Nockolds, relieved in the operating theatre, ran the officers' ward and a small below-waterline ward where the badly shell-shocked patients were housed. She was everywhere, working well into the night like everyone else. Ralph Izzard, the war correspondent for the *Daily Mail*, who often sailed with us, wrote of her: 'A rare, inspiring, imperturbable and supremely capable woman who never seemed to tire.'

Randolph Churchill, the war correspondent of the *Daily Telegraph*, also sailed in the *Maine* from time to time. We didn't see him much – he spent most of his time in the Master's cabin. He wrote a blistering report on the conditions and inadequacy of the *Maine*'s resources during this war period. The waterline ward required that the portholes should be secured when at sea and, as the temperatures there registered 90° to 116° Fahrenheit – since the wards were over the main generators and had no air-conditioning or washing facilities – there was a marked resemblance to Dante's *Inferno* as we descended the ramp to cope with some 80 to 100 battle-soiled and dehydrated walking wounded.

In spite of the lack of normal, basic nursing conditions however, the wounded were so grateful just to be able to lie down in comparative safety to sleep. Jugs of water and lime juice, known as 'limers', were placed in strategic positions and the patients were sedated because of the noise of the ship's engines below. But it is the cold of Korea that I will remember. Although we never stopped working, our bones were chilled. Rum was drunk hot with orange juice at midday. It warmed us up temporarily.

At the other end of the ship, and a deck above, the critically injured were amassed; the dying in free-swinging cots to lessen the effects of the ship's pitching. It was generally accepted that all those with penetrating abdominal wounds should have colostomies; all chest wounds should be treated with some form of underwater seal drainage, and head injuries, especially of the neck region, should undergo a tracheotomy.

On admission to the ward, and sometimes at the gangway, every plaster was bi-valved and every soldier with a wound or burn had an intra-muscular injection of penicillin, in the morning and the afternoon.

In those days this life-saving drug was prepared in a suspension of beeswax – quite diabolical to draw up speedily into the syringe. Our dental officer and his assistant came to the rescue; they toiled from bed to bed and from one end of the ship to the other, and each evening began all over again. They somehow achieved this in addition to attending to the intricate jaw and facial reconstructions which presented themselves on each trip.

As far as nursing sisters were concerned, the dressings seemed endless and the added nightmare of discovering maggots in the wounds, inside plaster and under scalps (and even first colostomy dressings produced thousands of these horrors), made our work doubly traumatic. The wounded were given basic first aid and perhaps some sort of emergency surgery before they came to us. They all had luggage labels tied to their wrists with whatever drugs they had been given written on one side of the label and what treatment they'd had on the reverse.

We saw some sad sights. Some of the Americans would shoot themselves in the feet on purpose. But, if they were not in desperate need of immediate care, they were left in the field. That's when the flies descended on them, the maggots and the gangrene got in and one or two lost legs.

We also had a number of British soldiers in with napalm burns and they were angry because the Americans had bombed the wrong hill. From time to time Americans and British were almost in neighbouring beds and the occasional fracas broke out. Patients were trying to fight each other with drips in their arms and tubes coming out of their noses. We were so busy we didn't even have time to stop them.

Often their wounds weren't fatal but they were very traumatised with tiredness and lack of fluids and they were utterly weary. They'd had time to think about what they'd been through and sometimes they were silent – they turned their heads away and would not talk. They were all so young.

But with just rest, fluids and food, most of the patients showed a remarkable improvement after their short stay with us. Then they were transferred to their next medical care haven, either in American or in Commonwealth base hospitals in Kure or Osaka.

Sadly, we did not have our own chaplain, but one sailed with us occasionally to join a destroyer or frigate flotilla. Many men died without the comfort of the last rites of their church or a final blessing. Nor did we have a lot of time to hold a dying man's hand. We could stay for a few minutes and then our attention was needed for someone else.

Americans do not bury their dead at sea or on foreign soil, but return the corpses to their homeland. So their dead had to be laid aft, and because of the heat, precious ice had to be placed over them at two-hourly intervals. The overworked dispensary leading-hand had to perform this unsavoury task, but was helped on occasions by the war reporters to whom we were 'giving a lift'.

The organisation for receiving patients in Osaka was highly efficient. They were disembarked speedily to a fleet of waiting ambulance and medical coaches. The dead went first, covered with a flag of their country, while appropriate music was played by a military band on the quayside. It was a sad moment for all.

Immediately after this, when all the patients were ashore, more feverish activity of a different kind continued in the wards. Beds were stripped and disinfected and when fresh linen was delivered on board (since our ship's laundry could cope only with uniforms), the beds were made up in preparation for the next convoy. A bag containing toilet necessities, playing cards, writing paper, magazines, packets of cigarettes and sweets, supplied by the American Red Cross, was placed inside each locker. Only after completing this task could the medical staff sleep – and often it was for twenty-four hours.

Returning to Pusan very early on in the war we were awakened at first light one morning by the sound of bagpipes. We saw, quite close to us, a light fleet carrier and, on the flight deck, the outline of troops in battle order. They were the Argyll and Sutherland Highlanders who were about to disembark. It was a chilling moment for us as well as a poignant re-enactment of the start of battle rituals of long ago.

In the late August of 1950 a new situation met us every time we arrived in

Pusan. Sometimes the hospital trains disgorged not patients, but hundreds of white painted coffins which were then loaded on to store ships returning to the USA.

Occasionally the quayside was strewn with air-dropped pamphlets and there were air raid alerts when all ships in harbour dispersed at top speed, while the *Maine* remained fully illuminated with her Red Cross and Green Bands aglow.

One nail-biting incident happened when an ammunition ship broke her typhoon buoys and careered out of control in harbour. She was brimful with high explosives and she missed us by inches. Her captain was highly commended for the way in which he handled his ship. We were the only ship not fleeing towards the open sea. That was one of my few moments of fear; it was probably the only time we were really frightened apart from the time when unidentified planes were flying overhead while we were well lit up.

The situation on land was now very serious indeed, and on approaching Pusan, we were told that it would be our last journey to load wounded on board because the North Korean and the Chinese armies were only thirty miles away. We could see the red glow and flashes behind the hills.

We waited until all the wounded had embarked. To make a tragic situation even worse, news of Osaka being devastated by a typhoon caused us to divert to Tokyo. When we dropped anchor, the typhoon was so fierce we were unable to land our patients, so we set sail for Yokohama with a full load.

Another two days at sea in dreadful conditions only added to the misery of the already distressed troops but by now, perhaps due to Randolph Churchill's article, two much-needed extra nursing sisters arrived together with more sick berth staff. The port became busier and, to our relief, the arrival of the US hospital ships *Repose, Haven* and *Consolation*, greatly cheered us. These superbly equipped, purpose-built ships, of similar patient capacity, boasted 20 medical officers, 41 sisters and 130 sick bay staff. Compared with our six medical officers, six sisters and about 50 sick bay staff, it was undoubted bliss. Thus the *Maine* was able to leave the war zone and take some badly wounded and seriously burnt British soldiers from the Argyll and Sutherland Highlanders and the Gloucester Regiment to Hong Kong. However, the common danger we all shared forged a strong esprit de corps and lasting friendships which, even today, are remembered, and not least among the South Koreans themselves.

In 1950 the First Sea Lord, Lord Fraser of North Cape, said: 'One of Britain's most useful contributions to the United Nations effort in the Korean War has been Her Majesty's hospital ship *Maine*.' How could we have foreseen, on joining this floating hospital in 1949, the ultimate role of the ageing twelve-year-old vessel which was to be our home and workplace for the next two years.

LIEUTENANT DEREK 'PUG' MATHER, RN

I was captured in Korea during the first launch of the New Year's patrol, on 3rd January 1953. Our target was dive-bombing bridges in an area called the *So-Ho* region. By then I had done altogether eighty-seven missions. There were two or three bridges to attack. The Flight Commander and his number two made the first attack and got one with their bombs. We went off to do some armed reconnaissance and then I and my wingman, Lieutenant Ted Anson, took the next bridge.

Unfortunately the enemy was waiting there. It was a flak trap. They got me at the bottom of a dive with, I think, a 76mm shell under the engine. I had just enough time to call up and say that I had been hit, and I was pulling up to gain a bit of height, and then my Seafury blew up. The engine came off, and the tail, and I was going down in half an aircraft. I tried to get out and appeared over the side in the conventional manner and the next thing I knew I was floating down in my parachute. We did not have ejector seats. Theoretically you jettisoned the canopy which took a bit of the side of the cockpit away, you stood up in your seat, put your backside and the parachute over the edge and kicked over in a backwards somersault. Apparently I did all that but I don't remember it. Fortunately I got out. It was between 1,000 and 1,500 feet at the most. I can remember floating down, while soldiers on the ground were firing up. I had bought a Remington 45 automake and had some ammunition for it. We were issued with Webley.38s but the 45 was a much more accurate weapon. I let go one magazine of that and, by the time I was close to the ground, I swiftly threw it away. I landed in the snow and that was it. I was captured straightaway.

They took away my aircrew watch, but were not terribly belligerent. They didn't wear rank. These were North Koreans. They marched me away from the area and we holed up overnight. The next day we were walking up a river bed, then arrived at a bridge which was being attacked by Fireflies. My flight didn't know whether I was alive or not. They had seen me go down so there was a reasonable chance. Subsequently they put in 'Leopard' Troops – these were cloak and dagger people who did a landing on the coastline and infiltrated the enemy lines – and they reported back that I had landed, had been captured, and had been seen alive.

I was very worried and frightened. Nobody had been returned. The briefing that we had before we went out to Korea was that there were prisoner-of-war camps like the old German Stalag Luft. But these weren't. One was kept to oneself, in solitary confinement, for about three weeks or more. I was moved partly walking, partly on the back of a truck; overnight one was just taken into a Korean peasant's house with your guard and that was it – no-one spoke English.

Finally I ended up in a place called Paks Palace which is north of Pyongyang, the capital of North Korea. It was a big clearance centre and there I was handed over to the Chinese. There I met British army prisoners as well as some USAAF, which was reassuring. This was after about four weeks. I was just eating or dozing during that time. In that sort of climate you only eat twice a day, at first and last light. You had rice and little else. I was well built, was physically fit, rather plump and suffered no illness.

At some stage they took our uniforms away and I was given Chinese type clothing: the padded cotton stuff which I then had for the rest of the time. We went through a period of interrogation. Interrogation had been talked about. I had, by sheer chance, missed doing an escape and evasion exercise which was just bad luck, but it was probably not realistic anyway because little information had filtered back. They were asking general questions. It was not until years later, when I used to lecture on resistance to interrogation, that it came home to me that they were just probing for any information to fit the intelligence jigsaw pattern to use against somebody else. There were few specific questions. They wanted to know about ship formations, for instance, but you could keep away from that sort of topic. They didn't particularly like the name, rank and serial numbers reply, particularly because in the navy officers we didn't have serial numbers. We gave them minimal and useless information. We weren't considered to be prisoners-of-war, we were enemies of the Republic of China. They were also trying to get germ warfare confessions and things like that and a mixture of military intelligence and all the while giving us political indoctrination. I didn't take this very seriously because I thought it was ridiculous. You would think it was a waste of time to try to convert one person to being a communist. But that's what they wanted to do. One of my interrogators was a graduate of the London School of Economics. He knew more about the British political scene than I did. Like most of my age group I was slightly apolitical.

There were various types of interrogator, the nice ones and the ones who put on the pressure; they alternated. Anything to try and keep you unstable which, under those circumstances, was fairly easy to do: you had nobody to talk to and nobody to discuss with and so almost welcomed interrogation because at least they were speaking in your language. Occasionally they allowed me books, mainly Russian ones with English translations. An exception was *David Copperfield*, because they reckoned that Dickens would have been an ace communist if he had been alive at that time; another was Marx's *Das Kapital* and all sorts of others: Zola, Thomas Moore's *Utopia*.

Obviously, though, time goes on and interrogation keeps going on, and you don't know how long it is all going to last. They took away our cold weather protective clothing. It became rather cold and then later on we cleared out of that camp and moved out towards the Yalu River but then we were put in solitary confinement. This was not unusual, in fact some of the prisoners said in some ways you were probably better off than being in a camp as they were not all that pleasant. I had to learn to be on my own and try and pass the time by myself. I was held in solitary until the war was over in September, for about six months.

They were slowly moving us up north. Part of the time I sat on one wing of a jeep and another prisoner sat on the other with a guard and a petrol drum between us. It was like that too when we slept overnight. Passage of time was difficult to tell. They would take over a room of a Korean house, a mud shack, and you and your guard were there. You had your own guard, although they changed occasionally. I knew a few odd Chinese words. Do you want food? Or, it's time to go to bed?

The Chinese varied between those who had been in the front line themselves and those who had marched straight down from the mainland, who were pretty ignorant and basic. The ones who had been in the front lines were slightly more compassionate. But they were terribly brainwashed in their appreciation of what we were like, which was rather humorous in a way. They showed me a piece of soap and because they had a pretty basic existence themselves they thought they were doing me a great favour by giving me a bar of soap to wash with. They assumed that we, because we were soldiers or airmen fighting a war, were also deprived of such things.

I lived in a fairly small room and I worked out that if I walked so many thousand times across this I might do a mile. As time went on I was allowed outside my hut. I was in an area in which a lot of the people were in solitary confinement, and when we were allowed out we weren't permitted to talk at all. There was one time when a band was walking along singing *Sarri Mare* (a South African song) because some prisoners were South Africans who had been flying Mustangs. One chap not far away from me heard this too and he was looking at me. He was wearing an RAF blue belt. He was trying to point to himself with a bit of sign language. I knew that the RAF weren't out in Korea, so I thought it was strange. In fact he was called Olaf Burg who was of South African birth, had joined the Royal Air Force, been sent out to Australia to 88 Squadron and then been shot down.

I did wonder if all this was going to end or where it was going to end. The situation had been relatively deadlocked for eighteen months or more before I got there. The chances were that it would go on that way. There was no news. The lowest point, however, was the occasional shots I heard in the night, with the odd scream; immediately my mind started thinking the worst. One night I was called out and told to follow the guards out and to start digging a hole in the ground. I immediately thought, that was going to be a hole for me to finish up in. Luckily it didn't work out that way. I don't know why I was made to dig the holes, probably because it was part of the pressure. The interrogators were good at psychological pressure, which of course, affects people differently. But they didn't get many converts to communism.

Later on, the food seemed to get better, and then a Dakota came flying down the valleys late one evening. A door was opened - the aircrew were in the doorway shouting, but we couldn't hear them because their loud speaker had broken down. They were supposed to be broadcasting the news that the war was over. A few days after that I was moved out of the solitary area on the back of a mule cart and we were allowed to talk. That was very strange. Then we got close to the camp, lo and behold the prisoners started shouting, 'It's all right, the war is over.' It was a great relief.

We were put into cattle trucks by the Yalu River and came all the way back through Korea down to Panmunjom, where we were released to the United Nations. The guards were not very much in evidence. We were given cigarettes for the journey down. I had been reported by name as being positively alive by an American who had been medically repatriated some weeks before. That was the first sign. Up to then I was 'missing presumed killed in action'. That message was then passed to my parents and it was not very long before I was repatriated.

My captivity lasted from January to September. I felt great on my return. We were taken down to Sasebo and there was HMS *Ocean*. *Glory* had gone home and *Ocean*, where I had lots of chums, had come back out again. They gave me a cabin on board and we were issued with khaki uniform and I had a ball, free at last. There were only three naval people captured altogether. I was debriefed by the Royal Marines and then took passage in HMS *Unicorn* down to Hong Kong, the first part of my journey home. The only reaction I had to my imprisonment was that I was losing the feeling in my toes, which is an early sign of beri-beri or lack of vitamins. Physically I was very fit, the best weight I had been for years.

My parents came to meet me, and some of my old squadron. It was easier talking to the latter than to my parents.

When we got back we didn't have much counselling. I was sent on three months' repatriation leave. I was married by then so went back to my family. The leave was a waste of time because all I really wanted to do was get back to flying and to rejoin my old squadron.

CORONATION, 1953

SERGEANT ANDY LUCAS, RM

King George died in 1952 and we did the funeral. It was a sombre day, a cold day. We lined in procession somewhere around St James. The drums were muffled as he went by, carried on the gun carriage with his horse behind. Then, fifteen months later, we came up to London for the coronation of the Queen. We had training beforehand down in Portsmouth, all we seemed to do was stand at ease for half an hour and then stand at attention for an hour. This time we were lined up on the Embankment near Cleopatra's Needle. When I was a boy at George V's Jubilee in 1935, I was up there, on the opposite side.

What I remember most was all the troops coming down. The Mounties were the ones who really stood out, and the South African police on their horses. And of course the old Queen of Tonga, she was wonderful. She was a big woman and she sat in this open Landau, laughing and smiling and waving. It was pouring with rain, really coming down, but she didn't mind.

As the rain came down I could feel the blanco coming off my helmet. I had on my lovely number one suit with all the gold plate, and there was this blanco dripping down on it. But the crowd were all laughing, they didn't mind. The coronation reminded me of war-time, with all the people and atmosphere. When they'd all finished we marched through what was then the old Scotland Yard into Whitehall, and ended up facing Downing Street. Most of the people had been there all night. It was very friendly, a lovely sort of feeling. There was a lot of banter between us young marines, and the mums and dads and kids: it was like a carnival.

In those days we had that sort of atmosphere; I don't think we'll ever get that back. The war had only been over for about eight years. There was still rationing and people didn't have a lot of good clothes, not like they have now, but they had excitement in their lives. A lot of these young people had just come through a war and they hadn't seen anything like the celebrations afterwards, except on VE-Day.

NUCLEAR TESTING IN AUSTRALIAN WATERS

Captain John Gower, RN

The National Radiological Protection Board (NRPB) had found that there was no evidence that the cancers suffered by many of the 20,000 servicemen were caused by their roles as witnesses of the atom bomb trials on Christmas Island in the Indian Ocean during the 1950s and 1960s. My story is different. I commanded a ship which was twice required to steam through fall-out from exploded atomic bombs.

Early in 1956 I was working as Director of Physical Training and Sports and Portsmouth when I got a 'pierhead jump' to join HMS *Diana* at Devonport. Her captain had broken both his legs skiing. It was very awkward – as I had a wife and four children. Anyhow, I found this lovely ship being hastily fitted with a pre-wetting system. The cover story was that we were going to watch the atomic trials in Australia, but we all more or less knew something was up, as the whole crew had been through a week's Atomic Material Chemical Defence (AMCD) course.

We commissioned on 28th February 1956 with a west country crew, and a month later sailed for Malta via Gibraltar in company with the rest of our squadron – *Daring, Decoy* and *Diamond*. The Admiral of our squadron detached me on 12th April saying, 'Off you go.' I don't know if he knew what we were going to do – we never saw him again. Now we were on our own, ready to start training. We had to be at the Monte Bello islands (off the north-west coast of Western Australia) by 3rd May to take part in two operations, code named Mosaic I and II.

The Chiefs of Staff wanted to know what effect an atomic explosion would have on ships, their contents, equipment and men: this was *Diana's* role. How much radioactivity could a ship stand and still remain operational? None of us had any knowledge of the operation – it really was a story of the blind leading the blind. There were two or three scientists on board but at that time they were fairly green themselves. The political background to the situation was illuminating. Since the war the United States had kept her nuclear tests to herself, leaving Britain out in the cold. The purpose of all our tests at that time was to show Washington (and Moscow) that we were a full member of the nuclear club. Time was running out before a world-wide ban was to be imposed. Between October 1952 and September 1958 twenty-one atmospheric nuclear tests were carried out on the Australian mainland and off the coast, as well as at Christmas Island. The British Government wanted the hydrogen bomb, but it takes an atom bomb to detonate a hydrogen bomb, and the scientists had to perfect the trigger device. This was to be done at Monte Bello in 1956, and in order to ensure that they could detonate the H-bomb at Christmas Island in 1957 they had to do it fast. The scientists wanted to hold Mosaics in May and June – the Australian winter, when the winds should blow from the west. Forecasting was difficult anyway, and July would be too late since it was a dependably stormy month.

Twenty thousand servicemen were involved, many of them National Service youngsters, mostly stationed either at Christmas Island or in the various offshore islands near the Australian coast or in the Pacific. Three hundred of them were the officers and men on HMS *Diana*, who were ordered to steam deliberately through the two atomic fallouts. The MOD was confident that radiation from the tests would have 'no measurable effect' on those taking part. They said this in 1953 and they were still saying it in 1983.

On 3rd May we arrived, anchoring three miles outside the parting pools as our draught would not allow entry. The Commodore of Task Force CTF 308 sent some of his scientific staff over to report on the progress of our training, undertaken during the voyage. Their report read: 'General impression was everybody understood the basic problems and how to tackle them but they have fallen short in the apparatus and tools to do the job.' This was followed by the usual disclaimer: 'We cannot, however, assume any direct responsibility for the radiological safety of *Diana* since this is outside our terms of reference.' So doubt *did* exist. At least we were subsequently supplied with 600 overshoes and gauze face masks for all. All the time we were assured by the Ministry of Defence, oh no worry at all, and it is only forty years later when we are all in our sixties and seventies that these things are coming to light.

By the time we arrived we had steamed 11,000 miles in five weeks. There was a delay, so the Commodore allowed us a four-day trip to Fremantle for a well-deserved break. We were back at Monte Bello on 14th May in time for the first explosion, due to take place on 16th May. This was to be a 15 kiloton tower-mounted bomb located on Trimouille Island, code-named 'Hot Shot'. Incidentally the bomb dropped at Hiroshima was 13 kilotons, i.e. equivalent to 13 tons of TNT. On top of our other commitments we had to lower and anchor a whaler full of scientific recording instruments during each blast.

During the actual tests the entire area was cleared of shipping and everybody, including myself as captain, had to go down below into two citadels. The forward one accommodated 207 men, the after one 95. The only men not inside were the engine-room watch keepers. The pressure inside the citadels was immense; we were absolutely clamped down. We had our roentgen* meters at the ready and everyone wore a radiation film badge.

The immediate engineering object was to investigate the entry and expulsion, retention and distributions of radioactivity into machinery spaces and systems after fallout, and locate any subsequent problems. Because of this the engine-room, boiler room, evaporators, circulation pumps and no. 1 diesel generator were unmanned. We were using one propeller, one engine room, and one boiler room: the others were open to the air, as we wanted to see how much atomic nonsense would come in through the vents. When we got back to Singapore after the first explosion we had to have the boiler re-bricked, so it obviously had got in.

During the explosions we covered the mountings with canvas, as well as a canvas over laid over the bridge. We found the pre-wetting system took 15 minutes to get everything sprayed – it was a heavy drain on the firemain, but it was about eighty percent efficient. The only place not sprayed was the top of the mast and one or two other places like that. When one of my telegraphists had to go up later on to clear something in the mast he

* Unit of dose of electromagnetic radiation

found it was red hot because the spray hadn't reached there. Quite frankly we were all innocents.

We had to be down-wind in order to steam through the atomic fallout. So we weighed and proceeded, steaming towards the bloody thing – the wind was bringing it down as well so we were soon in it. We could steer from below using radar. The bomb exploded at 11:51, the ship went to action stations at 12:20, and to shelter stations at 13:05. The expected arrival of 95% fallout was 13:25, but our first readings showed us only on the fringe of the fallout. There was no real effect until 19:15, then the fallout continued until 21:00. The monitoring staff, fully protected, left the citadel at 21:35, switched off pre-wetting and took readings at selected positions on the upper deck, which were marked in white paint to increase night vision. The readings were mostly 5MR*. At 22:30 decontamination parties went out to hose and scrub the upper deck and external surfaces and all the canvas covering was ditched. The upper deck was considered safe by 01:00. We had no anti-gas pavement between the two citadels during this trial, although this was sorted out in time for the second bomb.

The four engineers had the most gruelling time. They had these big heavy suits attached to an air filter which when blown up made them look like with Michelin men. All the sweat would run down, and the suits rubbed raw patches on their shoulders. They were only able to do 35 minutes then they had to come up into the citidel for fresh air before going down again. They drank lime juice and ate salt tablets when they came up.

By the time they were let out the crew in the citadels had been enclosed for thirteen hours. They were suffering from the cramped conditions, humidity and excessive sweating (and, of course, no smoking). There was an obvious limitation on hot and cold drinks and action messing was difficult. Still the general feeling was of relief. No-one had dropped dead, although obviously we didn't know how much we'd inhaled. Initially some men suffered fatigue, faintness, headache, respiratory distress, abdominal discomfort and claus-trophobia. We had a very young Lieutenant doctor who'd never been to sea before – I don't think he knew much. He gave lectures which were intended to be reassuring rather than informative – remember the MOD edict that nobody would be at risk! We were also shown films (so far unreleased to the public) of Hiroshima and Nagasaki. I don't know where the air came from for the citadels – we weren't sucking in atomic air. There were monitors all round, we all had Geiger counters on us to measure the radiation and we carried gas masks. Otherwise we were in our ordinary working rig. At that stage we had no overshoes or gauze face masks.

* Milliroentgens

We recovered the scientific data from the whaler and sank her by ramming. While we were taking stuff off the whaler we wore protective clothing, although some lunatics still took their gloves off. We were then ordered to Singapore for a welcome break – the Aussies blacked us, wouldn't have us back. We arrived back at Monte Bello on 7th June having delivered stores to Christmas Island en route.

Then in we went to do the same old bloody thing, closing down and waiting. This was Mosaic II, code named 'flashlight'. The weather was fickle and there were several false starts. As the ship's company were beginning to get bored we staged every conceivable dog-watch pastime to while away the time. They seemed inclined to over-relax, and we gave lectures to remind them of the dangers of underestimating the task. It was just as well that we did. Unbeknown to us, Mosaic II was to be the biggest nuclear blast of all the twenty-one tests. In 1985, the MOD admitted that it had been 98 kilotons.

At last 19th June arrived and we were committed. We saw the flash at 10:14, at a distance of 97 miles. The fireball was twice the size of Mosaic I and it climbed a lot faster. The bang, when it came, was a colossal double-crack heard 200 miles away in Australia. We went to dinner at 11:30 and action stations at 12:20. The Task Force CTF 308 had signalled to expect fallout at 12:30 so we immediately went to shelter stations. Both citadels were pressurised by 12:45. The first traces of fallout were detected at 13:25 – by 14:40 we had recordings in excess of 10 MR but by 18:45 these had dropped to 0.4MR. At 21:47 we switched off pre-wetting and started monitoring, which took one-and-a-half hours, in darkness of course. Decontamination parties were released from citadels at 22:45 and, with their previous experience, took only ninety minutes. Everything was over by 00:25.

That second one was really horrendous. One of the nozzles on the quarter deck had got bunged up, and in that area we got a count of ten, while in other places it was 0.5. We just had to put ropes out, no-one was allowed there until we could go at it again the next day to try to get rid of it. Of course it was still radioactive. Inevitably of course people were poking around – they were curious.

Although the weather had to be right there was an urgent need to explode Mosaic II. The scientists had to get their trigger, but even so they took a big risk with the weather. Of course if they had not it would have been a great waste of time and money. The cloud began moving away from Australia but then changed and drifted back across the mainland. The Prime Minister of Australia was so angry at this that he signalled to the British Prime Minister: 'What the bloody hell is going on – the cloud is drifting over mainland.'

The trials completed, HMS *Diana* was released to go to Singapore before returning to her squadron in the Mediterranean, but instead we were diverted and held at Aden. The Suez Crisis was blowing up and obviously occupying the minds of the staff in the Mediterranean. After we had done all this the we thought at least we would get a 'Well done *Diana*, welcome back.' Not a bloody sausage. Our three month sojourn in Aden was another story. We assisted HMS *Newfoundland* to sink the Egyptian frigate *Domiat* on the first night of the war, then were overwhelmed for a week with seventy survivors. For this operation we were inundated by congratulations, one even from the First Sea Lord. Funny world.

In the New Year we were released to steam back to Plymouth round the Cape, clocking up 52,000 miles in the year. By then the Great British Public had forgotten our contribution, although another twelve tests were quietly sitting in the pipeline, seven of them megaton (equivalent to a million tons of TNT) and two kiloton. They wouldn't have been possible without Mosaic II.

The story doesn't quite finish there. The Chiefs of Staff had wanted to know what the reaction was on the men. What still puzzles so many of us is why on conclusion of the trials no effort was made to see what effect nuclear explosions had, both physiologically and psychologically, on the men who witnessed them and – perhaps more importantly – those who went right through the fallout. Yet there were no follow-up medical checks of any kind. From February to August 1957 *Diana* remained in home waters. This seems an appalling waste of a unique opportunity. I believe Mosaic II cost £1.5 million. Why not get value for money by testing everything – men as well as weapons? They did it in the USA. The answer given by the Prime Minister in 1983 was: 'No-one was exposed to any significant health hazard; therefore no tests were necessary.'

So what was the *Diana* doing at the time?

SUEZ

Captain Derek Oakley, RM

My two Troop subalterns, the regular Lieutenant Leslie Hudson and the National Serviceman Lieutenant David Westwood, along with Sergeant-Major Mick Casey, inspected the Marines, checking their equipment and ammunition and testing their radios. Of my five fighting sections all were National Servicemen who were to prove their worth that day and match their regular counterparts.

The order was passed to go down to the welldeck to embark in our Landing Vehicles Tracked (LVT). Each could carry up to 30 men, travel at about five knots in the sea and then run up the beaches on their tracks. At

0410 the bow doors of *Suvla* opened and the vehicles slowly churned their way out of the mother ship, amidst a deafening noise.

Circling in our pre-positioned assembly area like a gaggle of tin boxes wobbling on the broken surface, the Marines whispered quietly together. I looked at my watch in the gathering daylight. It was 0425 GMT. Our watches had been set to Zulu time, three hours behind local time, which made the whole operation seem uncannily inaccurate. I glanced at the men crouching or sitting in the well of my LVT, nervously fiddling with the slings of their weapons or the straps of their equipment. It was fast approaching the time to start the run-in to the beach. I looked round to see other LVTs of 'A' Troop approaching to join this tight circle, like young ducklings gathering around their mother.

The minutes ticked away and the sun's rays gathered strength. Then suddenly, with a terrifying roar that rent the stillness, the 4.5-inch guns of HMS *Decoy*, our parent bombarding ship, and her fellow destroyers, opened up as she steamed past parallel to the coast. This was our signal to start the run-in. The adrenalin began to flow, nerves tightened and a look of qualified satisfaction shone on the Marines' sunburnt faces. A last-minute government decision in London had limited the size of guns to be used for the bombardment to no larger than 6-inch. The French battleship *Richelieu* with her 15-inch guns, and the British cruiser with 8-inch, turned dejectedly away in the distance.

Below my feet the LVT engine roared into life and the Royal Armoured Corps driver turned the unstable craft towards the beaches. We were some 800 yards offshore but it would be only minutes before we touched down on the beaches, not knowing what reception would greet us.

After a week at sea, slowly churning our way across the Mediterranean from Malta, we would all be glad to get ashore. It was probably the slowest convoy since the days of Cleopatra. Briefings had been carried out on board our landing ships during that week, but it was only the night before landing that we had received new aerial photographs of our initial objectives, mostly obliques taken by the Fleet Air Arm. To our surprise and consternation we learned that, after passing through five rows of beach huts, there were more buildings than had been projected on the out-of-date street maps which had been issued to us. The obliques showed quite clearly that our first objectives were far larger than the two-storey buildings we were expecting. This led to hastily reorganised plans and a reappraisal of the timings. On deck we heard the dull throb of aircraft engines, presumably in support of 3 Para, who earlier that day had been dropped on Gamil airfield, some six miles to the west of Port Said. Bright flashes lit up the evening sky, reminding us that this was Guy Fawkes Night, but it was a restless sleep that most of us went to. I tossed and turned in the stifling heat of my non-air-conditioned cabin. HMS *Suvla* and most of the supporting ships had no such modern amenities. Most of the Marines slept with their weapons on the upper deck, snatching what solace they could.

A slight breeze ruffled the waves as we chugged slowly towards the beaches. To my left I could see seven other Buffaloes, with 40 Commando, in the distance, nearer to the town of Port Said, then our own 'A' Troop commanded by Troop Captain Hamish Emslie, who had served with the SBS and won an MC in Malaya. I turned to my right and there speeding across our bows were our two destroyers, HMS *Decoy* leading HMS *Chaplet*, their Battle Ensigns taut at their mastheads, almost obliterating their superstructures, with their guns pounding the shoreline.

With only 400 yards to go I could still see the naval shells bursting on the beach ahead. A couple of Seahawks swooped down from the cloudless sky and strafed the beach in front of us. It was exhilarating, yet frightening. With only 400 yards to go I felt the LVT tracks grind against the bar, grip the sand and we slowly and majestically lifted out of the water, increasing our speed as the sea grew shallower. We felt naked and exposed, and took cover against the expected enemy fusillade. But the Royal Navy had done their stuff: the rows of beach huts were mostly ablaze and the smoke obscured our view, acting as a screen before our final approach. There was no resistance here. Above the din of the engine I heard the occasional shot, reminding me that this was no exercise, but any local noise was drowned by the bombardment which had now lifted to the second block of houses. This was the restricted limit beyond which they would not be allowed to fire for fear of causing civilian casualties.

From then on we were on our own.

As we trundled up the beach Sergeant-Major Casey ordered the rear ramp to be lowered. The Marines prepared themselves physically and mentally for battle and I heard the signalman do his last-minute radio check. Fifty yards short of the road the LVTs stopped and the Marines felt the first soft touch of sand on their feet and fanned out in defensive positions prior to taking their first objectives. Lieutenant Hudson gathered his section around him. His first objective was a large oriental building with a huge solid oak doorway. Although there appeared to be no enemy opposition at this stage he took every precaution and called up the Assault Engineers with a pole charge. They lit the fuse and retired to a safe distance: A tremendous explosion rent the air and the huge door disintegrated in a cloud of smoke and dust. I watched with subdued amusement from across the road. As the smoke died away, I saw a small dilapidated Egyptian, obviously the caretaker, emerge from a ditch beside the road waving the key!

It was now 0535, and we noted with much satisfaction that 'C' Squadron,

6 RTR, with their Centurions, had now joined us. Our LVTs were refuelled and mustered in the lee of the seafront houses as 'C' and 'X' passed through us to take blocks of houses further inland. Many of the Marines took the chance to have a quick brew, as breakfast had been taken so many hours ago.

The CO, Lieutenant-Colonel Peter Norcock, called us together and briefed us for the next phase of the battle, a dash through the town in our LVTs supported by tanks to secure the Nile Cold Storage and the Port Said Power Station, on the southern outskirts of the town.

At 0630 we climbed back into our LVTs, this time leaving the rear ramps down for a quick exit if necessary. We turned into the wide street, my leading tank seemingly gaining on me and making me feel neglected. I felt a tug on my trouser leg and looked down. My driver was trying to say something to me. I cupped my ear. 'Sir, do they drive on the right or the left in this country?'

I could see the Cold Storage Building in the distance and, before that, our target. As we approached I warned the Marines to be ready to disembark, but to my horror the leading tank had not recognised the buildings and rolled relentlessly on. I tried in vain to call him on the radio. In theory and even in Malta, it had been easy to contact him, but now that we were here in earnest, the radio failed to work. I decided to follow him further south with the rest of 'B' Troop in tow. 150 yards down the road, the tank calmly turned left through the main gates of an Egyptian Army camp. To my immense relief it was deserted. My tank came to a halt and I told my driver to take cover behind a brick hut, the remainder of the troop with their accompanying tanks fanning out in defensive positions. Engines were switched off and suddenly there was silence. It was quite uncanny: no sound, no movement.

I waited, anxiously assessing the situation, pondering what to do. My signalman called up Commando HQ and explained our situation. I was relieved to hear that 'A' and 'X' Troops had taken our objectives with a minimum of skirmishing.

A quick 'O' Group was called and I planned to go back to the Cold Storage Building. Meanwhile, my subaltern had called up Rear Headquarters for a casevac helicopter for the Sergeant-Major, Corporal Peerless and Marine Caffrey who had been wounded when we were fired on during the dash through town down Rue Mohamed Ali.

By the time we had made our way back to the Cold Storage Building and taken up our defensive positions, we heard with dismay that a temporary cease-fire had been negotiated. We felt we were only halfway through our task. Once more a governmental decision taken far away in London had prevailed. Leaving 'A' and 'C' Troops in position I took my Troop back up into Rue Mohamed Ali, still being made uncomfortably aware that snipers would continue to pester us. We fed and watered ourselves in the comfort of the buildings which had been our first objective. It had seemed a long day, and as dusk began to fall our watches still only said 4.30pm.

LIEUTENANT DONALD MILLS, RN

Prior to the Suez Crisis of 1956 there had been a great deal of diplomatic activity which we listened to daily on the BBC Overseas Service. There had been a new urgency in our training and we started night-flying from HMS *Eagle*. We also spent a lot of time with the 'Ceeball's' (Carrier-borne Ground Liaison section). They were a small group of Royal Marine and Army officers whose job was to brief us on ground targets and, more importantly, to talk us on to a target in unfamiliar territory.

We exercised with the French fleet then eventually we moved to Malta to join up with three other carriers, *Albion, Bulwark* and *Ocean*. We managed to find a day where we could get together the air groups of all four carriers and hold a monster reunion. It was a unique occasion which never happened even during the Second World War. It included most of the front-line strength of the Fleet Air Arm.

If we were going to war, at least we would be amongst friends. The morale of the squadrons was high and we considered ourselves very much the elite of all Britain's armed forces. The days when senior naval officers looked down their noses at aircrew were long gone, and the value of carrier aircraft had been proved time and time again during the second half of the war and again in Korea. No. 897 Squadron had been trained to operate anywhere in the world and in almost any weather, and we had great confidence in our sailors. So apart from being scared stiff, all was well. At least, most of us, like myself, had been under fire before as a child.

The fleet put to sea and turned eastwards, operating together now, as a carrier force. As we went, we were given intensive briefings on the opposition, for at last we knew for certain that we had orders to re-take the Canal Zone as a guarantee for international shipping. The main worry was the Egyptian Air Force, which had had a number of Vampires and Meteors supplied by us when relations were still good, but the Russians had also sent some 400 aircraft with an unknown number of experienced instructors. The aircraft were MiG-15s, similar in performance to our Seahawks; MiG-17s, about which intelligence was skimpy, but they were probably faster and more manoeuvrable; and a bomber force of IL 28s which were of a similar vintage to the Canberra. The High Command was not prepared to commit ground troops against a hostile shore until the enemy Air Force had been eliminated or at least neutralised. The question was, 'Will they come up and fight?' and if so, would the pilots be Egyptian or Russian or both?

The plan was that, in the early hours of 1st November, the major Egyptian airfields would be attacked by the 'V' force of Vulcans and Valiants operating from Cyprus. We were to launch before dawn 'and clean up around the edges' of anything they had missed. Once the Air Force had been dealt with, our priority would switch to close air support for the Paras and Marine Commandos who would assault Port Said. The French would land on the east bank of the Suez Canal, supported by two carriers, the *Lafayette* and the *Bonhomme Richard*. We were strictly forbidden to attack any civilian targets, including lorries.

We had been issued with khaki trousers and shirts with rank badges so that there could be no accusations of being a spy if we had to bale out in enemy territory. We also had 'escape kits' with maps and a little bag of golden sovereigns to bribe the Bedouin tribes in the desert. In the 1920s and 1930s aircrew flying on the North-West Frontier called these 'gooley bags': the money was given to the natives in place of your balls being cut off. We also carried a .32 Webley in belt or leg-holsters to defend ourselves. On the night of 31st October there was a very subdued mood in the wardroom.

The next morning we were shaken awake at some ungodly hour, had breakfast, and went to our crewroom for briefing: on our position and the whereabouts of other friendly ships, the weather, especially over the target area; expected ground fire; and finally by Ray Rawbone, our CO and Lin Middleton (later to command the *Hermes* in the Falklands) who had taken over as Senior Pilot, because Keith Leppard had broken a leg and been transferred to the *Lafayette* as liaison officer.

We launched before dawn with some forty other aircraft, formed up and headed for the coast. Our target was Inchas, a large airfield to the west of the canal zone, known to be a base for the MiGs. Ray had impressed on us the importance of sticking with the formation and that stragglers were vulnerable. That morning I believe our battle formations were strictly text book! We crossed the coast near Aboukir Bay, the scene of Nelson's victory at the Battle of the Nile, and I can remember thinking, 'I wonder if he's watching.'

The weather was clear and the Nile Delta stretched out below with its green fields and towns, a stark contrast to the desert. We had no trouble in finding the target and after letting down could see the hangars and runways with rows of parked aircraft. We attacked with 3-in. rockets. As I climbed away again following the Boss, I suddenly realised that the sky was full of little puffs of black smoke. I thought, 'My God, they're shooting at me!' On my second attack, this time using the 20mm. -cannon, I saw a lot of winking lights coming from the airfield perimeter, but it was much later that I realised these came from anti-aircraft and small-arms fire.

We then reformed in good order and started the trip back to the ship, expecting at any minute to be attacked by fighters. As we crossed the coast 'tail-end Charlie' turned to make sure we were not being followed, thus giving away the position of the fleet, but all was clear and we landed without incident. At the debriefing, it was clear we had destroyed or damaged a large number of parked aircraft, but how many was a different matter. I had seen a MiG blow up, hit by one of my rockets, and claimed it, but in the general confusion of battle it is difficult to make accurate claims. What also became clear was that the 'V' Force attack, which was supposed to leave a smoking ruin for us, had been a total failure.

One of the main worries was that the Egyptian high command would sink ships to immobilise the canal. They were thought to have a ship standing by for this purpose at Ismailia, on the Bitter Lake, halfway down the canal. Our next mission, therefore, was to look for signs of movement and sink the ship before it could be moved into position. When we arrived over Ismailia we didn't spot a ship, so we went to the secondary target of Abu Suweir, an airfield in the canal zone, built by us during the Second World War. As at Inchas, we met a great deal of ground fire, but we destroyed parked aircraft and hangars. On the third mission, later in the day, we saw a ship being towed to block the entrance to the lake.

We circled the ship whilst Ray Rawbone assessed the situation. When he gave the order to attack I happened to be in a good position. For once, I got it right and sent my bomb more or less down the funnel. As I pulled out of the dive, I saw two enemy Vampires flash in front of me. I turned after them calling on the radio, but there was so much chat about the attack on the blockship that nobody heard me. Eventually, bearing in mind the strictures about wandering off alone, I gave up the chase and turned to rejoin the Squadron. When we landed on and were debriefed, Ray said I had almost certainly missed a chance to down two Egyptian aircraft but he was under-standing about my reasons for not doing so, and at least I had sunk the ship. Later that night there was a broadcast by the captain, followed by Ops, with a detailed account of the day's action. This was for the benefit of the troops who had sweated in the engine-room, the galley and the hangars without seeing daylight, let alone the enemy.

The next day we made another pre-dawn patrol, setting off in the dark to Cairo West, much further south than the day before. Cairo West airfield was the main IL 28 bomber base. The danger of a mass-attack on our fleet, or even worse on the landing force, was obvious but when we got there the birds had flown. A few aircraft were on the hardstandings, including some civil airliners which we left strictly alone. We learnt later that most of the IL 28s had decamped en masse out of harm's way to Luxor. They were never to appear. There was flak here, but this time we had flak-suppression Sea Venoms who made the first attack to keep the gunners' heads down.

That evening one of the escorts made a firm sonar contact with a submarine, and the whole force was brought to 'action stations'. We started to zigzag. Intelligence reckoned that the Egyptians had no subs but there was always the danger of the Russians joining the fray. The most likely explanation was that the sub was Israeli, as they had recently taken delivery of some French boats. The contact was lost and, after thorough sweeps by the escorts, action stations was stood down.

On the morning of 3rd November we launched again before dawn to attack Almaza, an airfield north of Cairo where large numbers of MiGs had been photographed the day before by Canberras. This time the Egyptians were waiting for us and the flak was far more intense and accurate. A few aircraft sustained minor damage, including mine, but miraculously nobody was shot down. There was a rumour that a French aircraft had been shot down near Cairo, and its crew torn to pieces by a mob, but I have never discovered if this was true. After three attacks, we had destroyed another batch of aircraft on the ground and, as I saw it disintegrate, I claimed an IL 28.

The next trip was to Gamal bridge. The bridge is part of a system of causeways and bridges that connects Suez with Alexandria and the other towns of the delta. It was the easiest route by which to bring in reinforcements, so it had to be destroyed before the landing to isolate the garrison. I am ashamed to say that we made a low-level bombing attack on the bridge and missed. My last trip of the day was back to the bridge but this time doing flak-suppression as, like Almaza, it was heavily defended. The bridge was finally demolished by a 1,000-lb. bomb from a Wyvern.

During the trip, I saw a convoy of lorries out in the desert, obviously on their way to reinforce the garrison. I went down low enough to see the soldiers, rifles and all, sitting inside. I climbed up again and called the ship on the radio to ask permission to attack, but was told the rule was firm – no attacking 'soft' vehicles as you never knew who might be inside.

The next day, the ship retired to the north to rendezvous with the fleet train and replenish with fuel, food and ammunition. By now we had flown several hundred missions and expended large quantities of bombs, rockets and cannon shells. The aircraft were standing up well but there were leaking hydraulic pipes, defective instruments and splinter holes and our sailors were working twenty-four hours a day to produce a maximum launch every morning. By now it was reasonably certain that the Egyptian Air Force was not going to fight but there was still the chance of a few determined pilots, probably Russian, causing great damage during the crucial assault operations.

That night, we had a comprehensive briefing on the next phase. The Israelis had broken through the Mitla pass into Sinai and were rapidly approaching the canal zone. This information was used to justify further Allied landings, on the grounds that fighting between Israeli and Egyptian troops would have resulted in serious damage to the installations and the certain blocking of the canal. The Israelis had agreed to stop ten miles east of the canal so that any units to the west could be considered hostile. The Paras were to drop at first light on to Gamal airfield and hold the western boundary of the zone. The Marine Commandos would then make an assault on Port Said with landing craft backed up by helicopters. At the same time, the French Foreign Legion would land in Port Fuad on the opposite side of the canal.

As the Marines approached the beach, we were overhead as a Cabrank. For a Cabrank, we orbited a convenient fixed position, checked communication with Ceeballs, and awaited events. I flew the first detail, which was to protect the landing ships and craft as they deployed for the assault, and this passed without incident. On the next launch, there was an urgent call for fire from the leading craft, and Pete Newman put a rocket through one of the windows of the Customs house to destroy a gun concealed there which was hitting the first wave. This was a prime example of how our weeks of training paid off.

We maintained the Cabrank all that day and the next but, although there had been some quite fierce resistance on the ground, this soon crumbled and the commandos controlled the town. Ships then moved in to land artillery and armoured vehicles which were to be used for part of the assault force.

Later that day, I was briefed to make a reconnaissance down the canal to see what was there as the army ashore was ready to break out of the perimeter and drive to Suez. Off I went, along with my no. 2 Gerry Maynard, at about 5,000 feet. We kept our eyes peeled for any movement, going down all the way to Suez on the west bank of the canal but could not see any activity that might cause trouble for the advancing troops. We turned back and flew up the east bank. This time we saw a squadron of tanks in the desert outside a village between Port Fuad and Ismailia. We attacked them, registered some hits, then I circled round with Gerry behind me to make another attack. I had a problem because my gyro gunsight had given up the ghost and so I had no proper aiming point in the cockpit. Even so, I got off a rocket and hit a tank which exploded.

To this day I am not sure what happened next but I think I must have been much too low because of the sighting problem. Something hit the aircraft and immediately my tank-fire warning light came on. I pulled up out of the dive, climbed to several thousand feet and prayed. With a tank warning you bale out immediately, as the aircraft could explode at any second, and there was indeed a nasty burning smell.

I made a conscious decision to stick with the aircraft for a few seconds more, as ejecting on top of some tanks I had just been attacking didn't seem like a good idea! I called a 'Mayday', gave my position, jettisoned my hood, then ejected. The seat functioned perfectly and, before I knew what was happening, my parachute had deployed and I was floating gently in a clear blue sky. I could see the tanks, still not far away and heading in my direction. The ground then came up much more quickly than I had anticipated and I landed with a thud, not helped by my attempt to get my pistol out in case. I was dazed by the impact, but managed to release my harness and consider my next move. Gerry was circling overhead, but I knew he would have to leave soon or run out of fuel. In the event, he just made it back to the ship.

There I was, some forty miles behind enemy lines, clutching my pistol and listening to the noise of the tank engines in the distance. I have never felt so utterly alone in all my life. My overriding emotion was not fear, but sadness that I would not see my family again. I thought of Drucie and our baby Helen so far away, but knew that at least they would have the support of loved ones. It seemed to me that my only chance was to move away from my parachute as soon as possible and try and avoid capture until nightfall, then head north towards our lines. I had no confidence that the Egyptians would act in accord with the Geneva Convention.

As I started to walk, my life really did flash before my eyes. At the same time, training made me check my assets. At least I had water, some food in the survival kit, money if I needed it (which seemed unlikely) and in spite of a backache from landing I was in one piece. It never occurred to me that help could already be on the way.

I had been walking for some time when I heard aircraft noise; there to my delight were four Corsairs from the *Lafayette*. Two of them flew off to the south-west, then I saw them dive at the ground in the direction of the approaching tanks. Palls of black smoke rose into the desert air and I realised that I had not been abandoned. The Corsair leader motioned to me to return to my parachute.

A few minutes later Seahawks arrived, attacking something in the desert to the east. Much later, I learnt that they had stopped an Israeli column by firing in front of them. The Israelis had seen what had happened and were on their way to pick me up. If they had succeeded I would probably have had a hero's welcome in Tel Aviv!

After about half an hour, the Corsairs waved goodbye as they had to go back but by this time there were three divisions of Seahawks stacked above me and anything that moved within fifteen miles was being attacked. I was lucky because there was a lull in the proceedings whilst everybody was waiting for the order to move south, so I had four carriers to look after me!

Eventually I heard the swish of helicopter blades in the distance, followed by the friendly face of Pete Bailey, the CO of the ship's flight, grinning at me from his chopper. He touched down, I climbed in and away we went to *Eagle*.

I was taken to the sickbay and given a check by the Principal Medical Officer. As I was sitting there waiting for the verdict, somebody handed me a letter which had just arrived. It was from my sister, Babs, always of left-wing views, telling me that I should not be fighting for my country because the whole campaign was immoral. I had just returned from what looked like certain death and could still hardly believe I was back. It was a long time before I could forgive her. Luckily I was cheered up by a signal from Keith Leppard on *Lafayette*, which said in effect, 'Trust you to be the first ashore – you owe the 14-ième a crate of champagne', a sentiment with which I fully agreed. The 14-ième Flotille of course were the Corsairs.

TRISTAN DA CUNHA

PETTY OFFICER DUDLEY JOHNSON

I had been sailing in HMS *Leopard* since August 1961 on a big exercise called 'Capex' which also involved units of the South African navy. *Leopard* was a Type 41 frigate, with 235 officers and men on board. In October we had just left Simonstown for another phase of Capex when we received an 'Operational Immediate' signal which said, 'Come back, we've got a volcanic activity.' This was on Tristan da Cunha, which is the principal of a group of small islands about 1,700 miles west of Cape Town.

We worked into the early hours of the morning of 10th October, loading the usual gear for emergency relief. It is an established drill: you put in items like tents and blankets and all sorts of supplies, food and medicines, which in this case came mainly from South African navy stores.

Luckily it was not bitterly cold – it wasn't the season – but during the five-day journey we learned that the population already had been taken off Tristan and put on a little island five miles away called Nightingale. Nightingale is only about five feet above high tide. All it needed was a rough sea and the island would become water-logged. There are no buildings there, or power, or anything, so the people were scared, frightened and wet. We had intended to pick them up, but they were lifted and taken to a Dutch liner which had been diverted from South America and was closer than we were. We were about a day out from Tristan and banging on as fast as we could when we met her. We rendezvoused in the dark but didn't stop, flashing them by lamp instead – we knew from the Admiralty that they had picked the people up. We watched them disappear into the musky dusk carrying their cargo of bewildered refugees to Cape Town.

Leopard's objective had now changed, because a Russian depot ship was hanging around Tristan da Cunha. She was a sort of ubiquitous trawler and had what looked like a million-and-a-half aerials, even to my expert eye. I used to sit and stare at these things wondering what they all did. Small as the island was, Tristan had full diplomatic status and, as such, possessed a wireless station and a full set of the machines and codes that are used to encrypt and decrypt diplomatic radio traffic, including a K017 machine which was then the standard operational machine used on all British military ships. The Russians, of course, were aware of this and hoping to make an 'Enigma'-like capture. For her part, *Leopard* had been instructed to salvage valuable equipment on the island and to destroy what could not be moved.

When we arrived the island itself was an amazing sight. Tristan is like the top of a mountain, with no port, only a shingle beach. Imagine a bleak, grey and desolate pinnacle of rock sticking out of the sea. We thought, how could anyone live on that? It was mostly uninhabitable, but there was a little area where it looked as though some god-like figures had taken a trowel and scraped out a place where there was a little soil you could grow spuds on and keep sheep. The sea was teeming; you could catch fish with a bit of silver paper on a pin, and that is the way they lived. Their life was idyllic really apart from the fact that it was bitterly cold. They had no germs because the wind used to blow all the time and they had little contact with the outside world. The only outside contact was a little tramp steamer which used to come out from Cape Town about once every two weeks with outdated newspapers. Once a fortnight they used to get 16 mm films of the latest things and show them in the village hall. Every house had its picture of the Queen and Prince Philip.

The volcano was quite spectacular, especially at night. Red-hot ash and boulders rolled and bounced down its sides leaving glowing scars visible twenty miles away. When we first arrived and started to look for smoke we realised that the island was quite tall, and that the volcano was right down on the shoreline, not more than 60 or 70 feet above the sea. The eruption had started as a smoking molehill in the vicar's garden and when we left thirty-six hours later it was still growing, a single mound of hot ash and lava some 400 feet high. At irregular but frequent intervals great clouds of sulphurous gases and smoke burst into the air.

On arrival plans swung smoothly into operation to embark personal belongings and valuable stores. Houses were systematically and carefully stripped of valuables and the salvaged articles transferred to the ship. We unloaded each house systematically and put their belongings in boxes – 'This box belongs to no. 11', or wherever. It wasn't a happy experience, everybody was sensitive to the fact that these were people's own things. We couldn't carry everything, but we took what we could, including the heavier gear such as diesels and power generators, and Met. and radio equipment. We lashed the heavy machinery down on the upper deck in the hope that we wouldn't meet rough weather on the way back. All in the hope that one day the people would return to the island.

We spent thirty-six hours there. There were lots of strange little moments. Two thirty-ton whales were courting there because the volcano was warming up the sea and of course fish like warm water – at least that is what we put it down to. The whales had barnacles on their backs, and were scraping themselves on the bottom of the boat near two fairly prominent propellers. We were fairly sure that this amorous pair beating themselves to death at the bottom of our boat were going to bend our prop shaft while we were getting shelled by these big hot rocks.

We had two unpleasant tasks to perform. One was the destruction of all the alcohol on the island, which would have been a nuisance to the Master of the *Tristania*, whose crew would be using the island for as long as they could. We broke tens of dozens of bottles from open cases, and took all the unopened cases back to the ship. They were to be stored under lock and key in the Wardroom Wine Store. For some unaccountable reason that day was the only one in my naval career when I actually saw Chief and Petty Officers carry anything. Imagine my surprise when I got back on board to find a huge number of cases in our mess. Presumably the carriers had been overcome with fatigue, stopped for a rest, and then set off again completely forgetting their cargo!

The other unpleasant task was the destruction of the island's dogs and fowl. The cattle and sheep could be left to fend for themselves, but the dogs would either starve slowly or turn wild and savage other livestock. The 'Great White hunter' of our shooting team was detailed for this task. His first target was a very friendly collie, which was hit in the rump – not what was intended. The remainder of the dogs got the picture at once and made off for the hills, never to be seen by us again. We did take two pups back on board, predictably named Tristan and Cunha, and they returned to the UK with us.

We spent thirty-six hours off the island in the middle of the roughest ocean in the world, during the only five days of good weather they had had that year. Had it not been fine and calm we would not have been able to land at all as there are no quays or jetties.

Whilst we were on the island the volcano created a new beach where there had previously been a cliff. Someone persuaded the captain, whose name was Hicks-Beach, to signal the Admiralty hydrographer for permission to rename the erstwhile cliff, Hicks Beach! Back came the signal giving approval but, sadly, the volcano had turned Hicks Beach back into a cliff again.

When we finally got home our loved ones caused us great amusement by showing us the 'eye-witness' type accounts they'd kept, which had been all over the national tabloids for days. We were intrigued by this as none of the British hacks were within 11,000 miles of Tristan da Cunha.

The story did not end happily. In the UK the islanders were settled at Calshot, near Southampton, where many died, having never been exposed to the flu virus. Eventually the older survivors were repatriated back to Tristan but many of the younger islanders decided to stay in the UK.

The *Leopard* was made custodian of the tattered Ensign which had flown over the island, until it was returned to Willy Repetto, the Chief Islander, prior to their returning home.

BORNEO

CORPORAL MERVYN JONES, RM

Operation 'Round Up' was put into action on 10th December 1962. The objective was to free several towns in northern Borneo including Brunei Town and Limbang, across the border in Sarawak which had been occupied by Kedayan rebel forces. I was a section commander of 6 Section in 5 Troop of 'L' ('Lima') Company, 42 Commando.

We arrived at Brunei airport, ready for our task which was to guard Government House. But the Gurkhas had re-taken Brunei Town by the time we arrived, so our task was changed to collecting as many large boats or craft as we could find on the river which runs through the town. We were able to round up two medium-sized landing craft, after which we moved to the Brunei Hotel and to a briefing on our new task.

Limbang had been captured by the rebels, and six European hostages had been seized, including the British Government agent – the 'Resident', Dick Morris – his wife and a nursing sister. There were indications that the hostages were to be executed on 12th December. The task was to recapture the town and save the hostages. Our Company Commander, Captain Jeremy Moore, set about finding landing craft. After we found them, the plan was as follows: there would be two landing craft used, in the first one would be 5 Troop and the second would include 4 and 6 Troops with two machine-guns in support. 5 Troop was to land under covering fire on a jetty which was in front of the police station where 4 Section would go ashore and act as a stop behind the station. 5 Section was to storm into the police station and capture it, while 6 Section was to give additional close covering support. The remainder of the company were to land further down river and sweep towards us through the town.

We left Brunei at 2300. Both landing craft crept away from the jetty and proceeded up-river to our destination. The river was very narrow and the going was particularly hard at times. The navy handled things very well, but we had some alarming moments; three or four times we found ourselves ploughing through the mud and of course our old friends the mosquitoes were giving us a busy time.

At 0545 Limbang came into view. There was some speculation among the lads as to what we were going to expect and I know we were all a little scared. For most of us these would be our first shots in anger, yet it still amazes me that no-one showed any signs of nerves and there were still plenty of wisecracks going around.

The first signs of life at Limbang were the lights which had been ablaze and suddenly went out. Whether this was due to the approaching dawn or the sound of the landing craft I don't know, but it made the atmosphere pretty tense. Then as we rounded the bend, the place suddenly sprang to life and there were men rushing out of buildings, closing windows and doors and running along the road. These presumably were rebels standing to, but no shots were fired.

The craft slowly made its way towards the small jetty in front of the police station, gradually increasing speed to ram the bank so we could go ashore. Almost at the same time a hail of bullets and a terrible noise broke loose. The rebels had at last shown their hand, killing two of our lads in the first shots. We immediately returned fire at a very rapid rate into windows, doorways and any likely cover.

The landing took place as planned on the jetty opposite the police station. With no hesitation 4 Section of 5 Troop leapt over the bows of the craft and ran straight over a road and up into the jungle. No. 5 Section didn't have it so good and were pinned down on the bank under heavy fire; 6 Section were still giving as much covering fire as possible and were also preparing to land. Our landing craft had drifted off the bank and was moving once again upstream past a hospital and a few scattered buildings until we beached once again and managed to get ashore. Here, as before, there was no delay in getting ashore, apart from a few lads finding themselves waist deep in thick mud and slime, at which they promptly aired their views with language befitting the occasion.

Immediately we fanned out along the road, rifle group on the left, bren on the right, and commenced 'fire and movement' back towards the hospital.

There was only one incident when the bren gunner, firing from the hip, hit two rebels with a burst of fire, killing one and wounding the other. On arrival at the hospital the rifle group were still on the left and moved in front of the building while the bren moved around the back of the place, clearing the rear.

Here we came under heavy fire from the hospital. The section was split up under this fire. The bren group and rifle group moved forwards to a small piece of dead ground past the hospital, while the remaining part of the rifle group and Troop HQ, who were close behind, soon cleared the hospital. To our surprise, although we'd nearly shot them, the hostages were singing, 'They'll be wearing bright green bonnets when they come.'

We managed to get all six hostages out of the way to the end of the building; meanwhile we were trying to get the section organised and back under control and also to locate the enemy who had fired upon us. Here we very sadly lost the troop sergeant and two of the lads of our section who were killed by shotgun fire. The two enemy were soon located behind a small privet hedge at the front of the hospital and killed immediately, after which we joined up with 4 and 5 Sections and re-organised.

The other two troops at the other end of the town had by this time secured their task and had the rebels on the run. In all it was a very successful operation and the determination of the lads, good training and very high morale showed all the time, especially when things were a bit rough. Everyone pulled together and there was no backing down. 5 Troop took the brunt of the casualties; we lost five dead and four wounded, all the casualties of the action save two.

'L' Company's action at Limbang changed the whole course of operations decisively. For the first time the enemy had come under intense fire. The news of the defeat of a strong rebel garrison by a company group spread like wildfire, and everywhere garrisons left their posts and withdrew into the jungle.

NORTHERN IRELAND

For security reasons, no names are given in those accounts. The Royal Marines first tour was in 1969.

MARINE, 45 COMMANDO

We got sent over to cover the Orange marches in West Belfast. We never saw them, we were too busy keeping the crowds back. In late June there'd been some shooting from the Ardoyne into a Protestant area, they'd hit a young girl and the Protestants were coming in to burn the place out. We were there to protect the Catholics, because they were having a rough deal, everybody agreed.

We were dropped off at Butler Street, on the edge of the Ardoyne. I said: 'Right. Nobody gets through.' And this crowd came round the corner and just kept coming and coming. And that was the most frightening thing – I mean, riots these days aren't riots – there were thousands of them and eighteen of us. We were all looking at each other waiting for the first one to run. I'd have been the second, but there was no way I was going to be the first.

We just stood our ground. We had a single span of Dannert wire across the street and we started firing CS gas, because we didn't have rubber bullets in those days. We had the old-style steel helmets with visors, the metal shields with which you could cover either your face or your bollocks – it was up to you – and the old green combat trousers and combat gear. That was one of the first big riots so we hadn't switched then, but after that we used to shove paperback books inside our socks. You didn't really notice when you were getting hit, but when you'd come out of it you'd be black and blue. And you couldn't get derigged because at that stage we were on immediate reserve, ten minutes for anywhere in Belfast and thirty minutes' notice for the rest of the Province.

That day every soldier in Belfast was deployed. There were no reserves. The only people left in the camp were the cooks and clerks. We were sixty eight hours in that one street, and there was a news item in the *Daily Mirror*, which doesn't normally like troops. Some civvie car firm was going on strike for extra money and a thirty-five hour week, and somehow they'd photographed our lads as we came back in at the end of the riot, and there on the centre pages was a photograph of a corporal in a stripped-down Land Rover: he was sitting on the tailgate and had been unfastening his puttees while he was talking to his mates, and he'd fallen asleep with his puttee in his hand, with the rain coming down. The comment was: 'On strike for a thirty-five hour week already earning twice the money these lads earn – and they've just come back after sixty-eight hours on the streets and they'll be back out again in twenty-four hours.'

MARINE, 42 COMMANDO

We used to go out on patrol every night and have a gunfight, every night, guaranteed. You'd go round next morning doing the daytime patrols and you'd get a character standing at a doorway saying, 'Get any of us last night? Try again tonight.' And you knew he would too. The politicians would come across from time to time on big visits, had to meet the soldiers, and so you'd be pulled off the streets. We were in a hide on a long operation, been in there for four days, when we got the word: 'Pull out. Get back in.' There was a big flap on, a patrol came round to pick us up, we go back in, and the only reason was to meet Whitelaw. And all he said was, 'What do you think of the situation?

You're doing a wonderful job.' And you weren't. You knew you weren't because people like him were stopping you.

SERGEANT, 45 COMMANDO

We arrived in Belfast in '81, just as the fifth hunger striker, McDonnell, died. We were due to take over the Falls at 0800 on 8th July, though to reduce the likelihood of the departing battalion sustaining a casualty on their last day we actually moved in at 0530. However, the official entry in the log said 0800, and at 0801 we had a contact in the Andersonstown bus depot – one minute into the tour. When Sands had died they'd burnt the buses out in Andersonstown, so we thought it a good idea to place a couple of bricks there in case they tried again. Myself and the bricks went into the depot when it was still dark. The manager arrived at half past seven and began showing the brick commanders and myself round while the rest of the lads waited in the office. As we were looking round the back gate area a white civilian car screamed into the yard, the men inside, two depot workers, gesturing behind and shouting, 'Close the gates, close the gates.' Immediately a transit crashed in, screeched to a halt, and about a dozen young boys piled out with crates of bottle bombs. We challenged them, told them to stop, cocked our weapons. A couple ran off, but the others started throwing the bottles at us. One of the brick commanders was hit and fell to the ground, and the other corporal challenged a guy about to throw a bottle. He fired, and killed him outright. The rest of them legged it then. We didn't fire again, just one shot.

We were always told and told and told not to shoot petrol-bombers, because they didn't constitute a big enough threat. But I'm a great believer that in the heat of the moment, in that split second you flick the safety catch off and fire, if you're sure in your own mind, then as a trained man you are right to carry out that action. However much Northern Ireland training may emphasise safety, the responsibility has to be the individual soldier's, rightly or wrongly, and on that occasion I thought the corporal was quite justified. When the bottles were being thrown we didn't know whether they contained petrol, or acid, or a petrol and sugar form of action, and we weren't carrying baton guns. In fact, the corporal got a GOC's commendation, and the coroner's court laid the blame for the lad's death entirely at the doorstep of the people who'd enticed these young people to attempt arson. And we later heard that IRA recruitment of eighteen-year-olds was cut substantially because of that incident.

THE FALKLANDS

Lieutenant John Boughton, RN

The Falklands conflict blew up on the day we were finishing for the Easter break and everyone had gone home except the instructors. On 1st May 1982 I got married, which was as planned, and about 9.30 that night there was a phone call from Culdrose telling me to return tomorrow. I wasn't surprised; everyone was very much aware that the possibility was there. They were running out of helicopters down south and basically had decided they needed another Commando squadron, so they looked at their resources and chose the Sea Kings because of their lifting capacity.

We went back on the Sunday to Cornwall and waited at home for the phone call and on the Monday afternoon I got a message that they were forming a squadron that afternoon. It turned out that they'd taken all the pilots they needed, nine pilots from the training squad, and had decided who could go. Bearing in mind my family commitments, they thought I should be left out. I was left out! I was desperately disappointed, but Sally, my wife, said I ought to volunteer, which I did – I really wanted to go. A phone call came on the Wednesday to ask me to help with some night flying, they were a man short; and then they told me to pitch up the next day as well. I was in! I was over the moon.

We left a few days later after re-equipping the planes, changing their colours and weapons. Some of us were on the *Atlantic Causeway*, but two crews and my boss were on the *QE2*. I was with Phil Sheldon on *Causeway* to begin with, but then he went on to the *QE2*. On the way down we had lectures from two Commando pilots on the *Causeway*, to teach us the basic skills that we didn't already know.

At first we went into San Carlos Water and were told to assist in unloading ships. We each had our own aircraft: eight guys, myself, a second pilot, an experienced crewman and five maintainers. We arrived at the end of the day through a snowstorm and landed right next to the Marine HQ which was at the San Carlos settlement. We shut the aircraft down and were promptly told to shift because we had landed on one of the landing sites that was going to be used at night! We moved the aircraft, got our tents up, and a sergeant in charge of the perimeter fence told us to keep our heads down because there were possible snipers in the area. We were outside the perimeter fence so if the Argentinian patrols came down, we were in their path, which of course made our day! My first night in the Falklands was spent sharing sentry duty with my team. We each had our own weapons which we had spent two weeks solidly re-learning how to use on *Causeway* on the way down.

In the morning we received some tasking but that was only to move POWs from San Carlos. They stank after being out in the fields, soaking wet and just generally unclean. That really surprised us.

There was tremendous friendly rivalry between the Commando helicopter squadrons and our own anti-submarine warfare squadron. As soon as the Commandos knew that some of the 'pingers', as they call us (because of the noise of the sonar), were coming ashore, we felt they were all looking for one of us to make a mistake. We were very conscious of that, especially as we were operating in an unfamiliar environment. We felt, at the time, that the taskers basically gave us the shitty jobs to see how well we did and, luckily, because we were all experienced instructors, our aircraft flying and general skills in the Sea King were possibly better than some of the 'junglies' because they were fairly new to the aircraft.

We'd come to understand the Sea King – it's a challenge. Unlike the Gazelle, which is like a racing machine, the Sea King is stable, solid, more like an aeroplane than a light aircraft. You need to spend a lot of time understanding it – it won't be hurried. Our appreciation of landing sites and map work wasn't up to speed, however; some of it was totally new and navigation over the sea is a very different skill, when you're talking about 30–50 feet altitude at 100 miles an hour, trying to evade rather than go in a straight line. We had to progress very quickly! Also, we weren't equipped in the best way. Our second pilots hadn't completely finished training so they could end up turning the map round in circles, which was a bit of a problem. Considering their inexperience, they did a good job.

On the third day we started being given different tasks to do, such as moving gun batteries from A to B. We were all getting the less complicated jobs, but we were still very conscious that we didn't want to make any mistakes. We were able to run our own show, with our maintainers, which included one or two petty officers and three juniors, and the actual esprit de corps was very strong when the rest of the squadron appeared. They had been shifting the Guards and Gurkhas from the *QE2* to the *Canberra* and a couple of other ships. So all of a sudden, from four aircraft of our own, we had ten Sea Kings.

On our first day we were told firmly not to go beyond a certain line. Then we were given the task of moving a whole gun battery ten or twelve miles beyond that line, which was a bit strange! I was the lead aircraft of eight and was carrying a 105 gun, which weighs approximately 3,500 lbs.

What with some navigational problems and the troops 'hiding' in the valley it took almost the rest of the afternoon to move the gun battery to Mount Kent, where it stayed for a week. Then we got the job of moving it further forward. In doing that we were shelled, for the first time. I was flying down the hill with a gun and Phil Sheldon, who was in front of me, had two mortars land either side of him and came back up the valley with a high-pitched voice on his radio! We were going down Mount Kent into a valley, then just up a small ridge, but as we came down this hill, hoping to disappear out of sight, using the terrain, the Argies were lobbing shells in roughly what they thought was the right area and they weren't far wrong.

As we arrived to put the gun down, all the gunners had taken cover in trenches but somebody leapt out of the hole and directed us to the position they wanted. It was certainly exciting. We received a bit of criticism from one or two of the Commando pilots about the way we were handling the aeroplanes. We were flying them to the limit but that was one thing we could do well. By that stage we were very much more up to speed, our navigation was better and we were learning what tasks to turn down. We'd had a very crash course and come through.

We were under a lot of pressure because the constant message coming through was very much to go – go hard. We'd had to be ready by a certain date but at the same time conserve our assets. It was planned, as far as we knew, to end on the day it did. We knew that Stanley was being reinforced every day, and we knew that the longer the Argentinians had to think about it, the more likely they were to try a counter-offensive. (Why they didn't do that, God only knows.) There were rumours, on a number of occasions, that there were troops being landed on the north point from San Carlos by Argentinian Hercules and they were going to carry out a counter-attack from San Carlos. In fact, there was a very, very strong rumour about that. There was a feeling that they were being dropped all over the place to come and have a go at us. I believe there would have been more lives lost had we dallied.

Two days before the *Galahad* tragedy, we'd taken the first troops up to Bluff Cove. 2 Para had made a phone call to Fitzroy and the residents there said the Argentinians had gone, so it was decided to snatch an advantage. Three Gazelles went in with a few troops, each armed for immediate attack with rockets. They landed at the settlement, found there weren't any Argentinians around and decided to reinforce the area very quickly. The next thing we heard was that the brigadier jumped into our senior pilot's aircraft and said, 'Get three of your aircraft together. I've got a special job for you.' So three of us were sent to Goose Green to pick up some troops. We didn't know what was going on at that stage, all we knew was that we had to take some troops to a grid reference which the senior pilot had and we didn't, so we just followed him. We arrived to find 2 Para fully rigged out and ready to go into battle – completely camouflaged, ammunition wrapped round as far as it would go and all quite psyched up. We thought we were just moving personnel. We got them in, and then we were given the grid reference, which was Bluff Cove. We were most surprised because, up till that morning, the brief before dawn was, 'No go past Goose Green'. We flew in cloud all the way, flying at twenty feet and very slowly because we couldn't see very well. We dropped 2 Para off on a ridge which was in fact being overlooked by Argentinian look-outs. As soon as they'd all cleared the aircraft, we disappeared off again, and we did that for the rest of the day and the next day.

On 8th June we were sent to move some equipment from the *Galahad* and *Tristram* in the morning, but when we got there the task was being carried out by other aircraft; so we were sent back to Goose Green, where we started moving the rest of the Guards forward. I had one of the Land Rovers under the aircraft and was flying at about fifty feet below on the ridge lines. It was a beautiful clear day. All of a sudden I saw four Skyhawks flying at very low level, all following each other, so I came up on the radio with a contact report, saying that there were four Skyhawks inbound towards Fitzroy. While I was doing that I descended to put the Land Rover down. First, I went into a quick hide, because I thought there might be some more fighters coming behind. I went into a small gorge, where I hovered for about two minutes, still with this bloody Land Rover underneath. Eventually, I came out of there and put it down in the middle of a field, next to a fence, so I'd know where to find it later.

As soon as I'd gone into the hide, I heard on the HF radio that there was an attack at Fitzroy, so I called Phil Sheldon who, I thought, was about ten miles behind me, and asked him if he'd accepted my radio transmission. He had, and I suggested he join me as soon as he could, to see what was going on. I got about a mile or two closer and could see the smoke coming out of the *Galahad*. I didn't realise it was a ship at that time, but I got back to Phil and told him to get there as fast as possible.

As my aircraft arrived, there were survivors in dinghies and smoke was pouring out of the back of only one ship – the other ship looked intact, I couldn't see any damage on it at all. We went straight on to the fo'c'sle with the hold open and smoke coming out. The blokes in the dinghies looked okay so we went to pick up the soldiers who were still on the ship. As soon as we came within about fifty yards we could see that the men at the front were pretty badly off: some of their clothes were still smouldering, others were jumping up and down to try and keep their circulation going, many had badly burnt hands and a few were just lying on the deck. There seemed to be a few able-bodied men who definitely knew what they were doing medically, and they were trying to sort out the soldiers who were injured. There was also the captain of the *Galahad*, who was excellent. He'd organised people to search the ship as best they could and was controlling everything.

All we did was winch up casualties as they got put on to the rescue strop. Normally we'd sit them down and strap them in as soon as they were in the aircraft, but in this case there wasn't time, so we just got them moving down the bus. I said to my crewman, 'As soon as someone comes in who looks badly injured, we'll take him directly ashore,' because it was only twenty seconds' flying time to a patch of fairly flat grass, which had been used as a landing point for ammunition. We knew about this because we'd taken a number of loads there. As soon as we picked up a badly injured man we went straight to the shore as fast as the aeroplane would go. We landed them next to anybody we saw and called them in to help carry the casualties out. By that stage 2 Para were already organised and a few stretchers had appeared. They then took the injured out of the aircraft, and that set the pattern. From then on, it was just straight off from the beach back on to the fo'c'sle. Radiowise, it was very quiet amongst the aeroplanes and the only thing one could hear was someone saying. 'Next,' which was to tell anyone waiting that they were getting the last bloke in. Everyone had decided individually that as soon as they got a badly injured guy on board they'd go and then call, 'Free space up here' or something similar. It was chaotic, but calm.

After the first run, when my aircrewman had his hands full, I sent my second pilot down the back to become another 'dragger in'. I just flew it on my own up front, which is no problem as long as you don't have an emergency. After we'd made four or five runs ashore, one of the other aircraft discovered they'd opened up a first-aid post in the middle of the settlement. From then on, we started taking the casualties there.

By that stage, the fire was very well set in and occasionally there were some large explosions, which was a bit hairy. We were sitting there in the hover, winching up these poor blokes. Hovering is all an art of watching for changes in your depth of field, or your perspective movement, and as soon as you see a change, you automatically correct to stop it. This is fairly easy if you're sitting over a nice big area where you can see all around you, but all we could see was three or four square feet of deck, because we were right over the fo'c'sle. The door of the Sea King, which is quite a long way back in the aeroplane, was the focal point. The door was over the bows while the cockpit was over the sea, out in front, which made it slightly difficult because I had to crane round to see. But I had a very, very good crewman in Leading Aircrewman Roy Eggleston, a young bloke but probably one of the best to have there at the time. He kept the whole operation going very well, telling me what was going on, with the occasional 'Ugh' because obviously the sights were pretty gruesome. He was also trying to keep me in the correct position, so very much of the success of the task was due to him, which was sad because when it came to the awards, of course the captain of the aeroplane gets the medal.

As the fire set in more and more, everything got worse, and you could see right down into the hold. The pillars that were supporting the deck down in the hold were completely wrecked. It was just like looking into a furnace. The ammunition started to cook off and that was, I think, probably the worst bit of the lot, because Eggleston was leaning out of the aeroplane, and he'd been shaken by these blasts – but he kept going. I had my window open and the first explosion was quite a smack against my face so goodness knows what it was like to be on the deck, because a lot of hot debris was flying out of the hold. I could see in my field of vision a few blokes who were just sheltering, waiting to be lifted off, and the captain who was walking up and down, obviously very concerned at this stage, trying to get everything sorted out. He used to come into my line of vision, which was that very small area of deck, and indicate the distance between the bottom of the aeroplane and the deck. I'll never forget him doing that – he really looked concerned. But of course Eggleston was indicating our height all the time. 'You're four feet above the deck. You're in a good position,' or 'You're fifteen feet over the deck – good position, hold that there.' I would ask him if we could move in a certain direction and he would 'talk' us into the best position. Certainly, working as a team was all-important. At our feet the men were being passed up from the deck. I'd told Eggleston that we'd go as low as we could so the men wouldn't have to spend a long time being winched up, so we were definitely quite low at times. It was the quickest way to get these poor devils into the aircraft.

At one point we had to pick up a severely injured guy who'd lost his leg just below the knee. He was brought out on a stretcher in trauma. They got the bottom of a pallet and wrapped some ropes round it, put the ropes on the winch and he was lifted up and then dragged in by the aircrewmen. The smell of burning flesh was awful. Normally, you have to shout to be heard without the intercom, yet I could actually hear quite a few of the casualties shouting out in pain. This was no bad thing, because if they could shout they must be in a reasonable condition, so you didn't worry quite so much. It was the guys who were really quiet that worried me.

I don't have a clue how long it took. We picked up the second from last man from the ship, Sergeant Naya of the RAMC. I'll never forget him; he was incredible. Eggleston said, 'Okay, the last guy before the captain is just coming up now.' I must have had about six or seven on board and I remember that when we landed in the middle of the settlement to offload them, the captain and two or three others came up and shook my hand and gave the thumbs up. But Naya came up and gave me a smacker of a kiss on my cheek. I was a bit surprised. He was the one guy I remember vividly. There was nothing I could say – he said it all. He'd done all he could and more, and I think he was overwhelmed with the thought that he had survived – not only that, but that others had survived because of our teamwork.

Captain John Coward, RN

In late March 1982 *Brilliant* was sailing quietly off the coast of Morocco on an exercise with Admiral Sandy Woodward. We went to Gibraltar for a week and on Sunday 29th March, at lunchtime, I was in the next berth to the admiral. He sent for me and said, 'It's the Squadron's Sports Day today. However, we've had to send a submarine from the UK towards the South Atlantic as a precaution. The cover story is that it's exercising with somebody and that somebody had better be you. So get out of here this afternoon and meet it.'

I ran in the veterans' race and, believe it or not, I won; but I hadn't time to wait for the prize and ran on down to the jetty where my crew had the boat waiting. As I climbed up the side the first lieutenant let go and we were off. Sandy Woodward had cut the sports and stood on the bridge of *Antrim* to see us off. 'See you in South Georgia,' we joked; and indeed it was prophetic. So I steamed two hundred miles straight out into the Atlantic.

I teamed up with Admiral Woodward and his frigates when they left Gibraltar on 2nd April and we sailed on down to Ascension Island. He told us to spread out, avoid being seen by passing ships, fuel when we could, and see him there. It was a shrewd precaution. We hung around for a couple of days gathering stores. At that stage the government was deciding whether or not to re-invade South Georgia, and trying to get the Task Force together back home. Then *Antrim*, *Plymouth* and *Fort Austin* were sent to South Georgia, and my force – *Brilliant*, *Glasgow*, *Sheffield*, *Coventry*, *Arrow* and *Appleleaf* – was ordered to steam off south towards the Falklands. We were told to go as fast and as far as we could until we ran out of fuel and then wait for the tanker to catch up with us, in order to establish a British presence as far south as possible.

Going south as spearhead of the force in this very bracing South Atlantic weather was exciting, probably the most exhilarating part of the campaign. Type 22 frigates are exceptionally good at going fast into weather and *Brilliant* averaged around 24 knots. The other ships didn't like it; *Arrow* was starting to crack and I had to send them a message, 'If you break down, don't worry – we'll leave you behind!' I used to get all the captains on board at nine o'clock each day to talk over what we were going to do. We thought we would be in action as a group of six against the Argentinian navy a month before a carrier arrived on the scene, so there was quite an atmosphere. We practised Exocet attacks until we were blue in the face, targeting from our helicopters all the way down. There was a Royal Marine detachment on board and I had them practising against *Glasgow* and *Sheffield*. When I told them we might get the chance to take or burn or capture an Agentinian Type 42, they thought I was mad!

We'd hardly settled down to that task when the South Georgia operation went wrong. The assault force lost their helicopters before they even started. I was signalled to take the troop-carrying helicopters from *Coventry* and *Sheffield* and rush off on my own. It was blowing like hell and, in running fast to South Georgia, *Brilliant* rode the gales exceptionally well. Until the Falklands Conflict the Admiralty had tended to dismiss Type 22s as little more than expensive yachts, but they emerged as one of the successes of the campaign for their missile capability and simply because they would go so fast in bad weather.

When I arrived at South Georgia our ships were well off the coast because they'd heard the night before that there was an Argentinian submarine, *Santa Fe*, in the area. Our helicopters joined up with those from *Antrim*, *Plymouth* and *Endurance* to range along the coast and they found the submarine almost at once, just as he was diving on his way out of Grytviken at dawn, having landed some commandos overnight to bolster the Argentinian base headed by Captain Astiz. The boys dropped bombs and torpedoes and damaged it quite badly, and the captain, shaken, turned back to the harbour and rammed the sub against the old base jetty.

The Argentinians in South Georgia capitulated when the firing really laid itself down on their heads, and the next morning the army asked me to get the submarine off the jetty in case it sank and blocked the harbour. The British Force Commander, Brian Young, had instructions to salvage it because of its supposedly high intelligence value, and he decided it should be put with the old whaling wrecks up beside the whaling station. It really was a horrible, old-fashioned piece of junk, in a terrible state, and I realised I'd have to use the Argentinian crew to help move it. So we gathered them up and I was given some Marines to guard them. I was worried they might scuttle it, which would have been a bold stroke for Argentina, blocking the harbour beautifully, but in retrospect I realise they didn't have the fight left in them – they were crushed, poor chaps, absolutely crushed.

I stood on the bridge as we moved off, the captain giving orders in Spanish. Suddenly he realised the sub was about to sink, and ordered the crew down below to blow out the tanks to keep the boat on the surface. The trouble was, down below it was dark and drippy, and the Marines thought the crew were trying to scuttle it, so a fight started. The first thing I knew there were shots in the air and an Argentinian was killed. Boats started coming out from the shore. The captain, I think, understood the situation and the Argentinian crewman was buried with full military honours. It seemed it was going to be rather an odd war – up to then nobody had been killed.

Almost immediately I embarked Cedric Delves and his SAS men and some Marines and rushed off to get them up to the Falklands. I joined up with Sandy Woodward and the main Task Force who, at that point, were starting to move into the Total Exclusion Zone. The Argentinians had a lot of Exocets spread around their fleet and we knew we had to win the initial Exocet encounter. Both sides were firing the same weapon from their ships which was a bit worrying since an Exocet is quite a successful fire-and-forget weapon if the right person fires it first. We weren't sure then if they were going to be as incompetent as we hoped, particularly their Type 42 Exocet ships, because we'd trained those ourselves at Portland and knew they weren't that bad. So we were much more concerned about their surface force than anything else; wrongly, as it turned out. The Total Exclusion Zone was dominated by the Argentinian air force, so there was bound to be trouble, and the trouble descended on *Sheffield*. From then on, as far as we were concerned, it was very much a shooting match. *Brilliant*'s principal job throughout the Falklands Conflict was bodyguarding HMS *Invincible* during daylight hours every day. Whatever else I was doing, I had to flash back and fall in dead astern of *Invincible* by first light, and HMS *Broadsword* did the same job for *Hermes*. Everyone was worried that an Exocet would flash out of the sky, and the Sea Wolf missile system on board the Type 22 frigates was the only weapon available that had a chance of shooting one down. Every dawn they thought they were about to be attacked, but in the event dusk turned out to be a much more dangerous time. We would close up at action stations an hour or so before dusk and wait anxiously while we heard the reconnaissance flights for the Exocet coming up. Then, when it was nearly dark, I would say to the ship's company, 'Right, that's it for the night, chaps, we hope!' and two minutes later the bloody alarm would go. The crew got sick of that!

On many nights we ran into the islands to drop off SAS, SBS and Marines or to collect them after daring deeds ashore. I had a marvellous boatman, Leading Seaman Gould, who really liked getting wet and cold – a tough character, the sort of bloke you'd find running a boxing booth. I gave him a wireless, and our fast boat used to flash him into the night, often on his own, to land or pick up the Marines. Once close inshore we'd direct him like a helicopter and tell him where the rocks were from the radar. His principal interest was the bottle of rum I'd leave in my pantry for when he got back, but we all thought Gould was pretty noble and he was mentioned in despatches. He is the sort of seaman Nelson relied on and just as good.

We had a great rapport with the SAS and regarded them as our special army. They were outstandingly brave. One night about twenty-five were being transferred across to *Fearless* when their helicopter fell in the water. About five SAS men were clinging to a small life raft that had inflated automatically and we brought *Brilliant* up alongside them. It was cold, dark, and rough, and they were in a terrible state with broken arms and legs and collarbones, and weren't wearing life jackets. One of my young Marines, Neat, dived in and prised them off the raft and swam them back to the ladder – he was also mentioned in despatches. I remember packing one of the survivors, an army sergeant in Delves's squadron, into our helicopter to send him back to *Hermes*. His arms and legs and neck were all bandaged up. 'You know,' he said, 'this is the fourth helicopter ride I've had in the last fortnight, courtesy of the Royal Navy. The first one fell on the glacier at Fortuna on South Georgia. The second one rescued me and then fell in the bleedin' Fortuna glacier again. Then I got in the one that fell in the water! I hope yours is under guarantee.' Quite tough lads.

The anti-aircraft requirements in the anchorage by day, running in SBS or Marines to the islands at night, and rushing back for the dawn action stations in the Task Force was tiring. But I had very good young officers and could safely go to bed and let them get on with it; they were totally capable. I never had a moment of worry over the ship's company. I'd talk to them every day to keep them informed of all I knew of the situation, and I'd arranged beforehand a signals link via our sister ship *Battleaxe* in the UK which kept our wives in the picture. In a very modern ship like *Brilliant* you are remarkably detached; it's lovely and warm inside and you know everything that's going on because you've got better radio and monitoring equipment than anybody else. It's also a slightly unreal world. Even action stations didn't quite break that, but it certainly got the adrenalin moving when you heard that general alarm – it really is the most hideous, horrible sound.

One night *Brilliant* went chasing submarines. I had received a typical Woodward signal: 'An aircraft has reported sighting a submarine twenty miles north of Port Stanley. Go find him and bring me back his hat.' I knew if we found him he'd be on the bottom, and the whole place was littered with old whaling ships. We would find something, ping on it and it would look about the size of a small submarine, so we'd fly a helicopter with a magnetic detector over it and yes, it would say, it's metal. But I didn't have enough bombs to cover each wreck, and very few helicopters with metal detectors on them. The place was also full of whales, which gave enormous echoes on the sonar. Every so often a whale would come up, give a little blow and a flock of seagulls would gather round, appearing on the radar as a quick flash. Everybody would say, 'Christ, it must be a submarine,' and we would launch a few torpedoes. All in all it was total frustration but, looking back, I've a feeling that one of those wrecks was the *San Luis*.

On 12th May Sandy Woodward sent us in to bodyguard the *Glasgow* with the Sea Wolf whilst he shot up Port Stanley. The aim was also to bait their aircraft out to try and shoot a few down – at that stage nobody had shot anything down. After *Glasgow* had been banging away for about half an hour it was quite obvious that somebody was going to be called out to thump us and, on the radar, we picked up two squadrons of their aircraft flying down over the mountains. Four of them then peeled out from the coast and started skimming out towards us in a tightly packed group, right down on the water. I said to *Glasgow*, 'You steer over here and I'll keep between you and them. Watch the Sea Wolf go!' and turned it on.

The Sea Wolf is an entirely automatic system designed to shoot down missiles fired at you at close range – as long as it's switched to 'FIRE' it'll go on its own. It went on its own and shot down three of the four aircraft with two missiles: the first missile took the first aircraft, the second took the second, and the bits from the second aircraft knocked out the third one, which flew into the sea. The fourth one dropped some bombs, which bounced over us. We didn't mind that.

Then the second squadron came at us, more spread out, and I said to *Glasgow*, who'd started firing his gun, 'Relax, don't fire – the Sea Wolf might think it's a missile. We'll do the same trick again.' The Sea Wolf looked at this lot, said, 'That is not a missile,' and went back to park. Things happened quite fast then and the Argentenians dropped bombs everywhere. Fortunately they nearly all bounced over us again, but one went straight through *Glasgow*'s engine-room and out the other side. It didn't explode, but it knocked out an awful lot of pipes and mucked up her fuel and compressed-air systems. We then thought that maybe this wasn't such a good idea – fifty per cent probability by the Sea Wolf wasn't what we'd expected. So I called up *Hermes* and said we'd come back out and try to persuade the Sea Wolf it had to do better. The problem was that the Sea Wolf is controlled by its surveillance computer system which was originally designed to recognise missiles, not aircraft. In order to see a projectile approaching against the background it was programmed to pick out something less than a football in size and to reject clutter and big things. So the things the Sea Wolf discriminated against had included these four aircraft flying in loose formation. The system was still in the experimental stage. We had on board an electronics engineer from Marconi, David Breen, who had been with us on Operation Spring Train off Africa in March. On the way south I received repeated orders to send him back to the UK because he was a civilian. So very reluctantly I'd transferred him to a tanker going north, asking him to pack his bags of spares and fly down to meet us in Ascension, which he did. He was absolutely first-class. He kept the Sea Wolf going, and being strafed by Mirages and the like didn't put him off at all! Once he had identified the problem he got on the telex to the team working on the computer at

Portsmouth and by the next morning they came up with a change in the software, telling the Sea Wolf that once it had seen one target it should engage it, and not take notice of any other distractions. We put that into the system.

The *Glasgow* went back to find the support ship *Stena Inspector*, to have a patch put over her side. But the bomb had done her a lot of damage and because at that stage Sandy Woodward thought there might be a stalemate lasting many weeks, he sent her back home to be repaired.

Brilliant's next big job was bodyguarding the Task Force at San Carlos. That morning, 21st May, I took up position out in the Sound on the gun line with *Broadsword*, *Ardent*, *Argonaut* and *Alacrity*. When things really started to get nasty and *Antrim* was bombed I moved in to be close to the *Fearless* and *Intrepid*. The aerial attacks were very, very fierce and we found ourselves virtually defenceless because the Sea Wolf wouldn't go at all. It had been all right in the Sound but in San Carlos Water, which is virtually a creek, its radar was seeing so much clutter and putting so many inputs into the computer that it was overwhelmed: the computer could handle thirty or forty inputs but not hundreds all at once. We felt frustrated and infuriated because we knew that if we could get the missiles away they were going to knock the Mirages down. The only other firepower we had on this almost brand-new ship were two absolutely useless Bofors, built in Canada in 1942! The only modification they'd had since then were electrical firing circuits instead of old springs, which virtually ensured that they hardly ever worked.

But it was well worth staying there because, halfway through the morning, it suddenly became clear that all the ships with fighter direction capability were miles too far away to do anything about the Argentinian aircraft, who were over San Carlos Water; *Antrim* could have hacked the problem if she hadn't got bombed. Our Sea Wolf was seeing them all right and First Lieutenant Lee Hulme, who'd been a fighter direction instructor back in the great days of the Fleet Air Arm, picked up the fighters coming in off the carrier and guided them in. Although the computer wasn't designed for this task, by reading off its print-out numbers Hulme managed to intercept seven Mirages and Skyhawks during the day. That evening I was handed a message from the carrier saying, 'All our pilots here are talking with great admiration about your First Lieutenant, who really made the day.' Lee Hulme was deservedly mentioned in despatches.

On the second day of San Carlos, *Brilliant* was hit, the first and only time during the campaign. A Mirage shot a string of 35mm cannon shells through our side which exploded inside. We weren't badly hit by many others' standards, just three men injured, but it was disastrous for our weapons system. The system came in from the water line right up to the Ops Room, through the Sea Wolf office, through the for'ard Sea Wolf launcher and peppered the wiring to all the electronics. In our wisdom we'd run the computer's myriad input channels right up the ship's side, so the whole system was now firmly out of action. We tried to fix it up as best we could, using everything we had on board, but it didn't work, so Sandy Woodward called us out to the repair ship. That night about thirty-five electrical engineers descended from the *Stena Inspector* and, under the guidance of David Breen, they bypassed the whole mess with a load of new wiring and got it working again, virtually overnight.

The chap at San Carlos who stuck out in my mind as a very tough egg was Pentreath in the *Plymouth*. That first morning it became obvious that *Plymouth* was more or less useless to the event, being an ancient ship with ancient radar and no very modern weapons. Pentreath's answer to that was to steam in defiant circles round and round *Fearless* and *Intrepid* just to show he was there, blazing away with his gun. About a week later I flew over the anchorage and he was still doing this – it was perfectly clear that sooner or later he was bound to be bombed, which he was, quite badly. It was magnificent defiance, but quite preposterous.

We continued bodyguarding *Invincible*, but of course after San Carlos the navy's role as a fighting force diminished. On the basis of first in, first out, *Brilliant* steamed up north soon after the Argentinian surrender.

Looking back, the ship and everybody in it had behaved exactly as expected, and the things that went wrong had done so for entirely predictable reasons. On the way north, the weather was very similar to when we went down– big sea, bright sky, lots of cloud, the same albatrosses, all very South Atlantic. I fell the crew in, in their best uniforms, and we had prayers for the dead, particularly for *Sheffield* and *Coventry*. Both ships had been part of my little squadron coming down from Ascension. Now we were going back without them and it seemed almost incredible that such fine ships had disappeared.

ABLE SEAMAN (RADAR) JOHN DILLON, RN

Before the bomb fell, everyone was laughing and joking. *Ardent* had already been under attack and we'd had to keep taking cover, which after a while was getting a bit boring. Then, at around four o'clock, we got an order to take cover and we thought it was just another false alarm. We all lay on the floor, but the next thing we heard was this big bang and everything went quiet. It just seemed like a dream, we couldn't believe that we'd actually been hit. I think the flight deck was hit and, as I was in the Damage Control Team, I got up with my mates to tackle one of the pipes that had broken and was starting to spray water everywhere. The dining-hall was starting to fill up with water so we got some buckets and started bailing. At the time it felt really good, you know, that we'd been hit; we could go home and tell all our mates. The next minute we were told to take cover again.

The worst thing about being below deck is that you can't really hear or know what is going on outside. You can hear all the gunfire but you don't actually know what is happening. Then there was a loud bang. We got up to assess the damage, then we were told to take cover again. There was another loud explosion and all I remember was waking up with this black smoke around me and all these people screaming and groaning. Most of the blokes down there had been killed. I was trapped under this wreckage with all these people screaming to get out. I thought, 'What's going on here?' It was just like a nightmare. All sorts of things started flashing through my mind; I got this image of my Mum at home doing the cooking in the kitchen, I imagined my sisters there, and my brothers at school.

I was dying; it was weird. I thought someone was just going to open a big curtain and there'd be a crowd of people watching us, like being on a stage. It all seemed so unreal – there was a pain in my arm, the smoke, just everything together, you know. I was trapped, there seemed no way out. I was actually dying. I was just going to say 'Forget it,' and wait there to die.

It was then that the images of my great heroes, like Bruce Lee and Silver Surfer, started flashing through my mind. I used to collect comics, hundreds of them; and I was fascinated by Kung Fu. Although I was hit in the back and it was difficult to move my right arm, which I was using most of the time, and all this thick, black smoke kept pouring into my lungs, I thought, 'I can't just lie here and die – I've got to do something. *They* would never give up. *They'd* have the will to survive and somehow get out in the end. *They* wouldn't give up until they were dead.' So I just kept pushing, and somehow, I don't know how, I got the girder off me and crawled out.

I tried to stand up but there was so much smoke about that I just kept close to the deck. It was then I realised that I'd shrapnel in my back but I soon forgot my own pain because there was someone lying beside me with a girder right across his head. I thought, 'I've got to get him out.' He was screaming for help. Water was pouring into the ship, I knew I was fighting time, but however hard I tried I couldn't lift the girder off. It really was tremendously heavy, so I had to leave him. I felt bad about it because I knew he must have died. I don't know to this day who he was.

I could hear a lot of other people screaming but I couldn't see anything because of the dense smoke. There was a small emergency light on the ship but even that was being covered up because the smoke was so thick; you could almost touch it. I thought to myself, 'I've got to get out – I can't hack it in here.' As I was going down aft to find a way out I heard this voice in the corner shouting, 'Get me out, mate.' I looked over and saw a man trapped in the wreckage. I thought, 'I've got to try and help him.' So I crawled over to where he was under all this rubble and said, 'Are you all right?' He said, 'Get this girder off me,' so I put my shoulder underneath and slowly managed to lift it so he could crawl out a bit. I could just see his hand coming out. He said, 'Go on, keep lifting it.' But because the air was so bad, I had to keep stopping to get my breath. I'd managed to lift it and he'd crawl out a bit until gradually he managed to crawl free. He looked a mess but I didn't realise how badly he was hurt.

The smoke seemed to be getting worse so that I could hardly see anything. We crawled about a bit trying to find a way out. I looked down aft and it was all black. Then I looked for'ard and there was a fire up there. I thought, 'I'd better try down aft.' I got halfway down there but the smoke was so thick I couldn't go any further. So I went back to the middle of the dining-hall and just sat there. I thought, 'This is it. I'm going to die.' Then I looked over at this Chief and I think he was praying, he was kneeling there, praying. I thought, 'We can't die now.'

I'd seen the fire up front and realised that if there was a fire then there's got to be air somewhere. So I crawled up towards the for'ard a little bit; the fire looked bad from a distance but all it was was some wires on fire. So I called the Chief over and said, 'Look, we can get out of here.' When I got closer to the fire, I saw this big hole in the bulkhead which I couldn't believe – a big hole like that and yet there was so much smoke inside the ship. I thought, 'Oh, great! At last some fresh air.' So I just stood as near as I could to the edge and started taking deep breaths. The Chief just followed me as I climbed up some steps because I didn't fancy jumping into the oggin – you know, the sea. We could've jumped in but I didn't know if anyone would have seen us. I suppose we were about twenty feet above the sea. We were used to jumps like that from training, but I thought, 'I don't fancy going in there because I'm bound to drown' – I was so weak from exhaustion.

I started looking for a way out. The Chief was inflating his life jacket so I thought he must want to jump or something. I tried to open the hatch but it was all buckled. I tried to use my other arm, but I couldn't do it because of my back, so I let that go, and just climbed down. I'd seen him inflate his life jacket, and I tried to inflate mine, but I couldn't because my throat was all burnt. So I just thought, 'Forget it. I'll jump in without the life jacket.'

The Chief then started walking across the bulkhead and I followed him. Suddenly he began to sway and, because he was so dazed, he fell into a hole in the deck. It was then I realised how bad he was; one of his fingers was hanging off and he had a big split all the way down his face. I thought,'Oh God, this bloke's going to die.' I'd never seen anything like that before. He didn't seem to know what he was doing, so I bent over the hold and said, 'Here you are, mate.' He grabbed my hand, and I pulled him up. That took some time as I was feeling pretty weak. He then stood upright, walked over towards the edge and jumped into the water. I knew he was trying to get away from the ship. He was calm though; it was surprising. He just jumped into the water. I looked down and I could see him, he was just drifting away. I thought, 'He's going to die unless I do something.' So I just jumped in beside him and got my injured arm and kind of hooked it around him; I couldn't move it any other way, I just hooked it around him and started swimming. We were swimming away from the ship, but I knew I couldn't last long, because I'm not a very good swimmer. I'm surprised at what I did in the water; I did all right. I don't know how long I was in the water, probably about ten minutes but that's a long time in the cold. It was a relief to jump in there though, it felt really cool to start with. But I had my boots on, and they're pretty heavy when you're trying to swim. To make it worse they had steel toecaps as well.

As I was swimming away from the ship I knew I wouldn't be able to keep it up for long. I kept shouting at the Chief to kick his legs hard because I was starting to go under. So a hundred yards away from the ship I just turned round and there was a warship. I think it was the *Glamorgan*. I thought, 'Oh great! It's going to pull us out of the water.'

At that moment I looked behind at the *Ardent* and all the back end was just full of smoke. I looked up for'ard and saw these blokes all lined along it in their red suits. I couldn't believe it because I thought everyone on the whole ship had been killed. I just couldn't believe that one half of the ship was all right and the other half was smashed to pieces. It was mostly the dining-hall that had been smashed up. Just seeing all those people up there . . . I couldn't believe it. They were all shouting because they were trying to direct someone down towards us. I looked up and it was getting closer. I started swimming pretty fast this time. I don't know where I found the strength from but I really swam hard and then I looked up again and the ship seemed to be further away! I thought I would never make it. The blokes on the ship were telling me to move away from it in case I got caught up in the props or something. But I didn't care at this time, I was just trying to get on to some dry land. But I was so tired and my arm was killing me. I couldn't hold on to the Chief any longer – I was slipping under the water and dragging him down as well. I thought, 'I'll let him go because at least he's got a life jacket so he'll be all right for a while.' So I let him go and he just started drifting away but he was almost unconscious by then. I started swimming by myself but I was really tired now.

Then I looked up and saw this helicopter and it was lowering this strop. I tried to reach the strop but I couldn't. They lowered it down a little bit more, and I was just about to reach it, and they flew off. I thought, 'Oh no, this is it. After all that I've been through, I'm just going to finally die,' and I just started going under. I began to sink – all I could see above was water. I didn't feel any pain or anything, just kind of relaxed. I wasn't even frightened as I quietly waited for myself to go to the bottom. It was all over.

The next minute this hand grabbed me from behind and it just lifted me out of the water. It was magic! This bloke had come down the hawser; he wasn't supposed to, but he did. He just picked me up and grabbed me. I thought, 'What a relief.' He just lifted me out of that water. He was a really good bloke he was. I owe him my life. He was Surgeon-Commander Rick Jolly. It was a very brave thing to do. I couldn't believe it; I was safe. Then he went down again for the Chief as well. He told me later how he'd seen me going down under the water, and wanted to try and save me. I was totally exhausted when he returned with the Chief and pulled him in beside me.

They flew us to the *Canberra*, and wrapped me up in this blanket because of the hypothermia. As they were carrying me down to the sick bay, I heard the tannoy call out 'Air Raid Warning Red, Air Raid Warning Red. Enemy aircraft on the starboard side and closing.' I thought, 'Oh God! I can't go through that again.' I just cried; I couldn't believe it. 'Not again, don't say I have to go through that lot again.' Everyone was running around with these life jackets. I've never been so scared in my life. I was lying on the stretcher on the deck. They all took cover beside me. One of the blokes got all these pillows and he covered me with them. All this within a couple of hours of them fishing me out of the sea. Thank God it all came to nothing.

Slowly I recovered; my back's all right now. It was sore for a couple of months but now it's all right. I think the smoke had a much longer-lasting effect. I keep getting colds and sometimes a smoky room triggers off memories – that's going to take a few years to get out of my system. What I do feel bad about was meeting Commander Jolly at Buckingham Palace. He came up and offered me his congratulations, but I didn't even know who he was. I felt really bad about that – he's a good bloke.

Although I'm not a strong Roman Catholic, I think what I went through has changed my ideas about God. I think about it a lot. I'm not even sure we've got a soul. If I had died I wouldn't have gone anywhere, I'd have just been in a relaxed state. I'd be nothing, you know, nothing, as if you weren't there. You'd just fade away. I don't know what helped me out there – I suppose I never will.

Rear-Admiral John 'Sandy' Woodward, RN

At HQ the business is cool-headed management. You are into careful planning and the assessment of chances; you have to disengage from the battle cries and the hot lead. You are always hearing first-hand reports of damage and disaster, and your job is to distance yourself because they are naturally highly emotive, almost confusion factors. If you don't distance yourself you can become frightened and distressed, and that will cloud your judgement. Despite your cares, you have to calculate the odds, the gains and the losses.

The decisions I liked least were when I had to send friends in harm's way when, of course, I couldn't go in myself; they were very uncomfortable. I remember ringing up the captain of *Alacrity*, Commander Craig, on the secure telephone to ask him to go through Falkland Sound at night. Before landing in San Carlos we needed to find out what was going on there, how difficult the passage would be by night, and whether the opposition had laid any mines. I said, 'I want you to go into the Sound, have a look round and keep them on their toes. If you find anybody, do what seems necessary. Come out the northern end and be back offshore with the battle group by dawn.' I wasn't going to tell him about the mines; I dissembled because I never wanted to put the frighteners on my captains any more than I had to. But Craig, bless him, saw through me straightaway: 'Oh, I expect, Admiral, you'd like me to go in and out of the northern entrance several times before I come home?' Realising I'd been rumbled, I replied, 'Well, that's quite a good idea, but why do you suggest it?' And he said, 'I imagine, Admiral, that you want to find out if there are any mines in the northern entrance.' 'Oh,' I said, 'it's funny you should mention it, but we would be very glad to know and we'll do our best to bail you out later if we can.' I thought it was a bloody brave thing to do: a small ship, thousands of miles from home, on his own and knowing damn well the risks involved, which in this case were high. I had already assessed that there was no other way to do the job, and, probably, so had he. He had seen instantly what I wanted and accepted it with humour. Fortunately, it all turned out well.

Throughout the campaign I was surrounded by such men, whom I knew and could trust, and by men who also knew me. One of the good things when doing the cool planning bit was knowing that others were doing it too.

Most days on *Hermes* my life settled into a routine, albeit a routine I'd never done before. With the management of a large force you're trying to build a picture of everything that's going on, and there was a mass of periodically repeated tasks to do in a fairly routine manner. You have to follow everything that's going on in order to find the odd thing because it's the odd feature that you're going to have to deal with. You must be ready for the unexpected that can come at you from nowhere, as it did to the poor old *Sheffield* in three-and-a-half minutes flat. I was often encouraged to go off and visit the other ships, but I never felt that was part of my job. I always thought that things could go wrong very quickly and to be absent from my place of duty on *Hermes* wouldn't be too sharp. For instance, when *Sheffield* got hit and the information came into our Ops Room, where we all were, one or two people were very badly shaken. Voices were raised and getting louder and one said, 'Come on, Admiral, you must do something!' I had to say, 'No. Leave it to the people on the spot. There's one frigate already there with a helicopter, and another frigate on the way. All we need to do is tell the chap who's there first to take charge of the on-scene action. If we get involved with the tiny detail we'll only bring the operation to a grinding halt.'

On the occasion there had been a near-panic reaction; people were pressing me to do something, when all we had to do was sit cool and calm. Panic is infectious. I've always been conscious that the way the captain performs his duty is vital to morale. Unlike a land force leader, you're comforted by the familiarity of your surroundings and the danger may be less immediate, but even when you're a hundred miles away from where it's actually happening and you're sitting in a large tin box with a low light, people still need to turn to the place where the boss is sitting to see what's written on his face.

The Ops Room on *Hermes* was about fifteen feet by fifteen feet with fairly low lighting in order that we could see the various radar screens and monitors. I had a funny little cabin just down the passage, about nine feet by nine, with a little bunk, a tiny table and a shower: a cell, really. About twenty people worked in the Ops Room checking the data with a Group Warfare Officer on watch, doing the minute-to-minute management of the battle group. Normally, comparatively junior officers would have held that position, which would have meant calling the admiral every few minutes to take a decision. I thought that I was likely to be down south for a long while and that, if called to make decisions that any captain could make, I would be running around all the time and incapable of doing the long-term thinking or planning. So I chose to change the system and co-opted Captain Buchanan and Captain Woodhead for the job. They worked twelve hours on and twelve hours off from late April until July and did marvellously well. Both captains were friends of mine and had worked with me before, so it was a very easy relationship, for me, anyway! I don't know how I would have got through without them.

I wasn't physically tired but, like everybody else, I was mentally tired from the strain. I realised that I could go on for a couple of months without any real exercise because I'd done that before, and I made a point of keeping myself as rested as I could. You can remain alert and in good, decisive, reactive condition for very long periods as long as you look after yourself, almost cocoon yourself. When I'd done it before, I didn't sleep for more than forty-two minutes at a stretch, and that was once in two months. You can only do it easily if you're used to it. You have to discipline yourself.

I used to find when I got back to my cabin after being in the Ops Room I'd sit down and say, 'Well, what about writing a letter home, or reading a book, or watching a chat show on the internal television?' Then I'd say to myself, 'Now, hang on a minute. Just think through yesterday again, or the day before. Think through what you intend to do next week and whether there is any way you can find a solution for that problem which has proved intractable so far. Just remember you're here to do a job. Go over and over things again.' So, in the end, even had it gone wrong, I would have been able to say to myself, 'Well, I did give it the absolute maximum amount of thought and time I possibly could. If in the end my solution was found wanting, well, so be it, it was wanting, but it wasn't for lack of effort.'

As manager of the organisation, there are lots of things you have to keep to yourself – you live with your responsibilities. I found my diary a great safety valve. You can get rid of the steam and hassle of the day and you feel better when you've done it. But no-one should take too much notice of what's written; often it's just the steam. Undoubtedly my diary was the main outlet for my feelings.

On the way south we didn't know we were going to war, but we might have been, so there were a lot of conflicting requirements on what I said. I had to convince the workforce, my own blokes, that we could do a good job and we had a good chance – you don't tell anyone they're going to lose, even if you think they are. Then there was the opposition: the message I wanted to pass on to the Argentinians was one of determination, efficiency and confidence. Bearing in mind the national characteristics of the Argentinians, I was slightly more pushy in what I said to them: my own workforce may not have been able to take it, but the opposition probably needed it. Then there was the home market to consider, ranging from the Prime Minister to the man in the street – they all wanted to hear something.

In the face of such demands and constraints the only safe answer was to say nothing but, of course, you're not allowed to do that. As a consequence I got variously interpreted and variously misunderstood. I most regret being reported as saying, 'What I expect is a walkover.' I know that sometimes you think you've said one thing and it's heard as something else, and I accept entirely that Brian Hanrahan, a very good, objective journalist, reported it the way he heard it. But what I actually meant was something quite different: I said I would much prefer a walkover, in the sense of a tennis match where your opponent doesn't turn up and you're given a 'walkover'. The press had a field day, *Private Eye* talking about the 'jumpy little bugger' saying 'it's going to be a walkover'. That caused a lot of trouble back home and I had to live with the repercussions for a while.

Obviously PR is important, but at the time I had rather more worrisome things on my mind. The thing is, it's not my trade. If I were an actor or a politician it would be different, but I hated the publicity, and still do. Going from captain of a ship to admiral of a whole group of ships means you go from being a bit-part actor to the lead, where all the lights are on you and the microphones are everywhere. I'm not a stage sort of person. I've always preferred to do my business from the edge. I therefore found the change to being an admiral and, indeed, an internationally known one, extremely difficult. I'd been rather pitchforked into the front of the limelight business.

Some of the men were very apprehensive about the probability of actually going to war. It was the biggest fleet of British ships to sail since South Korea and, of course, most of us had not seen active service before. I joined the Navy in 1946 at the age of thirteen-and-a-half, but I didn't go to sea until I was seventeen-and-a-half. The first time I'd really had to face the fact that I might have to go to war as part of my profession was during the Suez crisis in 1956. Up to then the Navy had been a way of life rather than a job where you might get killed in action. I had to try to explain this commitment to a lot of young people on the way south. One man's contract had expired a few days after we sailed, but as a fully trained man, I told him we had to keep him: one trained man was worth ten volunteers. He took it very well. Professionals have no choice other than to go along, and I must say that during the campaign I never had to exhort people to do things. There were always too many willing to go – I had to hold them back.

As we went further south there was a strong sense of time pressing, because the whole operation could only last for a limited period. We knew we hadn't got a forward base and therefore we would eventually run out of everything. I reckoned my ships were going to fall apart by the end of June, especially the aircraft carriers because we had none to replace them. We had replacements for most other things, such as frigates and destroyers, but we also were short of Sea Wolf systems and Sea Harriers; our force for long-range air defence was thus a very limited asset. For various reasons we actually couldn't have a landing force in before about mid-May and we had to be finished by 1st July, so there could only be a six-week period for the land battle. It was quite a close thing, as it turned out, because, of course, we finished in mid-June. Fortunately, Sea Harriers were quite plentiful because we didn't lose them, which was a relief, and the carriers continued satisfactorily, with *Hermes* running for over three months and *Invincible* for more than four. But the destroyers and frigates were really falling apart by the end, because they were the workhorses. On the last night, 13th/14th June, I agreed to give General Jeremy Moore four ships for naval gunfire support for the land forces, and unfortunately, because of damage and wear and tear, only one ship managed to turn up. Air defence systems were also badly affected by weather and action damage: on 14th June only about one-eighth of the systems was available to us. If the opposition had found us then, we'd have been in a very poor way.

I would say that there was one really low moment in the campaign. This was 25th May, which is the big Argentinian naval day; their aircraft carrier is even named after it. I wrote in my diary, 'They will probably do something today.' Then, later in the day, I wrote, 'Well, they don't seem to have done much, maybe we'll get away with it.' That was my mistake. Within the hour they got *Coventry*, and shortly afterwards *Atlantic Conveyor*.

As for the *Belgrano*, enough has been said on that subject to satisfy anyone, I'd have thought, but personally I have always been of the same view as the Argentinian Admiral Lombardo, who effectively called it the fortunes of war and no more or less than he would have done in the same circumstances.

The finest example of straight calm in the face of extreme anxiety that I can recall was shown by Bill Canning, the captain of *Broadsword*, at the time of the sinking of *Coventry*. He was on one of the high-frequency radios telling me about the situation as the attack occurred. I was about one hundred and ten miles away listening to what was effectively a running commentary. He was telling me what he was doing and suddenly said, 'I'm going to stop for a moment – something's happened.' There was a twenty-five-second pause and then he came back and continued describing what was going on, in exactly the same voice. During that break two bombs had passed straight through the stern of his ship. Remarkable cool. He just carried on in the same calm voice, even when *Coventry* was hit seconds later by the next wave of aircraft.

Another facet of character occurs to me. I don't much like talking about the campaign, and perhaps I should have known better than to ask one of my COs, long after the war was all over, what was the single, most important lesson he had learnt down there. I immediately added, 'No, don't answer that.' But he said, 'No, I will. I learnt to cry.' A fantastic thing for a young commander to say to his admiral; an honest and very courageous thing to say. I think a lot of people did learn to cry – it is, after all, a very important thing to learn.

I took a particular interest in the SAS raid on Pebble Island since I always felt, rightly or wrongly, that it was one of 'my' operations. It went very well despite some major difficulties and was completed in a very short time. One of the features was that it was rehearsed, very professionally prepared in five days flat. It's most unusual to go into an unreconnoitred area, working against aircraft not seen before on the ground and destroy eleven in the middle of a gale. It was a great success story – the biggest single disaster for the Argentinian air force. Later I flew out to Pebble Island in a Sea King and the memory of it is still very clear. Green fields similar to the north-west of Scotland, lovely cold, bracing wind, and there in the middle of this peaceful scene those eleven aircraft, looking almost undamaged until you got close. The bombs the SAS used had blown their centres out, absolutely wrecking them as far as flying was concerned but leaving the rest of the aircraft largely intact. They created, especially the Pucaras which looked like praying mantises, a surreal and uncomfortable image. Everything was fresh, brisk and clean apart from this dead, deserted machinery – quite symbolic.

The day after the surrender I landed on board *Fearless* on the way to meet General Moore at Port Stanley. General Menendez was on board and I was asked whether I would like to meet him. I decided I didn't wish to. I could easily have become extremely angry; the temptation was to say, 'What a bloody waste of time and valuable lives and limbs! Why couldn't you have bloody well given in on 3rd April?'

In Port Stanley General Moore suggested we went down to the airstrip to have a look at all the prisoners. General Moore and I, his colonel, his chief of staff and a young subaltern armed to the teeth, all packed into a car and we drove right on to the airstrip. It was the first time I had seen the Argentinians at close quarters, which was ironic, and it was a nervous moment; 5,000 men were there and we had only one properly armed bloke. I found myself a bit reluctant to unlock the car door but General Moore leaped out and off we went for a walk down the runway. He was quite right, they were docile, and I felt more than a little foolish.

Up until March 1982 I never dreamed we would go to war with Argentina. The whole emphasis of the armed forces is to be so patently good enough that it is not worth the candle for the opposition to take action against you. That's the thesis, the underlying precept of our lives. The concept of deterrence is important, and in the history of that funny little war we did in fact fail it. We withdrew HMS *Endurance* and it was read by the Argentinians as the final pull-out. They thought, 'There are only forty-odd Marines left, and as long as we don't kill them, the job will be done.' You can't entirely blame the Argentinians for not being deterred, but at the time we could not find it in our hearts to believe that the removal of *Endurance* was of any real significance. But that's the danger with deterrence – you don't know when the balance is being tipped until it's too damned late.

Nurse Jackie Hayward, QARNNS

I was on nights in an intensive care unit at Haslar Royal Naval Hospital near Gosport, when they told me I was going to the Falklands on Sunday – this was

Friday night! But I got my things together because I had volunteered and I wanted to go. My husband, who was in 42 Commando, was already down there. He later got a message from the matron to say that I'd arrived on the *Uganda*.

We were flown in an uncomfortable Hercules from Brize Norton out to Uruguay and were met at the airport by armed guards and searched on the plane. It was then it hit us that we were going to war. We had a police escort through the town and everyone stopped and stared at us. We joined a small hospital ship but the captain didn't know anything about us. He thought he was getting thirteen males, which is what he'd asked for on the signal; instead he got three females! We were soon transferred by helicopter, which was very exciting, to *Uganda* and became the first naval female nurses to be on a ship since the last world war.

We met up with *Uganda* at the Red Cross box, which was an agreed safe area, somewhere in the middle of the ocean. During the day we went into Falkland Sound and took out casualties but at night we had to go back and rendezvous in this Red Cross box with the other ships. We got on to *Uganda* after Goose Green and before the other major battles. When I arrived I was told that I was going to work on the intensive care unit. I'd worked on intensive care at Haslar but only for three weeks, during which time I hadn't actually got any patients! But at least I had become familiar with the machinery, which was a big help. The first day on board we were told to find our way about the ship. I'd never been on a big ship before and I was seasick, but not bad enough to keep me in bed all the time. I kept thinking about my puppy which I had left with a neighbour.

We were told to report to the ward. It was set in different watches and we started working four hours on and four hours off. Then, when we got lots of patients, things became too hectic and we got called back – casualties were coming in too quick for a normal routine. They tried six hours off and four hours on, but in the end we did four hours on and eight hours off, because we were getting so tired. When I actually started in intensive care there was only one patient, who was a Marine; the rest were on other wards.

Everything was fairly easy and really there was a bit of a lull – but the *Galahad* changed all that. I'd only seen one burns case before and that was an old lady who had fallen into a fire, which was quite nasty. At eight that morning, I'd just come off duty when I heard the call, 'All Hands to Flying Stations.' I sensed immediately something was very wrong. I went straight back away to my ward to see these horrifying sights – so many burnt and disfigured men, you couldn't recognise any of them. They looked like teddy bears, their faces were all terribly swollen, and they were in such pain.

There were Chinese men as well as ordinary men and you couldn't tell the difference, they were all black and swollen. Their burnt flesh left a smell which I'll never forget. The fire had singed all their hair. The clothing they wore protected them, but their hands and faces really got it. One was burnt all over, the only thing that was perfect was his feet – they were immaculate. I think he was going up the ladder when the blast hit the whole of his back. He came straight to us in intensive care. It was a horrible sight.

I remember Simon Weston, who was really badly burnt, coming through with another Welsh Guard. I was amazed because they were talking to each other, they were really so cheerful, it was unbelievable. I just stood there and looked at them, and thought how can you be so cheerful when you really hurt so much. He asked how everybody was, and had they seen so and so? This was because his face had swollen up so much that his eyes had closed and he couldn't see. He really was so brave. He didn't often show he was in pain.

That day *Uganda* took 159 casualties. The helicopters would land every five minutes and so many people would be brought off. The chaps that came were just so glad to be in bed, with clean sheets and feeling safe. There wasn't any noise of firing or people getting hurt – they were just there. Some of them looked so young.

Because they were so fit, they healed quickly. We had one who was really ill, but he never once blamed anybody, not did he blame the Argentinians. He was more worried about getting home to his fiancée, but he died. Then we had another one who was three beds away from an Argentinian and he would call him all the names under the sun. He said he was going to kill him but in the end they were all talking to each other. One minute they had been trying to kill each other on the battlefield and the next minute they're stuck in the same room together talking or trying to speak English or Spanish to each other. But the true Argentinian soldiers didn't really want to know. Yet some of the conscripts were only sixteen and they were petrified. They'd been told that once they got on board they would be tortured immediately, and the food would be poisoned. Because we were females, they thought it was a new tactic. But one who had been shot in the mouth on his eighteenth birthday underwent a tracheotomy – he was fantastic. In the end, when the Argentinians took him back, he cried because he didn't want to go home. He gave one of the sisters his rosary. It was ironic because another Argentinian had been shot on his eighteenth birthday and the same day one of ours who was twenty-one that day was also shot. They were both together. They cursed each other but then they apologised afterwards.

After the *Galahad* we took them from everywhere, wherever they were, we took them. The helicopters on the island used to fly them over to us. There were so many of the men that stand out, especially in intensive care. They each had their own particular way of showing how they were overcoming their pain. My friend Karen told me about one patient, a young Scots Guard's officer, Bob Lawrence. He was paralysed down one side and he used to sit there and joke about it. But I think he, like the rest, did it to keep his own spirits up. He also knew that he was going to meet the Queen so he was determined he was going to walk up and get his medal. But all of them had such really high spirits. In their own way they were determined that they were going to do something and get better.

There was one who had been hit in the leg and it was so badly damaged that the doctors said they might have to amputate. They gave him the choice and they let him phone his Mum and Dad and fiancée. He spoke with them and told them that to keep his leg he would have to go through years and years of operations. In the end he decided he wasn't going to have it amputated, he was going to keep his leg. He went home on leave on one of the hospital ships with a Portsmouth Bar on his leg, which pins and keeps his leg in plaster and holds the leg in traction. I didn't see anything more of him for a long time and then I came back off leave to his ward and it was lovely to see that his leg was healing. He was so determined that his leg wasn't going to come off and even more determined to walk up the aisle with a leg, with or without a plaster, and he did. That leg fixed lovely. Then, ironically, she hurt her leg on honeymoon and finished up in plaster! He was fantastic, he was; a tall bloke with dark hair.

There was another called Paul, who was only nineteen, who'd been hit everywhere but very badly in the back. He'd gone to theatre so many times but his only thought was to get home to his fiancée and their six-month-old baby. They were going to get married in the August but somehow before his last op he knew he wasn't going to get through and that was it – he just died. It cracked us all up because of the length of time we'd looked after him – he had six nurses looking after him. We did all we could for him. That night I went out and sat on my own on the flight deck. I think it was a big ship but it wasn't that big. Of course I used to let out a lot of feeling in my letters home. Letters are very important. The soldiers on the ward used to get upset if they didn't get a letter from their girlfriends. But in the end, those who got letters would share out their news – they were like a family really, all helping each other.

We did our best but we couldn't take away completely the pain they had. At night a lot of their memories would come flooding back. We had one young lad who had to have his leg amputated. In his dreams he would re-live the moment when he'd been hit and he used to wake up in agony because, even though his foot wasn't there, he would still feel the pain. He used to shout and wake himself up and we'd have to calm him down and talk to him. The others would be shouting out, 'Take cover, take cover', really re-living the whole thing.

When everything was over, my husband managed to get on board to see some people in his company who had been injured. He looked so drawn and as if he needed a good meal. We went down to my cabin to get him some washing gear. I'd got some things on a cupboard when the ship rolled and they fell and bashed on the floor. I turned round to say something to my husband and he was lying on the floor! He got up and told me it was force of habit and laughed it off. But it worried me, seeing that sort of thing. I don't know how I would have responded if he'd been badly hurt and I'd had to nurse him. Three of us had husbands down there and other nurses had their boyfriends.

A lot of people who lost an arm or a leg really needed to be convinced that their wife or girlfriend would still need them. They used to say, 'She won't want me any more now.' They were all right while they were together on the ward – all in the same boat. So we really had to try and convince them that they'd be all right, because they knew there would be a different world for them once they left the ship and had to face reality.

One lad on the ward had been on a ship that sank. I was with him when two enemy planes went over very close and he could hear them. You could see the fear in his eyes. I couldn't convince him that he was safe. How can you convince someone who has just been blown out on a ship by aircraft that he's all right? It took a lot of doing but we got him to realise that at least he was part safe, but it took a lot of doing. We could deal with the physical things, but the mental scars were something else.

I think it dawned on us when we all got back what we'd actually done. We had so much to do that we didn't have time to get frightened – but we used to get frightened for everyone else. It seemed ages before we got back to Southampton and that marvellous reception. There in the crowd I saw my husband who had arrived six weeks before me. It seemed funny, really, because all the wives were waiting for their husbands! I don't think I'd have missed it. I learnt a hell of a lot down there and met a lot of very brave people.

SEARCH AND RESCUE

Chief Petty Officer David Wallace, RN

I first joined the navy as a ship's electrician, but had also already trained as a ship's diver. One day I was watching these guys jumping out of a helicopter. I thought to myself, 'That looks interesting. I wonder what it's all about.' One of the other ship's divers told me that they were Search and Rescue divers.

I was eighteen at the time and thought, I'd have to learn how to jump, do a bit of first-aid, and that was it. So I put in for it and got it. It was only after I got into the training that I realised what I'd let myself in for. You were taught basic navigation, map reading, radio work and a little bit about aircraft systems.

The more physical side of the training involved winching and talking the aircraft into position to operate the winch, carrying out the pick-ups for the helicopter, and lifting loads. That basic training took twelve weeks.

Afterwards everybody departed to different specialisations. Some people went anti-submarine, some to the commando helicopters, some went on to Wasps, the anti-shipping helicopter which were on the back of frigates. I was the only one on my course who went 'Search and Rescue'. There were about twenty-two on my course to start with, which boiled down in the end to seven. It had and still has a high failure rate; about fifty percent and I nearly gave up at one stage myself because I thought I'd bitten off a bit more than I could chew. I was struggling with the academic side of it, the navigation during the pre-flight training before you could get near a helicopter. I went away to my mess that night and sat down and thought about it. I decided to get my teeth into it and go for it. Later on we had to go in front of a board for an interview. They told me I was borderline, that they had put me through as a training risk and that the rest of it was up to me. The shots fell for me and I took my chances while they were there.

I got my wings about four weeks after my twentieth birthday. At the time I was the youngest person to get his wings as an aircrewman, although other people have since superseded me. It took me a good three years to learn to slow down. As soon as that alarm went off I used to go hell for leather to the aircraft. I'd get inside and think, 'Right, what am I supposed to be doing?' I was an excitable kid then. The guys who are coming through now are all twenty-three plus.

The first job I ever went on, I got scrambled for a Hunter with an engine problem. He was making either for Saint Mawgan or Culdrose. I got into the aircraft and we lifted off. It was only then I realised I'd left my wet suit in the crew room, even though the chief had reminded me earlier to put it in the aircraft. Luckily I had my wet suit bottoms with me. In those days we used to have two men in the back of the aircraft; one to operate the winch and one to go down. Fortunately the guy with me was a diver as well and he had his wet suit with him, so we did a quick change-over. He became the diver and I became the navigator. That will always live with me; I've never left my wet suit in the crew room since that night. The Hunter landed safely, so that was a good end. And a good beginning for me.

My first official scramble which involved diving, was when four helicopters crashed in a massive mid-air collision. They were the Sharks Display Team, six gazelle aircraft – and they were practising display manoeuvres when two or three of them collided. One of the aircraft was hit with the rotor blades of another and two ditched into the sea.

At the time I wasn't duty Search and Rescue crew. I was in the canteen at the base when they asked for all the divers to report. We all went out, and got into the water, searching for the aircraft. I never found anything, but I must have been really close because when I came up I was covered in red specks of paint, and the aircraft was a dayglo orangey-red. I remember seeing all this paint coming past me under the water, but I never clicked as to what it was. Whether I was going in the right direction or further away I'll never know. There were two men in one aircraft and one in the other and all three were killed. We eventually found them: it was the first time I'd come across a dead body.

That was when I learnt about the force of very quick deceleration. I was on the surface of the water when one of the first pilots was brought up. The pilot's green suit and helmet were intact but he had lost his flying boots. The next one came up and his boots were gone as well. I couldn't understand why these boots – which came halfway up the shin – had come off. It wasn't until later, when I talked to the police and the fire brigade, that I learnt it was the same with car crashes. For some reason the massive deceleration force makes the feet and legs contract and the shoes or boots come off. Those situations were quite clinical compared to what I've seen since. There was no blood or apparent injury. When somebody drops two hundred feet down a cliff and lands headfirst, they don't land in the best position, nor in the best of states. That's the nastier side of it simply because it's so messy. Training can't prepare you for everything but it can help you into a clockwork motion where you just get on with it. Over the years I've learnt that, no matter who is picked up, it's better not to think of them as a person, but as an object that's got to be treated as such. It's very much like a fighter pilot who can't stop to think that the guy sitting inside the aeroplane he's going to shoot down is a human being. The personality side of it is taken away. Luckily, I've never had to pick up anybody I've known.

Sometimes it's not until later on that the shock of a rescue operation hits you. Probably the worst case for me was in 1989. A person had gone over a cliff and hit his head on a big rectangular stone at the bottom, corner on, from a height of two hundred feet. There was an inquest later where people were trying to pin the blame. They wanted to find out whether this person had been drinking beforehand – which we knew he had. The coroner wants all the details at the inquest but when the family is sitting there, you don't want to describe it all too graphically. However, you're forced to.

Another time we were second crew out in St Austell Bay. The first crew had been scrambled to look for a boat that had been overdue and sank. There was the father, the uncle and a three-year-old toddler with no life-jackets or anything like that. They'd gone out in one of these little pleasure motor-type boats, which had a massive engine on the back end. They opened the engine up when they were out at sea and the transaxle had completely ripped away because the wood was so rotten and the engine too powerful. They all got out of the boat and the father had hold of the little boy but then something started going wrong. The father's story was that he couldn't swim because the child started sliding down his leg, and so he couldn't tread water. He let go of his son for literally a second to try and get his trousers back on and the little lad disappeared.

The first aircraft was out there searching, and although they'd picked up the father and the uncle they couldn't find the young lad, so we went out and relieved them. Within five minutes we spotted him just under the surface of the water. That's not a slight against the other crew, we happened to be lucky because it's extremely difficult to find somebody in the sea. I went into the water, grabbed him, got him up and into the aircraft. We actually got him breathing again. It was brilliant. He was coughing and breathing very, very slowly, but breathing. Within five minutes, however, he stopped breathing again. I don't know why, but for some reason I've got an image of this little kid's sandal on his foot which always stays in my mind. Although they kept him on a life-support machine for a few hours, he unfortunately died.

The problem with the sea is that a lot of people can die of secondary drowning. Once they've taken water into their lungs, you can get out as much as possible, but the salt will stay there. Through osmosis, the salt will just pull the fluid from the tissue straight back into the lung, so the person drowns. I believe that's what happened to this young lad. They didn't have life-jackets on, which to me is criminal. Situations involving children can be heart-breaking, especially when it is a case of parents' lack of forethought. People don't think it will happen to them.

It's a tribute to the Royal Navy that the instruction we're given when we're young is enough to pull us through. When things start going wrong or just become sheer hard work, you don't think about it. You just get on with it and it works. A lot of people seem to think the services work like clockwork but it's not quite like that.

The *Muree* went down on 28th October 1989. I was on Second Crew that day, so at 8.30 am I was going to my stand-by position on a bleeper on the end of the phone. It was very, very windy and there was a bit of a job already going on. We could hear what was happening on the radio. The first pilot of that day's duty crew came in and sat down. We were mucking around like we often do when there's a wind up, and I told him I'd see him later on. He said, 'What do you mean?' I said, 'There's going to be a big job today!' He said, 'Yeah, yeah,' and off I toddled home.

I had a perfectly average day at home although it was blowing a hooley. I went out to walk the dogs around and watch the village football team playing.

The goalkeeper took a goal kick and because it was blowing a gale the ball ended up as a corner. This really tickled me. The next thing I knew the bleeper went off. Typically, I was nowhere near a telephone so I had to tear up the road in my Barber jacket and wellies a mile and a half to the telephone at home.

When I got in I learnt that the crew had been scrambled to a ship with about fourteen people on board but they needed a second aircraft just in case. I can remember diving into the car – my daughter Nathalie, who was two-and-a-half then, must have sensed the stress because she was crying, 'Daddy! Daddy!' I never leave the house without kissing them because it upsets them.

It took about three or four minutes to get to the squadron. One of the pilots was already there so we started making the phone calls. The Rescue Coordination Centre at Plymouth wanted to know if we had the second aircraft ready. We replied that we were just collecting the crew and they said, 'Right. There are forty people on board, not fourteen.' It was a totally different ball-game. Organized panic and hell let loose.

We have seats for ten passengers in our helicopters but we took a lot more. The first aircraft was on its way with 'Shiner' Wright on it. Everyone had arrived except for Stevie Dodd, the crewman. We couldn't get hold of him anywhere. He didn't answer his bleeper or his phone. Unfortunately for Steve, he'd gone to Texas Homestores that afternoon. They reckoned that the metal building shielded his bleeper from going off.

It's a tribute to the lads on Search and Rescue that, when we had a ring round, the first crewman I came to didn't hesitate: 'Nige, it's Wally. We've got a problem. There's a ship going down with a lot of people on board. Get your backside in.' He said, 'Yep. No sweat.'

So while Nige was coming in we were doing the planning: ascertaining the definite position of the ship, how many people on board and also getting the kit ready for the spare aircraft. We knew it ran south of Start Point because another aircraft was by now over the ship. It took us about thirty-five minutes to get there.

As we got overhead the front mast was down and she was taking waves over her bow. *Marie* was a freighter of 17,000 tons carrying railway spares and engineering equipment. The front of her was just crammed full of transport containers which are picked up by lorries. We think she had either hit something or that one of her hatches had come open and she had taken on water.

The first aircraft had winched off ten and the 772 squadron aircraft had taken 17 which left 13 to be picked up. My mate was already on the deck and had been helping to offload the crew. I decided to go down to help him. While I was sending the crew up, two at a time, Steve went up to the bridge and sent off a 'sit rep'. He could see that the ship was sinking and told them so. But we were confident we could get them off. We had got down to the last four when the ship started to go nose down. There was then an explosion and we reckoned the bulkheads had started to cave in. We got two more off. Then just as the strop came back she gave another lurch, but we managed to get the last two off. As the winch hook came back down for Steve and me the ship suddenly went up 60 degrees, nose down. Nige realised the hook wasn't going to reach us in time, so he signalled to us from the chopper to jump. I looked at Steve and he looked at me. I shouted, 'I'll see you on the other side.'

I saw that I had a clear area and then looked up at the aircraft and thought, 'Bloody hell! This is high.' It was ninety feet above the water. I just launched myself and jumped. We had different life-jackets on; I had taken an aircrew life-jacket because I didn't expect to be in the water. Shiner wore a diving type. As Shiner jumped, he lost his balance a bit and started windmilling with his arms. Just as he hit the water he was on the upstroke and a wave wrenched his arm. He didn't notice until a lot later on. I didn't even see him. I was on my way down watching the water get closer and closer. I hit the water and went under – which of course you expect. It went from white to green to black. I then decided to inflate my life-jacket so I pulled the inflation tube and the jacket just went limp on me. One of the reasons divers stopped using them is that they didn't inflate below seven or eight metres because the pressure in the bottles isn't enough to cope with the sea pressure. I realised I was about twenty-five feet under the water. I started kicking towards the surface. I was wearing training shoes because they're better on the deck than flying boots.

As you get closer to the surface the pressure comes off so the air starts expanding. My life jacket inflated so I came bursting to the surface. As I surfaced I could just about touch the ship and see it going past my shoulder. I was fascinated because it was clearly sinking. I don't know how but I found myself facing the ship. I looked up and all I could see was the back end towering above me. A stupid thing which ran through my mind was the old black and white film of the *Titanic* going down with the band playing. One of the last shots of that film is the back end of the ship as she's going down. It's amazing what your brain does at times of stress. Everything slows down.

My life jacket was fully inflated by then but since I knew I had to try and swim away from the ship, I had to get all the air out of it. At this point I thought, 'Oh sod it! Once too often – you have blown this.' I was watching the ship and I just stopped. It frightens and annoys me now that, once I had given up, I accepted the inevitability so readily. I remember looking up and saying, 'Sorry, Carol. Say goodbye to the kids for me.'

It gives me a lump in my throat even now. That was it, I was ready to accept it. Then suddenly I thought, 'Bollocks to this! You're not getting out of it this easily.' I turned on my front to try and swim but, because I was wearing socks and training shoes, I couldn't paddle the water properly. I stopped again and took my shoes off and started to pull my socks off but realized that I wasn't as far away from the ship as I should have been. I turned and swam like hell. Luckily for me and Shiner the sea was going away from the ship. I went some distance when something compelled me to watch the ship sinking. I reckoned I was far enough away so I stopped, turned around and watched her disappear under the water. I thought, 'Oh God. This is brilliant!' The water was being spouted up in plumes. Then I remembered the stories I'd read about ships in the Second World War, dragging everything behind them. So I swam for it, then suddenly the winch hook appeared right in front of me. While all this had been going on the boys in the aircraft were still working, terrified for us. I was never so glad to see a bit of metal in all my life. I grasped it and hooked myself on, looked up at the aircraft and signalled that I was all right. Nige and I made eye-to-eye contact over about forty or fifty feet. He looked as if he was going to winch me straight in and I motioned to him to stop. With my eyes and hands I was saying, 'Where's Shiner? Where's Shiner?' He obviously realised that I was all right but that I didn't know if Shiner could be injured or unconscious.

Nige stopped the winch. The wind and the twist in the winch wires turned me so I could see Shiner about twenty or thirty yards away. I hadn't been able to see him in the water because of the sea state. Nige took me over and put me in the water beside Shiner, who was all right. Between the two of us we both managed to get hooked on, gave the thumbs-up and got lifted out of the water. We just burst out cheering and laughing like a pair of kids – that was the adrenalin. The aircraft was topped up by now with ten people and the rest of the crew. There weren't enough seats for everybody. As we got into the aircraft I saw a couple of the crew sitting opposite the doorway whose eyes were like dinner plates after watching what we'd been through. I was standing there in my socks with no helmet on because I'd left it on board. If you go on a ship you take your helmet off to enable you to talk to people and then put it back on afterwards. When all this happened I couldn't be bothered with my helmet. I'd love to go down to that ship and see if my helmet is still in the same place. hours later. I didn't sleep properly for about two months after that. I used to wake up in a sweat, even crying a couple of times.

I went to work the following Monday morning and the press had really got hold of it by then. It had happened at about five o'clock on a Saturday night and so it had missed all the Sunday deadlines. It turned out that one of the Esso vessels which we'd asked to stand off had been taking photographs of it all. This was spread all over the news and then the TV cameras hit us and dragged us, quite willingly, off to Plymouth to appear on a show.

I received some nice letters from people and the RAF sent us a signal saying, 'Brilliant job. Well done.' There's always been this battle between the

RAF and the Navy, but really we think a lot of each other even though we take the mickey. One of the other squadrons who were nothing to do with Search and Rescue wrote a letter to the boss saying, 'These boys are what the Navy's for.'

A lot of people have heard about what one of the survivors wrote on his life-jacket on the way back. I still can't believe that the guy did this. I don't know whether he thought of it or learnt it as a kid, but what he wrote on the jacket and got them all to sign was this: 'To the angels who come in the guise of men. They have been chosen to perform the most profound of God's gifts – to save life. You are what the world's made for.'

THE GULF

LIEUTENANT-COMMANDER DAVID LIVINGSTONE, RN

I became flight commander of HMS *Gloucester* in early 1900, flying the Lynx helicopter. My observer was Martin Ford, otherwise known as Florrie. He is quite an adventurous sort of guy, very sociable and cavalier. In the air he had a lot of zip and fire, whereas I'm probably more reserved. This combination worked well; a bit of thinking and working things out, with that extra bit of spark and bravado. That Easter Florrie and I carried out a number of exercises together and built up a very good relationship. We had also formed an outstanding maintenance/deck crew of eight, led by Chief Petty Officer Paul Leeper, and the Joss – MAA Boyce. This great bunch were all masters of their trades – Florrie and I were lucky to have them in close support.

Coincidently, the *Gloucester* was due to go to the Armilla Patrol as the Gulf guardship anyway, so all the necessary aircraft equipment modifications for the hot weather and particular threats in the Gulf were fitted before September. When Iraq invaded Kuwait on 2 August, everything was brought forward. During this period my wife and I were enjoying our first holiday alone together for some years when we were interrupted by a phone call. I had to fly to Farnborough the following day to test some satellite navigation modifications. The urgency gave me a positive jolt – there was a sudden charge in the air and I realised that we were preparing for war.

The ship worked up in the Portland training areas and South West Approach for a short while. Then we sailed off around Gibraltar, across the Mediterrean and to Cyprus. Every day the tension was building, especially since we only had a very vague idea of how the military strategy in that area was progressing. We didn't have access to any daily papers so we were relying in large part on the World Service for information.

Sailing down the Red Sea, I had to fly into Jedda Airfield to pick up a spare part for our Vulcan Phalanx weapons system. It was a nightmare experience flying straight into air traffic control who didn't speak English and our helicopter navigation system was unaccountably inoperative. I flew over the eastern side of the huge airfield where the US Air National Guard was stationed with its KC 135 tankers. The enormity of the military presence there for the first time brought home the scale of military effort that was being prepared.

We were constantly receiving additional bits of kit, like infra-red camera systems and satellite navigation systems, literally as they were coming off the production line. There were tested at home and sent straight out to us, so we were trialling them on route; we were also getting up to speed with our weapon loading drills.

We sailed around Saudi Arabia, into the Arabian Gulf and more or less straight into the Maritime Interdiction Operations where we began patrolling the south-eastern end of the Gulf. The ship was given ten-mile square boxes to patrol. We, in the helicopter, did more long range work, depending on shipping traffic density. There were a lot of tankers which we had to investigate taking their names and interrogating them about their cargoes and destinations. Naturally some of them were less than cooperative.

We were in an operational theatre for the first time so there was a great temptation to fly too much. I don't think I got the balance right overall, I wanted to get the hours in the log-book before 'peace was declared' after which I'd be back to the peacetime norm. That went against us in the end, because by the time the shooting war actually started we were already fairly tired.

We used some of the time working up with the American helicopters, Sea Hawk SH60Bs from the USS *Bunker Hill* and the Aegis Class cruisers. We developed a cooperative tactic. The SH60B had an extremely competent aircrew, navigation kit and radar but no missiles or weaponry except for a solitary machine-gun. We, however, had air-to-surface missiles and our navigation radar kit was good enough, so we would conduct our own independent search operations but the Americans, with their better capability, would get better intelligence flow of information. Consequently they could just radio us if they needed us to engage a target they had detected.

Our American counterpart was the flight commander of the USS *Bunker Hill*, Jeff Reizinger. When I was talking to Jeff Reizinger once, he said to me, "My grandpa did World War II, my pa died in Vietnam, now this is my goddam war." Although when the *Gloucester* went off task for our stand-offs we'd hand over the development of the tactic to other British ships.

The flagship was HMS *London* whose staff aviation officer, Lieutenant Commander Collins, just let me get on with the job. Commodore Paul worked for our Commander Task Group, Commodore Christopher Craig, who was outstanding throughout as our godfather figure. He really looked after British interests, British lives and British risk. He was firm enough with the Americans to protect our proportional input and was universally respected as the ideal man for the job.

Progressively, through November and December, our patrol areas moved northwards and then came to a stop. I desperately wanted to start flying much further north off the Kuwait coast to survey the battleground. We started off twenty-nine north, which took us a little bit further than Bahrain and then, I think, to 29 degrees, 30 minutes north, but that was as far as they ever allowed us before shooting started and all this time a single Iraqi Type 43 minesweeper was laying mines close to Kuwait which would eventually cripple the USS *Princeton* and USS *Tripoli*.

The ship's Company were training hard with weapon drills, using the Lynx we regularly did an exercise with one helicopter flying as fast as possible against the ship to simulate Exocet. We would compress the time-scale so, essentially, the ship would have its radars turned right down until a safety officer saw us coming in at fairly close range. So everyone had to do injections as fast as they could. This drill would prove vital when the ship shot down the Silkworm – the Ops Room guys fingers were well-honed by that time.

We spent Christmas in Abu Dhabi, but our regular stop was a very neat little dockyard in Jebel Ali, and this turned into a miniature naval base. The harbour gradually began to fill up with more and more of the Royal Navy, and it became quite inspiring to watch more frigates, another tanker and Hunt Class minesweepers come in until there was quite an imposing collection. Christmas was a very poignant moment and a number of tears were shed during the day. I think many of us were wondering if we would see another Christmas, although, ultimately, nothing would be sure until two o'clock in the morning on 17 January.

In the lead-up to the war the *Gloucester* was in the midst of it. Drifting mines were being discovered, so the Lynx was carrying out regular mine searches, each time clearing an area of box of ten miles square. Looking for those floating mines was annoyingly tedious, but luckily we could tune into the World Service on our HF sets. We'd be conducting a mine-search with the UHF tuned into the ship, and the HF into the World Service.

And 17 January came along. We had two hours notice of the opening of hostilities. At about midnight on the 16th HMS *Gloucester* and HMS *Cardiff* came up into a line east to west approximately fifty miles north of Bahrain, along with four American ships, including the USS *Bunker Hill*. At about twenty to three the first cruise missile was fired.

It was a stunning night with visibility reaching for miles; a starlit panoply. Then in amongst this raw nature I saw the first cruise missile going from the line of ships. They salvoed these things, firing five to six off in fifteen to thirty seconds, and taking a few minutes to break in between. To begin with a few of the ship's company stood and cheered on the upper decks, shouting, 'Hooray!' or 'That one's for you, Saddam,' and worse, much worse. That show of bravado stopped very quickly, as the enormity of the situation dawned on the revellers.

The ship went into action stations about three hours later, anticipating a reaction of some sort, which didn't come. The first flights in war are very different from any other flight. The Lynx was tasked to go and pick up a spare part from *Cardiff* which was a hundred miles away on the other side of the Gulf. Of course, by that time, the visibility had deteriorated to about three kilometres. We knew that there were a lot of fingers on triggers by this time so we were flying around thinking very much of the good old blue on blue accident. The adrenaline was rushing; communicating with the ship, telling my position, careful not to buzz the American ship five miles away, thinking, 'Does he know who I am?' We were speeding back to the *Gloucester* with a little more confidence, when Florrie picked up a radar contact which we decided to go and investigate. We knew it wasn't one of ours, and all the merchant shipping had disappeared from the Gulf two days previously. When the last diplomatic mission had failed, the tankers had simply gone. We sped towards this tiny target – which could have been anything – and we found ourselves in our first real reconnaissance probe, 150 knots at about twenty feet above the sea. It was an Arab. dhow. By the time we got on top they were standing on deck waving white flags, as if surrendering and completely nonplussed.

The ship was now under the operational control of the Americans. Admiral Fogarty of the USS *Midway* was overall boss of the Gulf Naval forces, but the anti-surface warfare coordinator was in the USS *Paul F. Foster*. *Florrie* and I went to re-brief his staff, taking the helicopter and missiles with us to demonstrate our capability. All of a sudden they took a lot of interest. The Allies needed to be patrolling the waters further north because of a significant threat from fast patrol base coming out of the Kuwait and Iraqi waterways, Kuwait City, Mina Sa'ud and places like that, which could use oil rigs as cover before making a dash to their targets. There's a big belt of oil-rigs south-east of Kuwait City, including the Dhorra, the Hout and others which have given cover to this dangerous threat. If the enemy disappeared within that belt they'd be very different to pick out on radar again and could reappear only sixty miles from our ships, and with Exocet that's very bad news indeed. So we had to take the battle to the northern part of the Gulf, to get the enemy craft in the clear space between the coastline and oil-fields. It was a very tricky business, because on the map you see one or two oil-fields which are apparently aeronautically navigable, but in reality there are hundreds of rigs with disused well-heads poking up, which have been abandoned in the past, but could now possibly hide enemy with shoulder launched SAMS.

I persuaded USS *Paul F Foster* we should be moving northwards using patrol idea incorporating the integration with Sea Hawks. Once we'd proved we could fly up to the north and refuel on a couple of frigates they had around on the oil-rigs, we knew we'd have no problems. But it was very, very heavy on hours. I on occasion did seven hours forty-five in one sortie without getting out of the seat.

It was decided that the North Persian Gulf clearance operation was going to be Royal Naval Lynx, assisted by Sea Hawks and any other intelligence we could get together. The Americans loved this, because we'd just get on with it, and the *Gloucester* became responsible for programming the total Lynx effort. They gave the Lynx fleet, which now comprised of four aircraft from the *Gloucester, Cardiff, London* and *Brazen,* a set of grids which they wanted us to concentrate on, but essentially once we were up there, we were on our own. The Sea Hawks would give us the intelligence, if they had anything, but we were also talking to Nimrods, P3 Orions and anyone else that could help in our patrols. All this paid off on 29 January, at the time of Al Khafji when the aircraft from *Brazen* received information from the Americans that there was a convoy of small vessels looping around the coast. *Brazen* picked them up and we flew in to help. For some technical reason they couldn't get a lock on with their missile system, so eventually we took it on. Florrie and I fired the first missile of the campaign. The targets were only very small boats, carrying commandos or special forces, so we picked the biggest one. We fired at very short range from quite high up which was extremely uncomfortable because we felt very exposed being close to the enemy shoreline. We used the range of the missiles to our best advantage. Our missile did not hit our target, but it hit the water, just before impact with the boat. Analysis afterwards seemed to suggest that the target had been hit by shrapnel, but, in any event the aim had been achieved as the convoy broke for cover. *Brazen*'s aircraft got a missile off and there was a follow-on attack by RAF Jaguars, which arrived some time later. The convoy was decimated and scattered in different directions.

The real meat of the Lynx engagements came during the next few days with a friendly rivalry developing between *Cardiff* and the *Gloucester* as to who was going to get the next kills. By this time the *Gloucester* flight maintenance team was working full out. Those guys were living rough, sleeping when they could and constantly getting the aircraft ready for flight. The only time they had off was when I was airborne.

On 20 January we were doing a routine inspection of the aircraft, when we heard that the *Cardiff* Lynx had a hit, somewhere up the Umm Qasar waterway. I told the chief to hurry up and get us ready to get airborne, and pretty soon afterwards Florrie and I were up there through all the oil-rigs again, out into the clear water of the Persian Gulf which was becoming familiar territory to us. Florrie quickly spotted something out of place in the channel coming out of the Umm Qasar waterway. We told the ship by radio and thundered in to target at low level – visibility was only about 10 kilometres – and identified the ship as a TNC45; an Exocet-firing Kuwait ship which had been commandeered by the Iraqis. So we backed away, told the *Gloucester* and requested authorisation to open fire. Because of the Rules of Engagement in force we had to be very careful about not hitting our own side. We turned in and fired from well within the missile's maximum range and at a comfortable height. The first to go was the starboard missile and as I saw it fly away with it's booster ignited, but it seemed to be going in the wrong direction. It was so murky – the visibility must have been about five miles and we'd closed in on about three miles from the target, which was now directly ahead of the aircraft. The missile veered off five or ten degrees and I thought, 'Damn, it's a rogue missile.' I looked down and saw the missile heading towards the TNC45 so apparently it was a second ship on the nose of the aircraft, and it was the T43 minesweeper. We watched the missile as it hit home. The TNC45 subsequently sank – the first ship sunk in the Gulf War. We requested authorisation to fire again at the T43. We had range advantage and could do it at our leisure, and it was taking no evasive action. We later found out that the T43 burnt all the way through.

The PR advisor on the *Gloucester* had given us all hints about what to say to the media if we were ever successful, so when we were interviewed by the resident ITN team on board, Florrie came up with, 'I paddle the canoe,' (pointing to me, and 'He shoots the ducks.') Really all I wanted to do was go and debrief in the Ops room, dash down to my cabin and have one deep drag on a cigar. The media was very good in some respects – we were all agreed that it was vital for the Royal Navy – but on a personal level, when you're trying to focus, you don't really need it.

We reloaded and heard that *Cardiff* had now got a FPB57. We flew back up to the northern part of the Gulf where Florrie picked up another bunch of contacts: he seemed to have a nose for it somehow. We found one of these contacts on closing it, another TNC45. We asked for permission to fire which was duly given and away went two missiles. One hit the bridge area of the TNC45 and the next one went into the mid superstructure. That was our third successful engagement in one day.

I was sent to *Cardiff* who'd sailed north to get closer to the action. I remember that the captain of *Cardiff*, Commander Adrian Nance, met Florrie and I in the hangar and said, 'David, this is a great day for the Royal Navy, and for the Fleet Air Arm in particular.' Despite the rivalry between the two ships, it was a very moving time. We took one more trip up to the north with now new targets, during which time the *Brazen* Lynx had retired and been sent down south.

We went back to *Gloucester* and started to listen to it all on the World Service. It was a bit like watching an old film; 'This is the BBC Home Service. Today heavy engagements have been carried out in the North Persian Gulf. Enemy have been destroyed, there are no reported losses to friendly forces.' It was strange to think we were all personally involved in it.

The following day we were stooging around our usual stamping grounds again when a call came in requesting us to participate in a combat search and rescue mission looking for Iraqi survivors from the day before. We had dreaded being tasked on this type of mission because it meant going in rather closer to the enemy than we would ever have chosen to. We joined an airborne task force of two US Navy Sea King helicopters.

We decided there wasn't enough going on at the scene of the rescue so we went off and started our own patrol. Doing this we picked up a radar contact. We closed in on this and out of the gloom came the third TNC45. We asked the US Commander if there was any friendly contact in our area and the reply came back 'negative'. I requested permission to open fire and we delivered two missiles at it. We didn't see the first explosion, the second missile most certainly went in.

We were invited on board the USS *Nicholas* to meet their delighted captain. His ship had been patrolling a very exposed area around the oil-rigs so he was very keen to have every single threat removed. He let us into the hangar as we landed and said, 'Well done, 410.' They gave us free steak and chips which we ate as we flew back to the *Gloucester* – 100 miles to the south.

I don't think we could have done any better than we did in this series of engagements, that some would call the battle of Bubiyan Island. We could have done with more missiles closer to the action. If we had had a ship with a magazine of Skuas in the northern part of the Gulf, hidden amongst the rigs where the American frigates were, we would have killed our contacts so much quicker.

We carried on patrolling but our movements became more controlled. We were employed less flexibly than we had been, which was disappointing. Mines were becoming a bit of a problem and we were all getting very tired by that time. We flew over a hundred hours in January, in fact, in the whole of the seven months of the ship's Gulf War deployment we were in the air for over three weeks.

As part of the Allied plan, the Gulf naval forces were to poise for amphibious landings on the coast around Kuwati City. Even if the landings never went ahead, the presence of the Task Force would draw Saddam's attention away from the western desert, where the Allied punch was aimed.

The move north finally came and I've never seen anything like it. It seemed like the convoy to end all convoys. Battleships, carriers and other ships; it was awe inspiring flying down the line of them. We were in real minesweeping territory, and we had to protect the minesweepers which had turned, essentially, into capital ships – without them the campaign could not proceed. I remember the morning when USS *Tripoli* and USS *Princeton* were both hit by mines within about an hour of each other. The effect that these had on people was quite salutory.

Once we were allocated a target just off Kuwait City. We had great difficulties locking up our radar for some reason – they system wasn't particularly happy. It was about one o'clock in the morning and we had to circle around three or four times before we got our first missile away. It flew as advertised but we didn't see the explosion because it was dark. From what we knew on previous attacks, explosions were without flash or flame. It was the first time we'd fired at night – you have to keep one eye shut and hope for the best. We fired a second one at the same contact just to make sure, but when we did, air defence batteries in Kuwait City fired two SAM missiles at us. By manoeuvring the aircraft hard we avoided these but it was a close call.

In the early hours of 25 February the Iraqis fired a double Silkworm salvo at the naval task group from a site at Al-Fintas, south of Kuwait City. The first malfunctioned and ditched straight away. The second was probably targeted on the flash of the battleship *Missouri*'s guns. I don't believe it was ever going to hit its probable target, USS *Missouri*, but the *Gloucester*'s missile crew only had a small radar contact coming off the coast, and about a minute-and-a-half at that short range to destroy it.

The first inkling I had of it was when I was woken from a catnap. It was difficult to sleep properly because of all the adrenaline. I heard the hydraulics pump of the Sea Dart system start up with its high-pitched whine from the bowels of the ship. I jumped out of bed and was pulling on my boots when I heard the bang and whoosh from the Sea Dart, then repeated. I stumbled down to the flight deck but realised that the helicopter was powerless to do anything from that range anyway. The atmosphere was quite relaxed because there was nothing more anyone could do. You can't get airborne in one minute flat so we went down and looked into the blackness at the enormous shape of the battleship *Missouri*. In between us was the American self-defence flare floating on the water. Its heat is supposed to attract missiles. The battleship continued to loom in the distance and we realised that we'd shot the Silkworm down. A lookout had seen its sodium flare and watched it fall. Undoubtedly it was a bloody good shot.

The whole team had been outstanding. That same morning the *Gloucester* finally went off task. We had been up there in the north for such a long time and were all relieved to head off down south. The Americans were effusive about everything the Royal Navy did – over the moon about Sea Skua and thrilled with the accuracy of Sea Dart.

On the way back to the U.K. I felt tired and strange. It was the decompression from adrenaline, and fatigue. The aircraft was in a bad way because we'd had to let a lot of non-essential maintenance go. We later discovered a few cracks and other problems, but we had flown her the way an aircraft should be flown. She was a credit to Westlands and amongst others a very good aeroplane herself. The only time she broke down was when the starter button for the No.1 engine gave way through metal fatigue and dropped into the bottom of the aircraft.

None of it really comes back to me now. Only the smell of diesel, as if from an oil slick, will instantly conjures up images from that most exciting time. I didn't really see the enemy face to face – only one dead Iraqi face down in the water. They say we took out the entire fighting part of the Iraqi Navy with no fixed wing from America or the RAF. In the wider picture, the allied Navy group, of which Florrie and I were but a part, made quite a contribution to the Gulf War. The American carriers provided a considerable amount of bombing power, but in the end, the whole group helped the land campaign by taking Saddam's eye off the ball. Flexibility and sea power going hand in hand as usual.

LIEUTENANT STEVE MARSHALL, RN

When Iraq invaded Kuwait we were put on 72-hours' notice. We were always going to go out there, but, quite rightly, the Superintendent of Diving argued that we would be better off training in the UK rather than going out there. We actually arrived at Christmas 1990. Each of the three units of the Fleet Diving Group had a different role: my unit, half of which had to remain behind because of its United Kingdom commitment, were to counter any terrorist threat to the Royal Navy ships. We did that initially when we were at Jebel Ali in the United Arab Emirates. However, once the ships had sailed there was no threat anymore. So we then formed up with another part of the Fleet Diving Group which had come out and were basically responsible for airborne EODs – Explosion Ordnance Disposal, and mine clearance. We were part of the advance force which along with the American and Australian divers, would clear the shallow water in the event of an amphibious force going in. We were based on RFA *Sir Galahad* which had two SeaKing Mark 3s that had had their sonar stripped out of them. We had a team of twenty-four when a buoyant mine was spotted, and we would jump out of the helicopter and swim down on to the mine and dispose of it.

When the Iraqis started firing missiles at us all the ships did a strategic withdrawal. We went out about fifty miles and then turned around and came back in at night. We were right next to USS *Tripoli* and the *Princetown* and we were within a mile of them when they were both mined. I was on the bridge of *Sir Galahad* and for no particular reason was looking through binoculars at *Princeton* when I suddenly I saw this huge plume of water underneath her stern and almost instantaneously another one about quarter of a mile ahead of her. This explosion lifted her about six or seven feet out of the water. That was quite a sight. She ended up being towed out to Bahrain. *Tripoli* had been mined earlier and we put some divers onto her hull. We found a twenty by thirty foot hole in her bow caused by a locally made Iraqi mine which probably cost $100 to make! Had it gone off twenty feet further aft, she would probably had been in very serious danger. It just goes to show how cheap it is to do millions of dollars of damage to a ship. More to the point it slows everything up: you have to decide how much risk you can take with a ship. We also cleared some oil rigs which the Iraqis had taken over and cleared them of unexploded ordnance.

On the day of the surrender, when Kuwait was liberated, we moved ashore to Ash-Shuwaiba, the main port to the south of Kuwait city. Under the command of an American commodore we started clearing all the harbours, jetty installations and beaches of unexploded ordnance. There was a lot of Iraqi ordnance everywhere, unexploded bombs, damage from coalition air attack, it was just a mess. That was a tough time because we were living in metal containers on the dock where the Iraqis had been living in a few days earlier. We lived off American army rations for a while before getting some from our own ships.

The whole time was dominated by the blackness from the oil fires: in the middle of the day you needed headlights on the vehicles. At the end of the day we returned filthy, black. One of our team had fixed up a water heater and a makeshift shower and a huge barrel that you would sit in and have hot water poured over you. Then you got scrubbed down – almost like the old cowboy films! The worst working conditions came on land where you would be breathing in the fumes. Inside your nose and around your eyes would be black, and your eyes would stream from the pollution. Most days we dived as long as we could, sometimes eight to ten hours at a stretch. It was absolutely black: we had to go through six inches of glutinous crude oil. I had never dived in oil like that before. Because oil rots everything we had to clean the equipment in about three different solutions each time we came out. However it didn't interfere with the breathing equipment, although the shit and filth in which we had to work, as well as the unknown danger, did drain morale. Down in the bottom of the harbours were a number of dead bodies in varying states of decomposition. Crawling along the bottom you can't see two inches in front of you and suddenly you come across a body. The young lads had to deal with that which was not easy.

Another difficulty came from random gunfire by Palestinians sympathetic to the Iraquis. At the same time we had teams out in the surrounding area clearing beaches: there were a lot of anti-ship mines that had been washed up. To get to them you had to crawl through anti-personnel minefields clearing with a bayonet just like the old days, only then could you counter-mine or take the larger anti-ship mines apart.

A lot of the Kuwaitis wanted to return to their destroyed homes. So we were called on to clear them of Iraqi ordnance. The Iraqis leaving in a hurry would sometimes leave a grenade with its pin out between a stack of boxes of mortar rounds. So you had to be careful: you didn't move anything before you searched for booby traps. We also cleared a number of huge Kuwaiti tankers that had been commandeered by the Iraqis and had been hit by coalition missiles which hadn't gone off. We had to make them safe.

The whole fourteen weeks was very exhausting. The days were long and at the end the officers and senior NCOs needed to attend briefings with the commodore and compile necessary paperwork. That was the other biggest thing – constant work without any break, no relaxation. We had had very little rest for weeks. However on one occasion I sent about eight of the guys down to Bahrain for a couple of days in an RAF Hercules. A few people's tempers did get frayed during this time and there were a couple of instances which ended up with disciplinary problems. But these things happen. I found the biggest challenge was keeping the morale of the young guys going: we had been around longer – seen it, done it – but some of the young lads didn't look at it that way. They started to ask questions, 'When are we going home?' and, 'Is there any danger for us doing this?' That was a big challenge from a leadership point of view, keeping these guys doing the job. The satisfaction I derived was that we did the job and came out of there without having lost anyone.

Throughout my time out there, although I was only a lieutenant, I was elevated to a position of higher responsibility. It's a once in a lifetime's chance that you get. Senior officers would come ashore to see me to ask my opinion on how we were going to do something: as a lieutenant you don't normally get that. I was honoured to be in that position. No doubt we made some mistakes and looking back I can think of things I would have done differently. But expediency was also dominant.

The thing with explosive ordnance disposal is that your fate is entirely in your hands: if you do your job properly and take all the precautions necessary, in theory you won't be killed. The unexpected, of course, can always happen.

But it is a bit different from a soldier advancing on a position, he is in the hands of God.

The satisfaction for me was that once again the Royal Navy got out there, did the job and, in my view, did it on all counts better than any other navy that was there. We were a very small part of the American force; but from the naval point of view, be it from the mine hunters to the divers, to the destroyers, to the Lynx helicopters that were sinking all the Iraqi gun boats, we did better than anyone else. And I don't think anyone will ever do it better than us. The Americans might fly aircraft off carriers better than we do, but that's only because they've got them; but with regard to doing specialist tasks, we're as good as anyone.

Finally we were relieved and, like so many others before me, I arrived back at Portsmouth. My father served forty-five years in the Royal Navy and, although I have left the service, I still feel an immense pride. My son is going to join and I'm very proud of that.

Envoi

It is often said that sailors are sentimental beings, and there is a good deal of truth in the saying. But those that go down to the sea in ships are frequently cut off from life on shore for long periods, so it is not surprising if their minds run on these lines. This may no longer be so true, however, in this age of instant and constant communication, and the innovations of modern technology. The modern sailor is a very different type from my day; he is far less cut off from the world and his family, and his interests are far wider. But basically I have every reason to believe that he is the same human being.

For over my years at sea I have seen God's creation in all its splendour and in all its fearful power. I have watched in silent awe the mysteries of the Northern Lights as they shimmered and swayed in great curtains of light across the sky; the colours glowing and fading and changing from rose to yellow to white and green and back again. Or shooting across the sky in shafts of brilliant white light like some gigantic celestial firework display. I have waited for and seen the 'green flash' which occurs in certain atmospheric conditions – mostly in the Caribbean – just at the moment when the sun sinks below the sea horizon.

What dawns and sunsets I have witnessed; what tropical nights, when the stars burned so brightly in the black canopy of the night sky that you felt that you could almost touch them. The Southern Cross and other constellations wheeled to and fro with the movement of the ship as the phosphorescence in the water lit up the bow wave.

What tropical storms I have encountered, when the lightning flashed and crackled frighteningly all around and the rain beat down with an intensity that sucked your breath away. And then as suddenly as it came it went; the wind dropped to a gentle breeze and the stars shone with a fresh intensity.

I have stood my watches in the fierce Atlantic and North Sea gales when the ship lunged and plunged into the great seas. Their wicked crests shuddered throughout its length as the bows lifted and the water surged aft to the break of the foc's'le, bending stanchions like putty and pouring down into the waist and along the decks. I have clung to the life lines as the ship rolled her decks under and the water boiled past and tugged at our legs. Fought it out as one did in destroyers, numb with the cold and soaked to the skin, the ship labouring and struggling like a living thing under you. And the only hot food you could take was soup or ship's cocoa from a bottle as you held on with one arm to some fixture, and then fished in your pocket for a damp ship's biscuit or a hunk of cheese.

I have listened to the growl of the pack ice as it grinds and heaves and the bitter wind blowing the top off the crests racing past, hurling the frozen spray in your face. Then when the decks iced up and life was grim with the ship battened down and little to choose between the conditions on deck and the foetid air below. We ran for days on 'dead reckoning' feeling our way clear of the deadly growlers; capsized icebergs with little to show of their presence except a drop of a couple of degrees in the sea temperature as we approached.

How I have battled with that most insidious enemy of all seafarers – fog. Fog in all its aspects: the slow forming mist which gradually thickened and trapped you into thinking it wasn't really too bad until you suddenly realised that you were in the thick of it; the equally inconspicuous sort that waited for you to enter its clammy folds and find yourself in its octopus-like grip; the great rolling banks of fog that advertised their advance as they bore down on you, giving you time to place your fog lookouts in the bows, at the masthead and on the bridge wings, and close the water-tight doors. Hours when one crept through a silent world of frustration; eyes and ears straining and nerves taut – broken every two minutes by the whoop of the ship's siren. Surrounded by the calls of the other shipping coming from seemingly all points of the compass; such is the distorting effect of fog. I was schooled in those North Sea and channel fogs as a youngster and I shall never forget them.

And I have memories of the clear blue water of the Mediterranean when in those far off peacetime days we would stop ship and pipe 'hands to bathe', and plunging over the side float on the buoyant water, 2,000 fathoms deep, rising and falling on the gentle swell.

So much beauty, so much power, given for man to see and experience and to feel the might of the Creator who controls all things. But for sheer splendour I have never seen anything to equal the blue moon that shone in the South Atlantic that day in 1941. 'Once in a blue moon', that hackneyed yet only half-understood expression was common in my youth. But for me, and for some of those with me who saw it that day, it was an unforgettable experience.

We were on our patrol line in latitude 40 degrees south, hundreds of miles from land, cut off from the world and out of W/T touch (except at intermittent intervals). We had no radar and our only companions were the sea birds, the occasional whale, the dolphins and the flying fish. Then one morning at about 0530 my buzzer went and I was called on deck. It was quite light – the sun was about to rise. And there it was – low in the sky – a full moon of the most wonderful blue; heavenly blue – azure, watchet, call it what you will, but serene and resplendent in the clear and cloudless sky. I stood there lost in wonder at the Creator who could order such things, while the ship ploughed her way through the long low swells of the great ocean. The colour faded in the rays of the rising sun, and I turned and made my way back to my cabin.

> Captain Brian de Courcy-Ireland, RN
> who saw action at the Battle of Jutland,
> served throughout the interwar years
> and the Second World War and in the
> time of peace.

Index

Ranks are shown as in the extracts, not necessarily the highest achieved by the speakers. References in **bold** are to the accounts by those writers/speakers included.

2 Para, in Falklands 362–3
8th Army 196–7
40 and 41 Commandos 195
42 Commando 358–9, 383
45 Commando 357–8, 359
617 Squadron, 5
806 Squadron 65
815 Squadron 65, 69
819 Squadron 65
825 Squadron 82, 95, 118
887 Squadron 274
894 Squadron 274, 275
897 Squadron 346

Abdiel, HMS 81
Achilles, HMNZS, 1, 29, 30, 31, 34, 35
Activity, HMS aircraft-carrier 219
Admiral von Scheer, German pocket battleship 4, 29, 33
Aitken, Lieutenant Bob 207
Ajax, HMS, cruiser at Battle of River Plate 1, 29, 30, 31, 34, 77
    at Dunkirk 46–7
    at Haifa 315–20
Alacrity HMS 371, 377
Albania 68
    mining British destroyers 308, 312–14
Albatross, HMS, seaplane-carrier 34
Albion, HMS, aircraft-carrier 308, 346
Albrighton, HMS destroyer 159
Alexander, Albert Victor, First Lord of the Admiralty 224
Alexandria (Egypt) 69, 70, 170
    and the French 6
    Italian submarines in 191
Algiers 191
Almeria Lykes, USS, sunk 142
Amethyst, HMS incident 308, 321–5
Ancon, USS 241

Antrim HMS, destroyer, 366, 367, 371
Ardent HMS, destroyer 371, 372–6
Arethusa, HMS, cruiser 54, 241
Argyll and Sutherland Highlanders 331, 332
Ark Royal, HMS, aircraft-carrier 6, 18, 52, 54, 275, 310
    sunk 100–2
Armilla Patrol 393
Ashanti, HMS, destroyer 57
Ashigawa, Japanese cruiser 270–1; sunk 271
Atheltemplar, tanker, hit 168
Atlantic Causeway 360
Atlantic Conveyor, hit 381
Avenger, HMS aircraft-carrier 164, 166, 167, 168, 169–70
Azerbaijan, Russian tanker 131; hit, 133

Baines, Captain Eddie **138–9, 151–2**
Balfour, Lieutenant-Commander 242
Ban Pong camp 292–3
Barenfels, merchant vessel, sunk 206
Barham, HMS, battleship 7, 97–8; sunk 98
Barker, Marine Noel **255–60**
Barnham, Able Seaman Thomas, RN **73–6, 260–2**
Belfast, HMS, cruiser 212
Belgrano (ex-USS *Phoenix*), sunk 310, 381
Bell, F S 'Hookie', captain, HMS *Exeter* 31, 33–4, 36, 37, 38, 39
Berguis, Sub-Lieutenant Adam 287, 288
Berkeley, HMS destroyer 159
Berrill, 'Dapper' 82, 83, 84, 85, 86
Birmingham, HMS, cruiser 326
Bishop, Marine Bill **61–4**
Bismarck, German battleship 4, 82, 87–9, 90–1, 94, 95–6, 102
Blacker, Marine Stan **234–6**
Bligh, Captain (*Bounty*), advice 71–2
Bodham-Whetham, Rear-Admiral 164

Index

Bombadiere, Italian destroyer 181
Bonaventure, HMS depot ship 284, 286
Bonham-Carter, Admiral Sir Stuart 129
Bonhomme Richard, French aircraft-carrier 347
Borneo 355–7
Boughton, Lieutenant John, RN **360–5**
Bowdrey, on *Waimarama* 136; death 142–3
Bramham, HMS destroyer 138–9, 139, 147, 150, 151–2
Brazen HMS 397, 398
Bretagne, French battleship, sunk 6, 55
Bridge, Lieutenant John **197–202**
Briggs, Sub-Lieutenant Ken 287
Briggs, Ted, *Hood* survivor 92, 93, 94
Briggs, Lieutenant-Commander T V, **278–83**
Brilliant, HMS, frigate 366, 367, 368, 369
Brisbane Star, merchant ship 154
Brissenden, HMS frigate 319
Britannia, merchant ship, sunk 70
British Dominion, tanker 189
Broadsword, HMS, frigate 368, 371, 381
Brooks, Sergeant Terry **102–3**, 109–10, **292–4**
brothels, sea-borne 264
Brown, Signalman Jack 'Buster' **241**
Brown, Surgeon-Lieutenant Maurice **110–15**
Bulwark, HMS, aircraft-carrier 308, 346
Bunce, Leading Airman Donald, Fleet Air Arm **117–21**
Bunker Hill, USS aircraft-carrier 394, 395
Burnett, Rear-Admiral Bob 165, 168

Cairo, HMS light cruiser 135, 139, 141; hit 140
Calcutta, HMS 7, 77; sunk 81
Caldwell, Surgeon-Lieutenant Dick **26–30, 103–9**
Cameron, Lieutenant Don, VC 205, 207
Campbell, Lieutenant-Commander C H 'Jock' 131
Canberra, liner 361, 376
Canning, Bill, captain, HMS *Broadsword* 381
Cape Matapan (Greece), battle 68, 69
Cardiff, HMS 395, 397, 398
Cardigan Bay, HMS frigate 318, 319, 327
Carey, Sub-Lieutenant David 283; death 284
Carlisle, HMS 77, 78
Chaplet, HMS, destroyer 344
Charybdis, HMS, cruiser 136
Cheviot, HMS, destroyer 317
Chieftain, HMS, destroyer 317
Childers, HMS, destroyer 317
Churchill, Winston 187
    and U-boats 4
    and Far East 8
    and French Navy 55
    on *Prince of Wales* 102–3
    about *Prince of Wales* 104
    across Atlantic on *Prince of Wales* 108
Clan Ferguson merchant ship 140; hit 141

Coles, Stoker 2nd Class Vernon **18**; Stoker 1st Class **54–5**;
    Engine-Room Artificer **202–6, 287–8**
commandos, Royal Navy 191
    at Tobruk 171
    Sicily 192–4, 195–7
    D-Day 236
Concord, HMS 325
Conqueror, HMS, submarine 310
Conrad, Joseph, quoted xv
Consolation, US hospital ship 332
Consort, HMS, destroyer 321, 323
Coppeard, Ordinary Seaman Dick, RN **43–4**
Corbet-Singleton, Lieutenant-Commander C H, RN **47–51**
Corfu 312–14
Corfu Channel 312
Courageous, HMS 18–26, 81; sunk 20, 24–7
Courcy-Ireland, Brian de, Captain, RN **315–20**
    quoted xv, 406–8
Coventry HMS 366, 367, 372; hit 381
Coward, Captain John **366–72**
Craig, Captain Chris 377, 394
Crete 7, 68, 76–81
Cricket, HMS 61, 234
Cullum, Leading Telegraphist Percy **97–9**
Cumberland HMS, cruiser 279
Cunningham, Admiral Sir Andrew 7, 65, 69, 78
    on Operation Overlord 232
    on tradition 312

Daring HMS, destroyer 338
D-Day 1944 7, 232–53
Decoy, HMS, destroyer 338, 343, 344
Deucalion, merchant ship, sunk 138(2), 139
Dieppe, operation at 156–60, 163, 195
Dillon, Able Seaman (Radar) John, RN **372–6**
Dolphin, HMS, Gosport 70, 202
Donitz, Admiral Karl 3, 4, 5
Doric Star 30
Dorset, merchant ship 147, 151; sunk 149, 151
Dreadnought, HMS, submarine 309
Duke of York, HMS, battleship 5, 177, 211, 212, 213, 300, 301, 302
Dundas, Midshipman, *Hood* survivor 92, 93, 94
Dundonald, HMS, Combined Ops headquarters 155–6
Dunkerque, French battle-cruiser 1, 55
Dunkirk 2, 44–51
Dunstan, Marine Peter, RM **109–10, 288–92**

Eagle, HMS, aircraft-carrier 6, 65, 66, 136, 275; hit 136–7
    at Suez 346, 352
Edinburgh, HMS, cruiser 126–30; sunk 130
Electra, destroyer 92–3

Index

Elizabeth II:
    Coronation 337
    Spithead Review 1953 308
Emile Deschamps, French auxiliary naval vessel
    50
Empire Beaumont, merchant vessel sunk 167
Empire Heywood, merchant vessel 316
Empire Hope, hit 141
Empire Rival, merchant vessel 316, 319
Empire Stevenson, sunk 167, 168
Emslie, Captain Hamish 344
Encounter, HMS, destroyer 40
Endurance, HMS 367, 382
Enterprise, HMS, cruiser 54
Escapade, HMS, destroyer 39–43
Escort, HMS, destroyer 40
Esmonde, Lieutenant-Commander Eugene
    82, 95, 118, 119, 120
Exeter, HMS 1, 9, 29–31, 32–5, 35–9
Exodus, see President Warfield
Express, HMS, destroyer 110

Falklands War 310, 360–86
Fame, HMS, destroyer 57
Faulknor, HMS, destroyer 18, 54–5, 166, 202
Fearless, HMS, destroyer 368, 371, 372, 382
Fell, Captain W.R. 284, 285, 286
Fiji, HMS, cruiser 7; sunk 78
Fiume, Italian cruiser 69
Fogwill, Able Seaman Len 31–4
Fonda, Henry 301
Forbes, Admiral Sir Charles 18
'Force Q' 176
'Force Z', to Far East 8–9, 104
Foresight, HMS, destroyer 128, 129–30
Forester, HMS, destroyer 128, 129–30
Formidable, HMS, aircraft-carrier 68
Fraser, Admiral Sir Bruce (later Lord Fraser of
    North Cape) 165, 211, 212, 283, 301,
    302, 332
Fraser, Lieutenant Ian 'Tich' VC 283–7
Frobisher, HMS, cruiser 81
Furious, HMS, aircraft-carrier 136
Fury, HMS, destroyer 126, 131

Gardiner, Able Seaman Eric 144–6
Gazelle aircraft 361, 362
Gibbs, Commander E A 174–6
Gibbs, Petty Officer Airman Roy 271–3
Gick, Lieutenant Percy 100–2
Giulio Cesare, Italian battleship 6
Glamorgan, HMS, destroyer 375
Glasgow, HMS, destroyer 366, 369–70, 371
Glenorchy, merchant ship 142
Glorious, aircraft-carrier 2, 51–3, 65
Glory, HMS, light fleet carrier 327, 336
Gloucester, HMS, cruiser 7, 311, 393, 395, 396,
    398, 399
    sunk 78

Glowworm, HMS, destroyer 2
Gneisenau, German battle-cruiser 2, 4, 34, 52,
    117, 121
Godetia, HMS, corvette 183
Goose Green, Falklands 362, 363
Gossamer, HMS, minesweeper 49, 50, 128,
    129
Gould, Petty Officer Thomas, VC 121–3, 125
Gower, Captain John 337–42
Graf Spee, German battleship 1–2, 29–31, 33,
    34, 35, 36
Graham, Bobby, commander, *Exeter* 30, 33,
    37
Graham, Harry, captain, *Escapade* 40, 41
Grenade, HMS, destroyer 48
Greyhound, HMS, destroyer 7; sunk 78
Grouper, USS, submarine 297
Gueritz, Acting Lieutenant-Commander
    Edward 236–8; Lieutenant 312–14
Gulf War 393–403
Gurkha, HMS, destroyer 110–15; sunk 115

Haguro, Japanese cruiser 9, 282–3
Halsey, Admiral William F 'Bull' 301
Harrier, HMS, minesweeper 126, 128
Harvey-Jones, Lieutenant John 176–9, 267–9
Harwood, Commodore (later Admiral Sir)
    Henry 1–2, 29, 30, 31, 34, 35, 37–8, 170
Havant, HMS, destroyer 49
Havelock, HMS, destroyer 183, 185
Haven, US hospital ship 332
Hawkins, Acting Leading Seaman Eynon, RN
    189–90
Hayward, Nurse Jackie, QARNNS, 382–6
Healey, Denis 310
'Hedgehog' weapon 3, 222
Hereward, HMS, destroyer 7
Hermes, HMS, aircraft-carrier 9, 310, 347,
    368, 369, 370, 377–8, 380
Hett, Sub-Lieutenant (*Amethyst*) 324, 325
Hezlet, Lieutenant Arthur 16–17, 42–3, 202–3,
    269–71
Higgins, Ordinary Telegraphist Alan 126–30;
    Telegraphist 249–52
Hill, Lieutenant-Commander Roger 130–5,
    135–6, 137–8, 141–2, 143, 144, 146–8,
    152–3, 232–4
Hinton, Petty Officer James 242–4
Hipper, German battle-cruiser 134
Hollander, Able Seaman Leslie 144–6
Hood, HMS, battle-cruiser 1, 54, 55, 76, 82,
    86–7, 89–95, 321
    sunk 4, 80, 87, 88, 89, 91, 102, 108
    survivor 89–95
    losses from 94–5
Horton, Admiral Sir Max 4, 216
Hotspur, HMS, destroyer 81, 99
Howe, HMS, battleship 9
Hughes, Captain J H B, RM 231–2

Index

Humphryes, Signalman Frederick, RN 55–7
Humphries, Commander (Flying) Pat 'Wings'
    275, 276, 277
Humphries, Corporal Joe 195–7, 214–15
Hunt, Petty Officer Alf, RN 294–300
Hunt, Able Seaman Jack 183–6
Hussar, HMS, minesweeper 128

Illustrious, HMS, aircraft-carrier 6, 65–6, 67,
    68
Imperial, HMS, destroyer 7
Implacable, HMS, aircraft-carrier 272
Impulsive, HMS, destroyer 26, 164–9
Indefatigable, HMS, aircraft-carrier 272(2),
    273–8
Indomitable, HMS, aircraft-carrier 8, 104, 136,
    139, 271–2
Intrepid, HMS, destroyer 371, 372
Invincible, HMS, aircraft-carrier 368, 372, 380
Iraq, invasion of Kuwait 311, 393, 400
    defeated 400
Israel, destroyer 176
Israelis, and Suez War 349, 350
Ivanhoe, HMS, destroyer 49
Izzard, Ralph, war correspondent 329

Jackal, HMS, destroyer 81
Jackson, Junior Radio Operator John, MN
    139–40, 143–4, 147, 154
Jackson, Lieutenant Pat 81–6
Jaguar aircraft 397
Jamaica, HMS, cruiser 211, 212, 213
Japan 8–9
    versus Repulse, Prince of Wales 103, 104,
        105–6
    prisoners-of-war in 299
    operations against 267–8, 300–2
    surrender 302
Japanese:
    prisoner-of-war camps 289–94, 295–6, 299
Jaunty ocean tug 135, 137
Jennings, Lieutenant-Commander Richard
    29–31, 34, 38
Jervis Bay, merchant cruiser 4
Jewell, Lieutenant Bill 186–9
John Penn, merchant ship, sunk 167
Johnson, Petty Officer Pilot 51
Johnson, Lieutenant Bill 215–24
Johnson, Petty Officer Dudley 352–5
Jolly, Surgeon-Commander Rick 376
Jones, Corporal Mervyn 355–7
Juno, HMS, destroyer, sunk 77
Junor, Lieutenant Bruce 46–7

Kamikaze aircraft 9, 272, 273, 274
Kandahar, HMS, destroyer 78
Kashmir, HMS, destroyer 7, 78; sunk 79
Keeper, Able Seaman Arthur 144–6
Kellett, HMS, minesweeper 50, 241

Kelly, HMS, destroyer 7, 78, 79
Kentucky, merchant ship, 168
Kenya, HMS, cruiser 139
Keppel, HMS, destroyer 131, 133, 134
Kerans, Lieutenant-Commander (Amethyst)
    323, 324, 325
Kimberley, HMS, destroyer 81
King, Alison 228–9
King George V HMS, battleship 4, 96, 165,
    272, 274
Kingston, HMS, destroyer 78
Kipling, HMS, destroyer 78, 79
Kite, HMS, sloop 216, 218, 219, 220, 221, 222
Korean War 308, 325–8, 328–33, 333–6
Kuwait, invaded by Iraq 311, 393
Kwai river 291–2, 293

Lafayette, French aircraft-carrier 347, 351
Lamb, Lieutenant Charles 18–26
Lancashire, Surgeon-Lieutenant Roger, RN
    34–8
Layard, Lieutenant Frank, RN 12–15
Le Bailly, Lieutenant (E) Louis 76–81
Leach, Lieutenant Henry 210–13, Admiral Sir
    310
Leander, HMNZS Cruiser 312, 313
Ledbury HMS, destroyer 130–9, 141–4,
    146–53
Leggatt, Captain W R 237
Leggott, Petty Officer Pilot 51–3
Leigh-Mallory, Air Vice Marshal Sir Trafford
    118
Leopard, HMS, frigate 352–5
Lewis, Chief Engine-Room Artificer Trevor
    170–4
Li Wo, HMS 123; sunk 124
Lightning, HMS, destroyer 174–5, 176
Linton, Commander 'Tubby', VC 180
Lisbon Maru, Japanese freighter 297–9
Littorio, Italian battleship 66, 67
Liverpool, HMS, cruiser, 61–4, 315
Livingstone, Lieutenant-Commander David
    393–400
Lloyd, Bandsman George 124–5
London, HMS, cruiser 394
Lovat, Simon Fraser, 15th Baron 237, 248
Lowe, Chief Petty Officer Bill 86–7
Lucas, Marine Andy 336–7
Lützow, German pocket battleship 204, 205,
    206, 207, 210

MacArthur, General Douglas 301, 302
Macbeth, merchant ship, sunk 167
McIntosh, Midshipman Ian, RN 69–73;
    Lieutenant-Commander, 229–30, 253–4
Mackenzie, Lieutenant 121
Magennis, Leading Seaman Jamie 'Mickie'
    285–6, 287, 288
Magpie, HMS 219, 220, 221, 222, 223

Index

Maine, HM Hospital Ship 314, 329–33
'Major Martin' (the Man Who Never Was) 187–9
Malcolm, HMS 164
Malta 5–6, 7, 135
Operation Pedestal 135–54
'The Man Who Never Was' 187–9
Manchester, HMS, cruiser 139, 142, 147, 149, 150
Marshall, Lieutenant Steve **401–4**
Martin, Ordinary Seaman Ronald **252–3, 320–1**
Mary Luchenbach, merchant ship, sunk 168
Mason, Captain Dudley, (*Ohio*) MN **140–1**, 142, **148–51, 154**
Massey Shaw, fire float 50
Matabele, HMS, destroyer 57
Mather, Derek 'Pug', RN 333–6
Mauritius, HMS 231, 312, 313
Melbourne Star, merchant ship, 146, 147, 148, 152, 154
Mercury, HMS, Portsdown Hill 163
Mers-el-Kebir *see* Oran
Micklethwaite, Captain 171, 172, 173, 174
midget submarines 5, 203–6, 206–10
in Japan 283–7
new flotilla 287–8
Midway, USS 396
Millin, Piper Bill 248
Mills, Lieutenant Donald, **346–52**
Missouri, USS, battleship 301, 311, 327, 399–400
Mogador, French destroyer 55
Monte Cassino, marines at 214–15
Montgomery, Field Marshal Viscount Bernard 240, 245
Moore, Captain (later General) Jeremy 355, 380, 382
Morgan, Sub-Lieutenant Ivor **275–8**
Morral, Commander Dennis 399
Mountbatten, Lord Louis, Captain, commander HMS *Kelly* 78, 79; in charge Combined Operations 191, 195; on *Duke of York* 300
Murree, merchant ship, rescue from, 389–92
Musgrave, Surgeon-Lieutenant 277
Myoko, Japanese cruiser 285, 286

Nachi, Japanese cruiser 288
Naiad, HMS, cruiser 76–81; hit 77–8
Nairana, HMS, aircraft-carrier 219–20
Naya, Sergeant, RAMC 365
Neath, Lieutenant Ronald **300–3**
Nelson, HMS, battleship 18, 135, 136, 139, 211
Newcastle, HMS crusier, 327
Newfoundland, HMS cruiser, 308, 342
Nicholas, USS 398–9
Nicholl, Commander Rowley 236

Nigeria, HMS, cruiser 139, 141; hit 139, 140
Nimitz, US Admiral Chester W. 9, 301, 302
Noble, Percy, captain of *Quentin* 176
Norfolk, Lieutenant-Commander Bob 116, 117
Norfolk, HMS, cruiser 88, 90–1, 212
Northern Ireland 357–9

Oakley, Captain Derek, RM **342–6**
Oakley, Able Seaman Ken **191–4, 244–9**
Ocean, HMS, light fleet carrier 314, 327, 336, 346
Ocean Vigour, merchant ship 319
O'Connor, General Sir Richard 6
Offa, HMS, destroyer 131, 132, 133
Ohio, tanker 135, 139–40, 142, 147, 148–54
Oliver Ellsworth, US freighter sunk 166
Onslow, HMS, destroyer 168
Operation 'Corporate' 310
Operation 'Dukedom' 279, 283
Operation 'Mincemeat' 187–9
Operation 'Mitre' 281, 282
Operation 'Mosaic I/II' 338–41
Operation 'Overlord' 231–253
Operation 'Pedestal' 135–54
Operation 'Round Up' 355–7
Operation 'Source' 206
'Options for Change', 1980s cuts 311
Oran, Mers-el-Kebir, and destruction of French Navy 6, 54–5, 90, 174–5
Oregonian, US freighter sunk 167
Oribi, HMS, destroyer 126
Orion, HMS, cruiser 64, 77, 81, 312
O'Riordan, Surgeon-Lieutenant 314
O'Toole, Able Seaman Peter, quoted 306

Paladin, HMS, destroyer 279
Palestine 315–20
Palomares, HMS anti-aircraft ship 131
Panther, HMS, destroyer 174–5, 175
Parry, W E, captain *Achilles* 31
Parsons, Leading Seaman Tom **123–4**
Pathfinder, HMS, destroyer 174
Patton, General George S 189, 259
Pearl Harbor 105
Pebble Island, SAS raid 381–2
Pedestal Operation, 135–54
Peerless, Corporal 345
Pegasus HMS, seaplane carrier, 28
Penn HMS, destroyer 139, 147, 149, 150, 151, 152, 153
Perth, HMAS cruiser 77
Philip, Prince of Greece (later Duke of Edinburgh) 303
Phillips, Admiral Sir Tom 8, 9, 106
Phoebe, HMS cruiser 81, 136
Pimpernel, HMS, corvette 183
Place, Lieutenant Godfrey VC 205, **206–10**, 283
prisoner-of-war 209–10
Plymouth HMS gunboat 366, 367, 372

Index

Port Adelaide, merchant ship 14–15
Port Chalmers, merchant ship 152, 154
Port Line 15–16
Port Said (Egypt), Marines at 342–6, 350
Pound, Admiral Sir Dudley 8
Pozarica, anti-aircraft ship 131
President Warfield, (later *Exodus*) 317–19
Prince of Wales, HMS, battleship 8, 82, 87–9,
    90, 102–3, 104–7, 109
    sunk 9, 103, 108–9, 109–10, 123, 288, 321
    disasters before commissioning 109
Princeton, USS 295, 399, 401
Prinz Eugen, German cruiser 4, 88, 89, 90,
    102, 117
prisoners-of-war, British 74–6, 174, 235,
    255–60, 260–2
    escape 261–2
    German 265–6
    in Japanese hands 288–94, 295–6, 299
    escapees 296–7
    released 300, 302
    Korea 333–6
Provence, French battleship 6, 55

Queen Elizabeth, HMS, battleship 2, 94, 97,
    191, 281, 282
Queen Elizabeth II, in Falklands 360, 361
Quentin, HMS destroyer 176
Quiberon, HMS destroyer 174–5

radar 3, 178
    faults in 118, 124
    on submarines 253–4
    postwar 308
Raeder, Grand Admiral Erich 5
Raider, HMS destroyer 313
Raider E, armed merchant cruiser 70
Ramillies, HMS, battleship 4, 244
Rawalpindi, armed merchant cruiser 4, 56
Renown, HMS, battle-cruiser 2, 190
Repose, US hospital ship 332
Repulse, HMS, battle-cruiser 8, 104, 105, 106,
    107
    sunk 103, 107–8, 288
Resolution, HMS, battleship 54
Resource, HMS storeship 99
Reynolds, Sub-Lieutenant Dick **273–5**, 277
Richelieu, French battleship 9, 279, 343
Roberts, First Lieutenant, Peter VC 122
Rochester Castle, merchant ship 152, 154
Rodney, HMS, battleship 4, 18, 96, 135, 136,
    139
Roelich, Dorree *see* Spencer, Dorree
Rommel, General Erwin:
    in Africa 7, 174, 180
    and D-Day 239
Roxburgh, Sub-Lieutenant John **17**;
    Lieutenant **116–17**, **179–83**; Acting
    Lieutenant-Commander **254–5**

Royal Air Force:
    Battle of Britain 2
    losses at Brest 121
    and D-Day 240
    defence cuts 1960s 310
Royal Marines:
    discipline 25–6
    at Dieppe 158
    at Monte Cassino 214–15
    D-Day 234–6, 238–40
    in France and at Kiel 262–4
    in Singapore 288–9
    at Suez 308, 342–6, 350
    in Northern Ireland 357–9
    in Falklands 368, 369
    disbandment proposed 310
Royal Oak, HMS, battleship, sunk 26–30, 108,
    206
Russell, Guy, captain, *Duke of York* 211
Rye, HMS minesweeper 149, 151, 152

St Valéry, evacuation of troops from 45
Santa Elisa, merchant ship, sunk 142
Santa Fe, Argentinian submarine 367
SAS (Special Air Service):
    Falklands 368, 368–9
    raid on Pebble Island 381–2
    Australian 402
    Gulf War 402
Saumarez, HMS, destroyer 233, 312; mined
    308, 313, 314
Sayer, Telegraphist Air Gunner Les, Fleet Air
    Arm **95–6**, **169–70**
Sceptre, HMS, submarine 229–30, 253–4
Scharnhorst, German battle-cruiser 2, 4, 5, 34,
    52, 117, 121, 204, 205, 206, 207, 210,
    212, sank 213
Schofield, Brian, captain, *Duke of York* 211
Scotstoun, armed merchant cruiser 56
Scourge, HMS, destroyer 242–4
Scylla, HMS cruiser 165
Sea Hawk aircraft 344, 346, 351–2, 394, 396–7
Sea King helicopters 360, 361, 364
Sea Lion, HMS submarine 117–18
Sea Otter aircraft 226
Sea Scout, submarine 267–8
Sea Wolf missile systems 368, 369–70, 371,
    380
    qualities 370
SEALS 402
Search and Rescue 386–93
Seldon, Ordinary Signalman Les **155–60**
Seraph, HMS, submarine 186–9
Shah, HMS escort carrier 279
Sharpshooter, HMS minesweeper 168–9
Shean, Lieutenant Max 206, 287
Sheffield, HMS, cruiser 212, 366, 367, 368,
    372; sunk 310, 377–8
Sheldon, Lieutenant Phil 360, 361–2, 363

414

Index

Sherwood, Apprentice Mike, MN **14–17**;
   Midshipman, RNR **38–42**
Shin Se Maru, Japanese drumsteamer 298–9
Sicily:
   commando operations 192–4, 195–7
   scheme to put enemy off scent 187–9
Sikh, HMS, destroyer 170–3; sunk 173
Silkworm 395, 399–400
Simonstown (South Africa) 199
Singapore 8, 103, 104, 288
   surrender 1942 9
   base of Task Force 309
Sir Galahad, Royal Fleet Auxiliary 362, 363,
   383–4, 400–1
Sirius, HMS, cruiser 136
skoots, rector vessels (at Dunkirk) 46
Slack, Corporal Bernard **238–40**, **262–4**
Slapton Sands (Devon) 241
Smart, Captain Jack 205, 285, 286
Somerville, Vice-Admiral Sir James 6, 54
Sonar (formerly ASDIC) 3, 20, 164, 179
   postwar 308
South Georgia 366–7
Spaatz, General Carl (USAAF) 301, 302
Sparkes, Leading Airman 83, 84, 85, 86
Speedwell, HMS 49
Speedy merchant ship 139
Spencer, Wren Dorree **160–4**
Spithead Review 1953 308
Stalag-344 76, 260–1
Stalingrad merchant ship sunk 166
Starling, HMS frigate 216, 217, 218, 219(2),
   220, 220–1, 222, 224
Statesman, HMS submarine 279
Stone, Warrant Officer 200–1
Stone, Nursing Sister Ruth, QARNNS **328–33**
Strathallan, liner 175–6
'Stringbags' (swordfish aircraft) 67
submarines:
   life in 17–18, 43–4, 177–8, 180–1
   P614/P615 164
   with convoy 165
   German *see* U-boats
   one-man, Italian 191
   Far East 267–9
   see also midget submarines
Suez Campaign 1956 308, 342–6, 346–52, 380
Suffolk, HMS, cruiser 88, 91
Superb, HMS, cruiser 312
Sussex, HMS, cruiser 69
Suvla, HMS 343, 344
Svenner, Norwegian destroyer 243
Swift, HMS, destroyer 243
Swordfish biplanes 6, 42, 65, 66, 81–2, 102,
   118, 164, 166, 169
   on *Courageous* 20–3
   on *Victorious* 95–6
Swordfish Squadron 823 51
Syrtis HMS, submarine 205

Takao, Japanese cruiser 285–6, 287, 288
Tapir, HMS, submarine 254–5
Taranto (Italy) 6, 65–7
Taylor, Lieutenant Horace **58–61**
Temple Arch, freighter 164
Thetis, HMS submarine, disaster 17
Thorn, HMS submarine, disaster 17
Thrasher HMS submarine 121
Tilburn, Able Seaman Bob **89–95**
Tirpitz, German battleship 5, 133–4, 146, 204,
   205, 206, 207, 208, 210
Tobruk, action on 170–4
Torrens-Spence, Lieutenant Michael, **65–9**
Tovey, Vice-Admiral Sir John 165
Towers, Surgeon-Lieutenant-Commando
   Henry 277
Tracker, HMS aircraft-carrier 218
Transylvania, armed merchant ship, sunk
   56–7
Trenchant, HMS, submarine 269–71
Treves, Officer Cadet Frederick **136–7**, **142–3**,
   144
Trident missiles 309
Trident HMS submarine 17, 42–3
Trinidad, HMS, cruiser 124–6
Tripoli, USS 395, 399, 401
Tristan da Cunha 352–5
Tristania 354
Tristram 363
Tromp 279
tropical diseases 290, 293, 296, 297, 299
Troubridge, HMS 320
Truculent, 205
Trusty, submarine 177–8
TSR-2 bombers 310
Turnbull, Sub-Lieutenant F R A, RN 51
Turpin, 255

U-boats:
   operating from French Atlantic coast 2–3
   attacks on Russian convoys 131–2, 168
   Atlantic wolf packs 3, 216
   war against 3, 19, 41
   first sinking 19
   Type XXI 4
   frustrated in 1944 8
   sunk 218–19, 220, 221, 222, 223, 224
      U-486 255
      U-457 168
      U-88 166
   end of U-boat war 265–6
   postwar disposal 307
Uganda 383–4
Ulster 357–9
Ulster, HMS destroyer 274
Ulster Monarch, freighter 196
Ulster Prince, HMS, troopship 168
Ulster Queen, anti-aircraft ship 164
ULTRA decrypts 3

Index

Unbroken, HMS, submarine 206
underwater weapons, diving for 199–201
United, HMS submarine 179–83
United Nations, and Korea 325, 328
United States of America 4
   versus Japan 300
   and Suez 308–9
Uxbridge, RAF, mine 60

Valiant, HMS, battleship 54, 65, 78, 97, 191
Valiant, HMS, submarine 309
Valiant aircraft 347
Valona (Albania), attack on 68
Vampire aircraft, Egyptian 346, 348
Van Tromp, Dutch cruiser 231
Vanguard, HMS, battleship 309
VE-Day, celebrated 278, 300
Victorious, HMS, aircraft-carrier 82–3, 95–6,
   119, 136
Vigilance, tanker 184, 185
Vittorio Veneto, Italian battleship 67, 69
VJ-Day 301
Volage, HMS destroyer 308, 312, 313
volcano, Tristan da Cunha 353
Voltaire, armed merchant cruiser 73; sunk 74
Voracious, HMS submarine 179, 267
Vulcan aircraft 347
Vulcan Phalanx weapons system 393

Wacosta, US freighter sunk 167
Waimarama, merchant vessel 136–7, 139–40,
   142–3, 143–4, 144–6, 147, 148, 154
Wairangi, merchant ship, sunk 142(2)
Walker, Rear-Admiral 278, 280–1, 282
Walker, Anne, Air Transport Auxiliary 22
Walker, Captain D 215–25; death 224–5
Walker, Wing Commander Derek 225
Walker, First Officer Diana Barnato, ATA
   225–9
Walker, Rear-Admiral 'Hookey' 89, 94
Wall, Robert 19–20
Wallace, Chief Petty Officer David, RN
   386–93
Walpole, HMS destroyer 17
Walrus aircraft 226, 227–8
Warspite, HMS, battleship 6, 42, 78, 243, 244,
   252, 253
   history 320–1
   run aground 320–1
Wasp, US aircraft-carrier 273
Wemyss, Commander (*Wild Goose*) 219, 223

Wessex aircraft 401
Westcliff, HMS, shore establishment 234
Weston, Lieutenant (*Amethyst*) 322, 323
Weston, Simon 384
Westwood, Lieutenant David 342
Whirlwind aircraft 308
Whitelaw, William 358–9
Whitesand Bay 327
Whitham, First Lieutenant Bill 205, 207(2),
   209
Whitley, Bill 205, 207, 208, 209
Whittle, Chief Stoker, death 80
Whitworth, Vice-Admiral, W. J. 94
Wild Goose, sloop 216, 219(2), 220, 220–1,
   221, 222, 223
Wilder, Ordinary Seaman Dick **164–9**
Wilkinson, Lieutenant Thomas 123–4
Williams, Eric, official naval reporter **265–6**
Williamson, Lieutenant-Commander 66
Willis, Admiral Sir Algernon U 312
Wilton, HMS, destroyer 131, 134
Winter, Sub-Lieutenant Peter 68
Winton, Lieutenant John **325–8**
Wood, Bishop Maurice 246
Wood, Leading Sick Berth Attendant Sam **87–9**
Woodcock HMS, sloop 218, 219
Woodhouse, C H, captain HMS *Ajax* 31
Woodpecker, HMS sloop 216, 219, 220, 220–1,
   223, 224; sunk 224
Woodward, Admiral John 'Sandy' 366, 368,
   369, 371, 372, **376–82**
Woosung Fort, China 325
World War II, brief history 1–9
Wren, HMS sloop 216, 217, 219, 220
Wright, Ordinary Seaman Gordon 'Shiner'
   321–5
Wright, Captain Jefauld, USN 186
WRNS, numbers in 9

X-craft *see* midget submarines

Yamato, Japanese battleship, sunk 307
Yangtse-Kiang river, *Amethyst* incident 321–5
Yates, Surgeon-Commander 277, 278
Yokohama 302
Yugoslavia, former 311

Zara, Italian cruiser 69
Zarb, Petty Officer Cook Salvatore 314
Zeke, Japanese aircraft 274–5
Zulu, HMS, destroyer 170, 172; sunk 172